STANLEY
Dark Genius of African Exploration

Frank McLynn

TO JEFFREY SPAULDING

CONTENTS

PREFACE

Sir Henry Morton Stanley, greatest of the African explorers and one of the most fascinating of the late Victorian adventurers, has never received full biographical treatment. Neither Richard Hall's Stanley (1974) nor Frank Hird's H. M. Stanley. The Authorised Life (1935), the best of the biographies so far and the only ones to make use of Stanley's private papers, contains footnotes enabling the reader to check their treatment of the sources. Nor has any but a half-hearted attempt been made to probe the enigma of Stanley's psyche. Yet Stanley is surely a key figure in any history of European penetration of Africa. His impact on indigenous societies was profound and widespread: his travels took him over virtually the whole of Central Africa, for good or ill he founded the Belgian Congo as Leopold's servant in 1879-84, and he lives on in general folk memory as the man who found Livingstone and spoke the immortal words, 'Dr Livingstone, I presume?'

This biographical gap must be my excuse for dealing at length with the explorer. The years 1841-77 saw Stanley's most colourful exploits and although history may regard the foundation of the Congo Free State as his most important monument, his greatest feats as an explorer had been achieved by the age of thirty-six.

My list of acknowledgements must be headed by HM the Queen, for allowing me to examine the relevant documents in the Royal Archives. Mrs Stanley showed me round the Stanley mansion at Pirbright, and very kindly put a number of illustrations and other valuable material at my disposal. I owe a special debt of gratitude to the Warden and Fellows of St Antony's College, Oxford, for electing me to the Alistair Horne Research Fellowship in 1987, thus providing me with the resources to produce a more meticulous work than I could have done otherwise. Alas, the disinterested scholarly integrity of St Antony's was not in evidence in all quarters where I pursued my researches.

About ten years ago the Stanley family papers were sold to the Musee Royale Africaine at Tervuren in Belgium, and the museum's administrators pursue a policy of turning away all parties interested in inspecting the original documentation. Not even the intervention of the Belgian ambassador in London had any impact on the 'closed-door' policy. So much for the international community of scholars! It was fortunate indeed that the British Library possessed an almost complete microfilm copy of the exported manuscripts.

On a personal level I would like to thank my editor at Constable, Robin Baird-Smith, and, especially, my wife Pauline, who read the original script and made many helpful suggestions.

Chapter One

WHEN Henry Morton Stanley landed at Dover on 1st August 1872, in triumph after his famous meeting with Livingstone on the shores of Lake Tanganyika nine months earlier, he was appalled to find that his cousin and a half-brother from Wales were there to meet him at the dockside. The two relatives were already in an advanced stage of intoxication and mortified Stanley by drawing attention to themselves and to him. Bitterly he recorded in his diary:

What a welcome! Had these stupid newspapers not mentioned my name, the vanity of my poor relations would not have been kindled. Thus has my presentiment been realised on my first setting foot in England. They had already of course gained considerable éclat on the pier by their revelation of their relationship with me and a large crowd of quidnuncs, railway porters and others assembled to witness our meeting. I never felt so ashamed, and would have given all I was worth to have been back in Central Africa. What little Kalulu [Stanley's black servant] must have thought of my drunken relatives I do not know. There is no reason in the world why I should recognise them in public. They only bring to my mind too vividly my treatment, when I deserved something else than the scorn they gave me as a child, and any charity that they might have shown me then, might today have been remembered and returned with interest.

Yet Stanley's negative feelings did not end with bitterness, shame and disgust towards his family. The very mention of his Welshness was anathema to him, and this was not just because he was at the time claiming to be American bred and born. When Francis Galton asked him, in front of 3,000 people at Brighton on 18th August, to confirm that he was Welsh, Stanley confided to his diary his resentment at such curiosity in a British Empire that claimed to be a product of all races:

A person like myself with, such a miserable, unfortunate past cannot possibly find pleasure in speaking before people who have wined, and rather to the full, about his poverty-stricken childhood and indulge in maudlin grief over circumstances that were utterly beyond his control . . . What had I to do with my birth in Wales? It was only an accident that my mother did not prefer to stay in London when her pains informed her of the approaching event. Denbigh is only a day's journey for a pedestrian from the English border, and here these people are perpetually talking about Welshmen and Scotchmen and Irishmen as though these nationalities were foreigners to the English.

Repudiation of race and family comes close to a denial of one's real identity. It is no surprise to find that 'Henry Morton Stanley' is a pseudonym. What is more surprising is the discovery that all Stanley's legendary toughness came from a single impulse: a desire for revenge on life and mankind for his unhappy childhood. It was at once Stanley's strength and weakness that he surmounted early miseries that would have overwhelmed most mortals.

Our sources for Stanley's childhood are meagre. The problem for the biographer is particularly acute since the principal 'source', the Autobiography published by Dorothy Stanley in 1909, is largely a work of neurotic fantasy. Yet this has its compensations. While we must look elsewhere for the facts of Stanley's early life, the Autobiography is an extraordinarily rich seam to work for the inner Stanley and provides vital clues to his unconscious demons. To pin down the early years we must establish a 'dialectic' between the few facts at our disposal and the claims Stanley makes in the Autobiography.

The man history knows as Henry Morton Stanley was born on 28th January 1841 in Denbigh, Wales and was christened on 19th February in the parish church of St Hilary's. The name given to him at baptism was John Rowlands, after his presumed father. Rowlands was an Anglicised version of the Welsh 'Rollant'. For a long time this simple fact was unknown to the world. The plaque on his coffin at the memorial service in Westminster Abbey in 1904 gave 10th June 1840 as his date of birth and this was the date reproduced by the explorer Sir Harry Johnston in his panegyric. Johnston felt confident of his facts, since Stanley had spoken at length, and apparently freely, of his boyhood when he met Johnston on the Congo in 1883. The confusion over Stanley's exact date of birth was caused partly by Stanley's deliberate obfuscation and partly by the fact that he himself genuinely believed, until confronted with hard evidence in the 1880s, that he had been born in 1843.

The baptismal register records that the infant Rowlands was born out of wedlock to a twenty-six-year-old farmer called John Rowlands and a woman named Elizabeth Parry, born 1822, and thus aged either eighteen or nineteen. Little is known of the father's family but the little that is shows Stanley in that Autobiography as a first-rate fantasist. Despite his statement that his father died shortly after his birth, it is now known that John Rowlands actually died in May 1854, aged thirty-nine, of alcoholism. His life appears to have been an utter failure and he possessed none of the energies that had made his father a successful farmer. Stanley's paternal grandfather, another John Rowlands, died at seventy-four in 1856.

Since the bibulous John Rowlands has always seemed an unlikely father for the future great explorer, a local legend soon grew up that Rowlands had merely agreed to claim paternity to mask the true father, allegedly one James Vaughan Horne, solicitor, town clerk and Denbigh's deputy recorder. There is considerable irony here, for Home's own marriage was childless and he died at forty-six from alcohol-related causes (dropsy and liver failure).

We are on more solid ground in more senses than one with Stanley's mother. Stanley's maternal grandmother was the daughter of Andrew Roberts, who died in 1822 aged seventy-four. Roberts had five children: two sons and three daughters. One of his daughters, Mary, stayed on in North Wales to marry a Mr Davies when the Roberts family 'emigrated' to

South Wales. When Davies died, she married Moses Parry, then a prosperous butcher and grazier. With her Moses Parry had two sons (Moses junior and Thomas) and three daughters (Mary, Maria and Elizabeth). Elizabeth Parry was the mother of the man who would become H. M. Stanley.

By 1841, Moses Parry was in his late seventies and his family was dispersed. His wife was dead; Maria had married a man named Morris in Liverpool, Mary was already Mrs Owen. Moses junior remains a shadowy figure but it is clear that he was making some success in the paternal trade of butchery. Thomas had become the landlord of the Golden Lion inn. Elizabeth appears to have worked both in domestic service and in a bakery. But by the time of Stanley's birth Moses Parry himself had fallen on hard times. It was his proud boast that in his time he had provided dinners for a household of forty people, including servants and labourers. Whatever the truth of that, by January 1841 he was living in a small cottage in the grounds of Denbigh Castle. It was there that Elizabeth Parry came for her confinement, post-haste from London, as Stanley records.

Stanley was Elizabeth Parry's first child. She was to have four more children, all out of wedlock, two of them with a man she later married. This was exceptional even by the fairly relaxed standards of 1840s Wales and argues either for high libido or a degree of promiscuity bordering on amateur prostitution. There can be little doubt that this aspect of his mother compounded Stanley's shame at his illegitimacy and led to his later notorious difficulty in coming to terms with sexuality. His own portrait of his mother is far from flattering: 'a tall woman with an oval face and a great coil of dark hair'.

Immediately after Stanley's birth Elizabeth Parry departed for London and domestic service. Pregnant again in 1842, she returned to Wales to give birth to her daughter Emma. The young John Rowlands was left largely in his grandfather's care. They lived in the upstairs part of the primitive cottage on the green of Denbigh Castle; Parry's two sons lived below. Most of Stanley's early bonding was with the elderly male. There is no reason to doubt this part of Stanley's reminiscences: 'My grandfather appears to me as a stout old gentleman, clad in corduroy breeches, dark stockings and long Melton coat, with a clean-shaven face, rather round and lit up by humorous grey eyes.' Without question the child was a great favourite with the old man. Prophetically Moses Parry dubbed him 'Fy Nhyn dy Fodol I' - 'my man of the future'.

When he was four, Stanley began to attend school in the crypt of St Hilary's Church where he had been christened. But already the clouds were beginning to gather around him. Moses junior took a wife called Kitty, 'a flaxen-haired fair girl of uncertain temper'. Kitty made it clear that she had her eye on the upper apartments and could not wait for Moses senior to die. She began by forbidding the old man and the child to wander at will in the lower part of the cottage; they were only to descend on express invitation. Her opportunity to evict the unwanted tenants came when grandfather

Moses dropped dead one day in June 1846 while working in the fields. At once she persuaded the boy's two uncles (her own husband Moses and Thomas the publican) to board him out. For the rest of 1846 Stanley was placed in the care of Richard and Jenny Price of Bowling Green Cottage near Denbigh Castle. Richard Price combined the offices of sexton, verger and gamekeeper. The Prices were paid 2/6 a week for his board and lodging.

What Stanley remembered most about his time with the Prices was the dreadful bespectacled harridan who ruled the village infant school with a birch rod, the somnolent Sundays at the local Wesleyan chapel and the abnormal religiosity and superstition of Mrs Price. A particular trial was the Prices' daughter, Sarah, who inculcated her own morbid fear of demons and ghosts into her young charge. Fortunately or unfortunately, Stanley's osmosis with the supernatural was cut brutally short. The Price interlude came to an end in February 1847, but not before the Prices had dealt him a psychic blow greater than any fear of spectres or phantoms. By this time Moses Parry's other son, Thomas, had married. His new wife was of her sister-in-law Kitty's opinion that 2/6 a week paid for the upkeep of this unwanted bastard was money ill spent. It was decided to consign the young John Rowlands to the workhouse.

As is often the case with people who cannot bear the unpleasant reality of what they are doing, the Prices dealt with the matter in an oblique and underhand way. They did not inform Stanley of his changed situation. Instead, they told him he was going to live with his Aunt Mary (Mrs Owen) at her farm at Ffynnon Beuno. Richard Price, their son, took the boy on his shoulders and told him they were going to walk all the way. When the boy began to protest at the length of the journey, Richard used honeyed cajolery on him. After a long trek his treacherous guide set him down at an immense stone building. They passed through a set of iron gates. Richard pulled at a bell which the boy heard clanking noisily inside. When a hatchet-faced beadle appeared and pulled Stanley roughly inside, Richard turned the knife in the wound by telling the boy his aunt would be with him in a minute. The door clanged shut. Within minutes Stanley realised he was in the St Asaph Union Workhouse. In a paroxysm of tears he finally appreciated the depth of the deception. As he later remarked bitterly: 'It would have been better for me if Dick, being stronger than I, had employed compulsion, instead of shattering my confidence and planting the first seeds of distrust in a child's heart.'

It is difficult to overplay the role of this 'betrayal' in Stanley's psychic development. Saturday, 20th February 1847 remained a black day etched on his memory for ever. The generalised misanthropist and particular suspicion of all strangers has its origin in this shoddy episode of moral cowardice by the Prices and Parrys. To the end of his life this wound rankled. The poison was hot enough twenty-two years later for Stanley to record this impression in the 'autobiography' he wrote to his putative fiancée Katie Gough-Roberts:

This waif now became a burden, an annual expense (the amount of which is just one-tenth of the sum I yearly expend in choice Havannahs); the waif must be got rid of, but how? What a pity he did not die! Were murder a crime unpunished the waif would have been summarily disposed of... the moment the child Rowland (for so he was named) entered the workhouse he was estranged from the rest of the world; Cain's hellish mark was stamped on his forehead; a portion of Adam's sin and shame clung to him. For nine years the waif lived within the workhouse, uncared for by all relations, by all humanity, but cared for by providence and benign law. While in the workhouse the child Rowland was beaten, kicked, cuffed, sneered, jeered at and handcuffed as a workhouse brat - an illegitimate child. At an early age he became imbued with man's feelings. There can be no doubting the trauma of entry into the workhouse. But was life there quite the living hell Stanley depicts in the. Autobiography} There are grounds for thinking that Stanley, ever the obfuscator, shifted the focus from the ways in which the workhouse was a nightmare - ways not easily absorbed by his prospective Edwardian audience - to the areas where it was not. The real indictment of the workhouse system was that it was a breeding ground of promiscuity, vice and perversion, as the Commissioners of Enquiry into the State of Education in Wales pointed out. St Asaph's workhouse had been visited by the Commissioners a few weeks before Stanley had been deposited on its doorstep. They found it a nursery of female prostitution and male obscenity. Among the workhouse 'clientele' were prostitutes giving birth or recovering from venereal disease, young girls learning the tricks of the trade from their elder sisters, sodomites and other perverts. The children slept two to a bed, invariably an older with the younger, so that the already depraved corrupted the young. Because of their proximity to the adults, children saw them copulating and picked up their bawdy patois. The walls were paper-thin, so that a formal separation of adults from children achieved little. We may therefore conjecture that Stanley was at the very least sexually assaulted and manhandled even if he was probably not (for reasons that will later appear) the victim of actual homosexual rape.

A recital of all the evils of the workhouse would have been meat too strong for his Edwardian readers. Stanley in his Autobiography therefore concentrates on the kind of brutality they could accept: floggings and beatings of the 'character-forming' public-school type. In this recital the brutal 'heavy' is the workhouse teacher James Francis. Whether the few facts known about Francis altogether square with Stanley's portrait of him is, however, another matter.

If we for a moment place a bracket around the sexual area where the workhouse truly was an evil place, then it seems that Stanley's objective experience in the workhouse was not quite so black for him personally as he paints it. This is of course to say nothing of the way in which such a place would have been perceived by a boy of Stanley's sensitivity. Nor is it to suggest that St Asaph's was in any way a bed of roses. The monotonous diet of bread, potatoes, gruel and porridge (with meat just once a week), the shaven heads and 'hodden grey' of the boys and the striped cotton dresses of the girls, the fixed routine of bed at eight and reveille at six, everlasting unctuous Sunday sermons: all this was real enough. The crucial question was whether Francis was the sadistic monster Stanley portrays.

All the collateral evidence, and even some circumstantial pointers from Stanley himself, show that young John Rowlands very soon established himself as one of Francis's favourites. Francis soon discovered that the boy was good at arithmetic and geography, had a natural flair for music and a pronounced talent for drawing. It was related of young Rowlands that he loved wandering over a map of the world with a pointer and had the latitude and longitude of all principal cities in the world off pat. His excellent penmanship was early recognised. He was often selected by the porter to enter names in the visitors' book and to help the clerk's office with accounts. Thomas Mumford, a fellow inmate at St Asaph's and later a mechanic, remembered that when Stanley became head boy in the school, Francis would put him in charge of discipline during his absence; Stanley was quite equal to the task and would thrash enthusiastically any pupil who stepped out of line. Moreover, the wife of John Jones, the local painter, testified to Francis's special partiality for Stanley. Mrs Jones kept a cake shop in St Asaph in the 1840s. Whenever Francis received a shilling to spend on the workhouse boys, he used to visit her shop and bring young Rowlands (Stanley) with him to help carry the cakes back. Again and again he used to remark to Mrs Jones that he was sure the boy would be a great man some day.

Francis was at pains to promote Stanley's career at all points. It is likely that he condoned the boy's occasional truancies, as when the restless youngster stole away to his uncle Moses' house in Vale St Denbigh, only to be returned on the coach the next day. It has even been suggested that Francis might have encouraged Stanley to get out of the workhouse at the earliest possible moment and hinted at the career of schoolteacher instead of the likely manual work that loomed. One mark of Francis's efforts was the presentation to the boy of a Bible for 'diligent application to his studies and for general good conduct' made by Dr Vowler Short, Bishop of St Asaph's on 5th January 1855.

The story goes that the Bishop was much taken with young Rowlands' quick-wittedness and asked him what he wanted to be when he grew up. 'A bishop, sir,' Stanley is said to have replied.

Another hint that Francis was not the brute Stanley chooses to portray in the famous purple passages of the Autobiography was the fact, as Stanley himself concedes, that the schoolmaster tried to bring the boy and his mother closer together. For by 1851 Elizabeth Parry and her two illegitimate children Robert and Emma were themselves committed to the care of the St Asaph Board of Guardians. Elizabeth Parry and Robert were very soon discharged, but Emma stayed on until 1857 when she left to enter domestic service. In the brief time Stanley's mother was in the workhouse, Francis tried in vain to get her to evince some maternal feelings towards her first-born. First he pointed her out to Stanley who, hardly surprisingly, did not know her. 'What, do you not know your own mother?' Francis exclaimed. The sequel is described with great bitterness by Stanley:

I started with a burning face and directed a shy glance at her and perceived she was regarding me with a look of cool, critical scrutiny. I had expected to feel a gush of tenderness towards her, but her expression was so chilling that the valves of my heart closed as with a snap. 'Honour thy father and mother' had been repeated by me a thousand times, but this loveless parent required no honour from me.

All the evidence, then, shows Francis to have had Stanley's interests at heart. We need not conclude that the schoolmaster never beat the boy. Although the incident described in the Autobiography when Stanley was soundly whipped for pronouncing 'Joseph' as 'Jophes' has an apocryphal ring about it, there is good reason to think that the beating the boy received for illicitly feasting on blackberries is an authentic occurrence. Stanley speaks of 'a punishment so dreadful that blackberries suggested birching ever afterwards.' This is borne out in his later private diaries. During the Emin Pasha expedition in 1889 he records the following: 'Along yesterday's route ... we found several masses of blackberry bushes, and the luscious fruit recalled to my memory many an incident, some pleasant, others decidedly unpleasant, connected with blackberry picking.'

What do we know of Francis? He was a former collier from Mold who had lost his left hand in a pit accident and then been appointed schoolmaster at the workhouse. Schoolmasters in the 1840s were not required to have high academic attainments. When Stanley arrived at St Asaph's, Francis, then aged thirty-two, had been teaching for seven years. In 1863, i.e. seven years after Stanley left the workhouse, Francis was committed to the Denbigh Lunatic Asylum (North Wales Hospital for Nervous Diseases), where he died in January 1866. Francis's main qualification as schoolmaster was that he knew more English than other eligible candidates, even though the investigating Commissioners spoke of his 'very broken English'. Nevertheless, they praised his general pedagogic abilities; in 1856 he was granted an efficiency award and a wage increase. Local folklore also insists that when Stanley left St Asaph's in May 1856 Francis gave him a sixpenny piece as a parting gift.

This background knowledge is essential when we come to consider the most famous story about Stanley's childhood, the great purple passage of the Autobiography. According to this, in May 1856 Francis flew into a tempestuous rage because a deal table had been marked and no one would own up to the damage. He decided to birch the entire class, including Rowlands, the head boy.

The beatings commenced, 'How is this?' he shouted furiously as he came to Stanley. 'Not ready yet? Strip, sir, this minute. I mean to stop this abominable barefaced lying.'

'I did not lie, sir. I know nothing of it.'

'Silence, sir. Down with your clothes.'

'Never again,' shouted Stanley. What follows is his own verbatim account.

The words had scarcely escaped me ere I found myself swung upward into the air by the collar of my jacket, and flung into a nerveless heap on the bench. Then the passionate brute pummelled me in the stomach until I fell backward, gasping for breath. Again I was lifted, and dashed on the bench with a shock that almost broke my spine. What little sense was left in me after these repeated shocks made me aware that I was smitten on the cheeks, right and left, and that soon nothing would be left of me but a mass of shattered nerves and bruised muscles.

Recovering my breath, finally, from the pounding in the stomach, I aimed a vigorous kick at the cruel Master as he stooped to me, and, by chance, the booted foot smashed his glasses, and almost blinded him with their splinters. Starting backward with the excruciating pain, he contrived to stumble over a bench, and the back of his head struck the stone floor; but, as he was in the act of falling, I had bounded to my feet, and possessed myself of his blackthorn. Armed with this, I rushed at the prostrate form and struck him at random over his body, until I was called to a sense of what I was doing by the starless way he received the thrashing.

The sequel, according to Stanley, was that he fled the workhouse with his 'friend Mose in terror at the likely repercussions of what he had done. Despite its palpable similarity to Nicholas's famous thrashing of Wackford Squeers in Chapter 13 of Nicholas Nickleby, this tall story was, until very recently, accepted as the literal truth concerning Stanley's departure from St Asaph's in 1856.

It is of course an elaborate fantasy, as we can establish from independent evidence. Before 1851 no list of inmates at St Asaph's had been made out, merely lists of admissions and discharges. But from 1851 to 1856 detailed records were kept on the inmates and the name 'John Rowlands' occurs eight times. The last entry is dated 13 May 1856 and records against Rowlands' name 'gone to his uncle at the National School, Holywell'. Had Stanley in fact absconded following a fracas with Francis, this would have been recorded. Moreover, the 'Willie Roberts' whom Stanley earlier accuses Francis of having beaten to death seems to be a figment; there is no sign of any such person in the workhouse records.

A close chronological examination of Stanley shows how he eventually worked up this fantasy, which did not make its appearance until all principal eyewitnesses were dead. In conversations with his servant William Hoffman in the late 1880s, Stanley produced a story of a struggle with Francis in which the schoolmaster had slipped and struck his head against a table. The full-blooded thrashing has not yet made its appearance. It is also possible to appreciate the elements Stanley used in the concoction of this fantasy. His 'friend Mose' (Moses Roberts) was a real person who genuinely did run away from the workhouse, as the St Asaph's records show. But this event occurred on 24th July 1855, almost a year before the fictitious Stanley 'breakout'. Roberts had 'run away' entered against his name on the ledger - a very clear contrast with the entry against 'John Rowlands'. Knowing this enables us to discount the reality of the subsequent wanderings of the pair as recounted in the Autobiography, the visit to Moses Roberts' mother and young Stanley's application for help to his paternal grandfather John Rowlands.

The question then arises: why did Stanley find it necessary to make up such a story? In part it was the kind of tale beloved by Victorian audiences, in which innocence triumphs over evil. With his shrewd journalistic instinct Stanley would have realised that such a story was 'good copy'. In part it was an obvious fantasy of the powerless, transmogrifying impotence into control. But there are grounds for believing that the story was also a necessary outlet for the intense guilt and ambivalence Stanley entertained towards his grandfather Moses Parry. From Moses Parry and James Francis Stanley had received almost his only experience of kindness and compassion. Now Moses Parry was a one-armed man and Francis was similarly maimed, having lost his left hand. The loss of his grandfather in 1846 was for Stanley the 'end of Eden', marking a brutal transition to the reality principle. Yet the circumstances of Parry's death, as perceived by the young Stanley, were peculiarly calculated to instil a sense of guilt. Stanley describes them as follows:

There came an afternoon when, to my dismay and fright, a pitcher with which I was sent for water fell from my hands and was broken. My grandfather came to the garden door on hearing the crash, and, viewing what had happened, lifted his forefinger menacingly and said, 'Very well, Shonin, my lad, when I return, thou shalt have a sound whipping. You naughty boy!'

That very afternoon Moses Parry dropped dead in the fields. It is entirely plausible that the boy would have felt that he was in some sense the cause of his grandfather's death. In fact, unconsciously Stanley reveals his unease by the odd verbal usage he employs. Instead of saying that he dropped the pitcher, he says it 'fell from my hands' - a clear attempt to exculpate himself from the accident.

The sober truth, then, is that Stanley left the workhouse at the age of fifteen when he had come to the end of his natural term at St Asaph's. The discharge record is in error on only one point: the school at Brynford, half an hour's walk from Holywell, was run by his cousin Moses Owen. Elizabeth Parry's elder sister Mary was now widowed, having produced four sons. The eldest, Edward, was a railway official at Morley; the second son, Moses Owen, twenty-three, was the schoolmaster at the National School at Brynford. John, eighteen, was on the point of taking up a post as a railway clerk. David Owen, thirteen, helped his mother on the farm. Stanley's aunt Mary combined small-scale farming with shop keeping in the farmhouse called Ffynnon Beuno (St Beuno's Spring or Well) on the hill beyond Brynford hamlet.

Stanley's arrival at Brynford was not welcomed by his aunt Mary. Moses Owen had agreed to take the young Rowlands on as a pupil-teacher after an interview showed him to be a lad of exceptional intellectual promise. But his mother thought his decision unwise. In her opinion, Stanley's pedagogic apprenticeship would tie Moses down financially so that he would be unable to marry. The agreement was that Stanley would work for a month on Aunt Mary's farm until he had earned enough to equip himself with suitable clothes for school mastering. When the boy arrived at Ffynnon Beuno, his aunt received him coldly. Apart from thinking her son's action rash, Mary regarded her sister Elizabeth as the 'bad seed' of the family. She frowned on her numerous peccadilloes and regarded Stanley as the fruit of sinfulness. Mary's disapproval of her sister was especially acute at this moment. In the very month of Stanley's discharge from St Asaph's (May 1856) Elizabeth Parry gave birth to James, her fourth illegitimate child. Aunt Mary thought Elizabeth a dreadful example. She was a dedicated penny-pincher, obsessed with the idea that any departure from frugality would lead her to the workhouse like her younger sister.

With such views, not surprisingly she treated Stanley with glacial reserve. She displayed open favouritism to her own children. Her obsessive financial economies usually had Stanley as their overt target. In one area alone she was prodigal: the food she set before the household was always plentiful and of superior quality. Yet the sensitive boy yearned to break through the reserve and acquire the maternal love his own mother had denied him. When he failed to move Aunt Mary, Stanley came to think that he had merely exchanged one form of misery for another:

A young boy cannot be expected to penetrate into the secret motives of his elders, but though his understanding may be dull, the constant iteration of hints will not fail in the end to sharpen his intelligence. Thus it was that I came to perceive that my condition had not been bettered much by my abrupt exit from St Asaph. If in one I had suffered physical slavery, I was now about to suffer moral slavery.

After a month of mowing, ploughing, milking and churning Stanley had earned enough to buy his school clothes. He proceeded to Moses Owen's school, where he was to be monitor of the second class. From 8 a.m. to 4 p.m. Stanley instructed the boys in the subjects where he was their superior: English, history and geography. From 4 p.m. to supper-time he learned geometry, algebra and Latin, subjects in which the other boys harden edge, partly from Moses but mainly from his cousin's extensive library. A frugal supper of porridge and milk brought the day to an end. Then Stanley would read in bed. Since Moses questioned him about his studies during meals, Stanley estimated that he spent eighteen hours out of every twenty-four in the world of learning. A particular literary favourite at this time was Johnson's Rasselas. From this experience grew not just a love of books but a realisation that with books he could hold the harsh realities of the world at bay.

After a few months Stanley had easily established himself as the academic superior of the head boys. But his passage was not an easy one: on the one hand he was unpopular with his peers; on the other, he was beginning to arouse Moses Owen's envy and resentment. The boys sensed Stanley's intellectual distinction and his general difference and hated him for it. They were irreligious, loutish, bawdy, much given to crudity and obscene language. Worst of all, they had discovered the secret of Stanley's illegitimacy and used the knowledge to silence any remonstration on his part: They all appeared to have become acquainted with my antecedents and their general behaviour towards me was not dissimilar to that which the unconvinced show towards 'ticket-of-leave'. The gentlest retort was followed by expressions which reminded me of my ignoble origin. Often they did not wait to be provoked, but indulged their natural malice as from divine privilege. The effect of this was to drive me within my own shell, and to impress the lesson on me that I was forever banned by having been an inmate of the Workhouse.

On the other hand, once Moses Owen saw that his protégé might soon outstrip his own intellectual attainments, he began to undermine the boy's confidence by exaggerating his shortcomings and playing down his achievements. Aunt Mary, sensing that her son was beginning to turn against the unwelcome cuckoo in her nest, heaped coals on the fire. She continued to sap Moses' confidence in his own judgement. She was a much stronger person than her son and her campaign began to pay off. Yet instead of admitting that he had been wrong in his original decision to take on the financial burden of the young Stanley, Owen pretended that he had been right but that it was Stanley's subsequent performance at the school which was disappointing. The insincerity and bad faith involved in this increased Stanley's sense of the duplicity and treachery of the adult world, a sense first inculcated by the Prices' 'betrayal'.

After a nine-month 'cold war' in which Owen unceasingly sniped at Stanley's abilities, it was agreed that the boy should abandon his pedagogic apprenticeship and return to Ffynnon Beuno to work on Aunt Mary's farm. We know that the final breach was sudden: local folklore maintained that it came about when Owen peremptorily demanded that his pupil-teacher clean his (Owen's) boots and Stanley refused. But even at Ffynnon Beuno he continued to be a thorn in the family's side. Stanley got on well with the village locals and began to emerge tentatively from his shell. This irritated the members of the Owen household, even their maid Jane, and they at once proceeded to put the boy in his place:

My aunt was nothing lath to subdue any ebullience of spirit with the mention of the fact that I was only a temporary visitor, and my cousin David was quick, as boys generally are, to point out how ill it became me to forget it, while Jane used it as an effective weapon to crush any symptom of manliness. For more than a year Stanley endured this second-class status. His tasks at Ffynnon Beuno now centred on shepherding the flocks and serving behind the bar of the primitive inn his aunt kept in addition to her shop. Saturday night was a rowdy, carousing night, but even the most hardened drinker quailed at the thought of a tongue-lashing from the village termagant. When the cacophony in the bar became too great, the dark-eyed virago would appear from the back parlour and silence the revellers with an imperious glance. As he marked time, Stanley withdrew more and more to an inner life. He liked to walk in secluded spots where he could be alone with his thoughts. A favourite eyrie was the summit of the Craig, commanding a view over the Vale of Clywd.

Behind the scenes Aunt Mary manoeuvred to rid herself of the incubus on her family. A visit from her sister Maria, married to Thomas Morris in Liverpool, seemed to hold out a solution. The Morrises had a contact - or thought they had - in a Liverpool insurance office. It was decided that they would place young Stanley in a clerkship there. Once again there was a delay while the boy worked on the farm to earn suitable clothes for the interview. When no word came from Liverpool, Stanley wrote a desperate appeal to his uncle to save him from the anathema into which he had been cast by Aunt Mary's dislike. This is the only surviving letter in which Stanley signs himself 'John Rowlands'. The letter reveals that Mary Owen had accused Stanley of having botched his chances for employment in Liverpool by alienating his Uncle Tom Morris:

Dear Uncle, I sincerely hope I have not displeased you in anything, as my Aunt thinks I have done . . . They have not succeeded in finding me a situation at Mold Railway Station as the master was a very bad scholar and his health was very imperfect, and he was very unlikely to stay there long. Hoping sincerely you will return me an answer by return of post. I shall feel extremely obliged to you, so I remain,

Your very Humble nephew, John Rowlands.

The simultaneous reference to railways and schools is at once mysterious and interesting, as combining the two occupational ambits of the Owen family. Perhaps here we see some influence of John Owen, the only member of the family for whom Stanley had any time and whom he visited in Shrewsbury in late 1866.

Confirmation of the Morrises' willingness to take Stanley into their home soon followed. In August 1858 the seventeen-year-old journeyed to the Mersey from Mostyn Docks on a packet-steamer. Stanley records vividly the culture shock experienced by one who had never seen any town larger than Denbigh, and who was used to green, open spaces, when he confronted the noise and bustle and sheer size of Liverpool. Most of all it was the din and racket of city life that appalled him. He made his way to the Morrises' house at 22 Sheriff Street.

Stanley took to his uncle Tom; 'corpulent, rubicund, genial... he had the heartiness and rollicking of the traditional "sea-dog"' Tom began by getting his twelve-year-old son Teddy to familiarise Stanley with the city. Then came the day when Mr Morris had to make good his boast by securing the youth the longed-for insurance clerkship. Unfortunately this venture ended in disaster. When Uncle Tom's 'friend' Mr Winter put them off with a vague promise yet again, after twenty-one visits to his office, Morris exploded in anger, calling Winter a humbug and hypocrite.

Stanley was jobless and prospect less. When his interview suit and, shortly afterwards, his overcoat were taken to the pawnbrokers he got a very clear light on the finances of the Morris household. He began to tramp the streets of Liverpool, looking for work. He found a position in a haberdasher's in London Road at a wage of 5 shillings a week. He worked from 7 a.m. to 9 p.m. at shop-sweeping, lamp-trimming and window polishing. But after two months of this, he fell ill. After a week he returned to work, only to find that he had been dismissed in his absence and his place taken by a more robust youth. It was back to tramping the streets, all the way from Everton to the Docks. At Bramley Moore Dock he was taken on as a butcher's boy, with the task of delivering fresh meat to the ships berthed on the Mersey. He lasted just a fortnight at this, but learned enough to realise that it was possible to ship out for exotic parts as a cabin-boy. Meanwhile he was being overwhelmed by the hostility of the butcher's foreman by day and the spite of young Teddy Morris by night. The situation in the Morris household seemed to be the Owen scenario all over again:

Here also, as at Ffynnon Beuno, there was a wide distinction between children who had parents and those who were orphaned. For if ever a discussion rose between my cousin and myself, my uncle and aunt were invariably partial to their own, when called to arbitrate between us.

Faced with these twin evils, Stanley took the opportunity when delivering meat to the packet-ship Windermere, whose captain was David Hardinge, to propose himself as cabin-boy for a voyage to New Orleans. He was signed on at a wage of $5 a month. The resistance to his departure at Sheriff Street was token only. On 20 December 1858, a month before his eighteenth birthday, Stanley watched as the Windermere was warped out of dock, then towed to mid-river by a tug. The sailors hoisted topsails and by nightfall they were on the open sea, America-bound. What kind of general assessment can we make of the young Stanley as he departs for the USA aged seventeen? He was a youth obsessed with the different ways in which the world deemed him inadequate, fearfully ashamed of his own illegitimacy, his mother and much of the rest of his extended family, paranoid about diver's aspects of his 'betrayal', with a partial, Old Testament, view of Christianity, and a pronounced tendency to seek refuge from his ills in fantasy.

There can be no doubting the agony suffered by Stanley when he contemplated his 'low birth', illegitimacy and poverty. In the brief private journal he composed later to cover the first twenty-five years of his life, he was unable to write about his childhood experiences in English, but employed Swahili so as to distance the events from himself. Quite apart from his illegitimacy, Stanley had no proper experience of parenting. As he ruefully admits: 'I must have been twelve ere I knew that a mother was indispensable to every child.' His mother was cold and detached even when near him in the workhouse. Nor did his experiences with the Owens and Morrises provide him with a surrogate mother, for both Aunt Mary Owen and Aunt Maria Morris seem to have been as cold in their own way as Elizabeth Parry. Stanley was driven to use his imagination to reconstruct the likely affection existing between a mother and son, as in the fictitious embrace between Moses Roberts and his mother after the St Asaph 'breakout'.

The profound horrified recoil from his natural parents can be observed in a number of ways. Whichever man, John Rowlands or James Vaughan Horne, was Stanley's true father; it is significant that both were alcoholics and that Stanley remained abstemious and near-teetotal all his life. Likewise, the promiscuous sexuality of his mother contrasts with Stanley's own neuter-like abstinence from normal manifestations of erotic feeling. A certain misogynistic strain in contemporary Welsh culture did not help matters. We have already noticed, too, Stanley's desire to 'destroy' any actual person who might stand in a paternal relationship with him: John Rowlands, Moses Parry, and James Francis. All this makes Stanley a prime candidate for the 'Family Romance' syndrome - the neurotic fantasy that one's parents are an unknown, lost couple, usually kings and queens or other celebrities, quite different from the people purporting to be one's parents.

We have already seen that unconscious guilt figures largely in Stanley's psychological profile: guilt about Moses Parry and a profound shame about his mother's sexual promiscuity and his own sexual experiences in the workhouse. This feeling is likely to have been reinforced by the peculiar brand of Christianity the boy absorbed; Stanley himself explicitly links the notion of guilt with his early religious socialisation. The cloying religiosity of the close world of the workhouse made it peculiarly difficult to test the reality of a stark world of Heaven and Hell against the 'normal' world. What impressed itself on Stanley's mind was the Calvinistic sense of doom. Stanley throughout his life paid lip-service to the New Testament providential God. But his true deity was never Jesus Christ and the law of love; it was the wrathful smiting Yahweh of the Old Testament. Stanley always retained a powerful sense of Evil; what was hard for him was to see the operation of Good.

Stanley records that he had the most vivid nightmares involving ghosts and demons until he left St Asaph's at the age of fifteen. This was partly the damage done by the hyper-superstitious Sarah Price. It was also partly the fire-and-brimstone narrow Calvinism of workhouse dogma. One of the impulses drawing Stanley in later life to the conquest of the Dark Continent may well have been a desire to transcend the darkness within and to exorcise the (literal) demons whose images had been inculcated in childhood.

All of this psychic damage was bad enough. In addition, Stanley had to deal with feelings of inadequacy about his own physical appearance. The young Stanley was short-legged and short of stature and had a tendency to run to fat. During his time at St Asaph's he had to endure a deal of chaffing about this from adults. One suggested he should be put under a garden-roller; another stated that he would be in prime condition for eating after a month's stuffing on raisins. The young Stanley was not to know that the short-legged man is, in folklore, like Odysseus, traditionally gifted with cunning in recompense. It merely increased his sense of humiliation and his conviction that only power could change his destiny. The brutality later evident in Stanley's behaviour has one of its roots in the pain he experienced as a man of less than average height. But he is not alone in this. Similar over-compensation by small men has produced some of the worst authoritarian excesses in the history of the world: Caesar, Napoleon, Hitler, Stalin, Mussolini and Franco are well-known examples.

The result of all this was to produce a wounded, paranoid, hyper-suspicious personality, obsessed with notions of betrayal and with a tendency to self-pity. A contemporary description neatly encapsulates the physical and psychical aspects: 'full-faced, stubborn, self-willed, round headed, uncompromising, deep ... in conversation with you, his large, dark eyes would roll away from you as if he was really in deep meditation about half a dozen things besides the subject of conversation ... his temperament was unusually sensitive; he could stand no chaff, nor the least bit of humour.'

The self-pity and acute sense of having been betrayed at every turn could be exhaustively documented. Two citations from the Autobiography will suffice: 'Those to whom in my trustful age I ventured to consign the secret hopes and interests of my heart, invariably betrayed me.' And again: 'I regarded myself as the most miserable being in existence, deprived of even a right to love the land that I was born in. I said to myself: "I have done no harm to any living soul, yet if I but get attached to a field, all conspire to tear me away from it, and send me wandering like a vagabond over the unknown."

The early years left Stanley permanently scarred, bottling up a volcanic rage against the world. The outward signs of this rage were neurotic symptoms like his fetishistic regard for books and his fanatical neatness. Suspicion of everyone in the world led to compulsive secretiveness. It is from this combination of deliberate obfuscation and his own genuine ignorance of his origins that much of the confusion surrounding Stanley during his career derived. One of the astonishing aspects of Stanley's story is how little solid intelligence the public possessed about his early years during his lifetime. When Stanley returned from finding Livingstone in 1872, a veritable cataclysm of ill-informed rumour burst on the public. One author asserted categorically that Stanley's real name was Howell Jones and that he had been born on 6th November 1840. Despite the accuracy of Cadwalader Rowlands' 1872 account, Stanley successfully fought his corner and persuaded the public that he had been born and bred in the USA. The next upsurge in speculation was in the late 1880s during the Emin

Pasha Expedition. An anonymous letter in The Times confidently asserted that Stanley's real name was Owen and that he was born at Mold, Flintshire. Complacency signed 'One who knows', this farrago of nonsense was refuted a week later by one signing himself 'One who knows better.' Only in the 1890s did the main outline of Stanley's life become clear. But Stanley was successful in keeping much hidden. Yet it is hardly surprising that the identity of the man should so long remain obscure to the public, when its possessor remained fundamentally uncertain of it himself. The existentialist cliché about man constantly recreating his own identity has never seemed so apt as it does in the case of H. M. Stanley'.

Chapter Two

ANY idea that young Stanley had escaped from the determinism of life with his relatives into a new realm of freedom was dispelled within days on the Windermere. He learned he was not to be a cabin-boy but merely one more unit of sweated labour aloft. Giving him just enough time to find his sea-legs, the brutal mate soon had him swabbing the decks in heaving seas, Boston, the Windermere's home port, was legendary at the time for its 'death ships' and brutal officers. Moreover, Stanley learned from his fellow victims that the voyage to New Orleans was certain to be a one-way trip. Now at last he realised why Captain Hardinge had been so ready to sign him on. Hardinge and his officers ran a racket which involved pocketing the wages of their deckhands. Their method was simple. They made their young charges' lives such hell on board that the boys would jump ship at the first port rather than endure further brutality.

The routine savagery on board the Windermere was compounded by a conditioned reflex usage of oaths and obscenity. This was St Asaph's raised to a new power. The second mate, Nelson, really was the brute Stanley later accused Francis of being. Ever the survivor, Stanley set about finding protective cover. He ingratiated himself with the cook, Long Hart, who enthralled him with tales of storm-tossed rounding's of Cape Horn and voyages to Africa. He received less of the rope's end than three young Irish stowaways who were uncovered on the fifth day out and who lacked the wit to deflect the mate's worst excesses of brutish violence.

Gradually Stanley inured himself to the hardships of life at sea. He found a violent storm in the Bay of Biscay exhilarating rather than frightening. But he failed to establish any rapport with his peers - the below-decks seamen. This increased his sense of paranoia and his conviction that suspicion and mistrust should be his watchword:

From this date began, I think, the noting of a strange coincidence, which has been so common with me that I accept it as a rule. When I pray for a man, it happens that at that moment he is cursing me; when I praise, I am slandered; if I commend, I am reviled; if I feel affectionate or sympathetic towards one, it is my fate to be detested or scorned by him. I first noticed this curious coincidence on board the Windermere. I bore no grudge, and thought no evil of any person, but prayed for all, morning and evening, extolled the courage, strength and energy of my ship-mates, likened them to sea-lions, and felt it an honour to be in the company of such brave men; but, invariably, they damned my eyes, my face, my heart, my soul, my person, my nationality; I was damned aft, and damned forward. I was wholly obnoxious to everyone aboard, and the only service they asked of God towards me was that He should damn me to all eternity.

This sounds very like humbug. If true, it argues for a naivety astonishing in one who had been through the workhouse experience. More likely, it suggests that Stanley had not mastered the art of charm without sycophancy.

On the fifty-second day out from Liverpool, the Windermere dropped anchor off the mouth of the Mississippi. A tug took the vessel 100 miles up the river to New Orleans. From the wharves drifted the smell of green coffee, fermenting molasses, Stockholm tar, brine, rum and whisky drippings. Hundreds of ships lay alongside the quays. Multitudes of men of all races were busy sifting the barrels, hogsheads and bales. There was a chaos of horses, mules, drays and wagons. In places the freight lay in mountainous heaps.

Within minutes of docking, Stanley and a cabin-boy called Harry were the only crew members left aboard the Windermere. The rest had all dispersed to the crimp-houses, clip-joints and stews of New Orleans. At sunset the two boys finally got shore leave. Stanley and his companion reeled through the streets in a state of sensuous intoxication. After a while the street-wise Harry suggested that they enter a 'bar' for some refreshment. The naive Stanley agreed. When four young girls entered the room in their underwear, he realised he was in a brothel and fled in terror. Already the legacy of St Asaph's was such as to leave Stanley quaking in terror at any overt demonstration of sexuality.

Next day, finding to their surprise and anger that the 'Welsh monkey' was still aboard, Hardinge and Nelson tightened the screws to achieve their desired effect. They set Stanley to cleaning brass work, then found fault with his efforts and kicked and clouted him. It became clear that this was a war of attrition that the eighteen-year-old could not win. That night he emptied his sea-bag, put on his best clothes and, armed with just the Bible that Bishop Short had given him, stole ashore. He spent the night in a mound of cotton bales.

Next morning he set out to find employment for, as he remarked, 'the absolutely penniless has a choice of two things, work or starve'. On Tchapitoulas Street the sun was already hot at 6.30 a.m. Half an hour later he came to a warehouse billed as the property of Speake and McCreary, wholesale merchants. Lolling outside, reading a newspaper, was a bearded, middle-aged man in a dark alpaca suit. Taken with his air of distinction Stanley tried on him the Dickensian line, 'Do you want a boy, sir?'

The upshot was that after a quick literacy test the man took the 'boy' to his manager Mr Speake and Stanley was given a week's trial at $5 a week. Ensconced in an attic room in a respectable boarding house, Stanley exerted all his efforts during the week's probation. At the end of the week Speake told him that he was now permanently engaged as a junior clerk at $25 a month. After paying for board and lodging, Stanley was left with a monthly surplus of $ 15. To a former workhouse boy this was the wealth of Croesus.

By this time Stanley was learning something of his original benefactor. He was rather more than the 'agent' he had humbly described himself as; he was in fact a wealthy cotton broker with an established reputation in New Orleans. Dazzled by the reputation of his benefactor and by his many kindnesses, the youth decided to jettison his given name of John Rowlands in favour of that of his protector: Stanley. From 1859 onwards Rowlands was Henry Stanley, though the name 'Morton' took longer to be fixed.

As his protégé continued to make impressive progress as a clerk, Stanley senior increasingly took him under his wing. He began by inviting him to his house for Sunday breakfast. He introduced the young man to his wife; the couple were childless. Stanley was bowled over by the refinement and elegance of the first 'lady' he had ever known. But although husband and wife treated the young man as a son, ultimately the impact of Mrs Stanley was baneful. By putting her on a pedestal Stanley set up an impossible feminine ideal for actual women to match. He was in danger of falling into the trap of the Madonna/whore syndrome: there were 'women' like his mother and the other fallen creatures of St Asaph's and the New Orleans brothels; and there were 'ladies' like the wife of his benefactor. In this respect his own testimony is eloquent:

It was at this hour I made the discovery of the immense distance between a lady and a mere woman; and while I gazed at her clear, lustrous eyes, and noted the charms which played about her features, I was thinking that, if a lady could be so superior to an ordinary housewife, with her careless manner of speech, and matter-of-fact ways, what a beautiful thing an angel must be!

Gradually Stanley learned the true story of his protector, though he suppressed this in the Autobiography for his own self-serving ends. Henry Hope Stanley had been born in Stockport, Cheshire, which was why the Welsh lilt of the young vagabond had initially so intrigued him. His business career in New Orleans spanned the years 1838-78. He first came to the United States in 1836. After a short period in Charleston, South Carolina, he left for Texas where he married the first Mrs Stanley. Moving to New Orleans, they began by opening a boarding house on Dorsiere near Canal Street. His first wife died in 1843 without issue, but shortly before that the couple had adopted a three-year-old girl, Joanne.

Meanwhile Stanley senior's business career was thriving. He began in the cedar trade but soon diversified into sugar, cotton and iron foundries. By 1846 he was wealthy enough to make a trip back to his native England, where he met and married the fifteen-year-old Frances Meller. The woman who so entranced the young Stanley was thus twenty-eight at the time of the Sunday breakfasts. The entire Meller clan then followed Stanley back to New Orleans where they lived on Live Oak (Constance) Street in Old Lafayette (now the Fourth district).

Contemporary accounts describe Stanley senior as having a 'roast- beef' complexion and side whiskers with no moustache. He was said to give generously to charity but to have a tendency to switch business partners more often than was considered sound. His restlessness led him to move from cedar into cotton in a big way. In 1858 he operated a cotton-weighing business (the Mississippi Cotton Press) together with partners named Wright and Eager from offices at Exchange Place and Iberville (132-4

Exchange Place). By the mid-i850s he moved to a house at 904 Orange Street in Annunciation Square. In addition, he owned a huge plantation called Jefferson Hall in Tangipa Hoa parish near Areola. It was at Orange Street and Areola that young Stanley was to spend much of 1859.

The women in the life of Henry Hope Stanley seemed to have been singularly ill-starred. His second wife was also childless. When they adopted a girl, Annie, the experiment did not prove a success. Annie eloped with a suitor violently opposed by her foster-father. Meanwhile Joanne married and died young.

Given the fondness of both Stanleys for their young protégé, it was not surprising that Stanley was soon a son in all but name. Henry Hope taught him the business and gave him a responsible position on the Areola plantation. He also encouraged his self-education. Under his mentor's tutelage Stanley devoured Shakespeare, Byron, Irving, Goldsmith, Ben Jonson, and Cowper. But, as with Stanley's admiration for his adopted 'mother', a pathological element began to creep in. His obsession with books as the perfect barrier between himself and the physical world, especially the world of sexuality, became almost fetishistic: 'without them [his adopted parents], probably my love of books would have proved sufficient safeguard against the baser kinds of temptations; but with them, I was rendered almost impregnable to vice.' The other neurotic symptom in evidence in New Orleans was an obsessive tidiness, which first manifested itself in the months at the Speake store, before Stanley senior moved him on to Areola.

We can infer that sexuality gnawed away at Stanley in this period from a revealing story he relates in the Autobiography which, while unconvincing naturalistically, is of great symbolic importance. He tells us that in his early period in New Orleans, while still at Mrs Williams' boarding house, he shared his room and his large four-poster bed with 'Dick Heaton', ostensibly a Liverpool cabin-boy who had experienced the same sort of shipboard brutality as himself. Stanley noticed that 'Dick' never undressed at night and always shrank from touching him in the four-poster. Eventually the secret came out: 'Dick' was really a girl in boy's clothes and her name was Alice. We may conjecture that the proximate source for this fantasy was the Shakespearian comedies Stanley was reading at the time. But there is a more profound meaning for the fantasy. It is utterly implausible for a former inmate of St Asaph's to tell us, as Stanley does, that he knew nothing of female anatomy and had never seen a girl's breasts before. The true significance of the tale is Stanley's uncertainty about his own sexual identity.

Stanley was soon at home in the country of his adoption. He liked the cosmopolitan atmosphere of New Orleans and the absence of rigid social stratification based on externals of class like name, accent and education. The American myth of' log-cabin to White House' had an obvious appeal for a workhouse brat. But he was less happy with his adopted father. At first all went well. Stanley senior helped the young man to overcome his more obvious feelings of inferiority: 'I don't know', he said, 'what the customs of the Welsh people may be, but here we regard personal character and worth, not pedigree. With us, people are advanced not for what their parentage may have been, but for what they are themselves. 'So far so good. But there were from the earliest days signs that Stanley pre et fils were too alike in temperament to be really comfortable with each other. The taciturn Henry Hope reprimanded his 'son' for too much idle talk. He reinforced Stanley's feeling that books were to be used as an artificial barrier against 'low company' and the conversation of idlers. He was moody, and young Stanley found this hard to deal with. Most of all, he was short-tempered, like his charge, and this caused a lot of friction. 'A choleric disposition on his part would have been as a flame to my nature, and the result might have been guessed,' writes Stanley in the conditional, hinting at what actually happened.

Sometime around the end of 1859 or early 1860 a decisive rupture took place. The causes of the quarrel remain obscure, but the result was that Stanley senior sent his refractory protégé to work on a friend's plantation in Arkansas. Stanley's answer to this development was of a piece with his treatment of earlier father-figures: he simply 'killed off' his protector. At this point the Autobiography becomes a heady brew of deliberately confusing chronology and out-and-out fantasy. After paying a fulsome tribute to his adopted father, Stanley announces that his own departure for Arkansas followed the death of the second Mrs Stanley by fever and the subsequent voyage to Cuba by the grief-stricken Henry Hope. While he was in Arkansas, Stanley continues, he heard the dreadful news that his protector and father had died. In this tragic way ended his connection with the Stanley family from whom he had taken his name.

All of this is a tissue of lies. Henry Hope Stanley's wife did not die in 1859 but on 9 April 1878, aged forty-six, in New Orleans. Henry Hope Stanley himself dropped dead six months later (November 1878) at sixty-seven, at Foley Plantation, in Assumption parish on Bayou Lafourche. He left an estate of $130,000 but not a penny of it went to his adopted son. Henry Hope gave instructions after the quarrel in 1859-60 that Stanley's name was never again to be mentioned in his presence.

Even more astonishing than the pack of lies in the Autobiography is the fantasy Stanley concocted for his own amusement in his private diaries. Here he records a scene, as if it were actuality, in which he tearfully views his protector's corpse:

For the first time I understood the sharpness of the pang which pierces the soul when a loved one lies with folded hands icy cold in the eternal sleep. As I contemplated the body I vexed myself with asking. Had my conduct been as perfect as I then wished it had been? Had I failed in aught? Had I esteemed him as he deserved? Then a craving wish to hear him speak but one word of consolation, to utter one word of blessing made me address him as though he might hear. But no answer ever came, and I experienced a shiver of sadness, and then wished I could join him. There are many curious aspects of the 'death' of Henry Stanley senior. To lie to the world is one thing; to lie to oneself in the privacy of one's diary argues for serious neurosis. But there is more. Some unconscious guilt about this 'parricide' led Stanley to leave clues in the Autobiography that might suggest to the perceptive reader that his story of Henry Hope's death is false and that it was a quarrel that severed the relationship. Not for the last time the carapace of 'character-armour' with which Stanley shielded himself was betrayed by unconscious manifestations of self disgust and worthlessness.

Stanley's life in 1860-61 presents a tangled, deliberately obfuscated skein, of which only the main outlines are visible. He roamed the Mississippi and its lower tributaries: the Washita, Saline and Arkansas rivers. At various times he visited St Louis, Cairo, Memphis, Vicksburg, and Natchez. He learned the arts of the bargees and flat-boatmen. Later he ventured farther afield, to Cincinnati and Louisville: 'at one time I was profound in the statistics relating to population, commerce, and navigation of the Southern and South-Western states.' The Autobiography is full of stories of derring-do on the Mississippi, armed robberies, knife fights, duels between gamblers, some of which Stanley may have witnessed but which assuredly lost nothing in the telling. It is not easy to determine whether these journeys were part of his duties on the Arkansas river or (more likely) periods of self-assigned furlough during which Stanley picked up odd jobs as he went.

The Arkansas episode itself is obscure both in provenance and in chronology. Stanley tells us that he went to 'Major Ingham's plantation in Arkansas partly as a result of Stanley senior's precipitate departure to Cuba', partly as a result of his patron's desire to expand the business up-country - Stanley cannot quite decide which story he wants us to believe. The sober truth is that he was sent there in disgrace as a form of 'internal exile'. Within weeks he had quarrelled bitterly with the plantation owner - in Stanley's version because he objected to the brutality of an overseer. Bearing a letter of introduction, Stanley then moved on to a store at Cypress Bend on the Arkansas river, owned by a German-Jewish trader named Altschul. Altschul took him on as a clerk and junior salesman. This formed the basis for another Stanley fantasy, when he later claimed to have worked for a salary of £200 p.a. at this time.

There was one major problem about Cypress Bends. It was in Arkansas's swamplands. Malaria and ague were everyday hazards. Stanley quickly succumbed to fever. The attack began with a violent shaking, followed by a congealed feeling as though his blood was iced. After a couple of hours' shivering, clutching at hot-water bottles and swathed in blankets, Stanley was overtaken by twelve hours of delirium and a coda in the form of exhausting perspiration. After one bout he found that his weight had sunk to 95 pounds. It was here that he first learned to take quinine in a dosage of five grains every other hour from dawn to noon. Even so, Stanley later admitted that these Arkansas fevers had done nothing to prepare him for the far greater ravages of African disease.

The prickly and mercurial poor whites of Arkansas took some adjusting too, but Stanley was helped through his swamp baptism by the geniality of the senior salesman Cronin. Cronin, a New York Irishman, very soon attenuated the prejudices against the Irish that Stanley had learned from his workhouse mates. A heavy drinker, accomplished ladies' man and born salesman, Cronin possessed all the extrovert charm that Stanley lacked and envied. His larger-than-life personality swept all before it and overpowered the dour and hostile swamp folk. Eventually Cronin fell foul of Altschul when his employer discovered the extent of his informal harem among the black slaves.

The attack on Fort Sumter in April 1861 opened four years of bloody conflict in which more than 600,000 were to lose their lives. Feeling himself aloof from the Civil War, Stanley saw no reason to do anything but continue in his comfortable niche at Altschul's store. He felt contemptuous of the southerners who were hoist on the petard of their own code of honour and chivalry and smirked at those who enlisted in the southern armies simply because they could not endure the scorn of Dixie womanhood. He remained on the sidelines as the locals organised themselves into a company called 'the Greys'. He might well have brazened out his failure to volunteer to bear arms, even in face of a white feather. Then a female cousin of his friends the Gorees hit on a lucky idea. She sent Stanley a parcel containing a petticoat of the kind a black lady's maid might wear. This was meant to be a simple symbol of cowardice. But its powerful effect on Stanley was precisely that it tapped into fears and uncertainties about his own sexual identity. He hesitated no longer. That very afternoon he signed on for the 'Dixie Greys'.

It did not take him long to regret his hasty decision. 'Enlisting in the Confederate service, because I received a packet of female clothes, was certainly a grave blunder,' he recalled. In July 1861 the Greys were ordered up to Little Rock, where they were sworn to the service of the Confederate States for twelve months and issued with knapsacks and heavy flint-lock muskets. The swearing ceremony was presided over by General Burgevine, later to serve with 'Chinese' Gordon in the Taiping rebellion.

What Stanley found hard to come to terms with was not military discipline but anomie: what he calls 'this curious volte-face in morality', whereby what was illicit in civilian life was now permitted and encouraged, where the murderer became the hero. Rigorous physical exercise on forced marches had the effect on Stanley that his African explorations were later to have: he lost weight rapidly. In a 'state of nature' Stanley always had a tendency to run to fat; but the Spartan regime and diet of Little Rock soon slimmed down the sleek young men of Cypress Bends: Stanley records that by the end of 1861 he possessed a waspish waist, which measured a little more than two hands.

By the end of August basic training was completed. The Dixie Greys were shipped across the Arkansas river. Immediately a typhus epidemic invaded the camp and carried off large numbers of his comrades. Stanley blamed the loss of life on incompetent generalship. Southern generals, he found, were very good at strategy and organising commissariat, but were indifferent to the health and well-being of their men. No preventive measures or prophylactic diets were prescribed, so that disease in the army camps was rampant. Stanley remained unaffected and toughened his constitution by bouts of underwater swimming and diving in the Arkansas river. Then the Greys were ordered to the western front on the other side of the Mississippi. It took them until the beginning of November to reach the theatre of war.

On 7th November they observed, but did not participate in, the battle of Belmont, in which the Federal General Grant defeated the Confederate General Polk. Then the Greys were entrained at Columbus for Cave City, Kentucky, where they arrived on 25th November 1861. Here they remained quietly until February 1862, still without a taste of active combat. Doubtless because of his fear of contact with young women, Stanley boasted of his appeal for the older female and how, using the skills he had acquired when dealing with the difficult Aunt Mary, he was able to wheedle eggs and other delicacies out of farmers' wives. During the long winter Stanley won the plaudits of his peers by his skills as a forager. A daring raid on a Unionist farm secured his company a dinner of roast pork for Christmas. More tedious, however, was the resolute philistinism of his peers. Stanley had to read his Bible in secret for fear of taunts from his fellow troopers: 'and I was as ready to deny that I prayed, as Peter was to deny Christ.'

The period of 'phoney war' came to an end in mid-February. 350 miles of forced marches took the Confederates to Pittsburgh Landing where, on 6-7th April 1862, the dreadful battle of Shiloh was fought. Stanley witnessed the appalling carnage at close quarters on the first day and probably owed his survival to being taken prisoner early on the second morning of the blood-letting. There are some grounds for thinking that Stanley might deliberately have got himself taken prisoner by advancing too far too fast and thus blundering into the Federal lines. He himself explained the curious circumstances of his departure from the battlefield as an over-reaction to an imputation of cowardice from his officer.

'With my musket on the trail I found myself in active motion, more active than otherwise I should have been, perhaps, because Captain Smith had said "Now, Mr Stanley, if you please, step briskly forward!" This singling out of me wounded my amour proper and sent me forward like a rocket.' He found himself surrounded by blue uniforms and was roughly ordered to drop his gun. To his intense chagrin he was a prisoner. After Shiloh we enter a period of obscurity in Stanley's fife, where verification of his own account becomes impossible. There is a discrepancy between the Autobiography and the unofficial 'autobiography' he wrote to Katie Gough-Roberts in 1869. However, both versions agree that he served time as a prisoner of war at Camp Douglas near Chicago. It is in the sequel that the accounts diverge.

From Shiloh Stanley and several hundred other Confederate prisoners were taken by steamer to St Louis, where they arrived on 13 April 1862 and were sympathetically received by the Missourian locals, who had come within an ace of declaring for the Confederacy the year before. But the 'rebels' were soon removed from this friendly ambit to the heard and of the industrial North. The railway took them to a converted cattle-yard in the Chicago suburbs which masqueraded under the formal tide of Camp Douglas. Within the square enclosure hundreds of prisoners were herded. There were sentry-boxes every 60 yards along the walls. The guards had orders to shoot to kill anyone crossing the 'dead-line' - a perimeter denoted by a line of lime-wash. The prisoners were housed in barn-like structures of planking, each about 250 feet by 40 and accommodating between two and three hundred men. The total prisoner muster in the camp was about 3,000.

Restricted to just 30 inches of space in their bunks, with nothing to do, nothing to read and no scope for physical exercise, the prisoners began to waste away and drop like flies. Dysentery, typhus and vermin were endemic. The iron rations compounded the problem. The death-toll began to mount. Sick men could be heard at night, praying for death to take them and relieve their suffering. Many of the invalids were so debilitated that they fell into the primitive latrines while answering calls of nature and lay there for hours, moaning and inhaling the miasmata, until they were hauled out. Every morning wagons came to collect the carcasses of the deceased, much as if they had been joints of 'New Zealand frozen mutton'. In Stanley's recollection, the horrors of Camp Douglas equalled the more-trumpeted atrocities visited on Federal prisoners at Andersonville.

The only human rapport Stanley established in the camp was, first, with a fellow Confederate named W. H. Wilkes, nephew of a US Navy admiral, and, more importantly for his own survival, with the camp commissary Shipman. Stanley's tenacity as a survivor allied to his 'driven' determination to surmount all obstacles led to Shipman's appointing him a camp trusty, with responsibility for issuing rations and taking roll calls. It was Shipman who suggested to Stanley that the only way for him to avoid joining the daily swelling throng of the dead was to volunteer for the Union armies. According to Stanley, he wrestled heroically with his conscience for six weeks before falling in with the suggestion. This period of agonising is implausible, for it would mean that Shipman uniquely singled out Stanley for rescue immediately on arrival at Camp Douglas. The plain truth is that Stanley almost certainly accepted with alacrity an offer that released him from his living hell. That there is guilt about the way he evaded the fate of so many of his comrades can be inferred from the 'autobiography' he provided for Katie Gough-Roberts. Here he provides an heroic version of his escape from Camp Douglas. According to this, after three months, he broke out on a dreadful rainy night. Dodging the bullets of a dozen sentries that whined around him, he escaped by plunging into a river and swimming to liberty 'once more a free man and for the fourth time on the world'.

On 4th June 1862 Stanley took the oath of allegiance to the North and was drafted into the 1st Regiment, Illinois Light Artillery. The real Stanley, as opposed to the mythical persona portrayed in the Autobiography, would have felt no moral scruple about such apostasy. Ruthlessness and lack of integrity were to be hallmarks of the future great explorer. But neither Shipman nor the Union gained much from persuading Stanley to change sides. The pent-up virulence of Camp David dysentery almost immediately overwhelmed him. No sooner was he back in the war zone, at Harper's Ferry, than he collapsed and was rushed to an army hospital where he was pronounced unfit for active duties. On 22nd June the Union army discharged him. He was weak and penniless, but this was not an age of sentiment, above all not in wartime.

The sick man staggered off into the wilderness, clothed only in a pair of blue military trousers, a dark serge coat and a 'mongrel hat'. He could not walk 300 yards without pausing for breath. As he lay in the open under the stars, Stanley could perceive the sensation of internal bleeding. It took him a week to stagger 12 miles, half-way from Harper's Ferry to Hagerstown. Near to death, he collapsed at the Baker farm, 3 miles from Sharpsburg. He was unconscious for three days.

He awoke to find that he had fallen among Good Samaritans. He was in a clean bed, with fresh clothes on his back. The family nursed him back to health with a careful diet and allowed him to convalesce by sitting in their orchard. When he had recovered, Stanley helped the farmer gather in his harvest. He stayed with the Bakers until mid-August, building up his strength for the ordeals ahead. Stanley's mind had now concentrated on the thought that his four years in the United States had been an unmitigated disaster. Perhaps it was time to return to the land of his birth and try his luck there. He accepted the farmer's offer of his rail fare to Baltimore, where he could find a ship. Baker drove him to Hagerstown and put him on the slow train to Baltimore via Harrisburg.

On arrival in Baltimore Stanley sought out the fiancée of his fellow-prisoner W. H. Wilkes, possibly with a view to financial assistance. Nothing came of the interview. Stanley then found a temporary job on an oyster schooner. The accidental drowning of the captain brought that episode to an end. A few weeks later Stanley found what he was looking for: the opportunity to work his passage across the Atlantic. He signed on with the sailing-ship E. Sherman for a month's voyage to Liverpool.

Once in Liverpool, in November 1862, Stanley set out to walk the 40 miles to Denbigh. He was very poor, his clothes were shabby and a recrudescence of Camp David fever left him in poor health. But he was buoyed up by the thought that he was now a man, with battle honours. Surely this time his mother would welcome him with open arms and the memory of their workhouse encounter would be expunged. There was, too, the thought that her material circumstances had improved. Stanley had learned from the Morrises in Liverpool that his mother, now forty, had married Robert Jones, father of two of her children, on 20 August 1860 at St Asaph. Jones had given up his job as a plasterer to take up the tenancy of the Cross Foxes Inn at Glascoed near Abergale.

What followed was one of the searing experiences of Stanley's life. His mother received him coldly, grudgingly provided him with a single night's lodging and gave him a shilling next morning to take him back to Liverpool. There is some suggestion that Elizabeth Parry (now Jones) was suffering from depression because of the recent death from meningitis of her son James. At any rate she told Stanley that his arrival in such clothes and without means disgraced her and her husband in the eyes of the neighbours. She added this warning: 'Never come back to me unless you come better dressed and in better circumstances than you seem to be in now.'

Stanley was so choked with emotions of rejection and rage that he could not bring himself to record in his diary anything more than the bare fact of his rebuff; only in the Autobiography did his wife reveal some of the trauma he experienced. Such a profound wound cut the ground from under his aspirations for a new life in Wales. He decided to return to the New World. He obtained new clothes and £16 from 'relations of his second father' (this presumably refers to Henry Hope Stanley rather than his stepfather Robert Jones)

From November 1862 to August 1864 the Stanley trail goes cold. Just a few cryptic diary entries enable us to track his progress. 'December 1862. Ship Ernestine. New York.' is followed by the occasional jotting indicating service as an able seaman in the Merchant Navy, generally on voyages between Boston and Mediterranean ports: Mentone, Palermo, Cette. That he got a close look at Barcelona during 1863 is demonstrated by two separate entries from two different diaries. 'May 1863, Barcelona, Barque Jehu, naked night. Barracks of carabineers.' And again: 'Wrecked off Barcelona, crew lost, in the night. Stripped naked and swam to shore. Barrack of carabineers. . . demanded my papers!' It has been convincingly demonstrated that these two accounts blend faulty memory and deliberate fantasy (we have already noted that Stanley had no problem about lying to himself). In the first place a 250-ton Boston vessel, arrived in Barcelona in June, not May. Secondly, and more importantly, it was not shipwrecked. The truth is that Stanley deserted his ship in Barcelona harbour by diving into the sea with a pack. While swimming to land he lost this bundle, containing his clothes. A sentry found him on the shore and locked him in the case for the night. He was then released and made his way through Catalonia as a vagabond. Once across the French frontier he was arrested at Narbonne, freed shortly after, thence worked his passage back to the USA.

In October 1863 Stanley gave up seafaring for a time and tried his hand as a lawyer's clerk. His employer was Judge Thomas Irwin Hughes of Brooklyn, a notary public who lived at 313 Ryerson Street. Once again Stanley's talent for finding employment that ended with a melodramatic flourish was in evidence. One night the judge, in a rare state of intoxication, tried to murder his wife with a hatchet; Stanley had to restrain him. The reward for an outsider's intervention in a marital quarrel was the usual one: the next morning the judge's wife turned on Stanley and raved at him for smoking in her house.

The record for early 1864 is equally vague. The diary entries hint at another Merchant Navy voyage, this time to the West Indies; but confusingly other accounts place Stanley in Hughes' offices at Cedar Street, Lower Manhattan. It seems to have been under the influence of an acquaintance (possibly a former employee) of Judge Hughes, who met Stanley first at Cedar Street, that he took the momentous decision to re-enter the Civil War for the third time. Louis R. Stegman was on leave from Sherman's army and argued the federal cause eloquently, as well as the possible rich pickings to be made in journalism." When Stegman returned to active service in Georgia, Stanley decided to put his service in the merchant marine to good use by enlisting for three years in the Federal Navy. Ironically, immediately on joining up on 19th July 1864, he was entered as a 'landsman' (non-sailor).

Exhortations and cajolery from Stegman (who was the same age as Stanley) notwithstanding, the decision to re-enter the arena of fratricidal blood-letting seems odd in the light of Stanley's earlier experiences. The reason he gave to journalists later - that he was in danger of arrest by the Federal authorities as an escaped prisoner - is pure nonsense and depends for its effect on the suppression of the true story of his departure from Camp David. The explanation almost certainly lies deeper and has to do with the imperatives of a man of action. As Wassermann has postulated, Stanley was driven by a constant need for momentum in his life: 'his thoughts are relevant to actions and not to other thoughts." The catch is that the more one lives for action alone, the less is one capable of discrimination about which actions are valuable; hence the near-mania of the Alexanders, Napoleons, Caesars and Cromwells. So although Stanley's apparent reasons for re-enlistment seem tenuous, at a deeper level they make psychological sense.

Stanley's first ship in the US Navy was the North Carolina. The rank of 'landsman' was an inferior grade to sailor so that there is a certain mystery about how Stanley was entered under this heading. Even more surprisingly, Stanley's first work aboard ship was as a cook; Stanley apparently took pride in his alleged prowess as a short-order cook. After three weeks, Stanley was transferred to the Minnesota at Hampton Roads, Commodore Joseph Lanman commanding. Here his superior handwriting was noticed and he was made ship's clerk. It was while he was discharging this duty that he made the acquaintance of a fifteen-year-old youth, Lewis Noe, who had recently enlisted in a fit of bravado and was employed as ship's messenger. Noe is a key figure in Stanley's life in more ways than one. Although Stanley and his powerful friends later went to great lengths to blacken his character, Noe was a truthful witness whose testimony always emerges well from any testing against unimpeachable sources.

As messenger Noe was in daily contact with the ship's clerk and was able to observe Stanley closely. All his observations tally closely with other recorded impressions. Stanley was always very tactful when dealing with the powerful, but was cold and aloof with his peers. He scarcely spoke to anyone in a social way and sat by himself and read whenever he had the chance. He was an excellent penman, could write a dozen different kinds of hands, and could forge anyone's signature within seconds of seeing it.

From Noe's evidence we can appreciate the nature and extent of the fantasies Stanley wove out of his basically unadventurous period of service on the Minnesota. Some of his exaggerations are harmless enough, as when he expands being ship's clerk under a commodore into being the private secretary of an admiral and securing promotion as an ensign at a salary £350 p.a. But some of his lies are more serious. Stanley claimed that after four months he was transferred to the USS Ticonderoga. Noe denied that such a transfer ever took place; the US Navy records bear him out. Not content with this fictitious 'promotion', Stanley proceeded to turn himself into the hero of the late naval battles of the Civil War. Here it is important to be meticulous in the separation of fact from fantasy. On 20th December the combined naval armour of the Federal fleet bombarded Fort Fisher, North Carolina, which guarded the entrances to the blockade-running Confederate port of Wilmington. After a desperate struggle, the Federal Navy was beaten off. Stanley observed the action from the Minnesota which was engaged on the outer fringes of the action and wrote up his perceptions in colourful prose - his first sustained act as a writer.

In January 1865 the US Navy returned to the assault. By this time, according to himself, Stanley had been transferred to the Ticonderoga. But Stanley was neither on the Ticonderoga nor in any way involved in this second battle. This did not prevent him from concocting his most elaborate fantasy yet, in which he becomes the hero of the entire engagement. In Stanley's version, he swam 500 yards under fire and tied a rope to a Confederate ship, so that the Ticonderoga was able to secure her as a prize.

It was in fact precisely the inaction on board the Minnesota and the lack of a proper stage on which to parade his talents that led Stanley to desert in February 1865. By this time Stanley had taken the young Noe under his wing. He bestowed on the youth the signal favour of showing him a photograph of Elizabeth Parry; he told Noe he was the only person in the world to whom he had shown it. Stanley outlined his plans for getting free from the irksome three-year naval indentures. The two of them would make all ready and dress in their civilian clothes. Then they would put on their sailor suits over the 'civvies' and simply walk through the dockyard gate with a pass signed by the commodore, which Stanley would forge.

The opportunity came when the Minnesota put in for repairs at Portsmouth, New Hampshire. On 10th February 1865 Stanley and Noe walked blithely out of the gates of the naval yard, flourishing the 'commodore's pass'.

STANLEY

Chapter Three

THE sequel to the desertion was not quite what Stanley had hoped. He had confided to Noe his ambition to acquire enough money for passage to the Middle East where they would surely make their fortunes. He proposed to raise the passage money by 'bounty jumping': he would 'persuade' Noe to enlist, then collect the bounty payable to anyone raising recruits for the Union army; Noe would then desert, Stanley would re-enlist him under another name at another recruiting centre, collect a fresh tranche of bounty, and so on, until they had raised the necessary sum. But when Noe visited his parents at Sayville, Long Island, and told them he had deserted, they were appalled and filled his head with the terrors of hanging if he was caught. In a panic Noe went out and joined the Eighth New York Mounted Volunteers under Colonel Pope. He used the assumed name Lewis Morton that Stanley had earlier suggested as the first of his bounty-jumping aliases.

Stanley was furious at seeing his plans lying in ruins. After vainly trying to persuade Noe to desert again (offering to meet him at a rendezvous with civilian clothes), he reluctantly concluded that the money he needed for his Eastern enterprise would have to be earned in some other way. For a short time he worked in the office of a lawyer called Lyon (or Lyons).While he was there, the Civil War ended, on Palm Sunday 1865. The following Friday was one of the most traumatic days in American history. Stanley noted in his diary in a typical juxtaposition of the sublime and the ridiculous: 'New York. Assassination of Lincoln. Great Excitement. Office of Evening Post.' The subtext of the last cryptic sentence was that Stanley was already making the rounds of newspaper offices, hawking the pieces he had written on the Fort Fisher bathes. Evidently the advice proffered was that it was a mistake to try to start at the top, that he should try to work his way up from the provincial press. Some time shortly after 9th May 1865, Stanley took the advice and set out for St Louis, where he had contacts from his Southern days.

In St Louis in June the editor of the Missouri Democrat was sufficiently impressed by Stanley's Civil War writing to accept him as an 'occasional' - someone whose freelance material would at least be considered and not consigned to the 'slush-pile'. He suggested that Stanley's best chance of obtaining 'good copy' was in the West. Stanley moved on. By late June he was in St Joseph, Missouri and in July had got as far as Salt Lake City. In early August he reached San Francisco after travelling over the high Sierras through the Donner pass.

We know little of Stanley's sojourn in California beyond the fact that he, like most nineteenth-century travellers, found the scenery bewitching. But he did not tarry there long. He doubled back to Colorado, spent a short while roughing it at Pike's Peak mining camp, and made a brief stopover at Denver City. 4th September 1865 saw him in Black Hawk City, Colorado, which remained his base until January 1866.

In Black Hawk City Stanley began as a day-labourer at $5 a day in the Lyons & Co. smelting works. He opened a bank account and began to save in earnest for his projected trip, now taking shape more clearly in his mind as 'Asia Minor'. Meanwhile he continued to bombard the Colorado newspaper with letters drawing attention to his literary abilities. Freemasonry was beginning to make strides in the Colorado mining communities; ever the opportunist, Stanley quickly set himself up as the head of a Templar's lodge.

Taking orders from an overseer was not, however, something that a man of Stanley's authoritarian personality could stomach long. His natural pugnacity soon surfaced. Fortunately for him, it won the attention of the Lyons management. A new quartz crusher had just been installed at the smelting works. The owner and his new superintendent, a man named Johnson, watched as the men shovelled quartz into the crusher. Aware of their presence, a burly foreman tried to impress them with his leadership qualities. He bawled at Stanley to shovel the quartz in faster. When the shift ended, Stanley challenged the foreman to a fight for the insult and offered him the choice of fists, knives or pistols. There was always something deeply frightening about Stanley when he was in this mood. The foreman evidently intuited that if he fought he would have to kill or be killed. He settled for an apology. When Johnson heard of the incident, he was so impressed that he invited Stanley to share his bachelor quarters with him. The arrangement lasted until Stanley left Black Hawk City.

Sometime around the end of January 1866 Stanley threw up his job at the smelting works and decided to try his luck in Central City. The Lyons contact secured him a job as a bookkeeper. He got on well with everyone in the business community, but already the itch for constant action was plaguing him. He was not getting on fast enough. He fantasised about going gold-prospecting in Alaska once he had learned the rudiments of mining and panning. According to one story, Stanley passed up an opportunity to join an Alaskan expedition because he was besotted by a Mormon's black-haired daughter, who rode into town occasionally for provisions. This seems to be another of Stanley's Madonnas that he worshipped from afar, for the story continues that the infatuation fizzled out when the Mormon family left for Omaha.

Feeling frustrated, Stanley abandoned bookkeeping when he got the offer of an apprenticeship as a printer with the Miner's Daily Register. This opportunity certainly seemed to take him closer to the journalistic fame for which he already hungered. But the editor did not pay his apprentice printers very much. Stanley was forced to alternate his printing with periods of prospecting. He began to work the Huff Lode in Central City. This was the time when he burnt his arm in an open fire as he was cooking a meal for his comrades. Nothing daunted, Stanley used the resultant scar as the raw material for a new fantasy: ever afterwards he told enquirers that the scar was the wound from an Indian arrow.

Stanley needed quick results, which his gold-prospecting was not providing. Printing, too, required sustained application for many years to yield fruit. Ever impatient and greedy for success now, Stanley conceived an audacious plan for a financial breakthrough, which he did not dare reveal even to his closest associates. But to achieve his end, he needed at least the passage money to 'Asia Minor'.

It was at this point that William Harlow Cook entered Stanley's life in a big way. Stanley had known Cook since his Black Hawk days, ever since Cook sent him a congratulatory piece on an article published in a Central City sheet. Cook, like Stanley, was an aspiring freelance journalist, but he utterly lacked Stanley's toughness, willpower and ruthlessness. Cook comes across in his reminiscences as an essentially negative personality, absurdly deferential to Stanley and credulous to a degree. Unlike Noe's testimony, Cook's 'evidence' is largely a rehash of Stanley fantasies or an endorsement of his lies. Such a companion, who automatically accepted Stanley's leadership and showed no independent spirit, was exactly what Stanley relished. He decided that he would take Cook with him on his daring 'Asia Minor' adventure. But first the two of them had to reach a standard of physical fitness necessary for the rigours Stanley saw ahead. He suggested, and Cook acquiesced in, a boat journey down the Missouri.

The first stage was to float down the Platte River in a flat-bottomed boat. The two men left Central City on 6 May 1866 and proceeded by stage to Denver. There Stanley supervised the construction of a boat for the 700-mile voyage down the Platte to Omaha. The timid Cook was aware that he was involved in a perilous project, since the melting spring snow from the mountains made the Platte a raging torrent at this time of the year.

They were both raw amateurs at navigating a flat-bottom in a river. They began the voyage by striking a tree in midstream but recovered and soon began to learn valuable lessons about currents and other aspects of river navigation - lessons that were to be put to good use many years later on the Congo. But on the seventh night out, they hit a large tree in midstream, which capsized the boat, spilling Cook and Stanley into the icy waters of the Platte. Here Stanley's abilities as a swimmer proved their worth. Even though the empty boat had been carried over the tree and downstream by the raging flood, Stanley managed to outrun it along the shore. At a suitable point he plunged into the waters and pulled the boat to the shore. The two of them then turned the boat upside down and slept under it, shivering in wet blankets.

Next morning Stanley again entered the swirling waters of the Platte, diving deep in hopes of recovering a prized rifle and revolver, but in vain. They trekked on wearily to Fort Laramie, in hopes of succour, but the military commandant took one look at their ragged and dishevelled state and put them under restraint as suspected army deserters. He did not actually arrest them but warned them not to leave the settlement until he had completed his enquiries.

Stanley was determined that all his plans would not be baulked by this pipsqueak captain commanding the garrison. He was not prepared to waste his hard-earned money on subsistence in Fort Laramie while the captain put the slow-grinding wheels of army bureaucracy into action. To a man of Stanley's aggressiveness, an army officer was no more formidable than the foreman at Black Hawk. Calmly he ate dinner in a small hotel in town, loaded up with provisions for the onward journey.

The captain had Stanley and Cook under surveillance and watched their preparations for departure. The two men returned to the hotel to pay their bill and depart. When they turned to leave they found the way barred by the captain. He glared at them. 'Do you want me to put you under arrest?' he challenged. Stanley fixed him with the look that so terrified Noe and Cook and replied, hand ostentatiously on revolver: 'Yes, if you have men enough to do it.' The captain knew this was no bluff and that blood would have to be shed. If the two men were not deserters, a full-blown scandal might erupt and his army career could be ruined. Like the foreman before him, he decided that discretion was the better part of valour. After a momentary hesitation, he stood aside and let the men walk out.

Stanley re-launched the boat and they continued downriver to Plattsmouth and Nebraska. Eleven days brought them to Omaha, reached on 27 May 1866. From there they took a steamer to St Louis, then carried on to New York by train via Chicago and Niagara Falls.

In New York they stayed for four days at the Richmond Hotel. Stanley visited Noe, with whom he had corresponded regularly from Colorado. He persuaded Noe's parents to allow the seventeen-year-old to accompany him on his proposed trip to Turkey. He smoothed over the parents' anxieties and convinced them that the desertion from the Minnesota had been no more than a youthful indiscretion. Wisely, Noe had not mentioned the 'bounty-jumping' proposal at home. To simple folk, Stanley's Asia Minor project seemed plausible. He argued that precious stones, diamonds and rubies, plus shawls and fabrics, could be picked up in Central Asia for next to nothing, then resold in the USA for huge profits. Noe's mother and father - and his influential sister - gave the scheme their blessing.

Next Stanley introduced Cook to Noe. The two did not get on. Cook had been Stanley's fidus Achates in Colorado, but he immediately sensed that Noe was more important to Stanley. From that moment Cook's antipathy to Noe was to be marked. But the trio at once set off for Boston, where they booked passage for Smyrna on a fruit ship, the E. H. Yarington, under Captain Mayo. They waited nearly a month in Boston (from 16th June on). The ship cleared from Boston on 10th July 1866.

The first shock for Noe on what was to be a deeply traumatic expedition was to find that Stanley expected him to work his passage across the Atlantic. The youth found this all the more galling since Stanley himself shipped out as a passenger and spent much of his time reading. Cook recalled that Stanley tried to improve his marksmanship by shooting at sea birds from the poop deck, but without any success. He also showed Cook some verses he had written. Cook's verdict was: 'If it did not reveal poetic genius, it showed at any rate that he had read history to some advantage.

'When the ship passed Trafalgar just before entering the Straits of Gibraltar, Stanley composed a poem on Nelson's victory, based on his own Minnesota experiences; to Cook this seemed slightly odd, as Stanley was forever dinning into him his admiration for Alexander the Great and Napoleon.

After fifty-one uneventful days they arrived at Smyrna (modern Izmir) on 28th August. Stanley entered in his diary his plans for a crossing of Asia that would take the three of them to China. But first he accompanied the captain on a visit to the US Consul. The consul was less than taken with Stanley's smart-alec riposte when he (the consul) asked Captain Mayo for details of his cargo. 'Missionaries and whisky,' quipped Stanley. On a more serious note, Stanley soon settled down with maps and charts and began to learn phrasebook Turkish. He appeared to have the flair of a linguist. Cook relates: 'He was soon able to speak it sufficiently well and this combined with his extraordinary intuitive perception made it possible to travel through the country without the aid of guides or dragomen, who are only so many leeches on the traveller.'

Stanley and his two companions left Smyrna singularly ill-equipped for a journey to China. After the purchase of two inferior horses and some cheap cooking utensils, the total Stanley war-chest amounted to no more than $5 gold; the entire stock was worth no more than $100. Noe was again reminded of his inferior status on the expedition by having to trudge along on foot while the other two rode.

Stanley wrote a detailed narrative of his Turkish adventure, in addition to his diary entries. The narrative conveys an admiration for the antiquities of Asia Minor combined with a lip-curling contempt for modern Turkey: 'the Turks are a degraded, semi-barbarous nation, ignorant and extremely superstitious.' The narrative abounds with admiring references to Alexander the Great, Croesus and Cyrus; Stanley confesses himself bowled over by the acropolis at Sardis. But whenever modern Turkey puts in an appearance, the sour note is evident: even Turkish women, Stanley remarks, are 'not as prepossessing as our American women'. At the town of Cassaba, reached on 6th September, Stanley was more interested in the way his horses munched the grass than in the everyday life of the locals.

Perhaps out of boredom Stanley indulged Noe in his tendency towards juvenile delinquency and even joined in himself. This disposition led to trouble with the Turks as early as the second day out. There was bad blood between Noe and Cook; Noe, encouraged surreptitiously by Stanley, decided to have a good laugh at Cook's expense. He set fire to some bushes near where they were camped and thoroughly alarmed the timid and circumspect Cook. When Cook saw Stanley laughing at his alarm, it deepened his feelings of hostility towards Noe. Stanley was cleverly playing off one of his minions against the other, ensuring that when he came to deal with Noe in his own way, he would have no trouble from Cook.

The trouble on this occasion came from the locals. The fire spread into a briar hedge and threatened to damage peasant property. The village police took Stanley and Cook into custody but Noe angered his mentor by decamping back towards Smyrna. The glib-tongued Stanley soon talked his way out of trouble in the village and browbeat the locals by brandishing his American papers. Then he and Cook doubled back to find Noe.

The fact that Noe had deserted them deeply angered Stanley. It gave him the pretext to work out his erotic fantasies on the seventeen-year-old. For by now even Cook had sensed something of the truth - that Stanley's attachment for this unprepossessing youth he called his 'half-brother' contained a repressed homosexual element. Unable to find an outlet for his erotic energies through heterosexual contact - because of his deep fear of women - and too deeply imprinted by the sense of sin he had acquired in a Calvinistic childhood to become an active homosexual, Stanley rationalised his problems by sado-masochism. The obtaining of sexual satisfaction by cruelty alone contained too large a ballast of guilt; it had therefore to be balanced in Stanley's psyche by a compensating masochistic element: redemption through suffering.

In his dealings with Noe it was the sadistic element that predominated. Stanley began his campaign to crush Noe's will by impressing on him that he was a servant pure and simple. To test his mettle, he sent Noe on some minor thieving excursions in the neighbouring villages. He told him ominously, 'Remember, you are here to do my bidding. If I tell you to cut a man's throat, you do it.'

It was shortly after the visit to Sardis that Stanley revealed his sexual hand. He and Noe were passing through a pomegranate forest; Cook was riding some way ahead, for Stanley habitually used him in this way as a scout. Suddenly Stanley got down from his horse, bound Noe's hands and then lashed him to a tree. 'I am going to give you the damnedest thrashing you ever had,' he told him. He ripped the shirt from Noe's back, then cut a switch from the grove, taking care to leave the knots in the wood exposed. Then he scourged Noe with the primitive whip until the blood ran. It seemed to Noe that the whipping went on for hours. As Stanley rested between strokes of the switch, he rehearsed the many occasions when Noe had angered him, some of them dating back to their service on the Minnesota. But the particular source of his anger seemed to be Noe's enlistment in New York without his consent. When the whipping ended, Stanley 'comforted' his victim by telling him that he had shown his mettle by taking it so well. Noe, with scabs from the wounds that did not heal for another five days, understandably found this scant consolation.

Why did Noe tolerate this behaviour? In part the answer is that he did not, for he tried to escape, was caught and scourged again. Stanley warned him that if he attempted to make off again, he would be shot down like a dog. But he also felt himself, at seventeen, in an alien land, whose language he did not speak and without weapons, to be powerless. Clearly he suffered from some kind of personality weakness, for he later confessed that with Stanley he was like the bird with the snake; the older man had absolute power over him as if he were hypnotised.

But Noe's ordeal was just beginning. The plan Stanley had evolved in his mind in faraway Colorado was now about to take shape, and the effeminate-looking Noe was to play a key role in it. In essence Stanley's plan amounted to provoking some kind of armed confrontation with the locals, so that he could claim afterwards to have been robbed of a large sum of money. He would then report the robbery in Erzurum, the largest city on Turkey's eastern border, adding the embellishment that his letters of credit on a merchant in Tiflis, Georgia, had also been stolen. He further hoped to produce fictitious credentials enabling him to raise a loan for the onward journey to Tiflis. By the time the Turkish bankers discovered the fraud, Stanley would be too far into Persia for it to be worthwhile for the bank to chase him.

After surviving so many perils in the United States, Stanley had grown over-confident of his ability to manipulate events and did not fully appreciate how dangerous his strategy was. On 18th September 1866 he was to learn about unintended consequences with a vengeance.

That afternoon as they plodded through the mountains in the autumn heat, Stanley thought he saw his chance and took it. They were near a dismal hamlet called Chi-Hissar, about 300 miles inland from Smyrna. Their horses were near to expiring from exhaustion. Cook was riding about a mile in their rear as his horse was faltering. Stanley told Noe that he had a plan for procuring fresh mounts but it would require his full co-operation and unquestioning obedience. After the recent flagellation experience, Noe was not disposed to cavil.

Very soon they came in sight of a Turk, riding one horse and leading another. He introduced himself as Achmet. Stanley said something to him in broken Turkish that Noe did not understand. Achmet motioned to a hollow basin nearby surrounded by hills. The three of them rode into the hollow and dismounted. Achmet strode up to Noe and began fondling his genitals. At this Stanley suddenly seized his sabre and smote the Turk a buffet across the head that made him stagger. The blow would have killed him but for the protection afforded his head by the pasteboard stiffening inside his fez.

Achmet struck back at his would-be assassin. Drawing his knife, he closed with Stanley, who soon found himself outclassed in this kind of combat and called out to Noe to shoot his assailant dead. There was some desperation in his voice: 'Shoot him, Lewis, shoot him or he'll kill me!' Mindful of Stanley's earlier words, Noe took aim and pulled the trigger, but the chamber was empty. Stanley had been using the rifle that morning for target practice and had neglected to reload it. Since Stanley was still yelling, 'Kill him!', Noe waded in and clubbed Achmet with the rifle butt. Again the Turk staggered but did not fall.

By this time Stanley's hands were ripped and bleeding from the struggle to keep the Turk's knife away from his heart. He rushed to his saddle bags to get his revolver. By the time he retrieved it, Achmet was at the top of the hollow and running for his life. Despite his marksmanship, Stanley failed to hit him with a couple of shots. Within seconds Achmet had made good his escape.

The sequence of events in the hollow from the entry of the trio to Achmet's escape is related almost identically in the two utterly independent extant accounts of the incident, Noe's to the New York Sun, and Stanley's in the unpublished 'Adventures of an American Traveller in Turkey'. The two accounts differ only in their interpretation. Stanley says he entered the hollow in all innocence; the next thing he knew, Achmet was making sodomitical overtures to Noe. Noe says that Stanley lured the Turk into the hollow with the promise that if he inspected Noe's person, he would find a girl in boy's clothing. According to Noe, it was Stanley's purpose to murder the Turk, gain possession of his horses, plead self-defence and then carry to Erzurum a story about how the Turk's comrades had robbed them of their money, which was how the shooting began in the first place.

There can be little question which version is more plausible. Can we seriously believe that a lone Turk would have asked two well-armed foreigners to turn aside into a hollow for some unstated purpose, that Stanley would have agreed, and that the said Turk would then make sodomitical overtures spontaneously? We must remember too that he had many companions nearby, as we shall see in a moment. The account Stanley provides in his 'Adventures' has the same whiff of fantasy as his many other 'true stories'.

As soon as Achmet had made good his escape, Stanley realised the deadly peril they were in. At this moment Cook trooped wearily in and Stanley put his astonished comrade in the picture. They turned back in the direction they had come from. But very soon whooping sounds and a cloud of dust at their backs told them that Achmet had brought reinforcements. A mounted chase commenced.

For four hours they careered wildly over the mountains. The exhausted horses frequently butted into each other in the attempt to keep their footing. They raced through dense woods and deep mountain gorges. At last they paused for rest in a 'deep dell enclosed on all sides by high mountains, whose summits everlastingly kissed the clouds'. In the clear mountain air the only sound they could hear was the distant tinkling of cowbells. Yet Stanley's instincts told him they were not yet safe. He urged his two comrades to one last effort; once over the almost perpendicular mountain wall ahead of them they would be truly secure.

The climb proved too much for the emaciated horses. One of them stumbled and rolled back down the slope, almost crushing Noe. They abandoned the horses and pressed on to the summit on foot. Triumphantly they sat on a grassy ridge, confident that the danger was behind them. Suddenly, as if from nowhere, Achmet and his companions rushed them, pinioned their arms, then trussed and blindfolded them.

Their captors led them down the slopes to a Turcoman encampment. At its outskirts Stanley began to feel real fear for the first time. Achmet and his men were joined by 'three hideous, ragged ruffians' who cocked their guns and swore by Allah that they would shoot the infidels. Just in time an old man waving a sword interposed himself and the three desperadoes moved sullenly to the rear. Then Achmet and the others tied their prisoners to a post and began shooting around them. The bullets whined dangerously near their heads. Just when Stanley was giving himself up for dead, the old man again intervened: At one time he hovered around us like a guardian angel with his drawn sword, again he energetically harangued them on the cruel, foolish course which they wished to adopt. Gradually his eloquence seemed to tell and we breathed free when hearing the word 'Hayde, Hayde' - 'Go ahead'. Although uttered harshly, they were none the less welcome.

The Turks ceased their 'target practice', untethered their victims and took them on to a village, which they reached at dusk. Their arrival caused the greatest excitement. A babble of yelling and halloing was counter-pointed by the firing of guns and the barking of dogs. Women and young boys came out of the houses and pelted the prisoners with stones and mud. One old man approached them with tottering steps and dealt Noe a number of energetic cuffs around the head. Piteously Noe asked Stanley whether they were to be killed. Stanley shrugged.

Next the prisoners were dragged to an open portico that seemed to double as a court. A sea of scowling faces confronted them. The old man who had cuffed Noe took the place of honour; Stanley observed cynically that the villagers deferred to him and called him 'Emir'. This patriarch and his council then proceeded to try the miscreants. Achmet was called to give evidence and pointed Stanley out with a show of great indignation. The council debated inconclusively what to do with the prisoners, then at midnight announced an adjournment until the next morning. The three Westerners were left in the hands of their captors.

The situation of Stanley and his two comrades was parlous. They were haltered with ropes around their necks, and thus in a state of semi strangulation, half-sitting, half-lying on the ground, out in the open, exposed to the cold night air and without any shelter or covering. But there was worse to come. The three ruffians who had caused Stanley such a frisson earlier in the day put in an appearance in the small hours, once the village had settled down to sleep. While two of them held a knife to Noe's throat and warned him not to make a noise, the third raped him. The others then took their turn at buggery, 'a crime common in Turkey but not fit to be mentioned to polite ears'. Stanley was not at first aware of the full horror of what was going on but 'I was awakened out of a fitful doze by deep, agonised, though stifled groans. They had no pity or remorse but one by one they committed their diabolical crime which is, I think, or I hope, unknown to civilised nations, especially Christian America.'

Stanley's mental turmoil was real enough. His graphic evidence suggests that he himself had not actually been sodomised in the workhouse, but the rape would doubtless have conjured memories of many lewd acts he had witnessed in St Asaph's. Even more poignancy, the Turks' actions brought home forcibly to Stanley the reality of the instincts towards Noe which he was suppressing and which had found their outlet in the bloody beating. The three ruffians were acting out a possibility he could not face.

Stanley's contempt for Islam was never so great as when, at sunrise, the three rapists turned towards Mecca to pray. Evidently the village council at this stage washed its hands of the whole affair, for Achmet and his men set about searching them and their effects roughly for money. They found none but offered to set them free for 1,400 pilasters. Then their captors hauled them back to the Turcoman encampment. They were given coffee while Achmet again harangued bystanders on the dreadful treatment Stanley had meted out to him. One old woman was so incensed by the tale that she broke through the ranks of the men and fetched Stanley a blow on the head that momentarily stunned him. One of the elders rebuked her for overstepping her social bounds, whereat she slunk away like a whipped cur.

Still undecided what to do with them, Achmet and his henchmen took them on, still bound, to a larger village. Here the three prisoners were released from their bonds and grilled on where they had hidden the money. All three swore there was no money. Achmet lost his temper, waved a sword menacingly over their heads and then hit Stanley hard on the hand with the flat of his sword in an effort to make him talk. This was another critical moment for Stanley. 'I now resigned myself to my fate and refused to answer any question whatever.'

Noe and Cook were more co-operative. After both had sworn a solemn oath to Allah that they were penniless, Achmet saw that he had but two choices: cold-blooded murder or a formal indictment before a magistrate. Once more he tied up his prisoners and set out with them for the town of Rashakeni.

This was a bad mistake on Achmet's part. Rashakeni happened to possess an intelligent governor who knew something of Western ways. In a dialectical contest a simple peasant like Achmet was no match for the educated, quick-witted Stanley. When both sides were called on to make their depositions, Stanley made verbal mincemeat of the opposition. He convinced the governor that the violence had started when Achmet and his comrades tried to rob them. For all that, the governor took a dim view of what he saw as Stanley's attempt to take the law into his own hands. He ordered that all parties to the dispute be chained and taken to the prison at Karahisar, five hours' ride distant.

At Karahisar Noe was again the butt of Turkish violence. When they arrived at the prison gates, there was a conversation between their escort and the prison porter, following which the porter struck Noe a blow that almost doubled him up. Noe appealed piteously to Stanley: 'Oh, Henry, I have been hit.' Stanley's response was typical. By his own admission, he could scarcely refrain from laughing.

The laughter was stilled when the three of them were thrown into a dungeon reeking with an intolerable stench and full of local riff-raff who surrounded them and began to take liberties with their private parts: 'You can imagine our feelings when surrounded by these people, who were too ready to induct us into their sodomitical practices. I really pitied the poor boy Louis, as he was mentally marked by these ruffians as that night's victim.

Providence intervened, for at that very moment they were taken to be interviewed by the prison commandant. He immediately saw that these were Westerners of higher status than had previously been represented to him. He re-housed them on their own in a better part of the jail. Next morning they were taken to see Raouf Bay, the governor. He was dressed in European clothes and for the first time Stanley was able to establish some true intellectual rapport. Raouf at once realised that there was an international dimension to the case. He decided to send Stanley and his companions to Bursa, where there were Turkish-speaking Americans who could represent them. Accordingly on 27th September 1866 the three men left Karahisar. Achmet and his minions were to be sent up to Bursa in chains when the trial started.

On 30th September they halted at Actumtael. Stanley recorded: 'We are all in excellent spirits, Louis especially. Entirely forgotten their dastardly barbarity committed on him.' On 2nd October they were at Klutrial, where they were well treated by a sect of Armenian Christians. On 8th October they arrived at Bursa and lodged at the home of an American missionary called Richardson. Richardson and his wife invited them to treat their home as their own.

On 11th October Achmet and his men arrived in chains and a preliminary hearing commenced. Since Stanley claimed that he and his companions had been robbed of 80,000 pilasters, yet only 40 pilasters had been found on the robbers, the Bursa magistrate decided that Stanley should swear a formal affidavit with the American consul in Constantinople. Stanley and his friends arrived there on the evening of 14th October, put up in the Hotel d'Orient and spent the next week drawing up a statement of their grievances.

The US Minister in Turkey at the time was the fifty-one-year-old Edward Jay Morris, who had been in post since 1861. He confessed then and later to finding Stanley's allegations puzzling on a number of counts. Stanley claimed to have had a large sum of money in gold and banknotes hidden in cartridge boxes plus a letter of credit on a Tiflis merchant for 200,000 pilasters (about $1,500). The gold alone was said to amount to $300. Morris thought it strange that his three compatriots should be travelling in Turkey with American coin, and even odder that Stanley should have had a draft on Tiflis drawn on a merchant in Maiden Lane, New York, since in his five years in Turkey Morris had never heard of any commercial intercourse between New York and Tiflis. Nor did Stanley increase the plausibility of his story by having a handbill printed in which he claimed to have been robbed of $4,000 in cash. He seemed as unable to decide exactly how much money had been 'robbed' as Senator McCarthy was later uncertain about how many Communists there were in the Eisenhower administration.

Stanley explained to Morris that as a result of the 'robbery' they were penniless. He asked Morris for a loan of £150 against a draft for that amount on his father, whom Stanley claimed was a rich lawyer at 20 Liberty Street, New York. Morris accepted the draft and paid Stanley the £150. Stanley then divided it among the three of them, but further alienated Noe by giving himself and Cook £59 each while Noe received just £32.

On 26th October the trio had to return from Constantinople to Bursa for the formal trial of Achmet and his comrades. Morris, who after some hesitation decided to back Stanley to the hilt, made a formal complaint to the Turkish government. The newspapers were full of the story of a 'barbarous attack on American travellers'. The affair threatened to become a cause celebre. The Turks, who in the prevailing international climate needed all the friends they could get, decided to conciliate the USA by indicting Achmet and the others for aggravated robbery and assault. The government accepted implicitly that if they found the 'robbers' guilty, they would have to pay compensation to the victims.

By 9th November Stanley, Cook and Noe had made their detailed depositions in Bursa and were free to leave. By this time they had overstayed their welcome with the missionaries and Mr Richardson had in any case requested them to leave his household. Stanley took Noe with him to Constantinople, leaving Cook to await the outcome of the trial and to send on any compensation payable. Once in Constantinople he did not bother to call on Minister Morris who had so trustingly helped him out, but immediately booked passage to Marseilles.

On 14th November 1866 Stanley and Noe embarked for Marseilles. There was a terrific storm in the Aegean, during which a man was lost overboard, then another violent gale after they passed Messina and entered the Tyrrhenian Sea. Sailing under the lee of Sardinia and Corsica, they arrived at Marseilles on the 23rd but were detained in quarantine for twelve hours before being permitted to land. They caught the 10.45 PM- train to Paris, arrived at Lyons next morning and reached the French capital after twenty-four hours 'on the cars'. After resting for three days at the Hotel de Dieppe, they caught the Newhaven packet and arrived in London late on 27th November. They at once took the night train to Liverpool.

During the fortnight's journey from Constantinople to Liverpool, the final breach between Stanley and Noe took place. Once back in 'civilisation' Noe complained bitterly about Stanley's treatment of him, about the beatings and the way Stanley's recklessness had led to the rape. The quarrel simmered on when they reached Liverpool. Stanley prevailed on Uncle Tom Morris and Aunt Maria to take Noe in while he went visiting his other relations in Wales; this time the Morrises had moved to 18 Davies Street.

Stanley had learned nothing from his experiences in Turkey. Undaunted by the fact that his fantasy world had brought him inches away from violent death, he uncoiled a further lariat of lies once in North Wales. After visiting his cousin John Owen in Shrewsbury, he called on his mother at the Cross Foxes in Glascoed to present her with a portrait of himself and impress her with the news that he was now an ensign in the US Navy. He developed the fantasy in an entry in the visitors' book at Denbigh Castle on 14th December: 'John Rowlands, formerly of this Castle now Ensign in the United States Navy in North America, belonging to the US ship Ticonderoga, now at Constantinople, Turkey; absent on furlough.' It was typical of Stanley's guile to interweave a truth (that he had recently been in Constantinople) with an egregious lie.

With the balance of the money he had inveigled out of Minister Morris, Stanley was able to cut a dash in Denbigh and sustain his fantasy of being a well-paid naval officer. The rest of his family were regaled with the same story. His cousin Henry Parry actually received a photograph of Stanley in naval uniform (presumably from his Minnesota days), signed 'Your loving cousin John Rowlands, 22nd December, 1866'. It is noteworthy that in Wales Stanley was still 'John Rowlands'. He gave a tea party at St Asaph's for the children as a sort of informal quid pro quo for a reference from the chairman, Captain Leigh Thomas. Quite what he was supposed to be doing soliciting for references at St Asaph's (and from Bishop Vowler Short and Squire Pennant at Tremerchion) if he had risen so high in the world is unclear. But it may be that some doubts crept in and that Stanley tried to get Noe to come down to corroborate his story, for Noe conferred with Uncle Tom Morris on the advisability of the trip, only to receive the chilling admonition by no means to venture there since 'if John got me in the mountains there, with his present feelings against me, I should never get out alive.' If ever Noe had thought that his morbid fear of Stanley and his capacity to commit any crime was some form of paranoid delusion, Uncle Tom Morris's words alerted him that others perceived Stanley in exactly the same way. Ever afterwards Noe and his family combined insensate hatred of Stanley with a genuine fear of assassination.

The one positive thing Stanley brought back from his trip to North Wales was a further reinforcement of his contacts with the Missouri Democrat. When Stanley happened to mention to the Bishop's coachman at the Palace Lodge that he had contributed occasional pieces to that newspaper, the coachman gave him the names of two relations named Ebbells who lived in Missouri and knew the editor well. Stanley had already decided that his future once more lay in the New World. On 7th January 1867 he returned to Liverpool and put up at the Commercial Hotel. Next day he went with Noe to visit the municipal museum and library, then on 14th January sailed for New York in the Denmark. The Turkish adventure merits further consideration, since it provides vital clues to Stanley's character and personality. Hitherto we have been able to convict Stanley as a liar, but arguably before 1866 his lies were 'inner-directed' rather than 'other-directed'. In Turkey for the first time Stanley gave unmistakable evidence that his lies were truly pathological, that he would bend the truth in all directions to secure his own ends, no matter who was hurt in the process. Moreover, although his ambiguous sexuality had clearly been a problem to him since adolescence. Turkey provided the first clear evidence of a 'solution' via sado-masochism.

First, the lies and the breathtaking criminality of the way in which Stanley proposed providing himself with money. It was the very audacity of his plan that guaranteed ultimate success, for although his story of the 'robbery' did not stand up to detailed scrutiny, the alternative scenario for men like Morris if they rejected it was too horrifying to contemplate. It was essentially the technique of the 'big lie': psychologically Morris was almost bound to believe that Stanley's story was in essence correct, even if it was ragged at the edges. It was simply inconceivable that there could be no truth at all in it.

Yet in his dark moments Morris must have allowed this possibility to surface. His own Secretary of Legation, Brown, told him bluntly that he had been a fool to trust Stanley, and Morris self-confessedly was hurt when Stanley left Constantinople without any further contact with him once he had paid over the £150. The sequel confirmed his worst fears. Morris sent Stanley's draft to his agent in Philadelphia, who reported back that no such person as 'Stanley senior' lived on Liberty Street. Morris would have been defrauded of the £150 had not the Achmet case turned out satisfactorily. Part of the affidavit Stanley had sworn to in Turkey contained an accusation of sodomy, which was proved against two of the rapists. The fact that the charge of buggery was sustained had a 'knock-on' effect on the rest of the indictment. Morris modified Stanley's compensation claim from $4,000 to the more believable $2,000 and accepted $1,200 the Turkish authorities actually offered. Out of the compensation money he repaid himself his £150.

Having taken no material loss, Morris, in retirement in Adantic City, was not disposed to get involved in a nasty wrangle in 1872 when Noe's accusations first surfaced in the American press. Noe correctly accused Stanley of a complicated larceny and of having defrauded Morris of £150. Since Stanley was by this time famous as the man who had found Livingstone, Morris naturally did not want to get into a bare-knuckle fight with Stanley and his protectors at the New York Herald. He therefore concocted the plausible story that he had advanced Stanley the £150 against the expected compensation money, though how he can have been sure the Turkish court would find in his compatriots' favour is not explained. More skilful cross-questioning from the rival Sun's reporter a few days later dug out the true story for anyone who cared to see it. Morris was forced to retract the categorical assurances he had made a few days earlier and admitted that he had sent the draft to Philadelphia for encashment.

Since we have established that Noe's allegations about Stanley's naval career in the Civil War and his larceny in Turkey are accurate, there are strong prima-facie grounds for presuming that his story of the thrashing Stanley gave him in the pomegranate grove is also true. In fact, Stanley himself admitted that he had given Noe a 'few strokes of a switch' allegedly for starting the fire in a 'valuable grove'. Noe successfully refuted the story by demonstrating that the ignited bushes were not a valuable grove and that Stanley had encouraged him to set them alight as part of the horseplay to tease Cook. Stanley's defence against Noe was twofold. First, there was vulgar abuse of a personal kind written by his acolytes but in no way answering the specific charges Noe made. Secondly, there was the 'corroborating' testimony of Harlow Cook. Cook's evidence is vitiated by the fact that he hated Noe and hero- worshipped Stanley and was not present at either the thrashing or the Achmet incident; furthermore, anyone reading the 'affidavit' he provided to enquiring journalists in 1872 will find it merely risible. The very speech and body-language described by the interviewer provide a virtual polygraph test of their own: 'A look of surprise but no quick answer'; 'Musingly "Yes, a considerable time"'; '"Well, I must think it over now" '; ' "I do not want to tell what I can at this time for more reasons than one."' The only surprise is that Cook did not plead the Fifth Amendment!

There would be many more beatings of servants and underlings in the future to lend credence to Noe's story. The true significance of the Turkey experience is the way it conflates the themes of lying and fantasy with those of sexual ambiguity and sado-masochism. Both strands were organically linked in the Stanley personality.

The deeper the neurosis, the more difficulty there is in distinguishing fantasy from reality. In part Stanley's lies were a product of his refusal to accept the facts about his childhood and early life. The denial of his Welshness, of his true identity as John Rowlands, his commitment to a 'Family Romance' were all part of this. Another aspect of the departure from reality is concerned with the need for constant action. A man in a frenzy of activity will be led increasingly into the realms of the preposterous. At a certain point the boundary between fantasy and actuality will begin to blur even in the perceiving subject. Another outstandingly gifted man of Africa spotted this aspect of Stanley: 'I never knew a European or any other creature who could lie like him. How can he tell truth from falsehood?'

Just as Stanley perilously straddled the twilight area between fantasy and reality, so did he inhabit the limbo between homosexuality and heterosexuality. Stanley was attracted to women, to their beauty and their compassionate qualities, but he could not integrate sexuality into his perception of them, except by the rigid Madonna/whore bifurcation. His relations with women therefore remained at the superficial level of idealisation and courtly love. Since he could only either worship or despise a woman, he could not have a female as a partner. The rough comradeship of men held out more hope of easy contact. There was no occasion to be shy or awkward with those who inhabited the same masculine world of action and violent adventure. At the same time, true equality with a man was also impossible, since a genuine equal would also be a potential rival for the esteem of the world. So Stanley chose men who were inferior to him in one way or another, in age, social status or, if it came to it, in will-power. Lewis Noe was the first of a long line that included Edwin Balch, Edward King, Frank Pocock, Albert Christopher- son and Mounteney-Jephson, to say nothing of Stanley's black or Arab servants: Selim, Kalulu, Baruti and the others. His homosexual feelings towards them remained at a passive level. If we are to dub Stanley 'bisexual' we must be clear that we are not talking about the active bisexuality of, say, the Ancient World. One obvious way to sublimate these contradictory sexual impulses is through the dominant/submissive polarity of sado-masochism.

Ambiguity, then, was the key to Stanley's personality. Mounteney-Jephson perceived something of this when he wrote of Stanley in the late 1880s: 'Half a white man, half an Arab . . . describes Stanley very well. All the falseness and double-dealing, the indifference to breaking his word, the meanness, brutality and greediness, are the Arab side. The wonderful dogged determination to carry through to a successful issue all that he takes in hand, his cleverness in mapping, writing, conversation etc. all belong to the European side. He has two distinct personalities, one cannot be too much admired and praised, the other is contemptible in the extreme.'

There is much irony here. Stanley denied his own Welshness, yet in pointing up the duality of the Welsh, he unwittingly provided a portrait of himself: 'A compound of opposites - exclusive as Spaniards, vindictive as Corsicans, conservative as Osmanlis, sensible in business, but not enterprising; quarrelsome, but law-abiding; devout but litigious; industrious and thrifty, but not rich; loyal but discontented.' 1867 was the year Stanley won his spurs as war correspondent. Originally hired by the Missouri Democrat as an 'occasional' on the strength of his unpublished Civil War jottings, he impressed them sufficiently to be taken on as a regular correspondent. His first assignment was to cover General Hancock's military expedition against the Southern Cheyenne. Later he reported on the peace conferences between the plains Indians and General Sherman and the other Peace Commissioners appointed by Washington: at North Platte (with the Sioux and Cheyenne) and at Medicine Lodge (with the Kiowas, Arapahoes, Comanches and Apache). During this colourful year on the plains Stanley made the acquaintance of many legendary figures in the history of the West: Generals Sherman, Terry and Hancock; Wild Bill Hickock and Custer; and the Indian chiefs Spotted Tail, Satank and Satanta. So successful was Stanley as a war correspondent that by the end of 1867 his pieces were in demand not just by the Missouri Democrat but by the big eastern newspapers, especially the New York Tribune and New York Herald.

In December 1867 Stanley presented himself at the New York offices of the Herald. By great good fortune (Stanley was always a lucky person), he found the proprietor James Gordon Bennett junior on one of his rare visits to his paper's headquarters. Bennett knew of, and was impressed by, Stanley's coverage of events in the West, but when Stanley proposed himself as a war correspondent in Abyssinia, Bennett scornfully replied that British imperial wars were of no great interest to an American readership. This despite the fact that the campaign promised to be a unique and sensational one. Ethiopia's emperor Theodore had taken a number of British subjects hostage in his mountain fortress of Magdala. When all diplomatic measures to secure the hostages had failed, the British reluctantly put General Sir Robert Napier, a hero of the Indian mutiny, in command of a powerful punitive expedition.

When Stanley insisted that there was 'good copy' in the war, Bennett, intrigued, asked what his terms were. Stanley replied that he would accept an assignment either as a Herald special correspondent, on salary and expenses, or as a freelance, payable by letter, in which case he reserved the option to send material to other newspapers. At that Bennett's face clouded over; the Herald shared with nobody, he said testily. But he suggested a compromise: he would be prepared to pay a very high rate per letter for exclusive rights to Stanley's reports, but Stanley had to pay his own passage and all his expenses. As an afterthought he asked what Stanley's experience was outside the United States. Stanley rattled off a long list of Mediterranean place-names which satisfied the dour proprietor.

Bennett then wrote to his agent, Colonel Finlay Anderson, head of the Herald's London bureau. Stanley made preparations for an immediate sailing to Europe, but first he took the precaution of securing letters of introduction by telegraph from Generals Grant and Sherman. With £300 in his pocket Stanley took the first available steamer from New York to Liverpool.

After crossing the Atlantic and making the necessary arrangements in London, Stanley sped to Suez, via Paris and Marseilles. The preparations of the British commander General Napier were already well advanced for the march on Theodore's capital of Magdala. At Suez Stanley took a momentous decision. He bribed the telegraph operator heavily to ensure that his copy was forwarded to London ahead of that of his journalistic rivals. Then he sped on to the Red Sea port of Annesley Bay in the Horn of Africa, where Napier was assembling his assault forces for the long inland march on Theodore's mountain stronghold.

Stanley arrived at Annesley Bay at the end of January 1868. For two months he marched with the British forces into the mountains and jungles of Abyssinia. On Good Friday, 10 April, Napier scored a spectacular victory over Theodore's forces in the plains below Magdala. The fortress was stormed, the emperor committed suicide. The British sacked Magdala before putting it to the torch.

There followed a gruelling march back to the coast in the height of the rainy season. By the end of May, having taken appalling risks and cut his safety margin to the bone and beyond, a lone-travelling Stanley was approaching journey's end, ahead of his fellow journalists. At Suez on 6th

June his first stop was the telegraph office, where he rewarded his accomplice and sent off fresh material. He was conscious of having scooped the field, but it was only when he travelled up to Alexandria on 26th June that he first realised what a sensation his despatches from Abyssinia had created. He had expected, after his bribery, to be first in the field. What he had not counted on was that his scoop would be such a sensation.

Immediately after Stanley's first batch of copy had been relayed from the Suez telegraph office the cable between Malta and Alexandria broke and was out of action for days. The consequences was that Stanley's copy was the first detailed news of the Magdala triumph and was the sole authoritative source for almost a week. So completely had Stanley slipped the field that his feat was regarded with incredulity. It seemed inconceivable that the first comprehensive intelligence from Abyssinia should be coming from a 'Yankee' journalist. He was dubbed charlatan and impostor. When, a week later, the despatches from the correspondents of The Times, Telegraph and Standard came in and confirmed Stanley's story, something very like a howl of indignation went up in London.

Stanley had now well and truly arrived as a war correspondent. He was immediately put on the Herald's permanent payroll. So great was the pleasure of Gordon Bennett junior at the discomfiture of his British rivals that he printed all Stanley's despatches at great length without cuts and taunted other newspapers with the superiority of its 'special' H. M. Stanley: 'Our readers will not fail to perceive the vast superiority in style of writing, minuteness of detail and graphic portrayal of event which the Herald correspondence possesses over the written accounts of the same matter printed in the London journals, of which we furnished specimens in the shape of extracts a few days ago.' As Bennett later admitted, it was Stanley's Abyssinian triumph that led eventually to his being chosen as the right man to 'find' Dr Livingstone.

In the balmy days of triumph in Alexandria, when the full scale of his achievement was gradually dawning on him, Stanley struck up an acquaintance with Douglas Gibbs, local manager of the Daily Telegraph. Gibbs was kind to Stanley, frequently entertained him to dinner, and praised lavishly his achievements in Abyssinia. Yet he was not without his eccentricities. Stanley arrived in Alexandria virtually broke, yet owed £200 from Finlay Anderson. When he approached Gibbs for a loan of £5, Gibbs turned him down, even though Stanley expostulated that he was good for a hundred times that sum and even though, as Stanley pointed out, Gibbs spent more than that on every one of the sumptuous dinners he treated him to.

Stanley now had to await word from his new employers as to his next assignment, so had time on his hands. He began by shipping 'Fayed' (the Arab horse he had bought from an aristocratic officer) and the groom to Liverpool. Then he went up to Ismailia for a week to report on the progress of the canal being dug at Suez. His report on this, though not commissioned, was published eagerly by the Herald. Another important contact Stanley made at this time was the Egyptian diplomat Hekekyan Bay, whom he met in Cairo, and to whom he introduced consul Cameron, one of the captives of Magdala.

On his return to Alexandria, on 17th July 1868, he fell ill and was in bed for several days with a fever. Men like Stanley are always impatient with illness, and will not accept the limitations to their actions placed on them by an ailing body. Barely recuperated, Stanley took himself off to a Mediterranean bay and decided to get back into shape by swimming. Since Stanley was an excellent swimmer, this would normally have presented no risk, but he reckoned without his weakened constitution. At first all went well: he plunged into the bay, felt invigorated and struck out strongly towards the sea. But after about 50 yards, he began to feel weak, then suddenly realised to his horror that he lacked the strength to return to the shore and so was in imminent danger of drowning. It so happened that the Reuter's correspondent, one Edward Viruard, was swimming nearby. Seeing Stanley in distress, he managed to life-save him back to the beach. 14 Years later, when Stanley was famous, Viruard claimed a financial 'reward' for saving his life.

The shock temporarily brought Stanley to his senses. This time he convalesced properly. It was just as well, for the orders that arrived from London on 7 August consigned him to another theatre of war. This time it was Crete, where the indigenous inhabitants had raised the standard of revolt against the Turks, seeking to emulate the 1828 example of the Greek mother-country. The Russians, always ready to discomfit the Turks in the 'Near East', had already sent aid to the rebels; American sentiment, too, was overwhelmingly pro-Cretan, and the Herald had been watching the build-up in hostilities with concern and interest ever since March. Reports that Turkish regulars had been decisively worsted on the island by Cretan guerrillas were the particular trigger for the sending of Stanley.

On 13th August Stanley left Alexandria for Crete, after a long rest capped by exhaustive sightseeing among the Alexandrine ruins. Turkish shipping embargoes plus the lack of any direct route from Egypt meant a roundabout itinerary, passing first by the lee of Rhodes. His first stop was Scio, a small seaport on the Turkish coast, in the Izmir area. While there he revived unpleasant memories by visiting the spot where Noe started the fire in the grove in 1866. Back at the Hotel Europe, he booked passage on a steamer bound for the island of Siros (Sira), on which he, an American and a Hong Kong lawyer were the only non-Greek passengers. Before he left, a contact named Alexandroff gave him a letter of introduction to one of the Siros bigwigs, one Christos Evangelides ('What a name!' Stanley recorded in his diary), a naturalised American.

On arrival at Siros at noon on 19th August, Stanley sought out Evangelides, a middle-aged man with a snowy white beard, and handed him the letter of introduction. Evangelides turned out to be another romancer of the Levison stamp, 'a Greek of Greeks', as Stanley put it, so the Herald reporter determined on keeping his sceptical distance. But Evangelides overwhelmed him with charm and offered to be his guide on the islands. He took Stanley first to visit Julia Ward Howe, author of the 'Battle Hymn of the Republic', not knowing that Stanley had had first-hand experience of the Civil War's 'terrible swift sword'. Then they went on to a seminary where Stanley made the mistake of commenting favourably on the good looks of young Greeks. Immediately Evangelides pounced and suggested that Stanley marry a Greek girl. The twenty- seven-year-old reporter's reactions, as confided to his diary, were of a piece with his combined uncertain sexuality and pedestal worship of the female:

Up to this moment it had never entered my mind that it must be some day my fate to select a wife ... yet the suggestion was delicious from other points of view. A wife! My wife! How grand the proprietorship of a fair woman appeared! To be loved with heart and soul above all else, forever united in thought and sympathy with a fair and virtuous being, whose very touch gave strength and courage and confidence! Oh dear! how my warm imagination glows at the strange idea!

Seeing the effect his words had had, Evangelides tried to press home his advantage and urged a Greek marriage all the more strongly. Stanley demurred on the grounds that he was a rover of the world and in any case had no money. Evangelides refused to take no for an answer and offered to be Stanley's proxy and to find him a nubile girl of unmatched beauty and character. Unfortunately the Greek's idea of what constituted these qualities was not Stanley's, for that very evening Evangelides proposed his unprepossessing daughter Calliope as candidate. Calliope's homeliness was such that it was difficult for Stanley not to burst out laughing in the paternal face.

Stanley returned to his hotel to bone up on the Cretan rebellion. There was plenty of evidence on Siros of the plight of the Cretan refugees, who were existing on food doles and hand-outs of clothes; an American missionary told him the story was the same on Naxos and Tenedos. But even while Stanley was revolving all this in his mind, the irrepressible Evangelides returned to the attack next morning by again proposing his daughter as Stanley's wife. The puritanical Welsh-American was deeply shocked: 'It is scarcely credible that a father would be so indifferent to his daughter's happiness as to cast her upon the first stranger he meets.' He made his excuses again, and spent the day of 22 August on a horseback excursion into the interior of Siros, reeling at the impact of a stainless sky and the 'wine-dark' sea: 'When I returned to the town, I quite understood Byron's passion for Hellas.' But Evangelides had not finished with him yet. That evening, while Stanley was taking his evening walk around the main square in Ermoupolis (Hermopolis), Evangelides again collared him and took him to visit a respectable middle-aged couple named Ambella in the residential quarter of the town. After some inconsequential banter 'in glided a young lady who came as near as possible to the realisation of the ideal which my fancy had portrayed .. . demure .. . wrapped in virgin modesty. Her name was Virginia and well it befitted her. She is about sixteen, and, if she can speak English, who knows?'

Stanley's way of thinking and talking about Virginia Ambella reveals his limitations as a serious suitor, even by Victorian standards. But there was nothing frivolous about the Ambella family's attitude. To his great uneasiness, Virginia's mother then cross-questioned him about his attitude to marriage in general and Virginia's suitability as wife in particular. Stanley was shocked at this matter-of-factness and lack of reserve. His embarrassed blushes rivalled those of the maidenly Virginia. But no amount of winking and nodding could shake Evangelides' 'astonishing effrontery'. Stanley was glad to get out of the house and back to his hotel.

Yet clearly he was left with mixed feelings, corresponding to his deeply ambivalent psyche. On the one hand he was profoundly attracted by Virginia's physical beauty. On the other, he must have known that, in terms of a serious relationship with a woman, he was merely shadowboxing. Yet he allowed Evangelides to lure him back to the Ambella household next morning, when further verbal fencing went on between Stanley and the determined matron. The mother accused him of excessive shyness. When they left the house, Stanley complained to Evangelides that he felt he was being 'bounced' into a marriage; why all the rush? Evangelides shrugged and said it was the Greek way. Stanley countered that he knew no Greek and little French, while Virginia knew no English and little French too; what sort of a basis was that for partnership? Evangelides responded by declaring that the Ambella family was well off. They parted, and Stanley noticed him going back to the Ambella house: 'What an extraordinary people!' he confided to his diary.

Evangelides came back later that day to say that the Ambella parents had agreed to a marriage with their daughter provided Stanley made a formal proposal for Virginia's hand. Stanley replied that, since he was setting off for Crete next day, that hardly seemed a sensible procedure. But eventually Evangelides wore him down. He composed a formal letter of proposal. The jubilant Greek bore it away and returned in the evening with news that the Ambellas would give him a formal answer when he returned from Crete.

The sheer artificiality of this 'romance' emerges most clearly in Stanley's diary for the 24th, when he was at sea, heading for Crete. Although Virginia was in his thoughts, his affections were under control and he was disposed to leave matters in the lap of the gods. The calmness of the sea and his position as the only non-Greek passenger aided his detachment. He had, in any case, other things on his mind, for the war zone was looming. That afternoon the ship anchored in the bay of Iraklion, dominated by the Venetian fort lost to the Turks in 1569. After three hours there, the ship ran along the coast to Rethimnon, reached at 9.30 that evening. It was after midnight before the final stretch of the journey, to Khania, was accomplished.

At Khania they encountered a rigorous customs search, so that it was about 7 a.m. before Stanley got clear of the port. He pressed on immediately to the nearby village of Kalippa, where he was to introduce himself to Mr Stillman, the US consul. Stillman proved to be a tall, thin, nervous man of about forty. He had literary ambitions and wrote articles for journals and was out of his depth in the Cretan rebellion, though constrained to continue in post in order to support his large family; as Stanley remarked, 'I fear he will be fit only for a madhouse if he lives here much longer.'

Evidently Stillman took to Stanley-perhaps it was the common interest in literature - for he stayed with them for a week, compiling data on the rebellion. But he showed no hurry to venture near the war zone; the diaries are full of entries on sea-bathing, sightseeing and overnight stays at ancient convents. Part of the problem was that Stanley was in the wrong part of Crete. After the success of Omar Pasha's 'blockhouse' system, the Cretans under Gogoneus decided to abandon the western provinces of Crete. On 31 August Stanley decided that the Cretan rebellion was a bore, that there was probably better 'copy' on the Greek mainland. The Stillmans saw him off on a ship bound for Siros.

The vessel ploughed through a ferocious Aegean gale that left Stanley unconcerned. He stayed in the ship's library and read Marryat's Percival Keene. After retracing the exact outward journey, Stanley arrived back in Siros at 3 a.m. on 2nd September. He made his way to Evangelides' house for an early breakfast, but on learning that there was no news yet from the Ambella family, at once embarked on the Eunomia bound for Athens. After stops at Kithnos and Kea, the Eunomia arrived at Piraeus at 9 p.m. Stanley hired a carriage for the drive to Athens and by midnight was ensconced in the Hotel de L'Angleterre.

He slept late next morning but was still in time to report a great day for Athens: the baptism of Prince Constantine, heir-apparent to the throne. A lavish banquet was laid on for the poor of Athens on the plain of Zeus the Olympian and before the temple of Theseus. The particular interest for Herald readers was the participation of US Admiral Farragut in the celebrations. He had arrived two days earlier at Piraeus with the Franklin and the Frolic and kindled Cretan aspirations with a rousing speech to 3,000 of their exiled fighters.

After writing his despatch for the Herald, Stanley was in no particular mood to move on. He spent five days sightseeing the classical antiquities before departing for Siros. On arrival there on the morning of 9th September he was greeted effusively by Evangelides, who informed him that his suit for Virginia's hand was successful and the marriage as good as concluded. A visit to the Ambella household confirmed this. This time two of Virginia's brothers and a sister were present, and it was obvious that Stanley was being scrutinised as a prospective brother-in-law. A tentative date for the marriage was fixed for the following Sunday. It was arranged that Stanley would have his first meeting with Virginia alone that very evening.

At last Stanley came to his senses and realised the enormity of the step he was about to take. Thoroughly frightened, he hinted to Evangelides that there were things in his past life that would not bear close examination. The hint worked. When Stanley returned to the Ambellas that evening, he was allowed to talk to Virginia alone; he recorded that his misgivings were temporarily dispelled by the touch of her hand and the moistness of her eyes. But Mrs Ambella was now setting new conditions: after all, she told Stanley, they knew nothing about him and before surrendering their cherished daughter to him they ought to know something of his background; she hoped that he would not be offended if the marriage was put off while she took up references. Stanley's reply clearly hints at his own divided emotions: 'Well so be it,' I said, 'though I am sorry and perhaps you may be sorry, but I cannot deny that you are just and wise.' His ambivalence comes through even more strongly when he reflects on the dinner he gave the Ambella family at the hotel de l'Amerique in Siros on 11th September: 'It is as well that I go away shortly, for I feel that she is a treasure; and my admiration, if encouraged, would soon be converted into love, and if once I love, I am lost! However, the possibility of losing her serves to restrain me.'

Stanley's initial actions certainly suggest the ardent suitor. He suggested to Mrs Ambella that she take up references from the Missouri Democrat in St Louis and from the Egyptian authorities in Cairo. He himself wrote to Hekekyan Bay to put him in the picture. The letter is revealing as its lifts a corner on his true feelings towards the Ambellas. After describing Virginia as 'a Greek girl steeped in poverty but famous for her beauty', he goes on, 'She is cursed with rather obnoxious parents but I risk all to marry her ... I have offered to settle on the poor girl the sum of $50 per month as long as she lives, but those parents are avaricious and want more.' So far as one can tell, the statement about Virginia's parents is utter nonsense, but the significance of the letter is that Stanley is already preparing an escape route for himself and a 'justification' for the marriage's failure.

12th September 1868 was the last full day Stanley ever spent with his Greek calf-love. He dined with the family again and enjoyed Virginia's demure company and her lady-like talents on the piano: 'We are convinced that we could be happy together, if it is our destiny to be united. 'Next day he left for Izmir on the Menzaleh. He found his regrets at parting keener than he expected but 'what must be, must be'.

There was a day's stopover in Izmir, during which Stanley again rode out over part of his 1866 route. On the 16th he put to sea once more. Passing Samos, Rhodes, the ship hugged the coast of southern Turkey, then headed down the coasts of modern Syria, Lebanon and Israel. Stanley managed shore excursions at Mersin, Iskenderun, Latakia, Tripoli (Syria), Beirut and Haifa. At Port Said he was able to report good progress on the Suez Canal, before coming to journey's end at Alexandria. There he found a cablegram from Finlay Anderson ordering him to Spain to cover the recent revolution. To buy some time in Alexandria while he sorted out the Virginia affair, he wired Anderson for further instructions.

STANLEY

On 26th September, the day after his arrival in Alexandria, Stanley wrote to Hekekyan Bay to thank him: 'I hope you gave me a good character to my inamorata, otherwise I gravely affirm that there is but the slightest chance that I will succeed. 'That afternoon he received a cable from Anderson to proceed to Barcelona via Marseilles and to wire London for precise instructions from the French port. Next day Stanley wrote to Evangelides and Mrs Ambella that he could not now return to Siros without a definite unequivocal 'yes' to his marriage proposal. On 28th September he left Alexandria for Marseilles on the Said. He never saw Virginia Ambella again.

The 'romance' with this young Greek girl may seem an insignificant affair, half typical Stanley insincerity, half a case of his not knowing his own mind (or heart). But there is more to it than that. The Virginia Ambella episode is deeply revealing of the inner Stanley, both of his sexuality and morbid fear of women and of his neurotic compulsion towards lies and fantasy. The real reason the affair petered out was that Stanley wished to act out a psychic fantasy of suffering, wherein it was always his fate to be rejected by women. This was to mask the fact that, for him, a total loving relationship with a woman, including sexual intercourse, was the ultimate horror. In a word, Stanley had to set up situations where he would be rejected so that he could console himself with a martyr logy of suffering. He tried various ploys to get himself turned down by the Ambellas: he had no money, he had a lurid past, he was too shy to court a wife, and so on. But the crafty Ambella matron called his bluff. She insisted on sending for references. Stanley correctly foresaw that his reputation was not of the pearliest in the American West and that this was the place to direct Mrs Ambella. Unfortunately for him, though he was correct in thinking that the people of Omaha were not especially disposed to give him a 'character', he did not foresee that they might deal with an enquiry from the Ambellas by simply ignoring it, which is what they did. As the Hekekyan Bay, he did what Stanley asked him to. The consequence was that the Ambellas received one very satisfactory reply on their prospective son-in-law and 'no reply', suggesting that their letter had gone astray in the wilds of the American West. Now quite satisfied, they wrote to Stanley to set a definite date for the wedding.

Stanley then tried a different tack. In Siros the Ambellas had countered his objection that he had to prove the world to make a living by pointing out that, in addition to the large dowry Virginia would bring with her, they would find Stanley a comfortable well-paid sinecure in Greece. Stanley now wrote to say that he found this proposition offensive to his honour as a man and that it would be necessary for Virginia to live with him in the USA; the dowry arrangement left an unpleasant taste in his mouth, as it suggested that in Greece it was the practice to sell off their girls. As expected, this drew an angry response from the Ambellas. A letter in halting English, signed 'The Brothers' and 'The Parents', rebuked Stanley for his animadversions on the 'venal' Greek culture and reiterated that there was no question of Virginia's being allowed to go to live in the USA; if Stanley wanted her as a wife, he would have to settle down in Greece.

This provided Stanley with the excuse for inaction he needed. And the discussion about money provided him with further ammunition for his later self-justifying 'reason' why he had not married Virginia Ambella. In 1890 he produced a wild fantasy that it was he who had been expected to provide a 'dowry'. According to this tall tale, Stanley was actually in church on the day of the marriage ceremony, fully intending to take Virginia as his wife, when her father asked through an interpreter for the 'bride price'. What was that, Stanley asked. The interpreter explained that it was the custom in Greece for the bridegroom to hand over a large sum to the bride's father as compensation for the loss of her services and the expenses of bringing her up. When he heard this, Stanley left Virginia standing at the altar, drew aside with the father and the interpreter and said indignantly, 'Sir, I came here to marry, not to buy, your daughter!' It was typical of Stanley's inattention to detail that he was completely unworried that the most superficial research into Greek customs would expose the story as bogus.

That the Virginia Ambella episode had a profound importance in Stanley's inner world can be gauged from the way he allowed it to affect his outer life and career. The arrangement for reporting the Cretan insurrection had been that Stanley would sniff the air for a month before reporting back to Anderson from Alexandria. Because of his absorption with the Ambella affair and the cul-de-sac he ran into in western Crete, Stanley's copy during August-September had seemed remarkably lacklustre after the purple passages from Abyssinia. Aware of the anticlimactic effect this was having, Stanley set out to remedy the situation with an entirely imaginary slice of war correspondence. According to this, he left Siros on a Greek blockade runner on 7th September and proceeded to Aghia Rumeli on the south coast of Crete. After dodging Turkish cruisers, Stanley landed on the Cretan coast, then made his way up into the mountains of the interior. Gruelling route marches took him to the guerrilla camp at Askyfo, whence he accompanied the Cretan irregulars on an assault on a Turkish column. Superior mobility won the day for the Greeks, and twenty-five Turks were killed in an hour's bitter fighting near Rethimnon. After this battle Stanley made his way back over the mountains to Aghia Rumeli, from where he took ship directly to Alexandria. The Herald gladly published the thrilling tale of derring-do witnessed by its own 'special'.

The trouble is that Stanley was nowhere near Crete on the dates (7-18th September) when he was supposed to be accompanying the gallant guerrillas. On these days he was either in Athens or Siros or on board ship in the Aegean. Moreover, he claimed to have taken a direct service from the south of Crete to Alexandria, when everyone knew there was no such service. The entire exciting episode is a fiction, expertly cobbled together with copious circumstantial detail from the mass of information Stanley had acquired on his passage through the islands. This was Stanley's most audacious application of the facility for 'bilocation' he had already employed in the American West. But it was typical of Stanley's near inability to distinguish fantasy from reality that his private accounts (on which he based his claims for expenses to the Herald) told the same story as his bogus despatch. Once again, we observe Stanley as a devotee of the 'coherence' theory of truth.

The fact that Stanley played such a dangerous game means that he was neglecting his professional duties because of his conflicting feelings over Virginia Ambella. A close reading of the diaries during the Siros period reveals not just a profound ambivalence over Virginia - who seemed the avatar of purity, virginity, modesty etc. (therefore Stanley could allow himself to idolise her) - but an 'over determined' impulse pushing him in her direction. It is of great significance that Stanley twice visited the scenes of 1866, and that Greece was at war with Turkey. Since the association of Turkey would be with Noe's homosexual rape, which in turn confronted Stanley with the reality of his homoerotic feelings, what more natural than that he should turn to a Greek female, virtually the polar opposite of Turkish sodomy, to expunge these feelings?

At any rate, by October 1868 Virginia Ambella was already in effect a closed book. Stanley now looked ahead to Spain, where the nymphomaniac Queen Isabella II had just been expelled by a coalition of liberal military officers in a convulsion compared by The Times in London to the French Revolution. General Prim and Admiral Topete, the ringleaders, landed at Cadiz on 19th September and then set up a provisional junta under Francisco Serrano, Duke de la Torre, before proceeding to Madrid on 7th October. Events in Spain had a particular interest for the New York Herald, since the USA was at loggerheads with the Spanish over the rebellion in Cuba. Spanish attempts to suppress the Cuban insurgents were perceived as a breach of the Monroe doctrine.

On 6th October Stanley reached Marseilles, after being delayed two days in the Straits of Messina when the ship broke its steamer shaft. After receiving confirmation from London, he boarded the Estremadura for Barcelona, which he reached on 8th October: 'The city has not changed since I saw it five years ago,' he noted. On the 10th he travelled to Madrid via Zaragoza to begin his assignment in earnest. He put up at the Hotel los Principes in Puerta del Sol and renewed acquaintance with many old press faces from Abyssinia, including Henty of the Standard, Next day he secured an interview with General Juan Prim y Prats, architect of Queen Isabella's overthrow.

Stanley found Prim grave, reserved, meditative and not impulsive. A Catalan, he had the high cheekbones and broad space between the temples that Stanley claimed were typical of the Celts. Prim was in civilian dress, as he had been a few days before when he arrived in Madrid. He received Stanley with great cordiality and freedom and spoke of his mission to regenerate the nation. Stanley ventured to remark that the new Spanish government could count on the friendship and sympathy of the USA as evidenced by Washington's swift recognition of the new regime in Madrid. Prim expressed his pleasure at this and said that the bad old days when the Spanish military took the law into their own hands were over. He had already suppressed the Jesuits, abolished the Moral Guard, the feudal police force, and was reforming the Army with a view to cutting down costs and surplus numbers. He had already called a municipal election under universal suffrage.

They proceeded to speak of Cuba. Stanley had already taken it as a good omen that Washington's portrait had replaced Isabella's in Barcelona's town hall. Prim agreed that the Spanish people felt very warmly towards the United States and he was well aware that the reactionary regimes of Europe (especially the France of Louis Napoleon) were trying to inveigle Madrid and Washington into conflict over Cuba. He hoped the appointment of the liberal Admiral Topete would be read as a reassuring sign. Stanley came away convinced that Prim was a true patriot and libertarian. His programme of universal suffrage, freedom of worship and association and the press, plus decentralisation plans constituted for the Herald reporter 'a bill of rights that if enforced will give to Spain a degree of liberty to the person and to the world generally such as few nations in the world possess', would lead to emergence from the seventeenth to the nineteenth centuries, and in general make Spain great again.

Stanley prepared to interview other Spanish notables. Suddenly he received a message of recall to London. In some perturbation he hastened away. Was Bennett displeased with him? It was true that there was another senior Herald reporter in Spain, but the degree of interest in Spanish affairs entertained by the US press surely meant there was scope for him as well. What was the explanation? Anxiety gave him wings. Travelling via San Sebastian and Bordeaux, he was in Paris early on the morning on 15th October and in London the same evening.

An interview with Anderson next morning did nothing to clear up the mystery. He was very fulsome about Abyssinia, but otherwise acted in an enigmatic way that Stanley found sinister, especially when the Colonel suggested they should defer their discussion until tomorrow. However, next day all became clear. Bennett had heard that the famous Dr Livingstone, who had disappeared years ago into the heart of Africa, was now approaching the Zanzibar coast; he wanted his star 'special' to go out and interview him. Stanley consented, but requested a few days' leave first, which Anderson granted.

Stanley sped to Denbigh, to give his mother the good news that he had made good and was therefore a fit person to receive at the Cross Foxes. Once again we can perceive how deep was the trauma of his rejection in 1862. There is something poignant in the way he deluged her with photos and presents: a head of the Emperor Theodore and other trinkets from Abyssinia that he had saved from the flood in the Sooroo pass. In North Wales, too, Stanley made two other important female contacts. He struck up a rapport with his half-sister Emma, who had left the workhouse to enter domestic service a year after Stanley's own departure from St Asaph's. She was particularly taken with John Rowlands' metamorphosis as H. M. Stanley. Emma later married a tanner, Llewellyn Hughes (on 1 August 1872). When she bore a second daughter (on 26th January 1875) she called her Emma Stanley Hughes. This kind of hero-worship was already foreshadowed in the autumn of 1868. T 0 the irritation of the Parry aunts (the same who had forced the child Stanley from the Denbigh Castle cottage into the workhouse), Emma insisted on calling herself 'Emma Stanley'.

The other female contact was even more significant. During his time at the Cross Foxes Stanley spent most of his time writing and did not mix with the locals. For relaxation he went walking in the woods. But one day he was persuaded to accompany his mother into Denbigh. There they ran into the wife of a local retired barrister named Gough-Roberts, for whom Elizabeth Parry had sometimes done domestic work. On the mother's arm was her daughter Catherine, then aged nineteen. From this casual meeting much future heartache would come.

Always with Stanley, contact with the female called forth an opposite and countervailing response. Doubtless feeling some of the Virginia Ambella sort of stirrings after the casual encounter with Katie Gough-Roberts, Stanley at once went to Mumford's corner shop and suggested to the Mumford parents that their seventeen-year-old son might want to accompany him on his global travels; this would 'make a man of him'. But young Mumford was too comfortable where he was, so Stanley made enquiries at St Asaph's itself. He identified an outgoing workhouse boy for whom he proposed the same future, but when the Board contacted his mother, she became alarmed at Stanley's intentions and refused permission.

It was characteristic of all Stanley's travels that he needed a young male as companion, protégé and amanuensis. But for the moment he was thwarted and had to return to London to make the journey out to Africa alone. On 23rd October he left London for Alexandria, travelling via Paris and Marseilles. By the end of the month he was in Alexandria, but switched his base to Suez to be in touch via his old friends at the cable office with all the latest news on Livingstone. On the 10th Bennett sent him further instructions: use your own judgement but on no account send despatches on the Indian telegraph as this would alert the opposition.'

On 12th November Stanley, who hoped to interview Livingstone, had a foretaste of Scotsmen when he met John MacGregor, then forty-three, already famous as the pioneer and populariser of canoeing in Britain and designer of the 'Rob Roy' canoe. It was scarcely a meeting of minds or spirits. MacGregor scornfully referred to Stanley as 'this active little Yankee'. Stanley's contempt was as amused, though privately recorded: 'His fondness for canoeing reminds me of my youthful passion for aquatics when at New Orleans, but it seems strange to me that a mature man should still retain his boyish love.' Interestingly, when Stanley did eventually meet Livingstone, the subject of MacGregor, whom Livingstone knew, came up again.

By 17th November, still with absolutely no news of Livingstone, Stanley decided to travel to the other end of the Red Sea and take up station at Aden, ready, if the occasion arose, to cross the Indian Ocean to Zanzibar. Four days later he arrived at Aden, which he found a depressing hole: 'a strange place this, fit only for a coal depot'. Although he did not share Anderson's belief that Livingstone would emerge on the coast, he wrote a confidential letter to Francis R. Webb, US consul at Zanzibar, explaining his mission and asking for a cablegram if Livingstone was reported. Meanwhile, finding that the local British officials and bureaucrats seemed to have no other interest than getting drunk, Stanley kept himself to himself and started to complete his self-education. Apart from scores of geographical guides, he devoured mainly the classical authors: Josephus, Herodotus, Plutarch, Homer and Virgil; 'without them the time would be tedious in this extremely warm place.'

In December Stanley crossed to Berbera on the Somali coast. He amused himself by donning Arab dress then, having had himself photographed as 'Khan Bahadoor', he sent the photo and a covering letter to Lewis Noe, thus breaking a silence of nearly two years. He also sent a despatch to the Herald, recounting all the various Livingstone rumours. This fitted quite well into Bennett's plans as he had already begun insidiously to fan the flames of interest in the great explorer among his American readers. However, to give the despatch more cogency and 'news value', Bennett changed the dateline from Aden to Zanzibar and held up its publication until Stanley was well and truly launched on the 'find Livingstone' exploit.

Back in Aden Stanley whiled away the dull days with an extraordinarily ambitious programme of reading: Tickell, Cowper, Fletcher, Dryden, Pope, Murphy, Milton, Ben Jonson, Massinger, Spenser and, always, Shakespeare. Helvetius also took his fancy, and for lighter reading there was the copy of A Christmas Carol given him by a friendly sea-captain en route from Aden to Rangoon. He also began compiling a biographical dictionary, mainly of early Church fathers and other figures from the Ancient World. His notes on history prefigure the discoverer to come: 'Hengist, Horsa, Alaric, Attila and Captain Smith were doing the same tasks of leading men from overcrowded countries to strange ones where plenty was to be had.' In his commonplace book, under 2nd January 1869, he writes of the agonies of trying to give up smoking. Since the Civil War days Stanley was seldom seen without a cigar or cheroot in his mouth.

January 1869 was another month in the doldrums. The diary entry on New Year's Day is that of a sour and depressed man: 'What is happiness . .. happiness is not to be secured in this world except for brief periods.' Stanley finished his book on the Abyssinian campaign (which was to wait another five years before publication), and explored Aden and its environs with a view to the future implications of the Suez Canal. The sheer boredom of his life and the continuing absence of news from Zanzibar soon cracked his New Year's resolution; by 7th January he was smoking again. At length a letter arrived from Consul Webb, scouting the idea that there was any chance of Livingstone's coming to Zanzibar. Finally on 1st February his recall came through: 'I am relieved at last,' he notes joyfully.

On 2nd February he embarked on the auspiciously named Magdala for Suez. The pent-up stress of the preceding three months - inactivity was a peculiar torture for a man like Stanley, who lived for action and action alone - found expression in a virulent fever that kept him confined to his cabin for three days. When he ventured forth on the 6th, his reactions to shipboard life were those of a crusty old colonel; he found fault with everything, and particularly resented the extras in tips and 'contributions' levied by ship's officers and crew on any and every pretext. But this sensibility did not enable him to make common cause with the testy veterans of India, who were interested only in alcohol: 'at lunch the most usual topic is beer ... the subject is also a weariness to me. Why cannot they take their drinks in silence? What does it matter to me which one is their favourite.' Then he adds archly: 'At dinner the topics are more varied. They range from brandy and soda to champagne.'

After a slow seven-day passage up the Red Sea, the Magdala reached Suez. Stanley immediately made for Alexandria, where he dined with Douglas Gibbs and intuited that Mrs Gibbs was in love with another man. But, finding nothing else of interest there, after five days he doubled back to Cairo. He capped a six-hour afternoon journey with a, for Stanley, rare binge on Irish whiskey. In Cairo he visited the circus, went sightseeing and waited for further orders from London, depressed and dispirited. Cairo was not his kind of town: 'I always feel out of place in any town or country that has in it the least of anything approaching to French tastes.' In addition, he found the food and rooms at the Shepherd's Hotel execrable. He further punished himself by reliving in his mind his three-month exile in Aden and rehearsing all the likely reasons why his book on Abyssinia would not be published. Once again the stress of inactivity brought on another dose of Aden fever, which even Stanley by this time recognised as partly psychosomatic in its triggering: 'Heavens, what a punishment it would be to have no object or aim in life!' he exclaims.

On 17th February his prayers were answered and he was recalled to London by a cable whose curtness upset him: 'It is so brief that I fancy the Herald is disappointed with me.' Typically, Stanley then confided to his diary that he was hardly to blame just because Livingstone had not revealed himself to the world; he railed at the injustice of being in disgrace when he could not alter events or change destinies. The residue of unconscious guilt in Stanley shows itself clearly in the need to exculpate himself not only against charges that had not yet been made nor would be made, but even against those it had never occurred to anyone to make.

On 19th February Stanley made another long journey from Cairo to Alexandria and embarked on the Pelusi for Marseilles. Despite his strictures on life at Cairo, he felt a pang of regret as he saw the palm-tufted strand fade from view and he realised that it would probably be many years before he saw Egypt again (as with so many things, Stanley was wrong on this score too). There was little to interest him on the Mediterranean voyage, except the curious fact that many young Abyssinians were, in the wake of Theodore's defeat, being taken to London to be 're-educated' as missionaries (they were already Coptic Christians). On 22nd February the Pelusi anchored for two hours in the Bay of Messina; Stanley went ashore and had a coffee. Then it was Marseilles, Paris and London, where he arrived on 26th February.

There were changes at the Herald bureau. It turned out that it was Finlay Anderson, not Stanley, who was being recalled in disgrace to the USA. Anderson was extremely bitter about Bennett's arbitrary behaviour, but Stanley cynically observed that there was no smoke without fire. Though at one level sorry to see Anderson go, he still harboured a grudge that, because of Anderson's negligence, he had arrived in Egypt from Ethiopia to find himself penniless.'' At the beginning of March he learned that he himself was still in high favour. Anderson's replacement, Douglas Levien, told him that he was to go to Spain to report the revolution there on an extended stint at £400 a year.

1869 was to be a crucial year for Stanley in many years, both in his inner and outer life. He himself had some intimation of this, for when on the Pelusi he reflected on some very different rites of passage: There is a period which marks the transition from boy to man, when the boy discards his errors and his awkwardness, and puts on the man's mask, and adopts his ways. The duration of the period depends upon circumstances, and not upon any defined time. With me it lasted some months; and though I feel in ideas more manly than when I left the States, I am often reminded that I am still a boy in many things. In impulse I am boy-like, but in reflection a man; and then I condemn the boy-like action and make a new resolve ... I am still a boy when I obey my first thought; the man takes that thought and views it from many sides before action ... I want work, close, absorbing and congenial work, only so that there will be no time for regrets, and vain desires, and morbid thoughts. In the interval, books come handy. .. though there is much wisdom in them, they are ill-suited to young men with a craze for 97 action. But in these reflections perhaps Stanley was overdoing the discontinuity between man and boy. In all essentials, including physical appearance, John Rowlands was father to H. M. Stanley. All the mature attributes - high intelligence, great ambition, physical courage, administrative flair, dauntless willpower - were discernible in the alumnus of St Asaph's. At fifteen he was the height (5 feet, 5 inches) he would remain. As to the rest the continuity is best established by a comparison of two descriptions, respectively of the fifteen-year-old Rowlands and the Stanley of the 1880s: Full-faced, stubborn, self-willed, round-headed, uncompromising, deep ... in conversation with you, his large dark eyes would roll away from you as if he was really in deep meditation about half a dozen things besides the subject of conversation ... his temperament was unusually sensitive ... he could stand no chaff nor the least bit of humour.

The second description, having established his height and weight (180 pounds), goes on: 'but he was far from being fat. His flesh was all solid flesh, evenly distributed, and, I fancy, his muscles weighed nearly as much as the fleshy covering. Anybody could see at a glance that he was a man of wonderful muscular power. His chest was broad and deep and his legs made one think of a couple of short posts, so solid did they look. His face was - and of course is - a face marked in every line with determination. His eyes are small, near together, and have - or, at least, had - the look of a tiger's ... he always struck me as being a rather moody sort of fellow, who disliked crowds, lived largely within himself, and didn't care to talk much, except with his intimates. He is not exactly what you'd call a vain man, and yet, when I last saw him, he apparently had a pretty good opinion of himself. No doubt he had good reasons for his opinions, but he was rather fond of using the personal pronoun and was inclined to be a little dramatic whenever opportunity offered.'

All physical descriptions of Stanley emphasise the short stature, the stocky, barrel-chested frame, and the piercing basilisk eyes (pace the second description, they were certainly not small). But the good opinion Stanley undoubtedly did hold of himself was in conflict with a countervailing feeling of being inferior and worthless. Stanley credited the world with a kind of X-ray vision, whereby it could penetrate the carapace of cosmopolitan urbanity he had armoured himself with, to perceive the workhouse brat within. His abnormal sensitivity on this score often threatened to topple over into outright paranoia. The English upper classes were a particular focus for his suspicion, and an incident at Suez in 1868 reinforced his worst fears. On a sightseeing trip Stanley took two young English aristocrats under his wing, entertained them and massaged their gaucherie and culture shock. To his utmost mortification, in the hotel at Suez, through the paper-thin walls that separated his room from theirs, Stanley heard himself being mocked and ridiculed in a way that seemed to him wildly incompatible with the kindness he had showered on them. Not only did this incident breed a morbid fear of and distaste for the English oligarchy; it also weakened his self-esteem and, at the unconscious level, reinforced his determination to punish himself the next time he met a woman to whom he was attracted. The opportunity came sooner than he expected.

ON 3rd March 1869 at the Queen's Hotel on the Strand, Stanley had an unexpected visitor. Catherine Gough-Roberts, the girl he had met the previous autumn in Denbigh, appeared with her lawyer father. It seems that Thomas Gough-Roberts, the father, had spotted a future 'winner'. When Katie remarked at home on Stanley's air of distinction and quiet confidence, her parents discussed the possibility of an alliance between their money and the fame of the Herald's star 'special'. The upshot was the visit to London.

Gough-Roberts peer did not beat about the bush but came straight to the point. Having ascertained that Stanley did indeed entertain a high opinion of his daughter ('plump and good-looking' was Stanley's private estimate), he proposed a dowry of £1,000 if he took Katie to wife; naturally, Stanley would first have to propose and be accepted. Stanley explained that he was due in Spain at the end of the month, so this would have to be a whirlwind courtship. Roberts, who had been drinking heavily, agreed to let matters take their course.

Having nearly been caught in the net of the Ambella family, Stanley was much more cautious this time. Though attracted by the idea of the marriage, he bore himself coolly. To his diary he confided his real thoughts on the matter, which show him far from encoded by obvious passions: When a well-to-do solicitor of our native town is so frank and so good-natured as to be oblivious of St Asaph, it must be that he thinks more highly of me than I can persuade myself to do. One of my secret aspirations has been to be able to wed some fair-haired girl of a silent and amiable disposition, whose affection for me would enable me to forget the ills of life and live up to that ideal we must all have at one time or another thought to be blessedness.

He dilates on the advantages of the promised money: 'Any other way is immaterial and not likely to call up the rapture of love. However, it will be no harm to let the affair proceed ... it may be that Fate had chosen this singular way of conquering my reserve, for I know no man less forward than I in the presence of a woman.'

For a few days Stanley got to know Katie while he made preparations for his Spanish assignment. With typical thoroughness he armed himself with books on Spain and its history. His commonplace book shows the shift of interest. Notes on Helvetius, Virgil's Georgies, Mecca, the Koran, men who murdered their relations and the difference between the Ancient Greeks and Old Testament Jews give way to entries on Spain of which the following (13th March) is typical: 'Spanish Republicans from being Catholics became atheists.' But the same commonplace book shows a rival interest, perhaps best signified by the following entries: 'faithful wives', 'vengeful women', 'what has been done for love of woman' plus a list of 'heroic women' including Joan of Arc and Emma, daughter of Charlemagne.

While he pondered what to do about Katie Gough-Roberts, Stanley switched his attention to two other women, his mother and half-sister Emma. At last he was in a position to show his mother what a figure he now cut in the world and to wipe out the memory of the 1862 humiliation. He sent for the two women, lodged them in his hotel overnight, then took them to Paris for two days of sightseeing. This was the Paris of Offenbach and the gaite parisienne, basking in the false light of the penultimate year of the Second Empire. The two simple Welshwomen were bowled over by it: 'Mother is in raptures with Paris - the life in the boulevards, the Bois and the imperial palaces. Emma, I observe, is too full of thoughts for much talk.' We can infer what some of those thoughts might have been, for it is clear from later events that Emma decided, now that her beloved half-brother had come into money, that no other daughter of Denbigh was going to be allowed to enjoy it.

Typically of Stanley, he does not appear to have mentioned Katie Gough-Roberts to his mother, but only Virginia Ambella, safely in the past, for he records the following: 'I gathered from the old lady that she has been cherishing the thought of being able to mate me to one of my own countrywomen, with the view to saving me from being snatched by some "vile foreigner". She does not scruple to exaggerate the virtues of British girls nor, though she is not acquainted with a single "foreigner", does she hesitate to express her opinion that foreign women "though pretty enough, goodness knows and perhaps rich and all that" do not come up to her standard of what wives should be according to her.'

On the second day in Paris Stanley took his two women to the Louvre before going on to dine at the Cafe Vefour. The idea of Elizabeth Parry and Emma in the Louvre conjures memories of the wedding party in Zola's L'Assommoir. On the nth they returned to London, and next day Stanley put them on a train for Wales, but not before, in his usual manner, making a meticulous note of what the entire excursion had cost him.

Back in London Stanley continued his preparations for Spain. He also kept the Livingstone business on the boil with another letter to Consul Webb in Zanzibar. But most of all his thoughts ran on Katie Gough-Roberts. His emotions tightened to the point where he was prepared to tell all about his early Welsh experiences. The way his mind was working can be inferred from the entries in the commonplace book: 'filial affection' (18th March), 'the sins of the fathers visited upon the children' (21st March). Finally, on 22nd March he took the plunge. In an immensely long letter he begins by declaring his love for her, then admits his illegitimacy, the horror of his early life in North Wales, and the searing experience of St Asaph's workhouse. In this section of the letter Stanley is careful to tell the truth, as it could easily be verified by the Roberts family. But when he comes to his public life, Stanley at once lurches into lurid fantasy. The Ticonderoga story is resurrected, this time with the embellishment that after the Civil War Stanley served on her on a round-the-world cruise; he finally obtained a furlough at Constantinople in December 1866, whence he came to Wales.

But the lies get worse. First Stanley claimed to have been on a salary of £350 a year while on the Ticonderoga. Then this was supposed to have risen to £600 p.a. with the Missouri Democrat. 1868, in turn, was allegedly packed with travel. There was no dreary sojourn in Aden, no absurd love affair with Virginia Ambella. Instead Stanley ran together past and future travels by claiming to have visited Arabia, Zanzibar, Egypt, Crete, Greece, Turkey, Syria and Persia and to have dined with three kings: the Sultan of Turkey, the Viceroy of Egypt and the King of Greece; 'he is known over all America as a traveller, a gentleman and an author.'

Doubtless this absurdly mendacious boasting might just have passed muster with a young, ingenuous girl from North Wales; there was always method in Stanley's madness, as he made a point of lying about his private life to the public (who could verify his public life) and about his public life to private individuals who lacked the intellectual sophistication to falsify his tall tales. But his absurd claim to have £5,000 in the bank plus a 140-acre farm in Omaha argues for his poor estimate of Katie's intelligence, since simple arithmetic would have exposed the hollowness of this hyperbole within minutes. The searing, conflicting emotions he entertained about Katie, which we shall examine later, must have made him careless.

Affecting insouciance about the £1,000 dowry, Stanley ended his long epistle by stating that what he wanted was 'not a pretty doll-faced wife but a woman educated, possessed of energy.' He then peremptorily asked for a definite answer to his proposal before the following Wednesday when he was due to set out for Spain. But the Roberts parents felt they were being rushed into the marriage; they suggested that it would be better to wait until after Stanley finished his stint in Spain, when a proper wedding could be arranged. Stanley affected to be disgruntled by this reply, but at an unconscious level it was the answer he wanted to hear.

On receiving this reply, Stanley left London for Paris, to meet Gordon Bennett for the first time since December 1867. Bennett confirmed his Spanish appointment and spoke very flatteringly not just about the Abyssinian coup but also of his letters from Crete and Suez. It was therefore in good spirits that Stanley arrived in Madrid, on the last day of March 1869, ready to report the new order in Spain.

He spent just over six months in Spain, reporting the birth-pangs of the new republic, threatened by fissiparous elements within its ruling elite and from Right and Left by, respectively, the Carlists and the Radicals. Until the final month Stanley's duties were far from arduous. He had the leisure to read omnivorously; he taught himself rudimentary Spanish (Stanley was never a great linguist); and he sent back competent, but prosaic political reports. He came into his own only with the great Radical insurrection of October 1869 which convulsed southern Spain. There was particularly bloody hand-to-hand fighting between the Army and leftist irregulars in the cities of Zaragoza and Valencia, and Stanley's exciting eyewitness copy showed that he had lost none of his skill as a war reporter.

On his return to Madrid in late October he found a cable from Bennett summoning him to Paris on 'important business'. He spent the next six days putting his affairs in order, then on 27th October took the train to Paris.

The story of how James Gordon Bennett junior commissioned Stanley for the famous journey to 'find' Livingstone is one of the best-known items of Stanley's. According to Stanley's own published account, he made his way to the Grand Hotel in Paris, located Bennett's room, knocked on the door and identified himself as H. M. Stanley. There then ensued the following celebrated conversation.

'Where do you think Livingstone is?'

'I really do not know, sir!'

'Do you think he is alive?'

'He may be and he may not be,' I answered.

'Well, I think he is alive and that he can be found and I am going to send you to find him.'

'What!' said I. 'Do you really think I can find Dr Livingstone? Do you mean me to go to Central Africa?'

'Yes; I mean that you shall go and find him wherever you may hear that he is, and to get what news you can of him and perhaps "delivering himself thoughtfully and deliberately," the old man may be in want; take enough with you to help him should he require it. Of course you will act according to your own plans, and do what you think best - but find Livingstone!'

Stanley then mentioned that the expenses of such an expedition could top £5,000 - the cost of the 1857 Burton-Speke endeavour. Bennett was not a bit abashed.

'Well, I will tell you what you will do. Draw a thousand pounds now; and when you have gone through that, draw another thousand, and when this is spent draw another thousand, and so on but find Livingstone!'

Whether the conversation actually took place exactly like this is doubtful. It was natural for Stanley to dramatise everything, and from the early 1870s, even in his private diary notes, he went in for the recording of 'verbatim' conversations. Some of these accounts have the ring of authenticity; more often, though, they seem designed to show off the wit, wisdom and infallible judgement of H. M. Stanley. What is certain is that Bennett gave his star 'special' a roving commission to find Livingstone. In order to make sense of this singular assignment, we must look more closely at the career of both seeker and sought.

David Livingstone was born into poverty at Blantyre, Scotland, in 1813. By great moral strength he secured himself an education as a medical missionary, and it was with the London Missionary Society in the late 1830s that he became 'Dr Livingstone'. He went out to South Africa in 1840 as a missionary, but his passion for exploration (self-aggrandisement, his enemies said) gradually led him to become impatient with the slow, tedious life of a saver of souls. His 'missionary travels' of the late 1840s, when he discovered lake Ngami, were really disguised explorations but, although Livingstone never made a single clear convert, he continued to assert that his journeys were necessary for the propagation of the Gospel. Whatever his true motivations, he gradually established himself as the most powerful European propagandist yet for the 'civilising' of Africa.

Livingstone lacked both the financial resources and the human qualities needed to lead large expeditions but, ironically, it was the very small scale of his travels that struck a chord in British hearts, since he seemed to be a latter-day Pilgrim battling against the Apollyons and Vanity Fairs of the 'Dark Continent'. His crossing of Africa in 1854-6 from Luande on the west coast to Quelimane (in modern Mozambique), accompanied by a mere handful of devoted African servants, fired the imagination of Europe.

He returned to England as a famous man. His Missionary Travels became a best-seller. He was the lion of Victorian England.

But Livingstone's very success led him into debacle. After severing his connection with the London Missionary Society, he led a large expedition to the Zambezi, which opened up Lake Nyasa and the Shire River (modern Malawi). On this expedition were the supposed advance forces of a huge missionary effort in southern Africa. But Livingstone's own psychological problems led him into violent conflict with his European subordinates. The expedition was a colossal failure, and when it was recalled in 1863, Livingstone vowed to travel no more with white men.

Under the auspices of the Royal Geographical Society, Livingstone set out on his last African journey in 1866. His mission was to settle the dispute over the true sources of the Nile that had led to the famous controversy between John Speke and Richard Burton. He started from Zanzibar in March 1866, pressed westward as far as Ujiji on the shore of Lake Tanganyika, then penetrated the Manyema country as far as the River Lualaba, which he thought was probably the headwaters of the Nile. Mutinies among his men and his own illness compelled him to abandon the exploration of the Lualaba and return to Ujiji. Livingstone, then, was at Ujiji in 1869, then away on the journey to the Lualaba until 1871.This fact is of crucial importance in understanding Gordon Bennett's remarkable hunch that the 'finding' of Livingstone could well turn out to be the journalistic scoop of the century.

What of Bennett himself? Born in 1841 (the same year as Stanley), he was the son of a Scottish journalist from Banffshire, who emigrated to the USA and in 1835 brought out the first number of the New York Herald,}® In 1866 Bennett senior turned over the management of the Herald to his son. 'Jamie' shared both his father's dislike of England and his Irish mother's distaste for the USA. His upbringing had been a disastrous mixture of pampering and instability, since as soon as his father made his first million, his mother decamped for Paris. 'Jamie' spent his young years in an ambience of fantastic wealth, surrounded by sycophants, but without adequate parenting. Forever commuting across the Adantic between Paris and New York, and by 1869 enjoying an income of a million dollars a year, James Gordon Bennett junior oscillated between alcoholism and a fanatical desire to outdo his father by making the Herald an even greater sensation in the world.

'Jamie's' was a severely fractured personality, and at this level there was an affinity between him and Stanley. When in his cups, Bennett was impossible. He would go on stupendous alcoholic binges, pick fights with strangers in bars, drive his carriage through the streets of Paris like a maniac, shedding his clothes as he went, so that he arrived home naked. Usually Bennett silenced all protesters by buying them off, but sometimes he went too far even for his millions to protect him. On New Year's Day 1877 he capped all his wild exploits by urinating in the fireplace at his fiancée's home in New York. This brought him a horsewhipping from the (at once former) fiancée's male cousin, and banishment from the few segments of polite New York society from which he was not already ostracised.

But as a businessman 'Jamie' was peerless. He pioneered the 'New Journalism' (soon to be known as the 'yellow press'): celebrity interviews, lavish illustrations, society gossip, salacious news. Much of the Herald's success was based on its 'Personal Column' advertisements - a guide to every prostitute in New York able to publicise her wares and in particular to the brothels of Bleaker Street and Sixth Avenue. To scoop his rivals it was 'money no object' to Bennett. He thought nothing of transmitting long despatches across the Atlantic by expensive cablegram and had a fleet of yachts permanently cruising the sea lanes on the New York approaches, ready to intercept steamers and send on the latest eyewitness interviews from European travellers.

The dark side of Bennett was less well known. He had all the capricious cruelty of the tyrannical child of arrested development. He was not above sacking his entire senior staff on a whim or putting his best reporters through the most agonising hoops just to test their loyalty. When Stanley knocked on the door of the Paris hotel in late October and a dressing-gowned Bennett invited him inside, Stanley had good reason for trepidation.

On the face of it, Bennett's interest in Livingstone and Africa was decidedly odd. To Bennett the blacks were 'niggers', as a column heading describing Grant's New Year's Day reception in 1870 made clear: describing the arrival of the sumptuously dressed Alexander Tate, Haitian ambassador to the USA, the headline ran 'A Gorgeous Nigger'. Bennett was much too cynical a man to have any real interest in what Livingstone was trying to do in Africa. Yet Bennett was a journalist of genius. Not only did he have an uncanny understanding of the kinds of stories a mass public would go for, but he also knew the precise optimal moment to break those stories. 'Jamie' had been following the agonised 1869 correspondence in The Times on the whereabouts of the 'lost' Livingstone. His famous intuition told him that here were banner headlines in the making. The hour of the 'Dark Continent' in news value seemed about to strike, especially as international news was in a doldrums period.

Yet if Bennett had decided to throw all the resources of the Herald into an expedition to search for Livingstone, it still remains to explain why he had chosen Stanley. Tall, angular, dark, with a long face and drooping moustache, 'Jamie' was the physical opposite of Stanley. Moreover, Stanley loved literature, art and history, and made this plain in his copy. The philistine 'Jamie' hated and detested aesthetes and intellectuals. Furthermore, Stanley's Abyssinian triumph and his rise to fame had been the work of the now disgraced Finlay Anderson, and it was Anderson who had originally suggested Stanley for the Livingstone assignment.

The plain truth was that Bennett had wanted to give the assignment to another reporter, Randolph Keim, but could not contact him immediately in the USA and was too impatient to wait for him to cross the Atlantic. And there was something to be said for Stanley. His rugged individualism and lack of any aristocratic polish appealed to Bennett; doubtless he could see in Stanley's gimlet eyes the same suspicious ruthlessness that stared back at him from his own mirror. And he had already proved himself on an African assignment. So Stanley, then, it was. Bennett ordered him to go to London and make his detailed plans with Levien, the head of the bureau there.

But first he made a stipulation that most clearly evinced his journalistic flair. In order to screw the tension from the missing Livingstone up to its highest notch, he told Stanley to delay his search for Livingstone for a year. Bennett guessed that the current debate about the famous explorer would die down for a while, only to burst out later with even greater strength. When that happened he wanted the Herald correspondent to be on hand to shake the world. 'If the Grand Lama of Tibet "shuffles off this mortal coil", a reporter of the Herald is present in the death chamber to feel the pulse of the dying sovereign,' one of Bennett's competitors remarked sneeringly. But to Bennett that kind of scoop was a source of pride.

Bennett took a well-calculated gamble. He would send Stanley on a long trip through Asia as far as India. If by that time Livingstone was still missing, Stanley should launch an all-out effort to find him. If Livingstone meanwhile emerged at the African coast or was discovered by some other European, Stanley would abandon the Livingstone mission and proceed to China.

The first port of call on the Asian trip would be the Suez Canal, due to be formally opened on 17th November; the Herald had 'trailed' this event in August. Stanley had little time left if he was to be in Suez on schedule. On 29th October he crossed to London to confer with Levien. The bureau chief promised him a £600 letter of credit, plus further supplies of money in the future, and spoke rapturously if sycophantically about Bennett's 'positively Napoleonic' conception. He also advised Stanley not to conceal from Herald readers the failure of the Suez Canal, if indeed it turned out to be the flop predicted by its detractors. Levien later sent Stanley a written summary of their conversation.

The next day, 30th October, saw the decisive resolution of the 'romance' with Katie Gough-Roberts. From Paris Stanley had wired father and daughter Roberts to meet him in London. On a cold autumn Saturday the three of them met and tried to make sense of the tangled relationship. Stanley, knowing such an offer must surely be refused, proposed an immediate marriage by special licence followed by an Egyptian honeymoon while he reported the opening of the Suez Canal. Katie's father demurred at such precipitate action. Either Stanley stayed in England and allowed a decent interval to elapse, with banns called and a proper wedding planned, or the marriage would have to be postponed until he completed this latest peripatetic phase of his career. Stanley remonstrated that he had no choice. The canal opened on 17th November and unless he was there to report it he would very soon be jobless; you did not trifle with a man like Bennett. Stanley tried to explain Egyptian affairs and found Katie utterly ignorant on the subject. More worryingly for his immediate and ostensible project, she seemed cold and aloof, hardly surprisingly in view of the violent mood-swings evinced in Stanley's letters of 'courtship'. It was left that the situation would be reviewed when Stanley returned. He continued to write to her spasmodically during his Asian travels and in April 1870 was still talking of imminent marriage, possibly in India. His final letter was dated 7th October 1870 at Bombay. But by this time the saboteur in his own unconscious had done its work well. Stanley finally secured the rejection he had unconsciously sought. Tired of his indecision and sensing that she was out of her depth with this particular psychological cripple, Katie accepted a proposal from one Urban Rufus Bradshaw and married him on 22nd September 1870, before Stanley wrote his last letter to her in Bombay. She bore a son in August 1871 and a daughter in February 1873. There is evidence, too, that Stanley's own unconscious masochistic urges had a conscious ally. His half-sister Emma was madly jealous of Katie Gough-Roberts, both because Emma's identity was now bound up in Stanley's and she feared the coming severance, and because she saw the supply of money and fringe benefits from Stanley about to dry up. She managed to get herself taken on as a servant in the Gough-Roberts household and set about an insidious destruction of the relationship. First she hinted that Stanley was already secretly married. When this ploy did not work, she intercepted Stanley's letters to Katie. One of them was later found floating in a water butt where Emma had thrown it.

The fact that Stanley had unconsciously willed his own rejection did not prevent him from being bitter and outraged at the conscious level. After his death, when Lady Stanley was trying to threaten, cajole or bamboozle his love letters out of Katie, her agent wrote to Mrs Bradshaw (nee Gough-Roberts) as follows: 'You are aware that up to his last hour he regarded your long past act as an unspeakable betrayal at a time when he was daily passing through the valley of the shadow of death.'

Stanley also ran true to form in his bisexual rebounding. Immediately after the unsatisfactory interview with the Roberts, he took the night train to Paris, then spent Sunday and Monday trying to persuade the Balch family to allow young Edwin to accompany him on his Asian travels. When this request was, predictably, refused (the boy was still only fourteen), Stanley subtly began to transfer his affections to another young man, Edward King, a fledgling journalist who saw him off on the Marseilles express at the Gare de Lyon. As with Noe, Stanley did not discard his displaced favourite all at once; he wrote to Balch from Malta, but swiftly thereafter his correspondence and sentiment petered out.

From Marseilles Stanley crossed to Alexandria, covered the opening of the Suez Canal, sailed up the Nile as a guest of the Khedive, then explored the Holy Land. Thereafter he visited Odessa, the Crimean battlefields, Constantinople and Trabzon (Trebizond). He proceeded through Russian

Georgia to Baku on the Caspian. Entering Persia at Rasht, he made a 1000-mile sweep through Tehran, Isfahan, Shiraz and Persepolis, where he slept in the ruins and carved his initials on a temple pillar. He debouched at the Indian Ocean at Bushehr, then took a steamer to Bombay, where he arrived on the first day of August 1870. Nine months of continuous travelling had yielded some colourful travel writing but to what ultimate purpose? It was as well for Stanley's mental equanimity that when he arrived in Bombay he found that the hunt for Livingstone was still on and that he would not be condemned to journey to China or seek out the High Lama in his Tibetan fastness.

STANLEY himself once noted the Duke of Wellington's remark that he never knew a good-tempered man in India. The hero of Waterloo's apophthegm would not have been refuted by a scrutiny of Stanley in Bombay in August-October 1870. After he had completed the first half of Bennett's 'budget of instructions which I look upon even to this day with dismay' Stanley's frustration was at a high point as he alternated the writing of seventeen letters on his travels with the assembling of rifles, revolvers and ammunition for the plunge into the Dark Continent ahead. While he spent his days at the Bycalla Hotel with furious scribbling, he also kept an ear open for the unlikely chance that a ship might call at Bombay which was sailing to Zanzibar direct. He was, as he expected, disappointed. When his preparations were complete and the epistles to the Herald all written, he was obliged to book berths for himself and Selim on the Polly, under Captain Petherick, bound for Mauritius, where he hoped to secure onward passage on a vessel making for Zanzibar from the Far East.

The Polly left Bombay on 12th October. For thirty-seven days it rolled, pitched and yawed on the vast Indian Ocean, making very heavy weather until it picked up the south-east trades on 3rd November. Stanley alleviated the boredom by overeating and reading: Fenimore Cooper was a favourite on this voyage. There were just two noteworthy incidents on the way to Mauritius. William Farquahar, the first mate, drew himself to Stanley's attention by thrashing a young deck-hand called Charlie on the starboard watch. The incident recalled Stanley's own treatment when a boy on the Windermere; it helps to account for his later treatment of Farquahar. Secondly, Stanley left a rare record of one of his dreams - a vital clue to the elusive inner man. He dreamed that he had entered Purgatory from above through a large aperture in 'the sky dome' and that a male companion of 'beautiful face, form and figure' had touched him while he sleepwalked. The content and symbolism is too obvious to need interpretation.

The news of Katie Gough-Roberts' 'betrayal', which caught up with him a little later, reinforced Stanley's sexual anxieties and brought on one of his bitterest attacks yet of sado-masochistic reviling of the sins of the flesh. The early days in Zanzibar are full of fulminations against sexual intercourse in general and miscegenation in particular.

On 18th November, wafted by a spanking breeze, they passed Round Island and anchored at Bell Buoy in sight of the main harbour of Mauritius. Next day they spent a day in the island's principal town, Mahebourg, and on the 20th inspected the Pamplemousse botanist. November Stanley engaged first mate William Lawrence Farquahar from the Polly to be his chief of porters in Africa, but on condition that his pay would commence only on departure from Zanzibar.

On the morning of 22nd November they set sail for the north in the brigantine Romp, bound for the Seychelles, 1,200 miles due north. Sharing the captain's table was an ordeal for Stanley, since the master, 'a fidgety... superstitious and most selfish fellow, was a Creole with a chip on his shoulder, who thought that Creoles spoke better French than Parisians and that all Englishmen and Yankees were desperadoes. The combination of his company and the impotent lolling of the Romp in the doldrums was calculated to reduce a man like Stanley to despair. His lamentations sound like Captain Ahab on the Pequod in pursuit of Moby Dick: 'Oh insufferable ennui! Ah, torment of an impatient soul! Whatever is the value of a sailing vessel in the tropics! My back aches with pain, my mind becomes old and tends to dotage with these dispiriting calms.'

On 7th December they sighted Silhouette Island 50 miles away to the north, then Make Island next day. But it was the evening of the 9th, 'a fine moonlit night', before they made landfall at St Anne's Island. And still Zanzibar was 1,000 miles away due west. Stanley's urgent enquiries revealed that the only vessel going to Zanzibar was an American whaler, the Falcon, whose captain was Isaiah Richmond of New Bedford. The problem was that Richmond was adamant that he wanted no passengers on his ship. Stanley spent all day on the nth, pleading and blustering with Richmond to no avail. He finally won over the dour New Englander by revealing in desperation what his true mission was, and selling it as an opportunity for Yankees to steal a march on the 'limeys'. But Stanley's ordeal was not quite over. Next day was spent haggling over the passage price. It was a battle of the giants between two penny-pinchers. Richmond agreed to take Stanley's party for $150, provided Selim helped the steward in the galley. When Stanley tried to beat him down to $125, Richmond shut off the bidding with the unanswerable retort that Bennett was rich enough to pay the going price.

On 14th December Stanley, Farquahar and Selim went on board and learned that the Falcon had already been twenty-eight months away from her home port. A further day was spent waiting for the calm to die away. They then made very slow progress out through the islands of the Seychelles group before running due west on latitude 5, cruising for whales. On 23rd December Richmond took Stanley with him when he visited a fellow whaling captain on the Hecla. That was the sole incident that alleviated the tedium apart from a false alarm of 'Thar she blows' as they were eating their Christmas turkey. Once again Stanley became fretful and fractious with the boredom, especially when rough squally weather began to retard their already slow progress: 'Am unwell from sheer inactivity and overindulgence in smoking,' he recorded the day after Christmas.

Stanley found a focus for his frustrated rage in Farquahar. In his diary he railed at the Scotsman's laziness. When he asked him to make an oilskin coat for him, Farquahar demurred, on the perfectly reasonable grounds that his salary had not yet commenced. Stanley riposted by bringing up the advance he had paid him at the Seychelles. Soon Stanley became angry that Farquahar was not showing him due deference: 'Mr Farquahar's conduct became so unbearable that I spoke to him about it, at which he gave signs of being considerably astonished. Apparently he had forgotten the position in which we stood towards each other. Had I permitted his unwarrantable conduct to proceed further without comment, it would have spoiled him completely and rendered him unfit to be my companion.'

Stanley's feud with Farquahar continued into the New Year. On 2nd January he ordered the ex-mate to make Selim a pair of Turkish trousers. After much grumbling about having to indulge the absurd tastes of a 'damned barbarous nation' the Scotsman reluctantly made one pair. When Stanley asked him to make another, Farquahar indignantly threw down his needle and thread and said he had done enough for one day. Stanley privately vowed to settle the score.

On 4th January Captain Richmond promised them they would see land next day. As the reality of Zanzibar loomed, Stanley began to fret about the viability of his assignment. If Livingstone had already found the source of the Nile and proceeded to follow its course, there would be nothing left for his would-be 'finder' but to return to China, as ordered by Bennett. That was unthinkable, for already Stanley had had enough of maritime existence to last a lifetime: 'My long imprisonment at sea on shipboard I shall not readily forget.'

Zanzibar came as a relief and a revelation. After standing off the island on the evening of 5-6th January, not daring to approach the sound in darkness, Richmond landed his passengers next morning. Stanley was enchanted: 'one of the fairest gems of Nature's creation ... of all the islands I have seen it is the most perfect for the comfort of 20th March.

The next two days, when Consul Webb, his only contact, was too busy to see him, enabled Stanley to put his initial reactions to the test. The island of Zanzibar, 46 miles long and between 9 and 19 miles in width, was a low-lying, green and naturally fragrant land: as Stanley sailed along its coast prior to landfall his nostrils were assailed by natural scents and his eyes ravished by the variegated greens of mango, tamarind, bombax and cocoa palm. But the sweet sensuousness of nature soon yielded to man-made pollution. Anchorage at Zanzibar was a mere 400 yards from the town, and the harbour area was a forest of masts and sails: the (as yet) occasional European ship mingled with Arab dhows and a variety of small craft, slaving vessels and wood carriers.

The town of Zanzibar rose from the beach in a crescent form, 'white, glaring and unsymmetrical'. In the centre of the first line of buildings was the tall, whitewashed house of Zanzibar's sultan, Prince Barghash bin Said. Then there were the shore batteries and, to the right of them, the houses of the foreign diplomats and residents. To the left of the batteries were a number of sheds roofed with palm fronds - the Zanzibar Customs House. To the left of this again was the unfinished wooden palace of the Sultan and his harem, and the residence of his Prime Minister. Beyond this began the suburb of Melinde - the residential area for Europeans - which abutted the unhealthy Malagash inlet. Back from the shore, the indigenous quarters of the town were dominated by white light and blazing heat - the plentiful shade of the European suburb was absent. Everywhere was the amber-coloured dust of copal and the orchilla seed, the sweet fragrance of cloves and the stale sweat of hordes of slaves. The smell of decay was pervasive: festering sugar-cane debris, rotting orange and banana peelings, human refuse. In the business sector spicy smells and the odours of fruit, oils, peppers and cloth were counterpointed by swarms of flies. The pullulating population was supported by agriculture in the fields around. Here was an abundance of manioc, cassava, Indian corn, millet, sesame, plantains, mangoes, oranges, limes, pomegranates and jack fruit trees.

Commercially Zanzibar was both an entrepreneur's paradise and the cockpit for intense Anglo-American rivalry. A shrewd businessman had no particular difficulty in quadrupling his capital, especially in the ivory trade, since prices increased exponentially between the interior and Zanzibar. Until the close of the Civil War it was mainly the Americans who benefited from this unique investment opportunity. In a trade conducted mainly from New York and Salem, Yankee businessmen brought in annually some $3,500,000 worth of brandy, gunpowder, muskets, beads, cottons, brass-wire, chinaware, and especially 'Merikani' sheeting cloth, and departed with some $3,000,000 of ivory, gum-copal, cloves, hides, cowries, sesame, pepper and coconut oil. But in the late 1860s the Americans' near-monopoly began to be challenged by the British and Germans; by the time the Suez Canal opened in 1869, the US share of trading tonnage dipped alarmingly.

Added to this commercial rivalry was a political antagonism between the British and Americans. The Americans suspected that the British drive against the African slave trade masked a desire to absorb the independent principality of Zanzibar into an African empire and that the anti-slavery crusade itself camouflaged much more mundane economic interests. The two consular representatives on the island reflected the different styles and official aspirations of the two English-speaking nations. The US consul was the thirty-eight-year-old Francis Ropes Webb, also director of the Boston firm John Bertram & Co., and now in the third year of his Zanzibar consulate. The British political agent was Dr John (later Sir John) Kirk, vice-consul since 1866 and soon (1873) to be consul-general, in which post he remained (except for leaves) in Zanzibar until 1887. Kirk was primarily a diplomat, not a trader; he had served with Livingstone on the Zambezi expedition in the 1850s.

These two men were to be key players in the drama of Stanley's search for Livingstone. When Stanley arrived in Zanzibar, it was bad enough that he found no news at all of Livingstone. But he was stupefied to find that, with just $8 in gold left after fourteen months' travel, there was no letter from Bennett awaiting him to confirm the verbal orders in Paris and hence no money. In desperation, on 8th January he threw himself on Webb's mercy and asked him to pledge his personal credit of between $20,000 and $40,000 to the Livingstone expedition. It was fortunate for Stanley that he had already on several occasions established his credentials by letter and that Webb knew Gordon Bennett's interest in Livingstone was a long-standing one. Although Stanley's petition was, on the face of it, a very tall order financially, Webb agreed, on two conditions: Stanley would stay at the US consulate until his departure for the mainland so that Webb could protect his investment: and he would allow Webb to make all the preparations for the expedition with Sultan Barghash; Webb in turn would 'sell' the expedition to the Sultan as a way in which the Zanzibaris and Americans could turn the flank on encroaching British imperialism.

With the agreement secured, the two of them made their way to the Sultan's palace for a formal audience. Webb was fussily anxious that Stanley should not breach any of the rules of court etiquette and kept whispering instructions to him, reminding him that at no time should he turn his back on Barghash. Stanley was contemptuous of all this protocol, and also of the banality of the Sultan's conversation, but he played along with Webb, and was well rewarded at the outcome. Barghash gave him letters of introduction to Said Bin Salim, governor of Unyanyembe and a veteran of the two Speke expeditions. Another important letter of introduction was to the influential sheikh of the interior, Bin Nasib.

Next, without revealing what his true intentions were - only Webb of all the people in Zanzibar ever knew their true scope - Stanley made friends with the American mercantile community and began to amass a combined arsenal and warehouse at Webb's house: cloth, beads, wire, tar, canvas, tents, utensils, even two boats (one 25 feet by 6 feet, the other 10 feet long by 4V2 feet wide), which he stripped of their boards and then dismantled into sections that could be screwed together.

One of the necessary preparatory tasks was to cut up cloth for tents and canvas for saddles. Inevitably, Farquahar soon began to complain of the magnitude of the task, so Stanley looked around for another sailor with relevant experience. His choice fell on John W. Shaw, recently discharged mate of the USS Nevada. Shaw was a British sailor who had arrived in Zanzibar with charges of mutinous conduct hanging over him. The captain of the Nevada insisted on imprisoning Shaw and three other men in the Zanzibar Fort, saying he would neither pay them nor take them back to the USA. Webb investigated the charges and found them groundless; clearly the captain was merely trying to avoid paying the 'mutineers'. Forced to take them on to the USA the Nevada's master 'solved' his problem dropping the four men overboard in a longboat 7 miles off the coast. Now although the mutiny charges had been shown to be false - and on Webb's advice the captain was arrested on arrival in the USA – in terms of mercantile marine service there was a question mark against anyone who had been involved in such an incident. It was Shaw's knowledge that another ship would be hard to find that induced him to sign up with Stanley as Farquahar's Number Two.

With two white lieutenants in his employment, Stanley next had to engage porters, soldiers, bearers and their overseers from among the racially mixed wangwana or 'Zanzibaris' - the devoutly Muslim products of Arabo-African miscegenation. The two principal 'captains' engaged - at $80 a year and with a coveted uniform thrown in - were Bombay, a Yao former slave and veteran of the Speke expeditions, and Mabruki. Others of the 'old faithfuls' from the Burton, Speke and Grant ventures signed on at $40 a year apiece: Uledi, Ulimengo, Baruti, Ambari. The expedition gradually began to take shape: men, donkeys, provisions, barter goods, all increased in number throughout January.

But if Stanley enjoyed the best possible relations with the Sultan and his officials, and with the American community, he found the British on the island hard to take. The English missionaries were a particular irritant, especially their nominal overlord, Bishop William G. Tozer, who had achieved the singular distinction of withdrawing the Universities Mission to Central Africa from the mainland. Tozer, a High Church man, liked to go around Zanzibar dressed in priestly purple and fine linen and the sight of him for Stanley 'acted upon the Yankee as a red cloth on an insane bull'. But Stanley was not alone in his distaste for Tozer; Livingstone felt it too, and it was their common antipathy to Tozer and his High Church posturing that was to forge yet another bond between the Welsh reporter and the Scottish explorer.

Stanley's attitude to Tozer and his acolytes was one of mild contempt. Kirk was another matter. The 'Zambezi doctor' evoked in Stanley an immediate visceral antipathy. Each man seemed immediately to recognise the enemy in the other. Both were larger-than-life figures with a will of iron, arrogant and autocratic. Dr Kirk seldom inspired middle-range emotions. Those who came into contact with him either fell under his spell or detested him cordially. So on top of the coolness existing between the British and American communities, and between Kirk and Webb, there was placed a fresh layer of personal animosity between Kirk and Stanley. The full extent of his was not yet manifest, but the latent tensions were evident at their very first meeting on 9th January when Stanley caught Kirk directing a 'broad stare' in his direction. Later in the evening Kirk drew Stanley aside, ostensibly to show him a gun but really to talk to him about Livingstone, for Stanley had made it known that as a Herald reporter he was interested in any titbits of gossip about the great Victorian hero; he did not of course reveal to Kirk that his mission was to 'find' Livingstone. Kirk told him that Livingstone was a difficult man to get along with. Stanley, trying to be casual, asked what would happen if he accidentally 'stumbled' across him in Africa. Kirk replied: 'To tell you the truth, I do not think he would like it very much. I know, if Burton or Grant or Baker, or any of those fellows were going after him and he heard of their coming, Livingstone would put a hundred miles of swamp in a very short time between himself and them.' The idea that he was in search of a misanthrope did nothing to lift Stanley's spirits.

Moreover, what Kirk had to say about Livingstone at the second meeting was not encouraging: 'He [Kirk] gives me a very bad impression of Livingstone. I am told he is a hard man to get along with, is very narrow minded. Has had no personal quarrel with him but he has always had trouble with his companions. He thinks he ought to come home now and permit a younger man to go in his place.' These words, when later reported to Livingstone (for naturally Stanley made a point of repeating the conversation as part of his campaign to discredit the British consul), would whip him up into a frenzy against Kirk.

For the rest of January Stanley laboured away at the difficult task of assembling a credible African expedition. He had a number of meetings with Ladha Damji, the Sultan's customs master, in order to expedite Barghash's orders. He made the acquaintance of a man who was later to be important in his African work, an American bureaucrat, Augustus Sparhawk. He chafed at the suspected dishonesty of his agent, the nineteen-year-old local entrepreneurial talent Sewa Haji Paru. He had further meetings with the Sultan. He arranged how his porters would carry their loads (68 pounds per man). He learned about local currencies and the per diem payments of dhoti or cloth: how many yards of the various cloths to take, and how many beads (the currency preferred by some tribes) and of what colour. Most of all he learned from Sheikh Hashid about the most prized currency of all: wire, the thickness of telegraph wire.

By 5th February 1871 he was ready to cross to the mainland. As a parting gift he received two horses: one from the Sultan, the other from William Goodhue, a Salem merchant. But on the morning he was due to sail the dhows across the straits to Bagamoyo, Stanley found both Shaw and Farquahar missing. He tracked them down to a bar where they were both hopelessly drunk and insisting they did not want to cross to the mainland. Stanley threatened them with imprisonment for breach of contract and defalcation (they had already spent their advance of salary) if they did not immediately embark. Reluctantly the two went aboard.

As his flotilla crossed with bellying sails to the expedition's starting point at Bagamoyo, Stanley felt grounds for guarded confidence in the progress he had made so far. In a single month he had spent $8,000 of the advance extended by Webb against Bennett's wealth. On the first night in Bagamoyo his spirits were still further lifted by a noble dinner given him by the priests of the Catholic Holy Ghost Mission. This French order had been engaged in evangelical work in Zanzibar since i860, and Bagamoyo since 1868. Its father superior Anton Horner decided to open the prize vintages in the missionaries' cellars for this special occasion when the Herald correspondent, Dr Kirk and Captain Tucker of the anti-slavery cruiser HMS Columbine would all be present. Kirk had come over to the mainland on a shooting expedition with the French consul Charles de Vienne, and Tucker had seized the opportunity to request that he be included in a few days' 'sport'.

The dinner that evening was a truly splendid affair. But Stanley spoiled the fathers' generous gesture by his later cynical references to the occasion and by insinuating that the missionaries did a little too well for themselves, overlooking the fact that they were merely trying to impress their distinguished guests and that the array of fine wines did not represent their usual fare: 'The champagne - think of champagne Cliquot in East Africa! La Fitte, La Rose, Burgundy and Bordeaux were of first rate quality, and the meek and lowly eyes of the fathers were not a little brightened under the vinous influence.'

The 'vinous influence' also enabled Stanley and Kirk to get along well enough that evening. But next day Stanley found further evidence to fuel the animus he felt towards the British consul. For years Livingstone had been dependent for survival in Central Africa on supplies sent from Zanzibar by his erstwhile comrade Kirk. Yet Kirk's attitude to getting these supplies through to Unyanyembe, the great entrecote in western Tanzania, was dilatory to say the least. In November 1870 Kirk had despatched to the mainland £1,000 worth of goods supplied by the British government in a fit of anxiety and guilt about Livingstone. Instead of crossing to the mainland and making sure this vital convoy got under way for the interior, Kirk sent it across with a seven-man escort, five of them slaves. For onward transportation to Unyanyembe, at least thirty-five porters were needed, yet Kirk did nothing about recruiting them. The almost inevitable upshot was that when Kirk and Stanley came over to Bagamoyo in February 1871, Livingstone's relief caravan was still loitering on the coast. To save face Kirk then had to improvise hurriedly to get at least part of the supplies despatched inland.

The tension between Stanley and Kirk increased when Stanley remonstrated about the inept administration of Livingstone's supplies. Kirk coldly informed Stanley that he would change his tune when he experienced African conditions at first hand and prophesied that his two horses would not last a week in the African bush. Stanley got his revenge by a derogatory report about Kirk's marksmanship during the mainland 'shoot'. Since Livingstone was later to accuse Kirk of gross dereliction of his official and moral duties towards him, it is worth establishing at this stage that Stanley's accusations had substance. Kirk's many later defenders asserted that Stanley's secrecy was largely to blame: had he revealed his true intentions, Kirk could have sent the caravan to Ujiji under his aegis. But this argument will not hold, since it ignores the political realities of Anglo-American rivalry discussed above. Even had Kirk suspected Stanley's true designs, he would not have entrusted goods funded by the

British government to an American and an overt ally of consul Webb. Nor can naivety be pleaded in Kirk's defence: he, of all people, knew Africa and its delays - indeed he boasted of this knowledge to Stanley. We are left with the inescapable conclusion that, for reasons unexplained, he did not exert himself on Livingstone's behalf. Livingstone's later fulminations against Kirk are usually dismissed as the semi-paranoid ravings of a disappointed old man, who was being egged on by Stanley. But there was rather more substance to his criticisms than that. One explanation is that Livingstone was actually right, that Kirk bore an obscure, possibly unconscious, grudge towards him from the Zambezi days. Kirk had often got the sharp edge of Livingstone's tongue in those disastrous days and had parted from him on bad terms. One Kirk diary entry, dated 18th September 1862, is particularly significant: 'I can come to no other conclusion than that Dr Livingstone is out of his mind.'

Yet in Bagamoyo the issue of Kirk was a deferred item, not an immediately pressing one. All Stanley's time was taken up with the problem of finding sufficient pagazis or porters for his great exploit. The great cholera epidemic of 1870 had claimed so many lives that potential bearers were avoiding Zanzibar and the coast. For two months Stanley wrestled with an obstacle that threatened to wreck his expedition before it even got started. 'My life at Zanzibar I thought hard, but my two months at Bagamoyo a convict at Sing Sing would not have envied. It was work all day, thinking all night; not an hour could I call my own.'

In these two dead months at Bagamoyo Stanley also received his first education in the complex realities of African politics. At the level of technology reached in Africa in the early 1870s the porter was 'the camel, the horse, the mule, the train, the wagon and the cart of East and Central Africa. Without him Salem would not obtain her ivory, Boston and New York their African ebony, their frankincense, myrrh and gum copal.' Yet these crucial carriers, the Nyamwezi of what is now central Tanzania, were themselves divided politically into numerous small states. Overlaying the economic problem of short-term shortage of pagazis were political problems deriving from kinship, suzerainty and territoriality.' Yet at the very time Stanley was being held back by a mesh of delaying factors, his anxieties were rising daily. These were twofold, that the rainy season was approaching, and that, in the light of Kirk's remarks, Livingstone might decamp if he heard a white man was looking for him.

Stanley's frustration and anger over the long delay found a focus in the hated nineteen-year-old Sewa Haji. Stanley itched to take the dazzling young entrepreneur down a peg or two by a thrashing (preferably a flogging) for the many suspected peculations and financial irregularities, but Sewa was just too good at recruiting pagazis, who were hard to find even when paid well above market rate - Stanley's hiring bills in February-March 1871 came to $2,000 worth of cloth. And the young agent did give him one piece of invaluable advice: to send out his caravan in detachments, both because the chiefs of the interior were more likely to attack a large 'threatening' body and because, even if pacific, they would demand larger tribute or hongo.

Accordingly Stanley sent out his first two detachments, the second under Farquahar. He particularly wanted Farquahar out of the way, as the ex-mate had spent his time in Bagamoyo drinking heavily, whoring, and quarrelling with Shaw. Finally, by the end of March, Stanley was ready to leave himself. In all his detachments Stanley could count 192 men but in his own column, far the largest, he had (apart from himself, Shaw, Selim and Bombay) twenty-two soldiers and eighty-two pagazis. With them they took twenty-seven donkeys, two horses (including the bay which Stanley rode out of Bagamoyo), fifty-two bales of cloth, a boat, seven man-loads of wire, sixteen man-loads of beads, three loads of tents, four loads of clothes and baggage, two loads of cooking utensils, three of powder, five of bullets and cartridges, three of instruments and luxury items, and twenty loads of boat fixtures. The armaments of the expedition were also impressive. They comprised one double-barrelled smooth-bore No. 12, two American Winchesters ('sixteen shooters'), two Starr's breech-loading carbines, one Jocelyn breech-loader, one elephant rifle, two breech-loading revolvers, twenty-four flintlock muskets, six single-barrelled pistols, plus a quantity of axes, swords, daggers, hatchets and other weapons.

Altogether Stanley and his men took 116 loads, or 8V2 tons, of material into the interior of the Dark Continent. Stanley's very first expedition was already the largest ever to set out on a journey of African exploration. This fact was often underscored uncritically by later writers, who saw only the financial resources available to Stanley. They did not see that the very scale of Stanley's expeditions imposed its own logic, so that he could not afford to be as slow, methodical or flexible in his methods as his rivals. The Royal Geographical Society might send out explorers in a spirit of dispassionate discovery, but a hard task-master like James Gordon Bennett wanted fast dramatic results for his huge financial outlay.

As he left the suburbs of Bagamoyo behind, Stanley noticed that his expedition was already the object of much excited attention. Africans left the fields where they were planting and sowing to see the parade of soldiers and pagazis pass by. Stanley pretended, for the benefit of his Victorian readers, to be scandalised by their absolute nudity: 'compared to which Adam and Eve in their fig-leaf apparel must have been en grande tenue.' The expedition defiled up the narrow shaded lane, flanked by two parallel hedges of mimosa, that led inland from Bagamoyo. But soon they were clear of populated areas and approaching their first obstacle, the Kingani River. Here, after cutting down trees with axes to make a bridge over the feeder tributaries, Stanley's men ferried themselves across the main Kingani without difficulty.

Next day at dawn the kudu horn sounded and they breakfasted in the half-light. Stanley waited until the last straggler had left camp, then galloped to the head of the column, leaving Shaw to bring up the rear. On the western side of the Kingani, the terrain improved. No longer muddy jungle, it resembled the sward surrounding an English mansion. The trail led smoothly upwards towards a forest-clad plain, topped with occasional ridges from which panoramic views could be obtained. There was wild life in abundance: pigeons, jays, ibises, turtledoves, golden pheasants, quails, moorhens, crows, hawks, pelicans, eagles, as well as monkeys, antelope, steinbok, kudu, giraffe and zebra. Stanley tried out his .44 calibre Winchester rifle on the swarms of basking hippopotami but made no more impression on their hide than if he had used sling-shot. But since Stanley hated any kind of failure as if it were evil itself, he had to satisfy himself by killing one of the pachyderms with the No. 12 smooth-bore; as he himself admitted, this was purely a matter of 'sport', since his party was not in need of meat.

Stanley's prodigality was soon punished. On 27th March they were at Rosako, still in parkland, but now the supply of game was drying up. Already the sixth detachment was lagging behind, so he called a halt while Bombay went back to energise Maganga, the captain of the rearguard. It was four days before Bombay returned and a further four days before Maganga arrived. During the enforced rest, the expedition came close to collapse. Stanley's men began to sicken with fever and to desert. Stanley himself played with fire by allowing the tsetse flies he was examining to bite him, unaware that they carried elephantiasis and sleeping sickness. This incident is illustrative both of the primitive state of tropical medicine then prevailing, and, more particularly, of the appalling ignorance regarding the tsetse fly. But while Stanley experimented with flies, it was his horses that succumbed, not himself. The Sultan's horse dropped dead, and Stanley, in his present state of 'scientific' curiosity, carried out an autopsy. Despite the evidence, he remained adamant that it was some rare worm, not a horse fly that had killed the horse. Next day the bay that Goodhue had given him also died. Again Stanley evinced a certain morbidity by insisting on cutting up this carcass too. On top of these disasters, the heavens opened and the rainy season proper began. When Stanley was troubled with the nauseous stench of an anteater, which he had to dispatch with the Winchester, it seemed that his cup was running over.

At Rosako Stanley went through the first, and in many ways most serious, mental crisis of the Livingstone expedition. His two horses were dead, donkeys were starting to die, his sick list lengthened daily, and already the caravans he was not personally directing were falling behind. Worst of all was the realisation that the detested Kirk was right, that Stanley had severely underrated the risks and pitfalls ahead. Kirk had jeered that only a professional explorer could find Livingstone, and here was Stanley, not yet a week out from Bagamoyo, having to confront his own serious misjudgements and inadequacies. If he was so clearly wrong about the viability of horses in Africa, might he not also be wrong about the feasibility of the entire Livingstone expedition? It was symptomatic of his state of uncertainty that while hunting in the bush, Stanley himself got lost and retraced his steps back to camp only with great difficulty.

As with many people like Stanley, who habitually inhabit the twilight area between sanity and madness, the possibility of failure imparted renewed strength. Rage fuelled his determination to succeed; with the dedication of fanaticism, he decided to divest himself of all human weaknesses and become a man of iron. The change in Stanley's attitude was evinced in two ways. Normally, his propensity to beat and flog manifested itself towards those who were potential or putative rivals in one sphere or another (Noe, Sewa Haji); towards those who did not purport to be his equals he was complaisant. But now he decided to beat and flog all who did not meet his standards. And he decided (albeit unconsciously) to make Shaw the particular butt for his anger. Since Stanley's personality was being stretched to the limits of its capabilities, it is not surprising that many normally latent dark impulses began to surface. In this particular case it was a sadism directed primarily at an exponent of heterosexual promiscuity, for Shaw's various dalliances had long troubled Stanley and excited his wrathful contempt.

Moreover, Shaw was already a marked man in Stanley's conscious mind, for two reasons. In the first place Stanley found him humourless and inordinately vain and a bad influence on Farquahar. Secondly, Shaw had alienated Stanley by referring to the Zanzibar Arabs as 'niggers': 'he fully showed the uneducated Anglo-Saxon's ineptitude for travel and intercourse with other races.' As they began to climb up on to the East African highlands through the monsoon rains, and Shaw's complaints grew more vociferous, Stanley subtly increased the pressure on him and gradually edged him towards breaking point. He put Shaw in charge of the baggage cart during a trek through a fetid jungle on the way to Msuwa. For three days Stanley railed at him when he arrived late.: 'Shaw was in charge in the cart, and his experiences were most bitter, as he informed me he had expended a whole vocabulary of stormy abuse known to sailors, and a new one which he had invented extempore. He did not arrive until two o'clock next morning, and was completely worn out.' When Stanley had been mounted on his bay, Shaw rode a donkey. Now he walked while Stanley rode the donkey. Stanley's donkey-riding can be seen both as part of a new realism and as a desire to put Shaw in his place: he would never allow him to do exactly what he did.

At Msuwa, on the plateau, they halted for a day while Uledi and Ferrajji were sent in pursuit of Khamisi, who had deserted with two goats and Uledi's personal possessions. It was part of Stanley's plan to stop at the regular caravan stations, situated on the outskirts of villages, where goats, chickens and other food could be obtained. The usual pattern, as at Msuwa, was that the village and encampment would be surrounded by a protecting palisade. The drawback about these stations was that they were insanitary and fever-ridden, crawling with fleas, tsetse flies and malarial mosquitoes. The net consequence was that Stanley unwittingly further debilitated his manpower, since whereas in the bush his porters would certainly have been bitten, they would not have been constantly re-infected, nor would there have been so many noxious bacteria from human filth.

At Msuwa too Stanley had his first real taste of the tribute or hongo system, when he gave the chief two doti. But he salved the 'humiliation' he felt over this - for Stanley had not yet reconciled himself to African realities - by impressing the villagers with the firepower of his Winchester and breech-loading revolvers. On10April the expedition quit Msuwa and pursued the road to Kisemo, passing a chained slave-gang heading east as they went. At Kisemo Uledi and Ferrajji returned with the runaway Khamisi. His recapture provided a suitable cautionary tale for the other men. Uledi and Ferrajji related that they had rescued him in the nick of time from the Washensi people who were just about to kill him. Stanley summoned a court of eight bearers and four soldiers to decide what to do about the deserting Khamisi. Since the prestige of the Wanyamezi was diminished by his absconding, the court ordered a flogging; as presiding judge Stanley decided that the twelve jurors and Shaw should administer one stroke of the birch each.

Stanley involved Shaw in the administration of 'justice' as a way of reprimanding him for not preventing straggling. He tightened the screw on the luckless sailor in another way. Since Stanley had been accused by local tribes of 'bad medicine' in reading printed words from a book, he manoeuvred Shaw into lifting a 'sacred stone' out of the caravan's path to insinuate to his Zanzibari followers that the real Jonah on the expedition was Shaw.

On 12 April they reached the western edge of Ukwere at Mussoudi. Beyond lay the territory of the Wakami. Here they halted one day to replenish supplies before beginning the descent from the plateau into a valley of changing scenery and sable loam soil where plentiful sugar-cane, Indian corn, egg-plant and cucumber were grown. So far they had met only peaceful tribes, and the rumour was that the people Stanley called Wakami were no exception; any warlike propensities had been hammered out of them by the impact of the slave trade.

On 14 April they crossed the Ungerengeri River and began climbing out of the valley through a forest of tamarind, tamarisk, acacia, mimosa and mparamusi. Thence they ascended the southern face of the Kira peak and proceeded into the valley of Kiwrima. Stanley's hard driving meant they again overtook the fourth caravan at Mullaleh. To his chagrin it was full of sick men, hardly surprisingly since Stanley's detachment was the only one that carried modern medicines. More importantly to him, Stanley met a man who claimed to have seen Livingstone at Ujiji a year ago. This was Salid bin Rashid al Manzuri, who had helped Burton greatly during the 1856-8 expedition.

Encouraged by this definite news of Livingstone, Stanley prepared for the four marches that would take him to the great stone city of Simbawenni. But during a two-day halt he confronted two problems that would plague him to the 'city of the lions' and beyond. One was that the Luguru peoples he was now meeting were much more 'insolent and aggressive' than any tribes encountered hitherto. The other was Shaw. When Stanley took him to task for driving the donkeys across gulley's breast-deep in water, when prudence dictated unloading them first, Shaw exploded and called Stanley an over fastidious ingrate, a slave driver whom it was impossible to please. Shaw capped his remarks by stating that he would resign as soon as he met a caravan going back east. Stanley replied that he was free to do so, but he (Stanley) would retain all his effects against the advance money paid in Zanzibar. At this Shaw relapsed into a sullen silence.

18 April saw them outside the great stone fortress of Simbawenni (the site of modern Morogoro), whose population Stanley estimated at 3-5,000. Here Stanley was obliged by torrential rains to halt another four days, while he pondered in alarm the great mortality among the donkeys in the caravans. Simbawenni had been founded by Kisabengo, a Spartacus-like leader of runaway slaves, who died in 1867. His daughter was named for the fortress itself ('lion-like') and had established herself as a power in the land. She now sent to Stanley for tribute, which he refused on the ground that Farquahar had already paid it. For the moment she bided her time and contented herself with sending her people to stare at Stanley's caravan.

The four days outside Simbawenni were a nightmare. There was a constant downpour: 'a real London rain - an eternal drizzle accompanied with mist and fog.' Selim broke the trigger of Stanley's gun and nearly blew his own head off. Stanley himself was attacked by a fever that recalled the 'ague' of Arkansas and he was forced to dose himself experimentally with medicines. Worst of all, the caravan camp itself was a hotbed of malaria. Then filth of generations of pagazis had produced a plague of insects: red ants, centipedes, wasps, beetles; 'in short the richest entomological collection could not vie in variety and numbers with the species which the four walls of my tent enclosed from morning until night.'

On the fifth day the rain ceased long enough to allow them to wade through the Stygian mire to the flooded river-bank. They then crossed the river by a very unsteady suspension bridge and found a comfortable camp at the foot of the Usagara mountains, 5 miles to the north-west of the river crossing. On the morning of 24 April Stanley caught his cook pilfering for the sixth time and ordered Shaw to flog him as an exemplary punishment. Unfortunately, the cook's comrades saw the flogging as grotesquely unfitting for such a petty crime and helped him to decamp to Simbawenni. Stanley then sent three soldiers to bring the runaway back, but they were captured by the Sultana of Simbawenni, who took away their guns and chained them, then repeated her demand to Stanley for tribute. This presented him with a ticklish problem of credibility. Fortunately, some Arabs under Sheik Thani who had visited the Herald caravan passed on to the Sultana the canard that Stanley had guns with an effective range of a half a mile. At this she changed her tune and released her prisoners, retaining just two guns as a face-saver. The cook who had precipitated all the trouble was later found murdered.

The incident with the cook outside Simbawenni heightened tensions in the caravan. Bombay, who had earlier been reduced to the ranks for failing to get the stragglers into camp before midnight, now regarded Stanley as a madman, unlike Burton or even Speke, who had knocked his front teeth out in 1862. Shaw, too, who had been involved both in the initial flogging and then the retrieval mission to Simbawenni, started to realise just how dangerous was this man with whom he had signed a contract.

Between Simbawenni and Rehenneko, their next major objective, loomed the dreadful Makata swamp. There was an easier circuitous track that would have taken them to their destination, but Stanley was obsessed with the need to make sure the first three detachments were already well ahead of them, and not festering at Rehenneko. His methods had been unusual from the very first. Normally explorers did not travel in the rainy season - and it had rained every day since Stanley left Bagamoyo - but his impatient fanaticism would brook no delay.

So into the Mataka swamp they plunged. They marched 45 miles in five days, knee-deep in water and black mud. Fever, smallpox and dysentery assailed them. Shaw, Selim, the soldiers, the dog Omar all went down to one strain or another, the dog fatally so. Stanley suffered from fever, then from dysentery; including his spell in bed at Rehenneko he had lost 40 pounds in little more than a week (reducing from 170 pounds to 130).The men trekked on because they were more afraid of Stanley and his whip than of the swamp and floods ahead. Stanley here first showed clearly a trait that was later to become notorious: his habit of abandoning the ailing and sick. He left behind one man dying of smallpox then had the Pharisaic effrontery to justify his action by claiming that he did so 'lest they commit the barbarism of leaving him unburied when he was dead'. He topped this mouth-stopping arrogance by likening the situation to that of a man falling overboard during a hurricane, forgetting that a hurricane is a natural force and that the only force driving these particular men was his own demoniacal will.

That was not his only moral blemish during these agonising days in Makata. Although Stanley would always call a halt if he was dangerously ill, as he demonstrated later on the expedition, he showed no such consideration for anyone else. If another white man fell ill, Stanley immediately rationalised the inconvenience as 'malingering'. When, therefore, Shaw appeared at the point of death with fever in the swamp, Stanley simply pressed on faster. His grotesque injustice to his two white comrades can be seen from an example of unconscious irony when he simultaneously castigates Farquahar for his performance so far on the expedition and boasts about his own 'Sisyphean labours' in the Makata swamp, failing to see that those same labours had already been performed by Farquahar ahead of him. Stanley's published account of the passage from Simbawenni to Rehenneko is singularly revealing; it must be one of the few occasions when a public figure reveals himself more clearly in his published writings than in his private journal:

The first of May found us struggling through the mire and water of the Makata with a caravan bodily sick ... Shaw was still suffering from his first munkunguru (fever), exhibiting himself under a new phase - a phase none of the pleasantest. Besides delivering himself of certain desires not at all complimentary to the Expedition within our hearing, he seemed to assume by degrees the character of a chronic hypochondriac, which, at all times an unlovely character, is positively hateful to the mtongi (leader) of an African expedition battling with swamp and rain, with a sickened caravan. . .MabrukSaleem, a youth of lusty frame .. . laid himself down on the marshy ground, professing, while imitating a man who vomits, his total inability to breast the Makata swamp, but a plaited thong vigorously laid across his naked shoulders expunged the seeming nausea from the stomach; Abdul Kader, the Hindi tailor and adventurer .. . was ever ailing.. . but ever hungry. 'Oh God!' was the cry of my tired soul, 'were all the men of my expedition like this man I should be compelled to return, but not before taking summary vengeance upon the whole of them.' The virtue of a good whip was well tested by me on this day... and I was compelled to observe that when mud and wet sapped the physical energy of the lazily-inclined, a dog-whip became their backs, restoring them to a sound - sometimes to an extravagant activity.

At Rehenneko (near modern Kilosa), Stanley halted for four days to recover from his own fever, a luxury he would never allow to others in his expedition. At last the rainy season came to an end, so that the worst seemed over. But now came news from ahead that Farquahar was seriously ill. Stanley was angry with Farquahar both for this 'malingering' and (unconsciously) because Farquahar too had conquered the 'incomparable sufferings' of the Makata swamp, so that Stanley was not 'first'. Since he was too ill to write himself, he ordered Shaw to compose a letter.

Shaw composed an illiterate screed, to which Farquahar, now seriously ill, was only able to scribble a few incoherent lines in reply. Stanley later reproduced both letters, to show the 'impossibility' of his two white assistants, without explaining the desperate pass to which Farquahar's health had come. 'Callous' is a mild word to characterise Stanley's observations:

However ungrammatical and misspelt the above note [from Shaw] is, it is far more intelligible to me .. . than the reply which was received from the third caravan .. . this was the precious response I received to an anxious inquiry as to the condition of himself and his caravan. Had the man been stark crazy he could scarcely have incited anything better calculated to confuse one ... in short the letter is incomprehensible to me unless the man Farquahar is hydrophobically insane. We may note in passing a typical Stanley ploy: condemn person X, then condemn person Y even more vehemently by giving faint praise to the already damned person X."

When Stanley recovered from his fever, he went on ahead to Kiora to learn the true situation with Farquahar. He found him grievously ill from dropsy and elephantiasis. But what concerned Stanley more was

Farquahar's overgenerous payments to his porters (six bales of cloth) and the fact that all his donkeys were dead: 'An Arab proprietor would have slaughtered him for his extravagance and imbecility, but I had no other course but to relieve him of all charge of such goods.' As for Farquahar's ghastly illness, that merely elicited from Stanley a prime example of the sadistic mentality: 'As he heard my voice, Farquahar staggered out of his tent, as changed from my spruce mate who started from Bagamoyo as if he had been expressly fattened by the Wabembe of the Tanganyika, as we do geese and turkeys for the Christmas dinner - as interesting a case of hypertrophy as Barnum's fat woman.'

Stanley's attitude to Farquahar was despicable on just about every count. There was no word of either gratitude for the sterling job the Scot had done in such dreadful conditions, or compassion for his tsetse- induced state. Instead Stanley coldly quoted the proverb 'Set a beggar on horseback and he will ride to the devil'. Nor can Stanley be absolved on the grounds of being a mere psychopath, for he was capable of extreme compassion for his 'dark companions' and for animals, as the following stricture on Farquahar shows: 'I had given him a capital Zanzibar riding-ass... which he had ridden to death. He had never condescended to dismount from the moment he left one camp until he arrived at another, and, not knowing how to ride, he had see-sawed from side to side until the poor animal's back was so chafed that it soon died.'

Both Shaw and Farquahar were now in need of a sustained rest, but Stanley insisted on pressing on at once. They began to ascend the Usagara mountains. From Kiora the united caravans wound along the banks of the Mkondoa River, compelled constantly to cross and re-cross the stream because mountain spurs blocked the way. Since Farquahar and Shaw were only just able to sit on their donkeys and had no energies left for anything else, the column began to get strung out. Eventually Shaw was left far behind. Stanley sent him word to catch up, then sent a stiff written note. When no answer was received after four hours, Stanley's patience snapped and he rode back along the trail, to find Shaw and the rearguard 2 miles from camp.

For two days and nights Shaw had been grabbing what sleep he could in the open, since his tent and equipment were at the front of the column with Stanley. None of this weighed with Stanley who was simply enraged that he found 'Mr Shaw was riding at a gait which seemed to leave it doubtful whether he or the animal felt most sleepy.' Stanley at once ordered him to dismount, ill though he was, and walk the rest of the way to the camp, on the grounds that the donkey needed to be taken back at a brisk pace to be loaded.

But the alleged need for intemperate haste was waived next day when Stanley called a halt while his 'police' went in search of a deserter. The hapless Shaw and Farquahar were able to sleep undisturbed while Stanley took himself off on an exploration of Lake Gombo. But the retrieval of the deserter precipitated the three white men into a new phase of their running personal crisis, for the runaway, a Hindu handyman, was a personal friend of Shaw and Farquahar. From the surliness of their attitude at mealtime that night, Stanley knew a storm was imminent, but he was perhaps unprepared for its violence. Immediately on seating himself at the supper table, Shaw launched into a vituperative attack on his leader. He started by claiming that their food was not fit for a dog, then broadened the indictment by saying that Stanley had systematically breached the terms of their agreement, the latest instance being his insistence that Shaw walk to camp instead of riding the donkey. He ended with a flourish: 'I feel as if I would rather be in hell than in this damned expedition!'

Stanley hit back angrily. The two men had had exactly the same food as he had; as for the donkeys, it was very clear that in a few days they would all be dead. 'Have you considered well your position? Do you realise where you are? Do you know that you are my servant, sir, and not my companion?'

This was too much for Shaw. 'Servant, be damned!' he exclaimed. At this Stanley sprang up and knocked him down. Shaw staggered to his feet and faced his tormentor. 'I tell you what it is, sir,' he muttered, 'I think I had better go back. I have had enough and I do not want to go any farther with you. I ask my discharge from you'

This was playing into Stanley's hands. At once he ordered Bombay to strike Shaw's tent and carry it and his baggage 200 yards from the camp. When Bombay had completed the task, Stanley told him to put Shaw's gun and pistol in the same place. When Shaw calmed down, he realised he had made a bad mistake, for he could not survive in the wilds alone in his present debilitated condition. He had to play for time and obtain food, water and shelter while he decided what to do next. At sunrise he went to Stanley and made a grovelling apology. Knowing he had the whip hand, Stanley made a show of gracious acceptance.

The desertions, sickness, and terrible rains made Stanley decide to wait another day before moving on to Mpapwa. He therefore returned to Lake Gombo to shoot grouse. While he was gone, Shaw and Farquahar conferred on the most effectual way to rid themselves of their tormentor. They decided on a desperate expedient. They would murder Stanley, proceed to Mpapwa to buy food and spread the word that their leader had been killed by hostile tribesmen, then return to Zanzibar and safety. It was a hare-brained scheme. Had the two men been in full possession of their mental faculties, they would have realised that the wangwana were too loyal to Stanley for their assassination bid to succeed. There was the further snag that Farquahar, an excellent shot, was too ill to do the shooting and it would have to be performed by Shaw, an inferior gunman.

That night when Stanley returned from the lake, the two men put their scheme into operation. The minute Stanley had finished writing his notes and extinguished his lamp, there was a loud report and a bullet tore through his tent, missing him by inches. He snatched up his revolver and rushed out of the tent. He found Shaw pretending to be asleep but with the tell-tale weapon lying alongside him. Shaw sat up and rubbed his eyes drowsily, but Stanley bent down, picked up the gun and found that the barrel was still warm. He thrust his finger into the barrel and withdrew it black with gunpowder. Grimly Stanley asked Shaw if he had recently fired it. Shaw hastily improvised a story of having seen a thief pass his door. Stanley fixed him with his withering basilisk stare and said coldly: 'I would advise you in future, in order to avoid all suspicion, not to fire into my tent or at least so near me. I might get hurt, you know, in which case, ugly reports would get about, and this perhaps would be disagreeable, as you are probably aware. Goodnight.'

Stanley knew very well that there had been a murder attempt, but violence did not appal him as it would most men. He was content that he had a hold over Shaw, for he now had witnesses to an attempted homicide. Shaw, by contrast, was likely to have been in the deepest despair after bungling the assassination. If he attempted to desert now, Stanley could send word to the authorities in Zanzibar to have him hanged. As for Farquahar, Stanley knew perfectly well that he had been an accomplice in the plot, so decided to take his revenge by abandoning him at Mpapwa. Although he promised to pay a headman to look after him (he did not), in Farquahar's state abandonment was tantamount to a death sentence. Farquahar was far too ill to care, and was overjoyed at the prospect of rest when Stanley sent him ahead on a donkey, surrounded by solicitous porters, to Mpapwa.

On 17 May the expedition marched up a dry river bed to the foot of green mountains, where lay the great caravan town of Mpapwa. Already many caravans were strung across the welcome shade of forest covering the slope of the foothills. Stanley ascertained that Farquahar was ensconced in a nearby village and that his fourth detachment in the van was well on the way to Tabora. He retired to his tent for his first full refreshing sleep for a month.

Next day he ran into Sheikh Thani, the Arab leader who had aided him at Simbawenni. Thani had overtaken him by the simple expedient of travelling by the direct route. He believed in travelling with long rests and recuperations and exhorted Stanley to feast on the produce of the caravanserai: fresh milk, sweet potatoes, beef, mutton, honey, beans, sorghum, grain and nuts. After fifty-seven days on a diet of tough goat and matama porridge, Stanley needed no second bidding.

Thani also introduced him to a man with even more recent news of Livingstone: Sheikh Abdulla bin Nasibu. Nasibu painted a picture of a portly disciplinarian, a 'heavy grubber' feared by his men. A few days later another Arab, Amir bin Sultan al Harthi, one of Barghash's favourites, asserted that Livingstone was still at Ujiji.

This was exciting news, and Stanley made fervid preparations to move on as soon as possible. But Thani counselled caution and urged at least three days' solid preparation. Ahead of them lay forced marches, necessary to avoid the bleaching sun of the waterless plains of Ugogo and the notoriously belligerent Wagogo. Only the very largest caravans or those too small to be worth plundering risked crossing their tribal areas; all others went in convoy. Thani suggested that Stanley join a caravan under Sheikh Hamed.

Stanley deferred a definite decision, but spent two days collecting supplies, mending broken equipment, buying livestock, repacking loads. He spent the days while his men worked climbing the mountains behind Mpapwa. Then he told Thani he could wait no longer. At night in his tent he was being plagued by white ants and earwigs, a special source of terror to African travellers, ever since Speke had an eardrum pierced when one of them burrowed into his auditory canal. Faced with thousands of earwigs as companions at night, Stanley felt that henceforth locusts, fleas and lice would hold no terrors for him. Speke's fate was uppermost in his mind: 'My intense, nervous watchfulness alone, I believe, saved me from a like calamity.'

So Stanley dashed off ahead of the Arabs, exhorting them to catch up with him at the camp at Chunyu. But his haste was costly. Within four hours twelve donkeys died from drinking the brackish water at the camp - water so notoriously bad that the Arabs never allowed their baggage animals near it. The men too suffered nausea, bellyache and 'an unconscionable irritability' from imbibing the noxious fluid: 'The water had the flavour of warm horse urine and mud.'

Stanley's departure from Mpapwa effectively sealed Farquahar's fate. Stanley went through the motions of believing that the Scotsman's chances of recovery were good. When the headman at the village where Farquahar was 'convalescing' requested that an interpreter be present, Stanley sent him Jako, the Hindu whose desertion at Lake Gombo had Henry M. Stanley aged twenty Stanley relaxing on the downs above Brighton, August 1872, just before doing battle at the British Association meeting Stanley in 1874, at the time of the 'romance' with Alice Pike Stanley with his gun-bearer and servant Kalulu ■mm Stanley's party on the lower Congo, 1877. The earliest known photograph of Mutesa, kabaka of Buganda

Stanley entering Bagamoyo, May 1872, with Selim and Kalulu 'Image-making'. A formal pose with Kalulu, London, 1872 James Gordon Bennett, proprietor of the New York Herald Livingstone in 1864, on his last visit home 'Dr Livingstone, I presume' precipitated the confrontation between Stanley and his two white lieutenants. He also handed over enough cloth and beads to pay for Farquahar's keep, plus a special issue of cloth to be made over by Jako as a present to the headman if Farquahar recovered. But Stanley must have known that without medicine Farquahar could not hope to survive, and he later revealed his true sentiments by describing his doomed comrade as an incubus: 'Farquahar had become the laughing stock of the caravan from his utter helplessness to do anything at all for himself.'

Too ill to realise fully what was happening to him, Farquahar lingered just five days after the big convoy left Chunyu before succumbing. Farquahar was the first of many victims of Stanley's hard-driving, callous brutality. Although Stanley had never divulged to him the true object of the expedition, Farquahar had actually performed manfully in blazing the trail past Simbawenni, through the Makata swamp and up into the mountains before falling to the infection-aggravated diseases of the tsetse. Naturally, it was beyond Stanley ever to admit that any of his lieutenants had done well.

The question arises, why did Stanley think it necessary to take on Shaw and Farquahar in the first place? Doubtless he was misled by the example of other African explorers (Livingstone excepted) who never travelled into the interior without white companions. But he should have reflected that these were always handpicked comrades. Rather than picking up men from the bars of Zanzibar or the forecasts of 'hell ships', Stanley would have done better to employ an experienced African guide. Yet Farquahar's death was more than a mistake. It was a harbinger of things to come. The death rate among whites who accompanied Stanley to Africa would always be terrific. Farquahar in the vanguard blazed a trail for those coming after him in more senses than one.

7

DESPITE the many travails encountered so far, Stanley's descriptions of Usagara were sufficiently enticing to stimulate German would-be empire builders to look favourably on this part of East Africa, with its relatively docile Sagara people. Nobody ever made the same claim for Ugogo, the land through which the expedition conducted its next nine marches. The Wagogo were 'the Irish of Africa, clannish and full of fight'. All caravans passing through their territory had the simple choice: pay or fight. The Wagogo controlled the scarce water supplies that alone made travel across their barren plains feasible; strategically situated between the Masai and the Hehe, they were for a time a major force in East African politics. Most caravans were content to be mulcted rather than face ferocious armed opposition; it therefore cost Stanley $ 170 to get through to Unyanyembe.

Stanley was in no position to argue with the Wagogo. Desertions and deaths among his pagazis and the loss of seventeen donkeys had reduced him to an auxiliary position in a mighty caravan led by Sheikh Hamed. Stanley was in the rear of the convoy with Sheikh Thani, providing a powerful screen of riflemen for the travellers. From the Arabs he acquired a further tranche of expertise in African trekking. The route of a caravan, he learned, was not a single track but a number of different divergent roads, and the skill lay in choosing the right one for the prevailing season. During the rainy season a caravan leader would choose the route that avoided low-lying ground. In the dry season he would travel on the most direct route between one waterhole and another.

It was now high dry season, and the first part of the trek was a seventeen-hour slog across 30 miles of waterless terrain - what Stanley called 'the fiery plain'. The country abounded in game but was 'as safe from our rifles as if we had been on the Indian ocean'. The rigours of this journey brought on another attack of fever. Here, as ever, Stanley was lucky. If the Arabs benefited from his riflemen, he gained from being under their tutelage. With an invalid Stanley in his care, Shaw alone would have turned back to Mpapwa; even worse, the cross-grained valetudinarian Stanley might well have lost his temper with the inquisitive, aggressive Wagogo, possibly with fatal results. As it was, Sheikh Thani's men nursed Stanley through a delirium on the first afternoon. His fever dropped during the night and he was at the head of his column when it set out again at 3 a.m. on the second day.

At 8 a.m. on 1st June they crossed an invisible dividing line between thorn-tree desert and fertile crop country and at once tasted the legendary arrogant aggression of the Wagogo. At the village of Mvumi there was almost a riot. The Gogo people had allegedly never seen a white man before and alternated between stupefied staring and embarrassed laughter. Stanley had not yet fully adjusted to the culture shock of Africa that had been partly responsible for the demise of Farquahar; in addition he was only semi-recovered from fever. The staring of the Wagogo infuriated him, but his anger served only to attract larger crowds of onlookers. At last, in fury, Stanley picked out the most 'insolent' bystander and thrashed him with his donkey whip. This intemperate action could well have precipitated a general melee. Indignant Wagogo pressed closer to Stanley, taking care, however, to keep out of range of his flailing whip. A very nasty situation was finally contained with the arrival of Thani, who calmed Stanley and pointed out the impracticability of trying to shoot it out with the well-organised locals. Stanley tried to dig in his heels, but a timely recrudescence of fever removed him from the arena.

Thani was not well pleased with his ally's truculence. After all, Stanley's expedition was sui generis, but they, the Arabs, had to live and deal with the Wagogo on an ongoing basis. When Stanley recovered again, Thani talked him round to paying the detested tribute. Stanley once more relapsed into fever and doctored himself with heavier and heavier doses of quinine; his one turn of good fortune came when one of his soldiers shot dead a large hyena that had been disturbing his sleep and terrifying Shaw and Selim with its ululations.

On 4th June Stanley felt well enough to travel on, but the 'humiliation' inflicted on him by the Wagogo continued to fester. The sadomasochistic equilibrium in his reactions can be seen in the mixture of an (impossible) desire to wreak vengeance on his oppressors by wholesale bloodshed and a countervailing impulse towards redemption through suffering: 'Ugogo is to the white traveller what Vanity Fair was to Christian and his friends. It is an ordeal to prove of what stuff he is made of. He will be tempted a score of times each day to draw a bead with his rifle on some of the yelping, taunting savages who prance alongside him.' To salve his violent feelings, Stanley got his own back on Thani for his 'weakness'. He marched to the next village of Kiddimo and promptly paid the hongo demanded without demur, thus disturbing the fragile barter economy built up so painstakingly by the Arabs and making things more difficult for future travellers.

That was not the end of the Arabs' problems with Stanley. He continued to adopt a confrontational posture with the troublesome Wagogo. At Nyambua he took his lash to them again; at Mukondoku he adopted the tactic of laughing at them. Once again, it took a council of tribal elders and Arab sheikhs to pour oil on troubled waters. Another problem arose from the intermittent shivering fever Stanley suffered from all the way to Unyanyembe, which meant that he recorded the journey only intermittently while he dosed himself with quinine, waking from restless tossing to espy the endless herds of elephant, rhino, zebra, antelope and giraffe before succumbing again. Not only did this increase Stanley's short-tempered propensity to solve irritants by force; sometimes, as at Mizinza, it led to the entire convoy's coming to a halt, since Stanley was too ill to continue.

There could scarcely have been a greater clash of temperaments than that between Stanley and the caravan leader, Sheikh Hamed. Stanley was naturally pugnacious and disposed to cut corners, brooking no delays (except when he himself was ill). Hamed was a small, dapper, finicky, nervous man, whose anxiety to avoid trouble seemed only to attract it the more, as at Nyambua when a careless slip led him to pay extra tribute, while Stanley who had physically assaulted the Wagogo got away scot-free. Moreover, Hamed was a Shylock in business and the wearying negotiations with the Wagogo over hongo reduced his nerves to tatters.

Stanley's insistence on resting a day at Mizinza pushed Hamed close to breaking point. The reason was that at the previous village his two prize donkeys, valued at $100, had wandered off and been impounded by the local chief. The chief then claimed ransom money of $25 to compensate him for the grass the donkeys had eaten! After protracted negotiations a hongo of 36 yards of cloth, on top of the normal tribute of 60 yards, was agreed on. To make up the loss thus sustained, Hamed decided to crack on at a blistering pace, hoping to save on food for men and beasts. But after just one day of Stanley-like progress, Stanley fell ill and demanded a day's halt at Mizinza. Beside himself with frustration, Hamed announced that he was going on alone. Stanley appeared to acquiesce, knowing that Hamed was too timid to advance without the white man's firepower.

Chafing over the enforced delay, Hamed next tried sleight of hand. At Mukonduku, on the western border of the Gogo country, there was a choice of three routes to Unyanyembe. There was a long, rough northern route that skirted settlements and meant reduced Kongo. There was a short and dangerous track; there was also a middle itinerary known only to Stanley's men. At first Hamed opted for the northern route to save money, but his porters mutinied and he was obliged to promise them he would go by the short route. Stanley, however, was adamant that he would follow only the middle trail. Hamed appeared to accept this and set off along the middle track, intending to branch off on to the short trail desired by his porters. Stanley, who was checking the direction of the column with a compass, spotted the manoeuvre and gave orders that any of his porters following Hamed would be shot. Thani followed Stanley on to his chosen route. After an hour they saw the chastened Hamed plodding along in their rear. Without Stanley he had feared to try conclusions with the Kiwyeh warriors along the 'short' trail.

They started up the escarpment, its sides scored with erosion and covered with thorn trees and bushes. It was a difficult climb: 'The ascent of the ridge was rugged and steep, thorns of the prickliest nature punished us severely, the acacia horrida was here more horrid than usual, the gums stretched out their branches and entangled the loads, the mimosa with its umbrella-like top served to shade us from the sun but impeded a rapid advance.' At the summit a road ran straight through the jungle to Munieka. While trekking along it, the humiliated Hamed expunged his wounded feelings by picking a fight with Thani.

As the caravan pressed on beyond Munieka, the plentiful water supply put the column in unusually good spirits. The prospect of a nocturnal halt in the wilds, with no village at hand and in the cold night air of the plateau at 4,000 feet above sea level, did not damp their spirits. They were pleased to be well clear of the Wagogo and had as company only the jungle ruins of a Stonehenge-like set of standing stones. But Hamed had been plotting his own revenge on Stanley. Waiting until all were asleep, at about 1 a.m. he suddenly ordered his herald to sound the kudu horn. The entire encampment rose up and rushed to arms, thinking they were under attack. A march commenced in the darkness, which Stanley did not try to interrupt as he was unsure of the true situation. As soon as he ascertained it, he ordered his men to throw themselves down in the first village to resume their interrupted sleep (it was now 3 a.m.).

In the morning they learned that Hamed had moved on to the next village, some 7 miles farther on. Stanley quickly caught him up, to learn that the Arab's fabled ill luck had struck once again. Not only had his favourite girl in the harem died of smallpox but his three body-servants had absconded, taking all his best clothes. In his attempts to find the runaways, Hamed lost further time and ended by falling behind Stanley and Thani. But now the smallpox epidemic was tearing such swathes through Thani's followers that the Arab had to excuse himself from further hard marching. Stanley paused for a day to revictual, then plunged off into unknown country, but not before he had used the whip on his men, who hated the idea of parting from Thani. During the day's rest, he had been overtaken by Hamed who pressed on without taking on fresh supplies. This was a bad mistake, as ahead of the convoys stretched the Tura forest, uninhabited since the Tabora Arabs had burned down all the local settlements after a revolt. Where the forest merged with the first plains of Unyamwezi Stanley caught up with the Hamed caravan. After beating off an attack by thieves on the encampment, the two parties travelled on together to Tabora.

The ravages of smallpox on his party put Stanley into a rare state of despondency during the march through Tura, and the monotony of the terrain did not improve his temper. His cook tendered his resignation, but asked to accompany them to safety in Tabora. Stanley replied that the man must either work all the way to Tabora or disappear into the forest then and there. When the cook replied that he could go no further because of the incubus of two donkey saddles he had to carry, Stanley took the whip to him for his 'impertinence'. Another man asked permission to retire into the forest to die quietly of smallpox but Stanley insisted that he carry his load until he dropped. This was the wrong moment for the chief porter to suggest that the men be given a bonus for all their forced marching. Stanley rounded on Bombay violently and said that the men would be rewarded in Tabora but not before. To underline the point he laid around him with the donkey lash.

The trail through Tura was criss-crossed by elephant and rhino tracks and they even met the occasional band of local elephant hunters. Such was the received opinion that elephants could be the only business of men in the Tura that when Stanley encountered Hassan, son of the Arab governor of Unyanyembe, it was difficult to persuade him that Livingstone, not a giant tusker, was Stanley's quarry. But Hassan, who had met Livingstone, was able to provide an interesting description (of mixed accuracy) of the great man: 'He is a very old man with a beard nearly quite white, has the left shoulder out of joint by a wild beast' (clearly a reference to Livingstone's famous encounter with the lion in Mabotse).

As they came closer to Tabora, the number of Arabs they met on the trail began to increase. One invited him to eat outside his tent, as his harem was lodged within. Another treated him to an excellent chicken curry and regaled him with a rum story about Lake Victoria: how it was a salt-water lake fed from the sea. Soon Stanley was at Rubuga - a flourishing town in Burton's time, but now gutted and occupied by nomadic squatters. Kigwa too was desolate, with burnt-out houses and overgrown fields, like Rubuga a victim of abortive revolts against the Arabs at Tabora. Only at Shiza, the last camp before Tabora, was life normal; the chief there killed a bullock and gave a feast in Stanley's honour and provided a 5-gallon jar of beer for his men.

Having reached Tabora, Stanley had grounds for cautious self-congratulation. He had marched 525 miles in eighty-four days at 6V4 miles a day, as compared with 134 days for the same distance on the Burton/Speke expedition and 115 days on the later Speke/Grant exploration. But Stanley would undoubtedly have been stupefied if anyone had told him that his progress in the next three months would be precisely nil. Stanley did not realise that he had blundered straight into a war between the Tabora Arabs and the most powerful Nyamwezi chief Mirambo and that the theatre of war barred the way to Ujiji.

In his first three days in Tabora, the Arabs did not see fit to tell him.

They wanted his succour in the war but feared to reveal their hand too openly. So to begin with they treated him like a prince. He was assigned a tembe in nearby Kwihara: a large, strong mud house, one-storey, with a flat roof and a single door, with walls 3 feet thick. Inside the hallway to Stanley's rooms was guarded day and night by men with loaded guns; the detail was under the direction of the giant Mabruki, the veteran of the Speke/Burton and Speke/Grant expeditions. In his early days in the tembe Stanley feared natural enemies more than human, for Tabora was a notorious centre for Tanzania's 114 varieties of snake, including the dreaded black mamba.

The Arabs now prepared to gull Stanley into military support. The governor began by laying on a sumptuous banquet, in which course was piled on course over a period of hours: 'Just when I began to feel hungry again, came several slaves in succession, bearing trays full of good things from the Arabs; first an enormous dish of rice, with a bowlful of curried chicken, another with a dozen huge wheaten cakes, another with a plateful of smoking hot crullers, another with pawpaws, another with pomegranates and lemons ... After these came men driving five fat hump-backed oxen, eight sheep, and ten goats, and another man came with a dozen chickens, and a dozen fresh eggs. This was real, practical, noble courtesy, magnificent hospitality, which quite took my gratitude by storm.'

The Arabs followed this up by laying on lavish spreads for his men, to encourage them to follow their master into any and every venture. While they caroused, Stanley found himself with time on his hands. Strolling around Tabora, he was 'casually' invited in to a council by the Arabs, who had of course planned every step. Here at last they came to the point that was exercising them. Would Stanley participate in an attack on Mirambo? They were confident that they could defeat the Nyamwezi chief within fifteen days, and this was a consummation to be wished by Stanley, since Mirambo's forces at present barred the way to Ujiji. Stanley listened to the arguments adduced by Said bin Majid and his son Soud. They seemed plausible enough. Lacking a detailed knowledge of the complex politics of Tanzania, Stanley was not to know that he was being inveigled into a particularly desperate endeavour. Nor did the Arabs realise that they were pitting themselves against one of the great African warriors, a man who in fourteen years would conquer all lands from Tabora to Lake Victoria to the north, Lake Tanganyika to the south, and Lake Rukwa to the south.

It was left that Stanley would rendezvous with the Arab forces once he had engaged new men and then proceed with them to the battlefront, leaving the tembe and its stores under heavy guard. But almost immediately after the conference with the Arab leaders, Stanley was struck down with a virulent fever that came close to killing him. It was five days before he was able to move out of his bed, and he then immediately sustained such a violent relapse that he once more hovered on the threshold of death; in his hallucinated state he passed in review the main events of his life.

It was 29July before Stanley was fully recovered. In the meantime open warfare had broken out between Mirambo and the Arabs. Sheikh Said bin Salim had already taken the main Arab army out of Tabora. Stanley ordered Shaw to distribute powder, balls and thirty rounds to each of their soldiers, then headed north to Zimbiro, where he made contact with his allies. Three days of stubborn irregular warfare and skirmishing brought the combined Arab /Herald army to the outskirts of Mirambo's stronghold at Wilyankuru. There Stanley conferred with Said bin Salim and Soud and suggested firing the long grass around the village to prevent an ambuscade. Salim brushed aside Stanley's suggestion and confidently sent his son Soud and 500 men into Wilyankuru for the coup de grace. Mirambo appeared to flee in terror, departing at one gate as Soud entered by the other. Soud's men looted and sacked the stronghold and staggered out on to the Wilyankuru/Zimbiro road at the other end of the town, laden with ivory. Suddenly Mirambo's 400 men arose from their ambush in the long grass and slaughtered them to a man.

When this news reached Stanley and Said in Zimbiro (a handful of slaves still in the town escaped the slaughter), the panic was almost absolute. The only Arab leader to retain presence of mind was Khamis bin Abdulla al Barwani. Stanley, who had felt his fever returning on the second day of the campaign, was in his sickbed when the chaos and confusion in Zimbiro engulfed him. His men were swept up in the general panic. Both Shaw and Bombay lost their heads, and Stanley would have been abandoned if he had not forced one of his soldiers at gunpoint to fold his tent and accompany him. He came on Shaw in the act of saddling a donkey with Stanley's own saddle, quite prepared to leave his employer to Mirambo's mercies. Selim sprang at Shaw, wrenched the saddle away from him and ordered Bombay to prepare Stanley's donkey. For a moment Bombay stood transfixed with fear, then snapped to and obeyed the order.

Stanley assembled a small party, then set out, ill as he was, for a twenty-four hour forced march. With him were Shaw, Selim, Bombay, Mabruki, Chanda, Sarmean and Uledi. They got to Mfuto, half-way to Unyanyembe, at midnight, before Stanley considered it safe to slacken their pace. Mirambo was in no hurry to follow. It was ten days before his forces appeared at Tabora. In the meantime his 1,500 Watuta or Negroni under Mtambalika with 1,000 guns, assisted by the ruga-rugas or professional mercenaries of Unyamwezi, spread havoc and destruction on the road to the Arab capital and picked up an arsenal of discarded ammunition and abandoned tents left behind by the fleeing Arabs.

Meanwhile most of the Arabs in Tabora opted for abandoning the settlement completely. Even though it contained some opulent houses, like that of Amrani bin Masudi, the town was really a glorified collection of tembes, each surrounded by a fence. Stanley had no choice but to stay and fight it out if he was ever to get to Ujiji. He fortified his tembe at Kwihara, distributed his 150 defenders around embrasures in the walls and laid in five days' supply of water. He estimated that he had enough ammunition and food to withstand a month's siege, so ran up the American flag and waited.

When Mirambo's hordes arrived at Tabora, they carried away vast quantities of cattle, ivory and slaves and put the town to the torch. Fully one quarter of it caught fire and was gutted. There was little resistance. One of the few to display personal courage was Khamis bin Abdallah, who sallied out with his son, five Arab followers and eighty slaves to do battle with the ruga-rugas. But the slaves immediately deserted and the seven Arabs were cut down in a hail of bullets. Mirambo's men skinned them, cut off their genitals, then boiled skin and genitals up into a gruel which they used as a kind of gravy with their dish of goat and rice. Panic-stricken refugees began to stream out of Tabora to refuge at Stanley's tembe at Kwihara. At their ditches and embrasures the defenders stood ready; Stanley was determined on a kind of last-ditch Rorke's Drift avant la lettre. Professing quiet confidence, he wrote on the evening of 23 August: 'We have passed a very anxious day all in the valley of Kwihara. Our eyes were constantly directed over the saddle which connected the two hills separating Kwihara from the plain of Tabora.'

But the attack did not come. On the morning of 24 August Mirambo and his followers departed as suddenly as they had arrived. Mirambo was thought to have withdrawn because he feared a counterattack on the return to Urambo. Besides, with another victory under their belts, his men were so laden with booty that they would have been as vulnerable to an Arab backlash as Soud's men had been outside Wilyankuru. Also, Mirambo realised that his men did not have the equipment for a long siege of Stanley's heavily fortified tembe; the longer the siege and the shorter their provisions grew, the more they would be exposed to the likelihood of a successful Arab sortie.

As soon as Mirambo had withdrawn, Stanley went up to Tabora and tried to rally the Arab survivors. He found them confused and broken in spirit, fearful that Mirambo would return to attack them once he had secured his booty. On 26 and 27 August he attended Councils of War with the Arabs, at which their lack of ability or desire to open the Ujiji road was evident; indeed many of them talked of withdrawing permanently to Zanzibar. Stanley railed at their indecisiveness and lack of resolution:

Alas! all my fine spun ideas of proceeding by boat over Victoria Nyanza, thence down the Nile, have been totally demolished and scattered by this war with the black Napoleon. Already I have been here over two months and there is every prospect that I shall be two months longer because the Arabs take such a long time to make up their minds, to arrive at a decisive conclusion.

Once again Stanley had miscalculated badly. Not only had he backed the wrong horse in assisting the Arabs in their war for the control of the Ujiji caravan route, but he had placed all future European travellers in potential danger from Mirambo, who now regarded them as the Sultan's allies. His decision was widely thought to have ended all hope of finding Livingstone;

Mirambo now stood like an angel with a fiery sword between the doctor and his would-be rescuers. The other consideration was that the news of the Mirambo war, and Stanley's participation in it, alerted all intelligent observers to the fact that Stanley's mission was to find Livingstone, not to explore the Lufiji River as he had claimed.

Stanley returned to his tembe and began the task of hiring extra porters. Whatever his critics said, he was determined to press on to Ujiji, even if it meant going it alone without the Arabs. One consolation he derived from his frustrating last month in Tabora was the company of Kalulu, a seven-year-old Lunda slave given him as a present by one of the Arabs. Stanley made him his personal servant and chief butler. Kalulu was one of the most important in the long line of young male companions Stanley felt the need to have at his side; very soon he supplanted Selim in his master's affections, and there is much evidence thereafter of a running rivalry between the two boys. Stanley was delighted with the newcomer: 'He understands my ways and mode of life exactly. Some weeks ago he ousted Selim from the post of chief butler by sheer diligence and smartness. Selim, the Arab boy, cannot wait at table. Kalulu - young antelope - is frisky. I have but to express a wish and it is gratified. He is a perfect Mercury, though a marvellously black one.'

But if Kalulu was a source of comfort for Stanley, the boredom of his daily life at Tabora fuelled the impotent rage within. Once more he turned on Shaw as the butt for his frustrated impulses. After Mpapwa Shaw had a respite from Stanley's worst excesses: Stanley was ill most of the time on the road to Tabora and his gamesmanship with Thani and Hamed absorbed the remainder of his destructive energies. Shaw was much more successful in dealing with the aggravation of the Wagogo and Stanley even allowed himself to appreciate Shaw's attempts at humour when dealing with the staring of the Gogo people: 'Shaw said "These must be the genuine Agogians" for they stare - stare! My God there is no end to their staring.' For a time Stanley even tried to establish friendly relations with Shaw and rubbed out many of his diary animadversions on his companion. In response to this new geniality Shaw unfolded a series of tall tales: he had been at four levees of the Queen of England, was the son of a naval captain, had been studying Malay since the age of seven, had been in the Metropolitan Horse Guards and had lost£5,000 when buying himself out, was a devoted admirer of monarchy and aristocracy.

But after the incident at Zimbiro when Shaw tried to escape and leave Stanley to his fate, the earlier hostility returned. Stanley's journals are full of complaints about Shaw's laziness and malingering. Stanley responded by a show of open contempt for Shaw's intellectual powers. 'Shaw is a sentimental driveller with a large share of the principles of Joseph Surface within his nature. He is able at times to kindle into an eloquent rash about the vices of mankind, particularly those of rich people ... he is very angry, though, with me, because I laugh at him, and has just opened a sentimental battery on me which makes me almost cry out with vexation that I encumbered myself with such a fool.'

Soon Shaw's very presence and his physical mannerisms were grating on Stanley and kindled within him sadistic fantasies of beating and flagellation. 'Piff-puff at his nasty pipe. Hear him breathe! You would think he was dying; but he is not even sick. He told me only the other day, that he knew every trick of old sea-salts, when they wished to shirk duty at sea. I am sure he is practising a trick on me. This intermittent fever! I know every stage of it; and I feel convinced he has not got it. Of one thing, I feel sure, that if I took a stick, I could take the nonsense out of him.' And again, on Shaw's 'hypochondria': 'I know it proceeds from nothing else than a sick ennui. If I had recourse to the stick, I could cure him in less than ten minutes of all this annoying by-play.'

On Shaw's side, the more he learned of Stanley, the more he became convinced that he had signed up with a dangerous maniac. This conviction was reinforced when Stanley, in an attempt to establish a true rapport, divulged the true objective of the expedition. So far from reassuring him, this news terrified Shaw and precipitated him into a near mental collapse at the thought of the dangers and hardships to come. Disappointed at Shaw's reactions to the 'good news', Stanley decided to turn the knife in the wound. When news of Farquahar's death came in, Stanley taunted Shaw with weakness. 'There is one of us gone, Shaw, my boy! Who will be the next?' Shaw was out of his depth with this sort of thing and his clumsy attempt at retaliation in kind merely increased Stanley's hatred for him. On the last night at Kwihara, when Stanley was delirious with fever, Shaw made the mistake of creeping into his room and enquiring archly who was Stanley's next of kin since 'even the strongest of us may die'.

The troughs and crests in Stanley's moods while he waited at Kwihara, his alternating exhilaration as he hired wangwana for the onward journey at triple the normal rate and depression as he observed the Arabs' inertia, the joy caused by Kalulu on one hand and the anger induced by Shaw on the other, fed into his Herald despatches, so that even his geographical descriptions seemed to exhibit a kind of manic-depression. His analysis of Nyamwezi and the Usukuma country to the north of Tabora oscillated between a euphoric celebration of its potential for Europeans and a gloomy deterministic pessimism.

On the one hand, Stanley portrayed Nyamwezi as a paradise, far superior to the jungle plains of Ugogo, the forests of Unyanzi and the plains of Tura and Rubuga. From a vantage point it looked like a succession of blue waves in an ocean of forest; hills of syenite dotted the prospect, like islands in a sea or crenulated fortresses. Around the rocky hills were fields of maize, holcus sorghum, millet, vetch, sweet potato, manioc; herds of sheep, goats and hump-backed cattle. Especially in the south, there was an amazing profusion of game: elephants, buffalo, zebra, eland, hartebeeste, zebra, springbok, blackbuck, wild boar, lions, leopards and hippos. But on the other, he asserted that the climate and vast extent of the terrain (it extended over three degrees of latitude) made it deadly for Europeans: 'Supposing it were necessary to send an expedition such as that which boldly entered Abyssinia to Unyamwezi, the results would be worse than the retreat of Napoleon from Moscow.' Yet he was later to state that it was Usukuma which first opened his eyes to the potential of Africa for Europeans!

The other aspect of Stanley's ambivalence touched a peculiarly raw nerve. Mirambo had defeated him, so it was necessary subtly to downgrade the fighting qualities of the Nyamwezi warriors. Suddenly we find that his tormentors the Wagogo are the superior fighters: from a despicable rabble they become 'a bumptious full-chested, square-shouldered people' by comparison with whom the Nyamwezi are negligible. 'The Arabs never dream of arming the Wanyamwezi as escorts, as they are utterly unreliable. A Mgogo boy with a spear in his hand would be sufficient to make a legion of Wanyamwezi tremble.'

The truth is that Stanley in his limbo at Tabora and Kwihara was in a state of depression where he was not able to get a clear fix on the reality of his situation and thus jumbled up solid objective observations with illusory subjective perceptions; he admitted that the border-line between illusion and reality was becoming so hazy that he began to think that Livingstone was simply a figment of his imagination. The way out of such a seeming impasse for Stanley was always through the brutal exercise of willpower. He forced himself to transcend the seemingly insurmountable.

By September Stanley had enough porters to travel on without the Arabs. But he noticed that whenever he mentioned his intended departure for Lake Tanganyika, the Arabs always declared adamantly that to go on alone through a war zone was suicidal. Stanley came to see what their real game was when he overheard Sheikh Thani saying farewell to another traveller making for Ujiji. It was quite clear that the Arabs wanted Stanley's firepower to aid their war against Mirambo. The conviction hardened when he heard that Sheikh bin Nasib was extremely angry with local guides who had given him information concerning the Ukononzo road. When Stanley pressed hard for a letter of introduction to the Arab governor of Ujiji, the upshot convinced him that the Arabs might be prepared to go to any lengths to keep him at Tabora. He found himself vomiting and nauseous after a meal the Arabs had given him, and became convinced they had poisoned him, not with the intention of killing him but of keeping him as an invalid at Kwihara. This was the wrong tactic to try on a man like Stanley. He responded by telling the sheikhs that he had no intention of waiting another six months and was about to set out, whether they approved or not.

Sheikh bin Nasib retaliated by spreading a rumour that an attack by Mirambo was imminent and that he would be using the levies of the Bende from the shores of Lake Tanganyika. But Stanley learned from independent sources that Mirambo had in fact been driven off with losses from the town of Mfuto. He was just about to implement his final preparations for departure when his men were stricken with a fresh attack of smallpox. Baruti died at once; the languishing spirits of the others were further cast down by rumours spread by the Arabs of the dreadful state of the roads ahead and the infestation of the country by mga-rugas. The smallpox epidemic threatened to achieve what the Arabs could not: destroy all hope of an onward march to Ujiji. One by one the expedition members succumbed to its onslaught. From 4th September on Selim and Shaw were ill almost continually until the final departure. This time even Stanley was forced to admit that Shaw's illness was real and he dosed him with two grains of morphine.

This fresh blow to the expedition brought Stanley close to breaking point and saw his unconscious sadism at its very worst. Stanley's young male companions were ever the focus for the repressed homosexual side of his personality, and it was just at the time of the smallpox attack that Selim was being replaced as his personal favourite by Kalulu. This is the explanation for a truly revolting demonstration of brutality on 11th September. In a lucid interval on that day, before relapsing into delirium, Selim mixed himself a dish of milk and sugar to sustain himself through the crisis. Now Stanley's standing instructions laid down that he and he alone had access to the sugar. When Stanley learned what Selim had done, he ordered a flogging, smallpox or no, not only for the theft but because Selim lied about it. The humbug about lying from a professional liar is revolting enough. But to beat someone brutally who was already gravely ill with smallpox passes belief if we postulate a man of normal sensitivity and integrated responses. Anyone who doubts the pathological nature of much of Stanley's drive, and the aetiology of that pathology, will need to provide a 'normal' explanation of the dreadful events of 11th September 1871.

By 15th September the worst of the epidemic was over. Stanley announced that he would leave for Ujiji on 20th September and to this end began to distribute the loads for his pagazis. He took on another thirty wangwana to replace those lost in the war with Mirambo and through smallpox and reduced the impedimenta of the expedition to a bare minimum. Following the announcement, his men spent the night in a funeral celebration, dancing and singing the names of their dead companions and consuming vast quantities of liquor. On 17th September Stanley followed the usual custom before a great journey and gave a feast for his thirty-three soldiers: a roast sheep, fifteen chickens, 45 pounds of beef, 80 pounds of rice, eight large loaves of bread, corn, eggs, butter, sweet milk and a 20-gallon jar of the local brew.

On the eve of his departure Stanley himself went down with fever. His men were delighted. Overcome with trepidation at the dangers ahead, they now consoled themselves that the march to Ujiji would be abandoned. To their horror Stanley insisted on departing anyway. On 20th September the expedition trooped morosely out of Tabora, on a south-westerly track that Stanley reckoned would take them away from the theatre of war. The dispirited pagazis consoled themselves with the thought that their master, now delirious from smallpox, would have to return within a couple of days anyway. When the 'man of iron' began to defy their expectations, they started to desert. Stanley thundered that he would use a slave-chain on all deserters. To show that he meant business, he had his soldiers round up a couple of the runaways and placed them in fetters.

If the porters and soldiers were terrified at this leap into the unknown, unsupported by the Arab caravan, Shaw now plunged into terminal mental collapse. The morning of 20th September saw enacted another pitiful scene which Stanley reproduces as follows.

'Now, Mr Shaw, I am waiting, sir. Mount your donkey, if you cannot walk.'

'Please, Mr Stanley, I am afraid I cannot go.'

'Why?'

'I don't know. I am sure I feel very weak.'

'So am I weak. It was but last night, as you know, that the fever left me. Don't back out, man, before these Arabs; remember you are a white man. Selim, Mabruki, Bombay, please help Mr Shaw on his donkey and walk by him.'

After proceeding about 500 yards, Shaw fell off his donkey and pleaded to be allowed to return to Kwihara. Stanley refused. For the next two days he kept Shaw on the go, propped up on his donkey by the soldiers. On the third and fourth day Shaw proved unable either to dismount or to stay on the beast. Stanley was enraged: 'this little by-play of Mr Shaw's was getting too frequent.' When the porters rushed to help him, Stanley ordered them to leave Shaw be. Shaw lay for an hour on the ground in the full sun. Eventually Stanley approached him and asked him if he did not feel rather uncomfortable. At this Shaw sat up and wept like a child. Stanley takes up the story.

'Do you wish to go back, Mr Shaw?'

'If you please. I do not believe I can go any farther .. .'

'Well, Mr Shaw, I have come to the conclusion that it is best you should return. My patience is worn out... You are simply suffering from hypochondria. You imagine yourself sick, and nothing, evidently, will persuade you that you are not. Mark my words - to return to Unyanyembe is to die!'

'Ah dear me; I wish I had never ventured to come! I thought life in Africa was different from this. I would rather go back, if you will permit.'

Why did Stanley acquiesce now, when he had been so adamant throughout that the unwilling Shaw be dragged ever farther into the heart of the Dark Continent? Stanley himself in his diary presented his decision as bowing to the inevitability of Fate, after six months of absolute uselessness on Shaw's part. But more likely, Stanley now felt confident that to reach Ujiji he did not need Shaw and would thus be the sole white man to greet Livingstone. Failure with Shaw no longer implied ultimate failure on the expedition. It is also possible that, for all his bluster, he realised that Shaw was now seriously ill and he wanted him to die away from the expedition, where he would not be an inconvenience. But he made the grand gesture of giving Shaw the keys to the store cupboards at the

Kwihara tembe and sent him back on a litter, so that he could not later be blamed for his death. Whatever the case, within days of returning to Kwihara Shaw died.

Yet Shaw was not Stanley's only problem. Any slight relapse into fever was the signal for his men to desert in droves. Stanley sent back to Tabora to purchase from Sheikh Nabib the longest slave-chain he possessed. Then he offered Bombay and Chowpereh a new cloth for every deserter recaptured. Fourteen out of twenty were retaken and flogged, then chained around their necks. Stanley swore up and down that whatever the 'bleeding hearts' of Exeter Hall might say, he would always thereafter use the whip and the slave-chain while travelling in Africa. As an added disincentive to desert, he pressed on into the unknown by forced marches. But, as ever with Stanley, he could not resist a final self-justifying flourish to vindicate his treatment of the deserters: 'these men were as much bounty jumpers as our refractory roughs during the war, who pocketed their thousands and then coolly deserted.' When one recalls that it was Stanley himself who in 1865 was encouraging Noe to be a bounty-jumper, this sentence is truly breathtaking for its hypocrisy and, once again, suggests a mind unable genuinely to distinguish truth and falsehood.

The last days of September were disheartening ones for Stanley as he penetrated the forest separating Unyanyembe from Ugunda. Wave after wave of lengthy rectilinear ridges stretched ahead of him: 'Woods, woods, woods, forests, leafy branches, green and sere, yellow and dark red and purple, then an indefinable ocean, bluer than the bluest sky. The horizon all around shows the same scene - a sky dropping into the depths of the endless forest, with but two or three tall giants of the forest, higher than their neighbours, which are conspicuous in their outlines, to break the monotony of the scene.'

After a seven-hour trek through the forest they came to the capital of the new district of Ugunda, ruled by the Nyamwezi chief Muli- Manombe. Ugunda was a strongly-palisaded, turreted and impregnable fortress, but it could provide no fresh porters. Then they made long marches through the territory of Manyara, a region infested by tsetse flies. The chief initially held himself aloof but was induced to trade by the carrot of doti and the stick of a demonstration of Winchester power. They proceeded on a long forest march under a hot sun to the Gombe area, the most famous hunting grounds between Bagamoyo and Lake Tanganyika. The prospect put Stanley in good spirits. Commenting on the giant myukus (sycamores) in the forest, he wrote:

When daylight was dying, and the sun was sinking down rapidly over the western horizon, vividly painting the sky with the colours of gold and silver, saffron and opal, when its rays and gorgeous tints reflected upon the tops of the everlasting forest .. . infusing ... the exquisite enjoyment of such a life as we were now leading in the depths of a great expanse of forest, the only and sole human occupants of it - this was the time .. . when we all could produce our pipes and could best enjoy the labours which we had performed ... I am contented and happy, stretched on my carpet under the dome of living foliage, smoking my short meerschaum.

The sensuous euphoria induced by the forest again led Stanley to query the existence of Livingstone, then to accept it and wonder whether he was alive or dead. But the remarks he penned about Livingstone seem to have a deeper resonance, relating to his own psychic drama: 'Why is man so feeble and weak, that he must tramp, tramp hundreds of miles to satisfy the doubts his impatient and uncurbed mind feels?'Once arrived at Gombe creek, Stanley set about replenishing the expedition's meat supply. The Gombe area teemed with game of all kinds: buffalo, giraffe, zebra, waterbuck, pallah, stembock, wild boar, warthog, springbok, gemsbok, blackbuck, eland, as well as lions and hippo. The first day Stanley brought back two buffalo, a kudu and a wild boar for his men to feast on. On the second day he added four guinea fowl and five quail to his 'bag' of a zebra, two boars and three buffalo. Stanley's only complaint was that the Winchester cartridges supplied by a New York ammunition company were far inferior to the English cartridges provided by Eley of London. Whereas all the cartridges in the English double-barrelled smooth-bore fired, only a fifth of those in the Winchester 15-shooter were effective.

On the third day at Gombe Stanley's men requested a further halt to allow them time to dry the meat for the journey ahead. Stanley consented, on condition the lost time was made up later. After a lunch of antelope steak, hot corn-crake and Mocha coffee, he set out for the chase again with his two gun-bearers Kalulu and Majwara. They passed flocks of honey-birds, perpusillas, fish-eagles and bustards, but for Stanley they were small beer. Soon he came on a herd of grazing zebra. Although Stanley claimed that he hunted game out of necessity and not for sport and that he felt sorry for the animals he was obliged to kill, it is hard not to detect a cruel, gloating quality about his thoughts at this moment, at odds with the overt sentiments:

It was my option to shoot any of them. Mine they were without money and without price, yet, knowing this, twice I dropped my rifle, loath to wound the royal beasts, but, crack! and a royal one was on his back, battling the air with his legs. Ah, it was such a pity! but hasten, draw the keen, sharp-edged knife across the beautiful stripes which fold around the throat and - what an ugly gash! - it is done, and I have a superb animal at my feet. Hurrah! I shall taste of ukonongo zebra tonight. As so often when reading Stanley, the word 'humbug' hovers tantalisingly in the air. Stanley never truly felt sorry for the animals he shot. By pretending pity he makes obeisance to Victorian pieties, but when he is off guard, he reveals his true feelings. Often he wounded an animal, and the sole disappointment recorded is that the beast escaped.

It was perhaps an unconscious intuition that he had given himself away in that passage that makes Stanley go on to develop the theme of nature 'red in tooth and claw', with himself as much a potential victim as the zebra. He claimed that after shooting the zebra he was just about to take a dip in the cool waters of the Gombe and had waded ankle-deep into the water preparatory to diving when suddenly a huge crocodile shot to the surface yards away from him. However, Stanley's diary makes no mention of this incident - surely inconceivable if he had really had such a close brush with death. It seems to be a subsequent extrapolation from the later, genuine crocodile incident on the Malagarazi.

The three days by the Gombe were like an idyll in Lotus-land, but they were rather too enjoyable for Stanley's purposes. When he sounded the kudu next morning for a day's march, he found he had a mutiny on his hands. The ringleaders were Mabruki and the giant (6 feet 4 inches) Asmani, his brother. Stanley ordered Asmani at rifle point to lead his men out on the march. Asmani hesitated and seemed about to cock his own gun at Stanley in an act that would surely have brought his death from the trigger-happy explorer. For a moment the two men faced each other in a Wild West shoot-out posture. Suddenly Mabruki rushed in and knocked his brother's weapon to the ground. Mabruki then pleaded with Stanley to forgive Asmani. Typically, Stanley felt no appreciation for Mabruki's statesmanlike action but merely felt irritated that the guide's diplomacy had removed the pretext for flogging both of them. Baulked of his main prey, and in no way self-critical that it was his own fanatical hard-driving relentlessness that had provoked the mutiny, Stanley looked around for a scapegoat. He decided to whip Bombay on the specious grounds that he was really the secret organiser of the mutiny.

I at once proceeded about it with such vigour that Bombay's back will for as long a time bear the traces of the punishment which I administered to him as his front teeth do to that which Speke rightfully bestowed on him some eleven years ago. And here I may as well interpolate by way of parenthesis that I am not at all obliged to Captain Burton for a recommendation of a man who so ill deserved it as Bombay.

Again, this is vintage Stanley. First, the self-righteous brutality; then the introduction of another explorer to mitigate his own excesses; then the gratuitous slipping of the knife between the shoulder blades of a third explorer.

After this Stanley got his thoroughly cowed expedition on to the road to Marefu. They marched for five days through the monotonous forest of Ukonongo, through ruined villages, devastated by the ruga-ruga. There was plenty of wild fruit along the way and they encountered the largest herds of buffalo yet seen. Stanley admired the way his men could make a fire by rubbing a hard stick in the palm of their hands, but he was even more impressed by the honey-bird (indicator indicator), which guided humans to the nests of wild bees so that they could eat the honeycomb and the grubs when the nest was chopped out.

At Marefu they learned that they had edged closer than intended to the war zone and that the road ahead was blocked. Stanley's party fell in with an Arab embassy on its way to the Watuta to try to secure their services in the conflict with Mirambo, but the road to the Watuta lay through the war-torn territory of Chief Nyungu Ya Mawe. The only other road was the scene of a civil war among the Wavira. The head of the Arab embassy, an old man named Hassan, lacked the qualities for his mission. When Stanley suggested joining forces and striking north-west, instead of following the intended track south-west, the elderly Arab was horrified at the thought of a march across uncharted country.

Nothing daunted, Stanley plunged on: 'made a most determined march to avoid sleeping in a jungle infested by the Ruga.' As they crossed the mountainous ridge of Mwaru, the vegetation grew more varied: new types of fruit appeared, including the mbura (parinari curatellaefolium), the tamarind, the mtonga (mix vomica), like an orange, the wild plum (syzigium jambolanum). This plentiful fruit restored their health. The only serious invalid in the party now was Selim, whom Stanley was treating with Dover's Powders after he had drunk brackish water. However, what Stanley did not reveal in any of his published accounts was that Selim had only imbibed the tainted water after Stanley castigated him for over-drinking his water ration.

But still the trekking itself was gruelling. They survived a forest fire that roared on to them, even though Stanley feared his men would drop their loads and bolt. They passed through many charred and deserted villages, victims of the war between the Wakongo and Wavira. In one of them nine bleached skulls, stuck on top of a pole, told their own lurid story. Despite the war, the area teemed with game: buffalo, rhino, giraffe, ibises, fish-eagles, pelicans, storks, spoonbills, flamingos, ptarmigans, guinea fowl. Stanley shot a nimbi antelope for meat, and later caught sight of his first herd of wild elephants - the species that for Stanley truly deserved the title 'king of beasts'.

Ascending a ridge on to a plateau they came out of the forest and into the village of Mrera. Here Stanley called a halt for three days. This was one of his more humane decisions, for Selim by now hovered near death and his men were exhausted. At Mrera, where every tribesman seemed to possess a musket, they learned that they were still heading into the war zone so Stanley once again shifted tack to the north-west. Selim was recovering well - fortunately, since they now faced another long forest march. They camped at nights in ravines near quagmires of mud then continued zigzagging north-westward through the hill country at the base of the Kasera mountains. Sometimes Stanley sank up to his neck in the Stygian ooze of the mud churned up by elephants, rhino and buffalo: 'I had to tramp through the oozy beds of the Rungwa sources with my clothes wet and black with mud and slime. Decency forbade that I should strip and wade through the marsh naked, and the hot sun would also blister my body.' His sole consolation was a sighting of the rare sable antelope.

At last they emerged on to easier terrain, blessed with plentiful game. On 21st October they camped by the Mpokwa River, whose banks were clothed in sycamores, giant tamarinds and mvules. Next day they crossed to the Mtambu River and soon learned from a bitter lesson the truth of the local lore that the dense undergrowth and tall grass around the two rivers housed troops of lions and solitary leopards. At night lions would come prowling and roaring around the perimeter of their encampment, only to retreat at dawn. The leopards were more daring. A herd-keeper was driving a herd of donkeys and goats to water through a kind of tunnel in the brake made by the passage of elephant and rhino. The animals had scarcely entered the conduit to the water's edge when a leopard leaped on to the back of one of the donkeys and fastened its fangs in its neck. Fortunately, it was at once driven off by the massed cacophony of a dozen braying beasts.

The next week was one of the worst on the entire journey. That Stanley's luck was turning, and not for the better, seemed evinced by the failure of his next hunting trip. After disturbing a troop of monkeys, he began to stalk a wild boar, leaving Kalulu behind one tree and his solar helmet behind another. Firing from 40 yards, he pumped several shots into the boar. The stricken beast charged past Stanley then dropped. As Stanley advanced to skin it, the boar seemed suddenly to catch a second wind at sight of Kalulu and the helmet. It rushed off into a thick brake where, since it was now getting dark, Stanley did not dare follow it.

Next morning they made an early start to try to pierce the ring of mountains that barred their way to the Malagarazi River. They progressed through 'increasingly sublime' scenery, including the peak of Makoma that reminded Stanley of Magdala. At night the lions continued to roar. Stanley attempted to fire his Winchester into the darkness at them but gave up when the American cartridges failed him once again. On 26th October he had to suppress another near-mutiny after he rejected the men's plea to spend a day shooting game. To 'encourage the others' he had Selim flogged on the flimsy pretext that he stole a mbemba fruit contrary to orders which brought on a second attack of dysentery (again Stanley had no qualms about beating a man while he was already sick).

At the village of Itaga they found no meat but only some grain and vegetables. Once again it was demonstrated that Stanley was wrong and his men right: they should have laid in a supply of game while they had the chance. The supposed two-day journey to the Malagarazi was stretching into a week; meanwhile every shot Stanley took at wild life, be it leopard or buffalo, seemed to miss. On the morning of 28th October an entire herd of buffalo blundered into their camp but realised their error and careered off before they could be shot. By now Stanley's lack of foresight had placed them on starvation rations. Everyone was desperately hungry and keeping going only on the peaches or mbemba they had collected in the forest. They were also journeying in the full heat of the sun, out of the shade of the dense woods. Since Stanley still had plentiful supplies of tea and sugar he tried to sustain morale by brewing up and distributing cups of hot sweet tea. On 29th October they camped at night in a valley among rocky plateaux and precipitous ravines. Next morning, as the famished men descended further into the valley, they came on lots of rhino tracks and buffalo droppings and soon after, to their intense joy, reached a village where food could be purchased in exchange for excessive doti.

Their ordeal by starvation was now over, for away to the Malagarazi stretched a succession of crop-filled fields. After just one day of rest and recovery, Stanley struck out for the river. But once again Stanley's refusal to take advice and his headstrong determination not to be put off by the locals led them into trouble. Before they got to the Malagarazi they had to negotiate an extensive and treacherous marsh:

Fancy a river broad as the Hudson at Albany, though not near so deep or swift, covered over by water plants and grasses, which had become so interwoven and netted together as to form a bridge covering its entire length and breadth, under which the river flowed calm and deep below. It was over this natural bridge we were expected to cross. Adding to the terror which one naturally felt at having to cross this frail bridge was the tradition that only a few yards up an Arab and his donkey, thirty-five slaves and sixteen tusks of ivory had suddenly sunk forever out of sight.

As the men got on to this 'bridge' it sank one foot into the water and covered their feet. A donkey came within an ace of crashing through the grassy 'ice' and it required ten men to extricate him. During this struggle the 'bridge' sank another two feet and Stanley fully expected to see all ten men and the donkey disappear into the depths. Finally on the other side, they commenced a series of steep descents to the banks of the Malagarazi itself.

But at the river Stanley found that he had the 'insolence' of the local chief Nzogera and his son Kiala to deal with. Kiala extracted tolls from travellers for ferry rights over the Malagarazi. To square him, Stanley had to part with six doti of cloth and a quantity of the precious sami-sami beads, the most desirable form of East African currency. This settled both the hongo and the hire of canoes for crossing the river.

The second day of November was spent ferrying the men and stores across the 30-yard ferrying point. This was not as easy as it sounded for, as Stanley pointed out: 'I would prefer attempting to cross the Mississippi by swimming rather than the Malagarazi. Such another river for crocodiles, cruel as death, I cannot conceive. Their long tapering heads dotted the river everywhere, and though I amused myself, pelting them with two- inch balls, I made no effect on their numbers.'

At first all went well, except that after two canoe-loads had been landed at the other side Kiala appeared with a request for a further two doti. Stanley granted this grudgingly but warned the chief that any further extortion would lead to bloodshed. Eventually all the men except Stanley and Bombay were on the far side of the river. It now remained to get their two remaining donkeys across. Around sunset Stanley's favourite animal, Simba, was driven into the water with a rope attached to his neck. He reached the middle of the river where the water was no more than 15 feet deep when a crocodile seized him by the throat. Chowpereh and the others pulled frantically on the rope and the donkey's struggles were terrific. One crocodile could not have availed against the combined pulling of the rvangwana, but as Stanley recorded laconically in his diary: 'there must have arrived other crocodiles for the poor animal suddenly sank like lead.'

Stunned at the audacity of the saurians, for Stanley was certain that the very noise of the activity would keep the reptiles at bay, he abandoned work for the night, saddened at the loss of his favourite donkey. Next morning the one remaining donkey swam across without being attacked; Stanley's men attributed this to the charm they placed around the donkey's neck, but he himself, more detachedly, pointed out that in the early morning crocodiles liked to sunbathe on the shore.

At the first village on the other side of the Malagarazi Stanley received the exciting news that a white man had recently arrived at Ujiji from Maniema. Convinced that this was Livingstone, Stanley prepared to make a forced march to Ujiji at once. But there was a snag. The direct route from the village of Isinga ran through the scene of a bitter civil war between two Uvinza pretenders. Stanley decided to risk the two day- march through the Ha territory, although he had been warned by the Arabs that this was the one tribe he should avoid.

The Ha were one of the most powerful and warlike confederations of East Africa. Divided into six chiefdoms, they levied hongo well above the going rate on any traveller foolish or intrepid enough to cross their territory. It was into the Ha chiefdom of Luguru that Stanley now plunged, and once again his fanatical determination to press on through unknown terrain, whatever the local lore said of its dangers, brought his expedition inches away from disaster. In two days among the Ha, Stanley was mulcted of half his expedition's goods; if matters had continued thus, there would have been no point in his meeting Livingstone at Ujiji for he would have been denuded of all his effects.

The problem started when Stanley's column was intercepted on the road by the Ha chief Mionvu, who invited the expedition to rest at his kraal. Stanley, suspecting treachery, refused. In an atmosphere of high tension negotiations for the tribute commenced while the column lay drawn up at the ready on the road. Stanley's inclination was to shoot it out but his men argued that this would be suicide; they were just forty-five men against thousands of Ha warriors. Despite hard bargaining from 6 to 10 p.m., Stanley was obliged to agree to the extortionate hongo of eighty-three doti, in return for a promise that no more tribute would be exacted during the passage through the Ha chiefdoms. Stanley fumed at the humiliation. As he put it in his despatch to Bennett: 'The next time you wish me to enter Africa I only hope you will think it worthwhile to send me a hundred good men from the Herald office to punish this audacious Mionvu, who fears neither the New York Herald nor the Star Spangled Banner.'

But there was worse to come. Next day, despite Mionvu's assurances, Stanley was again stopped on the road, this time by Mionvu's brother, who insisted on tribute of twenty-six doti. When Stanley objected, citing Mionvu's promise, his brother replied witheringly that Mionvu had no right or authority to bind his fellow chiefs in that way. Stanley agreed to the tribute and decided to rest that night in the Ha village while he pondered his next step. Since there were four more chiefs along the line of march, it did not require great arithmetical talent to work out that by the time he had emerged from Ha territory, he would be destitute.

Desperate cases called for desperate remedies. In the village Stanley consulted with his guide about possible ways out of the Ha territory that would avoid population centres. The guide found a friendly slave - formerly the property of his old associate Sheikh Thani - who agreed to show them a way to Ujiji that avoided all human contact. His price for the information was twelve doti and he insisted that his stratagem could work only if Stanley had complete control of his party. Brushing aside the possibility that the slave might betray them, Stanley concerted his measures. At dead of night, at 2.30 a.m. on the morning of 7th November, Stanley and his expedition members made their several ways past the huts where the Ha slept and to the village gates. In bright moonlight they struck south, then turned west, parallel to the main road but about 4 miles inland from it.

At dawn they hit the Rusugi River. They were all hungry and the banks of the Rusugi teemed tantalisingly with buffalo, eland and hippo which they dared not shoot. While crossing the Rusugi, one of the women in the party became hysterical and began to scream at the top of her voice. To prevent her alerting the Ha and causing panic among his men, Stanley struck at her with his whip but had to lash her nine times before her voice subsided. His men solved the problem by gagging her with a cloth and tying her hands. Even so, there was some evidence that they had been spotted and that the Ha would even then be raising the alarm.

Crossing the Rusugi, they struck north-west through a jungle of bamboo, leaving no trail. At 1 p.m. they reached Lake Musunya. After ten hours of non-stop marching, Stanley ordered a cooking halt, then they plunged into the bamboo again and spent the night shivering silently without fires perilously close to a Ha settlement. At dawn the next day their guide made a mistake and nearly took them into a Ha village. An alarm was raised, but Stanley dissuaded pursuit by slaughtering all the goats and chickens the expedition had with them and leaving them on the road for the Ha to gorge on.

A long march that day and a further one at night finally took them out of Ha territory, across the Mkuti River and into Ukaranga and the Bende people. They had marched at the rate of about 4 miles an hour (an incredible achievement in Africa), in desperate hunger, forced to trek past amazingly tame herds of eland, buffalo, elephant and rhino without firing on them, lest the shots betray their presence.

At Ukaranga his coming at first caused panic, since the townspeople thought the expedition was Mirambo and his men. But they soon recovered and received their unexpected guests cordially. Next morning Stanley ordered the American flag unfurled; he himself donned his best clothes:

'My helmet was well chalked and new piggeries folded around it, my boots were well oiled and my white flannels put on, and altogether, without joking, I might have paraded the streets of Bombay without attracting any very great attention.'

The expedition set out in good spirits for the final leg of the journey to Ujiji. After two hours, from the summit of a hill, they caught their first glimpse of the breathtaking Lake Tanganyika. From the western base of the hill to Ujiji was a three-hour march but 'no march ever passed so quickly'. They crossed the Luiche River with its tall matete or elephant grass. At last they stood on the summit of the final hill in the overlapping folds that ran down to the lapping lake water. Ujiji was directly below them.

They began to enter the town. Where the suburbs started, Stanley ordered his men to commence firing. The guide blew his clangourous horn. The Stars and Stripes fluttered in the breeze. Bende tribesmen and Arabs came rushing up. Suddenly a black man was at Stanley's shoulder, speaking in English.

'How do you do, sir?'

'Hello, who the deuce are you?'

'I am the servant of Dr Livingstone,' the man replied, then rushed off like a madman.

As the throng of Arabs got bigger, Stanley threaded his way from the rear of the column to the front. All at once he was confronted by a knot of Arabs, at the centre of which stood a pale-looking, grey-bearded white man, dressed in a red woollen jacket, wearing a navy cap with a faded gold band around it. The two men raised their hats.

'Dr Livingstone, I presume?'

'Yes.'

'Doctor, I thank God I have been permitted to shake hands with you.'

'I feel thankful that I am here to welcome you.'

THE meeting between Stanley and Livingstone at Ujiji, just after midday on an autumn Friday in 1871, is one of the most celebrated incidents in all modern history. Unfortunately for Stanley, his absurdly stiff 'Dr Livingstone, I presume' caught the popular imagination in the wrong sort of way and became a music-hall joke. We are entitled to ask then, whatever possessed him to produce such a potentially risible greeting at such a moment?

Stanley never denied that he had spoken the famous four words, and usually explained disingenuously that he could not think what else to say. In fact the formula was the result of a good deal of agonising and soul-searching. The man who could brave the terrors of Africa, its fevers, crocodiles, snakes and savage tribesmen, was mortally afraid of rejection. Kirk's words came back to haunt him: that Livingstone would bitterly resent another white man coming to see him. As he later explained it: the newspapers described him as worthy of the Christian world's best regard; privately men whispered strange things of him. One that he had married an

113

African princess and was comfortably domiciled in Africa; another that he was something of a misanthrope, and would take care to maintain a discreet distance from any European who might be tempted to visit him. Not knowing whom to believe, I proceeded to him with indifference, ready to take umbrage.

This account is borne out by Stanley's private diaries. He confessed that he originally intended to stay in Ujiji no more than a day, just long enough to get a letter from Livingstone, acknowledging receipt of the stores and confirmation that the Herald reporter had 'found' him. He had no intention of risking being slighted or humiliated. After all, apart from Livingstone's reported misanthropic proclivities, he was an 'Englishman' (Stanley's phrase) and in Abyssinia and after Stanley had had enough of the peculiar foibles of the upper-class Englishman to last him a lifetime. In addition to his fears concerning Livingstone's individual reaction and those of Englishmen in general, Stanley had a third reason for his apparently austere pomposity: the conviction that any display of overt emotion in the presence of Arabs would lessen the prestige of the white man. The myth of the 'superman', increasingly required by the exigencies of imperialism, seemed, on Stanley's fallacious reading, to require the stiffest of stiff upper lips. It is perhaps significant that Stanley misread the situation in all three areas of motivation. Livingstone did not react as he had expected: Englishmen found Stanley's formality ludicrous; the Arabs formed a lesser, not a higher, opinion of European civilisation from the incident.

There is no reason to dissent from the general judgement that 'I presume' resulted from Stanley's basic lack of spontaneity in 'unnatural' situations where he could not be himself. Indeed he admits as much in a diary entry for November: 'What would I not have given for a bit of friendly wilderness wherein I might vent my joy in some mad freaks, such as idiotically biting my hand, twisting a somersault, slashing at trees ... these exciting feelings before appearing in the presence of Livingstone.' Yet it is also true that the latent content of Stanley's words, as opposed to their manifest content, speaks volumes of his unconscious turmoil.

Ironically, there was no need for Stanley's coiled-up hesitancy and self-doubt. He and Livingstone very soon discovered a natural rapport. After a few moments' general conversation Livingstone led him to his house. The two white men sat with their backs to the wall, while the Arabs took their seats on the left. After a short while, the Arabs, with what Stanley considered commendable delicacy, left them alone.

At once Stanley remembered the famous (or infamous) letter bag, originally dispatched by Kirk in November 1870 - the same which was languishing at Bagamoyo in February 1871, and which Stanley had later overtaken at Tabora and now brought on. At Stanley's invitation to open and read his long-delayed correspondence Livingstone demurred: Africa had taught him patience, he said; he had waited so long that it would not harm him to wait another day. In the meantime he would prefer to hear all the public news from Stanley. So Stanley started in. First there was the

Franco-Prussian war, the election of General Grant as US President, the laying of the transatlantic cable and the completion of the Union Pacific railroad; then came the events where Stanley had a more intimate connection: the Cretan insurrection, the opening of the Suez Canal, the flight of Queen Isabella, the Spanish revolution, the recent assassination of General Prim and the election of Amadeus of Savoy as constitutional monarch in Spain.

Suddenly Stanley remembered the bottle of champagne he had brought all the way from Bagamoyo for this exact occasion. He sent for the bottle, uncorked it and toasted Livingstone. The afternoon that followed Stanley remembered as one of the most pleasant of his life. Livingstone was genial and exuberant. He told anecdotes and jokes about his friends, particularly those who had accompanied him on his African travels, like William Cotton Oswell, William Webb, Gordon Cumming and Frank Vardon. He amazed Stanley by being able to quote huge chunks of Burns, Byron, Tennyson and Longfellow and disconcerted Stanley, who prided himself on his knowledge of literature, by being better informed on Whittier, Lowell and many other writers than the Herald correspondent himself, whose job it was to be au courant with matters American. So spirited and jovial was Livingstone that afternoon that Stanley suspected him of slight hysteria. 'You have brought me new life,' Livingstone repeated several times to him.

Stanley was not to know that Livingstone was speaking the literal truth. While away in Nyangwe the doctor had left all his trade goods and medical supplies in Ujiji with an Arab named Sherif, thinking they were in good hands. Sherif, a notorious drunkard and speculator, helped himself to Livingstone's cloths and beads to set himself up as a rich wastrel and sybarite in Ujiji, imagining that his 'benefactor' would not survive the rigours to the west of Lake Tanganyika. When Livingstone staggered into Ujiji half-dead in the middle of October, just two weeks or so before Stanley arrived, he found himself destitute. Sherif had wasted his entire substance on riotous living. Fortunately for Livingstone he had laid by an exiguous emergency supply of local currency with an honest Arab trader, but this represented just one month's subsistence. When Stanley arrived, half of the emergency supply was gone and imminent starvation stared the doctor in the face.

This helps to explain the gusto with which Livingstone tucked into the repast Stanley laid before him. Anxiety and shortage of money had combined to produce loss of appetite in the past terrible two weeks in Ujiji, but as Kalulu and Selim combined with Livingstone's cook to produce curried chicken, rice, stewed goat, meat cakes, yoghurt, honey and fruit, the doctor's reputation as a 'trencherman' seemed fully justified. Livingstone ate and drank his way through the afternoon's conversation. The two men talked animatedly until dusk.

Then Livingstone showed Stanley to his quarters in the tembe. The hut was a low, rectangular, thatched building with mud walls; it was about 45 feet long and 7 feet wide. There were two large rooms in front, which enjoyed an eastward prospect across Ujiji market-place and to the mountains down which Stanley had just travelled. Stanley had the right-hand room, Livingstone the left; there was a passage between them. To the rear of the tembe was Lake Tanganyika and on the front veranda (extended from the eaves and propped up by poles) was a combined office, study and reception room. Near the equator as Ujiji was, it enjoyed twelve hours of daylight from 6 a.m. when both men arose. Stanley enjoyed the unwonted luxury of a few moments' reflection in bed, scarcely able to believe that his quest was at an end and that Livingstone was found. His worry now was that the high spirits and joviality of the first day might simply be a flash in the pan and that Livingstone would revert to the curmudgeon his legend credited him with being. This was a particularly pertinent consideration, since he would have to 'come clean' this morning about his mission. Amazingly, in the euphoria of the first day Livingstone had not only not read his letters but had not bothered to ask Stanley what his business in Ujiji was.

For the first few minutes that morning Stanley's worst forebodings seemed about to be borne out. Over coffee Livingstone told him his news from the letters he had read after retiring last night. Stanley then remarked that Livingstone was probably wondering what he was doing in Ujiji. Livingstone replied that he had thought him an emissary from the French government until he had seen the Stars and Stripes but 'I did not want to ask you yesterday as it was none of my business.'

Stanley then confessed that his 975-mile, 236-day journey from Bagamoyo into the heart of Africa had been made explicitly for the purpose of contacting Livingstone. Livingstone claimed not to understand.

'Well,' said Stanley, 'you have heard of the New York Herald'

'Who has not heard of that despicable newspaper!' Livingstone answered tartly.

Stanley laughed. 'You will not call it despicable after you have heard what I have to say.' He then proceeded to present his mission as one actuated by pure philanthropy, pointedly not referring to 'scoops' or other newspaper practices. He outlined the resources he was prepared to make over to Livingstone to allow his work to continue and stressed that he had no desire to poach on Livingstone's preserves as a famous explorer; all he required was a formal letter of thanks for Gordon Bennett.

At this Livingstone recovered his animation of the day before. They spent a delightful morning swapping anecdotes. Livingstone confided that Stanley's coming had restored his appetite and zest for life. He told him how close to the edge of starvation he had come after Sherif's treachery. Stanley in turn recounted the zigzag progress of his quest for the lost explorer, how Bennett's order to go to Asia first was a signal example of God's providence, since otherwise they would not have been at Ujiji at the same time. Another joyous day closed with prayer; Stanley was having to revive the practices of his pious Welsh youth, for Livingstone insisted on grace before and after each of the three heavy meals he consumed that day.

The close relationship so quickly established never faltered thereafter during the four months the two men were together. Both Stanley and Livingstone were notoriously difficult and prickly individuals. On paper a successful outcome to their meeting would have seemed unlikely. For one thing, Livingstone's opinion of Americans was not high: 'Aye, they have a great population, viz. 21 millions of the greatest bores that the moon ever saw,' he wrote in 1852. For another, Stanley was a journalist and Livingstone had taken a roasting from the press after the death of Bishop Mackenzie on the Zambezi expedition. Stanley was prepared to storm off at the first sign of any affront from Livingstone. Yet the relationship prospered mightily. What, then, were the special factors contributing to this?

In the first place, neither was what the other assumed him to be: Stanley was no more an American than Livingstone was an Englishman. Both men were Celts, both born in poverty, both with a distaste for the upper-class Englishman. If Stanley had vivid memories of monocle aristocratic buffoons in Abyssinia, Livingstone for his part was still smarting under the humiliation of the terms on which the Foreign Office had granted him his consulship which he regarded as 'the most exuberant impertinence that ever issued from the Foreign Office'. The sense of inferiority that pervaded the men who had come a very long way socially, respectively from the Blantyre textile mill and St Asaph's workhouse, led them to make uncritical and unbalanced assessments of oligarchic patrons who took them under their wing; Livingstone's almost childish enjoyment of his lionising by London high society in 1864 was to find a later counterpart in Stanley's rather slavish bedazzlement by royalty in the person of Leopold of Belgium.

The two men also shared many points of similarity in temperament. Both were primarily journalists of genius. Livingstone's status as missionary and explorer was shaky. As a missionary he had made a single (later lapsed) convert and as an explorer his only undisputed discovery was Lake Bangweulu. What he possessed in abundance was a literary talent that made his readers feel that they had actually been in Africa and perceived the same things Livingstone had. In this way he made the Dark Continent the sensation of Victorian England and laid the foundation for his own legend.

On the other hand, both had the toughness and curiosity of the true explorer. Both were deeply religious - even though Stanley's God was primarily the Yahweh of the Old Testament while Livingstone followed Jesus and the law of love. They were brave, stubborn, prodigious in energy and intolerant of other men's weakness. Neither liked criticism or ridicule. Each was deeply sceptical of organised missionary activity; Livingstone especially shared Stanley's distaste for Tozer, whom he despised for basing himself on Zanzibar: 'The Mission in fleeing from Morambala to an island in the Indian Ocean acted as though St Augustine would have done had he located himself on one of the Channel Islands when sent to Christianise the inhabitants of Central England.'

On the debit side, the two men shared many of the same faults. Both had a pathological determination to be 'first' in their explorations and not to share the credit with associates; both habitually demeaned the achievements of other travellers in Africa. One of the causes for the many unexpected obstacles encountered by Stanley on his march from the coast was that he was determined to blaze a new trail to Ujiji and not simply follow in Speke's footsteps. Livingstone's experience on the Zambezi expedition rather uncannily pre-echoed Stanley's later career. They shared an inability to get on with other Europeans. Both were incapable of 'man management' and jealous that any other white man might try to steal their glory. A recent judgement on Livingstone vis-a-vis his European companions could also be predicated of Stanley: 'He was unconcerned for their interests and lacked insight into their problems. He viewed their illnesses as malingering, disagreement as insubordination, and failure as culpable negligence.'

The desire to be the first to discover anything and the refusal to share glory with other Europeans led both men to downgrade the contributions of their companions and, if necessary, to use lies to discredit them. It was bad enough that Livingstone failed to acknowledge the financial and exploration contribution made by the saintly William Cotton Oswell or the discoveries and travels of the Hungarian Lazio Magyar and the Portuguese Candido Cardoso. But it was even worse that he should lie about the Makololo missions and then traduce Roger Price in order to escape censure for having grossly misrepresented the situation with Sekeletu in Barotseland. At the limit Livingstone was even prepared to be as violent as Stanley. In 1859 he beat an insubordinate Makololo with a cook's ladle. Nine days later he thrashed a troublesome stoker, after telling Kirk he would 'break the heads' of any troublemakers.

Not insignificant, too, as a factor in the Stanley/Livingstone rapport was the fact that both men were below average height, so that there was none of the hatred and dislike that unbalanced men of short stature often feel for tall males. Both men, in fact, shared the compensatory drive often associated with physical smallness. Keltie of the Royal Geographical Society even claimed there was a physical resemblance between Stanley and Livingstone: 'In each the lower part of the face especially is almost identical, the same massive square jaw and firm mouth, indicative of unconquerable will, inexhaustible endurance, unflinching purpose.' But the similarities should not be pushed too far. Recent research establishes Livingstone as a victim of cyclothymia or hereditary manic depression. It was the cyclical nature of this illness that led to his worst acts of persecution against his European assistants, especially Richard Thornton and Thomas Baines. Stanley often felt depressed in the normal sense, but only when he was compelled to remain inactive for long periods. He never suffered from genuine depressive illness the way Livingstone did.

Stanley's outbursts of violence, his paranoia and persecution of his colleagues derived more from the 'will to power' than innate depressive tendencies.

Yet the overwhelming element predisposing the two men to forge close bonds was psychological. For Stanley, Livingstone represented the wise and benevolent father he had never known. For Livingstone, Stanley in an eerie way represented the return of the prodigal son. As a parent, Livingstone had not been successful. His eldest son Robert ran away to the USA, fought and was killed in the American Civil War. In the letter bag that Stanley brought on from Unyanyembe Livingstone received the first definite news of Robert's death from battle wounds. Yet the man who brought the news of the death of David's Absalom was himself a Civil War veteran. There were thus powerful impulses on both sides in the construction of a surrogate father/son relationship.

Such an interpretation of the relationship is no mere a priori speculation. Livingstone spent many hours discussing Robert with Stanley, almost as though he were bestowing on him the mantle of eldest son. His remark to Uledi at Ujiji is highly significant: 'I am very happy, you have brought me my child.' Stanley frequently referred to the paternal role Livingstone played towards him. When he was feverish in December, Livingstone was attentiveness itself: 'In an instant his tone changed and had he been my own father, he could not have been kinder.'

But perhaps the most extensive indication of Livingstone as surrogate father comes in Stanley's diary entry for 16th November, just six days after their meeting:

His manner suits my nature better than that of any man I can remember of late years. Perhaps I should best describe it as benevolently paternal. It is almost tender, though I don't know much about tenderness [italics mine] but it steals an influence on me without any effort on his part. He does not soften his voice or draw back his lips in an affected smile or mince his words or courtesy to my wish or will - but is sincerely natural and courteous with me as if I were his own age or of equal experience. The consequence is that I have come to entertain an immense respect for myself and begin to think myself somebody, though I never suspected it before. If it were other than perfectly natural with him, my conceit tells me I should discover it. It was all right to be acknowledged as someone by my own paid followers but when a man old enough to be my brother manages to convey it to me in every action, I get as proud as can be, as though I had some great honour thrust on me.

Soon Stanley learned to relax with Livingstone and lay aside his earlier fears of rejection. Their relationship gathered momentum. On the third day Livingstone took his new colleague to visit his Arab friends in Ujiji, then they walked along the lake shore, watching the long rollers breaking on the beach as if it were the ocean. Stanley asked the doctor if he did not feel like returning home. Livingstone replied that although he wanted to see his children again, he could not give up his quest for the Nile sources now, when he was just six or seven months away from providing a definitive solution to the problem. At first Stanley could not understand why the doctor had returned to Ujiji if that was his aim. Livingstone then carefully explained the circumstances of his men's mutiny in Manyema. This drew from Stanley a reflection on Livingstone's greatness: that if other men had explored as much as he had, they would be running to and from the coast to announce their discoveries, instead of doggedly persevering as the great Scotsman was doing.

They returned to the hut and Livingstone explained his future plans on a large wall map - drawn on a much bigger scale than anything Stanley had. Since it was a Sunday, Livingstone spent much of the rest of the day on religious services. He expounded a chapter in the Bible to a select group including Susi, Chumah and Selim. In the evening both men retired to write. The following day was spent in a detailed narrative of the Manyema expedition. Next morning Livingstone, in sanguine mood, proposed that Stanley accompany him back to Manyema to complete his work. This was a ticklish situation for Stanley. He did not quite know how to refuse without giving offence. Because he had presented the Herald expedition as a philanthropic concern, he could not reveal just how hard a taskmaster Bennett really was: 'from what I know of him, he would even begrudge the few days I must naturally stay here.'

Stanley replied that he was not a free agent: his mission had been to take supplies to Livingstone; now he would have to return to the coast for further orders. Livingstone's face clouded over at this reply. Then he brightened and said: 'I see how it is. You would come if you thought it would be permitted. Well, there is nothing like sticking to duty and I will not be one to tempt you.

They plunged into a discussion on Africa. Stanley said that he did not think he was cut out to be an African explorer. He found the African native peoples troublesome and ungrateful and confessed himself disillusioned on a number of scores since leaving Zanzibar: then there was novelty and excitement and he still believed in the power of kindness; since then the necessity for hard driving, the toll Africa took on the nerves and the constant need to dose oneself with quinine had turned him sour on the Dark Continent. Livingstone dealt with this gently. He said it was a great pity that few white men who came to Africa could look at it objectively and get beyond their own feelings; he expressed the hope that Stanley would come to look on the continent more kindly before he departed. Had he ever seen such natural beauty, such landscapes? Rather peevishly Stanley replied that he had seen many sights as impressive on his travels, and he was not even sure that parts of the scenery of the United States were not superior. There was an awkward silence until Stanley remarked conciliating that he could not dissociate Africa from fever: 'whether the cause is in me myself or the land, I fancy something of sadness in what I see.'

'I know what you mean,' said Livingstone. 'That is the bile. Nothing more than the effect of bile in your own system. As long as you look at

Africa with eyes of yellow bile, you cannot help but feel that.'

Overwhelmed by Livingstone's compassion and his own guilt about rejecting the invitation to Manyema, Stanley forced himself into a magnanimous gesture. Whereas he could not afford a year to travel to Manyema, he did not see how Bennett could object to a month's diversion. He therefore proposed that he and Livingstone make a trip to northern Lake Tanganyika to see if there was a river that flowed out northwards towards Lake Albert and the Nile; the entire trip would be financed by the New York Herald, To remove the least scintilla of a patronising role in their relationship, Stanley divided all his effects, clothes, medicines, trade-goods, food, into two heaps and then told Livingstone to choose whichever heap he wished and retain it as his own. He also informed Livingstone that he regarded the older man as the leader of the joint expedition. Stanley would not have deferred like this to any other man in the world.

Their first step was to acquire a suitable canoe for the lake-borne journey. Sayid bin Majid, the Arab 'grand seigneur of Ujiji, supplied them with a large craft that would carry twenty-five men and 3,500 pounds of ivory. Stanley's arrival had brought about a remarkable transformation in Majid's attitude towards Livingstone. Where he had previously seen him as a penurious old eccentric, a suitable object for charity and compassion, Stanley's coming had alerted the Arab to Livingstone's real importance in the wider European world.

On 16th November they set off, Livingstone in high hopes that he would find a route that would enable Nile shipping to penetrate as far as Ujiji. Apart from Stanley and Livingstone, the exploration party comprised sixteen rowers, Selim, Ferrajji the cook and two Wajiji guides. They had been warned that the trip could be dangerous and that the Warundi, previously victors over the Arabs in war, might not let them pass. At first the canoe rolled horribly because of overloading. Stanley made his men unload, jettison much of the cargo and then repack to make the boat manoeuvrable.

Once on the lake, whose shores reminded Stanley of the Turkish Black Sea littoral, Livingstone continued to beguile Stanley about the virtues of the African continent, and how the removal of the blight of the slave trade would transform a potential Eden. Stanley listened politely without agreeing. As so often in their four months together he and Livingstone contrasted strongly: it was respectively pessimism versus optimism, original sin versus perfectibility, the rule of force against the law of love, the Lord God Jehovah against Jesus Christ. Stanley's view was: 'I always feel that the fever is not far off, but if it were not for that, I think his influence and example and sweet patience and grand hope that everything will come out all right at last would have an effect on me.'

They sailed past Bangwe Island to Kigoma. The forested scenery was so spectacular that even the cynical Stanley was forced into exclamations of wonder; the natural beauty surpassed anything he had seen all the way from Bagamoyo to Ujiji. Livingstone was as enthusiastic as his young companion; six years' exposure to Africa had not jaded his appetite for the wonders of nature. Stanley continued enraptured: 'The lake was quite calm; its blue waters of a dark-green colour, reflected the serene blue sky above. The hippopotami came up to breathe in alarmingly close proximity to our canoe, and then plunged their heads again, as if they were playing hide-and-seek with us.'

At Niasanga, their first stopping-place, Stanley shot a dog-faced monkey, 4 feet 9 inches from nose to tail and weighing 100 pounds. Livingstone was out of action with diarrhoea, from which he was a chronic sufferer, so Stanley passed the time admiring the abundance of bird life: wagtails, crows, turtle-doves, fish-hawks, kingfishers, whydah birds, the ibis nigra and ibis religiosa, geese, paddy birds, kites and eagles.

A four-hour pull on the oars brought them next to the River Zassi, where the mountains rose sheer from the lake to a height of over 2,000 feet. Stanley found Zassi the most beautiful spot yet; surrounded by a group of conical hills, it surpassed even his hitherto favourite, Lake George on the River Hudson. On the fourth day out they came to Nyabigma, a sandy island in Urundi which offered a 20-mile prospect between the two capes of Kazinga and Kasofu. On the mainland he could descry an alluvial plain into which five large rivers fed; all the rivers were hedged by a thick growth of matete or elephant grass which formed an impenetrable jungle.

At Nyabigwa they prepared for a possible battle with the Warundi ahead and distributed ten rounds of ammunition to each man. Stanley shot another monkey and noted the same pipe-smoking phenomenon among the locals that he had observed at Zassi. At Mukungu, on the fifth day out, they received the expected demand for bongo. Stanley was fascinated to see how an old campaigner like Livingstone dealt with tribute. Sure enough, he proved an experienced negotiator and insisted on a sheep being brought to them before he paid the doti of two and a half cloths. Unfortunately his circumspection was not matched by his followers. The mateko or sub-chief brought a 3-gallon pot of sweet liquor for the two headmen, Susi and Bombay. The two men were soon gloriously drunk, and in the morning found that the Warundi had stolen all Livingstone's sugar, a bag of flour, 500 rounds of cartridges, ninety musket bullets and the expedition's sounding-line. Stanley was furious with Bombay: 'It was only the natural cowardice of ignorant thieves that prevented the savages from taking the boat and its entire contents together with Bombay and Susi as slaves.'

On the sixth day they coasted close to the low headlands formed by the rivers feeding into the alluvial plain. The streams that ran down the sheer mountain side to the lake formed a dangerous surf, capable of capsizing the boat and pitching them all into the crocodile-infested waters. Stanley was amazed at the fearless insouciance of his oarsmen, but their aplomb turned to over-confidence when they assumed that the next village after the headland of Kisunwe was one of the few hospitable spots along the lake shore. When the expedition tried to land it was greeted with threats, then with showers of stones.

At this point there arose the first clear difference in method between Livingstone and Stanley. Livingstone always believed in pacific settlement of disputes; Stanley's reflex action was to use force. Stanley begged the doctor to let him loose off a couple of shots at the stone-throwers. Livingstone's reply was stoical: 'What is the use? Let them be. We are safe. Let us bless God for that.' He placed his hand gently on Stanley's to calm him. Stanley acquiesced: 'I laid down the gun thinking what a pity it was that I should not send them home to meditate, and learn that some people had their wits about as well as they.'

Faced with this hostility, the expedition camped briefly at Murembwe point, which was protected on the landward side by thick jungle. Ferrajji brewed up Mocha coffee while Livingstone explained the unwonted belligerency as due to Arab raids. Then they pressed on towards Cape Sentaheyi, but darkness came on so that they were compelled to put in to another sandy strand. The fires they lit attracted interlopers, and when four more scouting parties came up to reconnoitre, Livingstone agreed with Stanley that this boded no good. After supper they pushed off again, just in time, as a sizeable war party was gathering. They rounded Cape Sentaheyi and after six hours' pulling at the oars put in to the fishing village of Mugeyo where they were allowed to sleep unmolested. At dawn they continued and reached the village of the friendly Warundi of Magala, having rowed 40 miles in eighteen hours.

Though well-disposed the Warundi of Magala reminded Stanley of the Wagogo in that they were 'profound starrers'. In the afternoon the mutare came and for two doti provided a very good food supply. He warned them, however, that if they proceeded they would become snarled up in one of Mukamba's wars, so that unless they intended to join one side or the other they should go back. But the lure of the Rusizi River, the hoped-for effluent that would lead them on to Lake Albert and the Nile, was too strong. They decided to persevere.

On the eighth day of the joint expedition, a violent storm overtook them while they were half-way between Urundi and Usige. Their canoe yawed fearfully in the wave trough. In terror they put about and made for the village of Kisuka, where they heard further rumours of local wars, of raids and counter-raids. Even more depressingly, their local informants were adamant that the Rusizi flowed into Lake Tanganyika. To fill the cup to overflowing, Stanley went down with a fever that made him a mere passenger for three days. The canoe continued passed the broad delta of Mugere to Mukamba's village, where Livingstone put Stanley in a hut and nursed him back to health with 'tender and fatherly kindness'.

Mukamba's people had never seen a white man before, but their chief was friendliness itself. The morning after their arrival, he appeared with presents of a sheep, a goat and an ox in return for nugatory hongo. He informed them that the Rusizi delta was just two days' journey away. On the second evening at Mukamba's, Livingstone's headman Susi again showed his liking for alcohol by getting hopelessly drunk and climbing into bed beside Livingstone. Thinking he was Stanley, Livingstone said nothing until the inebriate Susi pulled the blankets over himself, leaving Livingstone cold and uncovered. At this point the doctor discovered the identity of the culprit. In the ensuing hullabaloo Stanley was woken up. Left to himself, he would have set about Susi with a rod, but Livingstone simply gave him a perfunctory slap to wake him then rebuked him sternly: 'Get up Susi, will you? You are in my bed. How dare you, sir, get drunk in the way, after I have told you so often not to?' The crestfallen Susi slunk off, leaving Stanley to marvel at the doctor's Christian forbearance.

Next day Mukamba came to say goodbye. He loaned them a second canoe to get to his brother Ruhinga's country. It was unfortunate that shortly after Stanley and Livingstone's visit Mukamba died, so that the white man was then perceived as 'bad medicine'. Nine hours' rowing brought them to the head of the lake at Mugihema, the territory of Ruhinga. Cutting diagonally across the lake, the expedition gazed on the rich, flat country at the Rusizi delta, teeming with the finest herds Stanley had yet seen in Africa: goats, sheep and cattle in their thousands. The headwaters of the lake around the delta unfortunately abounded in less desirable creatures: crocodiles. To their great disappointment they discovered that the Rusizi incontestably flowed into the lakes, so that there was no question of an effluent that would take them on to Lake Albert and the Nile. Nevertheless, they contended themselves with the thought

that they were actually exploring a river that had eluded Burton and Speke.

On the second morning at Ruhinga's Stanley took ten strong paddlers and set off for another look at the Rusizi delta, almost as if he hoped that a second reconnaissance would after all reveal it as an effluent river. But it was even more abundantly clear on this outing that the Rusizi flowed into not out of Lake Tanganyika. Stanley found that it was nothing like so large as the Malagarazi; it surpassed it only in its infestation with crocodiles. Stanley then proceeded to a bay in the west, to which the mountains descended sheer, before returning to Livingstone at Mugihema.

Ruhinga, the chief, was not so dignified as his brother Mukamba but even more amiable and with a much better knowledge of the country. He provided the explorers with much valuable information about the country at the northern end of the lake; Stanley was able to determine from his intelligence that Lake Albert was nowhere nearby, so that Sir Samuel Baker's calculations must have been awry by some two degrees of latitude. Ruhinga also regarded the coming of the two white men as a good omen. He had been languishing from sickness and recovered at about the time of their arrival. Sumptuous festivities heralded his recovery. The women celebrated the event by smearing their heads and faces with flour; Stanley shot a brace of geese, a duck, a crane and an ibis religiosa to provide delicacies for Ruhinga's table. Ruhinga graciously reciprocated the gesture by sending the white men an ox, three sheep and some milk, from which Stanley's men churned butter - always a great treat in Stanley's eyes.

Ruhinga further showed his appreciation by sending the explorers a keg of his home brew and they responded by inviting him to take Mocha coffee. The first rain since Stanley's arrival at Ujiji also fell while they were at Mugihema. Their prolonged, enjoyable stay was topped off when Mukamba came on a visit to his brother and there was a further feast.

The only thing that marred their stay at Ruhinga's was illness. First Livingstone was laid up with bilious fever. No sooner was he recovered than Stanley went down with a severe attack; he remained at half-strength for five days and was unable to make a formal goodbye to Mukamba when he left on 5th December. But Stanley always remembered the nights at Mugihema as the time when he and Livingstone became really close. Livingstone was a fountain of anecdotes. He spoke at length about the famous Burton and Speke feud, of the 1864 Bath confrontation and of Speke's death (which the doctor was certain was accidental, not suicide). He told a hilarious story of how the freemasons had offered to make him a member in Glasgow on the grounds that membership would do him a lot of good in Africa! He spoke of how irritated he was by people who thought his refusal to lecture at a moment's notice derived from a desire for an enormous fee. One night after Livingstone had been out taking longitudinal observations, he and Stanley fell into a lively argument over the respective merits of Disraeli and Gladstone, Livingstone supporting Disraeli and Stanley Gladstone. Despite the warmth of the dispute, when an attack of Stanley's fever brought the discussion to an abrupt end, Livingstone at once reverted to paternal solicitude.

Stanley was so impressed by Livingstone and his instinctive rapport with and sympathy for Africans that he even felt ashamed of himself, and looked about for ways of proving that his own harsh methods were warranted. One night he found what he was looking for. Peeping through a crack in his hut, he saw Selim on his knees, with his head well back and his mouth under a dripping honey bag. The spectacle seemed an object lesson in mindless hedonism. Stanley was unable to resist the temptation to call Livingstone to witness the scene; the doctor turned away with a disgusted expression on his face.

On 7th December they quit Mugihema and pushed on to the boundary of Uvira. Ruhinga had told them that Usige was a district of Urundi and that all local chiefs were vassals of King Mwezi Kissabo the Fourth. But quasi-feudal bonds masked all kinds of differential local reactions. When camped within sight of the village of King Mruta, both Livingstone and Stanley agreed that they did not like the look of things. They decided not to stay in Kavima, but headed south in the teeth of a gale. They hid in a little quiet cove hidden by reeds, disembarked and built a thorn fence as protection during the night. At dawn after breakfasting on coffee, cheese and dourra cakes, they steered south from Kukumba point, intending to coast along the western coast of the lake for a while before crossing to Ujiji.

They found the western shores of the lake steeper and loftier than the wooded heights of Urundi or Ujiji. The mvule tree was much in evidence. They made about two-thirds of the distance to Cape Kabogi before camping for the night at a group of islets, one of which Stanley named New York Herald Island. On 9th December they came to the territory of the Wasansi at Cape Kabogi, on the coast of Uvira. They put in to nearby Cape Wasansi in the teeth of another gale and spent the night, unaware that the Wasansi took them for Arabs and hence as enemies.

In the morning, while his men prepared breakfast, Stanley was drifting back into a half-sleep when he was aroused from his doze by the words:

'Master, master, get up quick! Here is a fight going to begin!' He stumbled to his feet to see seven or eight of his people crouched behind the canoe with their guns primed, surrounded by a yelling mob. There was no sign of Livingstone; Bombay informed him that the doctor had gone off on an early morning reconnaissance with Susi and Chumah. Stanley quickly sent off two men to find him, but they had not been gone more than a few minutes when Livingstone himself arrived on the scene, to find Stanley sighting down his Winchester. Calmly Livingstone approached the mob ringleader and asked what the matter was. The man replied that the Arabs were traditional enemies of the Wasansi ever since an Arab grandee at Ujiji had beaten up one of their chiefs for straying too near the Arab's harem. Livingstone nodded, rolled up his sleeve, pointed to the colour of his skin and asked the Wasansi to take notice that he was a white man, not an Arab. This produced a great effect and the two ringleaders were beginning to subside when a drunken headman lurched into the arena, cut himself with his own spear and then claimed the 'Arabs' had wounded him. Again Livingstone's powers of conciliation were called on, and again he managed to persuade the Wasansi to disperse peacefully.

But Stanley had had enough. He ordered the tents struck, the canoes launched and the baggage stowed and implored Livingstone to come away. Livingstone acquiesced in this usurpation of his authority. They struck across the lake from Cape Lumumba and, after an eighteen-hour voyage over two days via Zassi and Niasanga, they arrived back at Ujiji on 13th December after a twenty-eight-day, 300-mile round trip. The return home could have been achieved faster, but Stanley was again taken with fever and Livingstone, out of compassion, obligingly headed the canoe for the nearest landfall on the evening of the 12th. The journey had been abortive in the sense that it was now clear there was no connection between Lakes Tanganyika and Albert but Livingstone still continued to cleave to the hope that Lake Tanganyika might yet link in some other way with the Nile, possibly via the Lualaba.

Back in Ujiji, which this time they entered quietly, without any firing of guns, but to the plaudits of the Arabs, Stanley marshalled his thoughts and impressions of Livingstone. He began the process of 'appropriating' Livingstone, presenting him as a man mistaken by the world, slandered as splenetic, misanthropic, demented, unscientific, uncommunicative, curmudgeonly, hypocritical, but uniquely understood and appreciated by

Stanley. 'God forgive them for such thoughts. In this prosaic age I have not heard of or seen a man more worthy of honour from his white brothers and I am certain I will die in that opinion.' On the contrary, argued Stanley, Livingstone possessed a unique charm, capable of affecting both African tribesmen and the hard-bitten Arabs of Ujiji, as well as all open-minded white men. Moreover, so far from being a po-faced dour son of the manse, Livingstone had a wonderful sense of humour and enjoyed a good laugh. He had the rare knack, too, of finding joy in another's good fortune, as when Stanley found telegrams from Paris and a letter from consul Webb awaiting him in Ujiji, to which Livingstone's response was, 'And I have none. What a pleasant thing it is to have a real and good friend!' Significantly, too, Stanley, who had attributed Shaw's downfall to his avidity for sexual intercourse with black women, praised Livingstone for not having taken an African 'wife', as the scandalmongers alleged. Stanley laid this particular rumour at two doors: that of the 'sex-obsessed' Burton and that of Kirk, a notorious retailer of gossip and tall tales.

Meanwhile Livingstone himself had to decide what his next step should be. There seemed to be a number of choices. He could try to link up with Samuel Baker in Equatoria by travelling via the Rusizi and Urindi to the Victoria Nyanza, thence through Unyoro and King Mutesa's country. He could return with Stanley to the coast, then home. Or he could set his sights on Manyema and the Lualaba, in which case the supplies Stanley had already given him were inadequate and he would need to come back with Stanley as far as Unyanyembe to pick up the next consignment of his trade goods and hire fresh porters. After a good deal of reflection, he decided to return to Unyanyembe and wait there until Stanley sent up fifty hand-picked pagazis from Zanzibar.

Next Stanley and Livingstone turned to the immediate question of the route back to Unyanyembe. They sketched out a route that would take them away from the war zone and out of the orbit of rapacious tribes like the Ha. First they would go south for seven days on the lake as far as Urimba; then they would cut across the uninhabited forests of Kawendi. Twenty days of marching should take them to Unkonongo, then they would head north for twelve days through Unkonongo and allow a further five days for the final stretch to Unyanyembe.

The rest of December was spent getting the expedition in shape. The first thing was to secure enough canoes for the week southward on Lake Tanganyika; then they needed an adequate supply of saddles and a flock of mulch goats to provide milk as they went, on the assumption that each goat would provide a pint of milk. To show his 'filial' deference, Stanley personally worked on a saddle for Livingstone's donkey so that the doctor could ride all the way to Tabora. Unfortunately, the 'trials' on the finished saddle were not propitious: Livingstone's donkey was evil-tempered and threw its rider several times, so that Livingstone was sceptical of his ability to ride the beast even with Stanley's saddle.

While he worked with Selim on the saddle, Stanley proposed that

Livingstone write a series of letters to the New York Herald (at a rate of £20 per 3,200 words) exposing the evils of the slave trade. Livingstone seemed doubtful whether enough Herald readers would be interested; Stanley, however, pointed out that such material would undoubtedly be syndicated, so that the doctor's pleas would reach a mass audience in a nation of nearly twenty-five million people.

On 18th December Stanley again went down with fever and remained more or less convalescent until Christmas, listening to the thunder and heavy rain lashing down on the lake. When Livingstone had finished his long prayer meetings, habitually ending with the reading of a chapter from the Bible, which he then translated into Swahili and expounded for his men, he would come and chat to Stanley about a variety of subjects: the detested missionaries on his Zambezi expedition, his campaigns against the slave trade, his early life in Scotland. He told Stanley that Lord Palmerston had once asked him what honour he would most like, to which Livingstone replied that he wanted nothing for himself but for Africa would like a treaty with the Portuguese outdrawing the slave trade. Palmerston abruptly changed the subject. Sometimes Stanley would be half-asleep when Livingstone came into his room, whereat Livingstone would begin to talk to himself as though to an audience. The first time this happened, Stanley asked with a start to whom Livingstone was talking: the doctor laughingly told him to take no notice, it was a habit picked up in solitude.

Ever afterwards Stanley treasured the golden memories of those magical evenings in Ujiji with Livingstone:

I never fancied myself more like a newspaperman than I did when at Ujiji with such an attentive listener as Livingstone. Then we sat until late in the evening long after the sun had set, long after the noise of ramblers and loungers of Broadway had ceased and long after the stars had appeared in the milky heavens above. I had something to say the whole time, something new to relate which drew from my listener sympathetic exclamations. I never thought I had such a good memory. A hundred events that I had already consigned to oblivion as things of no concern were recalled and dressed up as my fluency allowed.

The most sustained conversation Stanley held with Livingstone at Ujiji in December was on the 21st when Stanley had recovered well enough to be out of bed. An accomplished amateur drawer, he began to sketch Livingstone as he wrote up his journals. The initially desultory conversation developed in some surprising ways. As he sketched, Stanley noticed that the doctor had a curious habit of catching his journal whenever he changed the position of his legs, indicating some form of paralysis in his left arm. Livingstone explained that the injury dated from his celebrated mauling by a lion in Mabotsa in 1843. He asked Stanley to feel his arm. Stanley did as requested and perceived that the left arm was broken half-way between the elbow and the shoulder but joined in such a way that it felt as though the inner rim of the lower piece had been attached to the outer rim of the upper, resulting in an overlap of the lower half of the upper arm with the upper half of the lower arm. When the doctor stretched out his arms, Stanley could see that the left arm was considerably shorter than the right.

The gruesome story of Livingstone and the lion led the two men by association of ideas to talk of other encounters with animals dangerous to man. Stanley told the tale of Simba's being taken by crocodiles in the Malagarazi; Livingstone, too, had a fund of horror stories involving crocodiles. Stanley blurted out his feelings of extreme hatred towards the reptiles: 'Ever since [the Malagarazi] at every opportunity I have lost no chance to pour lead into them. I do not think I hate anything as I do a crocodile.' Even the normally gende Livingstone was disposed to agree: 'Yes, they are very cruel creatures and numbers of times they have caused me great grief.' They both agreed that there were some manifestations of the dark side of nature that it was difficult to adjust to.

Eventually Livingstone insisted on getting on with his work without interruption. As Stanley continued with his sketching, he noticed that, by contrast with himself who was thirty but looked forty, Livingstone was sixty but looked forty-five. He had cut off his beard when Stanley arrived and now shaved every day. His hair was still basically brown, though flecked with grey. His skin was much smoother and less wrinkled than when Stanley first met him six weeks before. He had discarded the scarlet jacket of coarse red flannelling that he wore at the famous meeting, and now wore a suit of dark Norfolk grey tweed that Stanley had bought in Bombay, but which had needed alteration as Livingstone was much bigger in the chest than Stanley.

By this time Stanley's feelings for Livingstone were clearly those of a son for an adoring father. Yet it was typical of his fragile core identity that Stanley had to justify the very obvious ways in which he was a different personality from his admired mentor. Livingstone's superior memory bothered Stanley, so he attributed it to the fact that Livingstone did not smoke 'so that his brain is never befogged even temporarily by the fumes of the insidious weed'. Naturally, Stanley could not bring himself to admit that Livingstone might actually have had a better natural memory or that he lived in his own inner world more harmoniously so could retain more. Still less could he have conceded that his own powers of retention were impaired by the need to remember all the lies he had told and make them coherent!

It emerged later that Stanley dreaded that if Livingstone had really got to know him, warts and all, he would have despised him, that he would have realised Stanley was fundamentally unlovable and unworthy of the doctor's esteem. Stanley therefore insinuated to his readers that Livingstone allowed his beloved Africans to take advantage of his kindly nature. This was Stanley's way of coming to terms with the undoubted efficacy of Livingstone's pacific approach to Africa, which Stanley envied but could not imitate. He summed up the differences between himself and Livingstone as follows:

I am more than ever convinced that the people at Zanzibar who pretended to know Livingstone and told me such extraordinary things about him must have been dreaming. He no more resembles their Livingstone than I do. My impression is that he would rather be killed himself than be compelled to kill another, even if he is a black man. At the same time on three or four occasions I think he has allowed himself to tell me incidents wherein he showed himself capable of a flaming anger. 'I came near shooting him' is an expression I have observed to escape him and the provocation was doubtless strong, but he has never done so, and if it came to the pinch my belief is he would resign himself to other alternatives rather than to it. I admire this as I say but I am afraid that I could not yield my life to every Tom, Dick and Harry who chose to demand it. The waste of good material for bad would strike me as wrong ... I wish to harm no one quite as little as the Doctor. The wish to do them some good is just as spontaneous in me as it is in him, but where we differ is, that whereas every instinct is prompt in me to resent evil or a deadly menace - he seems indifferent almost to carelessness. Perhaps the thirty years difference in age has something to do with it.

The relationship with Livingstone was the most significant of Stanley's life. He was arguably the only person Stanley ever respected, and certainly the only one to whom he was genuinely prepared to defer. Yet Stanley drew the line at accepting the doctrines and way of life of even such an impressive father-figure. The trauma of St Asaph's was too deeply etched. There is both sadness and defiance in Stanley's conclusion that Livingstone's modes could never be his: 'My methods, however, will not be Livingstone's. Each man has his own way. His, I think, had its defects, though the old man, personally, has been almost Christ-like for goodness, patience and self-sacrifice. The woodenheaded world requires mastering as well as loving charity.' 'Mastering the woodenheaded world' provides as concise a summary as any of Stanley's life project.

As the rainy season began and Stanley slowly recovered from his fever, he realised with a tinge of regret that the halcyon interval at Ujiji was at an end. The long trek to Tabora could no longer be delayed. They waited just long enough to celebrate Christmas, but their best-laid plans were ruined when the cook Ferrajji over-roasted the meat and burnt the custard.

On 27th December they left Ujiji in two detachments: Stanley and Livingstone went south by canoe while a shore party followed by land. Altogether forty-eight souls accompanied the two white men westward, including women and children. There were three canoes in the lake party. On his boat Stanley ran the Stars and Stripes up on the end of a punt-pole; Livingstone good-humouredly pretended to be jealous of the flag's eminence and managed to pin a Union Jack on a length of palm. The oarsmen were in great heart at the thought of returning to Unyanyembe and sang rousing songs while they pulled at the blades. Such was their gusto that the shore party driving the goats, sheep and donkeys, had a hard job to keep up with them.

The first stop was Ukaranga at the mouth of the River Luiche, which was flooded with the rains. They transferred the donkeys and goats to the canoes to get them to the other side. Next day, still striking south through hippo-infested waters, they paused briefly to take a cup of coffee and some sweetened vermicelli at the camp of one of Livingstone's favourite Arabs (Mohammed bin Garib); after eighteen hours' rowing they reached the mouth of the Malagarazi (2 p.m., 29th December), then waited three hours for the shore party to catch up with them.

The next day was spent transporting the whole caravan over the Malagarazi. On 30th December they carried out the same manoeuvre to pass the River Rugufu. Since this river teemed with crocodiles, Stanley assuaged his wrath towards the saurians by shooting one. They were now making for Urimba, a six-day trip by water with no prospect of food en route. Stanley therefore took the precaution of purchasing four days' rations for four doti. He and Livingstone were particularly solicitous about the shore party, which contained the women and children; this detachment had set out from Ujiji with eight days' provisions and now received another four days' rations. In addition, for this stage of the journey, they transferred the children and the weakest goats to the canoes and gave the luggage to the shore party. The precaution was necessary, for they were now striking into unknown territory, where no Arab or East Coaster had ever penetrated.

The days that followed were nervous ones. The canoes reached Urimba on 3rd January, after wasting much ammunition on the way by blazing away at hippos and crocodiles, not only to keep them away from their frail craft, but to alert the shore party as to their whereabouts. But at Urimba not only was no food available - the locals were themselves in a state of semi-starvation - but no one had heard anything of the land detachment. Stanley took Kalulu and his double-barrelled Reilly rifle out on a hunting expedition to get meat. He espied a huge herd of zebra and began to stalk them, but his stalk turned into fiasco as he found himself tangled up in a morass of low prickly shrubs. Then, when he tried to sight down his rifle, a swarm of tsetse flies alighted on the barrel and bit him on the nose. He managed to get off a lucky shot that downed a zebra, then capped his feat by bringing down a goose on the wing. Exhausted by his efforts, he lapsed into a semi-feverish state for a couple of days.

To show the land party the way, Stanley and Livingstone had run up an immense flag on a 20-foot long bamboo pole that was wedged on the very top of the tallest tree. On the third day at Urimba the exhausted land party came in. Livingstone waited until Stanley had recovered from his fever before ordering them on (on 7th January 1872). Then the united caravan struck east inland, through the Loajeri valley, still seriously short of food. Their luck held. That very afternoon Livingstone pointed to the other side of a deep crevasse. An immense cow buffalo was grazing there. Three well-targeted shots from Stanley despatched the animal; the expedition now had a meat supply. While Stanley and Livingstone dined that night on the tongue and other choice pieces, they tormented each other with talk of food: mince pies, buckwheat cakes, East River oysters.

It soon became evident that the expedition guide did not know the country he claimed to know, so Stanley put himself at the head of the caravan and steered it by compass. He led it across the swollen River Loajeri, through a gap in an arc of hills that teemed with game, especially zebra and buffalo, and on through alternating tall grass and beautiful parkland. Trekking through the tall grass was particularly exhausting for Livingstone, as it showered rain on the travellers at every step.

In the evenings they comforted themselves with wide-ranging conversation. Livingstone spoke with sadness of the death of his wife and his son Robert and with real passion when he touched on his two favourite topics: the abortive Zambezi missions and the Portuguese and Arab slave trades. He spoke of his many friends: James Young, a fellow medical student at Glasgow, Cotton Oswell, Murray, Frank Vardon. He declared his conviction that Gordon Cumming the lion hunter had built up the 'king of beasts' absurdly; Livingstone, who was in a position to know, felt that the lion's reputation far outstripped his reality. Stanley continued to marvel at his phenomenal memory and ability to quote from the poets, even though the only volumes he had ever seen on his shelves were the Bible, prayer books and religious concordances. Stanley noticed too that when it came to Africa Livingstone was more interested in ethnology than topographical geography. He was amused that Livingstone had little interest in the arts: 'Livingstone tells me that he has only been twice at a theatre in his life and would not give a sixpence to see the best play ever acted.' But he was delighted when the doctor, reminiscing about his early life as a missionary, suddenly took a sideswipe at his bête noire, Tozer: 'these weak, dandling creatures who call themselves missionaries . . . Tozer, bishop of Central Africa as hq is called, has not yet ventured upon his diocese. Central Africa indeed!'

But these pleasant camp-fire chats were interludes only in the grim struggle for survival in the wilderness. On 12th January, after crossing several ranges, the weary expedition confronted a raging torrent. To lift the men's spirits before battling with the flood, Stanley set out in the afternoon to hunt. But instead of small game, he ran smack into a herd of elephants. Stanley judged it wiser to retire than try conclusions with these forest monarchs, 'especially with a pea-shooter loaded with treacherous sawdust cartridges in my hand'. The day turned into a series of misfortunes. First he was stung by a wasp, then arrived back in camp to find that the men had eaten up all their reserve rations of dried meat. Three foodless days now yawned in front of them. As a finishing touch, at dusk that evening while Stanley and Livingstone were taking tea outside their tent, a herd of elephants rumbled by in the middle distance. Too exhausted for another joust with them, Stanley sent out his two wangwana hunters, who later returned, unsuccessful. Livingstone tried to comfort Stanley for his fruitless day in the bush by telling him tales of the great elephant hunters, underlining how difficult it was for anyone but an expert to down the great beasts.

On they went, up and down ridges, through torrents, in forests never before seen by white men. Despite the pleas of his pagazis, Stanley insisted on steering by compass and chart across the long series of longitudinal ridges that paralleled Lake Tanganyika. Livingstone had full confidence in his young companion. Stanley found time to comment on the extreme beauty of this country to the east of the Malagarazi and to marvel at the colonies of an unknown species of reddish monkey they encountered, but after six days of existing on mushrooms and forest fruit, his followers were exhausted. The very fact that the need for meat was so pressing seemed to affect Stanley's marksmanship adversely. On 15th January he had a good chance to make a killing among herds of hartebeeste and zebra, but over anxiety led him to shoot wide. Even such shooting chances came rarely because of the incessant rain and poor visibility: 'A thick haze covered the forests; rain often pelted on us; the firmament was an unfathomable depth of grey vapour.' Moreover, the presence of numerous lions, whose roaring plagued them day and night, disconcerted his Zanzibari hunters, who were apathetic even in face of a reward of five doti offered for each animal slain.

By 17th January they were all at the end of their tether. As always with Stanley, a mixture of anxiety and guilt brought out his worst side. It was his custom to walk in the relative cool of the morning, then ride his donkey in the humid heat of the afternoon. But because Livingstone could not ride his donkey he trudged all day long. Stanley's response to the situation was typical of him: 'To see the old man tramping it on foot like a hero makes me a little ashamed - and sometimes an unsavoury thought comes into my head that he does it to vex me. He must be a rider - having been in Africa - but it is an odd taste to prefer walking to riding. However, if he won't, he won't and there's an end don't.'

Yet relief was at hand. On 17th January they ascended a ridge in the beautiful rain swept parkland and were able to make out their old camp in the Mrera valley. Soon they were recognised and showered with congratulations on their safe return from Ujiji. The people brought food for the famished travellers: maize, sweet potatoes, beans. Livingstone was in poor physical condition: 'The doctor's feet were very sore and bleeding from the weary march. His shoes were in a very worn-out state, and he had so cut and slashed them with a knife to ease his feet that any man of our force would have refused them as a gift.'

Next day they pressed on, in better spirits after some solid food. Even though they were now in known territory, the guide managed to lose his way again, so Stanley reverted to leadership of the caravan. By now his shoes were as bad as Livingstone's. Yet he was cheered by the fecund change that had come over the land since his journey to Ujiji: 'the wild grapes now hung in clusters along the road; the corn ears were advanced enough to pluck and roast for food; the various plants had their flowers; and the deep woods and grasses of the country were greener than ever.' Livingstone was delighted with the profusion of plant life around them and insisted on stopping a few moments on the road to show Stanley the gum copal tree, the chilli and the sarsparilla plant. The lifting spirits of the party seemed vindicated by two events on the 19th: first they reached Mpokwa's deserted village and slept in the huts, two of which seemed to have been expressly prepared for their use; then Stanley succeeded in shooting two zebras, which provided over 700 pounds of meat or about 16 pounds per person. Stanley was especially delighted with his feat as he had dropped both beasts with his wrongly sighted O'Reilly rifle. The lean days seemed behind them.

Yet the zigzag nature of their fortunes was underlined next day when Stanley took aim at two separate herds of giraffe and succeeded only in wounding a female, which got away. Livingstone was at his most paternal over this incident and blamed it on Stanley's defective bullets. 'It was not the first time that I had cause to think the doctor an admirable travelling companion; none knew so well how to console one for bad luck - none knew so well how to elevate one in his own mind ... he was a most considerate companion, and, knowing him to be literally truthful, I was proud of his praise when successful, and when I failed I was easily consoled.'

The pendulum swung back next day when Stanley succeeded in stalking and killing a giraffe, fully 16 feet 9 inches tall, and weighing nearly 1,000 pounds. Stanley jokingly remarked to Livingstone that he wished the giraffe and zebra could be domesticated for, mounted on a zebra, a man could ride from Bagamoyo to Ujiji in a month. But again Stanley's see-saw fortunes were in evidence, for he went down with fever and was ill for three days. Livingstone nursed him and treated him with the 'Livingstone pills' - his own anti-malarial concoction of quinine, rhubarb, three grains of resin of julep and two grains of calomel.

The two factors of enforced rest, galling for a hard-driving achiever like Stanley, and the necessity to feel gratitude to a benefactor, clearly triggered the dark impulses within, for 27th January, the first day back on his feet, saw the only serious, albeit momentary, rift between himself and Livingstone. To make up for lost time Stanley cracked on the pace of his column towards Nisonghi. On the way they were attacked by a swarm of wild bees, who bit and stung unmercifully, turning the marching column into a wildly careering, panic-stricken mob. Stanley took two nasty bites on the nose and one on the finger during a pursuit of half a mile. Livingstone fared even worse. Ironically, because of his poor health and aching feet, he had finally been persuaded to ride the donkey. When the bees attacked, instead of bolting, the donkey rolled over and over on its side, exposing Livingstone to the full fury of the insects. For all his years in Africa, being so badly stung was a novel experience for the doctor: 'I never saw men attacked before: the donkey was completely knocked up by the stings on the head, face and lips and died in two days in consequence.'

On arrival in camp, Stanley sent some men back down the trail to assist Livingstone. They found him resting under a tree and offered to carry him the rest of the way. Livingstone reacted angrily: 'Get away with you - do you think I am a woman?' When this was reported to Stanley, he feared that Livingstone would be in a foul temper from the fall and the stings and would blame Stanley for having pressed on so fast. He ordered Ferrajji to prepare the best supper he could concoct and ordered Susi and Chumah to be at the ready, to pull off his boots and generally soothe him. While Ferrajji got to work on a meal of meatballs, custard and tea, Stanley asked his scouts to report to him the minute they saw the doctor approach.

Once they reported, Stanley hid behind a tree to observe. Livingstone limped slowly into camp and went to his tent, where Susi and Chumah washed his feet, then led him to the table where the aromas of Ferrajji's cooking were wafting around. Livingstone sat down and began to eat. Leaving ten minutes for the food to take its effect, Stanley sauntered over and said, 'Good evening' as though nothing had happened that day. Livingstone looked very grim at first but as he ate he began to relax, then allowed himself a diplomatic reprimand. 'Well, I thought you were going on to Unyanyembe without stopping. It is rather a long march is it not?' Stanley apologised and Livingstone allowed himself to be won round. 'Before long the doctor was in his usual sweet temper and we laughed over our misadventures. But a good hot meal is a great restorer of the spirits!'

They pressed on, across three streams to Mrera. The terrible rain that had dogged them all the way from Urimba continued. At Mrera they met an Arab caravan and learned the first full news of Shaw's death, which Stanley attributed to drunkenness and debauchery. Both Stanley and Livingstone were now beginning to suffer from food fantasies. They were no longer actually short of food, but they were starting to tire of the monotonous diet of salted giraffe meat, pickled zebra tongues, sweet potatoes, tea and coffee. Stanley was relieved to find that among Livingstone's human weaknesses was a concern for his stomach. Despite aching feet, fog, dew, rain and drizzle, Livingstone continued to gorge himself like a trooper. 'Among the blessings of this life I count meat, bread, good fresh butter,' Stanley noted in his diary.

Yet Livingstone was in good spirits on this latter part of the journey to Unyanyembe. He fascinated Stanley with his profound knowledge of Africana: trees, fruit, woodcraft, anthropology. He still took with him everywhere five exotic parrots he had acquired in Manyema. He confided in Stanley his excessive dislike of the Portuguese, and they found a common interest in etymology. Stanley retained particularly fond memories of the doctor's good humour during a five-hour march through a forest that seemed alive with elephant herds. There was just one macabre moment when, on passing a bleached skull in the depth of the forest, Livingstone expressed a desire to be buried in the stillness of such a forest. On an impulse, Stanley reverted to his Persepolis behaviour and carved his and the doctor's initials on a tree.

On 3rd February Stanley succumbed to yet another attack of fever, accompanied by severe pains in the back and loins. Livingstone dosed him with an emetic and gave orders that he be carried in a cot. In his lucid moments Stanley wondered whether it was his fate to follow Shaw to a Central African grave. Livingstone reassured him that this attack was merely due to the recent exposure to wet and damp; if he was going to die of fever, he would have passed away in Ujiji.

By the time Stanley recovered, they were once again at the rich game country of Gombe (7th February), and by the creek, still swarming with hippos and crocodiles. Seeing that they were now within a week of journey's end, Stanley sent Bombay, Ferrajji and Chowpereh on ahead to Unyanyembe to bring back medicines and letters. Since he knew Gombe to be a hunter's paradise from his visit on the outward journey, Stanley set off to add something to the cooking-pot. He saw a lion lurking in the long grass and tried to stalk it, but the big cat made off apace. Lions on land and crocodiles in the water were the bane of Gombe. Next day Stanley succeeding in shooting both an eland and hartebeeste but a pride of lions made off with the kill before he could retrieve it.

At Manyara they were very hospitably received and given a present of sweet potatoes by the chief. Stanley started to appreciate the force of Livingstone's arguments in favour of Africans: 'Here was an instance 175 of that disposition to sincere friendship with meritorious strangers which I ascribe to the chiefs in general in Central Africa where they have not been spoiled by the Arabs.'

By 11th February they were at the palisaded village of Kwikuru, now well into the original theatre of the war between the Arabs and Mirambo. During Stanley's absence the tide had turned in favour of the Arabs (but it was to turn again in Mirambo's favour in June). In particular, the Tabora sheikhs had taken heart from Stanley's exploit in opening the road to Ujiji and had resumed their caravans there. While Stanley and Livingstone halted a day to obtain provisions for the last lap of their journey to Unyanyembe, they discussed the doctor's future plans, once he had obtained his stores. Livingstone said he intended to strike south of Lake Tanganyika to the Lualaba and solve once and for all the question of the ultimate source of the Nile; he estimated that the journey would take him eighteen months, but to Stanley it seemed like a task that would occupy at least two years.

They fell to talking about the reception of Livingstone's work in England. Stanley said that he had seen many favourable reviews of Livingstone's book about the Zambezi; Livingstone replied that most he had seen were unfavourable. Stanley pointed out that Livingstone's reputation was unimpeachable and that if he had ever received bad reviews, this would have been because of the 'new journalism's' desire for 'good copy'. Livingstone's response reveals shrewdness: 'You are very kind, I am sure, but I am thinking that you have also a pretty way of saying pleasant things to one who is low spirited. I return you the compliment you paid me the other day.'

They marched on from Kwikuru on the 13 th. Stanley was again very ill and had to be carried, as he was unable to ride his donkey. He was in a sorry state at the end of the day's trek: 'I am in such a state tonight that I can neither lie down or sit quietly in one position long. Livingstone is calmly asleep. I am nervous and my head is very strange. I have the most fearful dreams every night - and I am afraid to shut my eyes, lest I shall see the horrid things that haunt me. I will go walk-walk-walk in the forest to get rid of them.'

Part of the feeling oppressing Stanley was a presentiment of evil. This seemed amply borne out when he arrived at Ugunda next day and met Ferrajji and Chowpereh, who had brought back a sheaf of letters from Tabora. The first one Stanley opened was bad enough. It contained all the recent news, including a graphic account of the bloody horrors of the Paris Commune, which drew from Stanley the comment: 'Oh France! Oh Frenchmen! Such things are unknown even in the heart of Central Africa.'

But the second letter he opened was even more of a bone-chiller. It was an irate communication from consul Webb to say that the cheque Stanley had left with him had been bounced by the Herald's New York bankers and that Bennett had disclaimed all responsibility for the expedition's expenses. After reminding Stanley of all he had done for him, Webb pointed out that he would be ruined if the debt was not repaid: 'I am distressed not only in my private capacity as a gentleman and businessman but also as a consular official.' Other letters confirmed the story of the bounced cheque. Stanley noted in his diary in great distress: 'There was not a doubt of it! Bennett was about to treat me as I had heard he had treated others of his unfortunate correspondents.'

Stanley's first instinct was to share his sorrows with Livingstone, but when he saw the look of quiet pleasure on the doctor's face as he read the long-delayed letters from his children, he did not have the heart to intrude his own problems. Crushed by the thought that he would have to pay off the entire debt out of his own savings, Stanley had no stomach for the other letters in the bundle. After about an hour he drearily opened the third letter from the Herald. It was from Zanzibar, dated 23rd December 1871, and contained a missive from London, date 25th September 1871, informing Webb that since Levien had now been replaced at the Herald's London office by Hosmer, the bureau was prepared to cash all drafts from Stanley.

Mightily relieved, Stanley chatted to Livingstone about the Franco-Prussian war and the Commune without revealing the emotional turmoil he had just lived through. Livingstone was in great form after the letters from his family. He commiserated with Stanley about his insomnia and confided that the long years in Africa meant that he could no longer sleep comfortably in a four-poster bed but tossed and threshed in it like a buffalo.

There were no further incidents on the march to Unyanyembe. They entered Tabora on 18th February in triumph, flags flying and guns firing, on the fifty-fourth day after leaving Ujiji. They went immediately to the tembe at Kwihara, where, it transpired, they had arrived in the nick of time. The headman Asmani sent by Kirk had been pilfering the stores and was discharged. Even greater depredations had been carried out by Said bin Salim, who blamed the obvious inventory shrinkage on 'white ants', but, as Stanley sardonically observed: 'the brandy bottles most singular to relate had also fallen a prey to the voracious and irresistible destroyers -the white ants - and by some unaccountable means they had imbibed the potent Hennessy.'

Stanley immediately got out his trade goods and made over to Livingstone the surplus not required on the journey to the coast: this included twelve bales of calico, fifteen bags of beads, thirty-eight coils of brass wire, a boat, bath, cooking pots, twelve copper sheets, trousers and jackets and, most importantly, a tent - for on the return from Manyema Livingstone had been without one. All in all, Livingstone now possessed four years' supplies; his only shortage lay in manpower.

They settled into a comfortable routine in the tembe which, compared with the hut at Ujiji, seemed like a palace. The tembe at Kwihara was already well on the way to acquiring legendary status as a 'hotel' for European travellers. The sensation that Unyanyembe, with its plentiful stores, was a semi-paradise after their recent sufferings seemed to draw substance also from the elements, for the teeming rain that had accompanied them all the way from Ujiji suddenly ceased and glorious weather supervened. Livingstone gave thanks after the first morning coffee by holding an impromptu religious service, attended by a surprising number of the men.

The last four weeks with Livingstone at Kwihara saw Stanley's relationship with his surrogate father at its deepest. Two days after arriving they decided to celebrate with a late Christmas dinner to make up for the one Ferrajji had spoiled at Ujiji. The after-dinner conversation showed the two men at their warmest and frankest yet. Livingstone gently chided Stanley for his excessive speed of marching, pointing out that he himself liked to do no more than 5 miles a day, so that he could make a thorough exploration of any aspect of the flora and fauna on the route that took his fancy. But to show that he harboured no grudge, he made Stanley his 'honorary son' by putting him in charge of his dead son Robert's affairs. He wrote to his daughter Agnes that all Robert's effects should be sent to Stanley in London, as the 'American' would be trying to find a secure resting place for her brother's bones at Gettysburg.

Stanley for his part recorded his pleasure that the doctor seemed to look much younger now than on their first meeting in Ujiji. This was mainly a matter of diet: Livingstone in normal circumstances had a voracious appetite, and Stanley estimated his weight at Unyanyembe to be around 180 pounds, though he could never persuade his mentor to weigh himself. He was a very close observer of the doctor. He noticed that whenever he was about to begin a story he always held up a crooked forefinger. There is a novelist's perception in his description of Livingstone in full flight. 'The loose front teeth which play while he talks add to the appearance of age a great deal. He uses humorous Scotticisms frequently ... he is full of sly jokes. When he begins one of his funny stories, I see how it is going to end by the gleam in his dark hazel eyes, the pucker gathering about his eyes - the uplifted forefinger.'

Every evening after dinner in the tembe Livingstone would discourse on some new topic that revealed further aspects of his personality. He complained bitterly about the Royal Geographical Society and its stinginess. They had not treated him well in any aspect of his life and work: they wanted basically to reap the benefits from his labours without making any financial outlay to support it. They would plagiarise his maps and doctor the letters he sent home so that they fitted in with the RGS view. The one good thing about the Society, for Livingstone, was its dinners; among the items in the 'gorgeous entertainments' the RGS laid on for its explorers were 'juicy marrow bones' and Devonshire cream. 'You will think of me when you taste those marrow bones at the Geographical and the Devonshire cream in London,' said Livingstone with a wistful smile.

But Livingstone's conversation was not all complaint and food fantasy. He embarrassed Stanley by placing Christianity firmly at the forefront of the daily agenda in Unyanyembe, plying the younger man with questions as to the suitability of the African for receiving the Gospel. Stanley prevaricated: spreading the Word would take a long time with 'such a stupid and wicked people'. Livingstone ignored the slur on his beloved Africans and asked how Stanley would go about the task of proselytising. It was perhaps typical of Stanley's habitual large-scale response to Africa that he suggested sending a thousand missionaries, all to be concentrated in the powerful hegemonic tribes. Inevitably, such religious conversations brought Livingstone back to one of his pet obsessions - the abortive Zambezi missions. Those years had thrown a chink of light on the Dark Continent, but the ineptitude of his comrades had allowed the darkness to descend again. Livingstone ended his long peroration on his incompetent toilers in the vineyard by quoting Burns:

See, yonder, poor o'erlaboured wight,

So abject, mean, and vile!

Who begs a brother of the earth To give him leave to toil!

Livingstone's monomania about his 'betrayal' by his co-workers on the Zambezi expedition eventually led Stanley to reassess his mentor.

Whereas at the outset he had been bowled over by the fact that Livingstone was a truly Christian man and not a misanthrope, after four months in his company Stanley started to think that he was perhaps incapable of true Christian forgiveness and not quite so perfect as he initially thought him. 'I have had some intrusive suspicious thoughts that he was not of such angelic temper as I believed him to be during my first month with him - but for the last month I have been driving them steadily from my mind.' However, he conceded that on the march back from Ujiji he had formed a balanced view and seen Livingstone whole, neither as misanthrope nor as subject for hagiography.

The slightly jaundiced tone with which Stanley recorded his impressions of his mentor in early March is explicable in terms of his own shame, for Livingstone had recently graphically demonstrated the supremacy of his own method of treating Africans over Stanley's. At Kwi- kuru, while Stanley was recovering from a bout of fever, he remonstrated with the cook for not cleaning the coffee pot properly. The cook, Ulimengo by name, retorted scornfully that he was used to working for Livingstone, and what was good enough for the 'big master' ought to be good enough for the Title master'. Enraged by this 'impertinent' reply, Stanley seized a club, fully intending, at his own admission, to brain Ulimengo. While his Zanzibari followers were restraining him, Livingstone walked into the scene of bedlam. 'Gendy, there! What is the matter, Mr Stanley!' he said kindly. Breathlessly Stanley blurted out his explanation. Livingstone lifted his hand, curled his forefinger and said, 'I will settle this.'

Livingstone then called Ulimengo before him and rebuked him publicly. Did he not realise that all the food and stores they had came from the 'little master' and they were all his mbengis (guests)? He went on to explain that Stanley was the real leader of the expedition: 'I am only the big master because I am older.' Ulimengo was so chastened by this that after apologising to Stanley he asked to be allowed to kiss his feet. Livingstone, doubtless not feeling that Stanley had acted entirely correctly, would not permit this. Having dismissed Ulimengo, he took Stanley aside and calmly got him to see the error of his ways. 'Come now, you must not mind him. He is only a half-savage and does not know any better. He is probably a Banyan slave. Why should you care what he says? They are all alike, unfeeling and hard.' The upshot was that that evening Stanley shook hands with Ulimengo and absorbed a signal demonstration that civil reprimand was preferable to the club or the whip. Unfortunately this was not a lesson that Stanley retained very long.

Any signs of less than saintly demeanour that Livingstone was displaying at Unyanyembe can in any case largely be attributed to Stanley himself, for it was in the tembe at Kwihara that he whipped up the doctor's anger against Kirk to curdling point. But it is important to be clear that Livingstone already had a jaundiced view of Kirk before Stanley came on to the scene. The fact that Stanley had an independent grudge against him simply allowed two separate streams of resentment to flow into one. Livingstone's bitterness towards Kirk had many causes. He blamed him for inertia and failing to exert himself sufficiently to make sure supplies and letters got through to Ujiji quickly. He censured him for using unreliable slave labour to escort his effects to Unyanyembe and for using incompetent or dishonest agents. And he suspected Kirk of trying to force him to return home before his work in Africa was done.

Within a week of meeting Stanley at Ujiji, Livingstone was bombarding his contacts in England with complaints about Kirk. As yet he did not make an official complaint, but in a letter to his daughter Agnes on 18th November he wrote the following: 'He has got by my influence to the top of his ambition - an acting consul and a political agent - husband of a wife and two children - and I may go to my grave before he will stir hand and foot for me.' Livingstone further objected to Kirk's reported remarks to Stanley that Livingstone's task was 'to clear up Lake Tanganyika from the must left on it by Burton'. Who did Kirk think he was? His attitude evinced all too clearly the unmistakable signs of the professional bureaucrat in thrall to the Foreign Office mentality - that same Foreign Office whose underling had so insulted Livingstone in London by his 'instructions': 'this was so insultingly nauseous from a mere jack in office that I never could quote it.'

But at Unyanyembe in February and March Livingstone publicly pointed the finger at Kirk. He was particularly infuriated by Foreign Secretary Lord Granville's remarks in the House of Lords: that all Livingstone's wants had been supplied. So far were they from having been supplied that it was only Stanley's advent that had saved him from starvation at Ujiji. Moreover, it was simply the chance observation of Livingstone's effects in Tabora that had led Stanley to lock them in the storeroom in the tembe. In addition, the entire Sherif episode was Kirk's fault. As far as Livingstone could make out, it was Kirk's intention to compel him (Livingstone) to give up and return to England, possibly with a view to getting hold of the precious research notes and publishing them himself. How else explain the incident at Ujiji when Kirk's hirelings had refused to hand over the Enfield rifles sent from Zanzibar for

Livingstone's use and Stanley had had to send an armed party to recover them? 'Dr Kirk's eagerness to appropriate the infamy of having told slaves to force me back is incomprehensible.'

Far the worst of Kirk's faults, in Livingstone's eyes, was having hired 'slaves' instead of free men: 'By some strange hallucination our friend Kirk placed some £500 of goods in the hands of slaves with a drunken half-caste tailor as leader ... it is simply infamous to employ slaves when any number of freemen may be hired!' 'Tell Kirk not to believe every Banyan's tale. It makes him a jape and not a disciple of David Livingstone.'

By the time Stanley was ready to leave for the coast, Livingstone had decided on two methods of humiliating his 'treacherous' former aide Kirk. In the first place, he wrote to the Foreign Office with an official complaint about the way his affairs had been handled from Zanzibar, which Kirk had no choice but to send on. Secondly, he ordered Kirk to hand over to Stanley the £500 sent out from London to fund his work and to assist Stanley in finding fifty new porters and supplies. This was an open snub, for it in effect announced to the world that Livingstone had no confidence in Kirk and had found someone else to supplant him.

But Stanley was also responsible for some more elevated correspondence from Livingstone, more in keeping with the popular image of Livingstone as saintly bearer of light in the Dark Continent. His pleas that Livingstone should write an open letter to the New York Herald in denunciation of the slave trade finally bore fruit. The right angle, Stanley hinted, was Livingstone's oft-expressed admiration for Abraham Lincoln.

Interestingly, the letter Livingstone wrote, shortly after Stanley's departure, was a melange of Stanley and Livingstone. It contained all Livingstone's passion about the evils of slavery and worked in his contempt for the present crop of missionaries in general and Tozer in particular. It then dilated on the affront to civilisation offered by the slave trade in an era of technological change, instancing all the examples Stanley had rehearsed to him (the Suez Canal, Pacific railways, railways in western Asia and India, the proposed Panama Canal, telegraph, steamships etc.). It finally exhorted all Americans to honour the memory of the 'good and great President Lincoln' by opposing the African slave trade as vigorously as they opposed slavery in Brazil.

The last weeks together in Kwihara were painful for both men, conscious of the imminence of separation. With no rain to hinder them, Stanley's men made rapid progress in the preparations for the trek to the coast. Stanley's packing was impeded by just one incident when a black fly crawled under his pyjamas and bit him. The bite became a boil which awoke him from a delightful dream and was so painful that he consulted Livingstone about it. Livingstone conjectured that the fly must have secreted an egg. He squeezed the boil, an egg sac popped out, and the pain ceased almost at once.

Stanley continued to press Livingstone to come home with him to restore his health, but Livingstone insisted that his work was not yet finished and if he had to die soon, he would prefer it to be in Africa. Stanley found something Arab-like in the way Livingstone seemed to subscribe to kismet or baraka: 'Livingstone takes life in the same cool and assured manner [as the Arabs] as if it had been whispered into his ears - the assurance of enjoying a few more decades. Strange people here. I wish I could have the same comfortable feeling about longevity, but my shrunken muscles and whimpering stomach urge me to leave the black man's land before another bout of fever lays me low under the sable soil of this malicious clime.'

For his part, as the time for parting drew near, Livingstone again proposed that Stanley accompany him to the Lualaba. Once more Stanley protested that it was impossible. Livingstone then pleaded with him at least to stay until after the next rainy season. But Stanley was now impatient to be gone: 'I have done my duty strictly by him and now another duty seizes upon me to sever us.'

Their intimacy deepened. Stanley, with his mania for neatness, was particularly impressed with the doctor's scrupulous care with his materials: 'his boxes appear like new, his compasses and instruments are in first rate order. His journals are clean and orderly kept - blotless - as if a copyist had been lately transcribing them.' More and more Livingstone confided in him, about his admiration for Lincoln (after whom he had named an African lake), about the chronic diarrhoea he suffered from (and which had nearly carried him off in 1854 on the way to St Paul de Loanda), about his grief for Manimokaya, his faithful servant and pathfinder to Manyema (who died in early March). Livingstone encouraged Stanley's project to write a book about the 'finding' at Ujiji and offered to help him find a publisher; he wrote a letter to the house of John Murray on his behalf. He sympathised with Stanley in his problems with the 'incorrigible Bombay' and quoted his favourite Scotticism: 'a stout heart to a stae brae'. Only one false note was struck during the month at Unyanyembe. Seeing him in one of his reveries, with brows puckered and right forefinger bent, Stanley ventured: 'A penny for your thoughts, Doctor.' Livingstone was momentarily disconcerted and irritated: 'They are not worth it, my young friend, and let me suggest that, if I had any, possibly, I should wish to keep them!'

At last their final Sunday together came round. Stanley finished packing the gifts for the Webbs of Newstead and the doctor's children, then attended the service, slightly longer than usual, where the congregation prayed for Stanley's safe arrival at the coast. Livingstone led the prayers then read the 35th Psalm and preached on it, referring to Stanley as his 'friend and brother'. Later, after breakfast, Livingstone outlined his proposed route to the Lualaba, and Stanley reiterated that the round trip would occupy at least two years.

Monday 12th March saw a farewell dance for the men. Livingstone sat up late finishing his letters, while Stanley went over to Tabora to fetch the Arab correspondence he had promised to take to Zanzibar. Then came the last day. The minutes flew by and Stanley felt sorely tempted to delay his departure. His time with Livingstone had been simply too happy and 'the farewell, I fear, maybe forever.' Livingstone came to him and thanked him fulsomely for all he had done and for saving his life in Ujiji. Such an expression of gratitude from a man he so admired was too much for Stanley. He burst into tears and sobbed 'as one only can in uncommon grief... his sudden outburst of gratitude, with that kind of praise that steals into one and touches the softer parts of the ever-veiled nature, - all had their indolence; and, for a time, I was as a sensitive child of eight or so, and yielded to such bursts of tears that only such a scene as this could have forced.'

As they folded up Livingstone's journal in several wrappings of cloth, Stanley broke the sad, embarrassed silence. 'Tomorrow night at this time you will be quite alone, Doctor.'

'Yes,' said Livingstone, 'this house will look as though a death had taken place. Had you not better stop until after the rains which are now nearly over?' Stanley shook his head. He had set himself a target of forty days in which to reach the coast and nothing, not even his love for Livingstone, would stop him.

On 14th March they were both up at dawn and ate a sad breakfast together. Then Livingstone accompanied Stanley a couple of miles to the slope of a ridge. As they walked together, he repeated his determination not to return home until he had found the true sources of the Nile. Stanley made a final entreaty to the doctor to come home. Livingstone declined. Then they looked back from the hill at the tembe where they had spent so many happy days together.

'My dear Doctor, you must go no further. You have come far enough. See, our house is a good distance now, and the sun is very hot. Let me beg of you to turn back.'

'Well,' he replied. 'I will say this to you: you have done what few men could do. And for what you have done for me I am most grateful. God guide you safe home and bless you my friend! And may God bring you safe back to us all, my dear friend! Farewell!'

They shook hands. Stanley saw a look of suppressed emotion in Livingstone's eyes and he came close to breakdown himself. 'March!' he ordered sternly to his men. The only way he could keep a dry eye was by putting space between him and Livingstone as quickly as possible. Finally he allowed himself a last look at his mentor. 'We came to a ridge and I looked back and watched his grey figure fading dimmer in the distance for a presentiment or suggestion stole into my mind that I was looking for the last time at him. I gulped down my great grief, and turned away to follow the receding caravan.'

For both men, it was the end of their most (one is tempted to say 'only') successful human relationship. Livingstone immediately went back and sent a postscript after Stanley to tell him, should he meet any more of Kirk's 'slaves' on the road, to send them back to Zanzibar. Livingstone had just one more year of life remaining but for the rest of it he continued to extol both Stanley's bravery and his filial qualities. 'Like a son' is the almost Homeric epithet Livingstone used thereafter whenever referring to Stanley. His opinion of Americans was miraculously transformed too (he still imagined that Stanley was an American). He habitually contrasted Kirk's 'lazy indifference' with Stanley's energy and courage, and encouraged his daughter Agnes to assist him in the writing of his book: 'it will in his hands do us no harm for the Americans are good and generous friends.' When Horace Waller counterattacked on Kirk's behalf and tried to drive a wedge between Livingstone and Stanley by asserting that the latter used the famous explorer to produce a best-seller, Livingstone simply bounced the criticism back: 'I am told by Kirk that Stanley would make his fortune out of me, if so he is heartily welcome, for it is a great deal more than I could make out of myself.'

Stanley was even more affected. 'In all fiction I know no moral hero greater than David Livingstone' was one of his milder later assessments. On the road back to Bagamoyo he reflected that if Samuel Baker deserved a baronetcy for naming Unyoro or Lake Albert, what did Livingstone deserve for discovering half a continent? 'Supposing that all west of the Hudson and Albany was all a blank unknown to us - crowd that with immense lakes and noble rivers etc. - and you will have some idea of what Livingstone has now done for African geography.'

But the pang of the first afternoon apart from Livingstone was the worst wrench Stanley had experienced since his sudden disappearance into the maw of St Asaph's at the age of six. The father-son motif appears in the diary entry written that evening: 'I felt very lonely all afternoon - as if I had but just parted with my own family. Pity that partings should be necessary... I never thought while being a victim to its fever that I should leave Central Africa with a pang but it was so, and only because of a white man ... I cried at parting with the good doctor. .. and I had to turn away rather suddenly.'

When he camped next day, Stanley felt so despondent that he wrote an agonised letter of longing for the lost 'father', so revealing of emotional hunger that Stanley, on reflection, did not send it. But it may stand as a fitting epitaph to the strength of what was on paper the unlikeliest of close relationships:

My dear Doctor,

I have parted from you too soon. I feel it too deeply. I am entirely conscious of it from being so depressed ... In writing to you, I am not writing to an idea now, but to an embodiment of warm good fellowship, of everything that is noble and right, of sound common-sense, of everything practical and right-minded. I have talked with you; your presence is almost palpable, though you are absent... It seems as if I had left a community of friends and relations. The utter loneliness of myself, the void that has been created, the pang at parting, the bleak aspect of the future, is the same as I have felt before when parting from dear friends. My dear doctor, had I not turned away from you quickly at taking our farewell I would have appeared weak and were not the Arabs present? Could they have understood my feelings? I doubt if you can understand them thoroughly but there I do you a wrong, and you will please forgive me.

Why should people be subjected to these partings, with the several sorrows and pangs that surely follow them? It is a consolation, however, after tearing myself away, that I am about to do you a service, for then I have not quite parted from you, you and I are not quite separate. Though I am not present to you bodily, you must think of me daily, until your caravan arrives. Though you are not before me visibly, I shall think of you constantly, until your least wish has been attended to. In this way the chain of remembrance will not be severed.

'Not yet,' I say to myself, 'are we apart' and this to me, dear Doctor, is consoling, believe me. Had I a series of services to perform for you, why then, we should never have to part. Do not fear then, I beg to ask, nay to command, whatever lies in my power. And do not, I beg of you, attribute these professions to interested motives, but accept them, or believe them in the spirit in which they are made, in that true David Livingstone spirit I have happily become acquainted with.

10

LIKE his short-legged prototype Odysseus, Stanley was aware that potentially the greatest danger to any enterprise occurs just near the end, when the safe anchorage is all but established. He therefore took the utmost pains to ensure that his journey back to the coast would be as risk-free as he could contrive it. While he had learned from Livingstone the advantages of being conciliatory and courteous to the tribes, he still believed in the big stick as much as the soft voice. Every night he loaded all his guns and placed a brace of pistols under his pillow. The boxes containing the cartridges were unscrewed and prepared for immediate action. In his mind he sketched out a variety of plans to meet all possible contingencies: night attacks, assaults by day, mutinies, desertions, epidemics.

Stanley was in a great hurry to get to the coast. He knew the rainy season was coming, he wanted to obtain the fifty porters for Livingstone, and he himself wanted to make an end of the expedition. There seemed a good chance that his estimate of a forty-day march might not be absurdly optimistic. They were marching back over terrain they had already traversed, Stanley was by now an old Africa hand and no longer the tiro he had been on the outward journey; most of all his men had their faces towards home and were motivated in a way inconceivable on the way to Ujiji.

Nevertheless, the blistering early pace of the march, through rat- infested Rubuga and Tura, past forests of baobab, had the wangwana straggling and complaining. By 20th March, in western Tura, with both rain and fever commencing, his men were begging to be allowed a halt. But Stanley would allow no let-up in his pace. Through the formidable river of Kivala they waded, on through the lotus blossoms of Ziwari and into the dense woods of the Wakumba people. The Wakumba were no military threat and habitually preferred to allow safe passage to caravans that carried firearms. And still the heavy rains beat down.

As they crossed the border between Ukumbu and Ugogo, Stanley was again subjected to the peculiar staring curiosity of the Wagogo when seeing a white man that had so irritated him on the outward trip. The other clear sign of Gogo territory was the gum-tree, which now joined the familiar thorn, tamarisk and mimosa. Ugogo in the rainy season was preferable to the scorched plain of June; now grapes hung thickly in clusters along their path.

At Kiwyeh they heard the booming and bellowing of war horns and braced themselves for an attack. But the din turned out to be the Wagogo sallying forth to do battle with Hehe raiders. The expedition watched rapt as the Gogo tribesmen gathered in the panoply of war: head-dresses of ostrich or eagle feathers, knee-straps and anklet bells, assegais, knob-kerries and shields. Then column after column swung off into the forest, more than 1,000 warriors in all. This was a sobering spectacle: Stanley realised how very little chance even the strongest caravan stood against a sustained assault by such numbers; typically it fuelled in him fantasies of bestriding Africa with 500 European riflemen.

Next day the fantasy of violence came close to reality. At Khonze, 'remarkable for the mighty globes of foliage which the giant sycamores and baobabs put forth above the plain', some renegade Wanyamwezi who had intermarried with the Wagogo attempted to extort cloth from them by a show of force. Stanley ordered his men to load their guns, then advanced on the leader of the hostiles, seized him by the throat and threatened to blow his head off if he spoke again. He then compelled acceptance of a very light hongo}

Light tribute was the surprising outcome of their progress through the much-dreaded Ugogo. At Kamenyi this was due to the fact that the chief had known Burton and Speke but at Mapanga, on 2 April, they had to live through some nail-biting moments. As they traipsed through the forest, they were suddenly accosted by forty yelling spearmen. Stanley pondered the inevitable losses in a fight between his forty guns and the opposing spears. He decided to negotiate. The leader of the spearmen asked what they meant by bypassing their village without paying hongo. In his best learned-from-Livingstone manner Stanley answered calmly that his caravan was in a great hurry to reach the coast; they did not stop for the simple reason that they were living on the breadline themselves and had nothing to offer. To his great relief, the leader of the spearmen started to laugh; why, he said, we are in no better position than you, for we were cutting wood when the call to arms came and we are in no mood to fight. To laughter all round a nugatory tribute was agreed. The spearmen accompanied them part of the way along the trail, while the leader explained that the Wagogo were reasonable people: they did not try to extort blackmail from those who had nothing.

Next the expedition passed Kulabi, penetrated a thorny jungle, then traversed a naked, red-loamy plain. Quenching their thirst on brackish water, they pressed on in the teeth of a storm and came to the territory of Mvumi, last of the Gogo chiefs. On 5 April they plunged into the wilderness and marched nine hours, past herds of rhino, quagga and antelope. With loud hurrahs they said goodbye to Ugogo and pressed on through the rain, which at least gave them plentiful supplies of fresh water.

On the 7th they entered Mpapwa in pelting rain, having come 338 miles in twenty-four days. They looked for the remains of Farquahar, hoping to bury his bones, but could find no trace of them. Next day Stanley noted the spot where his dog Omar had died. He was delighted with the progress they were making, largely attributed to the much lighter loads they, as a homeward-bound caravan, were carrying.

But the real force of the masika hit them once they entered the Mukondokwa valley. The rivers were now mighty brown floods, the banks brim-full, the nullahs full of water, the fields inundated. The rain cascaded down, causing a dramatic change in vegetation; this time the trails were covered with tall grass, higher than a man's head, intertwined in tangled heaps and swathes. On 11 April they spent five and a half hours crossing flooded fords before camping on a hill opposite Mount Kibwe at Kadetamare. The local chief was fond of strangers and to show his partiality sent them a 5-gallon jar of the local brew; in return Stanley gave him a generous doti.

On 12 April they got to the mouth of the Mukondokwa pass - the gateway to the tableland of the interior - 'after six hours of the weariest march I had ever undergone ... close to the edge of the foaming angry flood lay our route, dipping down frequently into deep ditches, wherein we found ourselves sometimes up to the waist in water, and sometimes up to the throat. Urgent necessity impelled us onward, lest we might have to camp at one of those villages until the end of the monsoon rains; so we kept on, over marshy bottoms, up to the knees in mire, under jungle tunnels dripping with wet, then into sloughs arm-pit deep. Every channel seemed filled to overflowing, yet down the rain poured, beating the surface of the river into yellowish foam, pelting us until we were almost breathless.'

Stanley noted in passing that Usagara would be the perfect base for a major missionary effort, since it unlocked Central Africa. But most of his time was spent in a literally breathless fight to survive against the fury of wind and rain and the jeopardy of engorged, overflowing rivers. 'This and the following day will long be remembered in the memories of the several members of the expedition for the fatigues and hardships incurred on those marches.' At night they battled with swarms of black, voracious mosquitoes while the rain pelted down unceasingly. By day they were starting to find the rivers unfordable because of the deluge.

A perilous river crossing by a tree bridge on the 13 th saw all of Stanley's ruthlessness on display. One of his bearers, Rojab by name, was crossing with the box containing Livingstone's journals and letters when he lost his footing and fell into a hole in mid-river. Miraculously Rojab managed to retain his footing but the risk to the precious box drew from Stanley an angry roar: 'Look out! Drop that box, and I'll shoot you.' It was of a piece with the 'little master's' methods that Rojab received no plaudits for saving the box; for his fumble he was cautioned never to carry valuable effects again.

To their chagrin this perilous crossing proved to be but a feeder to the main river, which boiled and seethed with wild, white churning waters. They constructed a raft from four trees, but it was immediately swept away in the roaring torrent and vanished into the whirling currents. Greater ingenuity was called for. They tied together a rope 180 feet long, then secured it around Chowpereh's body. Though swept downstream, he managed to reach the other side and lashed the rope to a tree. Then the expedition's members were hoist across the raging river in turn. But it was still too dangerous to risk the precious letter-box. Temporarily baffled, Stanley pitched two camps, one on either side of the river.

In the morning the river was still rising. Stanley cut two slender poles, then tied sticks across them to make a kind of primitive hand barrow on which a box could rest when lashed to it. He figured that two men swimming and holding a rope, with the ends of the poles on their shoulders, should be able to ferry across a 70-pound box. He then chose twelve of the strongest swimmers, fortified them with brandy and divided them into six teams, who relayed the box across the river with ease.

Seven hours' splashing through marshes and bogs brought them to Rehenneko. Stanley then ordered a four-day rest before they pressed on to struggle with the Rudewa and Itronga Rivers. A seven-hour forced march through slush, mud and mire, plagued all the way by gadflies, brought them to the edge of the dreaded Makata swamp. The only factor in their favour now was that the rain had stopped.

The crossing of the Makata was as much a nightmare as Stanley had feared. They began the crossing already exhausted, since clouds of mosquitoes had prevented any sleep before midnight; thereafter they were bitten and plagued so grievously that 'when the horn sounded there was not one dissentient among them'.

Into the Makata they plunged. They were up to their armpits, then up to their knees, then up to their armpits again, wading on tiptoe, supporting the children above the water. Beyond the swamp proper stretched a lake where four overflowing rivers converged. After sloshing through this for 6 miles, they came to the little Makata River, very deep at the centre and rising, with a current running at 10 knots. There was not a spit of dry land anywhere in the middle to rest a single bale of cloth. The tallest men waded into the 50-foot wide stream, half swimming, half treading water, probing and testing to find the shallow spots. Eventually they found a crossable route and waded back into the centre up to their necks to help the shorter and less able across. The crossing took two hours. They had entered the Makata swamp at 5 a.m. and it took them until 3 p.m. to get clear of it.

On 25 April they were outside Simbawenni. The swollen river had rushed on the city with tsunami-like ferocity a few days before and swept away the entire front wall of the proud stone city, causing the destruction of fifty houses and great loss of life. Once again Stanley had arrived at the right time, as he acknowledged: 'I consider our delay at Rehenneko to have saved us from much peril if not death. Everything so far associated with this expedition has turned out for the best.'

At Mussoudi too they found that the flooded rivers had acted like a tidal wave and swept away scores of villages with heavy loss of life. All that was left was debris and detritus piled high where there had once been houses. On they pressed through Kisemo and into a jungle, teeming with bird life and also with boa constrictors, some of them between 12 and 15 feet long. The plague of boas continued in the next jungle, beyond Msuwa, full of impenetrable thorn bushes and spear-headed cactus: 'could a bottle full of concentrated miasma be used, what deadly and unknown poison - undiscoverable - would it make. I think it would act quicker than chloroform and more fatal than prussic acid.'

In this dreadful jungle beyond Msuwa all of Tanzania's 114 varieties of snake seemed to have gathered in reptilian convention. There were boas in the trees above their heads and night-adders and cobras on the ground below. Stanley considered that this infernal forest topped the seven plagues of Egypt since, in addition to malaria, suffocation, miasma, stench, thorns under foot, spear cactus catching in clothes and bundles, and knee-deep mud, there were boas, poisonous snakes, scorpions and red ants to contend with.

On 2nd May they were at Rosako. Here at last they were within the Zanzibar ambit and Stanley was able to read back copies of the New York Herald from which he got his first glimmerings of the hostility his expedition had already engendered. He learned too that the exceptionally rainy season they had trudged through was but an echo of disastrous conditions off the coast, and that the mountains west of Simbawenni had actually protected them from the worst fury of the elements. A great hurricane had all but overwhelmed Zanzibar, destroying virtually every ship in the harbour.

Two days later they crossed the Kingani, which now resembled a sea, in canoes, and on 6th May reached Bagamoyo at sunset. They had covered 525 miles in fifty-two days. It was an outstanding achievement, overshadowed by Stanley's more famous journeys, but in technical rate-per-day terms arguably his most successful ever. If fear of the water often denotes fear of one's own passive tendencies, it is clear enough that this was one psychological disability that Stanley, with his compulsion for continual action, did not suffer from.

While Stanley trudged down a palm-fringed street of mud houses, a red-headed young man in topee and flannels hailed him from one of the better-quality white houses. 'Won't you walk in?' he said. 'What will you have to drink - beer, stout, brandy. By George, I congratulate you on your splendid success!' The young man turned out to be Lieutenant Henn, who had just arrived as part of an expedition (sponsored by the RGS) to relieve Livingstone.

It was the Mirambo war which jolted the RGS out of its previous complacency about Livingstone. It was clear that the road from Ujiji to the coast was blocked and there was a strong possibility that Livingstone's supplies had been destroyed; it was also obvious (or so it seemed) that there was no chance that Stanley, known to be in Unyanyembe, could reach the doctor. In one of its fits of periodic compassionate concern, the British public responded to an appeal for funds with £4,000. The RGS set up an expedition and appointed to its command naval Lieutenant L. S. Dawson, who had recently surveyed the Yangtse and the River Plate. Henn, Stanley's Bagamoyo host, had been named as his second- in-command. The third white member was Oswell Livingstone, aged twenty, the doctor's youngest son. In Zanzibar they also persuaded the Methodist missionary, the Revd Charles New, who had some experience of African exploration (he had recently climbed to the snow-line on Mount Kilimanjaro), to join the expedition. It was a pure fluke that New was in Zanzibar at all, for he had boarded the Abydos in Mombasa under the impression it was to sail straight to England. But no sooner had the expedition members crossed to Bagamoyo, on 27 April, than news came in that Stanley had 'found' Livingstone. Dawson at once took the view that there was no longer any point in his project, threw up the command and returned to Zanzibar. Over drinks in Bagamoyo Stanley further persuaded Henn that Livingstone needed no relief expedition, but only the fifty porters he was pledged to obtain for him.

Next day Stanley met Oswell Livingstone and put the same points to him. The young Livingstone dithered, then solved his vacillation by returning to Zanzibar to consult with Kirk. He finally decided to go home when a dispute between Henn and New as to who should now have the command (the older man with experience of Africa or the young naval officer officially designated as second-in-command) led both of them in turn to resign. Stanley felt that young Oswell was wrong. It was right that the now pointless expedition should be wound up, but that was no reason why Oswell should not accompany the porters back to Unyanyembe. Oswell later justified himself by saying that in his delicate state of health (he had a bladder complaint as well as attacks of malaria and dysentery) he could not face the swollen, waterlogged country between the sea and Ugogo. Kirk concurred in this wholeheartedly, but in going home Oswell was giving significant hostages to fortune, as well as valuable ammunition to Stanley in his later propaganda battle with Kirk.

While the fiasco of this RGS expedition was being played out, Stanley crossed to Zanzibar (7th May). He was greeted cordially by consul Webb and congratulated by Tozer and Kirk, as yet not suspecting the storm that was to burst on him. Stanley was startled, on looking into a mirror, to find that his hair was growing grey. He was almost unrecognisable, so much so that when he ran into his old friend Captain H. C. Fraser and greeted him, Fraser replied, 'You have the advantage of me, sir.'

Stanley at once discharged his men and rehired twenty of them for Livingstone's expedition. He parted on bad terms with Bombay: 'Stupid Bombay, though he had more than once expressed his scorn of dirty money was glad to take a present of $50 besides his pay.' Then he assembled fifty-seven men, all of whom were paid $20 in advance, and engaged a young Arab to head the caravan. Oswell Livingstone handed over clothing, provisions, money and fifty carbines from the stocks of the original RGS expedition. Stanley devoted extraordinary care to the choice of the fifty-seven, as on their performance his reputation with Livingstone would ride. He rejected Oswell Livingstone's Mombasa men and all obvious slackers and bounty jumpers; by the time he dispatched his party of sixty-four to Bagamoyo on 27th May he was well satisfied that Livingstone would have no cause for complaint.

By now Kirk had learned of Livingstone's displeasure with him and suspected Stanley of having put the doctor up to it. He had no choice but to forward Livingstone's letters impugning him to London, and (humiliatingly) to hand over the £500 to Stanley, but he swore that he would never do anything for Livingstone again except on a direct order from the Foreign Office. In private Kirk described Livingstone as a 'damned old scoundrel'; when told he planned to visit America after finishing his African work, he remarked caustically: 'I am now glad to think it is not likely to be for three years.' When Stanley suggested that Kirk might like to take charge of despatching the caravan for Livingstone, Kirk declined curtly as 'I am not going to expose myself to needless insult again.' Stanley had now laid firm foundations for one of the many bitter enmities of his life. Kirk immediately went over on to the counterattack. If there had been any problem in the arrival of Livingstone's supplies, this was mainly because Stanley's secretiveness about his true aims worked against the doctor's true interests; he also intimated that it was Stanley and Stanley alone who was responsible for the breakup of the Henn/Dawson expedition.

Nor did Stanley make any friends among the other Englishmen in Zanzibar. When he lectured Dawson on duty, Dawson stormed angrily out of the room. Oswell Livingstone was abashed by the lectures he received on filial responsibility. New, too, was irritated by Stanley's treatment of him. While admiring his energy and courage, he soon spotted that he was no angel and found his duplicity particularly trying: Stanley 'blames me for not doing that which he avers it was unnecessary for anyone to do and which he justifies everyone concerned in it for abandoning.'

Having completed the task he had promised to perform, Stanley wrote his last letter to Livingstone from Africa. 'Permit me to wish you joy of your plum pudding. And now, my dear and good friend, I have done to the utmost of my ability what I have promised ... All I can now, is to wish you the blessing of God, and the beneficent Providence who has watched over you so long.' The fifty-seven men arrived safely at Unyanyembe, and Livingstone later testified that all but one had given the most sterling service.

Stanley now had to reach the telegraph at Suez to learn what Bennett required of him next. He began negotiating with the owner of the steamship Africa to take him to the Seychelles to catch the Mauritius mail. The discussions were difficult, for the owner wanted $900 for the charter. Stanley intended to take New, Henn and Oswell Livingstone with him; he had offered Dawson passage, but Dawson was so angry with Stanley that he left on the Mary Away for the Cape of Good Hope expressly so as not to have to travel with him. But at last they fixed a price and the four men embarked (29th May).

The Africa rolled, pitched and lumbered along at a top speed of 7 knots in a most wearisome way 'but it is better than staying forever at Zanzibar'. They arrived at Port Victoria, Mahe Island in the Seychelles on 7th June, only to find that the French mail had left just twelve hours before. They rented a pleasant villa nicknamed 'Livingstone Lodge' at £30 a month, and there Stanley, New, Oswell Livingstone and a Mr Morgan lived, with Kalulu and Selim as servants, for a month while they waited for a ship (Henn stayed in a hotel).

The month in the Seychelles was an oasis of quiet and reflection for Stanley. He climbed the highest hill behind Port Victoria with Oswell Livingstone and returned exhausted, full of praise for the young man's pluck but puzzled by his excessive taciturnity: 'I cannot make young Livingstone out at all.' In the end Stanley concluded that Livingstone's excessive reserve derived from a deeply rooted suspicion and prejudice inculcated in him by Kirk for Stanley and all his works. Scornfully Stanley recorded how many young men seemed bowled over by Kirk, purely through their immaturity and inexperience. For Stanley, Kirk was a prima donna and a congenital liar and it was at his baneful door that the debacle of the abortive RGS expedition should be laid.

On 2nd July, Stanley, young Livingstone and the others were the guests of the British resident Hales Franklyn. Henn came from his hotel to join them and upstaged the other guests by playing the piano, singing Irish songs and making such a great hit with the ladies that Stanley was jealous: 'He is a star of the first magnitude, and I am naught, for I cannot converse with the fair sex, nor sing a song, nor play on the piano.'

On 4th July a ship came at last. They embarked on the Danube, of the Mesenteries Maritimes line, bound for Aden. One of their fellow passengers was Bishop Ryan of Mauritius and his curate, who also found young Livingstone silent as a sphinx 'as though he was offended at everybody'. On 10 July they reached Aden, where they were due to transfer to the French mail steamer from China, the Meikong. Stanley cabled for confirmation that he was to return to Europe and not go on to China. His cable crossed with one from Hosmer in London that in effect carried its own answer and set the seal on his achievement: Mr Bennett sends following. You are now famous as Livingstone having discovered the discoverer. Accept my thanks, and whole world. Recruit your health at Aden or elsewhere. Forward by special messenger Livingstone's letters and anything further you may have. Adept in addition assurance fellow correspondent that more splendid achievement, energetic devotion and generous gallantry not in history human endeavour. Hosmer.

Stanley now had the world-wide fame he hungered for, and would shortly have money too from his book on the Livingstone expedition. But what of his status as African explorer? What general judgement can we form on the basis of his first eighteen months as an adventurer and discoverer in Central Africa?

Stanley mastered the intricacies of African travel, the nuances of hongo, doti and porterage, with remarkable speed. He claimed to have learned all there was to know during the three months' march to Unyanyembe, after which it was simply a question of honing and refining his craft. Part of the judgement may be allowed to stand. Stanley had an extraordinary gift for knowing just how far he could push his pagazis and how much he could ask them to carry, before their discontent would boil over into outright mutiny. He also learned that the usefulness of donkeys in Africa was limited, as their loads would catch in the brambles, branches and thorn bushes along the caravan trails.

But Stanley as an explorer can be faulted in two areas: one venial, the other more serious. The trivial fault was a tendency towards hyperbole and journalistic 'expedient exaggeration': for instance, later travellers demonstrated that many of the accounts given in How I Found Livingstone were embellishments, since Stanley - located where he said he was - could not have seen the geographical features he purported to be describing as an eyewitness. Along with this went a certain sloppiness: describing a swamp as a 'pond', and so on. Part of this derived from his instincts as a journalist; he realised that too many scholarly qualifications and caveats would bore his readers. But another part came from his own temperament: Stanley was always too impatient, too concerned with achieving the grand effects, to be meticulous over small details.

Yet the inaccuracies in Stanley's travel accounts - and it must be stressed that there are few - had a deeper aetiology: his pathological desire not to share the glory with others, and to mock and disparage the discoveries and achievements of other travellers. Part of the difficulty of the outward journey to Unyanyembe was caused by Stanley's determination not to follow Speke's route but to blaze a trail of his own. Additionally, he was adamant that this achievement should be incontestably his own. So, although Farquhar was a trained navigator, Stanley deliberately did not use his skills. All Stanley did was use a watch and pocket compass to record the direction and duration of the daily march. There was no accurate astronomical plotting; in addition, Stanley's method of 'dead reckoning' was thrown out because he began his march during the rainy season, in a part of Africa where magnetic variation is notoriously high.

At every possible occasion Stanley tried to score off previous explorers, especially Burton and Speke. Some of his shots were wild, as when he claimed that the 'Kazeh' of Burton and Speke's narratives was unknown to the locals, only to be corrected by Verney Cameron who pointed out that Kazeh and Tabora were one and the same. Stanley's animadversions tempted his rivals to go over on to the attack. Stanley made lavish claims for the mineral wealth of Africa: 'underneath the surface but a few feet is one mass of iron ore, extending across three degrees of longitude and nearly four of latitude.' Joseph Thomson, the Scottish explorer and a geologist himself, called this statement 'the unrestrained exercise of fancy'. But sometimes the counterattack went too far. When Stanley said that Lake Ugombo was 3 miles long and 2V2 miles wide, Cameron commented that Stanley must have been dreaming. But the truth was that the two men had seen the same thing at different times of the year; seasonal fluctuations transformed the lake almost out of recognition.

Sometimes Stanley's geographical assessments were incorrect simply because at this stage of his African career his knowledge of Swahili was deficient. He simply noted down the phonetic equivalent of what he had heard, so that 'Nsisi' became 'Imbiki' and 'Ngererengeri' became 'Lungerengeri'. Two other associated problems were that many places were named after their current chief or after familiar objects. Stanley says he stopped at 'Mrefu' which means 'tall' or 'long', at 'Mtoni' which means 'river bed' and at 'Misonghi', which means a large, round hut. Another problem about Swahili was secondary meanings. His porters used the word 'Mkali' (hot) to describe the terrain between Ugogo and Tabora, when on his own admission it was not hot on the plateau. The probable explanation is that the wangwana were using the word in its secondary meaning of 'unpleasant' or 'difficult' as an anticipatory description of the rigours to corned Again, Stanley thought the local people had simply covered Farquahar's body with leaves, which was why he went to look for the corpse to bury it. But since the Swahili use the same word for 'grass' and 'leaves', what the people of Mpapwa meant was that they had grassed his body over, i.e. buried it. Similarly, Stanley was adamant that 'Unyamwezi' meant 'The Land of the Moon' whereas later scholars favoured 'The Land of the West'. On the other hand, Stanley is not as poor on proper names as some of his more astringent critics make out, and any deficiency in Swahili was something he certainly made up in later years.

By and large, though naturally subject to later corrections, Stanley's geographical observations were surprisingly accurate. When it comes to the peoples Stanley encountered, his anthropological flair is idiosyncratic. Stanley is good on the people who pose, or might pose, a personal threat to him and his expedition, and often made careful notes on the tribes who were friendly to him. But in peoples who posed no military threat, were distant from his line of march, or were known to him only by reputation, Stanley showed little interest. He was impatient with the complexities of tribal politics and, while he appreciated the significance of the Hehe, the Gogo and the Ha, he dismissed the crucial Kimbu peoples in one brief sentence. Nor was he much interested in the complexities of kinship, chieftainship or stratification in African societies. The fact that he was no precision also helps to explain why Stanley never realised, either on this expedition or any of his subsequent ones, the precarious knife-edge on which most African economies subsisted. Also, the reputation of African warriors tended to be made by their contact with European explorers. Stanley encountered Mirambo in dramatic circumstances, so the fame of Mirambo was placed before a wider audience. The Nyamwezi chief Nyungu, arguably as important as Mirambo, never had the same reputation because he never swam into the ken of the great explorers. In October 1871 Stanley narrowly missed meeting him on the borders of Mangala's Kimbu chiefdom (Iswangala Kamanga).

Yet if he showed no real interest in tribal organisation and politics, Stanley did manifest a genuine feeling for the black man, possibly because chieftains and porters were no threat to his personal prestige. He did not have to put them in their place as possible rivals to his authority or as claimants to new discoveries. Stanley always claimed that his experiences in the ante-bellum South were crucial in this regard. He despised the 'Yankee' notion of effortless white superiority over the black race. When consul Webb asked him in Zanzibar if he thought negro teeth had nerves, Stanley was not amused: 'As even then I had extracted about one hundred negro teeth to relieve my poor men from their tortures, my stare at Captain

Webb was sufficiently expressive.'

Under Livingstone's influence, too, he began to take a more positive view of Africa and to see it as a potential cornucopia, a further refuge for the 'huddled masses' of the world and a living refutation of Malthusianism. Here we may discern the experience of the West and the frontier as being decisive, rather than the South. The obvious obstacle in the way here was tropical disease: after all, Stanley himself had suffered twenty- three separate attacks on his first journey. No one knew better than Stanley himself the problem of the tsetse fly, even though the connection between insects and fever had not yet been made. It was Dr Donald Ross of the Indian Medical Service who finally showed that the deadly African fever was a virulent form of malaria transmitted, not by climate or 'miasmata', but by the anopheles mosquito. At the same time, Dr Walter Reed proved that yellow fever, another medical scourge, was also mosquito-borne.

Amazingly, even after all Stanley had written, majority opinion, including that of the explorer Thomson, continued to hold that the tsetse fly was unknown between Zanzibar and Ujiji. This conjured visions of the end of pagazis and porterage charges and a future of African travel based solely on ox-trekking. This consoling myth was finally exploded in 1878 when Edward Hore forwarded a specimen to Zanzibar and Kirk unhesitatingly identified it as the tsetse fly: 'it is established beyond all doubt that the line of road ... is swarming with the fly.' Stanley's response might well have been 'I told you so': he was in a good position to know what he was talking about for, aside from his personal experiences, Livingstone and Frank Vardon had encountered the tsetse in 1846-7 along the Limpopo; Vardon had actually brought the first specimen back to England. Later travellers in Tanzania recorded their incredulity that Stanley's assertions on the prevalence of the tsetse could have been doubted; exactly ninety years later a pair of adventurers following in his footsteps encountered a cloud of the insects almost exactly where Stanley had, at Maledita.

Yet it was not just in the general accuracy of his observations that Stanley showed himself to be an ideal African explorer. He was more capable than most men of reclusive self-denying existence. His sole 'vice' was chain-smoking; the familiar picture of Stanley is of a man puffing pensively on cigar or cheroot. He neither drank nor was sexually active. Nor did he sublimate his instincts in big-game hunting - an activity he despised. One of the items in Stanley's repertoire of abuse of Kirk was the consul's taste for hunting: 'When I started from the coast I remember how ardently I pursued the game; how I dived into the tall, well grass, how I lost myself in jungles; how I trudged over the open plains in search of meat and venison. And what did it all amount to? Killing a few inoffensive animals the meat of which was not worth the trouble. And shall I waste my strength and energies in chasing game? No, and the man who would do so at such a crisis as the present is the hardest part of exploration for some men (and this applies particularly to polar exploration) is the degree of instinctual renunciation it involves. In this respect Stanley's sexual personality was ideal. The alternation of redemption through the suffering of swamp, starvation and disease with the derivation of pleasure from the infliction of cruelty tends to make Stanley's journeys almost a classic story of externalisation. His own deep unconscious guilt meant that he himself could never be to blame for any mistake. He rewarded good work with grudging praise and bad work with the most stinging reproaches. No one reading his treatment of Shaw and Farquahar can doubt the sadistic impulse; the savage beatings administered to Selim and Bombay even while in the throes of sickness warrant the description 'lustful pleasure'. His habit-which was to recur in later expeditions - of leaving behind wounded or sick companions without taking proper thought for their safety goes beyond conventional ruthlessness. It must not be forgotten that all five white men who accompanied Stanley on his first two expeditions perished in the depths of Africa.

It has been speculated that Stanley obliterated all mention of his own sexuality in his published accounts of his travels as this would draw attention to the sadistic impulses of which he was himself dimly aware. But there is no mention of sex even in his private diaries, except routine denunciations of men like Shaw who, in Stanley's view, sacrificed their own well-being to the cravings of the flesh. Coupled with the cruel treatment of his companions and servants, the apparent absence of sexuality is itself circumstantial evidence for the fundamental personal ambiguity (at the sexual level, sado-masochistic) that we have postulated.

Other pointers are provided by Stanley himself. The fear of real human intimacy, as opposed to an idealised fantasy version, is everywhere apparent in his life and writings. On his expeditions Stanley habitually dined alone and slept alone in his tent. He had no sense of humour about himself and was hypersensitive to criticism. He expected people to dislike him and felt that every man's hand was turned against him: 'I make enemies every day of my life,' he observed. He was obsessed with the notion that his mediocre contemporaries sensed his greatness and conspired against him to topple him, out of the hatred felt by the nonentity for the man of genius. Exploration, notionally a means to an end, became an end in itself. 'I have had no friend on any expedition, no one who could possibly be my companion, on an equal footing, except while with Livingstone . .. though altogether solitary, I was never less conscious of solitude ... my only comfort was my work. To it I ever turned as a friend. It occupied my days and I dwelt fondly on it at night.' Such was the man who directed his steps towards Europe in July 1872.

ON 11th July the steamer Mekong arrived from China and Stanley and party embarked. At Suez he received orders to send on Livingstone's two letters for the Herald, ahead of his other despatches, so that Bennett could make the greatest possible éclat. The plan was for the letters to be copied in London, then posted to New York. Stanley was to come on slowly, so as to arrive in London fifteen days after receipt of the Livingstone letters. The timing was contrived so that Stanley would arrive in London just when the Herald's news burst on the world.

This placed Stanley in a dilemma, between his moral master and his material one. He could not disobey Bennett, yet he had given his word to Livingstone that no more than forty-eight hours would elapse between publication of the doctor's 'open letters' and the despatch of private correspondence to his family. To this end he had already booked passage to Marseilles.

At Port Said Stanley dismissed Selim with £33 severance pay after two and a half years' service, plus £2 passage money for the journey from Port Said to Jerusalem. Then he continued with Kalulu to Marseilles. The Meikong passed Stanley's old stamping grounds in Crete, then threaded its way up the Mediterranean past Messina, Rhegium, Sardinia and Corsica. They docked at midnight on the 23rd, and Stanley at once went in search of the London bureau chief George Hosmer, who had travelled to the south of France to meet him. At 2 a.m. he found him at his hotel, already asleep. Bleary-eyed, Hosmer staggered from his bed and roused the correspondent of the Daily Telegraph who was sharing a room with him. They obtained the best wine available at such an hour and sat up till morning toasting Stanley's success. Hosmer informed him that, owing to the special nature of his commitment to Livingstone, Bennett had decided to honour it, even though the cost of sending the despatches to New York by cable would be £2,000. This meant there was no longer any special reason for delay, since the Herald would now release its scoop in London on the same day as the reports appeared in the newspaper in New York.

Stanley spent the 25th and 26th buying appropriate clothes for his appearance in Paris, as he was still dressed in his rather shoddy Zanzibar outfit. Then on the 27th he and Kalulu took the train to Paris. When the express sped into a tunnel, Kalulu immediately crawled under a seat in terror, thinking that in the white man's country darkness fell instantaneously. When the train emerged into the daylight, Stanley persuaded the boy to come out, and Kalulu was just starting to regain his composure when the locomotive again roared into a tunnel. Kalulu gradually got used to this and lost his fear, but he remained disconcerted by the cacophonous whistling of passing trains and the 'flying countryside'. But by Lyons he was reasonably adjusted, and when they descended from the train to dine, Kalulu acquitted himself well with a knife and fork, his only mistake being to take an overdose of mustard so that his eyes watered. Stanley tried to remedy this with ice-cream, but Kalulu found this too cold and wanted to spit it out. Out of deference to the 'little master' he swallowed it. A warm-hearted French matron sitting opposite described the boy as a 'pauvre ange'

Paris, reached on the 28th, was a whirl of congratulatory luncheons and dinners. The day before, the first of Livingstone's letters to Bennett had been printed in the London Times and the Telegraph, and the scale of Stanley's achievement was starting to dawn on the popular imagination. The Americans in Paris particularly lionised Stanley and he was taken under the wing of US Minister Washburne, who invited him to breakfast with General Sherman. Sherman magnanimously rated Stanley's journey above his own march to the sea. Stanley repaid the compliment by asking Sherman if he had ever met him before. Sherman shook his head. Stanley then rattled off large chunks of the speech Sherman had delivered to the Sioux at the North Platte Conference in 1867, to Sherman's considerable astonishment.

On 29th July Stanley was at a banquet with eighty luminaries of Paris society. On the 30th he handed over Livingstone's Foreign Office despatches to the British Embassy; the somewhat frosty reception alerted him to a general British resentment that an 'American' had tracked Livingstone down. Perhaps in response to this, Stanley rather let his mouth run away with him, for he received a curt two-word message from Bennett: 'Stop Talking' - for Bennett, Stanley was in danger of playing his best cards too soon. It was hard for Stanley to remain silent, for his suite at the Hotel du Helder was thronged with callers. This was not to his taste. As he recalled wearily on the 29th: 'Already I have heard enough to make me wish that Bennett had not chosen me to seek Livingstone. I get no pleasure at all in these crowds of curious callers or in their grossly worded congratulations. I have a presentiment also that with this sudden fame that has come to me, the annoyances will be quite as great as any pleasure and profit that may be derived from it.'

His conviction that he was destined to make enemies every day of his life was borne out by a trivial incident at the hotel. Stanley was entertaining two guests when a card was sent in from the Reuters man, Edward Viruard, who had saved his life in 1868 when swimming in Egypt. Stanley sent word for Viruard to wait five minutes, but Viruard chose to take this as an insult and stormed off: 'He is too full of himself now to think of early friends.' The bitterness over this 'rebuff' was eventually to lead to Viruard to attempt blackmail on the man he had rescued.

But Stanley was often his own worst enemy. This was underlined on 31st July when Washburne and the American colony gave a farewell banquet for him at the Hotel Chatham. Nearly a hundred guests were present in the new dining-room of the hotel which had been specially refurbished for the occasion. It was a hot night, the hotel windows were thrown open, and a throng of onlookers in the courtyard beyond gazed in at the proceedings. Overcome by the occasion, Stanley allowed himself to launch into a violent attack on Kirk. It was particularly unwise to use an American venue for such a verbal mauling, for Kirk's powerful friends in London could now sally forth to his defence under the banner of patriotism and anti-Americanism, and there is no doubt that Stanley's performance that night further hardened opinion in England against him.

Stanley crossed over to England on the first day of August in sombre mood. The only thing that cheered him about Paris was Kalulu's sensational social success, particularly among Parisian women. A contemporary described the success as follows: 'Kalulu never allows his admiration to overstep his patriotism. His native Chambezi is ever to him the finest of rivers, and his description of its beauties and amenities represent it to be vastly more civilised than the most advanced districts of England. Since his introduction to French society his mental powers have been rather taxed but so far he has proved equal to the occasion. His first taste of wine, combined with the excitement of travelling by express, made him a decidedly hilarious companion.'

After the disastrous and embarrassing meeting at Dover with his uncle Moses Parry and his step-brother Robert, Stanley travelled up to London and ensconced himself in the Langham Hotel. To his mortification he found himself in a hornets' nest of controversy. Many London newspapers doubted his claim to have found Livingstone. Others queried or belittled the achievement. Stanley found himself the focus of a three headed beast of resentment. There was jealousy that an American newspaper correspondent had upstaged and humiliated the RGS Livingstone Relief Expedition. There was disbelief in his story because it emanated from 'that detestable newspaper'. There was animus from the English establishment because of his attacks on Kirk in Paris.

When it was first known that there was a possibility that Stanley might meet Livingstone in Central Africa, the attitude of the Royal Geographical Society was positive. The explorer James Grant, who had known Stanley in Abyssinia, had great faith in his ability to succeed. But the RGS line changed when its own expedition floundered into fiasco and especially when Dawson made his official report to the Society: 'Though I do not begrudge Mr Stanley his well-earned success, it would be distasteful to me, if not to both of us, to travel in company... I cannot but feel pain that he [Livingstone] should have adopted the course of forwarding his documents and correspondence through an American agent, and jealously avoided making known what his recent discoveries may have been to his former friend and fellow-traveller Dr Kirk.''

The response of the RGS was twofold. While Grant continued to foster the idea that Stanley had not in fact met Livingstone at all, Sir Henry Rawlinson systematically attempted to belittle the achievement. Grant's line was that the abandonment of the RGS expedition by Dawson and Oswell Livingstone was a bad mistake, since there was no proof that Stanley had found Livingstone. Rawlinson went much further. He coupled sarcasm at the Herald's expense ('our transatlantic cousins, among whom the science of advertising has reached a far higher stage of development than in this benighted country') with a clear attempt to demean Stanley: 'There is one point on which a little eclaircissement is desirable, because a belief seems to prevail that Mr Stanley has discovered and relieved Dr Livingstone; whereas, without any disparagement to Mr Stanley's energy, activity, and loyalty, if there has been any discovery and relief it is Dr

Livingstone who had discovered and relieved Mr Stanley. Dr Livingstone, indeed, is in clover while Mr Stanley is nearly destitute ... It is only proper that the relative position of the parties should be correctly stated.'

Such leads from Sir Henry Rawlinson and other RGS luminaries encouraged the worst excesses of the English press. When Stanley arrived at the Langham Hotel at the beginning of August, he found himself the butt of a sustained attack in the Standard, the gist of which was that he was a forger and a charlatan. After condescendingly declaring that Stanley's claims would have to be sifted by 'experts in African discovery' (to which Stanley in his diary rightly appended 'sic'), the Standard procedure to cast doubt on the American's account of his adventure on a number of grounds. Why did Livingstone not return with Stanley? Why did the doctor not communicate with anyone other than the New York Herald? Why had Livingstone not been relieved for four years and what had Kirk been doing all this time? Why had the RGS expedition turned back? Surely it was obvious that the letters purporting to be from Livingstone had been written by Stanley himself. They were not written in the true Livingstone style. How could Livingstone have such an extensive knowledge of American literature? And would he really have dilated on the feminine charms of the Manyema women? No, for any thinking man, Stanley's imposture was palpable.

These kinds of taunts were widespread in the London press. The Echo suggested ironically that perhaps Livingstone's letters to the Herald had been written by mediumistic means. Stanley dealt with the insinuations decisively. He appealed both to the Livingstone family and to Lord Granville, the recipient of some of Livingstone's most important private letters. Granville consulted with Lord Lyons, the British ambassador in Paris to whom Stanley had delivered Livingstone's Foreign Office despatches, and with his other officials, then wrote an authoritative letter to say that no serious doubt could be entertained as to the authenticity of the letters. On 2nd August Stanley met Tom Livingstone and handed over the doctor's private journals. Tom, who was much more like his father than Oswell, quickly perused the diaries then wrote a letter stating that the journals were 'his father's and no other's'. Corroboration from these two sources dealt the coup de grace to the theory of Stanley as charlatan/ forger.

But by now the third wave in the Stanley controversy was washing in to England, as Livingstone's letters revealed the depth of his bitterness towards Kirk and Kirk in turn mounted a counterattack. Livingstone's letter to Sir Roderick Murchison (the president of the RGS who died in 1871) was particularly incisive. He contrasted the 'lazy' Kirk with Stanley 'the good Samaritan' and the altruism of the American with Kirk's desire for salary and status as consul - particularly reprehensible since Livingstone had 'made' Kirk. Kirk had pleaded that the Mirambo war prevented supplies from getting through to Ujiji; how then had Stanley managed it? Moreover, while Stanley exhilarated the doctor by promising to obtain fifty fresh porters at Zanzibar, all Kirk could suggest was that

Livingstone should go home, as he was a tired old man, and let someone else finish his work.

In reply Kirk wrote to Lord Granville to point out that he had no such sum as the £500 Stanley pestered him for in Livingstone's name, that Stanley had wrecked the RGS expedition by insisting that Livingstone would receive relief only from Stanley himself, that he deeply resented Livingstone's 'grossly unjust and ungrateful' behaviour: 'I shall here add, as otherwise my conduct may be misrepresented, that Mr Stanley, in order to evade blame, if his men did not reach Unyanyembe in time, applied to me to see them started off after his departure from Zanzibar: this was positively and at once declined, and I informed him that I could not, after what Dr Livingstone had done and said, act in any but an official capacity.'

The dispute rumbled on and has never been wholly satisfactorily resolved to this day. Livingstone made partial amends to Kirk by telling Lord Granville that he regretted that Kirk should have taken the attack on Sherif as an attack on himself; he explained both to Granville and to Kirk that the nub of his complaint against Kirk was that he had allowed himself to be bamboozled into sending out slaves instead of free men. Kirk was later exonerated in an official enquiry by Sir Bartle Frere which, however, strikes one as distinctly unsolomonic in its judgement. After conceding that Livingstone's complaints were justified, and allowing that Stanley's efforts had alone saved him from destitution, Barde Frere concluded that Kirk was not to blame for the failure of Livingstone's supplies to arrive. This most unsyllogistic conclusion was not helped by the admission that 'Mr Stanley's own convoy would have failed to reach Ujiji but for his presence with it' for it was precisely the contrast between Stanley's energy and Kirk's fecklessness that Livingstone had been labouring. Nevertheless, many later historians have been content to accept Barde Frere as the last word on this affair, even though there are many issues in the anti-Kirk indictment it fails to answer or even to address. The fact that Stanley's methods were brutal, that he was an habitual liar, that he undoubtedly influenced Livingstone against Kirk, should not seduce us into the unwarranted conclusion that Kirk was beyond reproach.

The Kirk affair was also the proximate cause of Stanley's meeting with Livingstone's old associate Horace Waller. All Livingstone's letters to Waller were full of extravagant praise of Stanley; more worryingly for Waller, they contained many acerbic asides on Kirk, whom Waller worshipped as a 'man of Africa' second only to Livingstone himself. Waller was determined not to like Stanley, and on his visit to him at the Langham Hotel he found ample ammunition for his dislike. Waller was one of those Englishmen who had an exaggerated respect for the small change of social etiquette. When Stanley wrote to him from Paris to introduce himself, he protested that if he could have foreseen the enmity he would incur for going to find Livingstone, he would have thought twice about the assignment. Waller conveyed his reactions to Livingstone: 'Well, this was pretty strong from a man I had never written to, spoken to, and knew as little of as I did of Adam.'

Stanley for his part had good reason for coolness to Waller. Waller it was who had boasted that Stanley would fail in his quest for Livingstone since 'only the steel head of an Englishman could penetrate Africa'. Since reports of Stanley's denunciation of Kirk at the Paris banquet were now appearing in the English press, the omens for a successful encounter at the Langham Hotel were not propitious.

The meeting took place on Saturday 3rd August. Stanley began by trying to wrong foot Waller. He said it was a pity that Waller had not made an appointment. Waller replied that he had announced his intention to call on him in a letter he had sent to the Hotel du Helder in Paris. Stanley retorted that he had received no such letter. But a little later Stanley quoted a phrase from one of Waller's recent letters to The Times. This was a bad slip: Waller had written no letters to The Times and the phrase in question came from the letter to Stanley that he claimed he had not received. Waller moved in for the verbal kill. He pointed out that the quotation Stanley had used could only have come from Waller's letter to him. Instead of being taken aback at such exposure, Stanley simply shifted his cigar to the other side of his mouth and changed the subject abruptly.

Waller came away from the meeting shaken. Stanley had brushed aside his convoluted explanation about how he came to use the 'steel head' expression. When Waller taxed him with having called Kirk a traitor, Stanley simply denied that he had used that word. Waller sat down to try to discredit Stanley with Livingstone. He referred to his 'pretty strong' reputation in Abyssinia, narrated the 'barefaced lie' in which he had caught Stanley out and added: 'I confess, doctor, I did feel very sorry for you and very sorry for Kirk.' But he rather spoiled his defence of Kirk by suggesting that a Livingstone/Kirk imbroglio was an affront to Christianity and that the rift between them could have been compassed only by the powers of darkness. It was unlikely that Livingstone would ever see the man who had saved his life in that light. Waller compounded his tactlessness by hinting that the balance of Livingstone's mind might have been disturbed when he made his accusations against Kirk. ' But he did at least have the grace, in advance of Lord Granville and Tom Livingstone's pronouncements, to scout as absurd any suggestion that Stanley had forged the letters from Livingstone.

The destruction of the absurd canard that Stanley was a charlatan led many doors to open. The most significant was an invitation to read a paper at the Brighton meeting of the British Association on 17th August. There were also letters of congratulation from Agnes Livingstone and invitations to stay in aristocratic houses. Stanley's immediate problem was to find a publisher for his projected book on Livingstone. The doctor had given him the name of the prestigious house of John Murray, but Murray's irritated Stanley by not giving him an immediate reply. Harper's of New York made an early offer of 10 per cent on retail prices, but Stanley decided to accept the bid from Sampson and Low that guaranteed him 50 per cent of the profits with a £1,000 advance payment. The New York firm of Scribner and Low offered a further £1,000 for American rights, on condition that they shared illustration costs with Low's.

But as Stanley sat down to work on the book, he was disconcerted to find the rhythm of work vitiated by two things. One was the receipt of a letter from John Camden Hotten, recently a plagiariser of Mark Twain, which informed him that he would be working on a rival book on the 'finding of Livingstone' which he promised would not cover the same ground. Stanley was coldly angry: 'This man's consummate impudence is too astounding. Out of jail I did not suppose such men could exist.' The other, even more unsettling, barrier to uninterrupted writing was a spate of anonymous and begging letters and requests from his family for financial hand-outs.

A diary entry for 6th August illustrates the problem. 'My stepfather has now called on me at the Langham Hotel. I discover a disposition among the members of my father's family to indicate to me very plainly that having acquired this wearying newspaper fame, I must pay in cash handsomely to all and every member.' Again on 12th August: 'I have not only numerous public enemies but many venomous private enemies - whose bitter hate is excited because I will not satisfy their greed for gold. I lent £100 to mother and £15 to sister Emma and £10 to a cousin - but I seem to have a host of half brothers, cousins in Wales and Liverpool, uncles and aunts and a stepfather who have itching palms. There also seems to be an universal demand from Wales that I should discover myself freely to all the world - probably that Welshmen may share in the newspaper glory that surrounds me... I really do not know to what length my greedy stepfather will drive his wife. I offered to settle on her £50 as long as she lived, but she laughed at it and asked for double, which would mean a capital of £3,300 or thereabouts in the three per cent - which I have not got and which will take me perhaps a couple of years more to scrape together - and there are constant demands of me besides.'

But it was not just his family that tried to apply the bite. The anonymous letters were wounding but could be ignored - 'You detestable Welsh Yankee - what right had you to put your finger in our English pie.' The begging letters were more troublesome for, if ignored, they tended to graduate to blackmailing screeds: 'Ten guineas this day or look out for tomorrow's papers!' All kinds of people claimed kinship and hence financial assistance. The more subtle tried to elicit compassion. The most ingenious claimed a direct blood link. Nine separate women claimed to have been separated from their sons at an early age and were sure that Stanley was the lost child. Some of these women dogged his steps for years. On one occasion he had to call the police and on another the hotel staff had to eject a number of simultaneous competitors 'so fierce were they for my embraces'.

Apart from the Livingstone book and the plague of letter writers, Stanley had to prepare himself for the Brighton meeting. He suspected that the RGS was trying to discredit him with the press while being polite to his face, and that the public squabble between the Society secretary Clements Markham and the members of the failed Livingstone relief expedition (Dawson, Henn, Oswell Livingstone) was a Trojan horse to disguise the RGS's insidious campaign against their real target. Rawlin- son's excuse for why no one from the Society had met him when he arrived in London was lameness itself: 'I regret that you should have arrived in London at a time when all who would have been most desirous to welcome you had already left town or were on the point of doing so.' More suggestive, and more sinister, were the reports appearing in the newspapers that the RGS intended to 'pulverise' Stanley when he spoke at Brighton.

Stanley travelled down to the coast on 14th August as the special guest of Dr Burrowes, Mayor of Brighton. It was on Friday 16th August at 11 a.m. that he made his appearance before the Geographical Section of the British Association. Nearly 3,000 people packed into the concert room in Middle Street to hear his address. The 200-foot long hall, and the gallery that ran round its sides, were thronged with people. A row of VIP chairs at the front facing the stage (on which was hung a map of Africa) was festooned with scarlet cushions. Among the celebrities present was the exiled Emperor Louis Napoleon, the Empress Eugenie and the Prince Imperial, Stanley's patron Baroness Burdett-Coutts, the Bishop of Chichester and several Members of Parliament.

The official title of Stanley's address was 'Discoveries at the North End of Lake Tanganyika' but Stanley was encouraged to give a general account of his travels to find Livingstone. The idea was that this part of the meeting would be followed by questions, there would then be readings from Livingstone's letters and a geographical critique from Colonel Grant. The start of Stanley's speech was unpromising. Stage fright led him to make three false starts, and when he finally got into gear, the tone was not quite what the august gathering of scientists and geographers had expected. 'I consider myself in the light of a troubadour, to relate to you the tale of an old man who is tramping onward to discover the source of the Nile.'

Stanley then continued in the journalistic vein he was to make so familiar with the later publication of How I Found Livingstone. After a concise survey of his African journey and meeting with Livingstone he referred to the criticism that had been made of him in the press, by jealous foreigners and even by the RGS itself, and declared himself open for questions. Stung by the criticisms of the RGS, the president of the Geographical Section, Francis Galton, then arose to remind the audience rather tartly that they were gathered to assess new geographical discoveries in a spirit of dispassionate scientific enquiry and not to listen to sensational stories. This, naturally, angered Stanley and he decided to return contempt for contempt. When Galton, in a spirit of 'scientific enquiry', asked whether the waters of Lake Tanganyika were sweet or brackish, Stanley burlesqued the childish (and hence, by implication, insulting) question by replying that he could not hope to find nicer or sweeter water in the world with which to make a cup of tea.

This drew ripples of laughter from the audience. Much encouraged, Stanley set about his other critics. The Germans were simply jealous: 'I never yet heard of an Englishman who had discovered anything, but a Herr of some sort came forward and said that he had been there before.' This worked on the strong element of anti-German prejudice in the audience (especially with Napoleon III present) and provoked loud guffaws. William Cotton Oswell, the big-game hunter and Livingstone's first collaborator, got to his feet to say that whereas Livingstone was the true old African lion, the gentleman on the platform was the real true young African lion.

Stanley sat down, well satisfied. Then the. RGS launched its counterattack. Grant and Dr Beke criticised Livingstone strongly for identifying the Lualaba as a feeder for the Nile. Rawlinson pretended that there had never been any Society jealousy of Stanley. Worst of all, Galton asked Stanley if he would be willing to clear up the many speculations in the press about his nationality and origins. Incensed as much by the humbug of the RGS as by the attacks on his mentor and burning with indignation that his humble origins might soon be on display for the world to see, Stanley sprang to his feet and hit back angrily. He accused Rawlinson of drawing maps of Africa to suit his own prejudices then rounded on the 'experts'.

Colonel Grant says that Dr Livingstone has made a mistake about the river Lualaba, but I want to know how a geographer resident in England can say there is no such river when Dr Livingstone has seen it? Dr Beke, living in London, and never having been within two thousand miles of the spot, declares positively that Livingstone has not discovered the source of the Nile, whereas Livingstone who has devoted thirty-five years to Africa only says he thinks he has discovered it. I think if a man goes there and says 'I have seen the source of the river', the man sitting in his easy chair or lying in bed cannot dispute this fact on any grounds of theory.

Galton sensed that the meeting was getting out of hand and that a major scandal might be brewing. In some haste he closed the meeting but not before allowing himself the last word in his concluding remarks when he said with some asperity that a man in London might well have access to more information from books and maps than an explorer on the spot. Somewhat perfunctorily he proposed a formal resolution of thanks which was carried to loud cheers.

Stanley was assured on all sides that he had scored a triumph but he was nettled by the snide insinuations of the RGS, angry that they had doubted the word of his mentor Livingstone and, most of all, he smarted under the humiliation of Gabon's queries about his origins. He was in raw and vulnerable mood the following evening at a banquet held in his honour at the Royal Pavilion by the Sussex Medical Society. When called upon to reply to the toast, he began to speak of his admiration for Dr Livingstone. After so many years away from polite society, and used to haranguing recalcitrant tribesmen in a histrionic style with much arm-waving and body language, Stanley forgot the necessity to underplay to an upper-class English audience. In addition his physical appearance was unprepossessing and he seemed ill at ease in evening dress. The combination made Stanley appear a somewhat ridiculous figure to the assembled surgeons. As he rehearsed a dramatic confrontation with the Ha, one of the doctors burst out laughing. Stanley immediately unstoppered the magma of his wrath. The violence of his pent-up rage was breathtaking. Bitterly he lashed his audience. He was sick and tired of all the sneers and insults, the canards and innuendoes. If the English excuse was that they were not used to American ways, this was a singularly inappropriate argument for professional men to use. Did they ask a man's origins before they operated on him? Come to that, had Livingstone asked his nationality before welcoming him? No, enough was enough. To general astonishment, Stanley made a stiff bow and walked out of the room. It was only with great difficulty that the Mayor of Brighton persuaded Stanley to stay on to the end of the scheduled week of activities so that he could attend the formal civic reception.' The RGS tried to play down the consequences of their own boorishness. Grant wrote on 21st August: 'What sensations they have had at Brighton in the Geographical Section! and to wind up with Mr Stanley showing that he has a very thin skin. I am very sorry for the occurrence, though it is very laughable for, after his daring achievement, he need have feared no silly laugh from an ignorant listener. It is to be hoped that the newspaper report is exaggerated.'

The bruising experience at Brighton caused Stanley much private anguish, but publicly he retaliated by raising the temperature in his propaganda battle with the RGS. An obvious pretext was the new expedition being formed to succour Livingstone and the inevitable reflections this prompted on the failure of the earlier one. Stanley's technique was to insinuate that the RGS had chosen the previous expedition's personnel with insufficient care and that the expedition itself had ultimately been scuttled by Kirk." But his sniping backfired when he used the injudicious word 'daunted' to describe Henn's reaction to the area between Bagamoyo and the River Kingani. To avoid a libel action, on the ground that he had accused Henn of cowardice, Stanley was forced to backtrack hastily and publicly.

But he exercised no such restraint in going for the throats of the RGS grandees. In a letter to the Daily Telegraph he took on all his tormentors at once. Let it be understood that I resent all manner of impertinence, brutal horse-laughs at the mention of Livingstone's name, or of his sufferings ... all statements that I am not what I claim to be - an American; all gratuitous remarks such as 'sensationalism', as directed at me by that suave gentleman Mr Francis Galton .. . [Grant] chose to deliver himself of his unwise theories respecting Livingstone's discoveries . .. though Sir Henry Rawlinson is great in cuneiform inscriptions and Assyrian history, his ideas respecting Central African rivers and watersheds are wild, absurd and childish, to use the mildest terms.

Stanley's worst fear was that his origins and parentage would be exposed. When he went out to Africa he thought that Livingstone would be the only source of interest to the public but now he found to his horror that he was an equal source of interest to the public - which interest, however, he refused to indulge 'for I am sure that it was not to discover myself that Mr Gordon Bennett commissioned me to go to Africa, but to find Livingstone.'

Stanley was particularly enraged at the determined efforts of the Welsh to claim him as one of their own. 'Wherever I go, I find one or two more Welshmen who are determined to let the public know that I am a compatriot. Some of them claim the privilege of old friends, force an entrance into the anterooms of the lecture halls, and bawl out in long-forgotten Welsh a strange greeting. Then, perceiving me to be rather surprised at their barbarism, they slink away angered, protesting against what they call my pride.'

Stanley found that Welshmen could not forgive him for not proclaiming his origins from the rooftops, even though there was an unbridgeable chasm between him and all things to do with Wales, and not just in the mundane consideration that ninety per cent of the people he met abroad were superior in most things to the Welsh. They were also more congenial, 'were it only for the reason that they assisted me to banish from my mind the unpleasant recollections of boyhood - that sordid life that appears to me like a nightmare . .. there is no danger that I shall ever forget my parentless and abject condition in Wales, but I do not see the use of permitting myself to be branded with the hideous stigma.' He and the Welsh were poles apart: 'They cannot understand why I should not be proud of the little parish world of North Wales, and I cannot understand what they see to admire in it.'

To throw his pursuers off the scent, Stanley deliberately obfuscated his origins. He would mix a little truth with a lot of falsehood, or a lot of truth with a little falsehood, depending on his audience. One constant in his stories was that he was a native Missourian. Thereafter he varied the ingredients. The usual story was that he had been born in 1843 and had run away from Missouri to his early seafaring life. However, sometimes he claimed that the year of his birth was 1844 and that he had enlisted in the Civil War in 1862 at the age of eighteen. With amazing lack of concern for coherence he would at other times claim that he was eighteen in 1857 and had fought in the Indian Mutiny! But it has to be remembered that Stanley's main aim was to mystify and confuse, not to present a coherent story. He was fortunate, for in this period only relatively minor newspapers printed accounts of his origins that came close to the truth.

That his childhood and early life were Stanley's Achilles heel was quickly recognised by his bitterest enemies in the RGS. Sir Henry Rawlinson and, to a lesser extent, Grant were coming to feel that the continued wrangling with Stanley was serving merely to lower the Society in public esteem, but the hardliners, Clements Markham, Galton and W. Carpenter, were bent on a conspiracy to reveal the truth about Stanley's shame and illegitimacy to the world. Angered by the Daily Telegraph letter impugning the RGS, Markham took up the gauntlet on the Society's behalf and tried to put the upstart in his place. Some of the anger and dislike is evident in a letter Markham wrote to Stanley on 4th September, rejecting his claim to be a suitable recipient of the RGS gold medal on the ground that his geographical observations were not scientifically arrived at.

The way this correspondence developed is highly revealing of the public and private face of both men. Stanley retorted to Markham's patronising epistle by reiterating that he should have the medal, since Livingstone had promised him that such would be his reward; furthermore, he on his side would withdraw his uncomplimentary remarks about the RGS only when Galton apologised for 'sensational' and for doubting his nationality. He then proceeded with a spirited defence on his observations Markham replied emolliently if patronisingly: 'I am very glad you have done such good work by dead reckoning (as we call it at sea) next to actual observation dead reckoning is most valuable. I will also give you full credit respecting the map. I really mentioned that you were not a fractional observer with a view to explaining the reason, if the medal was not awarded to you and with no ill-natured intention whatever.'

But in private Markham fumed that Stanley was a blackguard, attempting to browbeat and blackmail the Society by using the magic aura of Livingstone's name. Stanley on his side was so angry with the initial supercilious letter that he leaked it to the Daily News, together with a running commentary mocking Markham's remarks. Then, in a wonderfully insolent touch, Stanley wrote to Markham denying that he was the source of the leak and urging him not to publish their correspondence. Markham bridled and ended a curt reply testily: 'I must remind you that when you write to honourable men and mark your letter private, it is quite unnecessary to urge them not to publish it as retaliation.'

Since Galton refused to apologise, Stanley renewed his attacks on him. But already the tide in the battle between Stanley and the RGS was turning in the former's favour. There were two main factors in this: the press backed the 'intrepid explorer' against the stuffy establishment; and Stanley received the irresistible accolade of Queen Victoria.

The volte-face in the press was largely the result of a brilliant campaign conducted by Bennett and the Herald. Gambling that Stanley would ultimately be successful in his quest for Livingstone, Gordon Bennett lashed the Herald into its worst frenzies of anti-British sentiment. First, it disingenuously claimed to know nothing of the Stanley expedition, and quoted Kirk's reports from Zanzibar as if they were red-hot news. When finally flushed into the open, the Herald claimed that its objective in sending Stanley was not a scoop but the promotion of civilisation, science and humanity and the enhancement of the prestige of the 'fourth estate'. It subtly advanced the notion - which was swallowed whole by Livingstone

169

himself - that in sending Stanley to Central Africa it had more interest in the doctor's welfare than the British government itself. Further to obfuscate his cunning purposes, Bennett sent out another 'special', Alvan S. Southworth, to 'find' Samuel Baker in the Sudan. Southworth's jingoistic Yankee sentiments were almost the mirror image of Waller's 'steel head of an Englishman' comments. It has to be conceded, too, that this kind of twisting of the lion's tail played a part in the RGS's anti-Americanism in August 1872.

The initial scepticism in England about whether Stanley had actually met Livingstone in Africa further played into Bennett's hands, in an era when Fenianism and the Alabama dispute meant that anti-British sentiment was already running high in the USA and especially in New York. Bennett stoked up the fires. Fie encouraged his rivals in their scepticism. In New York the Sun, animated by an ancient grudge between its proprietor Charles A. Dana and Bennett, duly obliged it. It was the Sun that published all Noe's revelations, but it went on to make the unwarranted inference that so many of Stanley's enemies made: that because he was a proven liar, nothing he said was true.

But the Sun's cynicism was a bagatelle alongside the propaganda advantage given Bennett by the attitude of the British press. He waited until the largest conceivable number had denounced Stanley as impostor, fraud, charlatan and forger before releasing Livingstone's confidential letter to him which contained such powerful circumstantial evidence of authenticity that all doubters were at once silenced. The Herald then counterattacked the RGS, stressing its ingratitude, its blinkered xenophobia, its myopic defence of Kirk, and its curmudgeonly refusal to give Stanley his due. This gave the British press pause. They had been

badly wrong about Stanley when they accused him of fraud. Perhaps their earlier unequivocal support for the RGS was equally misguided. Perhaps the real problem was that men like Sir Henry Rawlinson had feet of clay and were simply not big enough to admit it.

A further fillip to the pro-Stanley campaign was provided at the end of August when the journalist Winwood Reade wrote a withering critique in the Pall Mall Gazette of the mindless way British opinion had received the first two Livingstone letters. He pointed out that the canard that Stanley himself wrote the letters was untenable even on internal evidence. The objection had been that Livingstone wrote with an eye to human interest stories rather than as a dour missionary. But, said Reade, that was precisely the point. Everyone agreed that Stanley was not stupid, yet only a very stupid forger would make an error like that. An ingenious charlatan would try to get inside the notional Livingstone, and saturate his pronouncements with reverential allusions and references to the workings of providence. Only someone who had actually met Livingstone would know the truth which was, as Stanley pointed out, that the 'rollicking' quality of the letters was pure Livingstone since 'for genial, kindly humour, for keen sense of the ludicrous he might be editor of Punch'.

For all these reasons the RGS was already in full retreat in the battle for public opinion even before Windsor Castle took a hand. On 27th August, while Stanley was in the thick of newspaper stories about his nationality, he received sensational news. First there came a gift of a gold snuffbox from Queen Victoria in token of her admiration. The box was inlaid with blue enamel and bore the legend 'VR' in diamonds, emeralds and rubies. Then there followed an invitation to attend on her Majesty at Dunrobin Castle on 8-9th September.

Immediately Stanley sensed a changing atmosphere. On 4th September Sir Henry Rawlinson, who was to present him to the Queen, wrote a very conciliatory letter extending the hand of friendship: 'There may be very naturally a feeling of disappointment at your "having taken the wind out of our sails" and perhaps in some cases there maybe individual jealousy, but as far as I can judge the Geographers as a body . . . rejoice in the honours you are receiving.' Behind the scenes even greater activity took place. Lord Granville sent a confidential message to Markham and his fellow conspirators that they should on no account take any action that might redound to the detriment of the monarch, now that the gracious sovereign had seen fit to wrap Stanley in her mantle; any unwelcome publicity about the explorer would be received at Windsor with the greatest disfavour.

The prospect of an interview with the Queen saw Stanley through the nasty patch when Noe's revelations were being widely bruited and was instrumental in persuading him not to sue the Sun for libel. As yet, though, he was not disposed to accept Rawlinson's olive branch, since the president had not publicly recanted on 'sensationalism'.

On 9th September Stanley arrived at Dunrobin Casde, ancestral seat of the Duke of Sutherland, and dined that evening with Lady Churchill, while the Duke, Lord Granville and Sir Henry Rawlinson dined with the Queen. Once the sovereign had retired, the two parties met in the smoking room and began to discuss Gladstone and Disraeli. Stanley was appalled at some of the indiscretions committed by Granville, but was delighted to find that he had been assigned a better bedroom than Rawlinson.

The morning of the 10th was spent in receiving instructions from Rawlinson on how to behave at the coming reception. About noon Queen Victoria and Princess Beatrice entered. They all bowed, and Rawlinson introduced Stanley. Stanley was enraptured with 'this lady to whom in my heart of hearts next to God I worshipped'. To him she conveyed a definite charismatic aura; though aware of her own inaccessibility she was serenely proud rather than forbiddingly haughty. A ten-minute conversation on Africa ensued. Stanley was relieved to find the Queen even shorter of stature than he was himself, though with similarly unforgettable eyes which revealed 'a quiet but unmistakable kindly condescension and an inimitable calmness of self-possession.' The smallness of the sovereign recalled his aunt but 'what a difference between the subdued imperiousness and regal consciousness of one, and the sociable housewifeliness of the other'. The Queen asked why Livingstone would not come home and how long it would take him to finish his work. Stanley explained the situation. A second interview with the monarch took place, then on the third morning Sutherland whisked Stanley away on his private railway to Inverness, whence he caught the London express.

After the audience the Duke of Sutherland asked how Stanley had liked her. 'Splendid,' he replied. Sutherland then muttered something about the Queen being a good little woman who had a bee in her bonnet. Stanley's sentiments of rapt admiration were not however reciprocated by the sovereign and her entourage. Colonel Ponsonby found him 'rough looking' but very agreeable and an accomplished conversationalist with an unbounded admiration for Livingstone. The Queen herself was more critical and referred to the interview twice, in a letter to the Princess Royal and in her own journals. The letter contained the following: 'I have this evening seen Mr Stanley who discovered Livingstone, a determined ugly little man - with a strong American twang.' Even more interesting, as denoting the background research done by her intelligence departments on Stanley, is the journal entry: 'The Duke presented Mr Stanley, the discoverer of Dr Livingstone, who calls himself an American but is by birth a Welshman. He was, however, brought up in America and looks and speaks like an American. He has a very determined expression and is not particularly prepossessing.'

This seal of royal approbation largely silenced the critics. On his return to London, Stanley found a letter from Bennett, granting him the requested six months' leave of absence on full pay (£400 p.a.) on condition that Stanley crossed to the USA once he had finished his book, in order to milk the Livingstone story further. Stanley continued to scribble away furiously, ably guided by his editor Edward Marston. To economise on precious time he adopted a policy of sending Kalulu out to act as his proxy in response to social invitations. After one such tea, with Lady Franklin, Kalulu returned beaming at the way he had been petted and spoiled. Yet finding uninterrupted leisure for writing was still difficult. Fame exacted a heavy price at all levels, as when Stanley had to sit all afternoon for a partner from Madame Tussauds who came to make sketches for their planned wax model of him.

Stanley's enemies in the RGS had been thwarted in their more sinister designs by the bestowal of royal favour, but they still had many anti-Stanley options left to exercise. The principal one was the denial of the Society's gold medal, which public opinion now increasingly demanded for Stanley's achievements. Rawlinson was disposed to make the best of a sorry affair, but Galton, Markham and Grant remained intransigent. Markham's attitude is best conveyed in his unpublished history of the RGS:

I met Charlie Forbes, a great friend, who pointed down with his stick and said 'the Society is going down, down, down in public estimation.' I replied, 'Damn public opinion. The fellow has done no geography.' But Sir Henry Rawlinson was weak and got alarmed. When he consulted me about the medal, I said 'to give the fellow a jolly good dinner for finding Livingstone would be proper but it would be a desecration to give him a Royal award.' Nevertheless, the Council was specially summoned and Stanley was voted a Gold Medal several months before the time laid down by our rules.

Markham's opinion was shared by many RGS diehards. Dr Beke stated: 'As regards Mr Stanley, I think he is being overrated, just as he was underrated at first.' Grant's objections were especially vociferous. He reminded Rawlinson of the personal attacks Stanley had made on him and others (especially in the 27th August Daily Telegraph) and went on: 'If such a fellow is worthy of the honours of the Geographical Society, it must clearly follow that the safest way to Geographical honours is to insult the President and Council of the Society.' He suggested that if Stanley was to receive an award it should be one hundred guineas prize money and honorary life membership of the Society instead of a gold medal, 'for if you examine the list of gold medallists, Mr Stanley has not done enough to be ranked with any of them ... if Stanley has done any real geography, by all means let him be rewarded, but at this distance I cannot see what title he has to the distinction of our Society's medal.'

But Rawlinson had keener political antennae than the hardliners. He had access to the establishment, and he knew from his talks with Sutherland, Granville and others that the elite was concerned at the damage to Britain's reputation being caused by the RGS's apparently dog-in-the-manger recalcitrance. He ordered Markham to swallow his objections and make peace between Stanley and the Society. Markham therefore invited Stanley to dine with him at home, when Burton and Verney Cameron would also be guests. On arrival, Stanley was disconcerted to find that Markham used a system of signs to discriminate between his guests and indicate his differential preferences for them. Thus Stanley received one finger of the right hand to shake, Cameron, a naval officer, got two, while Burton was given an entire hand.

This was a dangerous game to play with the prickly paranoid Stanley. Although Stanley enjoyed the evening and got on well with Burton - 'Markham makes a kindly host in his own house - though outside he is somewhat uppish in manner' - Stanley did not forget the slight and dealt with it in two ways. First, to show the Society that it could expect no compromise from him in return for any honour awarded, he returned to his public indictment of Kirk. Secondly, he inveighed against Markham for allegedly supporting an anti-Livingstone clique and promoting a chimerical notion of ascending the Congo from its mouth to relieve Livingstone that way. Rather than wasting time on schemes that were impracticable, and would be undesirable to Livingstone even if they did work, it behoved the 2,500 RGS members to contribute £10 each to a special fund. With £25,000 at his disposal, a professional explorer could uncover all of Africa's remaining secrets.

It was now clear to Rawlinson and the Society that they had to accept

Stanley on his own terms or not at all. Stanley's indomitable will finally won the war of attrition. On 21st October, at a dinner given by the Council of the RGS, Stanley was formally made a gold medallist. Sir Henry Rawlinson made a conciliatory speech, defending the Society against the charge of having been cold and vindictive towards Stanley. He pointed out that the RGS had at no time aligned itself with those who claimed that Stanley had not found Livingstone. Mark Twain, who was present, was deeply impressed: 'Rawlinson stood up and made the most manly and magnificent apology to Stanley for himself and for the Society that ever I listened to; I thought the man rose to the very pinnacle of human nobility.' But Stanley, brooding and vengeful, did not see it that way. With the perseverance of monomania, he continued to harp away on the theme that Galton had never apologised for 'sensational'; accordingly, far from acknowledging Rawlinson's gesture, Stanley omitted all mention of it in his diary.

Royal audiences and disputes with the RGS apart, September and most of October were spent hard at work on the Livingstone book. Stanley used the public appearances to promote interest in Africa, as when he received the freedom of the London Turners' Company at the Guildhall and urged British expansion into the 'Dark Continent'. But before he left for the USA at Bennett's bidding, it was necessary for him to visit the land of Livingstone's birth. The tour of Scotland was a fairly complete triumph. There was little of the cavilling and sniping that had attended him in England. The Scots took him to their bosom as the rescuer of one of their greatest sons. Everywhere there were cheering crowds at railway stations, at every civic lunch there were ovations; the fact that he had twisted the tail of the English lion certainly did not dispose the Scots against him.

Stanley's first stop was Glasgow, where he noticed for the first time how typically Scottish Livingstone's physiognomy was. Next day he lectured in Hamilton and received the freedom of the city there. Here he met the extended Livingstone family, first the doctor's two sisters, who impressed him by the forcefulness of their personality (especially the elder one). In the evening he went driving with Livingstone's daughter Agnes, who had from the earliest days expressed her belief in him and who exclaimed after reading the letters from her father: 'Oh that man Stanley, if I had a crown of gold and gems I would put it on his head.' They struck up an immediate rapport, but Stanley's disdain for the 'common clay' was reinforced when their horses bolted after a political demonstration in the city centre and their carriage came near to overturning.

The lecture tour continued: Inverness, Aberdeen, Greenock, Paisley, Ayr, Helensburgh, Edinburgh. At Wemyss Bay he was the guest of the Scottish MP Grieve. Honours, freedoms, acclamations rained down on him. His lecturing technique was to tell the same basic story about his finding of Livingstone, then add different anecdotes on each separate platform: for example, at Glasgow he gave vent to his hatred for crocodiles, at Hamilton he concentrated on his previous American experience; in other towns it would be the Ha, or Mirambo that elicited the telling story. Whatever his experience at Brighton (and later in the USA), in Scotland at least there was no criticism of the style, content or delivery of his lectures.

After adding three further lectures (in Dunfermline, Liverpool and Manchester) to an already crowded schedule, Stanley returned to London to put the finishing touches to his book. But he could never steer clear of controversy for long. On 4th November he attended a great anti-slavery meeting at the Mansion House, at which the other speakers were Bishop Wilberforce and Sir Bartle Frere. It did not take Stanley long to upset his audience. He pointed out that the much-vaunted campaign against the Zanzibar slavers by the Royal Navy was less impressive when viewed at first hand, since the main result of releasing slaves from Arab dhows was that they were then indentured in the Seychelles, in effect exchanging one form of slavery for another. 'That is not true!' thundered the Lord Mayor. Stanley gave him one of his basilisk looks, repeated the charge, and said that Sir Bartle Frere, outward bound to Zanzibar on an anti-slavery mission, would shortly see the truth of it for himself.

By now word of Stanley's Scottish success had followed him south of the border and he was in demand as a speaker both in England and for later engagements in the USA. One public lecture in Maidstone afforded him particular enjoyment because of an incident on the train journey there. Stanley had hoped to have the compartment to himself but a typical English gentleman got in and struck up a conversation, not knowing whom he was addressing. The subject of Stanley came up. The gentleman described him as a Yankee rogue, 'the biggest impostor of the age'. Stanley let the man jabber away and soon discovered his prejudice to be the result of rabid anti-Americanism. As it happened, the man got out at the stop before Maidstone. Stanley kept him talking at the carriage window until the train began to pull away from the station, then handed him his card. In the light from the gas lamp Stanley was able to see the stupefied, incredulous reaction, which he found just compensation for the insult.

Both Bennett's urgings and the amounts of money being offered for his American lectures led Stanley to wind up his affairs in London as fast as possible. After a round trip London-Liverpool-Manchester-London between 6th and 9th November, Stanley booked passage for New York on the Cunard steamer Cuba and departed on the 9th. Within days of his departure How I Found Livingstone was published, more than 700 pages long, with six maps and fifty-three illustrations by himself. It sold by tens of thousands and was into its third edition by Christmas. Florence Nightingale famously called it 'the very worst book on the very best subject I ever saw in my life', and there is some truth in the charge. It is a volume marred by egocentricity. Stanley sustained his vendetta with Kirk in the book, and the long passages of self-justification were tiresome, but at its best, in its descriptions of the Mirambo war, the ordeal with the Ha, the crossing of the Malagarazi and the meeting with Livingstone, it deserved its phenomenal success.

The three and a half months Stanley spent in Britain in the late summer and autumn of 1872 have often been identified as the crossroads in Stanley's life, his period of simultaneous triumph and disaster. How accurate is this assessment? Is it true that in these months the potentially positive aspects of Stanley's personality were killed off for good, and if so, why?

There is some evidence that even at the physical level Stanley in 1871-2 crossed an invisible watershed. From a young man, he became a prematurely middle-aged one. There was still the same indomitable set of features: thick-set, well-knit, barrel-chested, deeply tanned with large, dark, intelligent eyes, a general self-assertive, aggressive, bulldog demeanour, the same evidence of decisiveness and determination. But his hair was rapidly turning grey. An early attempt to dye it turned into disaster when Stanley used a dye with an emerald hue and his hair turned green. He had to keep himself in hiding in his rooms at Duchess Street (to which he moved from the Langham Hotel at the end of August) to reverse the effects of the pigmentation, since an explorer with green hair would have excited universal derision. But the grizzled hair was only part of the ageing process. Whereas the younger Stanley was prepared, and almost too prepared, to take risks, the middle-aged Stanley began to approach African exploration with circumspection. He invented a special form of headgear - the 'Stanley cap' - out of some tent cloth or twill, lined with native grass and set off with the leather peak of an old cap. He had discovered that the 'regulation' pith-helmet was inconvenient, since when he threw his head back the helmet tipped over his eyes.

Yet if Stanley was ageing prematurely, his mental processes at this time were even more significant. A general feeling of disenchantment led him to violently anti-English feelings and a reassessment of his time in Africa. The disenchantment with the English particularly centred on their lack of fairness - exactly the quality they prided themselves on. Typical to Stanley's mind was the fabricated 'Stanley' dispatch that appeared in the Spectator in August. According to this fictitious 'report', Stanley was said to have told Livingstone that Horace Greeley would be Democratic candidate for the presidency in 1872. This was supposed to have drawn from Livingstone the following outburst: 'Hold on! You have related to me many stupendous things and with a confiding simplicity - I can peacefully swallow them down, but there is a limit to all things. I am a simple guileless Christian man and unacquainted with intemperate language, but when you tell me that Horace Greeley is to become a Democratic candidate I cast the traditions of my education to the winds and say, I'll be damned to all eternity if I believe it. My trunk is packed to go home but I shall remain in Africa, for these things may be true after all; if they are, I desire to stay here and unlearn my civilisation.'"

Having printed this nonsense, the Spectator then had the effrontery to 'refute' it as bogus, on the grounds that Livingstone would not have used profane language. But as Stanley pointed out, the 'story' was spurious on internal evidence; neither Livingstone nor Stanley could have known anything about Horace Greeley, since he did not announce his candidature until 1872. The true moral of the story, for Stanley, was that the English were cowards. Instead of the manly American tradition of settling disputes with pistols, the English resorted to calumny and slander. On his way through London to Abyssinia in January 1867 he bought an English newspaper and thought it more respectable than the hideous rags in the USA." But now he was undeceived. American editors might be bullies but 'his English contemporary is in my mind more like an old shrew with his venom-laden pen and his effeminate malice . . . their propensity to nagging at a man marks the unmanliness to which their excess of laws have [sic] reduced them.'"

The result of the sustained vilification Stanley endured in the English press in August 1872 left him permanently scarred: 'I am slowly discovering that this life with all its gay colour and glare only consists of an unusual amount of envy with the slightest tincture of real esteem ... I can count my friends on my fingers but my enemies are a host and command the entire press. Every mail also brings numerous proofs of English hate.'"This prompted two reflections: one that fame was an illusion; two, that the life of an African explorer, with all its hardships, was actually preferable to life in English society. On the first point, he noted: 'I have smacked my lips over the flavour of fame - but the substance is useless to me - as it may be taken away at any time. What a pity I did not go on to China without telegraphing Mr Bennett.' Again, contrasting the anguish of his life in England with the toil of life in Africa, he remarked: 'One brings me an inordinate amount of secret pain, the other sapped my physical strength but left my mind expanded and was purifying.'

Two things in particular seemed to strike deep wounds at the core of his identity during this period in England. One was the paradox that to taste fame as an international celebrity, he had to risk contumely arising from his 'base' origins. The worst ordeal of his months of fame was when someone at a banquet called for information on his early life. The other cross he had to bear was the sniping at Livingstone, his true 'father'. As well as being traduced as hard, morose, impossible and a hypocrite, Livingstone was frequently portrayed as 'something like an adulterer', a man who had married an African princess or retired into an Arab harem. Frank Harris, who had observed a white girl living in an African tribe, later asked Stanley if perhaps he had found Livingstone by tracking 'parti-coloured offspring' across Africa. Harris, who really did have the sex-obsession Stanley attributed to Richard Burton, was disconcerted when Stanley reacted angrily to the suggestion and dismissed the explorer as merely humourless. There was more to it than that. One of the reasons why Stanley regarded Livingstone as a true mentor and father was that he seemed in his daily life as chaste as Stanley himself. Stanley could therefore sustain himself with the thought that he was as 'normal' as Livingstone. Any suggestion that Livingstone might be a normal heterosexual male (and thus clearly unlike Stanley) caused him excessive anxiety.

Profound considerations merged with trivial ones. Part of the legacy of Stanley's deprived childhood was that he always fretted over the expenditure of money. Because his photograph was everywhere and he could not walk anywhere in London without being pestered, he was forced to travel by cab: 'Cab fares were a heavy tax though they cost less than running the gauntlet between the crossing sweepers, the sly kindred and lost Americans (all after money). When all these anxieties combined with the jealousy of other journalists and the resentment of the RGS, Stanley often found himself wishing that Bennett had chosen someone else to find Livingstone. The thought particularly impressed him the day he saw his name on a New York Sun banner headline. After ULYSSES S. GRANT, DRUNKARD Came HENRY M. STANLEY, VILLAIN, FORGER AND PIRATE. At this point Stanley confided to his diary in despair: 'I would willingly give them all [the newspaper cuttings] for a day of that boyhood when I was blissfully obscure. I once thought that a press notice of me was "Immortality", but alas, I have found that that kind of "Immortality" means only abject slavery.'

Some English observers agreed that Stanley had had a raw deal. As Stanley sailed away to New York, The Times recorded this verdict: 'We cannot think without shame and indignation of the conduct of the Royal Geographical Society in this matter.' But more usual was the response that Stanley's view of the RGS was typical Yankee chip-on-the-shoulder, like Nathaniel Hawthorne's complaint about Lord Lansdowne. If the RGS did not at first believe the story about the finding of Livingstone, why then, whose fault was this? What was the credibility of a known anti-British rag, the leading exponent of 'yellow journalism' supposed to be, after all? As for the Kirk controversy, Stanley had ultimately done himself more harm than good by plugging away at this theme, and in any case it had produced the 'spin-off' of the Bartle Frere mission to Zanzibar, for which the Herald was now shamelessly and mendaciously taking credit.

It would be a mistake to spirit away all the real anti-Stanley and anti-American feeling into the ether of Stanley paranoia. Much of it was real enough, but it should be viewed in the sort of perspective Stanley always refused to entertain. The first point was that there was nothing particularly personal in the bad treatment Stanley received. All explorers who came before English audiences could expect a bruising time. When the French explorer and discoverer of the gorilla, Paul du Chaillu, came to London in 1861 to address the Ethnological Society, a member of the audience queried his veracity as if he were a criminal on trial. The quick-tempered du Chaillu suggested that in his country such matters were settled by a duel. After a few more unsatisfactory exchanges, du Chaillu jumped over the benches to where his tormentor (one T. A. Malone) stood and spat in his face. When Malone appealed to the chairman, Chaillu yelled 'Coward' at him. Alongside this exhibition, the action and reaction at Stanley's lecture in Brighton was mild indeed.

Even more telling was the amount of support Stanley was able to enlist right from his earliest days in England. If we accepted Stanley's own account, we would have to conclude that he was indeed, in his own description, 'a perfect Ishmaelite, with his hand against every man, and feeling every man's hand was raised against him." But in fact very many notable English men and women rallied to his standard: Edwin Arnold, editor of the Daily Telegraph, William Cotton Oswell, John Murray the publisher, Lord Kinnaird, Sir Thomas Buxton, Lady Russell, Lady Jane Russell, Baroness Burdett-Coutts, J. B. Braithwaite the leading English Quaker and Mark Twain. Perhaps the most significant of all these friends were the Webbs of Newstead Abbey.

The Webbs were close friends of Livingstone, ever since Old Etonian William Webb met Livingstone on a hunting expedition in Africa. But the driving force in the family was Emilia, a woman in her late thirties with six children. Without having met Stanley she had an intuitive sense from the newspaper reports of the Brighton meeting of the kind of wounded, vulnerable being Stanley really was. She extended an invitation to him to stay at their splendid country seat of Newstead Abbey, 11 miles from Nottingham, Stanley accepted and was housed in the wing occupied by Livingstone himself on his last visit to Newstead in 1864.

Emilia Webb was one of the few women Stanley trusted. She had the rare gift of making acquaintances want to unburden their souls to her. Within a very few days at Newstead Stanley told her the 'shameful' secrets of his infancy. He behaved to her six children as a favourite uncle and romped with them in the woods in a most un-Stanley-like way. Stanley worshipped Emilia just this side of idolatry and was prepared to defer to her opinion in a way that would have been unthinkable with other women.

The underlying psychology of the relationship again reveals Stanley caught in the either/or posture towards women: either unattainable idol or carnal whore. The reasons for this deep-seated attitude derived ultimately from his promiscuous mother but had been reinforced by the culture Stanley grew up in, especially that of the American South where white women were idealised as 'ladies' while black women were regarded as carnal and seducible. Emilia Webb was the 'lost mother' as Livingstone had been the 'lost father'. That Stanley regarded her in a maternal light is clear from the childish petulance and jealousy he exhibited whenever she invited other guests to Newstead. Emilia intuited something of this for she remarked that a good woman would be the making of Stanley, 'only she would have to care for him enough' (in other words act like a mother).She herself was secure in Stanley's esteem, for as a married woman she was 'safe' - Stanley would never have to put his real feelings for her to the test by forcing them through the prism of carnality and thus compelling an integrated response (neither Madonna nor whore) towards her. So it was that the few days spent at Newstead in 1872 were as much an oasis in Stanley's troubled life as his months in Ujiji with Livingstone had been.

Ahead of him stretched more arid emotional deserts than he could imagine.

DESPITE the victory over the RGS, the completion of his book and the new-found friendship with the Webbs, the Stanley who boarded the Cuba for New York on 9th November 1872 was not a happy man. He confessed that the three months in England had been a turning point: 'All the actions of my life, and I may say all my thoughts, since 1872, have been strongly coloured by the storm of abuse and the wholly unjustifiable reports circulated about me then.' Stanley was in general the sort of person who ignores a hundred plaudits to worry away at a single insult, who dismisses the dozens of favourable developments to brood over the handful of unfavourable ones, who, child-like, remembers the wicked witch even when the fairy story has come through to a happy conclusion. But as a special source of anguish he had the myriad lampoons spawned by 'I Presume' to deal with. The (in retrospect) singularly infelicitous four words with which he had greeted Livingstone at Ujiji had entered the language and legend of England and coursed through the bloodstream of popular culture. 'Dr Livingstone, I presume?' became the last refuge of the scoundrel keeping failure at bay in the music halls. The October issue of Tailor and Cutter showed one dummy addressing the words to another. Stanley came to dread the time he would be introduced to new contacts: he could almost predict the 'Mr Stanley, I presume' that would be the inevitable response.

The exploit that had brought him fame and fortune and ushered him into the presence of the greatest man of his lifetime was to end, it seemed, because of a single error of verbal judgement, in everlasting mockery. Stanley's response was to harden himself and to stifle the few softening human impulses that remained. If Emilia Webb had made him look at a caring maternal woman in a new light, there was a much greater countervailing force at hand to fuel his misogynism. For among the audience at his last lecture in the Manchester Free Trade Hall was Katie Bradshaw, nee Gough-Roberts, now heavily pregnant with her second child by her architect husband. When Stanley departed after the lecture to the house of the president of the Manchester Chamber of Commerce, Katie took a cab there and sent in her card, asking for an interview. Stanley, angry not just at her 'treachery' but at the report that she had shown the 'unspeakable' John Camden Hotten the biographical letter he had written her early in 1869, refused brusquely and demanded the return of his personal letters. Bridling in turn, Katie told Stanley's valet that if he wanted them he would have to come in person to ask for them.

The memory of Katie's 'insolence' was obviously still smarting as Stanley crossed the Atlantic. He was in a violent temper, not just because of the slowness of the ship, but because its best quarters had been reserved for 'the ladies'. Not content with that, these pampered women then objected when he smoked in the public lounges and insisted he go on deck to indulge his vice. Stanley was livid: it was typical of the scheming ingratitude of women to allow the male sex to pay for their idleness in the most salubrious sections of the liner while humiliating them by insisting that they smoke under a canvas awning in a hatchway.

Stanley soon had a more concrete focus for his misogynism. As the most celebrated passenger on the Cuba he was seated at the captain's table, where he had a pretty young woman as a dining companion. At first all went well. The girl seemed captivated by Stanley's tales of Africa. Then, to Stanley's intense chagrin, one of their fellow diners, a young empty-headed aristocratic flaneur who spent his time smoking cigarettes and yawning with 'boredom', cut in. One day at dinner he mentioned that he knew how to make an exceptionally good salad and gave the recipe. The young woman at once transferred her attentions to him. Stanley simply could not understand how a stupid youth, with no conversation and not a single idea in his head, whose sole accomplishments seemed to be knowing how to make a salad and smoking cigarettes, could be preferred to the most famous man of the year. Insult was added to injury by the fact that the young fop wore a monocle; Stanley always had a violent prejudice against men with eyeglasses.

Stanley concluded both that women were impossible and that he could never be a lady's man. But the truth was that the young woman in question almost certainly picked up the essential oddity of his sexual persona; it was not so much that he did not know how to treat women, as that he frightened them by the impossibly high level of his expectations. Stanley's gaucherie with the female sex was usually attributed to his long absences in Africa, removed from polite society. But this was to make the symptom the cause. As a fellow journalist Thomas Stevens shrewdly observed: 'He would have been too scared to have seriously sought her hand, simply because she was young and beautiful. Mr Stanley thinks a lovely young woman a sort of wingless angel and a superior being who was made for rough man to admire at a respectful distance, but not to be approached too closely without sacrilege.' With Stanley, the Madonna/whore syndrome was part of a more general personality disorder, in which he simultaneously yearned for affection while taking steps to ensure that any real possibility for a close affectionate relationship was destroyed.

There was a curious sequel to this failed relationship. At a banquet in New York on his first night Stanley suddenly learned that his erstwhile protégée had fallen overboard when the ship was docking at the wharf and almost drowned. It was an uncomfortable reminder of the demise of his grandfather. Then the young Rowlands had wished that he might escape the promised beating, and, mirabile dictu, Moses Parry had dropped dead in the fields. Now, the vehemently hostile feelings he harboured towards the female sex had, almost, or so it seemed, brought about a young woman's death. Stanley at once rushed to her bedside where he was relieved to find her much recovered. But so great was his guilt that his reaction when she shortly afterwards married the monocled fop was mild.

On 20th November the Cuba arrived in New York. In the Hudson River was a Herald steamer bearing a 'Welcome Stanley' banner, which promptly took the hero on board and whisked him away; customs formalities were waived. His first stop on land was the Herald office, where he was irrationally miffed to find the reporters carrying revolvers. Stanley always liked the thought, when in polite society, that he was really a warrior who had the ultimate drop on the supercilious 'gentleman' who patronised him, by virtue of his superiority as a shootist. Armed reporters and sub-editors seemed to call this assumption into doubt; it was therefore necessary for him to browbeat the Herald staff with his superior knowledge of rifles to establish that he was really the 'top gun'.

But in worrying about his fellow hacks, Stanley failed to see where the real threat to him lay. By this time Gordon Bennett had begun to worry that he might have conjured up a sorcerer's apprentice. He was jealous of Stanley's fame, and resentful that it was Stanley, not the Herald and still less Bennett himself, who had got the credit for relieving Livingstone. His reporter's reception by Queen Victoria at Dunrobin Castle particularly annoyed Bennett. He himself despised the British and their monarchy, but he knew that the monarchy both enjoyed huge prestige in Europe and sold papers in America. Bennett brooded on the monster he had created. When he sent Stanley to find Livingstone, Stanley was a nobody. Now he was a celebrity, and all on Bennett's back. Bennett had conceived the expedition, financed it (albeit grudgingly), picked up all the associated expenses (such as the cabling of Livingstone's letters), and for what? He had not received so much as a syllable of thanks from the British while Stanley was lording it in London as if it were his own personal fortune that had made the discovery of Livingstone possible.

When he heard of the sums Stanley stood to earn from the exploit, Bennett was even more angry. Apart from the advance on royalties of $10,000 paid for How I found Livingstone, Stanley was to receive a guaranteed minimum of £10,000 for his American lecture tour, plus all expenses. It was a reasonable inference that Stanley might hope to net $50,000 in all, after all costs had been defrayed. For once Bennett agreed with English critics of Stanley. The discoverer of Livingstone would henceforth enjoy an income of at least £5 00 a year for the rest of his life, while the doctor himself, after more than thirty years in Africa, still had no salary from the British government, nor so much as a penny in guaranteed pension. This was a literally preposterous situation. But while Stanley was being lionised as the great American hero, it would be impolitic for Bennett to strike back at him. His chance for revenge, he decided, would come later.

Stanley's triumphant landing at the Battery was the signal for junketings on a scale far eclipsing those in Britain. A long caravan of carriages accompanied him in procession up Fifth Avenue to his hotel. His suite was inundated with reporters (the familiar chant 'Mr Stanley, I presume' predictably went up), and there were so many flowers in the rooms that at first he fancied himself back in tropical Africa. That evening he attended a banquet then went on to see a Broadway farce, King Carrot, which burlesqued the stuffed shirts of the RGS.

The days that followed were a period of unqualified success. He was the toast of the town: reception followed reception, banquet followed feast. Kalulu, dressed in page's outfit, was almost as much a sensation as his master; by now he had overcome his earlier aversion to European clothes. But the rich fare triggered a minor attack of African malarial fever, so that Stanley after a week decided to spend more time at home in his suite in the Fifth Avenue Hotel and to take greater care with his diet.

At the beginning of December he commenced the much-trumpeted series of American lectures. On the evening of 3rd December he appeared at Steinway Hall to deliver the first of them. All tickets for the four-lecture series had been sold and there was brisk business on the black market. Great things were expected, but they did not materialise. Stanley had made a number of bad judgements that worked against his success even before he opened his mouth. In the first place, on the advice of his agent, he had divided his speech into four parts, each part of the 'serial' to be given on successive nights. But, much more seriously, remembering how controversial his 'popular' Brighton speech had been, he decided both to discipline himself and make his material more 'scholarly' and to refrain from extempore speaking, as it was then that he seemed always to be carried away into indiscretion.

Also working away against ultimate success was the fact that in the first flush of the heady days in New York Stanley had already exposed his best cards. He had already delivered the thundering denunciation against the evils of drink in Africa that he had first unburdened himself of in England in August. And on 25th November at a dinner given by the Herald club he had repeated the flourish that had first brought the house down in Scotland. His trick was to start by saying, 'I may be called a forger . ..' then pause while he drew from his pocket the dark blue consular cap with the gold braid around it that Livingstone had given him as a keepsake at Ujiji before continuing, 'but I would like to know if I could forge Livingstone's cap.'

The Steinway Hall lecture began to a capacity crowd. Behind Stanley was a large map of Africa, the Stars and Stripes, and dozens of bouquets. To one side of the stage was a table laden with African weapons and artefacts. On the other side sat two guests of honour: Kalulu and Livingstone's brother John who had come down from Canada for the occasion. The audience buzzed with expectancy, awaiting a roistering evening, and perhaps more of the famous Stanley indiscretions and personal attacks. What they heard was an unpleasant surprise. Determined not to endure another Brighton, Stanley emulated the dry Teutonic academician at his worst. There was not a single anecdote, no levity, no jokes, simply a plethora of unpronounceable names that seemed to go on much longer than the actual one and a half hours. In so far as the lecture was controversial, it was merely because the content was unacceptably eccentric. A thumbnail sketch of African exploration from the days of Bartolomeu Diaz was followed by a 'proof' that Darwin was insane and that Christianity was bound to succeed in the Dark Continent. Stanley's delivery was poor: he could not be heard beyond the first ten rows and when after an unconscionable interval he glanced up from his prepared script it was to find that all but these ten rows had decamped. The remainder, too polite to depart, remained remarkably quiet and no sound of approval was heard to emanate from them.

This was disaster of the first magnitude. No more signal miscalculation could be imagined. As one student of Stanley has commented: 'It was as though he had indeed been touched with a curse which made him do everything backwards. The detailed scientific discourse which he gave at Steinway Hall ought to have been given at Brighton, and the light-hearted narrative offered to the Emperor ought to have been given in New York.' Yet this was just the sort of opening the brooding Bennett had been waiting for. He gave the nod to his reporter George Seilhamer to prick the Stanley bubble. If he could kill off the lecture series, Bennett would have evened scores with his 'uppity' employee.

The review in the Herald next morning was devastating. Stanley was 'intolerably dull ... his elocution is bad ... his manner of treating his subject was not such as to ensure a forgetfulness of his faults of oratory ... he talked commonplaces ... his anecdotes were spoiled in the telling ... his voice was pitched in a sing-song and doleful monotone . .. Mr Stanley has utterly mistaken the necessities of the platform... it would be cruel to him not to say so . . . Mr Stanley still betrays some of the vices which are the necessary blunders of the tyro. He speaks too fast in his eagerness not to bore his hearers, the consequence is that they sometimes fail to understand the force of what he has said... the subject matter was a trifle abstruse for his audience.'

Stanley tried to pull his chestnuts out of the fire. He had a brochure printed containing the following: 'Born New York City, 1843, ran away to sea, joined the Union Army, then became a war correspondent.' It was typical of this broadsheet's commitment to accuracy (for, apart from the war correspondent bit, every statement in it was false) that it also quoted Stanley's greeting to Livingstone as 'Dr Livingstone, I believe." But Bennett had done his work too well. When even the Herald admitted that its own man was a flop, there could be little incentive for the crowds to turn out. Although Stanley's second lecture was better delivered and stuck to the finding of Livingstone, the word had got about and the hall was only one-third full. The series petered out in fiasco. On the night of the third lecture, the dedicated handful of would-be listeners was turned away at the hall by a janitor who told them that the talks were cancelled as the box-office receipts were no longer even covering expenses.

This was disaster on a scale not experienced even in hostile Britain. The plain fact was that the organisers had badly miscalculated; what was wrong was not the lectures or their delivery but the fact that at bottom the American people, unlike the British, had no real interest in Africa. But Stanley, typically, saw the whole thing as a conspiracy, especially when he learned that Bennett, whom he suspected of having set him up, had suddenly quit New York in his yacht for Paris, significantly leering at Seilhamer as he walked up the gang-plank. But if Stanley saw his experience in New York as tragedy, New Yorkers saw it as farce. A ludicrous show at the Theatre Comique on Broadway called Africa presented African explorers much as Groucho Marx portrayed them sixty years later in Animal Crackers. Following the usual 'cast of thousands' portraying Mirambo, slaves, cannibals, concubines and other fictitious 'characters' the curtain rose for the last act, wherein Stanley met Livingstone at Ujiji. When the words 'Dr Livingstone, I presume' were pronounced the audience would collapse nightly into hopeless, hysterical laughter. By mid-December the Stanley saga was as much a joke as air-raid wardens in World War Two. The reductio ad absurdum was reached when a false Stanley appeared in Pittsburgh and was treated royally for two days as the guest of the city.

Severely wounded in his pride and self-esteem, Stanley left the Fifth Avenue Hotel and took rooms on East 20th Street. He now waited for the storm of ridicule to blow itself out. The New Year saw diary entries of the utmost banality: '1st January 1873. Called on Misses Battersby, 122 Madison Avenue. Called on J. G. Holland, the novelist and poet. Edward King of the Boston Journal left yesterday for Philadelphia.' Stanley kept his head down while the new star of the lecture circuit, Professor John Tyndall, received the accolades from the Herald that Stanley might have had but for Bennett's spite.

It was the middle of January before Stanley felt it was safe enough to venture into public again. The occasion was the Correspondents' Club in Washington. Since this was a tribute by fellow journalists he thought himself secure from the kind of public lampooning he had sustained in New York the month before. But he had misjudged the mood. There was still life in 'I presume', as Stanley learned to his very great cost. William Copeland of the New York Journal of Commerce composed a spoof epic poem called 'Stanlio Africanus' in which he worked in references to his friend L. A. Gobright of the Associated Press. After the banquet, toasts and speeches were over, Copeland was 'persuaded' to declaim his ode. It was fairly obvious imitation Longfellow but at the twelfth stanza the smoothness of the trochaic diameters, in the style of 'Hiawatha', was suddenly broken with the surprise staccato line 'Mr Gobright, I presume.' Like all catch-phrases, 'I presume' had already acquired humorous

connotations out of all proportion to its intrinsic mirthful worth. To Stanley's stupefaction, the banqueting room rocked with laughter. He slunk away to his hotel room, having endured the ultimate humiliation.

For three months Stanley, the stricken African lion, licked his wounds. In some ways the period January–March was the lowest point of his adult life. From being world-famous as the discoverer of Livingstone, he had now reached the pass where he dared not stir out into the public gaze, lest he endure another 'I presume' debacle. He worked on a fictional book, based on Kalulu, in which he transmogrified his servant into a young

African prince. Stanley was now almost completely in the world of fantasy. Bennett had had his revenge, more completely than he could ever have hoped or expected.

It is possible that Bennett deliberately left Stanley in limbo in the USA, hoping that further rebuffs and humiliations would be visited on the man who had stolen his thunder. If so, he was disappointed. After the bruising Washington experience, Stanley lay low on full salary and awaited the word from Paris. At last, at the beginning of April 1873, it came: Stanley was ordered to report to Bennett in Paris. 'I presume he thinks it is about time I proceeded to work again,' he noted. 'I think so too and infinitely prefer it.'

On 8 April Stanley began his eastward transatlantic crossing. As always, he chafed at the slowness of the Cunard vessels. In England he allowed himself a few days' leave with the Webbs at Newstead; Kalulu disappointed Stanley by failing to win a running race against Emilia's daughters. Once in London he left Kalulu in the hands of the Rev. J. Conder who ran a school in Wandsworth. Kalulu was quite an intelligent boy and within a month was making his first faltering steps at reading English; he could also write his own name.

On 2nd May, ironically the day after Livingstone died on the borders of Katanga, Stanley reported to Gordon Bennett at the Hotel des Deux Mondes in Paris. Bennett was in a vile temper, seemingly unmassaged by his reporter's humiliation in America. He made no mention of increasing Stanley's salary, even though, at £400 p.a., it stood at exactly the same level as in 1869 when he was a nobody. Stanley was forced to press the issue, to get an increase to £1,000 a year, but his bitterness towards Bennett for making no spontaneous offer was palpable. He was not to know that Bennett thought that, with his royalties and lecture fees, he had already been paid way above the market rate for the Livingstone exploit.

Though not mentioning money, Bennett quickly came to the point of the interview. Spain was again ablaze but this time the main threat to the government came from the Right rather than the Left. There had been many changes since Stanley was there in 1869. Prim had been assassinated in 1870, then on 16th November of that year Amadeus of Savoy had been elected king. His abdication in February 1873 signalled the collapse of the experiment with constitutional monarchy and opened the floodgates to power-seekers from Right and Left.

For four months Stanley divided his time in Spain between the Carlist uprising of Navarre and the radical challenge in the South. Then Bennett, realising that the Spanish agony was going to be more protracted than he had expected, recalled Stanley to Paris and gave him a fresh assignment: to cover the Ashanti war in West Africa. The Ashanti campaign was in many ways an epigone to the 1868 Abyssinian affair, with Sir Garnet Wolseley and his Highlanders playing the role of Napier and the Irish troops before Magdala. In technical military terms the campaign was another success, but after defeating the Ashantis and burning their capital

Kumasi, Wolseley hurriedly retreated, leaving the political context much as he had found it.

Stanley had arrived at the Gold Coast at the end of October 1873. The war was over by early February and Stanley left the 'white man's grave' with few regrets. When his ship put into Sao Vicente Island in the Cape Verde group on 25th February 1874, he learned of the death of Livingstone at Ilala near Lake Bangweolo the previous May. He became seized with the idea that it was his mission to continue Livingstone's work: 'Dear Livingstone! Another sacrifice to Africa!. . . May I be selected to succeed him in opening up Africa to the shining light of Christianity! .. . May Livingstone's God be with me, as He was with Livingstone in all his loneliness. May God direct me as He wills. I can only vow to be obedient, and not to slacken.'

Livingstone's death had been reported in Europe at the very moment Wolseley's expedition was getting to grips with the Ashanti. But still to come was the news of the astonishing nine-month journey Livingstone's servants Susi and Chuma had made across Africa, from Katanga to Bagamoyo. After finding their master dead at his bedside in a kneeling position, they had at once determined to take his body back to Zanzibar. First they cut out his heart and entrails and buried them in a tin box, so that the core of Livingstone would always remain in Africa. Then they dried the body in the sun for a fortnight, wrapped it in calico and fitted it into a cylindrical bark sarcophagus. The package was then sewn into a sailcloth and lashed to a pole that two men could carry. Under Susi and Chuma's directions, the whole Livingstone expedition then spent from May 1873 to February 1874 threading their perilous course back to Bagamoyo. The Foreign Office thereupon issued precise instructions. After a medical examination to establish that the body was indeed Livingstone's, the coffin was put on board the next mail boat for England, accompanied by another of Livingstone's 'faithfuls'Jacob Wainwright.

Stanley arrived in Lisbon on 9th March, and transferred from the Dromedary to the Garonne for the final leg of his homeward journey, to Liverpool. The mouth of the Tagus brought to mind the early Portuguese explorers of Africa, about whom he had lectured so disastrously in New York, especially Vasco da Gama. From Liverpool he proceeded to London and arranged to meet up with the Webbs of Newstead, who had Livingstone's last letter in their possession. Almost his first act on arriving at his favoured Langham Hotel was to write a long letter to Agnes Livingstone, setting down his impressions of her famous father. I was stricken dumb and I cannot give you a description of the misery I feel. How I envy such a father! The richest inheritance a father can give his children is an honoured name. What man ever left a nobler name than Livingstone? Written words, my dear Miss Agnes, however eloquent, would fail to express the sympathy I feel for you, and I feel too abashed by the subject to attempt it. The very name of Livingstone has a charm in it for me. I loved him as a son, and would have done for him anything worthy of the most

187

filial. The image of him will never be obliterated from my memory. It is so green with me when I think of the parting with him, that I almost fancy sometimes that it is palpable, and while I think of him I shall think of his children, more especially of his favourite daughter, and of the deep love he bore for her.

Stanley's secret resolution to complete the work of exploration started by Livingstone was further inspired by two things: on 6 April the Webbs arrived in London and handed over the doctor's last letter; and on the same day came reports that the latest attempt to chart the River Congo had failed. The question still remained unsolved: was the Lualaba the feeder for the Nile, as Livingstone thought, or did it flow into the Congo?

On 15 April the ship bringing Livingstone's body docked at Southampton. Four days earlier Stanley had travelled down with the Webbs to be on the dockside as a reception committee. The coffin came ashore to a twenty-one gun salute, was whisked away to London by special train, then lay in state for two days at the Royal Geographical Society. Tearful crowds filed past to pay tribute to Britain's greatest Victorian hero.

Then on 18 April came the state funeral in Westminster Abbey. A long train of carriages, including one sent by the Queen, filled Broad Sanctuary. Inside the Abbey was the greatest crowd seen since Prince Albert's funeral, with more than 900 reserved seats. The coffin was borne slowly down the nave. The congregation sang the 90th Psalm to Purcell's music. In front of the coffin walked Livingstone's two sons and his father-in-law Robert Moffat.' There were eight pall-bearers. Stanley was in the front row with Jacob Wainwright. Then came Waller, Kirk (on leave in England at the time), Webb, Oswell, Steele and Young. Behind the coffin walked the missionary Roger Price and Kalulu, dressed in a grey suit. In the congregation, seated next to the Prime Minister, were the two Livingstone sisters Stanley had met in October 1872, both of them on their first trip south of the border. The Dean (also named Stanley, as it happened) read the burial service. A wreath from Queen Victoria was placed on the coffin. The congregation sang Doddridge's 'O God of Bethel by whose Hand' to the tune by Thomas Tallis. Canon Conway preached the sermon. Then Livingstone's body was interred in the nave close to that of Marshal Wade..

Stanley returned to the Langham Hotel to ponder his next step. Whatever the sadness it occasioned, Livingstone's death at least opened up the possibility that Stanley's career might be rescued from the doldrums in which it had lain since 1872. Stanley was determined to be the man who carried on Livingstone's work in Africa, but the problem was how to bring this about. If he approached Bennett directly for the funds for a fresh expedition, the jealous Bennett would certainly turn him down. The trick was to force Bennett's hand.

Fortunately, one of Stanley's powerful friends had already come to the conclusion that Livingstone's work had to be finished and that only Stanley was capable of the task. Edwin Arnold (later Sir Edwin), editor of the Daily Telegraph, poet, orientalist and fellow of the RGS, was one of the few

Englishmen to have been completely won over to Stanley in 1872 Arnold persuaded the Telegraph proprietor Edward Levy-Lawson to put up £6,000 for an African expedition to be led by Stanley, on the understanding that Bennett and the New York Herald would match the figure pound for pound. Naturally, when Arnold mentioned the proposition, Stanley jumped at it. Now it was just a question of waiting for Bennett's answer to the cable inviting him to participate. Bennett was in a quandary. To agree would be to advance Stanley's career. Yet to refuse ran the risk that the Telegraph would find another co-sponsor; Stanley would simply resign from the Herald to head the expedition and both reporter and African scoops would be lost forever. Bennett felt that he had no choice. A terse and charmless 'Yes' was cabled across the Atlantic.

Five months' preparations now ensued for the expedition that was confidently billed by both the sponsoring newspapers as the greatest ever to be sent to Africa and the one with potentially the most sensational consequences; where nations sent armies, this project, backed by the despised 'Fourth Estate', would bring 'peace and light'. Offers of help from wealthy individuals and organisations flooded in. There was Angela Burdett-Coutts, one of the wealthiest women of the age and an admirer of Stanley since 1872. There was William Mackinnon, like Stanley a Celt and self-made man from humble origins, who had made a fortune from Indian commerce and founded in 1863 the British Indian Steam Navigation Company. His interest was particular, since in 1872 Mackinnon's company opened the first regular steamship service between Aden and Zanzibar. Then there was the Peninsular and Oriental Shipping Line, which made available various free facilities. The White Star Line gave Stanley free passage to and from America in return for the publicity. All in all, 'invitations to dinner and to parties and to spend a month or so in the country were so numerous that if I could have availed myself of them in succession years must elapse before any hotel need charge a penny to my account.'

Once news of the expedition was made public, Stanley was inundated with volunteers. He received more than 1,200 applications, 700 from Great Britain, 300 from the USA and about a hundred each from France and Germany, including three generals and five colonels. All the military volunteers had impeccable credentials but it was otherwise with the would-be civilian intake, which was distinguished by its extreme eccentricity. Many of them alienated Stanley at once by boasting of their 'street wisdom' and how they were 'up to every dodge', of how they had seen, done and knew everything. One madman proposed that he and Stanley should journey alone and unarmed through Africa, disguised as black men. Another suggested taking a tramway and a locomotive, of which he would be the driver. Yet another, a pre-echo of Kipling, suggested that he and Stanley set themselves up as kings in Africa. The most outré suggestion came from a man who claimed to be an expert in poisons and suggested that, instead of taking guns and ammunition or paying tribute to the 'nigger' chiefs, they would be able to poison them all as they went. Stanley reserved an especial contempt for the French and German applicants, many of whom offered as valuable attributes the ability to cook biftek or, even more idiotically, offered to interpret at the various 'hotels' at which the expedition would be staying during the crossing of Africa!

All of this evoked scorn and derision in Stanley. He inveighed at the mob of imbeciles who would 'take me up in balloons or by flying carriages, make us all invisible by their magic arts, or by the "science of magnetism" would cause all savages to fall asleep while we might pass anywhere without trouble. Indeed I feel sure that, had enough money been at my disposal at that time I might have led 5,000 Englishmen, 2,000 Frenchmen, 2,000 Germans, 500 Italians, 250 Swiss, 200 Belgians, 50 Spaniards, 5 Greeks, or 15,005 Europeans to Africa.'

However, Stanley did feel the need to take a handful of European companions with him. Typically, he decided they should all be from a lower social class, so that there could never be any question of a challenge to his authority. Three men only survived his severe winnowing process. One was Frederick Barker, a clerk at the Langham Hotel, who pestered and wheedled him until Stanley gave in. The other two were the Pocock brothers, two Medway sailors and fishermen recommended to him by Arnold; Edward Pocock, their father, skippered the Arnold yacht at lower Upnor on the Medway.'' They would be particularly useful to him, Stanley decided, because of their knowledge of boats. Among other innovations on this expedition he intended to take a specially designed boat, constructed by James Messenger of Middlesex. 40 feet long, with a 6-foot beam and 30 inches deep, of /s-inch thick Spanish cedar, the boat was in five detachable sections, each of 8 feet, on paper ideally suited for Africa's rivers. Stanley nicknamed this craft the Lady Alice, for reasons which he never publicly divulged.

The reason was particularly intriguing, for by the time the African expedition was announced, Stanley had embroiled himself with the third of his unattainable dream women. It was of the essence of Stanley's relationships with women that he had to light on someone who would reject him. This was because at the unconscious level he wanted to be rejected. At the conscious level this meant becoming entangled with women who were quite obviously unsuitable, in terms of class, culture or age. On 13th May at the Langham Hotel, he made the acquaintance of the Pike family. This was after the Livingstone funeral but a month before the announcement of the African expedition. At the time Stanley was in a fallow period, working night and day on the book that would become Coomassie andMagdala. But, perhaps significantly, Stanley had just been visited by one of the voices from his past. Virginia Ambella renewed contact, this time from an address in Athens, to indicate that she was still available as a wife. Stanley brushed the suggestion aside curtly: 'It is hopeless to expect that I can love again where that love was rejected in such an abrupt manner.'

STANLEY

The Langham Hotel was the most modern and spacious in London and as such a great favourite with visiting Americans. One of Stanley's fellow guests was a Mr Aronson from New York (whom Stanley did not like). On 13th May Aronson invited him to join his guests at dinner and Stanley, out of boredom, accepted. Two of the Pike girls were to be there, Nettie and Alice, daughters of Samuel N. Pike, a German-Jewish immigrant to the USA who had made a fortune out of distilling whisky in Cincinnati and built the Grand Opera House there. Nettie came to the table first. Stanley found her good-looking but rather 'fast': 'her hair was done up in what I believe are called frizzles, which is a lot of untidy hair hanging over the forehead. She had an enormous chignon, talked disgustingly loud.' Nettie got into a close conversation with Aronson, so that when Alice came and sat down, Stanley had her to himself for a long period. She was only seventeen but when he spoke to her, she turned her face around in a self-contained way that contrasted strikingly and favourably with the more volatile Nettie. Stanley observed her closely and his later jottings are revealing on what he considered desirable in a woman:

While her manner was constrained even to being frigid, the style of her hair and dress, diamonds and such, indicated 'fast' or inordinate vanity with over-much wealth to gratify it or absolve her from following what may be called good taste. Her eyes were of a bluish grey, were very large and seemed capable of expansion. Her mouth was large but well- formed, her nose had a certain Jewish fullness at the point with the slightest possible rise half way down. Her face was pallid, forehead was broad, temples prominent, her 'frizzles' however hung as thickly over the forehead that they marred what would otherwise have been a very attractive face . . . when she rose from the table I noticed her figure was very elegant. The carriage of her head indicated that she was cool and self-possessed and that if she does not know much of society she had a lower opinion of society than she had of herself.

Soon they were joined by Mrs Pike, a recent widow of about forty, stout and good-tempered. After dinner Stanley accompanied the Pike ladies to their suite of rooms at the Langham. During dinner the three women had declared great interest in his forthcoming African journey, but further questioning had revealed a woeful ignorance of African geography and, added Stanley waspishly, 'I fear of everything else.'

During the next few days Stanley's interest in Alice Pike was further enhanced by a series of meetings and drives in Hyde Park. He was attracted physically, while repelled morally. Alice, it was plain, was a coquette and a capriciosa. She had a number of suitors, among them an elderly judge called Mumford in St Louis. Another was a French nobleman, whose private letters she read out for the general amusement. Nettie, too, while admitting that she cared nothing for Aronson, encouraged him in his slavish admiration. Stanley's ambivalent reaction to this pair of flirts is well conveyed in one of his diary entries. 'I fear if Miss Alice gives me as much encouragement as she [Nettie] has been giving him [Aronson] lately,

I shall fall in love with her, which may not perhaps be very conducive to my happiness, for she is the very opposite of my ideal wife.'

A few days later this impression was reinforced. One morning he called to see the Pike girls at their suite, and Nettie was called downstairs to deal with another of her conquests. Stanley was left alone with Alice. Alice produced another letter from the French Count Portales, read out a section which was overly euphuistic and collapsed with laughter as she read it. Stanley was most disconcerted. 'It impressed on me the necessity of being very circumspect and I mentally vowed that she would never receive a declaration from me ... I have discovered that however pretty, elegant, etc she may be, she is heartless and a confirmed flirt.' The fear of being laughed at behind his back was in Stanley's case almost pathological; given that this was Alice's way, no worse choice of wife could be imagined.

Yet by mid-June, just when the African expedition was being confirmed, he entered the following in his diary. 'This day I saw my fiancée Alice, for so I must call her, depart from Liverpool by the Russia with her family for New York. She has sworn undying fidelity to me and our parting was very tender.' Clearly the physical impact of Alice had for the moment swept aside his reservations. As soon as he had tied up the London end of the expedition with Levy-Lawson and the Daily Telegraph people, Stanley found the excuse to follow Alice across the Atlantic in the alleged need to consult with Bennett in New York. With free passage given him by the White Star line, there was no financial impediment to the chase. On 24thJune he left Liverpool on the Britannic and arrived in New York on 4th July.

There was a strong contrast between the public and private parts of Stanley's American mission. Bennett went out of his way to snub the man who, he felt, had manoeuvred him into another African venture that would redound purely to Stanley's fame. After keeping him dangling for several days around the Herald offices with the usual lame excuses about being 'in a meeting', Bennett finally consented to see him at 10.30 a.m. on the morning of 8th July. When Stanley stepped into Bennett's office to speak, 'Jamie' cut him off brusquely, saying he was too busy to talk now - it would have to wait until Friday. As Stanley remarked, for once with understatement: 'This is rather an unkind way to receive one whom he is about to send to explore Africa.' When he did eventually manage to see Bennett, the proprietor simply handed him on to the editor Conway, who gave him his instructions verbally and conveyed the deep unhappiness of all at the Herald headquarters about the 'enforced' collaboration with the Daily Telegraph,

The quest for Alice fared better, or so it seemed. On Sunday 12th July Stanley signed a marriage pact with her at her home at 613 Fifth Avenue, the millionaire quarter of Manhattan, made fashionable by the Astors and Vanderbilts. 'We solemnly pledge ourselves to be faithful to each other and to be married to one another on the return of Henry Morton Stanley from Africa. We call God to witness this our pledge in writing.' The pledge was reinforced after a dinner on 17th July. They returned to the Pike house on Fifth Avenue and during an intimate talk in the parlour, Alice told him: 'You must hurry and do your work in Africa, and when the two years are gone, if you come to claim me, I will marry you, so help me God.' Alice explained that it was in deference to her mother's wishes that she had decided to postpone the marriage for two years, but that at the end of that time she would marry him with or without her mother's consent. After saying this, she raised her lips 'in tempting proximity' to his. He kissed her on the lips, eyes, cheek and neck and she kissed him in return.

Next day Stanley left New York for Liverpool on the Celtic. Alice repeated her vows and promised to write to him often. She and Nettie went down to the pier to see him off. 'I clasped her hands to bid her goodbye. She gave me such a look - a long, earnest, wide-eyed look, during which I thought that she was striving to pierce the dark, gloomy picture, but I turned away and the spell broke.' Once on deck he waved dismissively to tell them not to wait around. At the second wave, they moved off. 'Alice kissed her hand to me, and resolutely turned away, a seeming self-possessed maiden but hiding, I know, some pang at parting.'

Chapter Thirteen

BACK in London Stanley put the finishing touches to the expedition. Despite his experiences with domestic animals on the Livingstone expedition, he decided to take a quartet of dogs with him: a mastiff, Castor, a retriever, Nero, a bulldog, Bull, and a bull- terrier, Jack. These he sent ahead with the Pococks and Barker to wait for him at Aden. After signing formal contracts with Stanley on 4th and 5th August, his three white companions shipped out from Southampton on the Mongolia, bound for Aden via Malta, Alexandria and the Suez Canal. Stanley remained at the Langham to tie up loose ends, such as whether the British India Company could take the Lady Alice on from Aden to Zanzibar. Then in mid-August he left for Zanzibar on the BISN steamer Euphrates for Zanzibar.

The Pococks arrived in Aden on 2nd September and Stanley a week later, with the Lady Alice. Uniting the two parties, they sailed on to Zanzibar, reached on 22nd September. It was fortunate for Stanley that there was a skilled carpenter on board the Euphrates, for he found that the boat sections, instead of weighing a maximum of 120 pounds each (and as such suitable for being carried by two men) weighed anywhere between 280 and 310 pounds. It took the carpenter two weeks to remodel the sections.

At Zanzibar Stanley found many changes. Since he had been there last, in 1872, the Bartle Frere mission to the Sultan had succeeded in abolishing slavery on the island. Tozer had gone, replaced by Dr Edward Steere, a man universally liked and praised even by Stanley. Even better, Kirk was in England on leave and as Acting Consul and Political Resident there was Captain Pridaux, one of the Magdala captives. Stanley and his party stayed at the house of Augustus Sparhawk (now working for the Bertram Agency) in Shangani. Stanley was by now convinced he had made a wise choice with the Pococks, whom he found not just sober, civilised and industrious but very good singers and musicians.

He set about recruiting porters from among his beloved wangwana. Chowpereh agreed to join provided Stanley vaccinated his son against smallpox. Others of his veterans who were prepared to sign were Ulimengo, Rojab, Manwa Sera and Mabruki. The troublesome Bombay was not in any case available this time, since he had already accompanied Verney Cameron into the interior. But Stanley was able to recruit forty-seven of the men he had sent to accompany Livingstone on his last expedition. Additionally, he engaged a further 200, largely on the personal recommendations of his veterans.

Stanley spent a tedious first week in Zanzibar organising this greatest ever foray into the heart of the Dark Continent. He discovered that whereas barter goods had gone down in price in Zanzibar since 1872 because of uncertainties about the trade of the interior, the cost of porters had doubled. Stanley lost no opportunity in shifting the blame for this to his rival, attributing it to the 'somewhat inordinate liberality of the Cameron expedition'. He tried out his inflatable pontoon, designed by J. C. Cording of London to help in fording flooded African rivers, and made of thick India-rubber cloth. The only relaxation was horseback riding in the interior of the island every evening after dinner, or sightseeing. Yet, apart from the Mnazi Moya (One Coconut Tree) at Shangani Point, there was little enough to see - just a harbour filled with every conceivable kind of ship, from British warships to Arab small craft, sometimes as many as 150 at anchor together.

By the end of September Stanley had had enough. Leaving the final administrative details to Sparhawk, he took his companions over to the mainland to explore the Rufiji River. After several weeks' exploration, they returned to Bagamoyo and thence across the channel to Zanzibar. A further month on the island was necessary before the vast expedition was finally ready to depart. Stanley paid out £1,300 in advances to his wangwana; the formal contract of service, dated 15th November 1874, specified that the men of Zanzibar were to remain with Stanley 'for two years or until such time as he may require them or until such time as he no longer needs their services.' Stanley took with him into Africa 18,000 pounds of trade goods, arms and materiel - 8 tons divided into loads of 60 pounds each for his 300 porters. His three white companions toiled away at the boats to make them manoeuvrable and Weatherly on the treacherous African waterways. Barker and the Pococks timidly asked (and received) permission for a Union Jack to be flown, since this was an Anglo-American expedition. The simplicity of Stanley's two young fishermen is best illustrated by a visit to Zanzibar of HMS Thetis during which the crew put on a performance of The Merchant of Venice. It is quite clear from Pocock's diary entry that he had never before heard of the play.

At last all was ready. On 12th November 1874 six Arab vessels conveyed the expedition across the straits to Bagamoyo. But before the march could get under way there were problems. Stanley's men proved unruly and undisciplined. After one affray Stanley placed a dozen men under arrest. When his drunken followers continued to run amok, he called in the aid of the governor of Bagamoyo. But when his severity in turn threatened to make a bad situation worse, Stanley was reduced to asking the governor for lenient treatment for his followers. It became clear that the problems would be resolved only when Bagamoyo was left far in the rear. Stanley tried to encourage his men by pointing out that the 6o-pound loads would reduce to 30 pounds within the year.

The only point of interest for Stanley in Bagamoyo was to see the vastly increased rate of missionary activity there. But Stanley, never a friend to missionaries, criticised them for trying to take the African straight from barbarism to Christianity, without satisfying the intermediate stage of material want. For once, Stanley the hard driver was criticising people for trying to go too fast. The missionaries, in turn, remembering how Stanley had pilloried them in Hoiv I Found Livingstone, were wary. When Stanley returned to dine at the Holy Ghost Mission, the fathers made sure that this time there was no champagne, that the explorer was served only simple fare.

Finally, on 17th November, having secured six riding asses for the expedition, one each for the Europeans and two in reserve for the sick, Stanley was able to give the order to march into the interior. Many thought he was going to a certain death, but Stanley was unworried by this. As he wrote to J. R. Robinson of the Daily News: 'Now that I am face to face with inhospitable Africa there is something, it seems to me, which grinds out all hope of return. At the same time I cannot say that I feel any melancholy at the hopeless prospect, but rather a careless indifference as to what Fate may have in store for me. I say truly that I don't care whether I return or not. I have disciplined myself to look at my long journey in this light. If I return, it is well, if not, then it is well again, for I shall cease from being troubled or annoyed.' He ended by pointing out that Livingstone had preferred to die in Africa rather than endure the sustained hostility of people in England, and he himself felt the same way.

What light does this curious avowal of the death instinct throw on the relationship with Alice Pike? There are good grounds for thinking that both partners to the New York marriage 'contract' were acting in bad faith, Alice fundamentally unserious and caught up in the sentimentality of the moment, Stanley unconsciously willing his own ultimate rejection. There is something decidedly curious about a man who professes love for a woman, then disappears into the heart of Africa for three years. Equally, it is hard to take seriously the coquettish outpourings of a rather empty-headed seventeen-year-old for a dour thirty-four-year-old explorer. That the Stanley-Alice Pike romance was foredoomed becomes very clear when we examine the correspondence between them. Stanley's 'love letters' were better suited for the columns of the RGS Journal. Alice's letters are a farrago of social gossip and girlish chatter about dances, clothes, weddings and music lessons. She manages at once to convey the impression of being offhand about his deeper feelings and serious in her calculation that she will have a pretext for not writing to him once he heads into the Dark Continent. The restless tone of the letters makes it seem always unlikely that she would keep to the terms of the engagement.

On 13th October Alice writes:

My dear Morton,

I have not had a line from you in perfect ages, so wasn't I delighted on my return from a harp lesson to find, as I supposed a letter awaiting me . . . Although you have been kind in getting me so many pretty things you have been real mean about writing. You never write to me anymore and I just want to know why??? I am real angry with Central Africa.

Two weeks later she complains that she has not heard from him even though she writes every week. The level of communication is well conveyed by the following: 'I do love opera but I can hardly ever go, for Ma will not let me go out with gentlemen except one or two I have known for ages, or in a party.'

But most revealing of all is her reply to Stanley's farewell letter from Zanzibar.

Why did you not tell me you would be gone for more than two years? 1 did not expect you to be back on the very day or month, but I was hardly prepared for a whole year over the time. And suppose you are not home, then where will you be? Dead or still seeking the Nile? What a change these years will make in me! I will have seen something of the world by then, will I be changed for the better or not. I may be affected and proud and you will not like me at all. Then my past habits might change perhaps, I may be dead long before the three years have passed. We cannot tell. I might become very poor and have to support myself. I can do nothing but sing. I would have to go on the stage. I would be compelled to for there is nothing else I can do well. Of course you would be too proud to marry me, an Opera singer. If I should lose my money I would marry any rich man who would have me, to save myself from the stage . .. Don't for Mercy's sake, get jealous of Hall, he is the best friend I have, he is only twenty-one, I have known him ever so long. By this time you must know you will have no further fear from others. That is wrong what you said about they wouldn't like me unless I gave them some encouragement, it is natural they should like me. I give them no more encouragement than talking to them, singing and dancing, and it is really no fault of mine if they are conceited enough to think I will accept them, if they only ask me. I have the most horrid sore finger all blistered from playing the harp. I am getting along quite well with it, only I never practice.

The absurdity of such a letter, addressed to a man about to brave the dangers of unknown Central Africa, is evident. The fantasies of poverty seem particularly odious from the daughter of a millionaire. But instead of lamenting Stanley's inability to discriminate between immature women and those of greater emotional solidity, we should ask whether there was not method in Stanley's madness, whether he had not deliberately (albeit unconsciously) chosen an impossible object for his affections. We have established that Stanley in his oscillations between opposite polarities - sadism/masochism, homosexual/heterosexual - clearly manifested a schizoid personality disorder. The schizoid personality typically combines a desperate need for love with an equally desperate fear of intimacy. Stanley dared not make close contact with a woman for fear that any love given him would be withdrawn. Humiliated, unloved, despised, feeling himself the unworthy recipient of any apparent affection, Stanley constantly turned to African exploration as a means of re-establishing his identity. There is a motif of redemption by suffering both in the choice of Alice and in the penetration of Africa. The implausibility of an enduring relationship with Alice Pike, then, derives from something deeper than Alice's essential flightiness and frivolity.

Stanley's unconscious wish to be rejected was soon granted. On 11th January 1876 Alice married Albert Clifford Barney of Dayton, Ohio, himself the heir to a huge railway fortune. Nine months later she gave birth to a daughter. In later life she became a playwright and patroness of the arts. She and Stanley never met again. When she wrote to congratulate him on his emergence from Africa in 1877 she excused herself thus: 'You must know, by this time, I have done what millions of women have done before, not been true to my promise . .. No doubt before long you will think it a gain, for Stanley can easily find a wife all his heart could desire to grace his high position and deservedly great name.' But she began the letter with words that, in the light of Stanley's psychic turmoil, have an extra dimension of irony: 'Poor Stanley! How much you have lost, but your gain has been great indeed.' She could not have understood that the gain and the loss for Stanley were one and the same.

What were Stanley's intentions when he set out from Bagamoyo in mid-November 1874 on what would prove to be his greatest African expedition? In following the established caravan route at first he was partly trying to build up his men's confidence and partly trying to avoid the territory of the Masai, for whom he had an exaggerated respect. Once beyond the orbit of the Masai, he intended to strike north-westward to Lake Victoria to establish who was right about this great stretch of waterway. Speke thought Lake Victoria was just one vast lake, Burton thought it was a cluster of several smaller lakes, while Samuel Baker thought that Lakes Albert and Tanganyika were one and the same. The way to solve all this was to circumnavigate Lake Victoria and Lake Albert, visiting the great King Mutesa on the way, and possibly to end with a visit to Gordon in Equatoria - Gordon who had no interest in exploration as such. Finally - 'beyond this point the whole appears to me so vague and vast that it is impossible to state at this period what I shall try to do next.'

The first part of the march to Lake Victoria was something of a rerun of 1871. But this time it was the masika, and as they slogged through the familiar Usagara and Ugogo country, they had to endure deluges of rain. Christmas Day 1874 saw the four white men huddling in their tents in wet clothes and blankets while flash floods outside produced a torrent that could convert a plain into a swamp in fifteen minutes. They slurped and squelched through Ugogo, following a more northerly itinerary than in 1871, then crossed into Ukimbu, where no white man had ever been seen before.

Then they began to head north towards Lake Victoria. But at the village of Vinyata they became embroiled in sustained warfare with the hostile Waturu people. For a time it was touch and go whether the explorers would survive. In order to take the war to the enemy, Stanley divided his seventy effectives into four 'moving squares'. Unfortunately, the leader of one of these squares disobeyed orders; he and twenty men were lured out of range of their comrades and slaughtered to a man. Only quick thinking by Stanley prevented a second square from being overwhelmed. Learning from his mistakes, Stanley formed all his men into one bristling formation, resembling the Roman 'turtle'. His concentrated firepower then carried all before it. In a series of running fights the Waturu were completely defeated; the expedition could proceed in safety.

But victory had been won at a price. At the end of January' 1875 Stanley held a muster and found that half those who had started from Bagamoyo were dead. Apart from battle casualties, large numbers had perished from the aggravated effects of disease. Edward Pocock, who had caught fever on his first day on the African mainland and never recovered, died on 17th January. Among the wangwana there was a huge death-toll, from a plethora of illnesses: dysentery, bronchitis, pneumonia, ophthalmia, rheumatism, sciatica, asthma, dropsy, emphysema, erysipelas, elephantiasis.

Further gruelling marches had to be endured before they came in sight of Lake Victoria on 26th February 1875. Frank Pocock was the first to espy the distant glistening waters, thus becoming the fourth white man to see Victoria Nyanza, after Speke, Grant and Chaille-Long.' The porters burst into songs of joy at sight of the lake; universal joy was constrained only by the knowledge that Barker was now very ill with fever. A day later brought them to the small conical huts of the village of Kaduma on the lakeside, where they hired quarters. Euphoria was general at the thought of a long-earned rest. In 103 days they had come 720 miles from Bagamoyo - an average of 7 miles a day.

It had been a great feat of marching, but the human cost was extraordinarily high. Out of 347 persons with whom he had started, Stanley had lost 181 through battle, famine, illness and desertion. One white man was dead and another seemed likely to die. Against this was the rapport that Stanley had established with Frank Pocock, and Pocock with the Zanzibaris. Pocock had no feeling of racial superiority about him. He was full of praise for Manwa Sera: 'Such a nice man . .. like a father. When we were in a desert he went twelve miles among wild beasts for water for the white men, a turn I shall never forget.'

Frank Pocock wrote to his parents of his homesickness: 'I dreamed last night that I was at home eating fine things, but I awoke and found myself in Central Africa.' As they relaxed on the lake shore, Stanley too waxed nostalgic. He wrote to Alice Pike to tell her with pride that the Lady Alice had been carried 120 miles across Africa and spoke of his future plans. 'You asked me if we could not get married at once on my return, to which I answer that it shall be as you desire. The very hour I landed in England, I should like to marry you, but such a long time must elapse before I can see you that even to see your dear face again appears to me as a most improbable thing.' Unknown to him, Stanley's fantasy romance had become a true fantasy, as much a dream as Pocock's reverie of the Medway.

Chapter Fourteen

STANLEY allowed his men just one day of total relaxation. On the night of 28th February he gave a banquet and allowed extra 'pocket money' to Pocock and Barker in the form of beads and cloth with which to buy extra food. Next day he announced his plans for an immediate circumnavigation of Lake Victoria. To begin with he would take a small party north to locate the capital of Mutesa, King of Uganda. The rest of the wangwana were to be divided into eight squads of twenty men each, with an experienced NCO to guide each squad. All would be armed either with Sniders or percussion-lock muskets; the NCOs additionally would be armed with revolvers. Stanley gave specific instructions that in any armed clash with enemy forces during his absence, his men should open fire at a distance greater than 40 yards; the men of Ituru had shown what would happen if an enemy closed the range below this distance, when spears became as deadly as bullets. The dreadful casualties in the battle at Vinyata still preyed on Stanley's mind; he had come to realise that there were African warriors 'rivalling the Apache in ferocity and determination'.

It took Stanley just seven days to have the Lady Alice ready for its first real trial by water. He took with him ten men and large stocks of food (600 pounds of flour and 200 pounds of dried fish) to barter with the tribes. The local chief Kaduma was an alcoholic, so Stanley decided he would be useless as a guide on the trip north. But the tall tales his people recounted of the horrors to be encountered on Lake Victoria further demoralised the mangwana, who had already protested to Stanley that they were not sailors and knew nothing of boats. Stanley had to use a mixture of cajolery and browbeating to get the men he had picked into the boat. Even as they rowed away from camp on 8th March, the men looked back fearfully, sighed dolefully and hoped all the time for the signal to return.

Morale sank even lower as Lady Alice picked its way past Nathari Island at the mouth of the Shimeeyu River in the teeth of a ferocious gale. Next day the waters were as placid as a pond, but again nature intervened against them in the shape of a trio of hippos who rushed at them open-mouthed on the shores of Manassa and drove them off. The hippopotami of Lake Victoria were very aggressive and often chased the boat; on one occasion they bumped over the spine of a hippo, who bade fair to shake the craft to pieces. Being spilled into these waters was mortally perilous, since the lake was infested with crocodiles, which, to Stanley's interest, lived here in a state of peaceful symbiosis with colonies of monitor lizards.

They rowed east along the southerly shore of Speke Gulf, confirming that explorer's observations on Ukerewe, before turning north along the coast of Uriruri. They passed Ukara Island, later an especial haven for explorers of East Africa. So far they had met only Sukuma peoples, but as they paddled farther northward Stanley noticed a different dialect creeping in: the population was mixed, part Sukuma, part Shasti. They were finding it extremely difficult either to confirm or deny the Speke thesis that Lake Victoria was a single large waterway. For example, Stanley set down the Majita peninsula as two islands, did not spot that Baringo was a separate lake, and missed the Kavirondo Gulf altogether, as .it is shielded from Lake Victoria by an island. However, there could be no mistaking the fact that the people of Kavirondo were utterly different in language and culture from the Sukuma.

But along the northern coast of Lake Victoria they ran into their first group of hostile tribesmen. At Ngevi Island, the locals brandished spears at them but bolted in terror when Stanley fired warning shots in the air with his revolver. Next day they returned, to insist that the strangers visit their king. Stanley pretended to agree to this, then hoisted sail and swept past them. But a ferocious gale that night forced them to make landfall in the country of the Waruma. Something about their demeanour made Stanley suspicious and he ordered his men to stand ready.

Another gale, complete with hailstones, supervened the following night. Then, next morning, the Waruma attacked. Beaten off by a fusillade from the Sniders, they next launched a fleet of thirteen war canoes just as the Lady Alice was getting under way. To avoid conflict, Stanley allowed them to approach, but was forced to fire over their heads when they tried to seize the oars. Sheering off for a moment, the war canoes again came in close and the warriors taunted Stanley by pointing out the beads they had stolen during the land attack. Infuriated by this, Stanley opened up with his elephant gun, which at once smashed three canoes and killed four men. After he had holed the others below the waterline, the Lady Alice put about while their tormentors slowly sank in the water.

Making good speed, they entered Napoleon Channel (later Napoleon Gulf) and soon passed a great river flowing away northwards (afterwards identified as the Victoria Nile at Ripon Falls). They explored the Buvuma Islands at the entrance to the gulf. After failing to find Speke's Luajerri River, they sailed west along the northern shore of the lake, past Ikira, Kriva and Ukafu, and entered the territories of King Mutesa. They passed the word to the warriors who accosted them that they were bound for the court on an embassy. On 3 April the Kabaka's ambassador arrived in a flotilla of large canoes to accompany them on the last stretch. He wore a bead-embossed head-dress above which waved a long plume of white cocks' feathers. About his person was a long crimson robe and a snowy-white long-haired goatskin.

On 3 April they completed the last stretch of the journey together, 'the king's canoes making a fine appearance'. On 4 April they arrived at Mutesa's hunting camp at Usavara, where they were welcomed by the Katekiro, the Kabaka's prime minister; after being greeted by a volley of musketry, the strangers were feasted on chickens, eggs, bananas and sweet potatoes by 2,000 of the king's excited followers. Ten oxen and sixteen sheep and goats were slaughtered in their honour. Stanley himself was lodged in a special house. Stanley passed the Katekiro's interrogation with flying colours and both sides fell to mutual admiration. Mutesa's people seemed as different from the other denizens of Lake Victoria as Kansas whites from the Choctaws.

5 April 1875, the date of Stanley's meeting with Mutesa, was one of the decisive dates in the confrontation of European explorer with African indigenous power. It bore comparison with Moffat's meeting with Msilikazi in Matabeleland or Livingstone's with Sekeletu, the Makololo chief. A less happy precedent that might have been in Stanley's mind was the disastrous reencounter between Kabba Rega and Samuel Baker in Unyoro three years earlier. The actual meeting was certainly dramatic. Walking from his quarters, Stanley soon found himself in a broad street, 80 feet wide and half a mile long, lined with Mutesa's personal guards and servants. At the extreme end of the street sat the Kabaka in his house of audience. To the firing of guns, waving of flags and beating of drums, Stanley advanced slowly up the avenue. Mutesa arose, a tall, slender figure in Arab costume. He approached a few paces, held out his hand mutely, and the two men stood gazing at each other while the drums continued their deafening tattoo. Then silence fell. Mutesa sat down and invited his guest to follow suit.'

Seeing before him a 'most intelligent, humane and distinguished prince', Stanley was unable to recognise the Kabaka in Speke's unflattering portrait. Around thirty-four years of age (the same as Stanley), Mutesa deeply impressed him by his quiet dignity and his vast superiority in intelligence to the Sultan of Zanzibar. 'His face is very agreeable and pleasant, and indicates intelligence and mildness. His eyes are large, his nose and mouth are a great improvement upon those of the common type of negro ... his teeth are splendid and gleaming white.' A heathen in Speke and Grant's day, Mutesa now professed Islam. All his officers wore Arab dress and affected Arab ways. Taken by surprise at the level of civilisation at the court, Stanley rounded on Speke in his writings and accused him of luring him almost to his death by his inaccuracies; believing in Speke's portrait, he had come close to insulting Mutesa by offering him the sort of childish trinkets appropriate to the savage tribes of the hongo system.

Rapport between the two men was immediate. Next day Mutesa held a naval review to show off his power. Then he asked Stanley to demonstrate the force of his weaponry to the women of his harem. Getting off a lucky shot from a moving canoe, Stanley killed a crocodile stone dead from a range of 100 yards. Deeply impressed with this marksmanship, which he considered probably run of the mill with white men, Mutesa tried one of the rifles himself, but it fractured in his hands, and some very quick technical explanations were called for from Stanley to avert the suggestion that this was a bad omen. Once restored to full favour, Stanley penned this portrait of the king. In person Mutesa is tall, probably 6' 1" and slender. He has very intelligent and agreeable features, reminding me of some of the faces of the great stone images at Thebes and of the statues in the museum at Cairo. He has the same fullness of lips, but their grossness is relieved by the general expression of amiability blended with dignity that pervades his face, and the large lustrous lambent eyes that lend it a strange beauty, and are typical of the race from which I believe him to have sprung. His colour is of a dark red brown, of a wonderfully smooth surface. When not engaged in council, he throws off unreservedly the bearing that characterises him when on the throne and gives vein to his humour, indulging in hearty peals of laughter. He seems to be interested in the discussion of the manners and customs of European courts, and to be enamoured of hearing the wonders of civilisation. He is ambitious to imitate as much as lies in his power the ways of the white men. When any piece of information is given him, he takes upon himself the task of translating it to his wives and chiefs, though many of the latter understand the Swahili language as well as he does himself.

On 8 April the Kabaka's court moved from the hunting village to Mutesa's capital at Ugalla, a three-hour march away over rude roads. The highway improved dramatically just before the capital. As we approached the capital, the highway from Usavara increased in width from twenty feet to 150 feet. When he arrived at this magnificent breadth we viewed the capital crossing an eminence commanding a most extensive view of a picturesque and rich country teeming with gardens and plantains, and beautiful pasture land ... the vast collection of huts crossing the eminence were the Royal Quarters, around which ran several palisades and circular courts, between which and the city was a circular road, ranging from one hundred to two hundred feet in width, from which radiated six or seven magnificent avenues, lined with gardens and huts. Stanley was given a 'garden villa' of a marquee shape to live in. He was invited to the palace that very afternoon for the first of a week-long series of chats, during which the intimacy and mutual regard of both men deepened. Stanley had already seen that he could score a great publicity coup if he could declare to the world that the kingdom of Uganda was open for missionary work. He therefore continually urged on Mutesa the advantages of converting to Christianity. The Kabaka had no intention of apostasy from Islam, but he realised the advantages that could accrue to him, not least in the technology of war, from closer contact with Europeans. Accordingly, he pretended a deep interest in the Christian faith and expressed a wish to be converted. Stanley triumphantly made him a present of a Bible. Mutesa artfully questioned him on what was so good about the Gospel. Mention of the brotherhood of man, the equality of women and the absence of slavery produced a glazed look in the king. Then Stanley produced his trump. He claimed that there were eleven commandments; the eleventh, inverted by Stanley himself, ran thus: 'Honour and respect kings, for they are the envoys of God.' This was closer to the language Mutesa understood, and his features lit into a smile. He said that in that case he would certainly embrace Christianity.

Stanley was completely taken in and announced to the world that Uganda was a rich vineyard for England's missionary toilers. In London the call created a sensation, and eager acolytes flocked to the missionary standard, but Mutesa's later behaviour made it crystal clear that he had made the credulous Stanley his dupe. Here was a signal instance of one of the weaknesses in Stanley's personality. He was always prone to overrate his own persuasiveness and to imagine that he possessed the ability to win people round to his point of view. It did not occur to him, as long as they appeared deferential, that they might be gulling him.

There was a specific reason why Mutesa contemplated calling in the power of Europe to redress the balance in Africa. He was aware of growing pressure on his kingdom from the Egyptians in the north, especially since Colonel (later General) Gordon had become governor of Equatoria province. That pressure seemed to take a concrete form a few days after Stanley's advent when, coincidentally, an envoy from Gordon, Colonel Ernest Linant de Bellefonds, arrived in Ugalla. His coming illustrates the extreme complexity of Central African power politics in the 1870s.

In 1869 Khedive Ismail (whom Stanley had met that year at the opening of the Suez Canal) appointed Samuel Baker as governor of Equatoria - the area of the Upper Nile between Fashoda and Lake Victoria. His brief was to extirpate the slave trade and bring the headwaters of the Nile under Egyptian control. In 1870 Baker left Khartoum for Gondokoro, 'capital' of the province of Equatoria. Baker had been chosen as governor because of his earlier (1863) exploration of Lake Albert and the kingdom of Bunyoro, then ruled over by Kamrasi. Bunyoro was one of two powerful Bantu kingdoms in the lake regions, the other being Buganda. Buganda, on the north-west side of the lake, was the dominant power in the area during this period. When the Europeans first encountered the kingdoms, Buganda played the Inca to their conquistadores, with the rival state of Bunyoro as the Aztecs. In other words, the power of Buganda was on the ascendant while that of Bunyoro was declining.

In 1872 Baker, after a year of ineffectual blood-letting in a war against the slavers at Gondoroko, headed south with an army of about a thousand well-armed Sudanese and Egyptians, bent on the annexation of Bunyoro. Kamrasi's successor, Kabba Rega, had no intention of submitting to Egyptian rule. He forced Baker to make a humiliating retreat out of his kingdom, after coming within an ace of annihilating his invading army. In 1873 Baker resigned and was replaced as governor of Equatoria by 'Chinese' Gordon. I April 1874 Gordon arrived in Gondokoro, determined on southward expansion. His ambitious plans included exploring the Nile between Lakes Albert and Victoria with a view to steamer communication; occupation of the plateau between the two lakes; abandoning the Nile as a principal artery of communication between Cairo and Equatoria and its replacement with an overland route to the East African coast.

Clearly these plans posed a threat to both Buganda and Bunyoro. Militarily it might have seemed that Gordon lacked the capability to implement such grandiose plans, but the Khedive's attack on and occupation of the Sultan of Zanzibar's garrison forts north of Mombasa in

1875 showed that Egyptian will at least was not lacking. ' The Khedive was clearly a hothead. When he first heard of Stanley's expedition, he told Chaille-Long that the desire to complete Livingstone's work was merely the ostensible object of the Anglo-American expedition. Its real objective was to plant the British flag in Uganda. Accordingly the Khedive was keen that Gordon, Chaille-Long and his other lieutenants should beat Stanley to the punch. This was the genesis of the Linant de Bellefonds mission to Mutesa. Gordon was playing for time, hoping forlornly to get the Kabaka and Kabba Rega to negotiate away their territorial rights while he and the Khedive considered whether they really did have the resources for military conquest in Central Africa.

This explains both the much greater coolness with which Mutesa received Bellefonds, as compared with Stanley, and the sustained interest that Gordon and all his lieutenants showed in Stanley's movements in 1875-6. From Gordon's point of view, not only might Stanley's 'meddling' wreck his own designs against Mutesa, but Stanley, with his retinue of wangwana, had to be considered as in some sense the Sultan of Zanzibar's man and hence the enemy. Stanley's notion of meeting up with Gordon for joint action against the slavers was egregiously naive. Gordon made it clear that he would allow no Zanzibari soldiers on the soil of Equatoria. If Stanley made his way into the province, he, Gordon would send him politely on his way to Khartoum.

This complex background to the Bellefonds mission at Mutesa's court in no way diminished the pleasure that Stanley took in the Frenchman's company, largely because he was unaware of its wider implications. Bellefonds arrived in the Ugandan capital on 1 x April and at first mistook Stanley for Verney Cameron. That mistake corrected, the two men spent three stimulating days in each other's company. Bellefonds, at his initial interview with Mutesa, found himself having to confirm the truth of the Stanley version of Christianity. But afterwards: 'On leaving the king I went to breakfast with Mr Stanley, and we chatted together a long time, stretched out on our straw, smoking and taking our tea. These were for us happy moments - like a splendid meteor, the duration of which was like that of a shooting star. Each one of us found in the other a brother and opened his heart to him. Stanley told me about the fatigues and difficulties of his journeys, the hostility he had encountered among certain peoples whom he had been forced to fight - he gave me geographical information of the greatest interest.'

Stanley for his part was even more glowing: 'The meeting, though not so exciting as my former meeting with the venerable David Livingstone, at Ujiji in November 1871, still may be said to be singular and fortunate for all concerned. In Colonel Bellefonds I met a gentleman extremely well informed, energetic and a great traveller.' Their conversations ranged far and wide, over Mutesa, religion, the geographical details of Uganda and the Sudan, the future of Africa. They even swapped items of cuisine. Their opinions differed only on how to treat the Africans. Bellefonds was stiff and reserved with the Ganda people, while Stanley encouraged them to swarm all over his courtyard. It was good luck for Stanley that Bellefonds was a Protestant, against the run of probability for his countrymen, since he was able to tell Mutesa the same story about Christianity. The Kabaka was amazed that two men who had never met before could independently give accounts that squared with one another. It was a genuine loss to Stanley when he heard later that Bellefonds had been killed fighting the Bari on his way back to Gordon's headquarters. On his side the Frenchman paid full tribute to Stanley's already remarkable achievements since leaving Zanzibar five months earlier; if he were an Arab he would still be floundering through Ugogo.

On 14 April Stanley informed Mutesa that he had to return to see how his expedition was faring at Kaduma's. The Kabaka was sorry to see him go; his encounter with his fourth white man had left him both stimulated and content. With Bellefonds he returned to Usavara (Murchison Bay). There he said goodbye to the Frenchman and set off along the western shore of the lake, aiming to return to Kagehyi, where his men were camped, after a complete circumnavigation of the lake. Mutesa had assigned Stanley thirty canoes under the command of his admiral Magassa, but Magassa, a notorious prima donna, was not ready to sail on the 17th. He suggested that Stanley would do better to go on without him, while he assembled the promised canoes from the Sesse people. Taking some of the Ganda with him as an escort, Stanley set out to explore the 'Alexandra Nile' and the Ripon Falls on the north-west coast before sailing due south.

Once out of Mutesa's domains, Stanley began to encounter sharp signs of hostility. At Makongo on the coast of Urongora he was menaced by a war party. In face of such a welcome he withdrew to Musira Island 3 miles away. There he threw off the troubling company of his undisciplined Ganda escort by allowing himself the luxury of a quiet stroll in the woods. Next day Magassa's standard was sighted fluttering in the breeze; he appeared to have assembled the canoes promised by Mutesa. Stanley signalled to him to follow and cast off. Magassa acknowledged the signal and promptly ignored it. Alone again, Stanley put into Alice Island, where his men at once despoiled the local fishermen of their catch. To avoid bloodshed Stanley had to restore the stolen goods and compensate the fishermen. Camped in the shadow of a 50-foot basalt cliff, Stanley worked hard to establish good relations with the people of Alice Islands. The islanders were friendly enough but their prices were exorbitant. Stanley decided there were better pickings to be had elsewhere. After vainly waiting for Magassa until noon on 28 April, he set course for Bumbire Island.

They reached the island after sunset in another tropical downpour. They anchored under the lee of the island in the darkness and huddled there wretchedly all night, cold, hungry and miserable. Bumbire was a large island, 11 miles long by 2 miles wide, hilly, clothed in short grass and with a large population of some 4,000. As Lady Alice drew into the shore next morning, they were assailed with war cries. Stanley's inclination was to shove off again, but his men were hungry and he yielded to their blandishments.

No sooner had the keel of the boat grounded than the Bumbire people rushed it and dragged it high and dry on to the shore. Literally scores of tribesmen were needed to do this, as combined boat, crew and baggage weighed more than 4,000 pounds. Stanley's natural instinct was to shoot it out then and there. He raised his revolver to fire but Safeni, wisest and most diplomatic of his Zanzibari bodyguards, counselled him not to. Unconvinced, Stanley sat down in the stern sheets and awaited the crisis he was sure would break, for all around him the locals were yelling and screaming with demented fury.

Negotiations for hongo commenced amid this angry tumult. For three hours Safeni bargained with Shekka, the Bumbire chief. After viewing the cloths and beads on offer, Shekka retired to consider. He returned with a promise of food in return for large doti but immediately showed his treachery by ordering his warriors to seize the boat's oars. He then began again to talk emolliently, but Stanley guessed that it was only a matter of time before the Bumbire repeated the performance, this time with the guns. He continued to negotiate through Safeni, master of tongues and dialects. First he promised twenty cloths for the return of the oars, then offered to make blood-brotherhood with Shekka. Both offers were refused.

At 3 p.m. Stanley's worst fears were realised when Shekka and 300 warriors appeared in war paint at the brow of a hill no more than 300 yards from the Lady Alice. Presently drums were heard beating the call to arms. More tribesmen appeared daubed in paint. Shekka sat on the ground and began to exhort his people. When he had finished, fifty of the boldest rushed down to the water's edge to admonish Stanley to prepare his guns, as Shekka was coming to cut his throat. They bore off the Zanzibari drum as a trophy. While they were occupied in showing this triumphantly to Shekka, Stanley shouted to his men to push the boat into the water. With a desperate heaving effort, the eleven-strong crew lifted it off the ground and shot it into the water. The impetus of the craft into the lake bore them all quickly into deep water.

The Bumbire people, meanwhile, uttering a furious howl of disappointment and baffled rage, came running like dervishes towards their canoes at the lakeside. Stanley discharged his elephant gun, loaded with two large conical balls, into their midst. He then pulled one of the crew out of the water and told him to help his floundering comrades aboard while he kept the enemy at bay. He next fired his double-barrelled shot-gun, loaded with buckshot. The roaring explosion from this did terrible damage. The tribesmen fell back up the slope of the hill. It was now time to get Lady Alice out of the cove before the warriors manned their canoes and sealed off the exit.

Stanley ordered his men to tear up the seats and floorboards and use them as oars. They began to paddle away while Stanley picked off the most prominent of his pursuers with the deadly elephant gun. Among the first to fall victim was Shekka's war chief. On clearing the cove they were intercepted by two more canoes full of warriors, shooting out of another inlet. Stanley let them approach to within 100 yards before unleashing a killing fusillade from the elephant gun, now loaded with explosive balls. Four volleys were enough to kill five men and sink both canoes. The enemy sheared off, having taken casualties later discovered to be fourteen dead and wounded.

Yet even as they seemed to be reaching safety, Stanley's men came under attack from a wholly unexpected source. Two large hippos dashed on them open-mouthed. Stanley dispatched one at10yards' range and wounded the other. From the shore the watching tribesmen hooted with derision and frustration. 'Go and die in the Nyanza!' They salved their wounded pride by firing a few arrows at the vanishing Lady Alice; these dropped harmlessly into the water.

But the danger was not yet over. It was 5 p.m., they had four bananas between twelve men and had no idea where to go. All night, all next day and the following night they paddled, out of sight of land, battered by gales and surrounded by crocodiles ready to devour them if the storms capsized the boat. Even if they were wrecked on an uninhabited island, they would surely die of slow starvation. Stanley always regarded the day after the first Bumbire encounter as the most desperate of his life.

By the morning of 30 April the dozen-strong party had had just a third of a banana and a cup of coffee each since 10 a.m. on the 27th and had rowed sixty-eight hours in the meantime. Exhausted and in desperation they made landfall at 2 p.m. on an island christened Refuge Island by Stanley. The wangwana made a fire while Stanley and Safeni scoured the island for food. Stanley managed to shoot a brace of ducks; his men meanwhile had uncovered bananas and berries. That evening they feasted on duck, banana, berries and coffee: 'The tobacco gourd and pipe closed one of the most delicious evenings I ever remember to have passed.'

Next morning Stanley found himself feverish, the result of rain, famine and exposure. He rested a day on Refuge Island before the expedition paddled on through calamitous waters and freak waves in Speke Gulf to haven at Kagehyi. They reached home base after a fifty-seven-day absence to hear bad news on a number of fronts. Frederick Barker had died twelve days earlier, foaming at the mouth and breathing painfully at the end. Frank Pocock, who conducted the burial service, felt very lonely as the only white man in charge of 153 wangwana. He himself had been very ill with fever, which he tackled by lying on hot stones and drinking brandy. In addition, there had been a serious threat to the expedition from two different directions. First there was a conspiracy to attack the camp and pillage the stores, led by Kaduma's brother Kipingiri and Kurrereh, chief of Kyenzi. They tried to inveigle Manwa Sera into the plot, but he divulged it to Pocock, and the whole scheme aborted when Kaduma, for all his inebriation, decided to remain loyal to Stanley. Then fears arose among the men that Stanley would not return. The Zanzibari Msenna had declared that he would lead sixty members of the expedition back to Unyanyembe on 6th May; Stanley's timely advent nipped this scheme in the bud.

All in all, though, Stanley had grounds for his hearty congratulation of Frank Pocock on the way he had handled things in his absence, especially the way he had got on to such good terms with Kaduma. The wangwana were well fed and the differential dietary experiences of Pocock and Stanley revealed themselves in weights of 162 pounds and 115 pounds respectively; Pocock's complexion was the colour of milk while Stanley's resembled that of a Red Indian. Not surprisingly after his privations, Stanley went down with fever and was laid up for five days.

When he had recovered, Stanley learned with petulant impatience that Magassa still had not arrived with the thirty canoes promised by Mutesa. Having cleared up most of the problems relating to Lake Victoria, Stanley was eager to press on to Ujiji and Manyema, but the route westward was said to be impassable because of the continuing Mirambo wars. King Rwoma, lord of the Zinza state of Bukara from 1864 to 1895 (when he was killed fighting the Germans), an ally of Mirambo, was said to regard white men as 'bad medicine' on the basis of some tall stories retailed to him. A tentative overture was met with the response that Rwoma would fight him if he came that way.

Accordingly Stanley tried to obtain canoes locally for the passage to Uganda and thence westward. His first act was to send Pocock to treat with Lukongeh, ruler of Ukerewe, for the purchase of such canoes. Lukongeh was an amiable though wily ruler who managed to live at peace with the whites for years before the Germans defeated and deposed him in 1895. But Pocock was the first white man Lukongeh had ever seen. After promising him canoes, he kept him hanging around his kraal for days of infuriating delay. The mission finally aborted when Lukongeh made an offer of canoes with crews; Stanley had ruled this offer out in advance in his instructions to Pocock, for fear of outbreaks of fighting between the Ukerewe men and the Zanzibaris.

Stanley, who had been racked with fever during Pocock's absence - but had still managed to shoot an 11-foot long boa constrictor that slithered into camp - saw there was nothing for it but visiting Lukongeh himself. He crossed the Speke Gulf to the Ukerewe capital of Msossi and on 31st May came face to face with Lukongeh. The king received him on a knoll on a plain, seated on a throne, surrounded by hundreds of spearmen and archers. Light-coloured and affable, aged about twenty-eight, Lukongeh recalled Mutesa in his conspicuous robes of red and yellow silk and damask cloth. He proved as interested in matters European as the Kabaka (and professed the same 'expedient' interest in Christianity), even though he later admitted that Stanley lost caste when he told him that the USA had no king or queen.

Stanley came straight to the point. He wanted the canoes without strings, not subject to the whims of Ukerewe oarsmen. If that was impossible, he wanted a cast-iron commitment from the king that his men would take the

Anglo-American expedition to Uganda along the Uzinza coast. At first Lukongeh alleged that all his canoes were rotten and he did not want the responsibility for white men drowning on Lake Victoria. But when he came to Stanley's tent surreptitiously and saw the trade goods spread out on the floor, he became keen to trade and promised that he would have his canoes. He asked his guest for the magical powers of the Europeans; when Stanley refused, the king merely interpreted this as 'playing hard to get'.

On 6th June the king again visited Stanley secretly at night with his chief counsellor. He proposed that thirty canoes, with two oarsmen each, should accompany him back to Kagehyi on the pretext of accompanying the whole expedition back to Ukerewe. Once there, Stanley should seize the canoes and the paddles. This was the only way the king could accommodate Stanley's wishes, for if he ordered his men to Uganda, they would not even go as far as Kagehyi. But as an earnest of his good faith Lukongeh offered his nephew as a guide bver the perilous waterway to Uganda. So it was that next day Stanley returned to his base with twenty-seven canoes.

Once at Kagehyi, he ordered the wangwana to seize the canoes and oars. Then he issued an ultimatum: either the rowers could accompany them to Uganda or they could return home in relays; he would allow them just four canoes for the homeward passage. At this, and misunderstanding the presence of Lukongeh's nephew in the white man's party, the Ukerewe men sprang to arms. Finding themselves staring down the barrels of massed Sniders, they quickly desisted. None of the forty-five men volunteered for the onward journey to Uganda but accepted the four canoes for home relay.

Stanley now prepared to take two-thirds of the expedition across the lake to Uganda. He provisioned for a long voyage at a grain auction and recaulked and replanked Lukongeh's rotten canoes; the king, it seemed, had not been exaggerating when he said that his canoes might take the white man to the bottom of the lake. Yet on 20th June the expedition was ready to sail: 150 men, women and children were embarked, together with 100 loads of cloth, beads and wire, eighty-eight sacks of grain and thirty cases of ammunition.

The first day on the lake brought them close to utter catastrophe. Stanley was at first delighted with the way his men had picked up the art of paddling. But as they tried to 'island hop' among the Miandereh group, the waves began to make up and they found themselves rowing against an increasingly heavy swell as a light gale began to blow. Intense darkness overtook them; they paddled on in the inky blackness by the light of wax tapers. It was impossible for one boat to see another but they kept in touch with shouts and the measured, rhythmic plash and beat of oar and paddle. Now and then Stanley waved a flambeau through the dark wastes as a beacon. After three hours of this tentative progress, the first cries of alarm went up. 'The boat, the boat!' came the shout, as if from drowning men. Locating the sinking canoe, they could discern the heads of several men swimming away from the rotting wreck. Stanley ordered the men taken aboard the Lady Alice. A box of ammunition and 400 pounds of grain had gone to the bottom with Lukongeh's putrid canoe.

Half an hour later another canoe went down. This time five guns and four sacks of flour were lost. When the survivors were redistributed in the remaining boats, they brought the teetering craft to the very edge of capsize. If the winds increased in velocity all would be lost, for the Lady Alice was already up to its gunwales, with a complement of twenty-two men and thirty loads. Stanley altered course for the nearest of the islands. Across the Stygian gloom he bawled his latest orders. If any more canoes sank, the men were to jettison the cargo (but not the guns) and cling to the wreckage until he could devise means of rescuing them. If anyone lost his gun, he would be left to drown.

Almost on cue, two more canoes at once began to sink. After reiterating his orders, Stanley commanded his oarsmen on the Lady Alice to haul for the shore. An hour's heroic, superhuman pulling at the oars brought them to landfall on one of the Miandereh isles. Quickly disembarking men and goods, the Lady Alice set off into the lake to pick up survivors. Two of the most weathered canoes accompanied her. By this time there had been a veritable epidemic of sinkings. But the recovery rate of Lady Alice was superlative. All men, women and children in the water were brought to safety, and some of the rotten canoes were even refloated and taken in tow. All told on that dreadful night the expedition lost five canoes, five guns, a case of ammunition and 1,200 pounds of grain - a truly devastating setback palliated only by the absence of all human loss. Stanley conceded that his action in leaving men in the water for two hours, at the mercy of any cruising crocodiles, might have appeared inhumane, but he faced the possibility that the entire party could be lost in mid-lake if the Lady Alice had become overloaded and foundered.

After a halt next day to recaulk and patch up the canoes, they made their way gingerly to Refuge Island - a slow, careful seven-hour paddle. Stanley left behind the third of the party that could not be accommodated on the canoes with instructions to negotiate peace with the people of Ito and Komeh Islands, who had been hostile during his circumnavigation. These negotiations were successful and within days the whole party was reunited on Refuge Island, where Stanley was pleased to see his people going over every inch of their canoes in minute examination.

Leaving Pocock and Manwa Sera with forty-four men to construct a defensive stockade on Refuge Island, Stanley set out for Kagehyi to bring back the remainder of the expedition. He took the Lady Alice, seventeen canoes and 106 men. Pocock spent the time until his leader's return hunting and shooting crocodiles, for which species he had picked up Stanley's aversion. His men even managed to find a nest of fifty- two crocodile eggs on which they feasted - Pocock found them very indigestible, with the size and texture of a goose's egg.

Stanley's party meanwhile was caught in yet another storm, in which three canoes and thirteen men became separated. Two of them made landfall in Lukongeh's country, whence he returned them to Kagehyi; the other canoe and crew, after getting to land, deserted across country to Unyanyembe. On arrival at Kagehyi in July, Stanley made a fortunate purchase of a thirty-seater canoe he dubbed 'the hippopotamus'. But then he had to confront two ticklish situations in quick succession. First, a fight arose among the wangwana which left two men dead from stabbing. Kaduma and the Zanzibari NCOs decreed the death sentence for the two culprits, but Stanley intervened and commuted this to 200 lashes apiece followed by six months in chains. Next he was alerted that Kaduma had been listening to his brother Kipingiri and was disposed to acquiesce in a kidnapping of the white man. Stanley pre-empted this by not telling the chief when he was leaving, then shoving off before every last item had been loaded.

The journey back to Refuge Island was uneventful. The entire expedition was reunited on 11th July, and Stanley found that Pocock had wrought wonders of diplomacy with the locals. Once he tasted his firepower and saw the strength of his fortifications, Kijaju, ruler of Kome Island off the Zinza coast, made friendly overtures and brought gifts. The relief afforded by this good news allowed Stanley to relax; the pent-up stress burst out, prostrating him with a five-day bout of fever. But at least the seven days on Refuge Island put the expedition in good hearts. After exploring the island from top to bottom, his men had located copious supplies of fruit and wild dates. Stanley's real problem continued to be the canoes; after discarding the rotten ones he had only fifteen seaworthy craft left.

On 18th July, following a feast in honour of Kijaju, with frenetic moonlight dancing a feature, Stanley took the king's guides with him over to the uninhabited island of Mahyiga, the most southerly of the Bumbire group. Then he ferried the expedition over to this foothold in relays while he pondered what to do about the menace of Bumbire, on the flank of his route to Uganda. As they entrenched their camp, they were reconnoitred by their old enemies from Bumbire. Stanley addressed them through Kijaju's guides. He demanded that Shekka return the stolen oars; the Bumbire scouts replied that Magassa now had them and had taken them back to Mutesa's court. The rumour was current that the white man had been slain and Magassa believed it.

Attitudes hardened over the next few days while Manwa Sera gradually brought over every last man from Refuge Island. Another Bumbire canoe approached their redoubt on 23rd July and its occupants showed their contempt in the well-understood African way by throwing up water in the air with their paddles. Stanley decided on a draconian response.

In the feudal hierarchy of Lake Victoria, Antari, king of the Ihangiro, held his lands from Mutesa, while Shekka of Bumbire in turn was Antari's vassal. Stanley decided to use this hierarchy ruthlessly. Antari had received orders to provision the Anglo-American expedition from Mutesa and had passed these on to the people of Iroba, neighbours of Bumbire. Stanley took thirty-five heavily armed men to Iroba, placed their chief and two elders under arrest and announced that they would be released when Shekka was given up. The ruthless scheme worked. On the evening of 27th July the Iroba brought in Shekka and his two sub-chiefs; Stanley had to interpose himself to prevent his men from murdering the hostages.

Interrogation of Shekka revealed another twist in the skein. He told Stanley that Antari himself was preparing a large force to attack the expedition. Sure enough, next day a large force of Antari's men arrived to treat. Stanley allowed the armed envoys to land, under the watchful covering of Pocock and his riflemen. Antari's emissaries warned Stanley that in no circumstances would the king allow the expedition to proceed to Uganda. Stanley pointed out that he was the Kabaka's friend, reminded them of Antari's feudal obligations, and gave them until noon the next day to bring word of a safe-conduct, otherwise he would take Shekka and the others on to Mutesa to stand trial.

It is important to be clear that at this stage in proceedings Stanley's later justification for the attack on Bumbire held good: viz. that he dared not attempt the perilous passage to Uganda in rotting canoes with such an enemy on his flank. He was still thinking of the dreadful experience the night the canoes sank on the lake and running it together with his earlier armed clash at Bumbire to produce a hypothetical picture of unparalleled catastrophe. But this excuse ceased to hold good once large numbers of Mutesa's Ganda appeared in their war canoes to assist him. The first of these allies was Sabadu, with six canoes, sent by the Kabaka to learn the truth of Stanley's alleged death on the lake. Then there arrived eight more canoes under Mkwanda and two under Kytawa. Including his own force, his allies at Komeh and Ukerewe, plus the 250 Ganda arrivals, Stanley could now muster 470 fighting men, more than enough to overcome both Bumbire and Ihangiro. By the end of July his only worry was the food supply; he could no longer legitimately allege that he feared an enemy flank attack.

Stanley's justification for his assault on Bumbire was therefore bogus. But the later criticisms of him for gratuitous aggression missed the dimension of face-saving involved in the complex manoeuvres during these days of late July and early August. Confident of his overwhelming military power, Stanley sent a message to Antari, offering to release Shekka and the other prisoners in return for a token payment of five bullocks and a number of spears and billhooks. This was letting the Ihangiro king off very lightly, but Antari ignored the offer. After waiting for three days without an answer, Stanley was infuriated to receive a defiant message that Antari would attack the expedition if the prisoners were not given up at once. In Stanley's mind that settled matters. Sabadu and Mkwanda were still dubious about the benefits of an attack, but then the Bumbire people played into Stanley's hands. A Ganda reconnaissance mission sent to the island was repulsed, with one dead and eight wounded. Sabadu and Mkwanda at once threw in their lot with Stanley and agreed on a punitive assault.

4th August was the date set for the chastisement of Bumbire. At noon after a morning gale, a force of fifty riflemen and 230 spearmen set out in six large canoes and the Lady Alice. Twenty rounds each had been distributed to the riflemen, all handpicked Zanzibari sharpshooters. Stanley had rehearsed his warriors thoroughly in the planned tactics. He intended to feign a landing at a point where the sun would be shining in the enemy's face, then lure him on to killing ground under his guns. After two hours they pulled close to the 'hated isle'. The flotilla made as if to land, then rowed round the cove and, steering under the lee, entered a bay on the western side of the island. Through his field-glasses Stanley could see the heights of the hilly ridge crowded with his old foes. Panning along the shoreline, he also detected the main body of the Bumbire tribesmen in a plantain grove on top of the most southerly hill.

Having now enraged the enemy by exposing his battle plan, Stanley ordered his men to paddle slowly for the opposite shore of the bay, where there were bare slopes with short green grass, as if intending to make landfall there. The stratagem worked perfectly. The Bumbire warriors raced them to the shore to contest the landing. All this took about half an hour. At the end of that time there were knots of tribesmen poised around every conceivable beachhead.

Stanley came within 100 yards from the shore before forming battle line. He ran up both the Union Jack and the Stars and Stripes, then anchored the canoes together so that they faced broadside to the beach. He ordered a first volley fired at a group of about fifty warriors. Several at once fell dead and wounded. Seeing the danger of standing together, the tribesmen separated. Some advanced to the water's edge, slinging stones and shooting arrows; others retreated into the cane-grass, from which they discharged showers of arrows, all of which fell short. Stanley ordered the canoes to edge closer and delivered the next broadside from a range of 50 yards. A crashing, winnowing volley ripped the enemy ranks apart.

The slaughter was terrific. Frank Pocock was one of those who mowed down the 'savages' just out of bowshot: 'They were very thick on the shore but in ten minutes they were thinned [sic] from the fire of our rifles.' After an hour of the most excruciating pounding, the warriors began to withdraw on to the slopes, out of range. As a coup de grace Stanley again feigned a landing, then, as the Bumbire fighters raced back to close in combat, delivered a slaughterous volley that dropped them in their tracks.

Now the Ganda spearmen screamed and pleaded to be allowed to land to finish off the enemy. With supreme discipline Stanley restrained them. Instead he had the interpreter announce to the stricken Bumbireans that it would be ever thus if they attempted again to insult white men and they could enjoy a repeat performance next day if they wished. There was cruelty in the taunt, but it was not just Stanley's blood that was up. Both the Ganda and the wangwana whooped and yelled with triumph. Just two of their number had sustained bruises from the rock-throwing. On the shore they counted at least forty-two enemy dead and over a hundred wounded.

Maimed and lamed warriors could be seen limping off up the hillside.

They returned to base that evening in a state of euphoria. Next day Stanley embarked 685 souls for the voyage to Uganda. At 9 a.m. they were again off Bumbire and a warning shot was fired to call the people to parley. The enemy, now well and truly cowed, signalled that they had no further hostile intentions. Stanley announced that he was taking Shekka on for trial before Mutesa. 'Old Shekka the king viewed his island as he passed it with sad, regretful eyes, and at the sight of it I felt more than half inclined to land him on the shore and then and there forgive him. Had he shed one tear I should have done so, or had he asked me, but the captive king, though sad-looking, was mute and tearless.'

The news of the fearful chastisement of Bumbire travelled fast. For the next five days, as they plied along the coast to Dumo in Uganda, they were well received by excessively friendly chiefs. Arriving off the mouth of the Alexandra Nile at Dumo, having lost five guns and a case of ammunition and one drowned man when a canoe capsized, Stanley learned that Mutesa was now waging war against his old enemies the Waruma. Frank Pocock, it seemed, was destined never to lay eyes on the Kabaka. Once again Stanley left him in charge of the camp while he himself went on ahead. But his long detailed list of instructions, even down to fire drills, shows the perennial Stanley dislike of delegating authority. There is something irritatingly patronising about his parting words: 'As you value our success, our common safety depends upon your sleepless vigilance and diligence in my absence. P.S. My last words are: Watch and sleep not over your duty and it will be for your benefit in the future.' Pocock, as it turned out, found it extraordinarily difficult to maintain discipline during Stanley's absence. His bouts of fever made it impossible for him to obey his orders to the letter. Safeni's wife was egregiously insubordinate and insolent. There were daily squabbles over food. The wangwana tried to raid the arsenal for ammunition, against strict orders to the contrary.

Hastening to the capital meanwhile, Stanley found that Mutesa had already gone on ahead to the seat of war. For the rest of August Stanley marked time. He confirmed that the Ripon Falls were the only northerly outlet from the lake, and had the sad experience of burying Jack the bull-terrier after it had been gored by a cow; only Bull the bulldog was left of the original canine quartet. After pondering his next step, he concluded that the obvious wisdom of holding aloof from Mutesa's wars was outweighed by the thought of the future assistance the Kabaka could give them. Accordingly he decided to catch up with Mutesa at the war theatre.

There seemed even greater warmth in the Kabaka's greeting this time. Stanley was received in state by thousands of men standing in line. Mutesa made lavish promises of opening the area between Uganda and Lake Edward for his explorations. At the end of August Stanley watched as his protector reviewed his army, bound for the Waruma front. An estimated 150,000 warriors (Mutesa would never let Stanley inspect his muster- rolls) filed past the king, followed by some 100,000 women and camp- followers.

'Mutesa's face was covered with a whitish paste, his head was uncovered and he wore a blue check dress.'

Stanley raised the issue of his captives. Sabadu confirmed his story of Bumbire in every detail. Mutesa was willing to order the immediate execution of Shekka and the others, but Stanley argued that the recalcitrant Antari should be given time to ransom them. This unwonted compassion from Stanley was not unconnected with the Bible lessons he read to the king. Mutesa evinced a taste for theology and was particularly enraptured by the notion of angels. A quotation from the Bible on this subject led to an immediate order from the king that the entire 'Good Book' be translated into Swahili. Ecstatically announcing the ruler's sure and certain conversion, Stanley at once sent back to Pocock to have the copy of the Book of Common Prayer they had in camp sent 99 on.

But Mutesa's pragmatic reasons for 'conversion' soon became clear when he explained to Stanley that since the white man's technology was superior to that of the Arab, it followed that his 'magic book' must be superior to the Koran. This was a particularly urgent consideration to the king, since his war with the Waruma was not going well. Although Mutesa had overwhelming superiority on land, his enemy held the advantage on water and had just inflicted a humiliating defeat on the Buganda navy. 'Turn the other cheek' had not worked well; a peaceful embassy sent to the Waruma had been slaughtered to a man. It was in Stanley's interest in a double sense to assist the Kabaka in his war, both to restore Christian credibility and to enable himself to get away to Lake Tanganyika and the west.

Stanley therefore advised Mutesa to build a causeway to link the headland of Nakaranga with Ingira Island. But this was constructed ineptly. A determined attack by the Ganda on Ingira Island was beaten off. There followed four fiercely contested battles on the lake, with great loss of life. Although the Ganda showed greater battle skills and coolness under fire, they were consistently overwhelmed by the greater courage of the Waruma. In desperation Mutesa asked Stanley for his guns and ammunition. The request was refused, on obvious prudential grounds: 'because I should be as one committing self-murder.'

By the beginning of October the war had settled into a stalemate of attrition. Stanley made a final attempt to win the campaign for Mutesa by lashing together a number of canoes, building a platform over them and converting the whole into a sort of floating fortress. A bristling oblong stockade, 70 feet long by 27 feet wide, impervious to enemy spears, drifted towards the Waruma. After embarking 214 warriors inside the 'wooden horse' Mutesa presented the enemy with an ultimatum. The fortress was advanced to within 50 yards' range and the Waruma given the option of surrendering or being hacked to pieces. This did the trick. On 13th October the Waruma agreed to honourable peace terms.

Stanley's stock with Mutesa was never higher. The Kabaka pledged an escort of 500 spearmen for the expedition's journey to Lake Albert.

Stanley, absurdly overrating the extent to which the Kabaka's writ would run in Unyoro, felt that he had already as good as achieved his objective: 'We shall travel as safe as though we were in bed at home.' Mutesa he described as the most intelligent African he had ever known; his few faults were a susceptibility to flattery and (significantly in Stanley's book) 'he is too fond of women.' But relations between Stanley and Mutesa plummeted after a dreadful incident on 15th October. A fire mysteriously began in the Kabaka's camp; Stanley and the able-bodied escaped up the mountain slopes but hundreds of women and children were trampled or left to die in the conflagration. Stanley suspected Mutesa of having deliberately started the fire, in frustrated rage that his 'cowardly' armies had not been able to annihilate the Waruma, and let his suspicions be known. Such was the regard Mutesa entertained for him that he actually gave categorical assurances that he had not compassed or contrived the fire.

But Stanley was convinced that he had witnessed the dark side of his genial host, and determined to depart as soon as possible. On returning to Ugalla with Mutesa, he was delayed for a few days with another bout of fever. Then, after a formal leave-taking, he set out for Dumo, where he was reunited with Pocock after more than three months' absence. The entire expedition was in good heart at the tidings that Mutesa's warriors would clear passage for them to Lake Albert. Stanley ought to have been warned of the limitations of Ganda power after their poor performance against the Waruma. But buoyed up by the Kabaka's assurances he allowed himself to distrust the evidence of his senses. He was soon to pay dearly for this lapse of judgement.

STANLEY'S impact on Mutesa had been startling and his impressions of Buganda and its people very different from those of other early travellers. It remained to be seen whether he could make the same headway with Kabba Rega and Bunyoro. Seven days after his return to Dumo, Stanley commenced the march towards the rendezvous point with his Ganda escort on the Katonga River. Striking inland from Lake Victoria, they travelled through beautiful valleys of palm trees and villages rich in bananas. Smooth rounded hills were separated by broad grassy vales, teeming with game. They had to wade through many streams and swamps up to their waists in water, ever on guard against the numerous leopards in which this region abounded.

At Kikoma Stanley called a halt and waited for the man he had selected as guide to take the expedition on into Bunyoro. Mutesa had given him free choice, so Stanley had plumped for Sembuzi, one of the most intelligent Ganda chiefs, on whom the Kabaka ordained strict obedience to the white man. Stanley spent the time at Kikoma amassing meat supplies. In a five-day period he shot fifty-seven hartebeeste, two zebra and a waterbuck. The region was fecund with game, being largely void of human habitation both because of the large numbers of lions and leopards who were a threat to human life and because this was a favourite location for raiders from Ankole.

The one dark spot on Stanley's mental horizon was Frank Pocock's continuing propensity to fever. By now Stanley entertained a special regard for his one surviving white companion and he was beginning to regard him as a successful version of Lewis Noe or Edward King. Pocock's mixture of deference and efficiency suited the leader perfectly. 'Frank, you are the coolest man and the happiest I ever saw,' Stanley told him. To the Herald he reported, rather patronisingly: 'He did not look very promising as a companion at first; I thought him rather slow. He has a host of virtues and not one vice, nor shadow of vice. He is a brave, honest, manly, patient young Englishman.' Pocock for his part was gaining in confidence, fevers apart. He thought (with reason) that his disciplining of the men was more judicious than Stanley's and he was proud of the progress he had made in Swahili.

On 12th December guides arrived from Sembuzi. They then essayed the crossing of the Katonga River; it took an entire day and four separate journeys to force the Lady Alice through the reeds. They finally met up with Sembuzi at Ruwewa but the Ganda chief, already late for the rendezvous, further irritated Stanley by insisting on another five-day halt before pressing on to the general rendezvous at Langurwe. Stanley rationalised his impatience by telling himself that at least Frank Pocock could get over his fever. He took his gun and went shooting. There was a skirmish with a hyena on the outskirts of the camp, then he downed an eagle with a nine-foot wingspan.

Christmas 1875 was in many ways as depressing as the Yuletide the year before, but without the rain. At Langurwe, Stanley finally realised that he had been Sembuzi's dupe. Sembuzi had courted Stanley assiduously to get this position as the Kabaka's representative in the journey to Unyoro, but now, far from Mutesa's gaze, he acted more imperiously than the king himself. But Stanley was forced to grit his teeth and bear the impudence of this prima donna; the plain fact was that the Ganda outnumbered the men of Zanzibar twenty to one. The combined force numbered 2,270, with an effective fighting strength of 1,000, a hundred of whom had firearms.

On 2nd January 1876 this force finally crossed the frontier between friendly Buganda and potentially hostile Bunyoro. Stanley claimed to notice an immediate change in the terrain. North of the Katonga was rolling country crisscrossed by tributaries. But across the Bunyoro boundary, on the far side of the Nabwari River, this soft pastoral scenery gave way to rugged, mountainous country. Even the huts looked different, and while bananas were the staple in Buganda, here it was sweet potatoes.

For ten days they trudged through grassland, on permanent alert in case the Bunyoro people attacked. Even simple grass-cutting tasks required an armed escort. The unremitting tension was trying on the nerves. The valour of Kabba Rega's warriors was exaggerated by rumour: they were said to be capable of lying in long grass with their spears and shields then springing up in ambush like tigers. Fleet-footed as deer, they had also trained savage mastiffs to fight for them. Pocock later recalled:

'We travelled for several days, not seeing a single person. They had gone to earth for they are like rabbits, and they live chiefly underground. In time of war they put their cattle and women underground while the men fight. They have large dogs which they train to fight. They also dig elephant pits and holes to catch men. Several of our men were caught in them and went out of sight, but by screaming loud were heard and pulled out.' By 8th January they were on the east bank of the Mpanga River, at an altitude of 4,600 feet, the nights bitterly cold, with thick fog every morning. Ten hours' swift marching took them through an uninhabited strip of Ankole and back into Bunyoro in the district of Kitagwenda to the east of Lake George. On the way they passed through Uzimba, where the country looked like Switzerland, but where the people scattered at their approach and tried to pick off stragglers from the column. They took a few prisoners and released them on condition they went back to the local chiefs and advised them of the expedition's peaceful intentions.

On 11th January the expedition camped on a plateau 1,500 feet above Lake George, a small lake connected to Lake Edward by the Kazinga channel. With difficulty Stanley persuaded Sembuzi to descend to the lake with the sections of the Lady Alice and launch the boat. Immediately large crowds of Bunyoro warriors barred the way. Sembuzi asked leave for the expedition to pass through Bunyoro peacefully. The request was peremptorily refused. The men of Bunyoro pointed out that Kabba Rega was already fighting with the white man (doubtless a reference to skirmishes with Gordon's forward positions in Equatoria); it followed that the newcomers must either retire or fight. Kabba Rega was in alliance with Mutambukwa, king of Ankole, so fighting could have only one result. As the Wanyoro contemptuously expressed it: 'It is true you have come, but tell us how you will get away from here? Can you fly in the air? If not, think of tomorrow and sleep on what we have told you.'

To his anger and astonishment, Stanley realised that Mutesa's promises of safe conduct through Bunyoro and his 2,000 spearmen availed him nothing. Furiously Stanley lashed out at Baker and Gordon for their meddling: 'Ever since Sir Samuel Baker and his Egyptian forces provoked the hostility of the successor to Kamrasi, Unyoro is a closed country to any man of a pale complexion, be the Arab, Turk or European. Besides, Gordon's officers in the north frequently engage the Wanyoro whenever they are met, and thus the hate which Kabba Rega bears to Europeans is not diminishing.' Stanley was largely right. Kabba Rega objected to the presence of large numbers of Ganda from the rival Mutesa on his soil, wasting his substance, and he feared that Stanley's presence indicated a two-pronged attack from the white man, the whole engineered by Gordon, who was even then establishing military posts at Myuli and Masindi. But he did not want unnecessary bloodshed. He was prepared to let the expedition retire to the kingdom of Karagwe to the south.

At this resolute performance from the warriors of Bunyoro, the Ganda began to panic. Sembuzi announced his intention to retreat. Angrily

Stanley insisted on holding him to Mutesa's promise; if he would just get the Anglo-American down to the lake, the Ganda could depart, and good riddance. Sembuzi appeared to agree but then came back with word that lowering the Lady Alice to the lake was impossible: not only was there a sheer 50-foot precipice to the water but the enemy were massing in strength below.

Stanley was still confident that if Sembuzi would just stay with him for two more days, they could launch Lady Alice and find enough canoes for the rest of his party. He sent the wangwana out to find canoes. But at 5 p.m. on 12th January Sembuzi asked Stanley to attend a council of war. There, all the familiar arguments for retreat were rehearsed, and the decision to return to Buganda endorsed unanimously. Calmly Stanley tried to win the Ganda round. But he made no progress. Sembuzi reiterated that it would be difficult enough as it was to get back to Uganda in face of an enemy known to take no prisoners. To stay on even one day more was suicide.

At that Stanley's patience snapped and he railed at the Ganda angrily. He taunted them with being cowards, knaves and traitors. Failing to make any impression on them, he returned to tell his men that there was nothing for it but retreat prior to trying another route. So much for Mutesa's assurance that Kabba Rega would not dare to oppose him if he entered Bunyoro under the Ganda banner. 'Honestly I do not suppose I have been guilty of such a harebrained scheme as this before. Looking calmly at it now, I regard it as a great folly.'

Sullenly Stanley retreated, consoling himself with the new knowledge he had acquired about this utterly unknown region. They marched in compact formation, 500 spearmen in the front, 500 in the rear, with the others in a central cluster. Over the summit of Mount Uzimba they trekked and into the forest. They slept on the grass, hungry and tired, with fires burning all night to keep predators at bay. Sembuzi had to use the whip on his tired men to urge them forward. The Bunyoro tracked them at a safe distance, nudging and nagging the rear. Only once, on 15th January, was there a brief but furious attack on the rearguard, but this was beaten off without loss. At the Katonga Stanley and Pocock celebrated their deliverance by slaughtering a bullock and roasting it - their first meat for fifteen days.

Once across the border, at Kisweri, Stanley and Sembuzi parted company, on the worst of terms. Stanley sent a special courier to Mutesa, outlining the fiasco of the venture into Bunyoro and containing a detailed indictment of Sembuzi's conduct. He had added to his disloyalty in refusing to build a palisaded camp at Lake George by refusing to return three porters' loads of beads given him for carriage. Mutesa replied swiftly, since his prestige had taken a battering. He promised to provide 50,000 men to force passage through Bunyoro. He also informed Stanley that the recalcitrant Sembuzi had been placed in chains and all his property confiscated and ended with an assurance that he would do all he could to further the aims of the expedition.

But Stanley had by now decided that Mutesa's assistance was more trouble than it was worth. Henceforth, he decided, he would rely on himself and himself alone. His next objective was the kingdom of Karagwe. He pressed on southwards to the River Kagera, taking pot-shots at hippo and other big game in the tedious evenings. In February 1876 they crossed the half-mile wide River Kagera, adorned with spear grass, bulrush reeds and irascible hippopotami. On 25th February they were in Karagwe proper, at the Arab township of Kafurro, situated in a deep valley 1,200 feet below the tops of the surrounding mountains and at the source of streams flowing north and east to the Alexandra Nile.

Kafurro's Arab magnates were Ahmed bin Ibrahim, Sayd bin Sayf and Sayd Muscati. They explained to him the politics of the kingdom. Far from being a vassal of Mutesa, as Stanley had imagined, the king of the Haya state of Karagwe commanded the resources of the third important African state in the Lake Victoria region. Mutesa and Rumanika were linked as sovereign rulers in mutual defence treaties. Arab intelligence was first-rate. Ahmed bin Ibrahim had been in Karagwe twelve years and enjoyed excellent relations with both Rumanika, king of Karagwe, and Mutesa. Stanley asked about the prospects of penetrating westward from the state; Ahmed was dubious but offered to accompany Stanley to Rumanika's court to learn the king's disposition.

On 28th February Ahmed and Sayd bin Sayf accompanied Stanley to Rumanika's capital, across a lake the explorer christened Lake Windermere. Rumanika Stanley found even more impressive than Mutesa. Where Mutesa had a volcanic temper, and was nervous and intense, the soft-voiced Rumanika was placid, mild-tempered and kind. Dressed in a red robe, distinctive because of his Roman nose, Rumanika at 6 feet 6 inches towered over the diminutive white man. He was affability itself and gave Stanley leave to explore any part of his domains he wished. He provided him with guides and promised free subsistence.

Elated, Stanley set out with Pocock to explore the region north to Mpororo and south to Ugufu. They launched the Lady Alice on Lake Ruanyara (the one Stanley had dubbed Lake Windermere). After a boat race with Rumanika's men, they commenced the circumnavigation of the lake. Making their way through papyrus walls 9 feet wide, they spent the night among the reeds but were savagely attacked by a cloud of voracious mosquitoes. Rumanika was as good as his word on the subsistence, for Stanley recorded laconically in his diary: 'Food was reluctantly supplied gratis by poor population.'

After circling the lake, they entered the mouth of the Kagera, then descended the river, making careful observations all the way. They entered another lake, Ihema, on the Ruanda coast, outside Rumanika's orbit. Here, as the Arabs had foretold, they were greeted with hostile war cries. Stanley's contact with Ruanda-Urundi on 9-10th March was as fleeting as his twenty-four hours in Ankole two months before.

Next Stanley told Pocock to take Lady Alice back to Kafurro while he visited the hot springs of Mtagata- a two-day march. The relaxed journey to this famous Central African spa enabled him to appreciate the wealth of Karagwe. He counted 900 head of cattle in a single herd. Even more impressive was the abundance of game. In particular the rhinoceros seemed to have a special stamping ground here. On the first day he saw three white rhino and four black. His guides urged him to shoot one but, short of ammunition and not certain of getting in a killing shot, he decided not to court the well-known risks from a wounded rhinoceros. However, next day his men complained of the shortage of meat, and Stanley felt his credibility was at stake. Just before dusk he managed to creep within 50 yards of a double-horned specimen and get a shot through the ear. The pachyderm keeled over dead in an instant.

On 15th March he came at last to the fabled hot springs - a kind of Central African Lourdes: 'Male and female were seen lying promiscuously in the hot pools half asleep, while their itchy and ulcerous bodies were being half cooked.' Such was the stability and peace of Rumanika's domain that Stanley was able to remain at leisure at the springs for three days, with as much unconcern as if he had been taking the waters at a European spa. Ever the Victorian amateur scientist, Stanley bottled some of the water and took it away for later analysis, just as he had done six years earlier in the Dead Sea.

Arriving back at Kafurro on 19th March, Stanley spent a week in affable conversations with Rumanika before getting the king's consent to depart and a brace of guides for the journey to the south-west. Once again Stanley had mightily impressed an African potentate, so that traces of his visit lived on in local lore. But the idyllic interlude with Rumanika had momentarily made him forget the harsh realities of normal African travel. It was something akin to culture shock to find the chiefs on the Karagwe borders as hungry for hongo as ever the Gogo and the Ha were. As usual, Stanley's response to a demand for excessive doti was to press on in forced marches, hoping to find more amenable hosts. But famine in western Usui meant that four days' food ration now cost thirty-two doti of cloth. It was as well that he had acquired a new expertise as a rhino hunter and was able to kill three of the beasts for food.

Stanley was now entering the region of his 1871 expedition to find Livingstone. This brought problems. He shrank from another encounter with his nemesis that year, the Ha, and was hemmed in on another side by the hostile country of Ruanda-Urundi. He decided to strike south to the Malagarazi, hoping that his luck would hold and that he would miss Mirambo, just as he had missed the ruga-ruga chief's great rival Nyungu both in 1871 and in January 1875.

Now came famine and the rains. After being used to trading their cloths for goats, they found that not even millet was to be had for love or money. On emergency corn rations they struggled on, with morale lessening daily. As Pocock remarked: 'What is to be done except march to where we can get food, for the longer we stop here the worse it will be, although it is hard to march under a burning African sun for so many hours hungry, still it is better to go than to starve without a struggle.' On 6 April even the burning sun disappeared. As they traipsed wearily up a hill, a dreadful thunderstorm descended on them. The resultant floods forced them to plough through mud and water up to their waists. A feverish Stanley fell from his donkey into a quagmire and had to be fished out.

Still the hard-driving leader urged them on. He crossed the Nile/ Congo watershed, the dividing line between the basins of Lakes Victoria and Tanganyika, on xo April. Thenceforth their route lay away from the lacustrine territory of Lake Victoria, which had been their home since January 1876. They began to encounter increasing hostility. Chief Makorango sent an emissary to demand their presence. Stanley ignored this and got clear of the kingdom by two days of forced marches. This finally finished off Bull, last of the quartet of dogs. The hardships of these two days provoked another attempted mutiny, which he scotched by reducing the ringleader Msenna to the ranks.

Beyond the famine-stricken Usambiro district Stanley headed for the territory of Urangwa. He felt himself beset on all sides by hostile tribes, all with a reputation for levying prohibitive hongo. Beyond the mouth of the Akanyaru I dared not go, as the natives of Kishakka on the left bank and Ugufu on the right bank are a great deal too wild. I find that the long-legged race inhabiting the countries west of Uganda, Karagwe and Ui have a deadly aversion to strangers. The sight even of a strange dog seems sufficient to send them into a mad rage and paroxysm of spear-shaking and bow-bending. They are all kin to the long-legged mortals of Bumbiri, who sounded the war-cry at the mere sight of our inoffensive exploring boat floating on the Victoria lake.

After receiving a bullock from the chief of Urangwa in return for six doti, the expedition marched on to Serembo, only to hear the frightful news that Mirambo himself was approaching the town from the opposite direction. As he sat in a house once used by Speke, Stanley pondered the possible consequences of meeting the man he had fought against in 1871. A tumultuous welcome and the firing of 'Brown Besses' announced the coming of the black Napoleon. Learning that there was a white man in town, Mirambo asked for the symbolic token of the 'loan' of a gun and said he would not depart until he and the white stranger were friends. Stanley sent him a diplomatically worded reply, stressing that he was a man to be reckoned with. Tell Mirambo that I am eager to see him and would be glad to shake hands with so great a man, and as I have made strong friendship with Mtesa, Rumanika and all the kings along the road from Usoga to Unyamwezi, I shall be rejoiced to make strong friendship with Mirambo also.

On 22 April the two men came face to face. Stanley found Mirambo deeply impressive and very different from his reputation. Expecting someone like Mutesa 'whose exterior would proclaim the man's life and rank', Stanley found Mirambo's meek demeanour disconcerting and at first suspected that he might be the victim of a practical joke. Aged about thirty-five, 5 feet 11 inches tall, carrying not a surplus ounce of flesh, handsome, soft-spoken and open-handed, Mirambo was quiet and unassuming but amply conveyed the iron in his soul. Stanley liked to intimidate African chiefs by staring them out, but Mirambo met his gaze steadily - the first African who had passed that particular test. This, then, was the 'Frederick the Great' of Africa who had paralysed the Arabs in five years of warfare and consequently tripled the price of ivory. Mirambo explained his fighting methods. He liked all his warriors to be very young and unmarried, so that they could travel fast and unencumbered with women. After a long talk in Stanley's hut, Stanley returned the visit at Mirambo's that evening. Mirambo wore an Arab coat, tarbush slippers and carried an Arab scimitar. They made blood-brotherhood, outdid each other in the generosity of the gifts they exchanged and parted on the very best of terms.

Stanley later gave a fuller record of his impressions to Alice Pike:

Throughout all my travels in Africa I have not yet met such disinterested kindness as I have received from the great bandit Mirambo. He had 15,000 muskets with him, all handled by desperate fellows, but the minute their chief embraced me all the savages clapped their hands, and hailed me as a brother of their chief. Mirambo gave me oxen for beef and two mulch cows with calves, and gave me five men to guide the expedition to safety through his country that no stray bandits might molest us. He is tall, large chested and a very fine specimen of a well-made man. Mild featured, nose regular, small mouth and has a splendid set of teeth. He is as quiet as a lamb in conversation, rather harmless looking than otherwise, but in war the skulls which line the road to his gates reveal too terribly the ardour which animates him.

With Mirambo's 'safe conduct', Stanley pressed on with confidence to Lake Tanganyika, still through teeming rain. Able to browbeat the chiefs he met with the terror of Mirambo's name, he faced down the chief of Myonga who robbed Grant in 1861 and at Ubagwe upbraided the chief for his rapacity. Abashed by this eloquence from Mirambo's blood- brother, the chief became generous to the point of sycophancy. But if they could get food, they could not control the rainy season. Again they found themselves wading through mud and water all day long; on the worst stretches, they were up to their necks in water for hours. The men went down with fever, among them Pocock. It was a measure of Stanley's regard for Frank that he consented to spend four whole days waiting in a village for him to recover." The 1871 Stanley of Shaw and Farquahar would never have done so much.

At the beginning of May, learning of the ferocious reputation of the Watuta tribe, Stanley skirted their territory and marched south-southwest at great speed (a forced march of twenty miles) across an extreme strip of the territory. They came to the meeting place of the Gombe and Malagarazi Rivers, normally a plain, but a lake in the rainy season. Still bearing south-south-west they reached the stockaded village of Usagusi on 12th May, then linked up with an Arab caravan at Uvinza.

Uvinza, gateway to the crossing of the Malagarazi, was the scene of Stanley's 1871 confrontation with Nzogera and his son over hongo for the river passage. Rusunzu, the hawkish son of 1871, had now succeeded to his father's throne and proved as rapacious as ever. Having been paid one hongo for normal rights of passage through Uvinza, Rusunzu tried to mulct the expedition for an additional payment for the crossing of the swollen Malagarazi. Stanley pretended to open negotiations, meanwhile telling Pocock to assemble the sections of Lady Alice. Then, at the last moment, they launched the boat and got across without paying anything.

The route to Ujiji now involved a detour if they were to avoid the territory of the dreaded Ha. Strangely enough, the Ha were quite ready to sell food to travellers beyond their border, so that the expedition was well victualled for the journey through the wilderness between Uvinza and Ujiji; what seemed to drive the Ha into extortionate frenzies was the thought of strangers on their sacred soil.

On 26th May Pocock saw a mark cut in a tree by Verney Cameron's expedition. Next day at dawn they espied the waters of Lake Tanganyika from the top of a hill and at 3 p.m. in the afternoon they entered Ujiji, having travelled at twice the normal speed of Arab caravans since leaving Mirambo. Pocock estimated that they had now travelled 1,850 miles by land and 1,600 by water since leaving Bagamoyo.

Ujiji inevitably conjured nostalgic memories of the famous meeting with Livingstone nearly five years before. 'From the fact that the imposing central figure of the human group drawn together to meet me in Ujiji is absent, Ujiji in spite of the beauty of its lake and the greenness of its patterns, seems strangely forlorn and uninteresting.' The absence of Livingstone was not the only depressant. Ujiji was being so battered by the monsoon rains that its shoreline was 250 yards farther inland than in November 1871. Moreover, neither Stanley nor Pocock found a single line from home awaiting them. When a scouting party was sent east to Unyanyembe to see if there were any letters for them there, it promptly deserted. By now, not having heard from her in eighteen months, Stanley must have realised that his romance with Alice Pike had foundered. Not yet admitting this, he addressed her a cri decoeur. 'Heavens and earth, what trick is this fortune has played me? What would you have done in a like case, oh my Alice? Tear your hair, clothes, and shriek distractedly, run about and curse the Fates? I did not do anything so undignified, but I soberly grieved and felt a little discouraged.'

For a week Stanley was laid up with fever. Then, in June, he commenced a circumnavigation of Lake Tanganyika in Lady Alice, leaving Pocock in charge at Ujiji. First he sailed south, along the coastline familiar to him from the first part of the journey to Tabora with Livingstone in January 1872. By 21st June he was near Karema in country pullulating with game: elephant, buffalo, waterbuck, eland, zebra. 'They graze boldly along the water edge and up to this day I have succeeded in bagging three zebra and an antelope.' At Karema he added buffalo to the tally.

They came upon plenty of evidence of the recent presence of the dreaded Ndereh bandits: deserted villages, smoking and gutted settlements, mounds of human skulls. Soon they crossed Livingstone's route at Bisa on his last journey. Finding submerged islands and villages where the flood level of the lake had swept over them suggested to Stanley that, contrary to his hopes, there was no outflow from the lake - which later proved to be the case.

On 7th July they passed the Rufuvu River in a violent gale and three days later ran into elemental violence of another kind: with the cessation of the rains in mid-June the elephant grass, high and thick as cane, had become parched and dry as tinder and now sparked into flame; a tremendous forest fire roared around them on the shore.

Finally on 15th July they camped at the mouth of the Lukuga River. This was one of Stanley's principal targets on the circumnavigation. Cameron had claimed that the Lukuga was an outlet for Lake Tanganyika, but had not sailed all round the lake to verify his hypothesis. Content that he had asserted his supremacy as an explorer over Cameron, his rival as heir to the mantle of Livingstone, Stanley allowed himself to reveal an unwonted charming self: 'Let Cameron's friends, then, rest content, for in this letter I shall have to correct myself, Livingstone and Burton.'

Stanley then proceeded to 'tidy up' Cameron's findings. He met chiefs who had known Cameron and Livingstone, reported on the great changes in physical appearance of the lake since his own visit in 1871, and sent back reams of data on the local geography, fauna and flora. He was particularly intrigued by reports that the Lukuga linked eventually with the Lualaba, for the Lualaba was the key river of the entire Anglo- American expedition, which would unlock the final secrets of the sources of the Nile and Congo.

During the stay at the Lukuga they saw copious evidence of the slave trade against which Livingstone had preached so fervently. Slave caravans passed them, 1,200 strong; the mortality level among the slaves was astronomical and the survivors were weakened and emaciated. By introducing guns to the Wanyamwezi in exchange for slaves and ivory, the Arabs had in effect turned the whole Lake Tanganyika region into a kind of game reserve for slavers. The consequence was that all warlike tribes who resisted this slaving push were unwelcoming to strangers. On 27th July at the Nakasangara river, the Bembe people threw stones at them as a warning not to land. Farther up the western shore of the lake chief Kiunyu replied contemptuously to a request for grain: 'Are we slaves that we should grow grain for your use?'

When Stanley tried to proceed farther north up the western shore of the lake, war canoes began to pursue the Lady Alice. Stanley decided on one of his exemplary 'lessons' with the Winchesters: 'Six shots and four deaths were sufficient to quiet the mocking.' But the hostility of the people in this area made its impact. Reluctantly, he had to concede that his original ambitious project of striking out from Lake Tanganyika at Uzige to explore Lake Albert was impracticable. He heard rumours of Lake Kivu too, but all this territory to the west had to remain unvisited by Europeans for another twenty years.

On 29th July Stanley arrived back at Ujiji after a fifty-one-day, 810-mile circumnavigation of the lake. He found that Pocock had been ill for much of his absence; for the rest of the time he had been depressed, sickened by the everyday cruelty and the casual attitude to human life in Ujiji. A typical incident was when a woman drawing water at the lakeside was taken by a crocodile; Pocock could find no other reaction than a resigned shrug of the shoulders. But more serious from Stanley's point of view than Frank's state of mind was a smallpox epidemic that had broken out while he was away. The outbreak was now accounting for between forty and seventy-five deaths a day. Five of the wangwana had already succumbed and six more were seriously ill. But for the mass vaccination programme at Bagamoyo, the Anglo-American expedition would have been virtually wiped out; and it was the men who had evaded their shots then who were dying now.

Stanley faced a dilemma. If he ordered his men out of Ujiji, he might cause even greater mortality. On the other hand, to stay was to risk decimation. The decision was made for the leader when he went down with fever. He convalesced by writing letters to close friends and to Alice Pike. A letter to Edward Marston, his editor on How I Found Livingstone, enabled him to broach the subject of Livingstone, whose absence continued to haunt Ujiji. Think of the time when you first brought a splendid bit of pasteboard cover, rich in green and gold, whereon was stamped cunningly enough the pictures of two human actors in gold, saluting each other with doffed hats under the waving palms of Ujiji. Think of the reams of paper you have handled on which was written the word Ujiji. Can I think of Ujiji without thinking of Livingstone? Can I think of either without thinking of Marston?

The letter to Alice Pike was one of Stanley's longest-ever 'love letters'. He began by relating some persiflage from Kalulu about her being 'Stanley's girl' and reminded her that by now Kalulu was almost unrecognisable physically. He described the voyage of Lady Alice around Lake Tanganyika and said he thought of her on 4th July, wondering how differently that date would be celebrated in Philadelphia, especially in Centennial year. Then he came to the nub: I have not received one encouraging word from you or any living friendly soul since I left Zanzibar twenty-one months ago. But I do not blame you, the letters were no doubt detained somewhere on the road. Then, my own darling, if by that name I may call you, let us hope cheerfully that a happy termination to this long period of trial of your constancy and my health and courage await us both, that the time may come when we can both laugh at these silent gloomy days to me, both be amused at our experiences, various and different as they are, and that our after lives will never be marred by such a long separation. If one knew that such a happy time would certainly arrive, one might be happy enough now, but we do not know it. The Omnipotent has wisely kept us ignorant, but instead of the wisdom and foresight, he has given us some hopeful hearts and sanguine minds which sustain us equally well and better serve us on such occasions as this.

There are clear hints in this letter of the ambivalence characteristic of the schizoid personality: the hungry desire for intimacy coupled with the fear (or hope) that the writer will not be put to the proof.

At a muster held in Ujiji on 25th August Stanley found that of the 170 men still on his roll thirty-eight had deserted. Of the meagre force left he could trust only about thirty with guns. Morale was low at the prospect of an encounter with the Manyema cannibals. A quarter of the remaining wangwana had to be put under house arrest to prevent their deserting.

The first task was to ferry the expedition from Ujiji to the western shore of the lake. Pocock and the advance party left on 30th August and established base camp at Mtowa on the far shore; Stanley and the rearguard joined them there on 4th September. But there were three more desertions - something that particularly angered Stanley, as he had just spent £350 on six bales of cloth which were distributed to his men as incentive payments. Stanley sent Pocock and Kacheche back to Ujiji to retrieve the runaways.

Pocock's anger at the task assigned to him and his disgust with the routine brutality of Central Africa found expression in a confrontation with a slaver who owned the boat in which the white man crossed back to Ujiji. Finding himself packed like a sardine against the sweating bodies of hundreds of slaves, Pocock cleared adequate space for himself at gunpoint, at the expense of forcing dozens of slaves off the boat and into the bush, whence they decamped into liberty. Once in Ujiji the determined and cross-grained Pocock secured the aid of the governor of Ujiji and was soon recrossing Lake Tanganyika with his prisoners in chains.

Stanley was well pleased with Pocock's exertions, but his ego took another knock on 14th September when Kalulu himself deserted, only to be retaken next day. Stanley realised that it was the Arab settlements that provided the temptation to desert; before coming to Lake Tanganyika they had experienced almost no desertions. Accordingly between 16th September and 6th October he ate up the 200 miles to Manyema country, travelling at an average of nearly 10 miles a day. They passed the most astonishing variety of landscapes: conical hills, hot springs, wooded buffalo country (that afforded plentiful meat); then a long march from Kagongwe in Uvinza to Uhombo, remarkable for the fertility of its groves and its astounding physical beauty. 'It was the most delightful spot we had seen.'

They crossed the watershed between Lake Tanganyika and the Lualaba and entered the region of Manyema on 5th October. Manyema had a dual significance. In the superstitious minds of the wangwana it was the abode of ferocious cannibals. But for Stanley it was the land whose glories Livingstone had sketched for him at Ujiji in 1871, a land, the doctor had said, containing Africa's most beautiful women. Once into the Lualaba hinterland, they encountered the most spectacular scenery yet: 'It is a most remarkable region - more remarkable than anything I have seen in Africa. Its woods, or forests, or jungles, or bush -1 do not know by what particular term to designate the crowded, tall straight trees rising from an impenetrable undergrowth of bush, creepers, thorns, gums, palms, fronds of all forms, canes and grass - are sublime, even terrible.'

In this land Stanley heard his first stories of the mysterious pygmy race who hunted elephants with poison darts, and sighted his first grey Manyema parrot with crimson tail. He found that Livingstone's reputation everywhere in the area was of the highest - a fact confirmed to him by the chief of the Luama tribe Mwana Ngoi, who had known Livingstone during his penetration of Manyema. Contrary to Manyema's fearsome reputation, Stanley found the people of the area friendly, compassionate and humane. They told him stories of gorillas, but from the coughs and growls Stanley heard at night he conjectured that the apes in question were actually chimpanzees.

The aim of the expedition now was to follow the course of the Luama River, where Mwana Ngoi lived, down to its confluence with the mighty Lualaba and thence to the great trading town of Nyangwe. As they left the Manyema area they noticed that the friendliness of the native peoples they encountered rapidly vanished. Between Kabungu and Mtuyu the country was both populous and hostile. They had to proceed with caution, since an entire brigade could have been swallowed up in this country. The tribesmen on the banks of the Luama did not molest them, but followed out of curiosity, being particularly intrigued by their donkeys. They heard themselves being called by different names: sometimes wasambe- a word denoting those like the Arabs, who wore flowing costumes of cloth; sometimes nivema- whites.

On 17th October, beyond Mpungu, they came to the confluence of the Luama with the Lualaba. The 400-yard wide Luama emptied into the pale grey expanse of the Lualaba, almost four times as broad, winding slowly from the south and meandering in a vaguely easterly direction. Before launching his boats on the mighty stream, Stanley decided to visit the Arab post at Kasongo on the Lualaba bank. The lord of Kasongo and the overlord of the entire area 350 miles from the western shore of Lake Tanganyika to Nyangwe was the famous Arab slaver Tippu Tip, whom Livingstone had met in 1867.

Hamed bin Muhammed el Murjebi, known as Tippu Tip, born around 1840 to a family of prosperous Muscat Arab merchants, began his trading career at Unyanyembe under his father's aegis at the age of eighteen. The first Arab to penetrate the forest region west of Lake Tanganyika, by the early 1870s Tippu had a commercial and political empire based on slavery and the ivory trade. His political suzerainty over the 10,000 square miles of Manyema was based firmly on the firepower of his muskets, whose distinctive sound on firing was said to have provided him with his nickname.'

Though nominally subject to the Sultan of Zanzibar, all the Arab potentates of the interior (Unyanyembe, Ujiji, Manyema, Nyangwe) were in fact independent rulers. Far the most important was Tippu Tip. He possessed great political skills and was careful at this stage of his career not to embroil himself with his powerful neighbours, the Luba of Katanga. His commercial acumen was legendary; it was said that through the ivory trade he could convert an initial capital of $3 into $1,000. He had transformed the economy west of Lake Tanganyika from barter to currency; the standard unit of value and medium of exchange was the cowrie bead.

But most impressive of all Tippu Tip's achievements was the way he had transformed Manyema into a slave state that resembled Zanzibar in the pre-Bartle Frere era. As in Zanzibar, there was a three-tiered social system based on slavers, middlemen and slaves. The great slavers like Tippu inculcated aspects of the coastal culture, such as the use of Swahili as lingua franca, even though Arab culture and religion always ran skin-deep in Manyema. The key to the entire edifice of stratification was the wangwana or petits Arabes of the middle tier. Detribalised middlemen, recruited as adolescent males by the Arabs and ritually circumcised, the wangwana spoke a Swahili dialect called Kiungwana. Existing in a twilight world between freedom and slavery, the wangwana were the NCOs of the Arab slavers and controlled the local Africans on their behalf. Their relationship with the Arab overlords was rather like that of the Sicilian gabelotti to the landowners, and they were later to become the cornerstone of Leopold's control of the Province Orientale of the Belgian Congo.

Such was the power of the man Stanley met at Kasongo in October 1876. The anecdote Tippu Tip provides to illustrate their first meeting gives us clues to the character of both men. To overawe this formidable merchant of death Stanley boasted to Tippu that he had a gun that could fire fifteen rounds at once. When Tippu Tip asked for a demonstration, Stanley said it would cost $20-30, the cost of the ammunition. When the Arab gave an Islamically stoical shrug, Stanley relented and gave the desired demonstration of his firepower.

But the most important consequence of the meeting at Kasongo was the information Tippu Tip provided about Cameron, Stanley's putative rival for the charting of the Lualaba River. After leaving England on the would-be definitive RGS expedition, Verney Lovett Cameron had made a leisurely progress through Arica. In August 1873 he had stayed at Unyanyembe in the tembe that Livingstone and Stanley had made famous. It took him until December 1874 to reach Nyangwe, where he prepared for the descent of the Lualaba. But his men had refused to proceed any farther into the unknown Congo; they lacked sufficient canoes and were terrified of the ferocious reputation of the Upper Congo peoples. Tippu Tip himself had advised Cameron that the Congo was impassable; not even he, with his 'hordes', would dare to venture into those dark forests. Faced with this advice, Cameron abandoned his pursuit of the Lualaba and cut across to the west coast of Africa by an easier route taking him through Portuguese territory. This meant that the great task of charting the Lualaba still remained for Stanley to perform.

Since Tippu Tip had accompanied Cameron as far north as Nyangwe for an agreed sum, Stanley thought it might be possible to tempt him farther north as an escort in return for suitable largesse. But the Arab quickly turned his flank by showing Stanley his immense stocks of ivory, thereby demonstrating clearly that he did not need the money. Stanley tried a different tack and appealed to Tippu's prestige. Tippu replied that he would accompany him to Nyangwe as a favour, a gesture of friendship towards the white man. Even this decision caused ructions, as Tippu's lieutenants thought his magnanimity madness.

Stanley then questioned him about the Lualaba and the chiefs who lay along its banks. Tippu's best intelligence was that the Lualaba flowed undeviating northward beyond the ken of trading man. What about Munza, the grand chief of the Mangbetu? Why did Stanley want to know about him, Tippu asked. Stanley replied that he intended to travel north on the Lualaba to Monbuttu, then cut across west to the next watershed, be it the Nile or the Niger or the Congo.

The next days were spent in protracted and arduous negotiations concerning the exact conditions under which Tippu and his men would accompany the Anglo-American expedition. After exhaustive consultations with his lieutenants, Tippu Tip agreed to escort the expedition for sixty days in return for full subsistence for 140 men and a fee of $5,000. There were many conditions attached to the deal. Each camp should be no more than four hours' march from the one before; there should be a day's rest for every two of marching; the money should be payable even if Stanley abandoned his march before the sixty days were up.

While these tortuous negotiations were going on, Stanley discussed with Pocock their future strategy. There seemed no glory in simply following Cameron's southward route to the coast and besides, knowing Bennett, Stanley was sure the Herald would make difficulties over paying the wangwanas' passage back to Zanzibar from the west coast. Their best bet seemed to be to strike north, possibly returning to Zanzibar via Lake Victoria and Kagehyi. Even better might be the route via Munza's territory which would enable them to solve the Lualaba/Nile riddle and return via Gondokoro and Uganda, perhaps meeting Gordon on the way. First, however, they ought to try for a clear resolution of the north/south question. They tossed a coin to decide the matter: 'heads' for the Lualaba and the north; 'tails' for Katanga and the south. The omens were not good. Six times the coin came down 'tails'. When they tried drawing straws, long for the north, and short for the south, the short straws were drawn every time.

These academic lucubration's were interrupted by the news that Tippu Tip had agreed to the sixty-day march. A formal contract was signed, Tippu's men received an advance of cloth and their names were entered on the muster-roll of the expedition at the same rate as Stanley's men. Then for four days they marched through rolling, depopulated country full of ruined villages, sometimes through eight-foot high grass. To the east of them were the conical spurs of the Manyema hills; to the west was a rolling, marshy grassland extending to the Lualaba. The only incident en route was that Kalulu, newly restored to favour, was accidentally wounded by a loaded Snider.

They reached Nyangwe late on 26th October 1876. The farthest outpost of the Zanzibar Arabs, it was perched on a high reddish bank some 40 feet above the Lualaba. Stanley found it riven by factionalism and rivalry between the various Arab slavers based in the town. There appeared to be three main coteries under the domain respectively of Myinyi Dugumbi, Mohammed bin Nassur of Kassessa and Muhammed bin Said of Mamba Mamba, a relative of Tippu Tip. These three had carved up the local area and within a triangle hunted for blacks the way an English country gentleman would hunt for grouse, in a way that horrified Frank Pocock, already distraught at the experience of slavery in Ujiji.

But Stanley found two other Arabs more interesting. One was Abed bin Salim, one of the founders of Nyangwe, who found the discipline of Stanley's wangwana impressive after a march of 338 miles from Lake Tanganyika in forty-three days. The other was Abed bin Juma, who seemed to confirm Livingstone's idea that the Lualaba flowed into the Nile. Stanley also derived some bogus consolation from the peaceful demeanour of the Genia people on the left bank of the Lualaba. But it was a fallacious extrapolation as to what he would encounter later. The Genia were intrinsically pacific, and were also habitually left in peace by the Arabs, since their skill as boatmen made them useful.

During the week spent in Nyangwe Stanley and Pocock virtually rebuilt Lady Alice for the coming voyage on the Lualaba while they continued to ponder their route. Despite Abed bin Juma, Stanley was virtually certain by now that the Lualaba must feed into the Congo, since it was too mighty a river at this southern latitude to be a tributary of the Nile. But he was still undecided whether to follow the Lualaba to the sea or simply follow it north until it swung west before aiming for Munza's with the aim of linking up the spheres of discovery of Livingstone and Schweinfurth. There was much agonising on the point between him and Pocock until 'one midnight we resolved together that it was our duty to try it'. Pocock again tossed a coin and this time the decision favoured following the Lualaba.

But nobody could be certain where the Lualaba ended until its course had been traced. Stanley had earlier told Alice Pike that he would probably reach England in August-September 1877 if he emerged on the west coast, and some three months later if he came out at Zanzibar. Yet his letter to Edward King from Nyangwe revealed a fear that the Lualaba might, after all, be not the Nile but the Niger, in which case he would be lucky to emerge on the ocean before late 1879 b' 1880.

At the final muster on 4th November Stanley counted 146 of his own men, armed with twenty-nine Sniders, two Winchesters, two double-barrelled shotguns and thirty-two percussion-lock muskets. Though only forty of these were reliable shots, Stanley took comfort from the force of more than 500 that Tippu Tip had assembled. Stanley, wrongly as it turned out, could not see how a party nearly 700 strong could be opposed. They planned to travel in two detachments, a land party and a river squadron. The river section would have the advantage since, whereas a porter could carry 50-70 pounds for a maximum of 20 miles a day, a paddler in a trading canoe could transport 140-400 pounds a day twice that distance upstream and four times downstream.

Stanley and Pocock were now (save for a few last-minute wavering) definitely committed to following the Lualaba to the end, lead where it might. Stanley summed up his feelings on the eve of launching into the unknown. Should my opinion be confirmed I should by following the Lualaba so far north, be taking the expedition beyond all power of aid or supplies from any quarter. Such a long distance beyond all calculation would waste every article we could possibly exchange for food. If the mere purpose of this expedition was to cross Africa, with the utmost confidence I declare to you that I could reach San Salvador in six months from Nyangwe; but I should then, like Cameron, have left the question of the Lualaba just where Livingstone left it, to be discussed upon the grounds of each man's opinions. If I merely struck direct west for San Salvador, how could I presume that the Lualaba is the Congo, or that it is not the Congo but the Nile or the Niger - whichever it may be? I should forfeit all right to be heard upon the subject or to be considered as one able to confirm any of the theories broached upon the subject. This would be lamentable .. . But, as neither conjectures, dreams, theories nor opinions will make one positive geographical fact, I propose to stick to the Lualaba, come fair or come foul, fortune or misfortune; and, that I may not be driven back by force, I have recruited the expedition to one hundred and forty rifles and muskets and seventy spears. The desertions and deaths from smallpox at Ujiji had thinned my companions to such a degree that we should have been only a sop for a ferocious tribe ... it must be a very strong tribe indeed that can drive us back now. But what savages cannot do hunger may, if the Lualaba continues running so far north of the Equator. I have ample supplies for six months. Beyond that heaven knows what will become of us if we find ourselves at the confluence of these two rivers, the Lualaba and the unknown river, so far out of the way of supplies, with not a single bead or cowrie to buy food.

Nothing more clearly demonstrates the uncertainty of success entertained even by the man of iron himself.

Chapter Sixteen

IN the 'global village' near the end of the twentieth century it takes an effort of imagination to appreciate that in late 1876 the African region north of Nyangwe was completely unexplored and unknown both to Arabs and white men. Stanley and Tippu Tip were now entering the true 'Dark Continent' - where none but local tribesmen had ever ventured before. The very audacity of his attempt intrigued his followers, who oscillated between terror of the unknown and pride in the courage of the 'little master'. But Stanley himself displayed the insouciance that properly belonged to the unconscious rather than the rational calculation of odds: 'I believe I was made half indifferent to life by my position; otherwise I doubt if I should have deliberately rushed upon what I was led to believe - as my predecessors were - was almost certain death.' So convinced, indeed, were the Arabs of Nyangwe that the white man was bent on a suicide mission that they refused to supply him with canoes.

The great trek into terra incognita began on 5th November. The expedition marched 10 miles over a rolling plain covered with grass. Ahead of them stretched a black wall of tropical forest curving away to the south-east. Even Stanley was rather daunted by the prospect as he stole a last look at green and inviting Nyangwe. Next day they said goodbye to the sunlight and plunged into the forest gloom. Here Stanley made his first mistake. He allowed Tippu Tip's warriors, brandishing flintlocks and bows and arrows, to enter the dark interior ahead of him. These came to an abrupt halt when they encountered the tangled undergrowth of the forest, and those coming behind cannoned into them, throwing the line of march into chaos.

When order was restored, the expedition began to pick its way through 20-foot high undergrowth, fed by a feculent humus of fallen branches and rotten leaves. They marched in permanent twilight, soggy with dew under a fuliginous forest canopy, floundering through ditches formed by rivulets descending to the Kunda River. Their clothes were saturated with moisture. Stanley's white sun-helmet and dungaree felt as if they were weighted with lead. The atmosphere was stifling and sweat oozed from every pore. 'The path soon became a clayey paste, and at every step we splashed water over the legs of those in front, and on either side of us.' Although the main expedition made camp at around 3 p.m. the boatmen did not get into bivouac until dusk, as the sections of Lady Alice had to be driven like blunted ploughs through the depths of the foliage.

8th November 1876 was a date recorded in sorrow by the two white explorers. 'Through dense forest, at intervals we saw an open space, then plunged in the same deep vales and high hills of forest and bush as before,' wrote Pocock. Stanley's impressions were similar. The expedition crawled, tore and scrambled through the damp, dark jungle. The locals were surly and set spooked traps on which several of the men gashed their feet. Once on the crown of a hill they caught a distant glimpse of the Lualaba which seemed to the travellers like the promised land. Then back into the darkness they plunged, into a blackness so inky that Stanley could not see the words he scribbled in his notebook. They arrived in camp half-suffocated by the heavy fetid miasma of the forest. Stanley recorded the day's impressions.

Fearful time of it today in the woods - such crawling, scrambling, tearing through the damp cool jungles, with such height and depth of woods. Once we got a sidelong view from the limited growth of a hill over the wild woods around us which swept in irregular waves towards the Lualaba and of green grass plains on the other side of the Lualaba.

The next day saw more of the same. They tried to cut their way through the tangle with axes and billhooks, so as to clear a way for the boat sections, but they could make it neither wide nor straight enough, as so many forest giants lay prostrate across their track. Another difficult day's work in the forest and jungle. Our caravan is no longer the tight compact force which was my pride but utterly disorganised; each one scrambling to the best of his ability through the woods ... the path being over a clayey soil, is so slippery that every muscle is employed to assist our progress.

By the 10th, in the country of the Regga, the expedition was exhausted, so Stanley ordered a three-day halt. Since Stanley had insisted on following a track through the territory of the warlike Regga, Tippu Tip raised his rate for the job from $5,000 to $7,ooo. Such was the general despondency in the expedition that even the great Arab slaver's morale was low, and it seemed that money alone could palliate it. Certainly the folkways of the Regga were enough to demoralise the most sanguine traveller: so impregnable and secure were they in their forest fastnesses that many of them had never seen the Lualaba all their lives even though it was but 20 miles distant.

When they resumed the march, the straggling problem of the boatmen and the complete absence of food forced Stanley to head for the Lualaba and cross to the western bank. It was taking the twenty-four men bearing the boat sections twelve hours to march 6 miles, so that at this rate every other day would have to be spent resting. The march to the Lualaba finished off Stanley's penultimate pair of shoes; Pocock was already on his last. As he drew the final pair from his stores, Stanley pondered the prospect of barefoot marching on the Congo. It was not inviting, for, as well as the wealth of small grey white-necked monkeys in the trees around them, they encountered other less welcome forest denizens: 10-foot pythons, gigantic puff-adders, and armies of deep-brown 'hot water' ants.

At last, on 16th November, Tippu Tip's patience snapped. Not even the extra money could compensate for the daily agony. He complained of the length of the marches and pointed out that at their present rate of progress sixty camps could take a whole year to achieve. He therefore requested a dissolution of the original contract. Stanley doggedly held him to his word as an Arab gentleman. In that case, Tippu countered, after the sixty marches you must agree that I can take half the force back with me to Nyangwe. Angrily Stanley rejected this as nonsense. Not so, insisted

Tippu: without this number of men I would be torn to pieces by the tribes on my way back. He put it forcefully to Stanley that if he did not agree to an amended contract, he and his men would return forthwith to Nyangwe. Angrily Stanley raged at him. Four hours' march a day would mean that the sixty marches would be equivalent to less than thirty normal days. Tippu Tip seemed to him 'bent on breaking the agreement or making money'. But Stanley's position was weak and he knew it. If the Arab turned back now, the entire Anglo-American expedition would disintegrate through desertion. With supreme difficulty the two men hammered out a compromise whereby Tippu Tip would escort Stanley as far as Kima-Kima on the Rumami River.

On 17th November they left Uregga and entered the territory of Uvinza. On the river bank were the fishermen or Wagenya but ahead lay two warlike tribes, the Songola (Stanley's 'Wabwire') and the Kusu. 'We crossed several lofty hill ridges, separated by appallingly gloomy ravines, through which several clear streams flowed westward, and after a march of eleven miles north-westerly through the dark dripping forests, arrived at Kampunzu.' A 5-mile march through the forest west of Kampunzu brought them to a point at 3°35' south (41 miles north of Nyangwe) where the Lualaba proper ended and a new river began, which Stanley proposed to call the 'Livingstone'. Here the broad stream was 1,200 yards wide from bank to bank. They camped on the bank. The brown wave of the river flowed on, as gentle as a summer's dream, while Stanley contemplated the mysteries and dangers ahead.

That evening he harangued his men to the effect that destiny had led them to this confluence that they might follow the new river to the end. He asked for volunteers to follow the 'Livingstone' to its mouth. Only thirty-eight of the wangwana agreed to follow him; the other ninety-five sat tight-lipped. Tippu Tip and the other Arabs threw their weight into the balance, urging Stanley not to go on to certain suicide.

It was not long before the local tribesmen visited them. Stanley started to bargain for canoes, without revealing that he already possessed the Lady Alice. His overtures were received contemptuously. The Lualaba people told him he would first need a heap of cowrie shells a cubit high. Appearing cowed, Stanley gave secret orders that Lady Alice be made ready. Suddenly he launched it on the river to general astonishment. His sharpshooters trained their Sniders on the shore while Stanley commanded the Wagenya of the islands to appear in camp that evening to make blood-brotherhood. The Wagenya agreed to become blood- brothers provided the ceremony was carried out on their island territory.

Suspecting treachery, Stanley sent Kacheche and a company of men upstream, just four minutes away from the island, while Frank Pocock crossed over to make blood-brothers with the Wagenya. The precaution was justified: the relief force had to intervene quickly when the demeanour of the tribesmen towards Pocock turned nasty. Baulked of an obvious reconciliation with the recalcitrant Wagenya, Stanley decided to land his sharpshooters on the far bank so as to form a beachhead, pending the transfer of the entire expedition. He then floated down past the Wagenya village and called out to them that they were now between two fires, that resistance was useless. The Wagenya appeared to acquiesce in the fait accompli. The next step was to transfer the expedition to the far bank. On 20th November 458 souls with four donkeys and 150 loads of cloth and beads transferred to the right bank. Since the Wagenya still failed to co-operate, Stanley gave orders that all canoes were to be seized.

Next day they discovered that the Wagenya were using Fabian tactics against them, leaving their villages deserted and melting into the forest rather than co-operate. They left behind a series of man-traps for the unwary. Stanley decided to divide his force for the passage downriver. He and thirty-six crack shots boarded the Lady Alice and the few canoes they had acquired, while Pocock, Tippu Tip and the rest of the expedition tracked them from the bank. They floated down the Lualaba to the confluence with the Ruiki. Whenever they approached a village, the inhabitants fled, crying out, 'Wasambye, Wasambye.'

At 3 p.m. on 22nd November they came to the black and sluggish Ruiki, 100 yards wide. Since the land party would be unable to cross, Stanley awaited them here. He built a strong camp and set sentries. The locals offered them food, but it was clear that this was with the intention solely of ridding themselves of their unwelcome visitors.

By the 24th, when there was still no word of the land party, Stanley began to regret that he had divided his force. He decided to take Lady Alice 10 miles up the Ruiki in hopes of finding Tippu Tip and the others encamped there. He left behind a small 'holding' force to guard the camp. By 2 p.m., after ascending the Ruiki for 10 miles, Stanley concluded he was wasting his time and commenced the return to camp. At 3.30 p.m. they heard the distant muttering of gunfire. Rowing at full speed they came to the Ruiki junction to find it blocked by Wagenya canoes, full of warriors in war panoply who were pressing the camp garrison hard. They had waited until word came in that the white man had departed before pressing their attack on the camp, but then, fortunately, had delayed too long before assaulting it. Stanley arrived in the nick of time to save his beleaguered rearguard.

Finding the land party had now become an imperative. Stanley at once sent out Uledi the coxswain and five of the boatmen under cover of night to find Tippu Tip and Pocock. At 4 p.m. next day they returned with news that the main force had fallen foul of the even more formidable Kusu and had lost three men in arrow attacks. Four hours later Stanley was finally able to unite both sections of the hard-pressed and demoralised expedition. He then transported the entire party to the left bank of the Ruiki; an old man was shot by his bodyguard as he tried to repossess a canoe.

On 26th November the united expedition proceeded downriver to Nakanpemba. This time the land and river parties kept in close touch, by visual contact whenever possible, otherwise by drum-taps. The Lualaba was about 1,700 yards wide on this stretch. At deserted Nakanpemba they found rows of human skulls in the streets. Again the locals melted away and had to be taken by force for questioning. The expedition now no longer thought of barter but took whatever it could lay its hands on. In one village they appropriated fifteen goats, though this did not go far among 458 mouths. The diet was supplemented by roasting ears of Indian corn and manioc. Fatigue and food shortages were already depleting numbers, especially among the land division. The attacks came not just from smallpox and dysentery but also from ulcerated feet caused by the entry of thorns and serrated stakes into the soles and shins of the marchers. Stanley was forced to improvise a floating hospital for the sick by lashing together six abandoned and unsound canoes.

They glided below Nakanpemba at a rate of 1V2 knots. Soon they heard the dull murmur of approaching rapids. Stanley ordered the land party to camp for the day while he edged cautiously along the left bank to explore. His reconnoitring took him perilously close to an ambush mounted by about fifty canoes in a hidden creek close to the Lukassa rapids. The enemy canoes were based on an island between the two arms of the falls. Stanley landed ten riflemen and in a brisk skirmish drove his opponents off the island: 'It was most undesirable to have an enemy lurking in the grass or the reeds below the rapids.'

On returning to camp Stanley was alarmed to hear that Pocock had allowed four of his best men to shoot the rapids in one of the hospital canoes. They negotiated two of the falls but were predictably pitched into the water at the third. Though no lives were lost, three of the Sniders were borne away in the swirling waters. To add to this, the enemy canoes began to hover ominously close to the shipwrecked men until a rescue unit under Stanley and Uledi dispersed them. That evening Stanley upbraided Pocock angrily at the camp below the first rapids on the left bank 'with the noise of falling and rushing water all around us'. Yet his rebukes to Manwa Sera were even harsher, so acerbic in fact that the great Zanzibari captain stormed off to Tippu Tip's tent and vowed he would serve the 'little master' no longer.

Again Tippu Tip and the Arabs besought Stanley to turn back. He promised a definite answer next day, but upstaged them by portaging the boat and canoes around the rapids and ascertaining that there were no more falls ahead. They continued to float down the Lualaba until 5th December, making 4 miles a day. The land party again lost contact, but this time Stanley was less fearful as it contained 350 men and 120 guns. Stanley and the river party meanwhile continued unavailingly to make overtures to passing canoes. The Lualaba at this point would suddenly narrow to 800 yards if a large island lay athwart it, only to broaden again to 1,700 yards. It was characterised by many sharp bends with frequent dangerous whirls and broad patches of foam on its face. At night they camped at the communal market-places on the bank which no chief could claim as his own - most of them wide grassy spaces under the shade of mighty trees.

The river continued to run for most of its length in two broad streams, each about 1,000 yards wide, separated by large islands.

On 5th December Stanley's progress was halted by rainstorms and food shortages. At Ikondu he faced the first of the many river battles he fought during his progress down the Lualaba-Congo. As he explored the right bank of the Lualaba, he was greeted with a shower of arrows from a crowd of warriors he estimated as about 500 strong. An answering volley from the Sniders killed three of them and wounded several. In the afternoon battle was rejoined. After much blowing of horns and conches eight war canoes approached Lady Alice and issued a formal challenge. Stanley issued forth to meet them, with twenty riflemen and his elephant gun. A crashing barrage from the booming elephant gun quickly sowed confusion among the warriors. They panicked and fled. A few minutes later their would-be confederates, another hundred tribesmen in seven canoes, approached Ikondu from the left bank but, seeing their comrades in full rout, sheared off at once.

Victory on the water led to serendipity on land. Finding a large condemned canoe on the shore, Stanley gave his carpenters two days to patch it up and make it Weatherly. Twelve men with axes working flat out produced in forty-eight hours a viable monster canoe. This was a valuable bargaining counter for Stanley in his wrangles with Tippu Tip. It proved that a flotilla of 'super-canoes' could be built, capable of floating the entire expedition downriver and thus undercutting Tippu's pleas for a return.'' But if Stanley was now confident he could keep Tippu's party with him, he was shaken by the condition of the Arab's party when it came in on 8th December. Smallpox was making fearful inroads and would soon rage almost unchecked through the united party. In addition, the expedition was beset by dysentery, ulcers, itch, bronchitis, pneumonia, pleurisy, typhus, even cases of anal prolapse. Every day they tossed an average of three bodies into the river.

Yet it was as well that the two vanguard sections of the expedition were united, for on 8th December at Unya-Nsinge, a large town 4 miles below the junction of the Lira and the Congo, they ran into their stiffest opposition yet. In the afternoon fourteen large canoes came upriver and challenged the strangers to fight. Stanley drew up his men on the bank. At 50 yards' range the warriors loosed their poisoned arrows. They then attempted to land to use their short stabbing spears. Stanley waited until the keels were scraping the shore before giving the order to open fire. His musketeers performed terrible execution. The stricken enemy retired to a range of 150 yards, from where they continued to yell defiantly. Stanley decided on a sortie. With a handpicked crew, including Tippu Tip, he made a sudden dash to midstream in a canoe, tempting the enemy into close range. Then, at a distance of 50 yards, Stanley's sharpshooters unleashed a devastating barrage. The enemy retreated in a chaos of floating hulks and upturned canoes. The expedition had not lost a single man.

Stanley and Tippu dug in at Unya-Nsinge and waited for Pocock and the

third detachment to come in overland. It was the nth before this company
came in, having been engaged in running fights on the way and, like
Tippu's men, decimated by smallpox and disease. The smallpox was now
at epidemic level. Three rvangwana had succumbed on the march with
Pocock and new eight more died, including the three favourite girls in
Tippu Tip's harem. A further thirty were seriously ill on the hospital canoe.

And still there was no respite from the hostile tribesmen. Tippu Tip
spurned Stanley's offer of making the entire expedition river borne and
continued by land; Stanley took Pocock and Sheikh Abdullah (Tippu's
second-in-command) on board Lady Alice. On 14th December at Mutako
the river party ran into a well-planned ambush, beaten off at the cost of one
arrow wound: 'The Mutako natives made a first-class plan of attack, two
sides by water, one side by land, but it faded from their want of courage.
One canoe sufficed to drive the water party, and two canoes the land party.'

On the 18th they arrived at a market green between the island of Mpika
and the left bank. Again the war-horns sounded for battle, but a fortuitous
capture of the local headmen led to peace negotiations and the making of
blood-brotherhood. But this peace proved a false dawn. They continued
with confidence a further 10 miles by a channel between the river and a
long high island, with banks 80 feet above the water. At the end of this 10-
mile stretch the river widened to 2,000 yards. Just as they were about to
debouch on to this open waterway, Stanley heard the familiar ping of
arrows. One of the stewards on the hospital canoe fell transfixed. The
whizz of arrows showered uncomfortably near Stanley's head.

The expedition sheared off and landed at an untenanted market green.
Defences of brushwood fence were constructed. A shriek of agony rang
out from one of the wangwana followed by the crackle of Sniders. There
followed a cacophony of yells and war-horns, while arrows flew around
the defenders from all sides. They just had time to complete the defences
before Stanley's scouts returned with word that the enemy was
approaching in strength.

A savage combat now broke out. The warriors flung themselves forward
on to the killing ground in the 150 yards of clearing in front of the stockade.
Plumes of smoke arose from the embrasures as the defenders poured a
steady fire on their attackers. Uledi and Pocock were kept busy clubbing
would-be deserters from the wangwana back into position. At dusk, having
taken heavy casualties, the enemy retired but the night continued to be
punctuated by the din of ivory horns and the whizz and ping of poisoned
arrows. To sustain the sentries' vigilance, it became necessary for Pocock
and Sheikh Abdullah to pour kettles of cold water over their heads. At 11
p.m. a surprise attack was beaten off, but throughout the night the
depressing 'twit-twit' of falling missiles continued to aggravate them.

In the morning they breakfasted cautiously. Then Stanley reconnoitred
in the boat and discovered a large town just 500 yards away. This was
Vinya-Njara, 125 miles north of Nyangwe. The depth of the hostility they
had encountered now began to be explained, for Stanley's intelligence

revealed that the Vinya-Njara people had called in the bellicose Kusu warriors to 'eat up' the interlopers.

Stanley decided to occupy the southern village of the two that comprised the town, in order to provide rest and recuperation for the sick and a base camp for the daily-expected land party. Seventy-two men were now out of action with smallpox. Swiftly Stanley landed his forces and occupied the deserted southern village. He turned it into a defensive redoubt by constructing three stockades around the anthills that commanded the village, and felling trees to block the access trails. The Kusu responded by climbing tall trees and drawing a bead on anyone who showed himself in the broad streets. It became impossible for the expedition to bury its dead or attend to the delirious wounded.

Stanley responded in kind to this fresh threat. He sent four sharpshooters to climb the tall trees along the river bank and take out the enemy snipers. He himself pushed off from the shore in a canoe and by use of his field-glasses located the bowmen's main nests. A lucky shot managed to down one of the Kusu chiefs. Desultory firing continued all morning until noon when Stanley led a sortie that cleared the skirts of the southern village for the day. He then sent scouts to deploy in a crescent formation from beyond the ends of the village into the forest. Under this cover the rest of his men formed a line and began to cut down all the grass and weeds within 100 yards of the stockades. Next they constructed 15-foot high snipers' nests at each end of the village, so as to control all approaches.

When the Kusu launched their belated counterattack on 20th December, the strength of the new defences shook them. They retired to plan an assault in maximum strength. At noon the attack came. 800 warriors in canoes flanked them from the river while the bulk of the Kusu forces charged in from the forest. The task of containing these hordes fell to the twenty sharpshooters in the nests. Stanley, Pocock, Abdullah and twenty others received the attack at the riverside. The xvangwana behaved splendidly that day. After two years of gruelling discipline, Stanley could at last tell himself he possessed an elite fighting force.

A desperate struggle now ensued. The outcome appeared uncertain and the war canoes were massing for a landing in strength when sudden whoopings and ululations from the Kusu announced to Stanley that his land party had finally arrived. The enemy was now outflanked and outgunned. In rage and frustration the oarsmen threw water towards them with upturned paddles in the now familiar gesture of contempt.

The tide now turned in earnest. A large bribe of cloth secured the services of the forty original defenders for a daring commando operation to cut adrift the enemy canoes. Setting out at 10 p.m. on a rainy, gusty night, travelling with muffled oars, Stanley, Pocock and their elite squad achieved complete surprise and total success. Having cut adrift thirty-six canoes, they towed a further twenty-six back to camp. This was a crushing blow to the Kusu. When Stanley reconnoitred the enemy island base next morning in Lady Alice, he found they had fled. All that remained in the northern village now was a pitiful remnant who quickly made peace to avoid the occupation of their huts. Blood-brotherhood and the partial restitution of canoes secured a week-long peace, with no known enemy nearer to Vinya-Njara than 10 miles.

But if Tippu Tip's coming at the eleventh hour secured a great military victory for Stanley, it also marked the end of his co-operation with the expedition. The final march to Vinya-Njara had convinced Tippu of the madness of the exploit he was engaged in. His men had lost their way several times on the jungle trails, they were short of food, they were daily shrinking in numbers through smallpox. On the afternoon of 22nd December Tippu Tip informed Stanley that he intended to return to Nyangwe as soon as he had rested; this decision was non-negotiable.

The news ran through the camp like electricity. The tired and dispirited wangwana saw in Tippu Tip's decision a unique opportunity to escape their bondage with Stanley. Bondage it truly was in their eyes, since their interpretation of their contracts was that they had agreed to serve for two years only, and they were already well into their third year. At the prospect of mass desertion on the eve of his final breakthrough, Stanley's spirits began to quail. He sat depressed in his tent for some hours. Finally, on the evening of 22nd December he went to talk to Tippu Tip.

What happened next is disputed. According to Stanley he pointed out that Tippu Tip had not fulfilled the proper terms of their contract; however, he was willing to see him depart if the Arabs would help him force his wangwana into the boats. When Tippu demurred, Stanley threatened to denounce him before the Sultan in Zanzibar. Faced with this threat, Tippu simply passed the buck by threatening to shoot any of Stanley's Zanzibaris who tried to quit. Tippu Tip's own version is different, more subtle and more convincing. He suggested that the best solution was for Stanley to enact a charade. Stanley should harangue the men, warn of the wrath of the Sultan if they backed out, and insinuate that the Sultan would recoup the expedition losses from the Arabs if it was forced to turn back. At this point Tippu Tip would make an apparently spontaneous entry on the scene and declare that he was not going to take financial loss because of the cowardice of the wangwana. He and his levies would then force Stanley's men into their canoes.

However, some news of the intended comedy must have leaked out, for on 23rd December the wangwana learned that Tippu Tip intended to shoot anyone from Stanley's party who tried to turn back to Nyangwe. A delegation came to see Tippu on the night of 23rd December to point out that since their contracts had expired, they were perfectly entitled to return. Tippu repeated that he would not be ruined on their account and that he would shoot any unauthorised person who tried to return with him. The wangwana then lowered their sights and complained of Stanley's miserliness. To assuage this grievance, Tippu distributed nine bales of cloth which he then claimed back from Stanley as the price of success. He further promised that he would wait at Vinya-Njara a month to see if the expedition was turned back from the Congo.

According to Tippu, Stanley was overjoyed and jubilant at the success of the Arab's stratagem, and it is true that in the privacy of his diary Stanley later acknowledged his debt. In Stanley's version he rewarded the Arab potentate with a draft for $2,600 and a promise of a personal gift of $ 1,000 when he got back to London. In Tippu's version, the payment at Vinya-Njara was all in the form of promises, none of which were fulfilled. This left him with a legacy of bitterness against Stanley, who acquired the reputation in the Arab world as a master of double-cross and a man who did not pay his debts. There was a further reason for the hostility towards Stanley later manifested by Tippu Tip. Tippu swore up and down that no man could travel down the Congo and emerge on the Atlantic coast; the feat was an impossibility. When Stanley achieved the impossible, Tippu Tip's own reputation as a man of peerless wisdom suffered. There was an issue of credibility in Tippu's later pique against Stanley, as well as justified resentment against a man who would not pay his debts.

On Christmas Day 1876 Stanley announced to his captive wangwana that they would follow the river to the sea, wherever it led. He assigned his men to twenty-three canoes, each named after a Royal Navy East Africa cruiser. From now on the original Anglo-American expedition would proceed wholly by water, so that its speed would not be impaired by the need to wait for a land party to catch up. In the afternoon Stanley's men held an athletics competition against Tippu Tip's men. In one race Tippu Tip himself took on Frank Pocock over 300 yards and easily outstripped him. A dance by the men of Unyamwezi brought the festivities to a close. Next day Tippu Tip gave a farewell banquet of roast sheep to celebrate the departure of the 149 men, women and children who would go on with Stanley into the unknown.

THE morning of 28th December 1876 dawned wet and misty. So thick was the river fog that departure was delayed until 9 a.m. Stanley's men then began pulling slowly over towards the left bank, a mile above Vinya-Njara. Stanley remembered the occasion as the saddest day he had spent in Africa. To the sound of the thrilling farewell song of the Wanyamwezi we took our seats, and formed a line in mid-river, my boat in front. The influence of the song, whose notes were borne in wild and weird tones across the river, proved too much for my people: they wept as though they were nearly heart-broken. 'Children of Zanzibar!' I shouted to them. 'Lift up your heads! Cry out, Bismillah! and dash your paddles into the water. Let the Wanyamwezi return to Nyangwe and tell the tale to your friends, what brave men those were who took the white man down the great river to the sea. Gradually the beautiful elegiac notes of the song being chanted by Tippu Tip's men grew fainter, then faded altogether. The expedition paddled on despondently, in silence. They passed fourteen densely populated villages without incident. But at the confluence of the Kasuku on 29th December the war drums sounded and flotillas of pirogues dashed out from either bank. Stanley veered towards the left bank and engaged the enemy in a parley, thus taking his fleet out of range of the spearmen on the right. Then, at an appropriate point in the current, he allowed Lady Alice and the canoes to float under their own momentum. They were borne rapidly downstream past the gesticulating tribesmen on the left bank.

Stanley was perplexed by the unremitting hostility of the tribes and disconcerted by the perpetual cries of 'Niama! Niama! ('Meat! Meat!'), an alarming sign of cannibalism. At every curve and bend in the river the huge wooden drums sent ahead the message that strangers were coming, that fierce resistance should be mustered. Even where tribes were not cannibals, they entertained the fear that the strangers must be slavers. Stanley had no time to stop to explain his mission. He was racing against time, for both food and ammunition were short and the expedition daily faced perils that thinned their numbers. A storm on 30th December sank two canoes; two men were drowned and four guns lost. That meant seven guns lost since leaving Nyangwe. Out of the 143 souls left (apart from two asses, two goats and a single sheep), 107 were enlisted men on wages but only forty-eight now possessed guns. Of these forty-eight only thirty-two were good fighting men, so that the effective fighting force (with Stanley and Pocock) was just thirty-four. By this time, setbacks and disasters failed to spark the men into thoughts of desertion. They embraced fatalism which Stanley found moronic: 'They are terribly dull people to lead across Africa. They smoke banghy [hashish] until they literally fall down half-smothered.''

They continued past the confluence of the Urindi, hugging the right bank. At night they camped in dense low jungle, the haunt of elephant and hippo, where Stanley imagined their presence could not possibly be objected to. But he was wrong. Continual hostility forced them on, through rainstorms, past dark banks and low oozy mudflats and swamps, sometimes within an arm's length of elephant country - an impenetrable undergrowth of ferns, dates, palms, vines, capsicum, lianas, rattan leaves, camwood, bombax and teak. The forest hummed with the sounds of insects: ants, termites and mantises; Stanley allowed himself a jibe at armchair romantics who spoke of the 'silence of the forest'.

Armies of parrots screamed overhead as they flew across the river; aquatic birds whirred by us to less disturbed districts; legions of monkeys sported in the branchy depths; howling baboons alarmed the solitudes; crocodiles haunted the sandy points and islets; herds of hippopotami grunted thunderously at our approach; elephants bathed their sides by the margin of the river; there was unceasing vibration from millions of insects throughout the livelong day. The sky was an azure dome, out of which the sun shone large and warm; the river was calm, and broad, and brown.

1876 closed with yet another threatened naval assault from two wings, out of which Stanley again talked his way through the interpreter Katembo. New Year's Day 1877 they began well with three hours' peaceful progress: 'The morning was beautiful, the sky blue and clear, the tall forest still and dark, the river flowed without a ripple, like a solid mass of polished silver.' They glided past several settlements and shouted peaceful slogans, but this tactic backfired when their pacific sentiments were interpreted as weakness. A net was thrown across the river to catch them, as if they were game. A cry went up: 'We shall eat wajirva today!' The net infuriated Stanley. He hove to in Lady Alice, then allowed the war canoes to approach very close before opening up with his elephant gun. The enemy dispersed in terror at this awesome demonstration of firepower.

When the river broadened out to 3,000 yards, with no islands and no settlements, hopes were momentarily raised that the expedition might win a respite. But soon more islands funnelled the river, and they became involved in a series of short, sharp fights. On 3rd January they fought for three hours without pause, raking with bullets the combined forces of a powerful local confederation from both banks. During a lull in the fighting Stanley sent Katembo with shells as a peace offering for the chiefs, but they asked scornfully why they should settle for so little when they had the prospect of so much. Fighting was resumed. Stanley ordered his men to set up captured shields as bulwarks around the canoe; against their hide protection reed arrows tipped with poison clattered like hail. In reply Stanley ordered his men to load with brass slugs so as to overawe the opposition when they saw the fearful wounds such projectiles caused.

Katembo tried again to negotiate a peace. This time he was more successful. Inter-tribal rivalries were breaking down the confederation of war, with the less bellicose elements now disposed to negotiate. Taking advantage of the split in the opposition, Stanley revictualled and got his men to weave ropes out of lianas and convolvuli ready for the rapids the locals told them were just ahead.

But the hardliners in the confederation - the tribe Stanley called the Mwana Ntaba - had not yet finished with him. On the afternoon of 4th January they launched a fresh attack, in huge 50-foot canoes of a crocodilian aspect. Stanley got his boats into a line, using the shields as bulwarks as before. Holding fire until the enemy was no more than 50 feet away, they then commenced a rapid, stuttering fire. They poured volley after volley into the painted warriors and ended the conflict by ramming an 8o-foot canoe and pitching its occupants into the water.

Shortly after the battle the expedition came to another confluence, with a river Stanley later named the Leopold. Here the 2,500-yard wide Congo turned sharply to the north-north-east. At once they heard the roaring of the cataracts the friendly Kankore people had warned them about. They were in fact at the first of the seven cataracts making up what later came to be known as the Stanley Falls. Stanley Falls extended for 56 miles. The first, second, third, fourth and fifth cataract came so close together that they were distinguished only by the number of distinct waterfalls. Though Stanley did not know it at the time, a 9-mile overland journey could take him safely past all first five cataracts. Then came 22 miles of navigable waterway before the fearsome sixth cataract - an absolute fall on the left side and a set of barely passable rapids on the right. 26 further miles of navigable river led to the seventh cataract, where the Congo divided into four channels.

The first cataract at once posed unprecedented problems. At the Ukassa Falls in early December they had been able to float their canoes over the falls and pick them up on the other side of the portage. Here the waters were too turbulent. It would be necessary to drag the boats to below each fall. Yet even while Stanley pondered this problem, he was again assailed in the rear by the dauntless Mwana Ntaba. It was necessary to deal with them first. This time he improvised more skilfully. He landed a party under Manwa Sera, then turned his fleet broadside to the river. This meant that when the enemy came up to them, they would be caught between two fires. So it proved. A running fight from about 5.30 p.m. till dusk saw the warriors finally driven off. Landing by the lip of the falls, Stanley then had his men busy until 10 p.m. constructing a brushwood stockade.

5th January 1877 was a grim date in the expedition's calendar. In order to get his canoes to the foot of the falls, Stanley had to send some of his men to cut a 20-foot wide road through the jungle. He used the older wangwana on this task, keeping back the younger ones to repel attacks from the determined Mwana Ntaba, who were now in league with the Baswa tribe from below the first cataract. Remaining on the defensive until 10 a.m., Stanley then sortied and in a five-hour combat succeeding in flushing the enemy out of the woods around the falls. They saw the enemy no more for two days, but the victory had been costly. The expedition had taken casualties of ten wounded and two killed. Of this duo Stanley wrote: 'To prevent them becoming food for the cannibals, we consigned them to the swift brown flood of the Livingstone.'

Next the descent of the falls had to be compassed. Stanley ruled out the right-hand side of the cataract because of the enormous waves and decided to cut overland next to the left fork of the Congo. It took him no more than two hours to blaze a trail to the foot of the falls. Then he ordered his men to open up the trail to a width of 15 feet. Bringing the canoes as close to the lip of the falls as possible before landing them, he had them hauled overland along an expertly cut path through the tangle of rattan palms, vines, creepers and brushwood. The main obstacle was the rain and the fact that only half his force could be used; the other half remained above the falls on the look-out for the enemy.

By the afternoon of the 8th they had passed the first cataract. The temptation now was to race downriver but almost at once they heard the minatory roar of another cataract. As they hugged the left bank, they heard again the drearily familiar sound of drums, conches and war-horns. Between Scylla and Charybdis, Stanley decided to deal with the Baswa first before tackling the second cataract. He landed on the Baswa stronghold of Cheandoah Island and put the enemy to flight, hauling in an immense quantity of bananas, chickens and eggs as well as thirty goats.

From the cowed Baswa people they heard alarming rumours of a ferocious tribe of cannibals called the Bakumu, allegedly directly in their path on the left bank. Stanley's first inclination was to give them a wide berth but an inspection of the right-hand side of the Congo soon put paid to that idea:

The whole face of the river was wild beyond description and the din of its furious waves stunning ... we pushed a rotten and condemned canoe above the fall, watched it shoot down like an arrow and circle around that terrible whirring pool, and the next instant saw it drawn in by that dreadful suction, and presently ejected stern foremost thirty yards below.

The only way to resolve the dilemma was to confront the Bakumu, defeat them, then drag the canoes overland through the dense forest overlooking the second cataract on the left bank. On 9th January they left Cheandoah Island and made for the left bank. As they neared a creek, they virtually collided with a Kumu party in full war paint. After scattering them with a few volleys from the elephant gun, Stanley landed a party that flushed the remaining warriors out of two strongly defended villages and put them to flight.

Next day they portaged the canoes down the second cataract in relays. The route around these falls was especially gruelling and seventy-eight hours were needed to complete the task. One sensational incident punctuated their labours. Zaidi, a veteran of the Livingstone expeditions, was flung into the water when his canoe was smashed. Just as he was about to be borne over the boiling lip of the main waterfall, the wrecked boat snagged on a pointed rock, about a foot above the surface. Zaidi was left clinging to the point of rock just yards away from where the waters boiled over into the whirlpools below. Various attempts to throw him a rope or to send a canoe attached to the shore by rattan creepers failed ignominiously. Then Stanley called for volunteers. After some hesitation Uledi, coxswain of the Lady Alice, was joined by Marzouk the boat-boy.

Their comrades on the shore hauled on a length of cable while the two boatmen edged the canoe closer to Zaidi. They managed to secure a rope to Zaidi but then the cable snapped. The two men leaped for safety on to an outcrop of rock on the edge of the waterfall and pulled Zaidi to safety with them while the canoe was swept over the falls. Three men were now in a parlous position instead of the original one. 50 yards of boiling water and calamitous waves lay between them and their comrades. To the right of them was a fall 300 yards wide; below them was a mile of rapids and whirlpools. Dusk came on while rescue attempts were being made, so the effort was abandoned until morning.

At dawn Stanley ordered strong rattans to be cut in the forest. Then they fashioned extra-strong cables which were anchored on the bank and thrown across the foaming flood to the outcrop. There the three men secured the line to the rock and prepared to swing themselves over the water, hand over hand. After many anxious moments, especially when Marzouk's strength seemed to be ebbing, all three men winched themselves manually back to the shore. It was a great triumph of the moral over the material and another successful test of Stanley's sterling leadership qualities.

Stanley's luck continued to hold. The Kumu left them alone while they continued to negotiate the third, fourth and fifth cataracts. One portage involved cutting a road 3 miles long, while being stung by red ants and gashed by spear grass, trying to conceal their endeavours from the enemy betimes. Stanley noted in his diary: 'The men's backs are covered with blisters, while my scalp smarts as if wounded with a fine steel comb.'

No sooner were they clear of the fifth cataract, than they were attacked again, this time by the Asama people. Stanley counterattacked, dividing his force and landing on either side of the enemy. His tactical élan wrong footed the Asama. While they pondered their next move, Katembo's eloquence persuaded them to make peace. Stanley cunningly sent back the prisoners he had taken, laden with peace-offerings of shells and beads. Convinced of the strangers' pacific intentions, the Asama people made blood-brotherhood and supplied them liberally with food.

They resumed the voyage, still following the river north-north-east. On 19th January the expedition halted on the right bank on what was thought to be a market-place but within a minute a huge net had been thrown over them as if they were wild beasts. This kind of netting on the Congo always enraged Stanley. He ordered Manwa Sera to take thirty men and go upstream to set an ambush on the trail to the 'market-place'. Then he ordered the detachment he had kept with him to cut its way through the nets ahead of them. When the Wenya people saw this, they closed in for the attack, only to blunder into Manwa Sera's ambuscade. Stanley took two prisoners to guide him to the sixth cataract.

The passage to the sixth cataract was predictably disputed, so that it was 23rd January when they finally approached it, after running skirmishes with the locals. Their guides indicated a shallow channel 6 miles long that would take them through the sixth cataract. Despite the fact that this was, on paper, the most formidable obstacle in all the Stanley Falls, they got through without problems.

Later that day Stanley took observations and noted their crossing of the Equator. He decided to switch to the left bank. Suddenly his instruments indicated that the river was swinging decisively westwards. Here was the most powerful circumstantial pointer yet that the Lualaba really did become the Congo. But even while he congratulated himself, he heard the surge and thunder of the seventh cataract begin to sound in his ears.

The roaring of boiling waters was soon counterpointed with another, even more familiar, sound: the sonorous booming of war drums. Stanley pulled into shore and drew up his men in a crescent-shaped formation. He planned to hold the Wenya at bay while Pocock began the portage of the boats around the seventh cataract. He constructed strong defensive redoubts at a point where a kind of dyke separated the right bank from an inhabited island. The strength of this position seemed to dismay the Wenya. They began to pull their people off the island.

Stanley now had leisure to address himself to the seventh cataract. At this point the configuration of the Congo was thus. The river had narrowed from 2,000 to 1,300 yards; there was a 40-yard strip of water between the right bank and Wenya Island, then came 760 yards of Wenya Island followed by 500 yards of the main river. These 500 yards formed a spectacular waterfall, 10 feet deep, with 6-foot waves splashing up from it: 'Here was a stupendous river flung in full volume over a waterfall only five hundred yards across. The river at the last cataract of the Stanley Falls does not merely fall: it is precipitated downwards.'

While constructing the overland road for the boats, his men were attacked front and rear by the Wenya and lost one killed by a knife. A gallant running action held off the Wenya until the canoes could be re-launched at the foot of the falls. Finally, by the morning of 28th January they were clear of the last of the Stanley Falls, after a twenty-two-day nightmare period since 6 January. Away from the deafening roar they sped. Still the river ran north by north-west, confirming that this was indeed the Congo. The 2,000-yard wide river forked into two equal branches past an island at the confluence of the Mburra River. Stanley chose the right branch but had to exchange volleys with the locals before the expedition could camp in peace at the south end of the island.

On 29th January they floated on to a broad expanse of the Congo, now 2,500 yards wide, between high, steep, wooded banks. Here they were attacked by a new tribe (called by Stanley Yangambi) in full war paint, half daubed in white, the other half ochreous. After a running fight had failed to shake off their assailants, Stanley landed, constructed a boma and beat off a fresh wave of attacks on the shore. By now, after twenty-four fights, Stanley had perfected his defensive techniques. In each combat the women, children and other non-combatants would raise the sixty-four door-like shields in front of the forty-three riflemen, thus making them more effective than three times that number of undefended sharpshooters. The steersmen, likewise protected, were able to manoeuvre in the current in the course of a running fight. Stanley's real worry was ammunition. If the expedition had to fight its way to the mouth of the Congo, it would surely run out long before then. They would then be easy prey for the first powerful war-party.

The last two days of January seemed to confirm Stanley's worst fears. So far from lessening, the daily pressure seemed to be increasing. The strain on nerves of the constant drumming and conch-blowing could not be discounted. Stanley took to releasing his prisoners early to get some respite, as such release invariably brought a halt (albeit temporary) to the frenzied drumming.

Past the Ruiki River they floated, through perpendicular red cliffs 300 feet high, the enemy forever snapping at their heels. The banks were becoming lower. The picturesque cliffs, tall wooden ridges, and brown, red and grey bluffs seemed to have been dropped astern. At last they seemed to be emerging from the eternal forest as the river broadened to 3,000 yards, but all the wangwana were weary with the non-stop fighting. Even by clinging to the islands in the middle of such a broad river they were not safe. With cries of 'Niama! Niama' daily arising around them, they seemed to have a straight choice: fight or be eaten. Stanley's preference was for the right bank, which was still more forested than the left. By now the left bank was out of sight if they hugged the right shore.

But if Stanley thought he had worries enough, February was to provide the crown of thorns. The day began promisingly. In brilliant sunshine they continued to cleave to the right bank of the Congo, which was steep, high and crowned with woods. They made good progress until about 2 p.m. when they came to the point where the mighty Aruwimi emptied into the Congo. At this confluence the most awesome display yet of military might barred the way. Fifty-four huge canoes lay ready in battle formation, in two 'horns', half converging on them from the Congo's right bank, half from the Aruwimi. In the first ten 'super canoes' 500 warriors of the Soko stood ready to 'eat up' the Anglo-American expedition.

Stanley at once perceived what a deadly threat this was. This flotilla far surpassed in size and numbers anything they had encountered hitherto. First he had to calm his men's nerves, badly shaken at sight of such a huge armada. Four of his canoe crews immediately became panic-stricken and tried to pull away downstream. Stanley cut off their getaway in Lady Alice and ordered them back into line. He passed the word that any canoe attempting to desert would be holed by the elephant gun. Then he formed a defensive formation in the narrows between the Aruwimi and an island, ranged around Lady Alice. Eleven double canoes were anchored 10 yards apart, with Lady Alice 50 yards in the van. Again the shields were raised to form a bulwark. Nervously the wangwana fighting men fingered their Sniders.

Stanley ordered his men not to fire until the first spear was thrown. The fifty-four canoes began to swoop in on them, the two rows of paddlers upstanding, their bodies bending and swaying in unison as they chanted a blood-curdling chorus.

Down the natives came, fast and furious, but in magnificent style . .. their canoes were enormous things, one especially, a monster, of eighty paddlers, forty on a side, with paddles eight feet long, spear-headed and really pointed with iron blades for close quarters, I presume. The top of each paddle shaft was adorned with an ivory ball. The chiefs pranced up and down a planking that ran from stern to stern. On a platform near the bow were choice fellows swaying their long spears at the ready. In the stern of this great war canoe stood eight steersmen, guiding her towards us ... At a rough guess there must have been from 1,500 to 2,000 savages within these four canoes.

The wangwana discipline held up superbly that afternoon. In full confidence of victory the Soko shot past them in the first monster and launched a fusillade of spears. There was a cacophony of deafening drums, braying horns and triumphant ululations as the spears sped through the air, to bounce off or impale harmlessly in the shield wall. Then came a devastating broadside in reply. At such a short range, the Sniders dealt out death for every bullet. For about ten minutes a furious melee of close order combat ensued. Clouds of spears whistled and hissed around the defenders' heads but their rifles were already doing terrible damage. For a few minutes the outcome was uncertain; Stanley later confessed that the expedition was seconds away from being overwhelmed by sheer weight of numbers. Then the Soko broke and fled, unable to take such dreadful punishment any longer. Stanley lifted the stone anchors and gave chase. He carried the fight on to the shore, raided the village of the now demoralised Soko, and turned repulse into rout. His triumphant soldiers staggered back into the boats laden with trophies: not just food in abundance, but 133 pieces of ivory plundered from the Soko's 'ivory temple' (value $18,000) which Stanley gave to his men as prize money.

Following such a crushing victory, there was no further Soko resistance. After this, their twenty-eighth combat, the wangwana were all in. Moreover, Stanley was now seriously worried at the diminishing stocks of ammunition. He decided that thenceforth they must abandon the shore and glide down through the central islands. This seemed a feasible prospect, for the river after the Aruwimi junction was so broad that there were sometimes six distinct branches of the Congo, divided by islands.

What was the reason for the unremitting hostility along the Lualaba and the Congo? To a large extent it was a function of the hoary old cliché: 'failure to communicate'. Stanley was travelling too fast to be able to stop and explain his mission to every tribe he came across, especially as this would remove the element of surprise if it came to fighting and thus use up even more of the perilously scarce ammunition. Stanley himself showed some appreciation of the position of his opponents in his despatches to the Herald: The natives had never heard of white men; they had never seen strangers boldly penetrating their region, neither could they possibly understand what advantage white men or black men could gain by attempting to gain an acquaintance. It is the custom of no tribe to penetrate below or above the district of any other tribe. Trade has hitherto been conducted from hand to hand, tribe to tribe, country to country.

Moreover, though the extent of cannibalism on the Congo in this era has been exaggerated, it did exist, and faced with the constant cries Niama, Niama, it was probably more sensible for Stanley to shoot first and ask questions later.

For their part, the Soko were alarmed by reports of a powerful tribe descending the Congo, led by a man with a face as pale as the moon. Nor was there any record in Soko tradition of a tribe on the move with so many canoes, except for war. For that reason they fought at the Aruwimi. And if Stanley and the rvangwana got the fright of their lives when they saw this formidable armada waiting for them at the Aruwimi junction, the culture shock for the Soko was even greater. The coming of men 'with sticks which sent forth thunder and lightning' was (not incorrectly in the light of future Congo history) interpreted by them as the advent of evil spirits and the harbinger of bad days to come.

But the rationalisations possible later were no help to the beleaguered expedition in February 1877. For a time it seemed that many more battles would be their lot. Though the Congo was now between 5 and 8 miles wide and they were threading their way through a channel between a series of islands, they were not immune to hostile attacks. The Bemberri people refused to accept their peaceful overtures and replied with showers of stones and frenzied drum-beating. For all that, they did not attack but followed at a safe distance. For five days the drumming continued day and night, as the fugitives glided down narrow streams, between palmy and spicy islands, at risk from rocks, rapids, tribesmen and crocodiles. On the 7th the elements took a hand: heavy swells and howling winds buffeted the expedition, already weak from loss of food. And still the drumming continued day and night, driving Stanley to the brink of endurance. Near to despair he recorded in his diary: Livingstone called floating down the Lualaba a foolhardy feat. So it is, and were I to do it again, I would not attempt it without two hundred guns. The natives, besides being savage, ferocious to an extreme degree, are powerful and have means by land and water to exercise to great lengths their ferocity. I pen these lines with a half feeling that they never will be read by another white person .. . either bank is equally powerful, to go from one side to the other is like jumping from the frying pan into the fire. It may be said thus that we are now 'running the gauntlet'.

Stanley's desire to conserve ammunition now led him to cut his rate of progress down the Congo in the interests of coaxing and conciliating the tribes to allow him food and free passage without a fight. An especially anxious day was spent on 8th February negotiating for food with chief Rubunga of the Poto. The wangwana advised Stanley that Rubunga was stalling them, hiding away food supplies against the time of the fight. Stanley persisted in believing in the chief's good faith and was rewarded when Rubunga offered to make blood brothers and supply them with all the provisions they needed. The consequence was that for the first time in many weeks they could eat their fill - for food was cheap - rest free from anxiety, and get a good night's sleep.

Rubunga also sent on envoys to introduce the expedition to Urangi, the next settlement along. When they moved out on 10th February, Stanley was in high hopes that word of his generosity at Rubunga's would precede him. And indeed at first the chief of Urangi received them hospitably. Then on 11th February the mood changed. Urangi decided to try conclusions with them. Again Stanley was obliged to form his canoes into a square and demonstrate the firepower of the Sniders on contumacious warriors. When the expedition raised anchor, Stanley was again pursued from island to island until, at the end of their territorial range, the Urangi marauders turned back. But shaking them off had been costly. Manwa Sera's party lost the eighth gun since Nyangwe. This made forty-eight guns missing since they had left Zanzibar.

They continued gliding down through the Congo islands on narrow streams between palmy, spicy islands, full of cottonwoods, palms, guineas and tall cane. Unlike the Mississippi, the Congo appeared free of snags and sandbars. Gigantic trees on the bank were shrouded from full view by vines and creepers. Since the banks on this stretch of the river were only about 5-10 feet high, they were frequently flooded and mangrove swamps were the result. These swamps positively crawled with large crocodiles, and from the oozy miasmata issued forth armies of gadflies, mosquitoes and tsetses to plague the wangwana: 'The murmur of vast multitudes of these insects sounded during the night of our half-waked senses like the noise of advancing savages.' On the increasing number of islands they encountered a wealth of wildlife: storks, cranes, geese, flamingos, ibises, egrets, kingfishers, snipe. Lemurs and monkeys teemed in the trees and hippos and monitor in the river. Big game was represented on the islands by elephants and herds of red buffalo.

Yet if ever Stanley was tempted to daydream in the balmy, languorous humidity of the Congo, he was soon recalled to his present peril. On 13th February they rounded a bend suddenly to find themselves in the midst of a large cluster of villages. At once the war drums boomed and the horns sounded. To conserve ammunition, Stanley tried to float by without firing. The expedition was also dangerously light on weapons by this time, down to nineteen Sniders and twenty muskets (plus Stanley's personal arsenal). But the Marunja people sallied out in their canoes to meet them, and to his horror Stanley saw that they were armed with muskets. Fortunately their open-mouthed stupefaction at sight of Pocock and Stanley afforded a precious breathing space, so that firing did not commence until the expedition was almost clear of the village. In a 5-mile running fight the wangwana had much the better of the exchanges, but Rehani was shot dead.

Even so, 13th February seemed in retrospect a bagatelle compared with what came next - what Stanley called 'the fight of fights'. On the 14th they arrived at the first village in the huge Bangala settlement that extended along the right bank. Stanley steered in between two islands, hoping to float by without being seen, but the sudden sharp taps of a kettledrum dashed his hopes. At once Stanley withdrew his flotilla from the shelter of the islands and commenced a dash downstream. Bangala canoes came rushing out from the shore towards them. An attempt at pacific overtures by the expedition was answered with lead. The Bangala were much more dangerous than the Soko at the Aruwimi junction, for they possessed Ashanti-style blunderbusses, loaded with jagged pieces of iron and copper ore. This time there was a real doubt about whether the bulwark of shields would be enough.

This was the hardest-fought battle of them all. Sixty-three canoes assailed them at first and thereafter the Bangala fought in relays, with each successive village sending out its quota. The fight lasted from noon to just before sunset, during which time the expedition floated 10 miles downriver past the huge Bangala conglomeration of villages. It was breechloaders, double-barrelled elephant rifles and Sniders against Brown Besses loaded with slugs. Fresh supplies of ammunition had to be distributed to the wangwana riflemen. At first Stanley was fearful of the outcome. He counted 3x5 enemy muskets and knew that if the Bangala closed the range his tiny force would be outgunned. Fortunately, the Bangala were so impressed by the long-range deadliness of the Sniders that they kept their distance; they had never seen weapons that could kill so efficiently. The walls of their huts were riddled with bullets and many goats and unwary spectators were killed or wounded.

Around 2 p.m. Stanley began to fear the worst. There was no slackening in the enemy's impetus and the wangwana sharpshooters appeared off form that day. He himself for some reason seemed unable to hit any target. Just as he was beginning to despair, there came a turn-round in fortunes. Suddenly every shot from the expedition seemed to find its billet. Stanley finally found the range and every round he fired in the last hour of the battle found its mark. An uncertain combat suddenly turned into the equivalent of the turkey-shoots he had known from the deep South. The xpangwana drew inspiration from his accurate volleys. An extraordinary display of gunnery from all members of the expedition finally dropped so many Bangala into the water that the pulse of their assault weakened and they at last began to disengage. Their mistake had been to fight outside a range of 100 yards. Had they dared to come closer in, their numbers would soon have told.

The Bangala later explained their aggression by pointing out that they had never seen a white man before 1877, thought they must be envoys of the Ibanza or Great Spirit, but also considered them evil spirits because they were on the Congo. But the Belgian Coquilhat, who knew the Bangala well in the 1880s, thought their explanation should be taken with a pinch of salt, because of their known bellicosity. The missionary Holman Bentley concurred, 'Anyone who knows the people can have but one opinion; being there, he [Stanley] had either to fight in self-defence, or walk quietly to their cooking pots, and submit to dissection and the processes of digestion.'

The fight with the Bangala - 'the Ashantees of the Livingstone River' as Stanley termed them - was the most ferocious yet and boded ill for the remainder of the expedition, but though the thirty-first combat on the Lualaba/Congo it was destined to be the penultimate one. Seeing that the right bank had brought them so many hostile contacts, Stanley switched to the Congo's southern shore. For the next three days they were unmolested and heard no drums. The problem now came from the elements, for strong winds blew upriver every day and cut down their rate of progress; even a 2-foot wave could be dangerous to a canoe. The dry season (there was no rain between 12th January and 5th March) produced many mirages: a small crocodile basking on the bank looked as big as a canoe. At night they were prey to clouds of mosquitoes: 'few slept and continually was heard the flip-flap of branches from the poor tormented soldiers'.

On 19th February they reached the most enormous Congo tributary yet, greater even than the Aruwimi. Dubbing this the Ikelemba, Stanley found it to be 3,000 yards wide with a wine-dark colour that contrasted with the

Congo's whitey-grey. Again short of food, Stanley made a supreme effort of conciliation with the Ruiki tribe and succeeded in revictualling the 3i9 expedition. They continued to tack between friendly and hostile tribes, crossing and recrossing from right to left banks. But already Stanley was growing confident that he could escape further battles, for the river was now so wide and divided into innumerable channels (some of these individual channels were 5,000 yards wide) that escape from attacks would always be possible. Whatever the depredations from mosquitoes, ants, gadflies and tsetses, they could at least enjoy reasonable security from human predators.

They soon passed out of the territory of the Wangata or Bolumba peoples and entered the terrain of the Bolobo. The river grew sea-like - they could no longer see its banks but only the islands. Sometimes the islands disappeared and they could gaze out over an uninterrupted width of between 4 and 6 miles. At last their usual contact with the riverine peoples was of a peaceful kind. They had more to fear from the river itself, as Stanley recorded: 'A hippopotamus attacked a canoe and snatched a paddle from a man's hand and almost upset the heaviest canoe we had. I believe he was so ferocious at sight of the donkeys, believing they were young of his tribe.'

At the end of the month they reached the territory of the chief of Chumbiri. He was most friendly and made blood-brotherhood with Pocock. He warned them of a series of cataracts ahead, and offered guides to take them there, but wearied Stanley by continual changes of mind on the amount of doti he required: 'He is, though old and of a kindly aspect, a prodigious liar.' Yet even the friendliest tribes practised routine cruelty. A man condemned for witchcraft was tossed into the river, gagged and bound hand and foot. The executioner taunted him: 'If you are a magician cause this river to dry up and save yourself.' The victim was swept downstream by the current. A huge crocodile tracked him for a while, then rushed on him and dragged him under.

On 7th March after a long rest they resumed their voyage, but not before a 12-foot boa constrictor had crawled into the camp and caused a lot of commotion before being despatched. They were now into the rainy season and were lashed by fearful gales. They camped in the forest but had another encounter with a snake when a young boy was attacked by a python. His shrieks brought help and the serpent made off, but half an hour later reappeared to attack a woman. This time the wangwana killed it; the python pegged out at 13 feet 6 inches long.

These encounters with snakes were later read as bad omens by the Zanzibaris, for on 9th March the expedition was the victim of a surprise attack, 6 miles beyond the confluence of the Nkutu. A grim hour-long fight ensued, in which fourteen of Stanley's men were wounded. But this, the thirty-second combat, proved to be the last. Its unexpected nature was later unravelled by the missionary Bentley. The Bolobo told him that since all the tribes of the Upper Congo had fought the white man, their own credibility required it. Otherwise the Congo legends and songs would record that while others faced the white man's bullets, the Bolobo hid in the grass like women: 'We should be ashamed to travel or to trade, so of course we went.'

Having completed its great arc to the north, the Congo was now heading steadily south-west for the sea. The tea-coloured tributaries were changing the complexion of the river from whitey-grey to dark brown. The mainland was free from thick woods for the first time since Nyangwe. In their stead arose high, white cliffs with picturesque, precipitous shores. On the right bank were abundant herds of antelope and red buffalo, which Stanley dared not shoot for fear of arousing a general call to war. Then, on 12th March, the river broadened out into a kind of pool, surrounded by white cliffs like those at Dover. Stanley called the area Stanley Pool.

The next few days were spent in negotiations and blood-brotherhood ceremonies while Stanley attempted to unravel the complex politics of this densely populated area. What he learned about the river ahead depressed him. It seemed that henceforth his battle would be with the river itself, not the tribes. So it proved. South of Stanley Pool was a stretch of cataracts that made Stanley Falls seem like child's play. Having survived thirty-two fights and a thousand other perils, the expedition came close to disaster on this impassable stretch of waterway.

The Livingstone became straitened by close-meeting up-rising banks of naked cliffs, or steep slopes of mountains fringed with tall woods, or piles above piles of naked craggy rock; and presently swept impetuously down in serpentine curves, heaving upward in long lines of brown billows, sometimes as though ruffled by a tempest, or else with a steep glassy fall, or else thundering down steep after steep, tossing its waters upwards in huge waves, with their crests dissolving in spray and mist; or at another bend boiling round isles of boulders, which disported it into two branches with fearful whirlpools, with uprising whirling cauldrons; and as the magnificent river varied its wild aspect, so it raised its thunder, moan and plaint. At one time the rush sounded like the swash of sea waves against a ship's prow driven before a spanking breeze; at another time like a strong tide washing against the piers and buttresses of bridges, at another bit overwhelmed the senses, and filled the deep gulf with the roar of its fury.

They began the attempted descent of the falls on 15th March, lowering the canoes by hawsers through the boiling waters. The work was onerous. There was an ever-present danger of slipping on the wet rocks. Stanley himself tripped head-first into a 30-foot chasm and was lucky to escape with just a few rib bruises. The techniques tried successfully at Stanley Falls failed them here. Their best canoe 'London Town', 75 feet long by 3 feet wide was swept over the cataracts and lost. Even as they lamented this loss, two days later the canoe 'Crocodile' was swept over Rocky Island Falls. Six men were drowned, including Kalulu, who since Ujiji had been fully restored to Stanley's favour. For a fortnight Stanley scarcely penned more than a line in his diary, such was his depression.

Still Stanley did not desist from the impossible task he had set himself. Even though he admitted that 'the most powerful ocean steamer going at full speed on this portion of the river would be as helpless as a cockleboat,' he did not draw the obvious conclusion and abandon the attempt to follow the Congo by water. They were just 300 miles from the sea, and a 50-mile reconnaissance overland would have demonstrated conclusively that the Lower Congo cataracts were impassable. Yet he clung to his self-assigned task, with the result that in over four months they covered no more than 180 miles.

Was this fanaticism - the redoubling of effort when the rational goal is lost sight of? Was it a reluctance to abandon the Congo, in case some nitpicking RGS official later claimed he had not been all the way down by river? Was his judgement faltering after nearly three years of unremitting strain? Doubtless all of these factors played a part, but it is also possible to detect here an aspect of the masochistic redemption-through-suffering Stanley. When he was in this phase, the most likely sufferers were his white companions. Fortunately by this time he and Pocock had achieved an almost brotherly rapport that prevented Frank's being the victim of some sado-masochistic impulse. Pocock's patient stoicism, cheerfully submitting to Stanley's ever more desperate remedies, emerges clearly in his last diaries.

The terrible battle with the cataracts continued throughout April. Hauling canoes round rocky points by cable worked as long as the ropes and hawsers did not snap, which they frequently did. There were many narrow escapes from drowning. By 21 April they had come just 34 miles since mid-March. The best-laid plans were devastated by the elements. One canoe, being hauled by cable by no fewer than forty men, was yet torn from their grasp and sucked into a whirlpool. The problems of trying to control the boats with cables were intractable. Before us were long lines of brown white-topped breakers without any little indentation in the rocky shore to give us breath, so that the boat was urged along too rapidly and dragged the men behind too swiftly before they could secure their footing. Finally, to check the threatening hurried descent, the men were compelled to lie down on the rocks, but this was not enough. The boat dragged them over the boulders into the water.

Stanley described another incident when he was struggling for his life in the raging waters: 'Waves whirled around like a spinning top, diving into threatening troughs and swirling pits, then jostled aside, uplifted by another wave and tossed upon the summit of another, while the shore was flying by us with amazing rapidity.' And all this went on while the expedition was desperately hungry. Pigs and goats were plentiful but dear, costing three doti or a gun each. Economies were necessary, as they did not know how much longer they would have to remain on the river. The diet of yams, cassavas, groundnuts and bananas was far from balanced and contributed to the illnesses now becoming commonplace: ulcers, itch, dysentery.

Having come just 35 miles in thirty-seven days, Stanley tried a new tack and cut a portage through the mountains and then hauled the canoes over the hills to rejoin the river at Nsabi. There, having obtained permission from the local chief to cut down forest giants for timber, they built two new canoes: the 'Stanley' and the 'Livingstone'. But before these could be launched, Stanley had to deal with a fresh crisis. He had already caught some of the most trustworthy rvangwana out in petty pilfering from the expedition stores. But depredations from the local population were more serious, as they could precipitate another battle. He had long since warned his men that if caught stealing from the locals they would be surrendered to native law, which meant execution or eternal slavery. Even so, now that Saburi and Rehani were taken prisoner by the locals, he spent a whole day and $150 of cloth to ransom them, while issuing a warning that the next men found guilty would not be so lucky.

Towards the end of May they launched the 'Livingstone' and 'Stanley', having waited until the rainy season was over. The tempests in early May had been frightful; the level of the river had risen noticeably. For all their exertions, they learned that there were still another five cataracts ahead of them. Frank Pocock was now seriously ill with ulcers. His feet were inflamed and oozing with sores after going barefoot for four months, during which time he worked from dawn to dusk. His exertions in the past two months had been herculean, as his diary entries show.

16th March. Passed three rapids. Landed goods and let canoe down by ropes through roaring foam . . . Everyone very hungry.

28th March. Passed canoes down rapids and pulled them on shore.

29th March. Too dangerous to pass canoes in river, so had to pull them overland.

9th April. Halt to pass the canoes down. Got the largest canoe round the point with ropes.

12th April. Boat suddenly drops fifteen feet down a fall with Stanley in it. Had it been a canoe it would have been lost. The Lady Alice shot forward two miles in a few minutes. The escape was an act of providence.

30th April. This is the forty-seventh day of fighting with these rapids and likely to be fifteen or twenty days more.

Lady Alice''?, coxswain Uledi was not available to Stanley when they set out again, being under close guard after pilfering. Later Stanley submitted him to his peers for punishment, but he was such a beloved figure that two of them offered to take his punishment. In a Solomonic judgement Stanley freed Uledi, accepted the two others in lieu, then pardoned them. But while all this was going on, Pocock, unable any longer to walk, had taken over as Lady Alice's steersman. His inexperience brought them close to disaster when he took the boat on to the worst part of the rapids and she was holed on the rocks.

Making the usual one mile a day, the expedition reached Mowa. Here Stanley's habit of taking copious notes aroused the fears of the locals that this was 'bad medicine': it was an unheard-of practice, so must be a fetish or form of witchcraft. Stanley was requested to hand over his writings on pain of a declaration of war. Not wishing to sacrifice his precious notes, Stanley went into his tent and emerged with a pocket Chandos Shakespeare with a cover identical to his notebook, then publicly burned it to appease the Mowa people.

During the stay at Mowa Stanley scouted ahead and saw that there were more fearsome rapids to come. An attempt to shoot the rapids at Zinga was abandoned, after Stanley came close to being sucked into the central whirlpool. He hurried on ahead to parley with the Zinga chief, leaving word with Pocock to follow him overland, for the rapids were too treacherous. Stanley was by this time genuinely solicitous of Frank's welfare, and worried about his virulent ulcers. The quiet reliable uncomplaining Pocock had completely won him over. Stanley was prepared to accept him as a friend, if not intellectual equal, and loved to spend the evening with him, smoking and talking. He could not have imagined that, having come so far with him, Pocock was about to depart this life.

Stanley was in a good mood on the afternoon of 3rd June. His parley with the friendly Zinga chief had gone well. The expedition was already well within the orbit of European trade and the locals sold beeswax, indiarubber, palm oil and gum copal for beads; they did not fear the white man like the peoples of the Upper Congo. Well content with his negotiations, Stanley ascended an eyrie on the rocks and sighted his field-glasses upriver. He was alarmed to see an upturned canoe in the raging torrent of Masassa Falls, with three heads bobbing in the water.

Then the news came in. Three men were drowned, and one of them was Frank Pocock. Whether because he could not bear walking on his ulcerated feet or because as a Medway fisherman and expert swimmer he genuinely scorned the perils of wild water, Pocock had insisted on shooting the falls in a canoe. When the wangwana remonstrated and repeated the orders of the 'little master', Pocock jeered at them for cowardice. To save face, ten of the Zanzibaris joined Pocock in the canoe. In less than three minutes it was swept over the falls.

The canoe was in the middle of the great rolling billows with . . . flanks pitted with great whirlpools, into one of which the canoe was sucked bodily down to the bottom, and after a minute or so was shot up again with eight of the eleven that were in the canoe. Three out of the eleven were drowned and one of the three, to my surprise and my great grief was my faithful, honest, gentle Frank. Pocock's over-confidence in his abilities as a swimmer proved fatal. While surfacing Pocock struck his head on the bottom of the canoe and in his concussed state was drowned. His body was borne rapidly downstream, and eight days later a local fisherman found the bloated body of a white man - this was regarded as 'bad fetish'.

Stanley was genuinely grief-stricken, as the immediacy of his diary entry makes clear.

Alas, my brave, honest, kindly-natured good Frank, thy many faithful services to me have only found thee a grave in the wild waters of the Congo. Thy many years of travel and toil borne so cheerfully have been but ill-rewarded. Thou noble son of Nature, would that I could have suffered instead of thee for I am weary, oh so weary of this constant tale of woes and death; and thy cheerful society, the influence of thy brave smile, the utterance of thy courageous heart I shall lack, and because I lack, I shall weep for my dear lost friend. 'And weep the more because I weep in vain.'

Pocock's death brought Stanley close to nervous breakdown. The diary entries, full of illegible jottings, crossings-out and incoherent syntax, bespeak his deep distress. But he was jolted out of his depression by the catastrophic impact of Pocock's drowning on the wangwana. The stress of the via dolorosa over the rapids since Stanley Pool suddenly burst out. They mutinied openly, declaring that they would rather stay with the savages than follow a man whose payment was the wages of death. The truth was that the men of Zanzibar might respect and fear Stanley but they had genuinely loved Pocock. 'Mabuiki' - their pet name for Frank - ate from the same pot as them, he shared the same hardships, his justice was the merciful New Testament kind rather than Stanley's wrathful Yahweh variety. For three days they mourned the loss of Mabuiki in a prolonged wake of lamentations and ululations. Eventually Stanley grew jealous and resentful. He upbraided the wangwana-. 'Was he your father? No, I am your father; and would he have paid you your money in Zanzibar? No! I am the man you must rely on for your money, and now let us have no more crying like women.'

Stanley's resentment that the Zanzibaris valued Pocock more highly than him accounts for the changed tone of his communications to Europe and America on Pocock's death, where he was anxious to escape any hint of culpability for the tragic accident. After conceding: 'I feel his loss as keenly as though he were my brother,' Stanley told Pocock's father that his son's death arose from his contempt of water, for it was folly for a sick man with ulcerated feet to attempt to shoot Masassa Falls: 'The truth is that Frank died through his own rashness and his immense contempt for water.'

There followed a long delay at Zinga while Stanley tried to pull his demoralised and rebellious expedition together. His men were surly and refused to work. There were significant desertions. Without Pocock the entire chain of command broke down. If Stanley had failed to realise how much he owed to his second-in-command, he paid for the error now. In mid-June, still at Zinga, his depression found expression in a significant diary entry:

I have publicly expressed a desire to die by a quick sharp death, which I think just now would be a mercy compared to what I endure daily. I am vexed each day by thieves, liars and unconquerable laziness of the wangwana. I am surrounded by savages who from superstitious ideas may rise to fight at a moment's notice. Weeks are passing swiftly away and goods are diminishing until we have but little left, and at the rate we are going six weeks will suffice to bring us at death's door from starvation.

The worst days at Zinga were 20-22nd June. On the 20th thirty-one men under Safeni deserted without food, guns or ammunition, preferring to face the uncertain mercies of the tribes rather than continue with Stanley. Only great eloquence from Manwa Sera brought them back. Then on 23rd June the rattan cables they were using to haul the 'Livingstone' canoe clear of the Masassa Falls snapped, pitching the boat and two of the best expedition craftsmen to their death.

Finally, on 25th June, after an enforced halt of twenty-five days, they pressed on from Zinga with seven canoes and the boat. Zinga rapids was but the fifty-seventh in a series of seventy-four cataracts on the Lower Congo. The same agonising hauling and lowering around rocks and rapids continued until, by mid-July, the expedition was again in serious danger of famine and men were dying of dysentery. The wangwana responded by pilfering from the locals. This time Stanley's patience snapped. He refused to ransom a couple of the Zanzibar men caught red-handed by the Mata people. At this the other wangwana declared their intention of fighting to free their brothers. In that case, Stanley replied, he would press on downriver with all the loyal men and leave those who wanted to fight to stay and try conclusions with the locals. This was the last straw for Safeni, leader of the rebellious faction. By the end of July he was stark insane.

Finally, by 30th July the column, still wrestling daily with the cataracts and now openly maddened by hunger, reached Isangila. This was clearly the 'Second Sangalla' charted by Tuckey, which meant it was established beyond all doubt that the Lualaba became the Congo. At last Stanley gave the order to leave the river and proceed overland to the sea. The Lady Alice was left to bleach above Isangila cataract. The expedition ascended to the tableland and began to march across country to Boma, just six days away. But their ordeal was not yet over. The trail was thickly strewn with splinters of suet-coloured quartz which increased the fatigue and pain of the famished marchers. They managed just 8 miles before collapsing in an uninhabited valley and drinking from rain pools. Stanley now began to fear that his men would expire from starvation on the very last lap. He asked the chief of Nsanda to send a courier to Boma with a distress call for food, addressed to the Europeans at the trading post there. Signing the letter 'Stanley', he produced an epigone to his 'Dr Livingstone, I presume' gaucherie by adding a PS: 'You may not know me by name: I therefore add, I am the person that discovered Livingstone in 1871 - H.M.S.'

On 5th August 1877 Uledi and Kacheche departed with this message, guided by two of Nsanda's couriers. Stanley and the others trekked on wearily so as to be closer to the relief supplies. After narrowly avoiding an eleventh-hour battle over disputed hongo in southern Nsanda, they were overjoyed during the mid-morning march on 6th August to see in the distance Uledi and Kacheche returning with a caravan. They were saved. Eagerly they unpacked the goods and found all manner of luxury provisions: port, sherry, champagne, sardines, salmon, tea, jam, plum pudding. Enclosed was a letter from Messrs Da Motta Veiga and Harrison of the trading firm Hatton and Cookson, to whom Stanley dashed off an extravagant letter of thanks.

They gorged themselves on the unparalleled richness of the diet, then marched on refreshed. Three days' trekking took them to Boma on the Adantic coast. They entered Boma on the 999th day after leaving Bagamoyo. Stanley had come through the Dark Continent. His 999-day epic was the greatest feat in the entire history of the exploration of Africa and one of the greatest achievements in all exploration. The workhouse boy from St Asaph's now had a secure place in legend. As an explorer he had outstripped even Livingstone, his mentor. His was a name that would ever afterwards be mentioned with those of Cook and Columbus.

• CONCLUSION •

THE human head once struck off does not regrow like the rose,'
Richard Burton was warned as he set off for the forbidden city of -L Harar, whose ruler was reputed to behead all interlopers. 'Lord, let us kill this prodigy!' urged the officials and priests at the court of Mutesa when Speke arrived there in 1862, the first white man ever to reach Lake Victoria. Even the sandy David Livingstone, 'the father of the Africans' had to take up arms against hostile tribes on occasion. His fellow Scot Mungo Park was killed on the Niger while fighting off an assault with spears and arrows. first categorical refusal to accept the story by a biographer occurs in Hall, Stanley, pp. fantasy about Mrs Roberts telling him of his family and parentage and prompting him to go to his putative grandfather John Rowlands where he was rebuffed.'(Wynne-Woodhouse, p. 41.)

MOTTA Veiga and Harrison, the Hatton and Cookson agents at Boma, were staggered to receive, out of the blue, Stanley's despairing plea for food on 5th August 1877. But once they realised they were dealing with the man who had found Livingstone, and especially when the implications of Stanley's epic 999-day journey across Africa sank in, no expense was too great for them. Yet their hospitality at first met an uncomprehending response. Suffering from profound culture shock on re-emergence in 'civilisation', Stanley on arrival in Boma found himself unable to speak for several minutes as he regarded the sumptuous banquet laid out for him and his followers. He could not adjust to the demeanour and behaviour of white men. When the Dutch and Portuguese in Boma paid homage to him by carrying him in a hammock, he merely remarked coldly that it was an effeminate mode of travel.

But two days of being feted loosened up the misanthropic explorer, to the point where his hosts found him miraculously transformed from an uncommunicative recluse to a brilliant and witty conversationalist. On 11th August the expedition embarked on the Kabinda which took them out on to the broad Adantic and to the Portuguese port of the same name. The Portuguese housed their distinguished guest in a cottage overlooking the sea and set amid flowered gardens. Here the full force of culture trauma hit Stanley. Like many men who have achieved great things, Stanley discovered that the aftermath of success brought only melancholia and a sense of anti-climax. All seemed pointless and nothing worthwhile. His beloved Dickens now read like rubbish and the finest poetry appeared flat. The rvangwana too were afflicted by this ennui, depression and tedium vitae. Four of them, apparently in good health, died inexplicably at Kabinda.

At Kabinda Stanley met the Portuguese explorer Serpa Pinto, who was on the point of departing eastward for his own crossing of Africa. Serpa Pinto offered him onward transport on the gunboat Tamega, so after a stay of eight days that included a fresh round of banqueting, the Anglo-American expedition proceeded on 20th August to Sao Paulo de Loanda. There too they were generously treated; all 114 wangwana, including twelve women and some children, were lodged and boarded free until 27th September and the sick were tended in the government hospital. Stanley himself stayed in Serpa Pinto's house, discussing with the Portuguese explorer his projected route to Lake Nyara and Mozambique. The two men had wide-ranging discussions on the slave trade, but when Serpa Pinto tried to get Stanley to sign a document stating that there was no slavery in Portuguese territories, he politely declined. When Stanley later indicted the Portuguese for their role in the trade, the commonest reaction was to brand him as an ingrate in the light of the hospitality he had enjoyed.

Stanley now faced the problem of how he could keep faith with the wangwana and take them safely back to Zanzibar. He himself was offered immediate free passage to Lisbon, but he refused to desert his loyal followers. Just when it seemed that the only solution to the conundrum was another trek across the Dark Continent, the Royal Navy took a hand. Captain John Purvis of HMS Danae put in at Loanda with a small squadron and at once offered to take the expedition on board HMS Industry for the passage to Cape Town. On 27th September the expedition embarked. Once again they were the recipients of the utmost kindness and consideration. On 21st October Industry dropped anchor in Simon's Bay.

Stanley's bad luck in making maritime connections was again in evidence. It turned out that they had just missed the eastbound sailing of the Royal Mail steamer Natal, so the expedition had to wait in Cape Town for Industry to be refitted. Stanley was accommodated at Admiralty House while the authorities wired London for instructions. The wangwana were housed in the Sailors' Home.

The fortnight that followed was both interesting and restful. Cape journalists spent a lot of ink on the Victorian lion so unexpectedly in their midst. They found Stanley like Garnett Wolseley in appearance but much more charming and surprisingly gentle in manner and speech. His devotion to his faithful Zanzibari followers was noted. During the day Stanley made sure they were kept interested with sightseeing or attending British Army target practice. When he was the guest of honour at a Chamber of Commerce banquet, attended by the Cape Colony Prime Minister John Molteno, he insisted that the wangwana be brought into the room after dessert and their health drunk. Next day the entire expedition went on an excursion by train to Stellensbosch. Since this was the Zanzibaris' first experience of rail travel, they were as much astonished by the speed of the train as Kalulu had been in France in 1872. Stellensbosch was a glittering social success, marred only by the pointed absence of the pro-Kirk Sir Bartle Frere. But Lady Frere broke rank with her husband by giving the wangwana a gift of blankets.

The only cloud over the Cape Town sojourn was the opening ripple of the controversy over his methods in 1874-7 that was to engulf Stanley in England in 1878. The response from London, too, was disappointing. The Daily Telegraph and the Admiralty made common cause in urging him to return home immediately, leaving the wangwana to be taken home by Industry, The real fear in London was that the presence of the loud-mouthed and indiscreet Stanley in Zanzibar might upset delicate British relations with the Sultan. But Stanley was adamant that he had to see his men and women safely home. When Industry cleared Simon's Bay on 6th November for Zanzibar, to the accompaniment of fanfares and salutes from the assembled shipping in the harbour, Stanley was on board with his men.

They made slow progress through stormy weather and high seas to Durban (reached on 12th November). Industry also put in at Mozambique, where for the first time Stanley learned the unflattering reasons why London did not want him to proceed to Zanzibar. Then the ship beat up the East African coast and made landfall at Zanzibar on 28th November. There was great jubilation in the Zanzibari community at the return of their long-lost brethren; amid the euphoria of returnees and welcomers Stanley's stock rose very high. He further reinforced his reputation by paying off his expedition members meticulously and pursuing back claims for their pay while on the Livingstone expedition.

This involved Stanley in delicate negotiations with his old enemy John Kirk. Kirk made as many difficulties as he could in the way of a swift resolution of the 1872 contracts. While Stanley tried to mend fences with Kirk, Kirk responded with caustic malice. The tenor of relations between the two can be gauged from letters from Stanley to Kirk and from Kirk to the Foreign Office. Here is Stanley on 1st December: 'You are correct in your belief that it will give me pleasure to distribute these medals to the survivors of Dr Livingstone's last journey, but I assure you that it would be a still greater pleasure to be a mere witness while you personally distributed them.' Kirk's response to this was a spiteful despatch to London reporting Stanley's interview with the Sultan:

Stanley discoursed at length on the many collisions he had had with the native tribes, who seem everywhere to have given way before Snider rifles and repeaters.'

Once aware of the hostility from his old foe, Stanley kept his distance, mixed socially with Augustus Sparhawk and his coterie, and gave advice to the two expeditions that had recently arrived at Zanzibar for the purpose of penetrating East Africa - respectively from the London Missionary

Society and Belgium (under the auspices of the Association Internationale Africaine). It soon became clear that the wrangling over the 1872 contracts would take some time to resolve. Stanley therefore availed himself of the stateroom that William Mackinnon had booked for him on the British East India steamer Pachumba. After an emotional farewell from the wangwana he departed for Aden on 13th December.

On 23rd December the ship reached Aden and a week later anchored off Suez. Stanley disembarked and made his way to Cairo, where he was to be received by the Khedive. As ever, he made his base at Shepheard's Hotel. On 4th January he was received in formal audience by Ismail, who awarded him the Egyptian Order of Medjijeh. But next day came a meeting that meant much more to Stanley. Ex-president Ulysses S. Grant, Union commander during Stanley's baptism of fire at Shiloh in 1862, arrived at Alexandria on 5th January 1878, en route to Cairo and the Nile. During a three-day sojourn at Alexandria, Grant asked to be introduced to Stanley. The introduction was easily effected, for John Russell Young, managing editor of the New York Herald, was accompanying Grant and his wife Julia on a round-the-world tour and Bennett had suggested that Young might meet the returning Stanley somewhere in the Middle East.

Accordingly, on the evening of 5th January Stanley sat down aboard Grant's yacht in Alexandria roads to a dinner of twelve covers. Stanley accounted it one of the proudest moments of his life to be the guest of honour, seated on the right-hand side of America's greatest hero. Grant toasted his fellow-American's achievements in the Dark Continent. A thin and grey-haired Stanley answered with great charm and tact. Next day Young saw him depart for Brindisi and Europe.

At Brindisi Stanley was pressed to make a detour to Marseilles to receive honours that that city proposed to shower on him. The prime mover in this scheme was Alfred Rabaud, president of the Marseilles Geographical Society, a man with business interests in Zanzibar.

Stanley acquiesced and arrived in Marseilles on 13th January. Next day he attended a civic reception in his honour and received three gold medals from local geographical societies. A vast crowd accompanied him next day to the station for a repeat of the rail journey to Paris that had so enthralled Kalulu in 1872. At the Gare de Lyon a vast and enthusiastic crowd greeted him. Throughout 15-22nd January he was feted and lionised, the toast of Parisian society.

Stanley was swept unwillingly into a heady social whirl. Banquet followed reception and reception followed soiree. The publisher Edward Marston caught up with him at the Hotel Meurice, then accompanied him to a reception in the Parc Monceau, where the elite of Paris 'fair women and brave men' had gathered to pay him tribute. Stanley walked down a long avenue of his admirers with great reluctance, looking more like a chained lion at an exhibition than a conquering hero.

There followed honours from all the French geographical societies and a massive reception by the chocolate baron M. Meusnier, which Stanley left early. By the end of the week Marston found him at the end of his tether. He used his boredom and tedium vitae to advantage to conclude a favourable agreement on the publication of a book to be called Through the Dark Continent. The final reception in the Parisian social round, at the Hotel du Louvre, found Stanley depressed and suffering from severe feelings of anti-climax and loneliness. He remarked bitterly to Marston: 'What is the good of all this pomp and show? It only makes me more miserable and unhappy.' He was relieved to steal away across the Channel and ensconce himself in London at 30 Sackville Street.

What were the main consequences of Stanley's epic 999-day crossing of Africa? Apart from the personal career consequences to himself, his unique feat of exploration can be considered under three main headings: its impact on Africa, its contribution to geographical knowledge, and its effect on Stanley's reputation.

We have already had occasion to mention the impact of Stanley on individual African societies, but something more needs to be said about the way he affected the general political ecology of Central Africa. Basically, his effect was twofold: he increased European interest in Africa as a possible focus for exploitation; and, albeit unconsciously, he tightened the grip of the slavers on the area.

Stanley's arrival at the court of Mutesa seriously unsettled the balance of power in the Uganda/Equatoria region. Much of Gordon's gubernatorial period in Equatoria in 1876 was taken up with speculation on Stanley's intentions. He saw Stanley as a rival, someone in the service of the Sultan of Zanzibar, who planned to plant the Zanzibar standard on Lakes Victoria and Albert. Gordon aimed to beat him to the punch by setting up the Egyptian flag there instead. This was the reason for the expedition of Romolo Gessi, who in April 1876 circumnavigated Lake Albert in the teeth of heavy gales. Gessi penetrated Unyoro and raised the Egyptian flag at Magungo. This confirmed Mutesa's worst fears: that his kingdom might be menaced by an alliance of Gordon and Kabba Rega; therein lies the real explanation for his excessive cordiality to Stanley, for he planned to harness the Anglo-American expedition as a counterweight to the putative threat from Bunyoro and Equatoria. Naturally, when Stanley disappeared south as suddenly and mysteriously as he had come, all the political actors in Uganda and its environs were nonplussed, Gordon not least.

But although Stanley was not destined to be a short-term military factor in Central Africa, in the long term his influence was enormous. His spectacular progress from one side of the Dark Continent to the other excited the interest of the most heterogeneous groups: missionaries, speculators, imperial expansionists. Missionaries were drawn to Africa not just by Stanley's explicit call for proselytising in Uganda but by the undreamed-of opportunities revealed by his perilous passage of the Congo in 1877. There was considerable irony here, for Stanley's attitude to missionaries was at best ambivalent and at worst downright hostile.

What Stanley's epic 1874-7 journey did show clearly was the enormous fortune to be made from ivory and slaves. Although the first ivory seekers and slave traders from Zanzibar first reached the Upper Congo basin in the late 1860s (there are traces of elephant hunters on the Uele River in 1867), it was Stanley's 'Through the Dark Continent' expedition that truly unlocked the region. In doing so, the expedition also exposed the weakness of potential indigenous resistance. Backward African societies produced only a limited agricultural surplus, so that even a minor impact like that of the Anglo-American expedition produced local inflation and imposed a severe strain on resources. Nor did it escape the notice of ivory hunters and slave traders that the apparent wealth of the invaders often aroused the cupidity of regional warlords. This gave an opportunity for corruption and co-option to the looters. Moreover, as Stanley himself recognised, the demoralising effect of his firepower was such as to make the Congo peoples less inclined to resist the Arab slavers when they appeared on the scene.

While European capitalists were debarred for obvious reasons from benefiting from the slave trade, no such consideration applied to ivory. East African ivory, and later that of the Congo, was soft, ideal for carving, and in great demand in Europe for knife handles, piano keys, billiard balls and to satisfy the Victorian love of ornate decor and furnishing. Ivory inlay work ranged from ivory-handled umbrellas to snuffboxes and chessmen. In Latin countries ivory was used in many articles: fans, fingerboards for Spanish guitars, keys of Italian accordions, carved boudoir articles. There were flourishing ivory-carving centres at Dieppe, St Claude in the Jura, Geislingen in Wurtemberg and Erbach in Hesse, specialising in the production of miniature ornaments, statuettes, crucifixes, mathematical instruments, book covers, combs and serviette rings. Ivory was also used for false teeth until porcelain came in the latter half of the nineteenth century. In the USA it was particularly favoured for piano and organ keys and especially for billiard and bagatelle balls, to the point where the USA took 80 per cent of the soft ivory exported from Zanzibar in 1894. Because ivory is elastic and flexible and can be cut into almost any shape, nothing was wasted from the tusks. Scraps and even dust could be used for Indian ink and ivory jelly. Not surprisingly, therefore, the opening up of the vast elephant herds in the Congo and Sudan soon led to the near-extinction of the unfortunate animals. By the late 1890s most of the Congo herds had been 'shot out' and Leopold's state had to turn to wild rubber as its principal resource.

The only apparent deterrent to would-be interlopers in Central Africa was the plethora of tales of cannibalism that abounded in Europe. Quite how widespread this practice was in the Congo region and what its effects were is a much disputed question. Some have even claimed that the whole notion of cannibalism was a myth, and that the legend arose from misunderstandings by explorers and missionaries, misunderstandings often actively abetted by local chiefs who tried to discourage Europeans from trading with rival tribes by spreading the canard that they were cannibals.

A second source of misunderstanding was the fact that in most of the languages of the area the expression for killing someone by witchcraft was 'eating'; hence statements about witchcraft were often construed as statements about cannibalism. Yet the argument cannot be pushed too far. It is true that stories of cannibalism have to be approached with caution, but the thesis of its absolute non-existence cannot be sustained. Not only is there simply too much evidence from European travellers whose evidence on other aspects of African culture is unimpeachable. More tellingly, modern African research itself confirms the existence of nineteenth-century cannibalism. So the armchair critics who scoffed at Stanley's accounts of Niama, niama ('Meat, meat') were being too clever by half.

This brings us to the question of Stanley's geographical discoveries in general during 1874-7. Curiously, although the charting of the unknown Congo was clearly Stanley's greatest achievement, British lack of interest in the Congo led the luminaries of the Royal Geographical Society to assess Stanley as a geographer mainly through the far easier circumnavigation of the great lakes of East Africa. The definitive settling of the Nile issue confirmed Speke's stature as an explorer, to the joy of his confrere James Grant. He described Stanley's circumnavigation of Lake Victoria as 'one of the most important and brilliant that has ever been made in Central Africa or indeed in any other country. Who amongst us would have had his energy? Who would undertake a cruise in an open boat to absent himself from his camp for fifty-eight days? Who would risk such danger to life and exposure to an African sun in the month of April? Who of us are able to guide, provide for, lead and attend to a little army successfully, and in the midst of all this, take their observations for latitude and longitude?' Sir Rutherford Alcock endorsed the sentiments: 'Mr Stanley had been marvellous as an explorer, but he had now shown that he was still more remarkable as a geographer. They would have to search far in the history of geographical discovery before they could find a man equally successful as an active explorer and as an intelligent observer.' Even the man most adversely affected by Stanley's discoveries, Richard Burton, put a brave face on things and claimed that Stanley's exploration of Lake Victoria vindicated both him and Speke, as it demonstrated that the big lake itself was fed by smaller ones.

Yet, inevitably with Stanley, there were critics even in the areas where he was on the strongest ground. Some of this was mere nit-picking, as when Edward Hore criticised Stanley for identifying the otters on Lake Tanganyika as 'water hyenas'. Others were able to query his maps and observations simply because they spent years in a region where Stanley had spent weeks only. Schweinfurth, for instance, thought that his astronomical 'fixes' placed the Congo too far to the north. His maps were found to be impressionistic rather than the work of a precisian.But, as so often, the great African missionary Mackay, who came to know Lake Victoria better than any other white man, had the last word: 'Stanley's charts are wonderful for the short time he had at his disposal, but extremely inaccurate so far as I have been able to test them.'

The truth surely was that all fair-minded explorers were prepared to concede the greatness of Stanley's achievement; Joseph Thomson vindicated his findings on the Lukuga, Harry Johnston on the Lakes and the Congo, and so on. It was generally conceded that the quest for the ultimate source of the Nile was a pursuit of a will o' the wisp or philosopher's stone. It was mainly his sworn enemies who found excessive fault. One can almost sense the smacking of the lips in Kirk's report on Commander Wharton's 1877 exploration of the Rufiji: 'Mr Stanley's description is now found to be exaggerated and inaccurate, nor did he succeed in reaching as far as Captain Elton's crossing at Mpembeno.' The other tactic for Stanley's enemies was too damn with faint praise or to insinuate that anyone equipped with his resources could have done as well. After stating that Stanley's charting of Lake Victoria alone would have entitled him to a very high place among African explorers, Sir Henry Rawlinson drew attention to the munificence of the Daily Telegraph and the New York Herald: 'such munificence far transcends the efforts of private individuals in the cause of science,' he added archly, in a self-congratulatory reference to the RGS.

But sometimes Stanley was his own worst enemy and deliberately drew the fire of his critics. He was accused of breach of etiquette by Sir Rutherford Alcock because he proposed to rename the Alexandra Nile which had already been explored by Speke and Grant, because he arbitrarily changed some of Speke's nomenclature and failed to carry Speke's Discovery of the Nile with him out of arrogant disdain. This, it was alleged, was because Stanley the journalist always needed some 'new discovery' to adorn his latest Herald despatch. In retaliation the RGS refused to rename the River Congo the 'Livingstone' Even worse in his enemies' eyes was his lofty contempt for Verney Cameron, whom Stanley charged with leaving the Lualaba question exactly where Livingstone had found it. This drew from Cameron himself the stinging barb that in order to descend the Congo he would have had to connive at Tippu Tip and the slave trade, as Stanley had done.

None of these criticisms made a serious dent in Stanley's reputation as explorer and geographer. It was left to later scholars to point to the flaws in Stanley's account of Central Africa: how he had at once underestimated the area of the Congo basin while overestimating its population. Nor could anyone but the closest student of Stanley appreciate how he had played down the achievements of two other white men. In Through the Dark Continent he makes no mention of having met the Swiss trader Philippe Broyon at Mpwapwa, lest any other European appear to share the limelight. And he suppresses the fact that during the march through Bunyoro Frank Pocock claimed to have seen a snow-capped mountain (probably Ruwenzori), lest some other white man later take the credit for what could turn out to be an important discovery.

In 1878 nobody seriously disputed Stanley's claim to be, on paper and in a purely technical sense, the greatest of African explorers. What seemed to contemporaries to vitiate his claim was the appalling brutality he had allegedly visited on the benighted savages of Africa. When it was proposed that the RGS again honour Stanley, all the pent-up fury and resentment towards Stanley in liberal and humanitarian circles, suppressed since 1876, burst out anew.

The casus belli between Stanley and his enemies was the attack on Bumbire Island in 1875. Stanley's original stance on this encounter was that the first attack on his party by the islanders justified his later retaliation: 'With such people as the Wanyaturu and Bumbireh what can a man do, for they will listen to no overtures of peace or amity.' But when his account of the slaying of forty-two Bumbire tribesmen was published in the Daily Telegraph, the Anti-Slavery and Aborigines Protection Societies jointly protested to the Foreign Office, pointing out that the use of explosive bullets was forbidden in civilised warfare and that Stanley's sole motive was revenge. They wanted a clear statement that the British government did not condone such behaviour. For all that, their own words were hardly the restrained ones of Christianity and civilisation, for they suggested that Stanley be returned to the scene of the crime and hanged there, with the expedition's goods being auctioned off to compensate the inhabitants.

There was little the British government could do. Stanley was (so far as they knew) an American citizen and the alleged atrocities had occurred in unexplored territory. But Kirk took great delight in sending on the Earl of Derby's admonition to Stanley that he had no right to use the British flag to give his actions a cloak of legitimacy. Since Stanley was already launched on the Lualaba by the time this was sent, not surprisingly the message never reached him.

But Stanley's own reports from Bumbire provided his critics with a field day. Burton wrote smugly to Kirk: 'Of course you have seen Stanley who still shoots Negroes as if they were monkeys. That young man will be getting into a row - and serve him right. I have, somehow or other, serious doubts how far his assertions are to be believed.' Yet Burton's strictures were mild alongside those of the socialist writer H. M.

Hyndman, who had begun a vehement anti-Stanley crusade in the Pall Mall Gazette in December 1875. At an RGS meeting on 13th November 1876 Hyndman tried to introduce a resolution censuring Stanley but was ruled out of order. Seeing the storm clouds gather, Stanley's friends in the Society tried to close ranks. Edwin Arnold stressed that no RGS gold medallist could conceivably be condemned unheard.

On 27th November Hyndman returned to the attack. He read some extracts from the Daily Telegraph to an RGS meeting and asked for an opinion on them. Sir Henry Rawlinson again ruled him out of order, on the grounds both that Hyndman was not raising an issue of practical geography - the Society's only remit - and that Stanley was not a member of the RGS nor even a British citizen, but simply a gold medallist. Another gold medallist, Henry Yule, then got to his feet to support Hyndman and chide Rawlinson for hiding behind points of order. The matter was settled when the influential figure of Sir Bartle Frere - no friend to Stanley - arose to request that the RGS move on to its ostensible business of Gordon and the Upper Nile, adding that Hyndman was wrong to raise such a contentious issue. The general feeling was that an honourable draw had resulted: the RGS had not censured Stanley but they had certainly scotched the idea that they gave Stanley unqualified approval. Sir Rutherford Alcock summed up: 'There was not, he thought, two shades of opinion as to the conduct of Mr Stanley. The Earl of Derby had well expressed the opinion of the whole nation when he said that the letters of the explorer had created a most painful feeling throughout the country.'

This criticism of Stanley was grist to the mill of Bennett and the New York Herald. Bennett had no fellow-feeling for Stanley, but he hated the British and this campaign against his star reporter gave him an opportunity to whip up the most virulent anti-British American chauvinism and to pour scorn on 'the howling dervishes of civilisation .. . safe in London.' When Stanley arrived at the Atlantic coast in August 1877, the Herald commented: 'This will greatly distress the philanthropists of London who will again appeal to the British government to declare him a pirate. Their humane but rather impractical view is that a leader in such a position should permit his men to be slaughtered by the natives and should be slaughtered himself and let discovery go to the dogs, but should never pull a trigger against this species of human vermin that puts its uncompromising savagery in the way of all progress and all increase of knowledge.'

There matters rested until Stanley's return to England in January 1878. To the fury of Hyndman, Yule and the other critics, the RGS proposed to welcome the explorer with open arms, to invite him to speak at the Society without asking for an explanation of his actions at Bumbire. Yule and Hyndman, abetted by Stanley's old enemy Horace Waller, protested bitterly to the Society and threatened to resign if the lecture went ahead. The duo found a receptive home for their anti-Stanley diatribes in the Pall Mall Gazette where they lucidly laid out the basis of their charges: for them the issue was not the bloody descent of the Congo, nor whether newspapers should finance African expeditions, nor even the use of explosive bullets or the British flag; it was purely the justifiability of the attack on Bumbire. Yule's indictment was made sharper by his testimony to Stanley's virtues. Stanley, he pointed out, had 'done great deeds and shown great qualities. Mr Stanley's faithful adherence to people who had faithfully served him, till he saw them safe home to Zanzibar is (for example) a rare and noble trait of character.'

In Zanzibar, Kirk, sensing that the time for vengeance had come, launched a full-blooded broadside against his erstwhile tormentor. All of Kirk's correspondents at this time received their share of Stanley- bashing. To the secretary of the RGS he wrote in warning: 'The RGS will make fools of themselves with that fellow once more no doubt . . . he has not wit enough to resist the temptation and learn a lesson that it did not pay before.' To Mackinnon, Stanley's friend, Kirk penned the following 'statesmanlike' lines: 'Stanley is now on his way home. He is the same old man as he was before, pugnacious, conceited and small-minded. He is a fool not to see that he has done enough to be above, and can gain most by dropping, all petty squabbles.' But to Waller, who concurred with him in finding Stanley detestable, Kirk urged caution: 'As to Stanley I see he is the lion of all lions and his position made -1 hope now you will do nothing to attack him, you cannot injure him and it will only make him ten times a welcome lion if he has a few detractors.'

But when Stanley swept all his critics before him in England, Kirk changed his tune and forgot his sage advice to Waller. Together with the Revd Farler of the Universities Mission to Central Africa he nagged away at the Zanzibari participants in the expedition until he was able to produce a farrago of slander and downright lies about Stanley. He alleged that the attacks on the Congo descent were gratuitous, that Frank Pocock took a black girl as his mistress and fathered a child on her, that Mutesa presented Stanley with a nubile slave girl as his mistress (anyone who knew Stanley would see the absurdity of that one), that Stanley kicked and beat a man to death and employed a permanent chain gang. The only solid indictment in Kirk's charge sheet was the assault on Bumbire. But Kirk worked himself up into a fine old lather and finished with a flourish: 'If the story of this expedition were known, it would stand unequalled in the annals of African discovery for the reckless use of the power that modern weapons placed in his hands over natives who never before had heard a gun fired ... the doings of Mr Stanley on this expedition were a disgrace to humanity ... his proceedings will prove one of the principal obstacles that the future explorers and missionaries will have to meet when following up his track.'

What particularly enraged Kirk was the way Stanley had swept over his enemies at a meeting of the RGS at St James's Hall on 7th February? Despite many protests and resignations from members, Stanley spoke to his own brief and even had the temerity to lash out at his critics. Once again, as in 1872, the intervention of the Royal Family had effectively crushed opposition. The Prince of Wales was present to hear Stanley dilate on his achievements in the Dark Continent. This muzzled would-be objectors, for it was considered unseemly and even indecent for anyone to disrupt the decorum and dignity of such an occasion by interventions from the floor. The press was particularly angered by what it considered a Machiavellian RGS ploy to avoid facing the vital issue of whether geographical ends warranted barbarous means.

On 10th February, at a grand dinner given in Willis's Rooms by the assembled Fellows of the RGS, Stanley returned to the fray. Point by point he dealt with the charges against him. He asserted that the attack on Bumbire was essential to protect his flank during the passage to Uganda, and moreover: 'Where I failed to make peace, Livingstone would have failed and where I have made friendships with natives I made firmer and more lasting friendships than even Livingstone himself could have made.' Lord Houghton presiding gently chided Stanley for raising the matter at all and stated airily that the views of a few malcontents did not represent the position of the RGS. But next day the Pall Mall Gazette ran a blistering leader, pointing out that in his arrogance Stanley still did not appreciate that he was condemned from his own mouth, that the sole source for the indictment against him was his despatches to the Daily Telegraph. The thesis of self-defence would not hold, for 'a European traveller penetrating into a country inhabited by savage tribes is, whatever the services he may be seeking to render civilisation, an intruder. He is not, as so many European philanthropists appear to suppose, the natural lord of the soil in mere virtue of his white skin. Its black possessors have a perfect right to resist his invasion if they choose; and should they do so, we entirely deny that as a "pioneer of civilisation" he is entitled in the name of this mission, to force his way through them by the use of elephant rifles and explosive bullets.'

The controversy rumbled on throughout 1878. Another old enemy, Francis Galton, ingeniously posed the question of the basis in international law for the levying of war by a newspaper correspondent. Stanley's friends and most of his fellow explorers rallied round him. Gordon hit the nail on the head when he said: 'He is to blame for writing what he did (as Baker was). These things may be done but not advertised.' Similarly, Baker turned the argument from self-indictment on its head: 'I always declared that the very fact of Mr Stanley's publishing the details of his various encounters with the natives proved that he must have considered them unavoidable - otherwise he would most naturally have concealed them from the public.' Predictably, Stanley was much more intemperate than his friends and allies. The flavour of his various 'apologies' can best be gauged from the following later outburst: 'He only wished he could get every member of Exeter Hall (headquarters of the Evangelical movement) to explore by the same route he had gone from the Atlantic to longitude 23. He would undertake to provide them with seven tons of bibles, any number of surplices, and a church organ into the bargain, and if they reached as far as longitude 23 without chucking some of the bibles at the Negroes' heads, he would.. \How cogent were the criticisms by Stanley's enemies? It was true that he could be found guilty of humbug for the frequent references to Jesus Christ and God while he mowed down Africans with superior firepower. But many of the charges against him were overstated and thus failed to stick. He did not deliberately recruit slaves for his expedition, nor did he encourage his men to loot, as Lugard later alleged. Criticisms of Stanley for brutality during the descent of the Congo are also wide of the mark, as here he was genuinely running the gauntlet. There remains the attack on Bumbire, for which Stanley pleaded military necessity. Unfortunately for him, the argument will not stand up, and we are left with the inescapable conclusion that Stanley attacked the island out of motives of revenge. At one level he had to reassert his power and credibility in the eyes of the wangwana and those of Mutesa's lieutenants. But at a deeper level the fountain of unconscious rage from his childhood bubbled over into a murderous assault on those who thwarted him. The 'blind hate' he ascribed to his critics is better laid at his own door.

The most judicious conclusion is that Stanley's critics won the argument on points. At the very best, as his friends and defenders saw, he was guilty of gross insensitivity. Moreover, there was a gaping hole at the very centre of the defences constructed by his apologists. Even if it was conceded that the assault on Bumbire was justified through military exigencies, this in turn raised the question of whether African expeditions themselves were justified at such a price. As the Saturday Review ironically put it: 'Perhaps the Geographical Society cannot exist without rivers, and it may be so noble an institution that all the horrors of war must be perpetrated rather than that it should perish.' Moreover, the one organ that could not logically defend Stanley for Bumbire was the Daily Telegraph, currently the scourge of the Turks for their atrocities in the Balkans.

The first six months of 1878, while Stanley worked away on the book that would become Through the Dark Continent, marked a watershed in his life. He gradually turned away from both England and the United States and towards Europe. England had failed him in 1872 when he returned from finding Livingstone and it failed him again now in the aftermath of his greatest triumph. In his own mind Stanley was the man who had achieved an epic river voyage of 1800 miles from Nyangwe to the sea, fighting thirty-two battles as he went - an 'Odyssey of wandering and an Iliad of combat' as Sir Grant Duff put it. But his enemies concentrated on the cost of the achievement: all his white companions dead, seventy-seven wangwana dead and sixty-two desertions. Stanley retorted that Tuckey had lost eighteen Europeans and eleven blacks in three months on the Congo, on the Peddie Niger expedition all the principals lost their lives, while in 1805 the entire Mungo Park force had been wiped out. Moreover, most English attention was in any case focused on Bumbire, not on the Congo River journey.

The attitude to Stanley in England in 1878 was at best ambivalent. True he was laden with honours: a second Royal Medal and Honorary Corresponding Membership from the RGS, the patronage of the Prince of Wales, decorations from the French and even a resolution of thanks from the US Congress. But in liberal circles he was regarded as a man of blood. The split in elite opinion was vividly conveyed at his February address to the RGS. While Sir Edwin Arnold's family stitched together four large sheets to hang in Burlington Hall during Stanley's address, there were 200 vacant seats in the hall, even though the Prince of Wales was present.

The other factor that depressed Stanley was that the Anglo-Saxon world showed no interest whatever in opening up and exploiting the Congo basin. Moreover, his association with James Gordon Bennett was also drawing to a close. Accumulated arrears on his salary from 1st August 1874 to 31st

December 1877 provided him with forced savings of £3416 13s 4d. - an almost princely lump sum by the working standards of the day. There was also the prospect of substantial sales from Through the Dark Continent, at which he worked assiduously from February to the end of May. In eighty days he averaged over fourteen pages of manuscript a day, producing a total of 1147 pages. The Stanley diary for this period is almost a blank. Consequently he was able to take a much more detached and relaxed view of Bennett's ideas for his future. In the field of discovery Bennett's true love was polar exploration, and in February 1878 he proposed to Stanley that he cap his African exploits by a dash to the North Pole. But when Stanley probed to see exactly what level of financial commitment Bennett was prepared to sanction, he found the old 'Jamie' niggardliness and petty jealousy at work. It was clear that not enough money was being injected to make the polar project a success. Stanley therefore resigned forthwith from Bennett's service.

Bruised by his reception in England, Bennett's attitude, and the blow to his prestige by the public revelation by the New York Times of his failure with Alice Pike, Stanley entered a limbo period until June 1878, comparable with the similar fallow time in early 1873. In 1873 he had been prised out of his lethargy by the Carlist wars in Spain. In 1878 it was again Europe that prised him from his dogmatic slumbers, this time in the seemingly unlikely guise of King Leopold II of Belgium.

2

MORE unlikely candidate as standard-bearer of 'civilisation' in the Dark Continent than the Duke of Brabant, Leopold II of the Belgians would be difficult to imagine. Overweight and bearded like an Old Testament patriarch, Leopold was a liar, swindler, lecher and master of Machiavellianism. This was the man who was to be the architect of Stanley's fortunes during the last half of his life, yet he as clearly called forth the dark side of Stanley's nature as Livingstone had elicited the good. The only characteristic Leopold shared with Livingstone was that they were both 'heavy grubbers' - Leopold indeed would regularly eat an extra entree on impulse just after consuming a heavy meal.

Leopold's interest in Africa was evident from the early 1870s but quickened after the meeting of the International Geographical Congress in Paris in August 1875. The Congress's Economic Subcommittee put forward a plan for colonising Africa by regrouping indigenous tribal organisation into communities headed by a handful of Europeans. Each of these European 'cells' could provide a controlling nucleus, leading the benighted Africans by their example and introducing modern production techniques. Leopold was excited by this idea: it involved direct control, not merely 'indirect rule' with a class of native collaborators. He was even more alerted to the possibilities in Central Africa when the French explorer Brazza suggested the establishment of an international organisation to compass the Economic Subcommittee's ends.

The dream of personal empire was born early in Leopold's brain. He knew enough about his own countrymen (with whom he was decidedly unpopular) to realise that they would not rise to some chimerical bait of economic opportunity, so decided to use sentiment against the slave trade to mask his ulterior designs. In May 1876 he crossed to England to consult with Africanists there, including Stanley's friend Baroness Burdett-Coutts. He encountered no opposition to his 'humanitarian' ideas in elite circles. Apart from high indignation about the slave trade, Leopold found two further encouraging signs during his British talks. One was an inclination to blame the Portuguese for all instances of exploitative behaviour in Africa. The other was a clear British lack of interest in the Congo area. Cameron's 'annexation' of the Katanga area in the name of Queen Victoria had been brutally repudiated by the Foreign Office: one official minuted against the proposal 'not in our generation'. Immediately the King of the Belgians tried to co-opt Verney Cameron. Hearing that the explorer was short of money, he offered to pay his fare back to Europe.

Elated by the discovery of a power vacuum at the very heart of Africa, Leopold next called an international conference in Brussels. This was a triumph of public relations. By brilliant stage-management, dexterous flattery and ego-massaging, Leopold manipulated his guests from each nationality to the point where they were prepared to fall in with his proposals. They acquiesced in his proposal to set up an international body to combat the slave trade and bring light to the Dark Continent. There would be an International Commission under a president and chairman (Leopold, naturally), to direct through an executive committee of four the various national committees, whose task would be to propagandise and fund-raise for the great 'humanitarian' work. The name of the organisation would be the Association Internationale Africaine (AIA) and its first job would be to establish bases at Zanzibar and the Congo mouth, with the aim of working from both coasts of Africa towards the benighted interior.

Immediately Leopold showed his contempt for legal forms. The chairmanship was supposed to rotate annually among the member countries and the International Executive Committee was supposed to be the decision-making body. This committee met just once, in 1877, promptly broke its own rules by re-electing Leopold to the chair and was never heard of again. The putative nexus of International Committee-Executive Committee-National Committees soon became a purely Belgian hierarchy with Leopold at the top. It was already clear that the AIA was a 'spurious exploring and scientific organisation'.

To finance his bogus association's work, Leopold turned to his favourite fund-raising ploy: lotteries. In early 1877 he proposed a lottery of $3,500,000: $2,000,000 for the association's work in Africa, $1,000,000 for the lottery winners and $500,000 for 'expenses'. But by this time Leopold was seriously concerned about British opposition to his designs.

The British government objected to the AIA on the grounds that suppression of the slave trade was a matter for nation-states, not private organisations; that the organisation was not under British control; and that, as in India, commercial activity would inevitably lead to colonisation. As ever, when he was concerned about his failure to sway British public opinion, Leopold addressed himself directly to the Royal Family.

Even at this stage some people saw what Leopold's game really was. Greindl, Belgian Minister in Madrid, correctly analysed the King's crude personal ambitions at an early stage - the giveaway sign was Leopold's frenzied opposition to the suggestion that a non-Belgian could ever be Secretary-General of the AIA. The most Leopold would ever concede privately was that the AIA was a Trojan horse for Belgian interests. The real problem for the King was how to divest himself of Belgium so that he could obtain a personal African empire. Fortunately for him, there was great opposition in Belgium to the AIA, especially from the Catholic Church, which suspected it of being a front for freemasonry. All that remained, then, for Leopold was to perform a feat of prestidigitation, so that an organisation ostensibly founded to combat the slave trade could be converted into the instrument for acquiring a personal colony in Africa. The wealth extracted from Africa, in turn, would enable him to convert the Belgian monarchy into an independently funded institution, owing nothing to Parliament. This was monarchy as capitalism - what has been termed the 'King Incorporated'. The key to this was continuous confusion, camouflage and obfuscation.

It was at this stage in his grand design that Leopold first began to take an interest in the achievements of Stanley and from June 1877 he watched with caught breath to see whether the explorer would emerge at the Atlantic. When Stanley arrived at Boma in August 1877, Leopold at once sprang into action. He took 'references' on the explorer behind his back, one from James Gordon Bennett, the other from Disraeli, who however replied that he knew no more of Stanley than what he had read in the newspapers. Meanwhile Leopold employed as special emissaries for the Stanley mission both Baron Greindl and Charles Sanford, formerly US Minister to Belgium during the Civil War. If he could recruit Stanley for his service, he would have brought off a considerable coup. Leopold was especially worried by the growing French interest in the Congo area.

Leopold's most extended reflections on Stanley were penned in November 1877 when the explorer was on his way back to Europe via the Cape and Zanzibar. Always a master of timing, the King told his Minister Solvyns in London that he wanted to interview Stanley as soon as the period of feting and lionising had subsided; if he liked the explorer he would give him money to establish stations along the Congo which would later be turned into Belgian settlements. Since the British would prevent him if he tried to use Stanley openly for the purposes of colonisation, it was important to present the mission as pure exploration. He added significantly: 'We must be prudent, cunning and ready to act . ... to procure for ourselves a part of this magnificent cake.'

The consequence was that from Alexandria to London Stanley was dogged by Leopold's agents, wheedling, insinuating, hinting. They were under orders not to make a formal offer of employment with the Belgian King as yet, until things had been cleared with Gordon Bennett. John Russell Young made the first approach on Leopold's behalf during the meeting with General Grant on 6th January 1878. When Stanley arrived at Marseilles, there to meet him were Sanford and Greindl, who again raised the subject of the work of the AIA. Sanford, an ex-Lincoln man, resurrected honest Abe's old idea that American blacks might be persuaded to emigrate en masse to a new state - Sanford hinted that Leopold's Congo state could be the place. Finally, in Paris Greindl and Sanford made Stanley a formal offer of service with the AIA, but he responded that for the moment he was still in the service of the New York Herald. But Stanley's indiscretion was notorious and soon the story of the offer was all over the Belgian press. Leopold took fright and temporarily ran for cover. It was agreed on all sides that the next overture to Stanley had better be through Solvyns, the Belgian Minister in London. Solvyns invited the explorer to lunch and found him not unwilling, in principle, to work with the AIA. Encouraged by this, Leopold used Sanford as an intermediary to make a second formal offer of employment. But at a meeting in London on 13th March Stanley informed Sanford that he could take no definite decision until he had completed the writing of Through the Dark Continent which he projected for 15th May.

When 15th May came and there was no sign of the book, Leopold tried to pressurise Stanley to come to a decision. He sent a message via Solvyns that if there was any further delay, the King would have to look for another explorer. Stanley replied that publication date was 10th June. When, then, could he come to Brussels, Solvyns persisted, since the King was close to striking a deal with another African explorer? The two men met for lunch, and Stanley agreed to travel to Brussels on 10th June, but he made it a point of understanding that he was in no mood to sign another long-term contract so soon after being released from harness with Bennett.

Leopold always combined shrewd manipulation with large slices of luck. When Stanley set out on 10th June for Brussels, he was in sombre mood after the bruising controversies over Bumbire and the refusal of the British to take the Congo seriously. As Sanford reported to Greindl: 'His late escapades in public occasions in England will not have added to his popularity or excited any denouement in his favour for employment on the part of the English, I would suppose.'

On 10th June Stanley and Leopold met for the first time. Both men took to each other. Stanley always liked people who acted rather than talked, and the King's vaulting imagination chimed with his own. Leopold, a shrewd judge of men's weaknesses, perceived that Stanley was just what he wanted. His intelligence had revealed the flaws in Stanley's nature. The mixture of self-pity, ruthlessness and indifference to the sufferings of his European companions made him the ideal agent for the King's Congo dreams. Stanley thought that all men's hands were against him; this would make him impervious to criticisms of his work in Africa, for he would conflate criticism of Leopold and his designs with criticism of himself. Obfuscation was again the key, for if Stanley was criticised, as he would be, he would not think to probe deeply into Leopold's true motives, being too concerned to justify himself. Leopold was a shrewd judge. In the Congo Stanley was to complain plan gently and vociferously about his mission but he never criticised its fundamental objectives.

During the discussions at the palace from 10th to 11th June, Stanley made his position clear. He wanted a railway built from Matadi to Stanley Pool to bypass the cataracts and thus open up the Upper Congo. Part philanthropic, part commercial, the Congo railway project should be financed by a Societe Internationale de Commerce. Leopold objected that a railway would be immensely costly: he had in mind spending $100,000 over five years, yet a railway would involve at least 12 million francs of 'upfront' money. But the King did not want to be too discouraging. When Stanley mentioned a tramway that would take steamers across the lower falls, Leopold feigned interest. He promised to take soundings among various European capitalists and especially the Rotterdam-based company Afrikaansche Handels Vereeniging, already trading at the mouth of the Congo.

To keep the explorer on ice, Leopold then had Greindl and other members of the Belgian elite wine and dine Stanley for a week before he departed for Paris. He did not reveal that he was proceeding as if Stanley were already netted. Baron Lambermont suggested to the King that the best way further to detach Belgian interests from the AIA was to use the 'international' posts to be set up by Stanley as commercial Belgian stations. Stanley would in effect be serving two masters. The chain of posts on the Congo would be the official AIA business but the parallel business of establishing Belgian trading stations would in the long term place everything in the Congo under Leopold's control. The incompatibility between the ostensible scientific and humanitarian aims of the AIA and the emergent commercial aims of the King was already beginning to worry Belgian statesmen of integrity like Emile Banning.

After Paris Stanley went on to take the waters at Trouville, Deauville and Dieppe before returning to Paris for a round of social engagements: at the Paris Geographical Society, the newly founded Stanley Club, learned societies and expatriate American organisations. He was based at the Hotel Meurice in the Rue de Rivoli and it was there on 15th July that Leopold cleverly despatched Greindl to make soothing noises about the Congo railway and keep the explorer's interest unflagging. But Stanley seemed both bored and exhausted. A dispute was currently raging between Mason and Gessi on one side and Samuel Baker on the other about the dimensions of Lake Albert. Despite Baker's support for him in February at the RGS, Stanley declined to become involved. At the end of July he quit Paris for a two-week break at the Hotel de la Paix in Geneva.

He bounded back to Paris refreshed in August, ready for a meeting of the Executive Committee of the AIA, attended by Greindl, Rabaud from

Marseilles, Beraud and Lodewijk Pincoffs, chairman of Afri- kaansche Handelsvereeniging, whose proceedings Greindl faithfully relayed to Leopold. The Dutch were now inclining towards the idea of a two-tier expedition, one to build a railway to Stanley Pool, the other to exploit the Upper Congo. This made Stanley draw back. When Sanford returned to Paris in September for further consultations, Stanley told him that he would have nothing to do with the Dutch project, as he did not want to be associated with a failure; only a permanent expedition was of any use, and this should be headed by someone who knew Africa intimately. By this time Stanley was clear in his mind what his own terms were. He wanted a contract of £1000 a year for five years, plus 400,000 francs for initial expenditure with 125,000 francs a year thereafter. Sanford managed to beat him down to 318,000 and 115,000 respectively. He also asked for, and obtained, a scheme for nine stations from the Indian Ocean to the Atlantic to be run by eighteen Belgian officers; the cost of this was to be £14,000 initial capital and £9500 thereafter in annual outlay.

On 1st October Stanley paid another visit to Brussels to confer with Leopold. The King put him in the picture about his AIA expedition to the East Coast, led by Ernest Cambier and Ernst Marno. Cambier had founded a naval station at Karema on the eastern shore of Lake Tanganyika. An English employee of the AIA, Frederick Carter, had the idea of importing Indian elephants and mahouts and testing their fitness for African travel by a trek from Zanzibar to Karema; if the experiment was successful, these elephants could be used to train their African counterparts. Stanley told Leopold bluntly that this venture was likely to founder, not least because he was using military personnel on a supposedly commercial endeavour. When the elephant experiment proved a failure and, even worse, when Carter and his British associate Tom Cadenhead later blundered into an African war and were killed by Mirambo's warriors, Stanley's stock with Leopold rose higher and the King largely abandoned the Zanzibar coast and switched resources to the Congo.

Shifting to the subject of the Congo, Stanley now agreed in principle to head an expedition to the basin, provided that its aim was the establishment of permanent posts, and not a purely fact-finding enterprise without any capital investment. He explained to the King that because of the shortage of porters on the Lower Congo the construction of three stations would take three years. The only proviso was that he should be allowed to finish the course of lectures on Through the Dark Continent for which he was contracted. Leopold agreed, provided Stanley stuck to his adventures and did not alert his audience to the lucrative possibilities in the Congo. On 6th October from Paris Stanley confirmed the arrangement to Sanford, asked that 25th November be fixed as the date of his contract, and sent on a handful of detailed maps of the Lower Congo based on Tuckey.

On 7th October Stanley left for London and the start of his nationwide lecturing tour. He went north first, vainly trying in Manchester and the other large industrial cities to whip up interest in the Congo. But the financial crisis in Egypt and the gathering storm clouds in Zululand made both public and financial communities wary of further African involvement. Only sublime oratory could have made a difference, and public rhetoric was never Stanley's strong point. After a brief rest with the Webbs at Newstead Abbey, he returned to London and Brighton, then headed north again for more lectures. Stanley was in sententious mood, as the following extract shows: 'How was Texas first peopled by Americans? How came Mackay to dare the long journey of Speke and Grant? What induced that young bank clerk lately to lure a small yacht to dare the ocean? What sent a man like Nicol Fleming to Spain recently? Fear of justice and fear in many forms drove the Egyptians to look beyond Libya and Nubia.' But in general the lecture tour was a dispiriting experience. After reading Through the Dark Continent Mark Twain declared: 'Stanley is almost the only man alive today whose name and work will be familiar one hundred years hence.' Although the book sold well, few other contemporaries agreed with Twain. Almost the only pleasing experience for Stanley was being able to salute the coming marriage of Alexander Bruce to Livingstone's daughter Agnes.

Meanwhile in Brussels a syndicate was finally formed to develop a railway and commerce on the Upper Congo. A dozen subscribers put in 450,000 francs: Leopold contributed 133,000, Afrikaansche Handelsvereeniging 100,000. This was followed by Stanley's signing a five-year contract with Leopold. He would receive £1000 a year in salary, and in return would not publish anything nor make any public statement without Leopold's consent. For the expedition itself he would receive £20,000 for the first year and £5000 p.a. for the second and third years.

When his lecture tour was over, Stanley hastened to Brussels to be present for the formation of a new body to be called Le Comite d'Etudes du Haut Congo (CEHC) - an allegedly philanthropic and scientific organisation with a capital of a million francs and fourteen subscribers. Flesh was put on the bare bones of the October syndicate. The Belgian banker Leon Lambert, the Afrikaansche Handelsvereeniging and the English businessmen William Mackinnon and William Hutton together raised 742,500 francs' worth of the 500-franc shares; Lambert additionally purchased 265,000 francs' worth as Leopold's proxy. But the question no one raised was whether the executive of the AIA had given permission for the formation of the CEHC. The answer was no - both in the sense that Leopold had engineered the demise of the Executive Committee and that he did not inform the AIA national committees. Seeing the blatant chicanery Leopold had exercised in this matter, Stanley impudently requested, and received, a total of £4000 paid in advance for the following two years. This represented his salary as the King's personal agent and his quite separate salary from the CEHC, for which the contract was not signed until 9th December 1878.

Another underhand development that afforded Stanley wry amusement was that Greindl had been replaced by Colonel Strauch, first as Secretary-

General of the AIA, then as chairman of the CEHC. Greindl, a man of too much integrity for Leopold's taste, was packed off in disgrace as Belgian Minister to Mexico. The monocled Strauch, 'a man of exquisite suavity and a thorough gentleman', was more engaging than Greindl but Stanley found him not remotely in the same class for intellectual and moral fibre. Stanley had his doubts about Strauch from the very beginning: he was 'nervous and fidgety - and too amiable in fact - and in an excessive amiability there is often weakness.'

On paper now the situation was that Stanley had a dual contract, with the King and the CEHC, and his task was to build three stations on the Lower Congo and meanwhile explore the commercial possibilities of the Upper Congo. If these proved satisfactory, two companies would be set up, one to construct a link between upper and lower rivers, the other to exploit the Upper Congo. But the suspicious Stanley already intuited that there was something odd about the whole set-up. He was therefore on the alert when the first meeting of the new CEHC took place on 9th December 1878.

His suspicions were borne out, though hardly from the quarter he expected. At the Brussels meeting on 9th December, adjourned from 7 Rue du Luxembourg to the Royal Palace, it was Pincoffs, head of the Dutch company, who made the difficulties. He proceeded to read extracts from pamphlets, including one from a Dr Peschuel-Loesche who had been on the recent German expedition to Loango, purporting to show that any Congo venture was doomed to failure. After a quarter of an hour of this, Stanley's patience snapped. He passed a note to Colonel Strauch to ask what the point of it all was. Strauch shook his head and passed the note round the table. All other members shook their heads, but all seemed to be in awe of Leopold and not to wish to break silence.

Ever the plain-spoken advocate of bluntness, Stanley interrupted Pincoffs' flow of statistics to ask what the purpose of this recital was. Pincoffs replied that it was necessary for the committee to hear the other side of the story, not just the rosy picture of the Congo Stanley painted. How so, retorted Stanley, since it is I not you who will be going to Africa? Let us hear some accounts from people who have succeeded in Africa, not those who have failed. Pincoffs bridled and said it might be Stanley's skin at risk in Africa but it was their money. Very well, Stanley bristled,

I resign here and now.

At this point Leopold made a hasty intervention. It would be better if Pincoffs read his statistics at another time, he suggested. Now in full flight, Stanley refused to be mollified and said his resignation stood unless Pincoffs revealed the true reason for this display of negative thinking. Leopold quickly adjourned the meeting for lunch. In private conversation Stanley then accused Pincoffs of having ulterior motives - possibly he intended to withdraw from the syndicate. Pincoffs protested that he had nothing to hide and invited Stanley to visit his offices in Rotterdam to view his operation for himself.

In the afternoon it was agreed that Stanley would prepare estimates and submit them to a further CEHC meeting on 2nd January. At the conclusion of business Stanley accompanied Pincoffs to Rotterdam. All the trappings of an important merchant were on display there, including a Dickensian partner, M. Kerdyks, who reminded Stanley of the Cheerybles. Pincoffs showed Stanley full documentation for the £8000 he had committed to the Congo enterprise. In that case, Stanley pointed out abrasively, your conduct at Brussels is even more inexplicable. Pincoffs' eyes flashed angrily at this and he declared that for two pins he would throw Stanley out for the insult. This was the wrong tone to take with the pugnacious Welsh street fighter. 'Take care what you say, sir,' he replied coldly, 'or in the wink of an eye I will give you something which will require you to muster your establishment for that purpose. 'For a moment both partners showed signs of going through with their threat; then the mood changed, all was smiles and they took their rambunctious guest to dinner. Stanley, however, retracted none of his accusations.

On 2nd January 1879 the CEHC definitely accepted all Stanley's plans and estimates and confirmed him as chief of the Congo expedition. The readiness with which they did so may seem surprising, but Stanley's detailed budgeting revealed him for the first time as an administrative talent of a very high order. He had thought through the implications of everything and had overlooked no detail, down to the smallest machine part. His estimates contained provision for three river-steamers, a steam launch, steel lighters, wooden houses in sections, haulage wagons, furniture, utensils and a plethora of tools: jacks, hammers, crowbars, lengths of rope, drills, etc. The hiring of personnel was more difficult, since the British government had vetoed the recruiting of labour in British West Africa. Stanley had at first thought of hiring Liberians, but Pincoffs advised him they would be impossible to obtain, so he fell back on his old faithfuls, the men of Zanzibar. As back-up he intended to ask the Dutch agent at Banana Point at the mouth of the Congo to recruit up to forty Kabindas for domestic work at the stations and between 75 and 130 of the elite West African labourers, the 'Kruboys' to stiffen the Zanzibari work-force.

Senior personnel were even more difficult to obtain. Sanford originally proposed the employment of fifteen American blacks in this capacity and Stanley seemed to accept. Later he changed his mind and asked Sanford to find him three US whites at a salary of $ 1000-15 00 a year plus passage money and medical expenses. In addition, remembering the Pococks, Stanley took on two young Englishmen named Kirkbright and Moore, neither of whom had ever been out of England before. The final act in the initial preparations was to charter the steamer Albion out of Leith for the voyage to and from Zanzibar.

On 3rd February Stanley made his final farewells in London and crossed to Brussels for the beginning of an enterprise that would eventually result in the Belgian Congo. On the evening of the 4th he dined privately with Leopold and found him charming, amiable and statesmanlike. No greater contrast could be imagined than that between the 6 foot 5 inches tall monarch with his bushy brown beard and immense wealth and the diminutive Welshman born into dire poverty with an almost fetishistic concern about being clean-shaven. But the two got on famously, each doubtless responding to the ruthlessness in the other. Leopold usually made no concessions to any man but he was so impressed by Stanley that he was on best behaviour. Instead of the usual gourmandising, he ate temperately. The bevy of houris was nowhere in sight; instead Leopold made a virtue of his love of exercise and Stanley remarked with wonder that the King seemed oblivious to the most freezing temperatures.

As yet, however, Stanley had not taken the measure of Leopold's cunning. He found the Belgians innocent and naive, for at the office of the CEHC there was a huge map of the Congo with all the intended stations marked in red squares. Since there had been such stress on secrecy, Stanley found this odd, and in any case the number of foreigners employed in the enterprise meant that it was surely known to Belgium's rivals in the area, especially France. In fact Leopold's intention was to draw attention to a 'secret' so that no one would fathom the real secret of his true future ambitions.

Stanley now received his orders for Zanzibar. He was to recruit upwards of sixty men there, find out what had happened to the Cambier expedition, and investigate the possibilities of a Belgian trade concession. There was a rumour afoot that the Sultan was prepared to lease his country for an annual rent to a trading organisation that would have a monopoly. Hearing that the Albion had reached Gibraltar, Stanley set out for Paris on 10 February with Pincoffs and Lambert. All three put up at the Hotel Meurice while they bought presents of gold for the Sultan of Zanzibar. On the 13th Pincoffs saw Stanley off at the Gare de Lyon, bound for Marseilles. The explorer was in sour mood. Complaints about Sanford's grammar and syntax alternated with animadversions on his travelling companion, a thirty-year-old Belgian army lieutenant, a man who lacked the intelligence to benefit even from careful coaching: 'as simple in all things outside his military duties as a schoolboy.'

Stanley was travelling incognito under the name of 'M. Henri' so when he boarded ship for Alexandria on 20th February he was disconcerted to find Laurence Oliphant among the passengers. Oliphant, a friend of Speke's, had attacked Stanley bitterly in the Cornhill Magazine during the 1874-7 expedition and Stanley was afraid he would recognise him. Fortunately a strong gale confined Oliphant below for the first three days of the voyage. Instead he listened to the fulminations of a Scottish Presbyterian minister against the royal princes of England: 'a very wicked pair'.

When the gale subsided, off Naples, Oliphant reappeared and sat down at table opposite Stanley, without betraying the least scintilla of recognition. He boasted of his travels in the East and mounted a vigorous defence of Burton as the African traveller, far superior to Baker. For the next few days Stanley engaged him in conversation and found him knowledgeable and witty. Suspecting that Oliphant might be playing the same trick on him and that he really did know who he was, Stanley set Dutalis up to bring up the subject of H. M. Stanley. Speaking in French, Oliphant denounced the explorer as nothing but a 'vaurien', a murderer and 'mauvais sujef. He added with consummate scorn: 'His mother is in a lazaretto in England.' In that case, probed Dutalis, how did he do so well that Queen Victoria gave him a diamond snuff box? Oh, said Oliphant, there was no denying his courage and intelligence but he was still a 'vaurien

Arrived at Alexandria, Stanley had trouble with the Customs because of the amount of gold and jewellery he was taking to Zanzibar. At Suez he found the Albion waiting for him and at once proceeded into the Red Sea. He was at Aden on 8th March where, true to custom, he engaged a 'slim young Somali boy' called Dualla, who had learned English as a cabin boy on an American ship. Ten days took them to Zanzibar on 18th March.

Stanley expected to have a fight on his hands in Zanzibar to recruit men for the Congo project. His old enemy Sir John Kirk had kept the cauldron of enmity simmering ever since Stanley's departure from the island in December 1877. Stanley had learned some of the details from Augustus Sparhawk in 1878 but now he learned the full unsavoury story. Kirk had made trouble on two fronts. First, he had plugged away at the stories of'atrocities' and sexual peccadilloes during the 1874-7 expedition, not hesitating to put words into the mouths of the wangwana. Then he had dragged his feet over paying the claims for back-pay and compensation by the men who accompanied Livingstone in 1873, even after Kirk's superiors pointedly advised him to settle quickly to avoid bad publicity - for Stanley was threatening to open an appeal fund in England.

In an attempt to anticipate Kirk's blocking of his request for manpower, Stanley made a point of visiting the Sultan on the day after his arrival. The Sultan was delighted with his lavish presents but startled Stanley by announcing that he was holding one of the 'old faithfuls', Uledi, prisoner because he had allegedly caused mutiny among the bearers of the Abbe Debaize. At Stanley's intercession, Uledi was eventually released into his personal recognisance.

Stanley also handed the Sultan a letter from Leopold, requesting assistance in an important endeavour. Kirk, who had his spies everywhere, had learned from one of the Albion's sailors that the steamer was scheduled to call at a number of African ports and inferred from this that Stanley's purpose was to return to the Lufiji River for further exploration. Leopold's own note to Kirk spoke merely of the training of Dutalis in African exploration. But after Stanley's second interview on 23 April with Barghash, the cat was out of the bag. It was clear now that Stanley's presence in Zanzibar was to do with recruitment, but for whom and what? Mackinnon? Leopold? Both? East Africa? The Congo? Since all of Kirk's intelligence network could give him no clear line on this, he reported to London that Stanley was influencing the Sultan against British interests. He was alleged to have told Barghash that he was surprised to find him still in place, since the British intended to depose him for their own ends.

The task of recruiting men for an unstated task was clearly not going to be the work of a few days. On the other hand, the dreadful state of relations with Kirk denied Stanley access to all congenial members of the British community on the island. So while Kirk elaborated fantasies on what Stanley was doing in Zanzibar, Stanley crossed to the mainland to reconnoitre the Wami River, in hopes that it might provide a short-cut to the interior, bypassing the Makata swamp. On 3 April he ascended the river in his steam launch and tried out the eighteen-oar whaleboat. A week later it became clear that the Wami did not answer his hopes, so Stanley put about and made for Bagamoyo where he visited old friends. On 13 April he was back in Zanzibar.

On the island he advised Lt. Cambier on suitable sites for posts on Lake Tanganyika. On 17th May Stanley and W. H. Hathorne, the American consul, had another interview with the Sultan, to the apparent satisfaction of both sides. Stanley got formal permission to recruit free men (but not slaves) in Zanzibar. Barghash for his part received a stern warning not to sell an inch of land to the British but to cleave to the USA for protection. The Sultan was so affected by this warning that when Stanley asked for a minor concession for Mackinnon's trading company it was refused.

Still Kirk fussed and fumed away about the real reason for his enemy's presence on the island. An attempt to suborn Dutalis failed when the lieutenant pleaded ignorance of his ultimate destination and suggested the Red Sea or the Juba. French intelligence was in no better case, .although the consul made an inspired guess that Leopold intended to place steamers on the Lualaba and build a railway on the Lower Congo. Kirk was deeply resentful and suspicious of Leopold. He wanted to be the great power on the east coast and resented the Belgians' 'intrusion'. Leopold repaid his mistrust in kind and made sure that Kirk knew nothing even of his Tanganyika activities.

Pending final resolution of the hiring of manpower, Stanley took the Albion on a cruise to Mafia Island and the mouth of the Lufiji, then re-explored the delta in a whaleboat. It was 30th May before he finally cleared from Mombasa for Aden. His visit to Zanzibar had produced mixed results. On the one hand he had recruited sixty men for the Congo, put a spoke in Kirk's wheel and tilted the Sultan in favour of Leopold and against the British. He also bore away with him to the Congo as chief station manager Augustus Sparhawk whom he had known since 1871. Finally, he had been reunited with Kamadi, whom he had last seen in 1877 at Kibonda when he left him a prisoner with the Lower Congo tribes for lack of means to ransom him. After two months of slavery Kamadi escaped to the southern shore of the Congo, thence to

the ocean, whence he made his case known to the US consul, and finally to Zanzibar via Madeira and the Cape. He arrived on the island just two weeks before the Albion docked and promptly re-enlisted with Stanley.

But on the debit side the news of the Belgian expedition to Tanganyika was not good. Dutalis, whom he left at Zanzibar, would do nothing until the more energetic Popelin arrived, and Stanley was frankly sceptical about Carter's elephant scheme. Greffuls, a representative of the Marseilles house Roux de Frassinet, was supposed to be the AIA's commercial anchor man in Zanzibar but was patently not putting his back into the work, through jealousy of the Belgians. And still there was the insidious bile and spite of Kirk, working away through the Sultan against ultimate success for Leopold; his latest ploy was to insinuate that the men hired for the Congo work were all slaves.

As the Albion beat up towards Aden, Stanley had time to reflect on the financial composition of the CEHC. The original subscribers had put up 652,500 francs and the rest had come from new subscribers, including his friend Baroness Burdett-Coutts whom he had personally persuaded to contribute £2000: Hutton of Manchester had put in £800 and John Slagg, president of the Manchester Chamber of Commerce, £500. There seemed every prospect of an increasing British shareholding in the enterprise, which might achieve for Stanley by other means his dream of a British Congo. It still rankled with him that his reward for trying to interest the British in the Congo was to be called a mere 'penny-a-liner'. It had even been thrown up at him that he was not British himself, but Stanley dared not take out British naturalisation papers for fear of divulging the secret of his origins.

But when he reached Aden Stanley heard news that destroyed his dreams for ever. The Dutch company headed by Pincoffs and Hendryck had failed, leaving debts of £450,000. The explanation for Pincoffs' odd conduct at Brussels the previous December was now clear. He had had no money and feared that on Stanley's arrival at the Committee he would be asked to produce the pledged £8ooo. A question-mark hung over the entire Congo project. But what was disappointment to Stanley was serendipity to the devious Leopold. He saw an opportunity to take personal charge of the whole operation. On 17th November 1879, unknown to Stanley, the CEHC ceased to exist. At the AGM on that day shocked shareholders learned that three-quarters of the initial capital had already been spent and the rest was needed to liquidate contracts already signed. Then Leopold made his pitch. Using M. Lambert of Rothschild's as a front, he proposed to shareholders that if they were prepared to dissolve the CEHC, Leopold would return their original investment to them, pay 5 per cent profit to them out of future income, accept any loss himself and take over personal control himself. A new organisation, the Association Internationale du Congo (AIC), was formed. Leopold was a step nearer his personal empire in Central Africa.

The failure of the Dutch company also had immediate consequences for Stanley's expedition. Leopold pretended that he could not really afford to send Stanley on but that he was afraid that if Stanley proceeded to Africa with diminished resources and later failed, he would claim it was the King's fault. Keeping up the charade of being sucked unwillingly into the Congo scheme, Leopold secretly summoned Stanley to Brussels for new orders, which would reveal for the first time something of his true ambitions. The message reached the explorer at Suez. It suggested that Stanley disembark at once, speed to Brussels for new orders and then rejoin the ship at Malaga. The Albion would meanwhile steam in a slow circle round the Mediterranean coast, so that no suspicions were aroused.

Stanley brusquely turned the suggestion down. It was too risky to leave his Zanzibaris on the ship: not only were bloody fights likely without his restraining hand, but a drunken indiscretion at any of the Mediterranean ports would blow the secret of the Congo enterprise. Instead he suggested a meeting with a member of the CEHC at Gibraltar. To Stanley's irritation Leopold sent Strauch.

At the Hotel Royal in Gibraltar on 8th July Colonel Strauch and M. Gazelot, representing King and Committee, briefed Stanley on the new situation caused by the collapse of the Dutch company. Pincoffs was reported to be working in Brooklyn as a cab driver. Strauch divulged to Stanley in a private meeting that Leopold's aims now went beyond the mere establishment of three river stations. He wanted a territorial concession in the Congo and looked forward also to a 'new Liberia' - a powerful black confederation; the black president would reside in Europe and hold his powers from the Belgian king. Real power would be in the hands of Leopold's agents in the Congo. Leopold claimed to be influenced both by the 'noyau dirigeant' idea from the 1875 Paris Congress and by the writings of Schweinfurth. Stanley was sceptical. Cession of land could only come after years of trading with the chiefs; as for a Liberia, that was beyond his abilities or those of any white man. But he promised to do his best, consistent with the original aims contained in his contract of employment; Liberias were matters for the future, and he must first confine himself to the immediate objective of the river stations.

Now for the first time Stanley began to appreciate the way the King's mind was working. He was prepared to fall in with Leopold's ambitions for a colony, especially now that the British had so signally rejected his pleas for a Congo under the Union Jack. The one thing Stanley did not grasp was that Leopold intended the Congo to be a personal fief, not a Belgian colony. 'The King is a clever statesman. He is supremely clever, but I have not had thirty opportunities of conversing with him without penetrating his motives. He has been more open with me than he would have been had I appeared as a British subject. Still he has not been so frank as to tell me outright what we are to strive for. Nevertheless it has been pretty evident that under the guise of an International Association he hopes to make a Belgian dependency of the Congo.'

The Albion continued on its way, surviving a fire in the Straits. Off Goree there was further damage to the ship's furnace, so they put into Sierra Leone. Here the confidential nature of the Congo mission was exploded. At every port they touched, Stanley remained below, incognito. His cover story was that he was ill with fever. But the unknown white man with a cargo of blacks inevitably excited suspicion of being a slave-ship, especially since Stanley's front-man Swinburne seemed too young to be the ship's real charterer. At Sierra Leone there was a suggestion that the ship might be detained. Then Stanley learned from Swinburne that the governor was the same Dr Rowe he had met with Captain Glover's forces on the Volta in December 1873. He sent Rowe a message, revealing who he was and asking Rowe to expedite matters, since he wished to remain incognito. Once the matter was settled he consented to dine with the governor and accompany him on a picnic on his steam-launch. His story to Rowe was that he was on a philanthropic and scientific mission to the Congo on behalf of King Leopold.

On 1st August they were at Anno Bom Island, where Stanley purchased fresh fruit and vegetables for his Zanzibaris. They were now very near landfall. 'While yet a full day's steaming from our destination, we observed that the ocean became stained; the blue changed to a muddy green, which in a few hours changed to a pale brown, while weeds and forest debris languidly rose and fell on the low, broad rollers.' On 15th August he was off Banana Point. There he found the Barga which had left Antwerp in June with the immediately essential materiel, four river steamers, wooden houses and the tools for the expedition. Augustus Sparhawk had almost finished unloading everything from the Barga. With him were the expedition's personnel: two Englishmen, Kirkbright and Moore; two Danes, Albert Christopherson and Martin Martinson; and five Belgians, Losewitz, Van Schendel, Gerard, Petit and the carpenter Jansens.

Stanley was now ready to begin the great work on the Congo that was to occupy the next five years of his life. He felt committed to Leopold, for the King had shown greater trust in him than he (Stanley) would have been prepared to extend to another man: 'His faith in me is very great and that in itself indicates a great heart.' But he had still not got the measure of the duplicitous Leopold. Even while the King purred emolliently in Stanley's direction, he was attempting to spread his bets. In August 1879, when Stanley was arriving at Banana Point, Leopold was entertaining the French explorers Brazza and Noel Ballay in Brussels, trying to persuade them to enter his employment. When this bid failed and Brazza used his intelligence on the Stanley mission to get a French expedition launched (Brazza himself left for Central Africa in December 1879), Leopold failed to inform Stanley that there was a rival in the field. Leopold also tried to recruit Gordon to work for his new AIA at the end of the year; the idea was that he would start working inland from the east coast. But Gordon turned the offer down. The lack of an international status for the AIA meant that he would have had to work under the Sultan of Zanzibar's flag and thus appear to countenance slavery. Stanley, who was always jealous of Gordon's reputation, was indignant at this flirtation. 'It is useless to cite Gordon to me,' he exploded. 'Gordon had all Egypt and the Sudan to draw men from and the Egyptian treasury to back him up. I have only £12,000 a year for three years.' The Gordon incident was to be but the first in a long line of incidents that eventually made Stanley regret having taken service with this severest of all taskmasters, whose ambitions increased daily but whose supply of money did not.

3

HE first few days at the Congo mouth were spent in putting the flotilla on the water. The Albion was to go with them as far as Hatton and Cookson's at Boma, where Stanley had arrived exhausted almost exactly two years earlier. Accompanying her was a motley assortment of craft. First was the paddle-boat EnAvant, made of steel with side wheels, 6 metric tons in weight and 43 feet in length. When the Congo became unnavigable, three wagons would be needed to transport it. Then there was the Royal, 30 feet long and 5 metric tons, a wooden steam-launch with screw propellers; the Belgique, a twin-screw steel steamer, 25 metric tons and 54 feet long; the Esperance, 6 metric tons, 42 feet long, a screw-propeller steam-launch; the jfeune Afrique, a smaller screw-launch; two steel lighters of 12 and 16 metric tons respectively; and a wooden whaleboat of 3 metric tons. After a few days of sumptuous Dutch hospitality at the Banana factory, this imposing flotilla made its way up the Congo mouth to Boma. On board the ships were 116 working men, as well as the whites. Sparhawk had managed to recruit thirty-seven West African Krumaners and eighteen Kabindas to supplement Stanley's sixty-one Zanzibaris The expedition also possessed 2000 cases of tools and equipment, weighing 80 metric tons.

From Boma Stanley took some of his party upriver to Mussoko for a reconnaissance in the Royal. Then he ordered the full flotilla up to Vivi, no miles inland from the Atlantic, where he intended to construct his first station. At Vivi a hundred men set to work with machetes, hoes, picks, shovels, crowbars and sledgehammers: 'At a signal we saluted the dawn of a new era with the inspiring sound of striking picks, ringing hoes, metallic strokes of crowbars, and dull thudding of sledgehammers, which rang out on the morning of the first of October 1879, brisk and busy betokening the manner and spirit in which we intended to prosecute the first great enterprise up the Congo.' Stanley appealed to the local chief to help him, but without any great hopes of success. To his surprise, the chief provided sixty-five labourers. Morale was high. Stanley's men cleared the summit of Vivi hill of scrub bush, rough stones and ant mounds, and laid the foundations for houses. Gangs of men with crowbars and sledgehammers prised large boulders over a precipice; smaller ones were pulverised. It was on such an occasion, when they saw him wielding a sledgehammer, that the locals first dubbed Stanley 'Bula Matari' - 'the smasher of rocks'.

Stanley's genius for organisation was everywhere in evidence. Alluvial soil was brought to Vivi from the Nkusu valley. One of the wangwana acted as policeman and checked the load to make sure the locals were not defrauding them on the weight of earth. The next stage was to construct a vegetable garden with a palisade around it and sow seeds: carrots, onions, lettuce, turnips, cabbage, beets, tomatoes. Every day except Sunday they toiled from 6 a.m. to 11 a.m., then again from I p.m. to 6 p.m. After three months and twenty-four days, although they had started in the hot season when Europeans were wont to drop like flies, Vivi station was completely constructed by 7th January 1880; painting and decorating lasted until 24th January. The first station stood gleaming on Vivi hill, 340 feet above the river, looking to Stanley like the Acropolis itself. Augustus Sparhawk was made the first station chief. His duties were to receive goods and correspondence from Europe, despatch them to the various camps, and organise caravans of porters.

The next station was to be at Isangila, 50 miles farther up-river, past an unnavigable stretch of falls and rapids. 50 miles of river meant a mileage of 520 for the expedition, for they had first to construct a road, then return to Vivi to haul the Royal overland with its boiler and machinery return to Vivi again to haul En Avant and then make the final round-trip to Vivi with thirteen wagons to convey the remaining boats and heavy impedimenta.

Finally they descended the Lulu valley to Ngoma village, then climbed half-way up the humpy mass of Ngoma mountain, finishing the push to the summit next morning. On the peak of Ngoma they could command a panoramic view of the river all the way to their target at Isangila. On 18th March 1880 work began, inauspiciously, with just 106 effective road makers. True, his white staff had received reinforcements, so that he now had fourteen of them either as officers, station administrators or sailors. But the Krumaners were proving disappointing; as soon as any serious work was demanded of them, they threatened to desert.

The work gang began by tracing the line of the road by means of flagstaffs bearing white cloth streamers. Stanley provided a tall stepladder to guide the bearers of a half-mile cord and reel through 10-foot high elephant grass. Such was his ingenuity and woodcraft that he actually made use of the tracks left by buffalo and hippopotami, indicating a flat surface ahead. Stanley had acquired a fund of knowledge about the hippo 'who, short, stout and asthmatic, is very apt to reject any great steepness if he can.'

They cleared stretches of road 15 feet wide and 2500 feet long in a single day. The fecundity of the tall grass was remarkable: between July and September it was invariably consumed by forest fires but by the following March was already as tall as a young forest. By recruiting more men from each settlement they came to, Stanley's men built 15 miles of road by 15 April, good enough progress to make their leader feel he could afford time off for a side trip to Yellala falls.

On 22nd April Stanley's men completed the first 22V2 mile stretch from Vivi to the Congo, skirting the Livingstone cataracts. On 4th May they hauled the Royal over the mountains to camp on the Loa. Thereafter they were engaged in the predicted toing and froing from Vivi, bringing up steamers, boilers and machinery. Stanley was out of action in early June, stricken with bilious fever, but by the end of the month he was back in Vivi on the seemingly never-ending shuttle. On 10th July he recorded that since leaving Vivi to reconnoitre Isangila in February, he had clocked up 966 miles, all to achieve a position just 22 miles upriver!

By September they confronted the 350-foot high obstacle of Nyongena hill; they mounted En Avant on a large steel wagon, ready for a one-in-four ascent. It was laboriously hauled to the top with block and tackle on 2nd November, then the same process was repeated with Royal, next day they did the same with the boilers, machinery and other impedimenta. Now they lay in camp, commanding a view of Ngoma mountain, weary with their Sisyphean labours and aware that Ngoma would be an even greater obstacle.

Suddenly word was brought that a white man was approaching. To Stanley's astonishment, this turned out to be none other than the famous French explorer, Pierre Savorgnan de Brazza. It seemed that Strauch and the other anxiety-ridden members of the CEHC were right after all and France had stolen a march on Leopold. For ever since Brazza left Liverpool for West Africa and the upper Ogowe River on 27th December 1879, Leopold and his acolytes had been deluging Stanley with warnings that the French might get to the Congo ahead of him. Irked by the implicit aspersion on his achievement so far, Stanley replied irritatedly to Strauch in February 1880: 'Relative to your information about the French expedition going over from the Ogowe river to Stanley Pool, or the missionaries going there, I beg leave to say that I am not a party to a race for Stanley Pool, as I have already been in that locality just two and a half years ago, and I do not intend to visit it again until I can arrive with my fifty tons of goods, boats and other property, and after finishing the second station. If my mission simply consisted in marching for Stanley Pool, I might reach it in fifteen days, but what would be the benefit of it for the expedition, or the mission that I have undertaken?'

Who was this man who burst so inopportunely on to the scene of Stanley's labours? Like Stanley, he was an 'outsider' in terms of the foreign power he represented. Italian by birth (in 1852), Brazza began his career in the French navy and from 1871 was in service off the coast of Gabon. In 1875 he set out on his first great African expedition, with the aim of discovering the source of the Ogowe. For three years he charted the Ogowe and Alima Rivers meticulously. On his return to France in December 1878 he read Through the Dark Continent and realised for the first time that the Alima was a tributary of the Congo, and that if he had pressed on for another five days he could have planted the French flag on that mighty river.

Brazza was intensely jealous of Stanley's achievements and also resentful that Stanley's battle-strewn passage down the Congo had had unfavourable implications for himself, as when he told his hosts he was in search of his white brother and they, thinking he meant Stanley, turned on him and forced him to flee for his life. Ever afterwards Brazza tried to present himself as a man of peace and a friend of the black man, in contrast to the negrophobic man of force Stanley, though this portrait was severely overdone. It was true that Brazza probably was a man of greater moral courage and had more genuine sympathy for the African. Success was not his only yardstick; moreover, he genuinely liked life in the wilds of Africa. Both men revered Livingstone, but if Stanley was to emulate, and outdo, his mentor's achievements in exploration, he never approached his moral stature. Brazza, a lesser explorer, was a worthier moral successor to Livingstone. But he was no angel. Like Stanley, he was devious, unfair to rivals and thought that he alone understood Africa.

In 1880 Brazza evidently decided that his slow, careful progress in 1875-8 and his solicitude for the sick was the wrong way to proceed if he was to beat Stanley in the race for the Congo. Ironically, his model was the 1874-7 Stanley expedition, the very model Stanley himself had abandoned in his new manifestation of colony-builder. In this new endeavour Brazza had the wholehearted backing of French Prime Minister Gambetta and Foreign Minister Jules Ferry. This time he followed the Ogowe and the Alima on to the Congo, raised the French flag at Stanley Pool, then began to descend the river to the Atlantic coast. He won the respect of local chiefs both by 'burying war' - flinging his cartridges in a hole and covering them with earth - and by leaving them a tangible memory of his coming. At Dakar on his way to the coast he had hired ten Senegalese, including a Sergeant Malamine Kamara, whom he had left at Stanley Pool as the French stakeholder. Malamine quickly gained great status in the eyes of the chiefs around Stanley Pool through his prowess as a hunter; he had brought with him the latest Winchester repeating rifle.

History records many instances of pairs of great explorers operating in the same time and space (Drake and Quiros, Cook and La Perouse) and often in direct competition (Scott and Amundsen, Peary and Cooke, Byrd and Amundsen). It was in this category that Stanley and Brazza fitted, although Stanley was incomparably the greater explorer. The traveller Delcommune described their meeting as an encounter of contrasts, the North against the South, the saturnine against the phlegmatic, the snow and ice against the sunshine. Stanley was tenacious, cold, energetic, hard, shrewd, observant, egotistical. It was not surprising then that both men were wary or that Brazza approached the meeting with circumspection.

Brazza came into camp with fifteen Gabonese sailors armed with Winchester repeaters. He was tall, wore a helmet and a naval blue coat, and his feet were swathed in brown leather bandages. Stanley, as always a stickler for sartorial matters, found Brazza's dress sense closer to that of Livingstone at Ujiji than anything else: 'Genius is often distinguished by some eccentricity. De Brazza's is for ragged clothes and going about the country without walking boots.' Stanley found Brazza of a very dark complexion: he could have been Italian, Portuguese or Andalucian. What impressed Stanley was his energy and 'uncontrollable vivacity'. Stanley welcomed him and ordered breakfast prepared, then sat with him all afternoon and evening discussing Africa, though conversation was difficult, as neither spoke much of the other's language. They discoursed on the Ambanghi tribesmen whom both had had trouble with in 1877,

Stanley at the confluence of the Mpaka, Brazza on the Alima. Brazza confided that he hated to travel with white companions, as they impeded progress by their timidity and irresolution. As they talked, Stanley took closer stock. The Frenchman reminded him in full face of Winwood Reade and in profile of Serpa Pinto. He was a great romancer, prone to hyperbole and exaggeration, completely out of kilter with the current taste for scientific, factual exponents of African exploration; Stanley remarked scathingly that if Brazza's printed stories were anything like the ones he told over the camp fire, 'African travellers will envy him his reputation and become so many Munchausens or Jules Vernes.'

Stanley was more attracted to Brazza than Brazza to him. The Frenchman wounded him by saying that it would take him six months to get past Ngoma mountain and four years to reach Stanley Pool. Moreover, he was far from straight with Stanley. Later he sneeringly contrasted his own superior methods to Stanley's. Stanley's men, he pointed out, were fed on rice and his mules on hay and oats, all imported from Europe; all his work-force was imported too. By contrast, he, Brazza, could not afford such prodigal expenditure, so used the locals on the Ogowe to good effect. Worst of all, he did not reveal to Stanley that even as he sat there yarning with him he had in his pocket a treaty, dated 3rd October 1880, from 'Makoko' of Stanley Pool, ceding him territorial rights on the north bank of the Congo at the Pool. When he later learned this, Stanley was aghast at Brazza's duplicity: 'That's impossible!' he cried in disappointment.

Part of the disappointment came from Stanley's own fantasy that Brazza might be the true male comrade he had sought in vain since Livingstone's death. That he was drawn to the young Frenchman is evident from his diary entry for 7th November 1880.

I sat hours with him this afternoon and evening and find my ordinary measurements unable to follow his illimitableness, and my senses are somewhat confused by the cataract of illusions. My eyes were fastened intently upon a kind of rapture that came and went with wonderful rapidity. What eyes he has, so reckless, glancing and flashing! And the store of ideas and clouds of figures which he flung upon my dazed senses as he represented the intrinsic value of the Congo to that nation which first asserted its right to it.

When Brazza left for Vivi on the morning of 9th November Stanley suspected from his laughing mocking spirit that he was concealing something. As yet, however, Stanley could report just three solid things about the Frenchman to the CEHC: one, he was a great yarn-spinner, in terms of both the number of elephants he was supposed to have shot and the number of chiefs won over; two, he had learned all of Leopold's most secret plans after his visit to Brussels; three, Brazza echoed his oft-spoken sentiments about the desirability of importing Chinese coolies. Of course, this cost money but as Brazza said: 'Who thinks of money in such a scheme as this? The Livingstone [sic] river is worth forty milliards to that company that opens it.' When Brazza departed, Stanley made sure by letter that

Sparhawk at Vivi and all his other contacts on the coast would treat the French party as honoured guests.

Then he turned to the obstacle of Ngoma mountain, determined to prove Brazza wrong. On 24th November he gave Lt. Valcke the task of blasting a road through the side of the 1500-foot mountain wall of quartz and sandstone, using dynamite. The ear-splitting success of this exploit confirmed his nickname of 'Bula Matari' with Africans. Next, by feeding selective titbits from his conversations with Brazza, Stanley was able both to browbeat the CEHC, in Brussels and to energise his own workers. Taunting the Committee with having been systematically hoodwinked by Brazza, who winkled out all their secrets when in Brussels, he praised Brazza's 'brilliant conception' of opening up a trade route to the Congo via the Ogowe and called him a Bismarck in diplomacy and a Moltke on the battlefield. He quoted Brazza's words as an implicit reproach to the Committee: 'You need five hundred men not one hundred. Your task is out of proportion to your numbers. You're in the position I was in on the Ogowe expedition when I could not build roads for lack of wagons.' This was Stanley at his dialectical best. Humiliated by Brazza's advent at Stanley Pool, when he, Stanley, had assured Brussels this was an impossibility, he turned the tables on the CEHC by insinuating that it was their parsimony that had brought about the debacle. Moreover, Brazza had arrived under the open auspices of the French government - and open Belgian involvement on Stanley's behalf was exactly what Leopold's duplicity and secretiveness ruled out.

Next Stanley turned to his work-force. Brazza had boasted that he was able to travel so much faster than Stanley this time because he brought sailors from French stations in Senegal and Gabon and used the tribesmen of Ogowe as porters. Stanley retorted that Brazza had had 600 porters and fifty canoes, whereas all Stanley had was his sixty-seven wangwana. When Susi (of Livingstone fame) heard this, he felt so ashamed for his compatriots that he got them all to volunteer to carry in ten days what had taken Brazza's porters fifteen.

At the end of December the expedition finally got to Isangila, after the most painful stretch of road-building any of them could imagine. They had built three bridges, surveyed mountains, filled several ravines and gorges with earth, and man-hauled all the boats. During the rainy season, the first bridge, near Vivi - two weeks in the making - had been swept away by the swollen torrent. The construction of Isangila station was entrusted to the two army engineers, Lt. Janssen and Lt. Orban, who had just arrived from Europe. Finally, on 21st February 1881, the expedition was ready to move on from Isangila. A year after leaving Vivi, at a cost of 2300 miles' marching, with six Europeans and twenty-two Africans dead and a further thirteen Europeans prostrate with fever, living on a Spartan diet of beans, goat-meat and bananas, they had circumvented the worst of the Lower Congo rapids. Stanley prepared for the advance on Manyanga, leaving Lt. Valcke in charge at Isangila.

On 21st February he launched the Royal and EnAvant on the Congo. Straining every sinew, they squeezed through the rapids at Kunzu; passage would have been easy if the ships had been capable of just an extra 2 knots of speed.

On 28th April Stanley took the whaleboat as far as Manyanga cataract. Manyanga he found a depressing place; moreover, the cataract barred the way and once again they would have to haul the ships overland for the journey to Stanley Pool. Next day Stanley negotiated with the local headman, who was at first unwilling to grant the land for the building of a station but finally grudgingly consented after a lavish gift of cloth and beads. Gloomily Stanley surveyed his achievements so far. In the previous seventy days he had covered 2464 miles in coming 88 miles upriver. Since first leaving Vivi they had spent 436 days on road-making, with a force of sixty-eight Zanzibaris and an equal number of local recruits and West Coast Krumaners, just to get 140 miles from Vivi, and still there were 95 miles to go to Stanley Pool.

But on 5th May Stanley, who had survived 200 fevers already, was attacked by the most powerful one yet. Despite dosing himself with 60 grains of quinine, he lost weight rapidly and soon hovered on the edge of death. For a whole week, from 13th May, he was unconscious. When he came to on 20th May, he was convinced that the end was not far off, so made his farewells to his comrades. But twenty-four hours of sleep took him past the crisis. By 30th May he was out of danger and by the beginning of June he was strong enough to sit in a chair under the awning of his tent. Yet ever afterwards he remembered the horrors of the worst fever of his life, when his head drummed and throbbed more insistently than the Congo tribes in 1877:

The mind drifted away and carried me to a world whose atmosphere was crowded with the most hideously wriggling things imaginable. When these became too hideous to be borne and swarmed about my face and seemed about to enter my nostrils - I made an effort to recover myself and they fled .. . presently I am at the entrance of a very lengthy tunnel, and a light as of a twinkling star is seen an immeasurable length away. There is a sensible increase in the glow, the twinkling ceases, it has become an incandescent globe. It grows large and it advances and I fancy I hear the distant roar. It is a train and it is approaching and the sound of its rush is appalling - and the light grows blinding. It is no more a star, nor a globe but a wide expanding circle of dazzling flames, and the roar is now so overwhelming that I fear I shall be caught in the tunnel - and in this fear I wake up again to hear once more the increasing loud drumming in the head. It is the drumming and the wriggling creatures in the atmosphere of the strange world - and that glowing light and appalling roar that will revert to my memory when I think of this fever.

Recovery was accompanied by good news. The German Otto Lindner had arrived at Isangila with new recruits: there were twenty-four at Isangila and forty-six at Vivi. Cheered by these tidings, the skeletal Stanley (reduced in weight to 100 pounds) put Lt. Harou in charge at Manyanga and ordered a road constructed around the cataract so that he could bring up more boats. He took Valcke, Braconnier and Mahoney and seventy men overland with him for the final difficult stretch to Stanley Pool.

Stanley showed his awareness of the difficulties to come by crossing the river to the south bank for the last stage of the journey to Stanley Pool. The newly-arrived missionaries crossed with him, thus abandoning the original attempt by the Protestant missions to work towards the Pool in echelon on both banks (the LIM were already on the south bank).Had Stanley simply been building a line of stations, as he consistently asserted in his book The Congo and the Founding of its Free State, such a manoeuvre would have been unnecessary. It was the hidden part of his work for Leopold, the trade in ivory, that made this necessary.

Stanley first reached Stanley Pool in June 1881 but it was the end of that year before his position there was consolidated. Not only was he caught up in tribal middleman politics between the Babwende and the Bakongo, but Malamine, Brazza's deputy, menaced him from the opposite shore of the Pool and threatened to subvert the local chiefs, so that they repudiated any territorial concessions signed with Stanley. This period of Stanley's Congo mission is of byzantine complexity. Much of it hinged on rivalries between and within tribes, particularly the alleged paramountcy of a chief called Makoko and the attempts to wrest his crown by a thirty-four-year-old old banditti chief called Ngalyema, who specialised in the ivory and slave trade. It was December 1881 before Stanley had his final showdown with this ruffian, and the occasion provided him with one of his favourite after-dinner stories.

Stanley suspected that, after many weeks of probing, Ngalyema's next action would be sleight of hand or treachery rather than a frontal assault on his camp. So, while asking Makoko to call a grand council to announce to all the chiefs of the Pool the concession he had made to 'Bula Matari', he made appropriate preparations. Makoko's edict had sensational results. Ngalyema's attempts to rally his neighbours against the white man failed dismally. He was turned down by his neighbours Mpila and Kimbe while another, Ngamberengi, asked him what he meant by taking up arms against his blood brother. Infuriated by this, Ngalyema decided to take the bull by the horns. With a small bodyguard he strode into Stanley's camp. Stanley tried to browbeat him by insisting on his right to enter Kintamo; Ngalyema angrily denied this right. When the chief seemed likely to lose his temper, Stanley sounded a gong and his wangwana surrounded Ngalyema's party and forced them ignominiously from camp.

It was typical of Stanley's penchant for fantasy that he later rewrote this incident as a moral tale demonstrating both the superiority of the civilised white man over the benighted black savage and his own Promethean omniscience. Stanley's fantasy version was that he had lured Ngalyema into an elaborate charade. When Ngalyema came into camp, Stanley had hidden the wangwana, armed to the teeth, in a nearby thicket: The encampment appeared deserted and Stanley sat yawning in his chair, apparently bored and listless. By his side was a huge gong. When the discussions with Ngalyema petered out into acrimony, Stanley made a point of asking the chief not to touch the gong as it was powerful 'fetish'. After a lengthy period of being tantalised, the foolish Ngalyema could no longer resist the temptation of summoning the spirit of the gong. He beat it and to his consternation a swarm of armed men suddenly came running at the double. Thus was Ngalyema convinced of the superiority of Bula Matari's magic.

By now more than a hundred new recruits had arrived at Vivi, including the first woman, a focus of great interest by the Africans. At Stanley Pool Stanley himself had 153 blacks, including x 17 workers. They set to work to construct the new station at Leopoldville. First they cut down 125 large trees - teak, redwood and plane - plus nearly 3000 small trees to build the blockhouse, terrace, gardens and village. By 10th January 1882 the frame of the blockhouse was almost complete and by the end of the month the whole project was well advanced. When the last nail was in place on the house, on 25th February, work began on an artificial cove, to permit steamers and other boats to enter the harbour safely at high tide. By the beginning of March the village was complete. The vegetable garden was already thriving and on 9th March trading commenced. Stanley inaugurated proceedings by buying two pounds of ivory for the price of six handkerchiefs.

Leopoldville station was a level earthwork cut away from the hillside, 300 yards long. Here stood the blockhouse. On the ground floor was a long clay magazine containing stores, where cloth and a variety of articles were bartered with the tribes for brass rods or mitakos. On the first floor was Stanley's apartment. Higher up the hill was a building for European staff, divided into seven bedrooms plus an eighth communal room for meals. The post dominated the lake like extension of the Congo called Stanley Pool, a circular basin 250 miles in extent.

Yet if the physical basis of Stanley's work was proceeding well, his presence at the Pool for the first three months of 1882 was necessary to prevent civil war as the chiefs at first feared that Stanley would ally himself with one of them to the detriment of the others. Ngalyema seemed well and truly cowed: Stanley reported him as being interested in obtaining wood for a coffin, almost as though he wished to concretise the death of his larger ambitions. And when he received his trade goods in return for the deed of land, he was described as like a child with a toy. But his son Ngeli, who had reproached Ngalyema for failure to cleave the oaths of blood-brotherhood, bade fair to outstrip his father as a troublemaker. Stanley had to address a stiff formal note in March about Ngeli's fourfold insolence and impertinence to 'Bula Matari'. Not until 9th April 1882 did Stanley formally renew his ties of blood- brotherhood with Ngalyema and then not until Ngalyema had concluded a big ivory deal.

The other problem was the French. When Malamine first saw Stanley firmly ensconced at the Pool, he was inclined to take a hard line and delivered a letter from Brazza, dated August 1881, 'to whom it might concern', protesting against the intended occupation of the north side of the Pool by any other European. But when he saw how masterfully Stanley had his hands on the levers of power in the Pool area, Malamine decided on the better part of valour. A visit to Kinshassa to show off the first steamer on the Upper Congo found Malamine among the friendly crowds who gathered to greet En Avant, Any further fire-eating tendencies on the part of the Senegalese sergeant were terminated abruptly when Leon Guiral arrived as his replacement.

By 19 April Stanley felt confident enough both about the impregnability of the Leopoldville post to tribal attack and of French intentions to continue upriver and found a further station. He set off with En Avant, the whaleboat and two canoes, making heavy weather for 'the powers of the little paddle-steamer were taxed to the utmost, towing the two canoes.' It took them an unconscionable time to get clear of Stanley Pool. First a rainstorm wet their fuel on the 20th and delayed their start from Bamu Island, a 14-mile long sliver of land teeming with elephant, hippos and buffalo. Next, they were hampered by the straining of the boilers, the excessive heat and the necessarily cramped posture of the passengers. The sole consolation was the staggering beauty of the scenery between Stanley Pool and Mswata. Stanley confessed he could never understand the contemporary passion for Scottish lochs, but he could appreciate any conceivable rhapsody on the Congo, whose splendours dimmed anything he had seen in the Americas from Belize to Omaha.

During the rest of April-May 1882 Stanley alternated between administration at Leopoldville and further forays into the regions of the Upper Congo in the hinterland of Stanley Pool. But on one of these expeditions, he went down with another serious attack of fever. He lost consciousness and remembered nothing until he found himself back in Leopoldville. He was not out of danger until 27th June, but even when on his feet again found himself suffering from chronic gastritis and incipient dropsy.

He took a decision. After three years' hard toil in the Congo, it was time to recuperate in Europe on a home leave. He had achieved his principal objectives and more: he had constructed a line of stations from the ocean to Stanley Pool and, most importantly, by his treaties with Ngalyema and other chiefs like Ngobila, he had circumvented the French and set Brazza's earlier opportunistic feat at nought. The initiative now lay firmly with Leopold and the AIA. Stanley turned his face towards Vivi, the Atlantic and Europe.

Chapter Four

STANLEY'S mood as he came downriver for his convalescent leave was sour. Apart from his serious illness, he was cast down by how little had been achieved at Manyanga, saw little to cheer him at Isangila, and on 8th July 1882 at Vivi received his worst jolt yet. There had been yet another twist in Leopold's complex skein. Finally heeding Stanley's pleas that Otto Lindner's administrative skills were too good to squander on the Loango expedition, Leopold had sent another German, the naturalist Dr Peschuel-Loesche to head up the Loango probe. Peschuel-Loesche and Lindner were old comrades, having been together on the abortive Von Falkenstein expedition into the Loango in 873-5 when, as Stanley contemptuously noted, the Germans spent £9000 to advance just 140 miles into the interior. Mysteriously, on arrival at Vivi, Peschuel-Loesche made no move to go up the Loango. The reason became clear when Stanley arrived at Vivi to announce that he was going to Europe on sick leave. It turned out that Peschuel-Loesche had all the time had an order in his pocket from Leopold, nominating him as Stanley's successor in the event of sickness or resignation. As Stanley cynically observed: 'No wonder the man never stirred but has waited to step into my shoes. He has remained here doing nothing since March of this year.'

By now inured to Leopold's secretiveness and duplicity, Stanley was not especially surprised that the King had not consulted him on this appointment, even after he had freely conceded Stanley's right to nominate his own successor. But as he briefed Peschuel-Loesche and was in turn put in the picture by the German on the monarch's latest thinking, it was clear that Leopold still imagined he could advance a number of Congo projects in echelon, despite Stanley's warning. The King still hankered after the opening of a second trade route that could not conceivably be disputed by the French. The Loango mission was designed to outflank Brazza and was regarded by Leopold as even more important than the unlocking of the Upper Congo. In addition Peschuel-Loesche was instructed to gain exploitation rights to all mines, forests, vegetable and mineral assets. But most of all, Leopold advanced his most full-blooded colonisation conception yet. Peschuel-Loesche was explicitly admonished to regard the British North Borneo treaties with the Sultans of Brunei and Sulu as models for the treaties he should make with the Congo chiefs; it was territorial concessions alone that would allow Belgian influence to survive on the Congo. In a word, Peschuel-Loesche had been ordered to implement the very plan that Stanley rejected as impracticable at Gibraltar in 1879.

Stanley was too ill to argue the point. A new era for the expedition seemed to be dawning anyway. New personnel had arrived in the form of Von Dankelman and Van de Velde. Valcke had just come in with the fresh force of 200 Zanzibaris. The wangwana whose three-year contract was up would be escorted back home by a roundabout route taking in St Helena by Gillis and Albert Christopherson, also departing after three years' service. As a first stage Gillis intended to accompany Stanley to St Paul de Loanda and see the invalid leader on to the first Europe-bound steamer. At this stage Stanley was thinking of convalescing in Madeira prior to coming to a final decision about his future.

At Boma on 15th July Stanley was met by Mgr. Augouard who thanked him for all his help. The meeting was cordial and prolonged. The missionaries of all denominations owed a lot to Stanley, but not all of them acknowledged it. Whereas the Baptist Mission paid tribute to his achievements and poured scorn on the canard that Stanley was invariably a man of force, the Livingstone Inland Mission made common cause with his critics in Europe. This was all part of a differential strategy whereby the BMS preferred to co-operate with Leopold, whereas the LIM set its face against the King and all his works. They alleged, truthfully, that Stanley and the Belgians merely used the missions for their own cynical ends. This ostensible generosity was all part of a general strategy dictated from Brussels of preventing the missions from getting their own land by a veiled threat that if missions tried to own their own territory, it would all be alienated to the Catholic missionaries.

Transferring from the Belgique (on to which he had been carried, so ill was he), Stanley boarded the steamer Heron for the journey to Ambriz, where he arrived on 17th July. Once again he experienced his usual bad luck with maritime connections, missing the mail steamer by hours. He pressed on to St Paul de Loanda for an enforced stay of a month. He was put up by Herr Niemann, agent of the Dutch House, and treated by a Dr Olivera for the dropsical swelling in the legs, the result of the latest bout of haematitic fever. After three severe bouts (27-30th April 1880, 5-21st May 1881 and 31st May – 9th July 1882), even Stanley's iron frame was beginning to buckle: 'another one like this would kill the best constitution unless there was a period of recuperation in Europe between.'

As he slowly recovered in the Portuguese port, Stanley could allow his mind to wander to the few occasions on the Congo when he had been able to bask in the luxury of an inner life. He continued to brood about the bad press he enjoyed in England. In 1880 in the House of Commons Robert Fowler and Dr Cameron had bracketed him with the missionaries of Lake Nyasa as a perpetrator of 'outrages' in Africa. Stanley was adamant that he never fought except in self-defence and that the locus classicus of his 'atrocities' - Bumbire - had been necessary for the 'credibility' of the white man. He continued to ponder the absurdity of the charges brought against him: to whom was he supposed to look for arbitration when attacked by the tribes of Ituru or Bumbire? Was he supposed to give up more than 300 lives 'without benefit of priest or prayer, at the first demand of a rabble of unreasoning savages who had obtained the land they lived in by force of arms? ... the sharp lesson we were obliged to inflict on the impudent Wasuma was just what a spirited Englishman would try to give a lot of burglars whom he found in his house, boasting of their exploit and holding their plunder to view.

His only fault, he concluded, was that his early training as a journalist had taught him to set down the truth as he experienced it. The British public did not want truth - it wanted homiletic parables to disguise its own humbug. In his mind he ran through all the examples he knew of shooting incidents involving Englishmen, including some well-known Africa hands: Verney Cameron and Mackay of Uganda. Then the piece de resistance, aimed at an old enemy: 'The British Consul-General of Zanzibar Dr John Kirk lately shot an Arab on that island. Neither accidentally or wilfully have I done anything of that kind.'

Yet in other respects the three years on the Congo provided evidence of a certain mellowing in Stanley. The award of a doctorate from a German university for 'services to civilisation' helped: 'I have had so much dispraise since 1872 that honours of this kind serve to keep up one's spirit.' It is hard to imagine the old Stanley lending a helping hand to an old adversary, yet when he heard that Pincoffs of the Afrikaanishche Vereeneging - his opponent at the acrimonious Brussels Committee meeting on 9 December 1878 - had fled to the USA to avoid arrest, Stanley sent him £50; he did, however, draw the line at helping him to get a job as there was something far from creditable and straightforward about the collapse of the Dutch company.

His fascination with the African continued undiminished. As part of his theory that one could match physiognomy with temperaments he had made a detailed physical study of Dualla, who was now accompanying him to Europe. His fascination with the nude African figure is more the sensuous delight of the artist than the lubricy of a homoerotic sensibility. Eyes above all fascinated him. He had used his own steel-grey orbs to stare out and face down some of the greatest chiefs in Africa, so was more than normally disposed to see them as the mirrors of the soul. He claimed to be able to read any man like a book by gazing into his eyes. 'Not even de Brazza could completely hide what moved least. The laughing devil stood in his eyes like a mischievous imp, toyed with the firm lines around them, lowered and raised the eyelids, stepped out with freedom in the iris, or contracted himself into a pinpoint far behind. He was there all the same, joyous and tricky.'

But perhaps the most impressive evidence of the mellowing process in Stanley was in his response to children. In November 1881, while awaiting the final showdown with Ngalyema, he noted the following: 'All this day small children have made themselves at home in my camp - and have gambolled for hours before my tent door. I have never seen such touching confidence displayed before in all my African experience. The sight of these tender naked little beings following my camp into the wilderness, and laughing in my face, and hugging my knees, just thrilled me.'

On 17th August after a month of inactivity and reflection, Stanley boarded the mail-steamer China for Lisbon. Its track lay through St Thomas Island, Prince's Island, Bulama, St Jago, St Vincent (Cape Verde

Islands) and Madeira - twenty-six days' steam on a very slow boat. If the human side of Stanley had been triggered by his enforced rest at St Paul de Loanda, exposure to actual human beings at once turned him sour again. He deplored the lack of discipline on the China and the failure to enforce the rules on the second-class passengers. 'These, permitted to leave their own quarters, and invade on the narrow (first-class) deck, expectorated, smoked, and sprawled in the most socialistic manner.' Another irritant was the insolent and offhand behaviour of the stewards and the failure of the Portuguese officers to do anything about it: 'An American or a British captain, with a few iron belaying-pins within easy reach, would have restored order in the most peremptory manner.'

By the time the China reached Madeira (17th September), which impressed him favourably, Stanley could walk a few paces. Four days later they were steaming up the Tagus and from Lisbon he preceded to Paris overland (arrived 28th September). By the end of the month he was in Brussels, ready to talk business with Strauch and Leopold. He caught the Comite largely unprepared, for they had assumed that he would return to the Congo from Madeira before taking European leave.

In his first interview with Strauch Stanley made it clear that his return to the Congo was unlikely. As he understood it, his contract with the CEHC had expired, and he had in fact provided the Comite with an extra eight months as a bonus. This was not the way Strauch saw it. He insisted that the explorer's personal contract with the King took precedence. This was still in being, therefore Stanley must return to the Congo at the earliest possible moment. The Belgians intended to find a replacement, but it had to be the right man; such things could not be done in a trice.

Stanley was mightily cast down by this interpretation of the contracts but, after all, Leopold had inserted a clause allowing him the option of renewal after the initial three years. The question was whether Stanley's health could stand up to another tour: 'I had intended to bid adieu to Africa for a few years at least.' When he went to see the King, Stanley was still undecided about whether to yield to the monarch's importunities; one of his physicians had advised him that a return to Africa was tantamount to signing a suicide pact. Leopold, who had so bitterly criticised Stanley behind his back and secretly negotiated to get Gordon as his successor, suddenly realised how vital the finder of Livingstone was to his long-term plans. To Stanley's face he was all honeyed charm: 'Surely, Mr Stanley, you cannot think of leaving me just when I need you?' After much cajolery, Stanley reluctantly agreed to resume his burden in the Congo on or about 1st November 1882, but on certain unambiguous conditions. First, there had to be a better understanding in Brussels of the true state of affairs in the Congo. Secondly, if his letters were bluntly expressed, this should not be resented in the AIA offices or attributed to malice - he must be free to speak as he found.

Warming to his theme now that he realised how badly Leopold needed him, he poured withering scorn on Strauch's tripartite orders (territorial acquisitions, ivory purchases and penetration of the Upper Congo). He could no longer tolerate contradictory orders, sometimes a dozen at a time 'as though I had qualified agents without number fit to perform them simultaneously.' He took the King through his Congo personnel one by one and underlined their shortcomings before reverting to the tripartite instructions from Strauch and rubbing the monarch's nose in it: 'Your bureau should have known that there was only myself capable of doing any one of these things.'

Next he rapped Leopold for having subsumed the CEHC in the AIC without informing him until 1881: 'When I started in 1879 I had one, order, which was to build three stations and land EnAvant on the Upper Congo. That was simplicity itself. But now we have developed into a political power, a commercial company and also an exploring and pioneering expedition.' That being so, it was imperative that there should be someone capable left in charge at Leopoldville when he ventured on to the Upper Congo; perhaps this could be Gordon or Captain Thys, Strauch's assistant. Leopold nodded sagely at each point Stanley made, however roughly, said that all would be done to the explorer's suggestion and proposed an adjournment.

In one compartment of his mind, Stanley knew well enough that Leopold was manipulating him into a return to the Congo. But he found it impossible not to admire the devious old reprobate. After dealing with so many African potentates, he confessed he was no longer much taken in by royal pomp and majesty, but for all that he admitted that there was something different about Leopold; the Prince of Wales was the only other royal personage who could put one completely at ease, and it was providential that it was Leopold, not one of the Rothschild's, say, who was opening up Africa:

He is now in his forty-seventh year in the prime of life. His long flowing beard is quite brown. There is not a wrinkle on his face .. . [He possessed] the inimitable courtesy and graciousness of a truly royal gentleman ... While coming down the Congo [in 1877] I dreamed of some young Rothschild undertaking the civilisation of the Congo basin and entrusting me with the task like that imagined Prince in Thomas Carlyle's Shooting Niagara saying 'There is the money you need. Go and fulfil your writ.'

On 3rd October Stanley put the King out of his suspense by agreeing to return to Africa, against the advice of his physicians. Leopold again promised to fulfil all Stanley's conditions, reiterated that the British Borneo Company was the crucial precedent for the Congo, then passed him on to Strauch. In a no-holds-barred heart-to-heart with Strauch, Stanley finally learned the reason for much of the mysterious behaviour by his employees in the Congo. It turned out that the volunteers had insisted on contracts specifying service to the Comite rather than to a named chief of expedition. Lindner and Peschuel-Loesche, it now transpired, had expressly stipulated that they were not to be part of Stanley's staff. Strauch tried to sugar this pill by saying that he was sure there was no objection to

Stanley personally, it was just that they wanted to be explorers in their own right. Stanley put his own gloss on the prima donna-ish behaviour of the personnel on the Congo: they all wanted to loaf about doing nothing while drawing huge salaries and writing articles for newspapers betimes. What sort of example was this? 'No black man will work unless he is supervised, and the white man also is a master in the art of shirking when left to his own will.'

On 4th October Stanley lunched with Leopold and sketched out his ideas for the second part of the Congo enterprise. An ancillary expedition should be sent into the Kwilu-Niari basin to outflank the French. Secondly, Stanley would select the men he wanted to serve with him but his name would be kept out of the contracts. Signatories would have to take an oath of loyalty to the expedition chief personally, rather than the Executive Committee in Brussels; only when they were on board ship at Cadiz would it be revealed to them that they had taken a personal pledge of allegiance to Stanley. Finally, the way to knock out Brazza and the French was to maintain the sort of secrecy that had been conspicuously absent in 1879. A. steamer would be chartered, loaded with trade goods, and taken from Antwerp to Cadiz. Stanley meanwhile would board an express and speed down to southern Spain while Brazza thought he was still in Paris. This would provide him with the three months' head start on the French he needed for putting everything on a proper footing on the Lower Congo. He could then take a flotilla on to the Upper Congo in full confidence that his rear was secure.

Before he left for London on 5th October, Stanley twitted Leopold for having contributed £1600 to the French branch of the International Association, which meant that the King had in fact financially staked his rival. But Stanley had still not got the full measure of his master's two-facedness. Two weeks before Stanley arrived in Brussels, Leopold had again entertained his rival Brazza at the royal palace, naively hoping to 'turn' the Frenchman to work for him. Nothing came of these talks, except that Brazza's suspicions of Leopold's ultimate designs were deepened. Brazza threw in the additional thought that Stanley's true allegiance was to the British and the Americans that he hoped ultimately to make the Congo an Anglo-Saxon enclave. Moreover, he insinuated that Stanley's return to Europe was mysterious. This chimed in with Leopold's own conviction that Stanley's 'illness' was bogus and that the real motive for his sudden return to Europe was to cross swords with Brazza.

These allegations were later to bear fruit, though there was not a shred of truth in them. Stanley had offered the Congo to the British on a plate in 1878 and they had turned him down. His activities on behalf of Leopold were generally perceived to be diametrically opposed to British interests in the region. This was a line assiduously peddled by the old enemy Kirk. As early as 1880 he warned Salisbury that the Popelin expedition, if successful in cutting a route through to Stanley Falls, would ensure that all the ivory of Central Africa would be taken down to the Atlantic coast; the east-coast ivory trade would become a back number. He repeated this advice frequently during Lord Granville's incumbency as Foreign Secretary, stressing that British interests required the extension of the Sultan's territories ever westward to block Belgian expansionism. When challenged on his intentions, Leopold assured the British that his stations were being set up solely for the interests of commerce and civilisation, that he had no political aims or ambitions.

Even a blind man could have seen that Leopold was lying. His assurances were worthless. Every time the King approached the Sultan of Zanzibar for permission to hire more men on the island, he assured him this was positively his last recruitment request. Then he would shamelessly break his word and wheedle around the Sultan again. Leopold indeed sat long hours with Strauch working out exactly how they could hoodwink the hapless Barghash. But he was deeply worried about the British. Already calls had begun to be heard from Stanley's friends, like Hutton in the Manchester Chamber of Commerce, for a treaty guaranteeing the neutrality of the Congo. This underlines the fact that Stanley and Leopold always had conflicting aims for the Congo. While Leopold was trying to manipulate entrepreneurs like Hutton (and through him the British government) for his own ends, Stanley genuinely wanted the British involved, in the hope that the Congo could yet become part of the Empire.

These irreconcilable interests might have had explosive force in late 1882 but for the intervention of England's old enemy France. Until 1882 Leopold had been lucky. The Eastern question, problems with Afghans and Zulus, and finally the collapse of Dual Control in Egypt had preoccupied the minds of British statesmen, so that Leopold was in effect given free rein in the Congo. Yet the very fact of British triumph over Arabi Pasha in Egypt, which edged out the former French partners, made France determined not to be outmanoeuvred on the Congo.

This determination coincided with the return of Brazza from Brussels - a Brazza armed with new insights into Leopold's true ambitions. The King was right to fear that if Brazza's view prevailed in Paris, his own schemes for 'humanity' (i.e. exploitation) in the Congo would be destroyed, as European conflicts were projected out into Africa; this would mean that he would be put to the unwanted expense of political colonisation. Although Brazza's official superiors in the French Navy Department were not keen on African colonisation, the Ministry of Foreign Affairs, in one of its periodic fits of anger against 'perfidious Albion', decided to publish the 'Makoko' treaties and present them for ratification. Some historians have seen the French ratification of the Makoko treaties as the true origin of the 'scramble for Africa'. But there can be no question about their immediate causality. Even Kirk admitted that jealousy of England was the motive for French ratification of these 'ridiculous' treaties.

The French action played into Leopold's hands in one sense. It allowed him to claim that he now had no option but to obtain sovereign territorial rights in the Congo to protect 'free trade' against French protectionism; in a word France gave him the excuse to do openly what he had all along been attempting surreptitiously. On 16th October the King told Strauch he was not satisfied with the terms of the treaties Stanley had made with the chiefs; an article must be added, ceding to Brussels sovereign rights over their territories.

The new French bearing also plunged Stanley personally into the maelstrom. Back in London Stanley was working on schemes for possible new senior recruits for the Congo, including the traveller Archibald Colquhoun and Verney Cameron (against whom, however, there was a question mark on the grounds that he drank). Suddenly there came an invitation from the Stanley Club in Paris to speak at a banquet. Stanley saw a chance to tarnish the image of Brazza. He was irritated by the way Brazza contrasted himself as the man of peace as against Stanley the man of war, the gende Latin saving Africa from the brutal Anglo-Saxon. Despite advice from Leopold not to go, Stanley hastened to his old watering hole at the Hotel Meurice in the Rue de Rivoli.

According to the usual version, Stanley bumped into Brazza on a Paris street and warned him that he was going to attack him in a speech at the Stanley Club banquet. But the true story emerges from Stanley's diaries. Brazza called on him at the Hotel Meurice and Stanley advised him that he intended to deliver the coup mortel that night at the Hotel Continental. Brazza asked if he could attend. Stanley replied that he could promise nothing since he was merely a guest himself. The two evidently parted on good terms: 'We had a good deal of talk of an amiable kind, because personally he is unexceptionable, has lots of good humour and is a gay raconteur.'

The banquet that night turned out to be a much grander affair than Stanley had expected. The cream of Anglo-Saxon Society in Paris was there. For once Stanley indulged himself in champagne, so that when the time came for his address after the toasts, by his own admission it went on too long. He then pitched into Brazza in no uncertain manner. Brazza, he said, was a combination of Lally, Machiavelli and Pizarro. His so-called treaty with the Bateke 'Makoko' was a thing of farce. His Makoko was not paramount chief of the area, so had no right to make the concessions he made. And what kind of behaviour was it to gull an illiterate into signing a treaty in triplicate, then giving Malamine, who could not read, a document requiring him to afford every hospitality to any white man who came to Stanley Pool while verbally instructing him to the contrary? This was Machiavellianism in anybody's language; it was the introduction of 'an immoral diplomacy into a virgin continent'. It would have been far better if Brazza had worked under AIA auspices instead of fomenting the narrow nationalism symbolised by the French tricolour. He wound up by saying that he could not join in the paeans of praise for Brazza. So far from bringing morality to Africa, Brazza was the serpent in Eden.

As Stanley worked up towards his peroration, Brazza handed in his card at the door and asked to be admitted. Stanley acceded to the request The

US Minister introduced Brazza, in full dinner dress, and had him sit down next to Stanley. A toast was called for and when Brazza stood up to reply there was a roar of approval from the fifty Frenchmen present. Brazza's riposte to Stanley gained from its restraint and its astringent wit. He could have pointed out that the references to the AIA were humbug, since this had been superseded by the CEHC and then by the AIC, of whose very existence Stanley was unaware until 188 x , So much for internationalism. He chose instead to ignore the 'international' dimension, as if it did not exist, and proceeded as if Belgian/French rivalries were a fact of life. The contrast between Stanley the conquistador and Brazza the peace-lover was drawn by sly innuendo. He ended his speech by ironically calling for the very international co-operation that Stanley had presumed in his remarks. Proposing a toast to international solidarity, each country under its own flag working together, he threw out the broadest possible intimation that Leopold's 'internationalist' pretensions were spurious. The verbal duel was generally considered a win on points for Brazza.

Stanley did not see it that way at all. He was so convinced that he had had the better of the encounter that he pooh-poohed the idea that it was 'bad form' for Brazza to come to the banquet uninvited and attempt to steal Stanley's thunder; not at all, he replied: the rivalry between the two helped him as it publicised his work in Africa as the successor to Livingstone. But next day he was taken aback by the ferocity of press attacks on 'Stanley, Albion's Trojan horse': 'What a vocabulary of abuse this polite nation has!' He had not realised that by coming to France at this particularly delicate time he had walked straight into the cannon's mouth. It was no exaggeration to point out, as the London Times did, that the French government was launching itself irresponsibly into the unknown in Africa on a wave of crazed public opinion and perfervid patriotism.

Stanley bounced back next day with customary buoyancy. He gave a breakfast at the Hotel Meurice for thirty guests, including Brazza, Edward King and John Hay, author of the Pike County ballads: 'We had a good time and de Brazza and I laughed uproariously at the consternation of some of the gentlemen at the Continental to whom his presence was unsuspected.' But Stanley was underestimating the fear and hatred entertained towards him by the French, who saw him as Britain's stalking horse, even as he pretended to work for Leopold. Ever afterwards Stanley was a particular bête noire in French Foreign Ministry circles.

The rivalry between Brazza and Stanley itself was soon transmogrified as a living symbol of the struggle between Britain and France, even though on paper the two explorers represented the French and Belgians respectively. To Brazza's discredit, his smiling countenance at breakfast at the Hotel Meurice did not reveal his true feelings either about Stanley personally or his intentions. Later he was to underline the canard that Stanley was acting as a kind of British fifth column in the Congo. He also described Stanley's outflanking of him in 1883-4 as a personal vendetta and stated that Stanley was no gentleman. Naturally his intrinsic dislike would have been accentuated by the Welshman's decisive upstaging of him on the Upper Congo in 1883. The barbed remarks at the banquet, which later found their way into print, did not help matters either.

On 22nd October Stanley crossed the Channel back to England to find himself once again a target for begging letters and leeching relatives. With a mixture of resignation and bitterness he recorded in his diary:

People have come to impute to me great riches. Nothing can persuade my poor relations and those who think they have a claim on me but that I am rolling in wealth. By the urgency of their appeals they affect to know my financial condition better than I know it myself. They began as early as 1872 when all my worldly wealth was carried in my pocket but the numbers of believers in my riches are now considerably increased. I was indeed in 1872 rich in health and spirits ... I am now somewhat richer in experience, with less health and spirits - and as regards money - of what avail is it to think of it when one has very little chance of enjoying any of it. If I did not think each time I was about to enter Africa that there were too many chances against my returning to England, I might indulge in the belief that I need not fear starvation but I am not half so rich as these begging letter writers affect to believe.

For a week he toiled away on the plans for phase two of the Congo operation. He sent a number of men to Brussels for Leopold to look over, among them Captain Grant-Elliott whom he docketed as 'one to note'. Colquhoun turned down the offer of a senior appointment. Verney Cameron, who was not as hostile to Stanley as might have been supposed, and wrote five times to him between 1872 and 1884, likewise declined to serve, eliciting from Stanley the waspish conclusion 'Cameron is of course impossible, not but what he is intelligent enough, but he is not of the stuff to work.'

The end of October saw him back in Brussels, suffering from tripleheader malady. His cardiac arrhythmia had returned, he was suffering from bronchitis and his teeth required urgent work. While he consulted physicians and dentists, he received a set of amended instructions, dated 30th October and 1st November. These clarified the contractual position of Lindner and Peschuel-Loesche vis-a-vis the main expedition, explicitly gave him the right to nominate his successor, and contained detailed orders on the push into the Upper Congo; particular target areas for the acquisition of territorial concessions were the stretch between Leopold Ville and Ikalemba and between the Bangala and Stanley Falls. There was also a sealed letter to the captain of the Harkatvay, a charter ship at Cadiz, which informed him that landfall would be advised by the expedition leader once they were at sea. Stanley then prepared for a leisurely journey to Cadiz via Paris or, as he put it to Edward Marston, 'to busy myself in southern Spain, in a genial climate, and get rid of bronchial affections and the misery of chest uneasiness.'

On 12th November he dined at the Hotel de Londres with his friends Mr and Mrs French Sheldon. He was planning to take the 8 p.m. express from

Paris to Madrid that evening. Over soup Stanley sustained a violent attack of the mysterious stomach bug that had first appeared at Manyanga. The attack was so severe that he could scarcely breathe. Stanley felt that if the pain had lasted a minute longer, he would have expired on the spot. A doctor was sent for and, after injecting morphine, debated with French Sheldon as to the aetiology of the illness. Sheldon was certain it was contraction of the pylorus, but the physician diagnosed acute inflammation of the stomach. Stanley's own interpretation (consistent with his tendency to paranoid delusions) was that he had been poisoned, but by whom? The French, Portuguese and Dutch were all plausible candidates, perhaps especially the Dutch, from whose house at Banana he had already received one anonymous death threat.

Though in intermittent agony, Stanley resolved not to stay in Paris but to press on; if he was to die, he preferred it to be in Madrid or on the Harkaway. He begged a syringe and vial of black morphine from the doctor, and was driven off to the station in a drowsy state. He boarded the Madrid train, but within minutes the effects of the drugs began to wear off and the dreadful pain returned. He wanted to shriek out in agony but, in true Anglo-Saxon stiff-upper-lip fashion, was afraid of making a scene. Yet in the end an inadvertent groan escaped his lips. A Spanish marquesa, who was sharing the compartment, asked Stanley's servant what was the matter. When it was explained, she came over and wiped his face and bathed it in some perfumed water 'and ministered to me with such feminine grace and assiduity that filled me with devout gratitude.' However, she could do nothing about the pain; Stanley's new manservant Illingworth had to spend the next thirty-six hours to Madrid intermittently injecting his master with morphine.

Once in Madrid the marquesa saw him to a carriage, which bore him to a suite at the Hotel Russie. Here for seven days he remained under the care of a doctor, occasionally rising from his sick-bed to fire off a telegram to Strauch about Brazza, the new employees in the Congo and even on one occasion, such was his attention to detail, concerning the measurements for planks of teak wood! But on the afternoon of the seventh day, to the Spanish physician's horror, he asked for his bill and made as though to depart. The doctor warned Illingworth that he was putting his master's life at risk. From the mulatto colour on Stanley's face, the physician inferred that he had picked up some unknown tropical strain, which he had then exacerbated by overdosing with drugs to combat it. He prescribed a milk diet for the explorer and warned him to keep off further medication if he valued his life.

Stanley swept out of the hotel, caught the express to Cadiz, arrived next afternoon on board Harkaway and ordered an immediate sailing. The captain just had time to obtain his papers. Then, at 11 a.m. on 23rd November, the ship cleared for the Congo.

Chapter Five

STANLEY arrived back in the Congo on 14th December 1882 to find all was chaos and confusion. The two German 'supremos' sent out by Leopold, Lindner and Peschuel-Loesche, had already decamped, leaving behind them an administrative shambles. For two months Stanley struggled manfully to pull the demoralised expedition together. Meanwhile he sent Lt. Van de Velde to take possession of the mouth of the Kwilu and the adjoining coastline. Van de Velde moved very quickly, and by February 1883 had secured a territory on both sides of the river mouth and set up a station called Rudolphstadt. Striking upriver in hopes of meeting another party under Captain Elliott, he signed treaties with the chiefs en route, then founded yet another station, Baudoinville, at the confluence of the Kwilu and Lumani.' By this time he was out of supplies and returned to the coast just in time to forestall a French gunboat which on Brazza's advice had been sent to take possession of the Kwilu estuary. On the coast there were rumours of a white man sick upstream. Van de Velde went upriver, found Elliott, nursed him through convalescence, then returned with him to Rudolphstadt. From here Elliott set out again to establish a further station (Grantville) midway between the Kwilu and the Loango. This effectively severed all outlets between the Ogowe, the Congo and the Atlantic; only Loango, claimed by the roving French gunboat, was excluded from the Association's sphere of influence.

Stanley put the final nail in the French coffin by sending Hannsens to set up a line of communication between the Congo and the Niari, so as to link up with the Elliott route. Starting from Manyanga in February 1883, Hannsens reached the upper Niari by the end of April and founded Philippeville. By these three brilliant operations Stanley completely turned the tables on Brazza. Not only was the Kwilu Niari route several times shorter than that by the Ogowe; without control of this valley, along which a railway could be built to Stanley Pool, the French post at the Pool itself lost much of its value.

Thus did Stanley refute all the simple-minded criticisms by Leopold's more intemperate officials. His patient, long-term strategy had paid off spectacular dividends. Late 1882 and early 1883 saw the neurotic fusspots of the Comite in Brussels working themselves into a lather about what would happen when Brazza returned to the Congo. What was his exact route? How could the Comite compete with the credit of 1,275,000 francs voted by the French Assembly for Brazza's work after the ratification of the Makoko treaties? Might not France be contemplating a military occupation of Vivi? All these fears were groundless. When Brazza arrived in Central Africa in February 1883 he at once saw that Stanley had beaten him. He proceeded to Stanley Pool, invoked the now useless and superseded Makoko treaties and reinforced French claims on the left bank of the Congo against the day they might be exchanged for the Niari-Kwilu valley. He then proceeded to write screeds of complaint to France for transmission to Leopold about Stanley's underhandedness'. Leopold and Stanley concurred in concluding that this revealed Brazza as a mere opportunist, devoid of real talent; a genuine 'man of Africa' would attempt to challenge Stanley on the Upper Congo.

After dispatching the three Kwilu-Niari expeditions, Stanley wanted to press on upriver at once. But his departure was delayed by an untoward event when Fontaine, Gillis's agent, shot Masala, the interpreter at Vivi station and a key local figure. Fortunately the wound was not mortal, but the local chiefs converged on Vivi to demand reparations and see how the great Bula Matari dispensed justice. They began by demanding a hefty fine of £430 worth of trade goods. When the alarmed Fontaine told Stanley he could not pay, patient negotiation was required from Bula Matari to get a satisfactory resolution. The fine was reduced to £24, the offending revolver was ceremonially broken into small pieces, and Fontaine himself banished forever.

At last, on 22nd January, Stanley was able to get under way. He departed Vivi with a train of ninety-five wangwana, ten Kabindas and thirteen locals. He was at Isangila on 31st January and arrived at Manyanga on 4th February. On the 7th the Royal was mounted on a steam-launch for transport overland to Leopoldville. Having got as far as the river Inkissi on 27th February, Stanley was dumbfounded to receive the news that Leopoldville station was desperately short of food. To him this made no sense, as all the way on the road to Stanley Pool he encountered nothing but abundant food and friendliness from the tribes. But his stupefaction was complete when he eventually reached Leopoldville after an overland march to find, instead of a prospering agricultural settlement, a station overgrown with grass. Everywhere he discovered evidence of grotesque ineptitude and incompetence. The scale of his officers' failure was breathtaking. The near-starvation had resulted from a total breakdown in communication between the white officers of the Association and the local black chiefs. Stanley reported to Strauch that the scale of decay at Leopoldville beggared description.

When he reflected that the station chief, Braconnier, had been vacationing at Vivi (and even thinking of 'going sick' to Europe into the bargain) while all this was going on, the magma of Stanley's volcanic wrath finally cracked its casing. Braconnier had not helped his own cause by calmly telling Stanley, as if it were an event on Mars, that in his absence most of the Kinshassa chiefs had declared for France. On 31th March Stanley peremptorily dismissed him as station chief and offered him a lesser position. When the Belgian denied his superior authority, Stanley dismissed him. Braconnier then added insolence to injury by claiming that Stanley had no power to dismiss him, that Strauch had given him an absolute and indefeasible power at Leopoldville and a promise that no civilian or military authority could displace him. Stanley reiterated that he was sacked and that he would use main force to keep him off Association premises.

Next he wrote a blistering letter to Strauch to explain the sacking. After all the complaints he had made about Belgian officers with their private contracts (literal privilege), here was the most signal instance yet of Strauch's utter folly in making stupid and vain promises behind the back of the expedition leader. He rehearsed the tortuous history of his relations with Braconnier and pointed out that he had already dismissed Braconnier once, in 1881, and then reinstated him at the Comite's wish. His (Stanley's) very credibility was now at stake; Brussels had to choose between him and Braconnier without further prevarication: 'I would rather beg my bread around the world than be a passive spectator of indolence and incapacity, coolly sitting down uninterested in this drama on the Congo.' In a further private letter to Leopold Stanley protested at the preposterous pledge Braconnier claimed to have from Strauch; one would have to go back to the 'old Jesuits' to find such an idea. He put the King firmly on the spot, as only Stanley could: 'Sire, I had either to discharge Braconnier or to discharge myself. If I have done wrong, Your Majesty will be pleased to reinstate M. Braconnier and also to recall me.' It is not difficult to guess which option Leopold elected.

Stanley's main aim on his second tour was the unlocking of the Upper Congo. He had settled Brazza and the French. But before he could proceed upriver he had also to square the troublesome Leopoldville missionaries and, most important of all, put the Association on a good footing with the Stanley Pool chiefs, Ngalyema especially. Relations with Ngalyema had reached an all-time low in Stanley's absence. On 8 April, when all the Kintamo chiefs called on Bula Matari for a conclave, Ngalyema complained bitterly and vociferously about the haughty and arrogant treatment meted out to him by Braconnier and the other Belgian officers at Leopoldville. But behind this tale of personal slight lurked a story of hard-headed political calculation. After the foundation of Mswata, Ngalyema feared that his position as an intermediary in the Congo ivory market was under threat. When he learned in January 1883 of the good relations between Opontaba and the Association he had tried to stymie expansion upriver by a food blockade which, however, was an ignominious failure. Until Stanley's arrival Ngalyema and Ntsuula teetered on the brink of open warfare. Also, chief Bankwa of Ndolo opposed the signing of a general treaty with the Association.

At first Stanley too beat in vain against the rock of Bankwa, who persuaded Ntsuulu against a general treaty. But his formidable advocacy, the sheer awe in which he was held by the chiefs, and his overpowering mixture of charm and power (aided not inconsiderably by his new European machine guns) turned the tide. A general treaty was signed, vesting sovereignty in the AIC over all regions west and south of Stanley Pool. Harry Johnston, who met up with Stanley again at Leopoldville, accompanied him (with Vangele and eleven Zanzibaris) to Kinshassa for the final showdown with Bankwa and left a detailed description of

Stanley's methods at the 'pow-wow'. Stanley, 'looking his most chief-like, with his resolute face and grey hair and sword of state at his side', dealt diplomatically with the chiefs. He announced that it was entirely for them to decide whether to allow 'their son' to build there. Dualla, the interpreter, 'argued and cajoled the black brothers of the "Stone Breaking" chief into concordance with his wishes.' Eventually Stanley decided it would be impolitic to build at Kinshassa for the moment, because of Bankwa's hostility. But the treaty he secured more than made up for the disappointment.

The treaty had a knock-on effect farther up the river, for Opontaba concluded his agreement with Janssen after visiting Mpila and seeing that Ngobila (on the channel) and Ngalyema (on the Pool) had established a commercial lead over their rivals Ngantsu and Ntsuulu. But Stanley as yet could still buy ivory only from the Tio, principally Ngalyema. His one great advantage as compared with a year before was that his men had opened a second caravan route from Matadi to Kinshassa, supplementing the original 1880-81 road, and had signed further treaties with chiefs and built more way stations.'

On 9th May 1883 Stanley's flotilla set out for the Upper Congo, carrying a party of seven whites and seventy-three blacks. Stanley penetrated into the areas he had first charted in x 877 - the lands of the Irebu and Bolobo - founding new stations as he went, at Bolobo, Mswata and Equator. After establishing Equator station - 757 miles from the Atlantic and 412 miles above Leopoldville - he returned to Leopoldville to consolidate affairs there. News that the local tribes had attacked and gutted Bolobo station sent him steaming hard up the Congo once more. He brought the Bolobo tribes to heel with a display of awesome power from his new Krupps gun, and returned to Equator station after an absence of a hundred days.

In October he made peace with his old enemies the Bangala and left his most promising assistant, the Belgian Lt. Camille Coquilhat, in charge of the station there. Resuming his journey, Stanley came at last to the confluence of the Congo and the Aruwimi, where the massive war flotilla of the Soko had fought him in January 1877. As with the Bangala, Stanley was able to conciliate his erstwhile foes, but in so doing made an alarming discovery. His epic descent of the Congo in 1877 had given fresh heart to Tippu Tip's Arabs, who by 1883 had broken through the physical barrier of Stanley Falls and established themselves on the Upper Congo. Near Stanley Falls he ran into the Arab slave traders. A caravan of some 600 persons was arranged as a primitive concentration camp. Faced with the Arabs' inhumanity and brutality, Stanley confessed he had to fight hard against an impulse to open fire. 'What a pity I did not bring up one of the Krupps! I could then have annihilated the camp,' he wrote regretfully.

Instead he settled for cool civilities and took his departure as soon as normal politeness allowed. In December he completed his targets on the Upper Congo by founding a station at Stanley Falls itself. The return journey found the travellers back in the Bangala territory by Christmas Day

1883, whence they proceeded to Leopoldville, arriving 20th January 1884.

On arrival at Leopoldville Stanley at once went down with a fever that lasted a week. He came round at the end of January to find the familiar catalogue of personal problems and queries from Brussels awaiting resolution. He was full of his usual grumbles. 'If Strauch knew anything about figures, I should not have to descend to these minute details, but whenever he has to touch upon numbers, I am under the impression that there is confusion in Brussels.' At the end of the month he wrote a doleful letter to Leopold, lamenting the strain on him caused by finite financial resources and maladministration from Brussels.

Not for the fortune of a Rothschild would I undertake to go through the same experiences I underwent in 1880-81-82. I perceive them looming up again in 1884 - gigantic work, endless contradictory orders - with insufficient means in my sixth year of service to haul a 30-ton steamer with two hundred men while the garrisons of thirty stations are crying out for food! ... It may be that ill-health makes me write so despondency. It is certain I am not the man I was in 1879 when I began the Congo work.

On 21st March 1884, after licking Leopoldville into shape and making further treaties with the chiefs of Stanley Pool, Stanley set off for Vivi, hoping to hear news of his successor. Visits to the stations at Manyanga and Isangila left him disappointed with their poor progress and decrepit state. It was difficult for him not to make pointed contrasts between the vigour of men like Vangele and Coquilhat on the Upper Congo and the lacklustre performance of his personnel on the lower river.

On 22 April he reached Vivi. His anger spilled over when he saw that things were no better here and that, in the vacuum without a proper leader, the young officers had simply had a good time and allowed the station to go to rack and ruin. There was further correspondence from Leopold. He had tried various possibilities for Stanley's replacement. At one time General Gordon was a strong candidate, but he had to drop out when the British wanted him for service in the Sudan. Finally Leopold signed a contract with Sir Francis de Winton, formerly an administrator in Canada (also a friend of Garnett Wolseley and a protégé of the Royal Family), making him Stanley's successor. De Winton was to arrive at Banana at the beginning of May; Stanley was requested to stay on until then to effect a smooth transition.

During his last month at Vivi, Stanley was able to catch up with the ever more complex international politics and diplomacy that were to make Leopold's Congo venture the trigger for a general 'scramble for Africa'. For by late 1883 the Congo had become the cockpit for a ferocious four-way struggle between Leopold's AIC, France, Britain and the Portuguese that threatened to suck in all the other great powers as well.

Even while Leopold and the French braced themselves at the end of 1882 for a final decisive round in the Stanley-Brazza bout, Portugal decided to take a hand in the Congo; it laid claim to the area on the basis of ancient explorations by the captains of Prince Henry the Navigator and their successors. This claim found many backers. The British attitude was that the best future for the Congo lay in a slow colonisation by Portugal. Paradoxically, the French had concluded that Stanley was really a secret agent for the British that Britain's aim was annexation of the Congo, that therefore they would do best to endorse the Portuguese claim. France was aware that the British had begun to push Portuguese claims in order to checkmate Brazza, and indeed the point was scarcely denied among the power-brokers of the day.

Stanley, meanwhile, after defeating the French in the race for Stanley Pool, was now coming to see Portugal - always for him the hub of slave trading on the African west coast - as the main threat to Leopold's work in the Congo. The great impediment to a meeting of minds between Stanley and Harry Johnston was the latter's partiality for the Portuguese. For Johnston, the French were the real enemy and Portugal a useful bulwark against their African ambitions. The Portuguese in turn responded by accusing Stanley of inciting the Africans against them.

What of Leopold and the AIC in all this? Leopold's difficulty was that he could not simply throw a Belgian hat into the ring by making an overt bid for a colony, for he had all along portrayed his activities in Africa as 'philanthropic', 'international' and 'commercial'. The plain fact was that the AIC was simply Leopold and his own personal moneys. Its capital was provided out of a fortune amassed by clever speculation, possibly in Suez Canal stock. For years now he had cleverly maintained his Chinese box structure of obfuscating fictions: AIA, CEHC, AIC - with the added element of mystification that many people confused the AIA with the AIC; naturally Leopold did nothing to enlighten them. Once Brazza spotted what Leopold's game was he encouraged Jules Ferry to flush the King out of cover by the ratification of the Makoko treaties. At a stroke the AIC's blue flag with golden star that had fluttered over more than 300 tribal villages by now when treaties with the Association had been signed, would have to be hauled down. For how could a sovereign power be opposed by a mere trading company? Come to that, how could the said company, whose flag was recognised internationally for trading purposes only, make binding treaties?

Leopold had wrestled with this conundrum in international law for a long time, which accounts for his obsessive interest in the Dent/Overbeck treaties with the Sultan of North Borneo and those of early settlers in North America with the aboriginal Indians. He had even hired two tame academics to find favourable precedents for him. The chosen duo, Sir Travers Twiss at Oxford and Professor Arntz of Brussels, cited the practices of the Teutonic knights and the Maltese Knights of St John.

But in early 1883 Leopold feared that all this logic-chopping was in vain, that the Anglo-Portuguese accord, which already seemed to place Vivi and Isangila inside a recognised Portuguese sphere of influence, might be supplemented by a Franco-Portuguese treaty that would return the north bank of the Congo and the Kwilu-Niari territories to France in return for a recognition of Portugal's sovereignty on the south bank. Further alarm bells rang when his agents informed him that Britain was thinking of recognising Portuguese sovereignty on both banks as a protest against the Makoko treaties. The King's first step was obviously to nip this in the bud. He organised a campaign through his friends in England, stressing the slavery aspects of Portugal to one group, its protectionism to another. There was an outcry against the proposal to recognise Portuguese sovereignty, both from free-trading business men like Hutton and Mackinnon, alarmed at the thought of Customs barriers, and from humanitarians appalled at slavery. Leopold even enlisted the Prince of Wales on his side. The campaign was successful. Following a passionate denunciation in the Commons by John Bright, the government was defeated on the issue and dropped the proposed Portuguese treaty in April 1883. An attempt by the Portuguese lobby to counterattack by portraying Stanley as Leopold's man of blood failed when Lords Fitzmaurice and Derby (who had been secretly won over by Leopold) feigned ignorance of the relationship between Stanley and the Belgian King.

It was at this point that Harry Johnston seriously disturbed the tenor of Stanley's relations with Brussels. Both men wanted the British to establish a political protectorate over the Congo, but disagreed on the agency, Stanley favouring an alliance with Leopold, Johnston opting for the 'traditional' Anglo-Portuguese friendship. On his return to England Johnston visited the Foreign Office and lobbied for consular posts on the Congo. The officials in turn quizzed him about his talks with Stanley in the Congo and his (Johnston's) later interviews with Leopold in Brussels. Johnston revealed Stanley's enthusiasm for a British Congo; as for Leopold, Johnstone opined that he was either 'marvellously simple or marvellously deep'. But when Johnston's overtures proved unavailing, he tried a more public, and more indiscreet, tack. In a letter of July 1883 Stanley expressed forcibly his view that to deliver the Congo to the Portuguese was to make over the Congolese peoples to slavery. Since Johnston emphatically disagreed with this, he sought a public platform to air his dissent from the views of Africa's greatest explorer.

The opportunity came at the Southport meeting of the British Association for the Advancement of Science on 24th September 1883. The secretary of the Geological Section praised Stanley as the man who was opening up 'the great road across Africa'. Johnston then got to his feet and read out extracts from Stanley's personal letter dated 23rd July. This made it abundantly clear that Stanley wanted a British protectorate in the Congo. Stanley's point was that someone would sooner or later take the Congo into its sphere of influence, and he wanted that someone to be Britain. At present, either Portugal or France with fifty men was stronger than the Association with 1000, for the international law issue of whether the AIC could resist a nation-state by force had not yet been cleared up.

The reaction to this in Brussels was a stupefied horror that Stanley in person now seemed prepared to enter publicly the domain of international politics. Leopold wrote to Stanley to gag him, reminding him that according to the terms of his 1878 personal five-year contract he had promised not to publish anything or give any information about his work in the Congo. It was therefore imperative for Stanley to request his friends not to publish any of his letters to them. The King's tone was that of gentle chiding, and Stanley replied in injured innocence that it had never crossed his mind that Johnston might reveal the contents of a personal letter. But Strauch chose to put a more sinister interpretation on Stanley's actions. Years later he alleged that Stanley's 'treason' almost cost Belgium the Congo, and that the situation was retrieved only because the Anglo-Saxon nation turned down the gift that Stanley handed them on a plate.

What is the truth of this? Once again the true villain of the piece turns out to be Leopold. By not revealing the full scope of his ambitions and insisting that his interest in the Congo was purely commercial, he cut the ground from under any serious indictment of Stanley. Stanley's action was perfectly consistent with Leopold's interests as he saw them and, more to the point, as he had been advised of them by the King himself. Stanley wanted a free trade area in the Congo of which British merchants would be the main beneficiaries. This was why his friends Hutton and Mackinnon supported Leopold in the Congo. They knew well enough that Portuguese or French rule meant protectionism and tariffs and they hoped for better from the King. Stanley was in effect calling in the power of England to protect Leopold's Congo against France and Portugal. It was not open for Leopold to claim that Stanley had cut across his political purposes since he had never told his 'agent in Chief what they were, or even that he had any.

Leopold indeed had every reason to be grateful to Stanley, for he used his fame as an 'American' in his successful bid to shore up his stake in the Congo with US help. He also used the argument, calculated to appeal to the descendants of President Monroe, that the Congo would be a second Liberia, another home of the free black man. General Sanford, who detested the Portuguese, was again a useful go-between in the process of winning over President Arthur. Arthur announced his support for Leopold in his annual message to Congress on 4th December 1883. He seemed confused about the difference between the AIA and the AIC but then he was scarcely alone in being mystified about that..

Leopold's instinct that another storm was brewing was shrewd. On 24th February 1884 Portugal triumphantly struck back with the signature of a new Anglo-Portuguese treaty acknowledging Congo sovereignty. Once again Leopold mobilised his friends in Europe, but this time the Foreign Office had had enough of his hypocrisy. The head of the Africa desk, Sir Percy Anderson, recommended that Leopold's real objectives be revealed to the world by the publication of the treaties he had made with the Congo tribes in which he acquired political sovereignty. This would expose to the anti-Portuguese 'bleeding hearts' that Leopold's entire operation was just a mask for a barefaced commercial monopoly. Granville took the bait and wrote a polite but firm note to Leopold, threatening to divulge his secret manoeuvres. But by this time Leopold could not be budged, since he had learned from other channels that France feared Britain was about to absorb the AIC so would oppose the treaty with Portugal.

Leopold went from strength to strength in his adroit playing of the French card. He offered Jules Ferry a 'special' deal in the Congo. The Strauch—Ferry statement of 23 April 1884 stated that the AIC would not cede any territory in the Congo but that if circumstances changed, France would get 'first refusal'. In return France would respect the Association's stations and territories in the Congo. Here Leopold was playing an elaborate game. France thought that Leopold did not have the military and financial resources to hold on to the Congo and that it would soon be French. This was also the British conclusion, so Leopold hastened to assure them that the droid de preference was purely theoretical. As the shrewdest modern student of the Belgian King has pointed out, Ferry had allowed himself to be gulled. If the territories of the AIC could not be ceded, then the French first option was meaningless. And because the other powers were prepared to guarantee the neutrality of the Congo against France, France had been guaranteed a right which she could never use.

There was thus a wealth of international news for Stanley to chew on as he sat disconsolately at Vivi waiting for his successor de Winton to arrive. He knew he was already a marked man in Portuguese eyes, though he was unaware that from the very earliest days Leopold secretly felt he could use Stanley's indiscretion about a British protectorate to turn the screws on the French. The Strauch-Ferry accord was the triumphant culmination of this tactic.

On 11th May de Winton finally arrived at Vivi. The two men got on well though the friendship was always more marked on de Winton's side. Ever afterwards if Stanley felt de Winton received undue praise for his work in the Congo, he would 'redress the balance' with a little well- primed character assassination. But in the month that remained before Stanley returned to Europe, de Winton was suitably deferential to the great explorer and listened attentively to his advice (dispassionate?) not to venture on to the Upper Congo but to base himself at Vivi, with occasional forays to Leopoldville. Stanley asserted his superiority over his successor by heading a gang of construction workers on their morning shift from 6 a.m. to 11 a.m. while de Winton slowly acclimatised. One morning he returned to find de Winton and his friend Dr Leslie resting under the veranda with novels in their hands, looking downstream and positioned so as to receive the Atlantic breezes. Stanley warned de Winton that they were sitting in the deadliest spot in Vivi, but de Winton simply smiled incredulously. This was a mortification to Stanley, who always hated to have his opinions questioned, but he soon got his revenge: 'The two gentlemen came in to lunch and laughed at my warning, but when dinner time came, neither of them was at table and the next day they had their first bout of severe fever.'

On 6th June, after a decent handing-over period, Stanley made his farewells and, accompanied by de Winton, made his way to Banana Point via Boma. On 10th June he embarked on the British steamer Kinsembo. There was a day's stopover at Loango, another at Gabon, and on 20th June the ship put in at Fernando Po, from which Cameroon was visible, 40 miles away. Here the ship needed to be refitted, so Stanley benefited from the week's delay by crossing to Calabar on the mainland and going on a three-day excursion upriver; he found it just like being on the Upper Congo. Re-embarking at Fernando Po, he was at Bonny on 28th June (where he picked up various scabrous anecdotes about Burton and Verney Cameron) and in the roadstead of the Bight of Benin on 2nd July. On the 5th they reached Lagos and on the 6th Quettah, where Stanley's sense of European superiority and his taste for flagellation both received a jolt: 'The local news at Quettah is that a white man has been sentenced to eight months' imprisonment for whipping a negro!'

12th July found the Kinsembo at Sierra Leone, after which the ship made good speed to arrive at Tenerife on the 20th. Here Stanley got into a furious argument with an Anglophobe French chauvinist, whose distorted view of 'perfidious Albion' Stanley likened to the English view of Americans. But the verbal passage of arms prompted some interesting reflections on the English from a Welsh 'outsider'. I have noticed that they would rather not say they were religious, or confess to saying their prayers at night. They would prefer not to say who were their parents or where they were born (!!!), or that they did not take cold baths, or that they are poor, or of mean origin, or that they have no acquaintance among the aristocracy, or that they do not agree with the wild opinion of the masses, or their press is licentious and intolerant. They fear ridicule, of [sic] being pointed out by their neighbours, of being mocked by sinners, and disdained by the worldly and slighted by public opinion. They would rather affect to be what others wish them to be in manners, dress, habits, but against the contempt of other nations they affect superb indifference and cold reserve, but we cannot tell Frenchmen our faults.

On 23rd July Stanley arrived at Madeira to find a telegram from Leopold requesting the earliest possible meeting in Brussels. It was time for him to reflect on what he had achieved in the Congo in five years and to prepare an analysis of the remaining problems.

At a personal level Stanley had achieved something that was to be momentous in its consequences: the foundation of what was later to be the Belgian Congo. He told Puleston in 1887: 'The AIA was the happiest time of my life and the opening of the Lower Congo was the most interesting.' Despite having notched up his African fever by 1884 and despite the carping of envious Germans who alleged that Stanley was a mere explorer who lacked the ability to organise a state, this is exactly what he had done. He had laid bare for greedy Europe to see the potential riches of the Congo: palm oil, used especially for cattle feed, gum copal for varnishes, vegetable oils for medicine and cooking, orchilla moss, iron and copper and, above all, ivory. Stanley had already alerted the West to the fortunes to be made from ivory on the east-coast route: $2 a pound in Zanzibar, $1.10 in

Unyanyembe and one cent in Manyema, where it was so commonplace that it was used for doorposts and eave stanchions. Stanley compared the lust for ivory to the Australian and Californian gold rushes, the mining boom in Colorado, Idaho and Montana and the diamond fever of Cape Colony, but he neglected to point out that it was his colourful journalism and passionate advocacy that was stoking up the lust.

In fairness to Stanley, it must be pointed out that he sometimes realised the Pandora's box he had unleashed on the poor elephants by his portrait of the Congo as a land flowing with milk and honey. In September 1884 he wrote to de Winton to approve his ban on elephant hunting by the Association, which de Winton had imposed so as not to alienate the tribes with 'sportsmen' shooting out the herds: 'Stop the shooting of the elephants, do not murder any more for the sheer pity of the noble beasts. Let the ground of the Association be sacred to the elephants. We do not yet know, but we may have use for them. 'In military terms he had laid the foundations for Leopold's later bloody and barbarous colony, though he can in no sense be faulted for these later developments. By the end of 1883 he had at his disposal one hundred white men, 600 blacks, eight steamers, twelve Krupps guns, four machine guns, 1000 rapid-firing rifles and over two million cartridges. For once Lady Stanley, usually a purblind hagiographer, hit the nail on the head when she summed up her husband's achievement in the Autobiography: The founding of the Congo Free State was the greatest single enterprise of Stanley's life. Perhaps nothing else so called out and displayed his essential qualities. Its ultimate fruit cannot be so clearly measured as the search for Livingstone, or the first exploration of the Congo, of those enterprises he was himself the Alpha and the Omega; each was a task for a single man, and the achievement was measured by the man's personality. But the founding of the Free State was a multiple task, involving a host of workers. He had not made the selection of his helpers, except the rank and file, and the rank and file did not fail him. It was his lieutenants, selected by others, among whom the perilous defect was found. Further, his undertaking, in its essential nature, involved dangers which it was doubtless well he did not wholly foresee, for they might have daunted even his spirit.

Yet Stanley's achievement should not be exaggerated. He was far from having solved all the problems he wrestled with in his five years. In October 1883 Augouard wrote depreciatingly about his own countrymen: 'As for this precious French territory of which so much fuss is being made in the papers, it is simply a joke and before the vote [sc. to ratify the Makoko treaties] was taken all the deputies and senators should have been sent out to Stanley Pool for a month to live on roots and water. 'But by the time of Stanley's departure, the French were striking back hard. Ballay settled at Ngantsu's in November 1883 and established a French station there. Paramount chief Iloo, with French help, compelled homage from Opontaba, Ngalioo and Ngantsu in April 1884.The struggle for mastery in the Stanley Pool area continued after the going of Bula Matari, with

Opontaba playing a key role.

The one area where Stanley seemed to have decisively eclipsed the French was on the Upper Congo; with the expedition seemingly becoming more English all the time in French eyes (exactly what Leopold wanted the world to think, hence the recruitment of Gordon, Goldsmid, de Winton, etc.), the enemies of France appeared to have a stranglehold on trade coming down the river. Yet even here Stanley's commercial success was limited. Indigenous ivory traders could only be dealt a death blow by the advent of a railway. As late as 1889 Europeans still bought only five-eighths of the ivory at Stanley Pool, while the traditional caravans accounted for the rest. Moreover, since rubber did not become an important state activity in the Congo until 1889, Tio caravans largely continued to enjoy their monopoly on the sale of rubber.

The great plus Stanley enjoyed on the Upper Congo was the calibre of his officers, especially Coquilhat and Vangele, whom he later identified as the two finest aides he had ever worked with. Yet even a good officer did not guarantee ultimate success. Since Glave's station at Lukolela did not try to control trade or buy ivory, it was notably popular with the indigenous tribes. Yet the Belgians abandoned both Lukolela and Bolobo in 1885-6 since the 1885 Berlin treaty deprived the posts of much of their raison d'etre.

The real 'shirt of Nessus' (to use a favourite Stanley metaphor) that the great explorer left behind him was the post at Stanley Falls. This brought closer the inevitable conflict between Tippu Tip's Arabs and the Belgians that was resolved only by full-scale warfare in the 1890s. The leader of the Arab caravan whom Stanley had met near the falls in late November 1883, Obed-ben-Salim, told Barghash of his encounter with Stanley and asked for further instructions: should he have opposed the building of the fort; was he culpable in neglecting the Sultan's interest by letting Europeans siphon away ivory by the western route? But he was really addressing the wrong person. Tippu Tip, while paying token fealty to Zanzibar, was the real power in the area and he soon made his presence felt. Late in 1884 he came in person to the post at Stanley Falls to teach the Belgians the facts of life in Central Africa. He told Arnid Wester (who replaced Bennie in July 1884) that he intended to pass Stanley Falls and proceed downriver despite the Belgian interdict on interlopers. Wester did not have the military force to stop him, so Tippu Tip openly tweaked Leopold's nose by selling slaves in the Congo state. The nominal suzerainty of Zanzibar was maintained for a while by the combination of Arab strength and Belgian weakness.

The situation continued tense. In 1885 Vangele and Tippu Tip had a firm but friendly confrontation over respective spheres of influence. Tippu Tip insisted that the whole of Africa from Zanzibar to Banana belonged to the Sultan. Vangele rebutted this by pointing out that Stanley claimed the Congo for Leopold by being the first to chart it, rubbing salt in Tippu's wound, for the Arab had told Stanley in 1876 that the descent was impossible. Tippu said his methods were Stanley's: if he needed food, he took it by force. Vangele replied that Stanley at least never pillaged ivory or burned villages to the ground and took slaves. Vangele clearly won the dialectical contest, but this solved nothing as Tippu Tip had the power. By late 1885 the missionary Grenfell found the Arab chief dug in and unprepared to alter his methods one whit. When Wester was replaced by Captain Deane, the Belgian attitude shifted from realism to aggression. This was folly, since for the moment Leopold could do nothing but fume over Tippu's flouting of his authority, But the thorn in his side particularly rankled, as he had already confided in Stanley that it was his ambition to extend the boundaries of the new state as far as Bahr-el-Ghazal to the west of the Upper Nile. The opportunity to score off an old enemy was too good for Stanley to miss. After pointing out that the Arabs on 'Belgian' territory had uplifted 1300 slaves and a million francs' worth of ivory on a single raid, he insinuated that the Arabs were being manipulated from Zanzibar: 'Kirk reflects this faithfully. The stoppage of enlistment of Zanzibaris is due to him, the instructions to the Arabs of Nyangwe and Tippu Tip by the Sultan are also due to him.' The British seemed to be threatening the Congo from both ends, supporting the Portuguese at the Atlantic and the Arabs at Stanley Falls; Tippu Tip remained the wild card, the maverick, the unknown quantity. The 'King Incorporated' now had so many balls in the air simultaneously that even for an expert juggler like him the game was becoming supremely perilous.

Chapter Six

ON 27th July 1884, by special dispensation of the owners, the Kinsembo put in to Plymouth to land Stanley on English soil. In Plymouth Sound a Times reporter boarded the steamer for an 'exclusive' with the reporter on his views on Gordon and Khartoum. Stanley declared himself against an expedition to relieve Khartoum - Gordon could get out any time he wanted to - but with the proviso that only the British government knew the full facts. Privately he poured scorn on the press for expecting miracles from Gordon and foresaw the tragedy that was to overtake Khartoum the following January: 'Nothing else could be expected from one who was supposed to come out to help me in my Congo work and wrote about killing slave traders in their haunts. Great piety is not always inconsistent with good sense, but I fear in Gordon's case he is more pious than sensible.'

From Plymouth he caught the train to London, where he found further requests from Leopold to come to Belgium with all speed. On 2nd August he met the King at Ostend. There, at the Hotel de la Fontaine, he was Leopold's guest for five days; a special cook was even employed to see that Stanley received the traditional English breakfast every morning. Each day Stanley had two long sessions with the monarch, including a detailed debriefing after dinner. The pace was such that Stanley was forced to telegram Sanford: 'Can find no time to write. Visitors, interviewers, business continually. Am so sorry. Thanks for your welcome.'

The talks ranged far and wide over the international implications of a Congo state, for even while Stanley was on the high seas, the story had moved on a chapter. Leopold had one solid achievement to his credit. His lobbying of the USA, making out the Congo to be a new Liberia, had paid off. President Chester Arthur was impressed by the trading potential of the Congo and thought it significant that the Association's chief executive officer was an 'American'. This was exactly what Leopold had hoped for. US recognition of the AIC followed on 22 April 1884 and there was enthusiastic support for Leopold's idea of a chain of stations from Zanzibar to the Atlantic.

But Britain, thinking that Leopold was in league with France, had set its face against the Association. Even more worrying was that Bismarck had now entered the African arena. On the one hand, he refused to ratify the Anglo-Portuguese treaty, which was therefore still-born. This was part of a process whereby the German Chancellor picked a quarrel with Britain in mid-1884 as a means of signalling to France that he wanted friendly relations; there was also the desire to call 'the Reich in danger' at the forthcoming Reichstag elections and to cripple the Anglophile liberalism of the Crown Prince. So far so good, as far as Leopold was concerned. But on the other hand the 'Iron Chancellor' soon sniffed out the Belgian King's duplicity and low cunning. When Leopold sent him his 'humanitarian' proposals to move into the Sudan so as to snuff out the slave trade,

Bismarck at once saw right through him and scrawled 'Schmndel in the margin against the humbug about slavery. His remarks on Leopold reveal him as one of the few contemporaries fully to have taken his measure: 'His Majesty displays the naive, pretentious egoism of an Italian who assumes as a law of nature that everything will be done for him for the sake of his beauxyeux and nothing of equal value asked of him in return.'

The German banker Gerson von Bleichroder, one of Leopold's business associates, warned him that he was alienating Bismarck by his duplicity; Germany wanted a proper trade guarantee in the event of recognition of the AIC as well as modest, realistic boundaries for a Congo state. This news arrived on Stanley's very last day in Ostend. He was on the point of departure when the King asked him to delay for a few hours to draw up a map with reasonable frontiers which would satisfy the Chancellor's insistence that the proposed independent state be forced back on to Congo littoral boundaries. This sort of thing was Stanley's forte. The map he prepared was so thorough and professional that Bismarck was at once won round. He informed the French ambassador in Berlin that there was now nothing to be lost by German recognition of the Congo state. At the beginning of September Bismarck sent Leopold an eight-page handwritten letter to confirm this decision.

But most of the Stanley-Leopold discussions in Ostend in early August had focused on the putative enemy: Portugal and France. The King reassured Stanley that the Johnston gaffe at the British Association had been forgotten; indeed Johnston had performed a useful service by coming straight to Brussels on his return to Europe and giving a clear tour d'horizon of the situation in the Congo (Stanley's need for Chinese coolies and so on). Moreover, he had applauded the way Johnston defended Stanley in the European press after he had been accused of subduing the Congo with a horde of savage, murderous wangwana. For once the King was giving a true account of his own reactions at the time.

Leopold was reasonably relaxed about the threat from Portugal now that Bismarck had given Lisbon the thumbs-down. Brazza was another matter. The King agreed with Stanley that Brazza could only be knocked out decisively when the AIC had international recognition. Until that time the situation remained as Stanley had described it for Mackinnon from Vivi in May:

So long as we have not a character recognised by European nations, de Brazza with his walking stick, a French flag and a few words in pursuit of the whites of Leopoldville is really stronger than Stanley with his Krupps and all material of war, faithful adherents, aid of natives, etc. We could easily defeat him and lay him gently down on the soil of his beloved Brazzaville. But what then? The affair is not settled. It has only assumed a greater importance and gravity. France might shriek out: What? - this unrecognised filibuster Stanley has laid hands upon the emissary of the French government and then the Sagittaire coolly steams up the Congo and seizes all our boats and shells us out of Vivi and blockades us, and of course then comes the deluge.

Since Leopold and Stanley saw eye to eye on all these matters, it was not surprising that he was able to relate that he had received an ovation at the end of his time in Ostend, 'though not in the noisy manner peculiar to England'. From Ostend he sped to Paris, to put up at his beloved Hotel Meurice in the Rue de Rivoli, while he pondered his next move. During his brief stop in London on 30th July he had been given the impression that his old quarters at 30 Sackville Street would no longer be available as the premises had changed hands. But so far he had been unable to find suitable apartments in London. Yet at the end of ten days word came through that his old domicile was after all available. He crossed to London, missing Sanford who had set out for the Continent to meet him.

His first task was to lobby Lord Granville to recognise the Association as political 'overseer' on the Congo. But Granville was non-committal. Though generally sympathetic, he had no wish to involve Britain in a war with France over a notionally important territory in Central Africa. So Stanley decided to appeal over the heads of the Foreign Office directly to public opinion. He sat down to prepare a series of lectures arguing for recognition of a new independent Congo state with no Customs barriers. Leopold pledged himself to support the lectures by getting the widest possible coverage in the English press, while cautioning Stanley not to 'over-sell' the Congo just yet.

Yet Stanley, a dedicated publicity-seeker, could never keep out of controversy. First he was forced to write to The Times to defend himself against a campaign of vilification in the French press, which alleged that while in Paris he was provocative and insulting to Brazza. Then he became embroiled with the Baker family in a dispute over the military performance in the Sudan of Lupton Bay and Baker Pasha (Sir Samuel's brother), whose army had been annihilated by the Mahdi. Leopold had to warn him to be quiet, as his outspokenness on these matters pari passu with a lecture tour on the Congo might lead to an accusation that the Belgian King was meddling in the Sudan.

Stanley's relations with Brussels now began to enter a period of uneasiness that was to persist for the next three years. He took it hard when his personal recommendation of Julian Arnold (Sir Edwin of the Daily Telegraph's son) as Strauch's secretary was ignored. In retaliation Stanley took his time about replying to Strauch's offer of a new contract from the AIC, offering an immediate £500 a year as a retainer while in Europe and specifying the future maximum time to be spent in Africa as two and a half years. In addition, the royalties from his proposed Congo book would be his, provided he published nothing without prior approval from Brussels. This douceur seemed less impressive when Leopold a few days later sent a sheaf of sentences to be omitted from Stanley's first draft of the book and suggested that the entire project would be better shelved until after international recognition of the Association, now a distinct possibility in the light of moves to organise a general Africa conference in Berlin.

While Stanley stalled on the renewal of his contract with the AIC, he kept up a correspondence with Leopold's secretariat about the proposed Congo railway, advised on British half-pay officers who might be suitable for service there, and kept in touch with his successor de Winton. A welcome relief from the toil of working on his speeches to be launched at British industrialists was the interview he conducted in Sackville Street to select another of the success stories of the Congo, Herbert Ward. Ward described the encounter as follows:

The room in which I was received impressed me as characteristic of the man. There were here no ornaments or bric-a-brac, nor were the walls hung with guns and trophies of the explorer. Everything spoke of earnest, tireless work; floor and tables bore traces of it, littered as they were with manuscripts, maps and scattered papers and pamphlets, while amid the confusion everywhere around I detected the famous Congo cap, which has figured in so many illustrations, thrown carelessly on a sideboard. Stanley began by expressing doubts about how the new recruit would stand up to the climate. Ward explained that he had been in Borneo, which particularly interested Stanley because of Leopold's obsession that the British treaties with the Sultan of Borneo formed a precedent for the AIC. His objections melted away: 'Well, after all, the Congo is a sanatorium compared to Borneo. 'On 18th September Stanley delivered the pilot version of his commercial speech to the London Chamber of Commerce. He spoke of the record of the AIC under its various manifestations, how it had unlocked the Congo to free trade, how a Confederation of tribal states would be good for business. The lecture was enthusiastically received. But ever at his elbow lurked the spectre of Brussels. For the Manchester speech, perceived as crucial, he had to submit his draft to Leopold, who returned it with deletions: there was to be no mention of the Anglo-Portuguese treaty and nothing critical said about Germany, for it was on Bismarck that Leopold now chiefly depended.

Stanley was beginning to find the pace of work punishing. As he explained to Mackinnon when accepting an invitation to his castle at Balinakill, he had engagements in Brighton from the 13th October, had three speeches to deliver in Manchester from 21st to 23rd October, then had speaking engagements in Edinburgh. In addition, he had to hold himself in readiness in case he was needed at the Berlin Conference in November which had hardened into a fixture. Despite being a fast writer, he was beginning to feel under unconscionable pressure. But the success of the three Manchester speeches, to the Chamber of Commerce, the Manchester Athenaeum and the Manchester Geographical Society, set the adrenalin flowing properly again. Addressing the Chamber of Commerce in Manchester Town Hall on 21st October, Stanley was on his very best demagogic form. He asked his audience to imagine a market for cotton vaster even than India, one where millions of Congolese might be wearing a cotton garment. Such was his advocacy that the Chamber of Commerce at once began to lobby the Foreign Office to back Leopold and the

Association The Manchester Guardian, which had been agonising over the implications for foreign relations with France and Portugal, was won over, though with reservations. Stanley told his friend James Hutton, president of the Chamber of Commerce, that 'he had been rather afraid Manchester had drifted into old fogeyism and senility. Her loud manifestations and eager expressions of gratification at the prospect of the new market prove the reverse.'

From Manchester Stanley proceeded to a short working holiday with Mackinnon at Balinakill. Mackinnon himself had visited Leopold in Brussels the month before to co-ordinate tactics. Then it was time to proceed to Berlin, if he was wanted there. But it was precisely this that was uncertain during October and early November. Leopold's deviousness and dog-in-the-manger attitude led to a diplomatic tangle which took weeks to sort out. The problem was that the AIC, having no standing in international law, could not be invited to the Berlin Conference. Stanley was an employee of the AIC, but the Americans, with justifiable pride, wanted such a distinguished 'fellow-American' on their delegation.

The American Minister at Berlin and the man designated as their representative at the Conference was John A. Kasson. On 20th October he wrote to Stanley as follows: 'Can you hold yourself at liberty to be present at Berlin a week before the meeting of the Conference on West African affairs and during its deliberations ... this action will be in harmony with the interests which you represent [a reference to Stanley's divided loyalties as between the Association and the USA].' As each delegate would also be allowed an associate, Kasson thought of Sanford and sent for him. A further US official, W. P. Tisdel, was also accredited as 'US representative to the State of the Congo'.

Now ever since the idea of the Berlin Conference had been mooted, Leopold had been wooing Kasson, but he did not want Kasson to put either Stanley or Mackinnon fully in the picture on US-Belgian relations. Kasson's invitation to Stanley cut across his scheming, and Leopold issued a hasty note of regret that Stanley could not be released to the US delegation. Perplexed, Kasson conferred with Sanford in London about this unexpected development. Sanford suggested turning the tables on Leopold by a theatrical coup de main while he was in Brussels with the King. He had Kasson cable him requesting Stanley's presence yet again; this gave Sanford the opportunity to break off his talks with the King and endorse the request. Leopold dithered and finally agreed, provided Stanley signed the new contract, which he had not yet done: Leopold thus revealed one of the motives for his dog-in-the-manger attitude. In a memorandum in early November he revealed other reasons. Stanley would muddy the waters at Berlin since it would be open to representatives of other powers to point out that one of the US delegates was scarcely a dispassionate debater of the future of the Association in the Congo; he was indiscreet and might reveal secrets; he did not get on with Kasson and was secretly strongly disliked by Sanford.

Meanwhile Stanley added another twist to the story by requesting leave of absence until the following spring to attend such conferences as would help his book - a clear indication that he personally wanted to go to Berlin. He offered to return to the Congo in 1885 provided that his AIC salary was raised to £1000 p.a. Sanford felt that the way to cut the Gordian knot was to ask Bismarck to invite Stanley, but at this all Kasson's diplomatic hackles rose: it was not for Bismarck to say who should or should not be in the US delegation and anyway Stanley had been invited as an expert explorer, not an official member of the delegation.

When Stanley pressed to know whether he was to go to Berlin, Leopold's officials stalled, on the fatuous ground that it was not yet clear whether such co-opted 'experts' would be welcome in Berlin. Stanley decided to cross over to Belgium to speak to Leopold in person. Meanwhile Leopold contested Kasson's position with the argument that since Stanley worked for the AIC, and the AIC had not been invited to the Berlin Conference, the invitation had to emanate from Bismarck. The subtext of all this was that the Belgians wanted Stanley at Berlin as their observer, not as a member of the US delegation, and considered it important that Kasson should acknowledge their prior rights over the great explorer. Leopold got his way and the request was forwarded to Bismarck.

Bismarck for his part saw good propaganda advantage to be gained from Stanley's presence in Berlin. He was a popular and almost legendary figure who would arouse enthusiasm in Germany for overseas ventures now that the Chancellor had decided to go for colonies and claim the fatherland's right to a place in the sun. He immediately replied with his permission. Leopold had no option then but to allow Stanley to proceed to Berlin, cautioning him, however, to be prudent and be guided by Sanford.

Kasson meanwhile had withdrawn his invitation to Stanley on grounds of AIC opposition. It took further cables and messages to sort out the mess. Not until 11th November was it crystal clear that Stanley would, after all, form part of the US delegation. As a quid pro quo Sanford and his wife talked him round to the idea of renewing his contract on the terms required by Leopold.

Before leaving for Berlin Stanley had to sort out his domestic arrangements. Dualla was falling out of favour, and Baruti, the boy from the Soko tribe he had brought back with him to be a second Kalulu, was proving far more intractable than Kalulu had ever been. One night when Stanley was absent, Baruti asked the explorer's housekeeper to give him a certain choice dish from the larder. When she refused, he became violent, seized her baby and rushed upstairs. At the landing he held the baby over the banisters and threatened to drop it unless his demand was granted.

This was the troubled context in which an American woman of Stanley's acquaintance introduced him to a seventeen-year-old apprentice of German descent at Sackville Street, one William Hoffmann, destined thereafter to be a constant and troublesome feature in Stanley's life. Hoffmann later gave an account of his introduction to Stanley. He was working on the

Congo book in his study and a bright fire was blazing. 'Well, my man,' said Stanley, 'can you speak German?' 'Yes.' 'Will you accompany me to Germany, as I am going to attend the Berlin Conference?' Thus did Hoffmann become Stanley's manservant. But the master-servant relationship got off to a bad start. At Charing Cross, when they boarded the Berlin express, Stanley felt hungry and sent Hoffmann off to buy some sandwiches. By the time he came back with them, the train had gone. Left penniless, Hoffmann had to get the stationmaster to wire ahead to the coast to say that he would be on the next train. When he caught up with his master, Hoffmann was treated to the special tongue-lashing Stanley reserved for feckless or incompetent servants of whatever rank.

Stanley and Hoffmann reached Frankfurt at 5 a.m. on 15th November and Berlin later that day. He put up at the Hotel Royal and started familiarising himself with protocol for the US delegation. Immediately there arose a clash of personalities between Stanley and Tisdel, who disagreed violently with his estimate of the economic potential of the Congo and claimed to know as much as Stanley about African affairs.

When Sanford took Stanley's side, Tisdel stormed off and quit Berlin without taking part in a single session of the Conference.

There was much to research and digest before the first sessions of the Conference got under way. Stanley was not privy to all Leopold's secret thoughts and devious manoeuvring but he knew that the key to ultimate success was Bismarck, who formally recognised the AIC on 8th November, thus at one level throwing down the gauntlet to the British championing of Portugal. At Berlin, Bismarck and Jules Ferry made common cause in resentment and suspicion of the 1882 occupation of Egypt by Britain. Bismarck and Ferry shared the conviction that without colonies they would decline to the level of a fourth- or fifth-rate power like Spain. Additionally in the French case l'honneur and Brazza's prestige were at stake.

But cutting across these political considerations were the economic ones. At this level free-trading England and Germany were ranged against protectionist France and Portugal, thus introducing contradictions into the pre-existing political alliances. Free trade benefited the great powers of the day, as it always does. The inertia of power was bound to secure an automatic advantage for the imperial giant (Britain) or its great industrial rival (Germany). Indeed Lord Salisbury later justified his imperialism as a pre-emptive strike against the endemic French tendency towards tariff walls. Protectionism is the reflex action of the ascending, declining, threatened or second-rate power; significantly in the twentieth century when the USA became the great power in the 1930s, Britain switched to protectionism.

After being introduced as a technical delegate for the USA, Stanley at once plunged into the Conference maelstrom. He argued for a broad commercial delta 380 miles wide from the mouth of the Loge River to 20 S, latitude, within which freedom of trade would be guaranteed, and argued that the same freedom should be established to within x° from the sea coast, from latitude s°N. up to and inclusive of the River Zambezi. As against the Portuguese desire for a much narrower outlet, Stanley suggested that the northern limit of the proposed free-trade area be placed at Fernan Vaz. In fact this proposal originated with the British delegation, but it was thought to have a better chance of success if Stanley, not the Foreign Office, introduced it. Stanley impressed his listeners with a lucid explanation of the two senses of the term 'Congo basin', geographical and commercial, the point being that a narrow geographical definition might well deprive the trade of the Upper Congo of its natural outlet. Kasson was especially impressed by the performance of his fellow delegate: 'He [Stanley] went to a chart suspended in a room, and immediately engrossed the interest of every delegate, by a vivid description of the features of the Congo basin; and finally of the country necessary to go with it under the same regime to secure the utmost freedom of communication with the two oceans.' But Stanley's definition was resisted by France and Portugal, and the limit was eventually set to the south of Fernan Vaz, at Sette Camma.

Not all participants shared Kasson's enthusiasm for Stanley's approach. The explorer's clear mind could not deal with the fudging and compromise so necessary to diplomacy. Because he lectured and hectored the delegates on the need for crystal clarity in the Congo and hence for formal agreements, official representatives felt themselves browbeaten into writing home for explicit instructions, so that the net effect of Stanley's interventions was to delay proceedings. Also, his air of omniscience irritated those with no particular axe to grind on the east-coast trade area, so that they tended to make difficulties just to put him in his place.

Stanley's overwhelming aplomb came from the knowledge that he had both Kasson's overt support and the secret backing of Bismarck. The fact that the Conference accepted the principle of a free trade area and to some extent went along with Stanley's definition of it was hailed by the explorer as a great triumph, and he entered his first major social engagement, dinner with Bismarck, in a mood of exultation. There was just one other guest that night (24th November 1884) - a Hamburg merchant named Woerrmann, member of the Reichstag and delegate to the Conference, a man mainly interested in West African commerce. Bismarck introduced Stanley to him as a glittering example of what a solitary hero could do to open up unexplored territory. Stanley's glowing mood that evening is evinced in his journal entry:

This evening I had the honour of dining with Prince Bismarck and family. The Prince is a great man, a kind father, and excellently simple in his family. The Princess adores him, says little and that always in a deferent [sic] manner. The Prince listens in a benevolently paternal way, pats his big dog or plays with his ears, with his pipe held negligently downward, which seems to me, when with an encouraging smile he leans towards his wife - a sign of the usual habits of husband and wife. I gathered by their attitudes and behaviour a better idea of their domestic life than I should by ever so much description. The Prince asked many questions about Africa and proved to me that in a large way he understood the condition of that continent very well.

Stanley later exaggerated his role at the Berlin Conference. In fact a large number of African issues were discussed on which Stanley had no knowledge or could contribute little - the Niger question for instance. It gradually became clear that Britain was prepared to recognise the AIC in return for opposition to the internationalisation of the Niger basin. And when Stanley did re-enter the fray, on 30th November, he seriously embarrassed Leopold by giving away too much about his ulterior motives in the Congo. He effectively revealed the plan for a railway by arguing that concessions for developing the infrastructure should be given to the actual occupiers in Africa, thus alerting rivals to what was in Leopold's mind. When the gaffe was pointed out to him later, Stanley rewrote the incident. His version in Congo simply states blandly: 'I made a speech about the religious and missionary enterprise in the Congo basin.'

So marginal was Stanley to the main proceedings that Kasson raised no objection when Stanley departed on the evening of 30th November to keep a long-standing engagement in Edinburgh. He paid a flying visit to the Foreign Office in London to report the growing entente between Bismarck and the British delegation, following which the Foreign Office instructed Kirk to use his influence with Barghash to recruit another 400 Zanzibaris for Congo service. Then Stanley sped on to Edinburgh for his speech at the inauguration of the Scottish Geographical Society. He was in Edinburgh on the 3rd and 4th, then Glasgow on 5-6th December.

This proved one of Stanley's least happy ventures. Stanley regurgitated his Manchester arguments, presenting the Congo as a cornucopia of commercial opportunity. His speech was full of commodities, prices and statistics. In the audience was the Scottish explorer Joseph Thomson, who was known from his published work to be critical of Stanley. He could not see the great trading future that Stanley outlined and at the banquet afterwards Thomson took the more famous man to task: 'I have to express the melancholy feeling I have for the last few days entertained as I listened to Mr Stanley, on seeing how the iron heel of commerce has entirely knocked romance out of African travel. There were days when there was romance in African travel, but the soul-less [sic] march of commerce has been gradually trampling out that, and we must apparently consider that the days of African romance are pretty well gone. It is pitiful that such should be the case . . . We have come to look upon the palm-tree, not in regard to its artistic effect, but upon the quantity of oil that it is to produce. If this sort of thing is to go on, I should prefer to go to the North Pole. 'When Stanley bridled at this portrait of him as a mere money-grubber, Thomson pressed home the attack in the Scottish press. He accused Stanley of being thin-skinned and lacking a sense of humour: 'It has been said that Scotsmen require a surgical operation to impart a joke to them. Are we to claim Mr Stanley as a countryman from the apparent development in him of this interesting peculiarity?' Privately he was much more caustic. In a letter to Bates at the RGS, Thomson developed the theme of his dislike: 'There is one thing certain, however, that they [the Scots] are not inclined to dance to Stanley's piping. Even in Glasgow the merchants are shaking their heads over this windbag that he has been trying to inflate and in Edinburgh the people have been quite delighted with the little bit of fun I had out of him. He has not made a single friend and has succeeded in repelling everyone by his insufferable egotism.'

Stanley was soured by his Scottish experience, even though he fulfilled his commitment by going on from Edinburgh to speak to the Dundee branch of the Scottish Geographical Society. But the scepticism and even hostility he encountered, so tellingly in contrast to his treatment in Manchester in October, scarred him. When he recalled the events in early 1885 he was especially bitter about the way the Scottish Geographical Magazine had highlighted Thomson's remarks and those of other hostile commentators: In old times we are told the Caesars in their triumphal chariots were accompanied by a skeleton that they might not forget in the midst of their triumph how vain after all were all these temporary elevations. My Scotch friends doubtless with the view to conveying a moral to me put forth my address, and my speech, and then show me my skeleton made more hideous by falsehoods. The moral is plain, the philosophy is good, but the taste and the spirit of it all is censurable.

On 9th December a chastened Stanley was back in London, where he dined with Mackinnon and an assortment of Foreign Office mandarins and other notables. Then he proceeded to Brussels, fortified by the news that the Royal Treasurer Gazelot had just informed him that his salary would be the £1000 p.a. he had asked for. In this roundabout way he learned that he was still in favour with Leopold, who indeed received him well and told him he was pleased with his performance at Berlin. The time in Brussels was spent plotting how to leak to the Foreign Office Minister Julian Pauncefoote the French design to take from Belgium all the coastal territory from Sette Camma to the Loango. Stanley reported his impressions to Sanford: 'I saw the King. He is pale, probably from confinement indoors, otherwise charming and polite as usual and in no way dispirited, so far as I can judge.'

While Stanley returned to the fine and dry weather of Berlin in December 1884, Leopold had at last decided how to prise England away from Portugal. Fearful that if he made the concession on the Congo basin demanded of him, he would simply be asked to make yet further concessions, he threatened to pull out of Africa altogether, leaving chaos behind. Since he had already signed the droit de preference with France, this would leave the Congo behind French Customs barriers, and this would have been the end result of the sinuous Foreign Office policy. As Stanley wrote to Hutton on 10th December: 'I am off tonight for Berlin. We are going to the wall sure, if England will not act with Germany. 'Leopold's bluff worked. On 17th December Britain recognised the

Association and, following a full meeting of the plenipotentiaries, Italy, Austria-Hungary, Russia and Spain followed suit. But still France and Portugal remained aloof. The French were pressing hard for the annexation of the Kwilu-Niari lands, on the grounds that the treaties signed by Stanley's agents were with vassals of Makoko and therefore invalid. Leopold was in principle prepared to cede these territories but only in return for an indemnity of five million francs. When the conference adjourned for the Christmas holidays, Stanley was therefore sent back to London for a further session of arm-twisting at the Foreign Office. In particular Strauch wanted immediate permission from the British to enlist 500 Zanzibaris and 350 Chinese coolies for Congo construction work, as well as a couple of hundred sepoys for 'policing' duties. This was urgent, since the contracts of service of many of those at the Congo posts were near to expiry and their departure before replacements arrived would entail the abandonment of all the hard-won stations at Vivi, Isangila, Manyanga, etc.

During the Christmas holiday break from 23rd December to 5th January, Stanley was back in London lobbying Lord Granville, stressing the absolute necessity not to allow French protectionism to ruin commercial opportunities on the Congo. He received an invitation to speak at banquets in German cities and Leopold, pleased with his tireless work with Granville, granted him leave to attend, provided he made no reference, even indirect to Brazza, for alienation of the French at such a crucial time could cost the King the Congo. Here again Stanley paid the penalty for his crepuscular status, always the man in the middle. While Brazza was a French national hero, Stanley was doomed to fall between the three stools of Belgium, Britain and the USA, each with a claim on him but none prepared to embrace him as a true son. His irritation found expression in a letter to Sanford, witheringly ironical about the necessity to mouth 'effectless . . . pointless . . . platitudes'.

On 5th January the Berlin Conference resumed proceedings and at once passed a resolution prohibiting the slave trade in the Congo basin; an attempt to prohibit the sale of liquor also was defeated. On the 7th Stanley was banqueting in Cologne, and on the 8th and 9th he lectured to enthusiastic audiences in Frankfurt and Wiesbaden. He was about to return to Berlin when Sanford advised him that the Conference was suspended for a week. Stanley stayed put on the Rhine: 'I do not see the necessity of yawning over dullness there, as I can do it with so much more freedom here.'

He was back in Berlin on the 19th for the banquet given by Bismarck for plenipotentiaries and delegates to the Conference. It was at this time that he met the future Kaiser Wilhelm in Potsdam. There was a general feeling by now that the final lap of the Conference had been reached, but the last days of January saw Stanley firmly in harness. On 28th January Sanford persuaded him, much against his will, to write a long letter to Bismarck criticising Portuguese policy in general and on Kabinda in particular. He made a speech to the Conference on the wealth and resources of the Congo which later attracted much criticism. In this he claimed that the population of the area was forty-three millions, and cited Wissmann, Schweinfurth and even Tippu Tip as evidence. In fact the best estimate of the Congo's population in 1885 puts it at between twelve and thirteen millions, but Stanley in mitigation could cite Brazza in his defence, for Brazza made a rough estimate of fifty millions. He was at one with Brazza too in his exaggeration of the wealth of the Congo. Stanley estimated the potential value of trade to be £70,000,000. Of course for this to be achieved a railway was needed all the way to Stanley Falls; Stanley dealt briskly with Sir Edward Malet's suggestion that a line from Vivi to Leopoldville alone would be enough. When the Netherlands delegate made the mistake of mentioning Cameron's name in connection with the suggestion that canals could be used, Stanley snapped back that this was only possible between Lakes Mantumba and Leopold, if the delegate knew where that was.

At last in early February, Bismarck and the British 'squared' France. Leopold agreed to cede the Kwilu-Niari territories for an indemnity and permission for the Association to run a six million francs lottery in France. The French concluded a treaty with the organisation on the very day that news of Gordon's death in Khartoum came in. It remained now only for the Great Powers to bludgeon Portugal into acceptance in return for a face-saving strip of territory to the north of the Congo mouth; without English support, now that Britain had thrown in with Bismarck, there was little else the Portuguese could do.

On 15th February Portugal signed the convention and on the 21st the French neutrality resolution was adopted. There remained the formalities, such as the recognition of the Association by Sweden and Belgium itself. Then on 26th February came the formal plenary session of the Conference with Bismarck in the chair. The Berlin Act of this date declared the Congo and its tributaries to be a free trade zone from the Atlantic to the Indian Ocean and the whole area was designated as neutral. All the powers were pledged to aid missionaries and put down the slave trade. The only worrying feature for Leopold was that an International Commission was set up to oversee Congo navigation and raise loans for its expenses, thus conjuring visions of a possible rival to the AIC. All in all it seemed a fairly sweeping triumph for Leopold and his henchmen. The one minor cloud was that although Sanford signed the treaty, it was never ratified by the USA. Already the Department of State was distancing itself. Senator Morgan wrote to Sanford at the conclusion of the Conference: 'I very much regret that Mr Freyling- Hausen [the Secretary of State] has been so reticent about the Congo. Not that I could feel neglected in the matter but because you and Mr Stanley deserved something better than to be carefully hid away from sight as if you had purloined Congo and were trying to deliver the country over to us or somebody else in a sort of illegitimate way. 'Stanley spent the dog days of the Conference putting the finishing touches to his Congo book. He had to forward each chapter to Brussels for

335

approval; Leopold got out his blue pencil and deleted all incriminating evidence. His primary aim was to cover his tracks but he also insisted that Stanley tone down what he had to say about the state of the expedition when he arrived back in Africa in December 1882 and that he omit the offending officers' names. 'Your book coming out after the close of the Conference must be written in a peaceful spirit towards everybody. You must not allow a single sentence, nay a single word to be written that would hurt the legitimate pride of any power. 'What general conclusion can we come to on Stanley's performance at Berlin in 1884-5? He had shown his usual mixture of fidelity to Leopold and indiscretion. Opinions of him were as varied as ever. One of the diplomats, Sir Rennell Rodd, noticed that Stanley always spoke with real affection about blacks but that there was something about him that belied his words." Leopold's quondam trusted adviser Emile Banning said that Stanley was hopelessly ignorant of the subtleties of diplomacy, that he exaggerated the wealth of the Congo and that his optimism, common to all men of action, was strangely at odds with his reiterated pessimism on the many obstacles to a Congo railway. But Banning did at least acknowledge Stanley as a peerless explorer: 'With incomparable fatuity M. Brazza considered himself as a rival to Stanley and the French pretended to take the comparison seriously.'

Stanley felt magnanimous enough after the conclusion of the hard slog of negotiations to reopen contact with Harry Johnston, now that the Portuguese gaffe had been safely subsumed in history. Humorously rehearsing the many barbarous epithets - 'pirate', 'murderer', 'forger' - he had attracted during his career, he again extended the hand of friendship to his young protégé: 'Let us both promise to begin - I to stop pirating, murdering and forging at once and for ever; you never to make a promise unless you mean it and when it is once made to pride yourself on keeping it forever.'

Yet if Stanley could relax, his royal patron could not. Once the Berlin Conference had welcomed the new state into existence, Leopold's next step was to get Belgium to confer on him the crown of the Congo. The snag here was that Article 62 of the Belgian Constitution forbade a Belgian king to accept the throne of another state without the two-thirds majority assent of both chambers of the Assembly. This was why Borchgrave warned Stanley not to refer in his book to Leopold as the sovereign of the Free State, since his status had not yet been clarified; instead the book should be dedicated to 'all friends of Africa'.

Leopold faced the humiliating possibility of being denied by his own Parliament what had been granted to him by the Great Powers. To convince the Assembly that there would be no conflict of interest, the King gave assurances that he would be absolute ruler in the Congo and that Belgium itself would be committed to nothing, neither money, administration nor military force. The Belgian nation was then faced with the choice of humiliating its King in the eyes of Europe or letting him have his way. The outcome was predictable. Only one deputy voted against the bill, but all who voted for made it clear that the Congo was purely Leopold's affair and would never return to the notice of Belgium. A modern writer has aptly summed up the resulting situation:

One feels obliged to re-emphasise just what an incredible arrangement this was. The Congo had not been taken as a colony by Belgium, nor was Leopold to rule it as King of the Belgians. A brand-new state had been created essentially by fiat out of a vast African territory, unbeknown to the overwhelming majority of the people who lived there. And a private individual, whom an even greater number of those people had never heard of, had been given that state to own personally and had been made its king. 'The sovereignty of the Congo is invested in the person of the Sovereign,' a Belgian lawyer of the time wrote. 'His will be resisted by no juridical obstacle whatsoever.' Leopold II could say with more justification than Louis XIV did: 'L'Etat c'est mot.' Leopold himself, somewhat later, put it even more bluntly: 'My rights over the Congo are to be shared with none; they are the fruit of my own struggle and expenditure . .. the King was the founder of the state; he was its organiser, its owner, its absolute sovereign.' Perhaps an American newspaperman at that time summed up this peculiar situation most succinctly: 'He possesses the Congo just as Rockefeller possesses Standard Oil.'

Chapter Seven

THE conclusion of the Berlin Conference and the beginning of the 'scramble for Africa' in earnest provides an opportunity for an overview of Stanley as 'man of Africa'. Though his last great African journey was still to come, the essential pieces in the jigsaw puzzle were already in place by 1885. Certain questions virtually pose themselves. What was the impact of Stanley on African society (and the Dark Continent on him)? How does he relate to the theme of imperialism in general and Leopold's Congo in particular? Given that he covered such vast areas (modern Zaire, Tanzania and Uganda), what traces did he leave behind him in African folklore? What sort of a reputation did he have and were there any legends of Stanley?

It does not take exceptional insight to perceive that Stanley was only truly himself when in Africa, that he assumed a heroic size there and shrank back to normal human dimensions when in Europe. After 1871, whenever Stanley was away from Africa there was a distinct impression of a man working at half-throttle, someone killing time and going through the motions. This throws into paradoxical relief Herbert Ward's judgement that the influence of Africa on Stanley was almost entirely baneful. Ward felt that experience in the Dark Continent reinforced Stanley's belief in the efficacy of brute force and naked power, gave him an excessively pessimistic view of mankind, and also influenced his prose style, since the habitually flowery speech of Africa fed back its colour into Stanley's own idiom, producing a tendency towards archaic language and euphuism.

But Ward missed one vital point in his assessment. Africa was Stanley's salvation, and not just because it enabled him to rise high and far from a Welsh workhouse to a knighthood, world-wide fame and great wealth. It had a therapeutic effect also. Stanley's struggle with the Dark Continent was an objective correlative of his struggle with the dark forces within himself. It is even possible to speculate that, like Conrad after him, he might have drawn a kind of sustenance from the Congo itself. And it is certain that Stanley introduced the Congo into European imagination as the quintessential symbol of the 'heart of darkness'.

There is another point that Ward failed to bring out, Stanley's pessimistic view of human beings and their capabilities was partly mitigated by his generally high opinion of the black man. Naturally this sympathy operated within the general context of the common Victorian notion of the 'effortless superiority' of the white man - it would be anachronistic to expect otherwise, and of the men of the nineteenth century arguably only Thaddeus Stevens in the USA attained to a genuine empathy with blacks. Stanley's real feeling for the indigenous African was paternalistic, as was Livingstone's, but there is in his writings none of the contempt and dislike that disfigure the work of Sir Richard Burton or Sir Samuel Baker. Even Joseph Thomson, who liked to pride himself on his peaceful progress through the continent, as against Stanley's conquest with Sniders and Remingtons, eventually came to embrace a form of racial prejudice more like Burton's sentiments than anything to be found in Stanley.

Stanley frequently singled out one or other of the wangwana for special praise: Uledi, Baraka, Wade Hefeni and many others are the subject of encomiums throughout his writings; particularly during his five years building the Congo Free State (1879-84) he often contrasted the superior intelligence of his African aides with the white flotsam and jetsam of Europe that was sent out to him.- Few things irritated Stanley more than references to 'niggers' or suggestions that the African was a benighted savage, incapable of normal human emotions. He described blacks as capable of great love and affection, with a full sense of gratitude and other noble traits. He found them in general clever, honest, industrious, docile, enterprising, brave and moral: 'in short equal to any other race or colour on the face of the globe.' As he wrote in his journal in October 1883, commenting on the Bangala chieftain's love for the grandson whom Stanley was holding for ransom: 'I have seen hundreds of instances which absolutely contradict that absurd statement of Monteiro that the Africans know neither love, affection nor gratitude. Monteiro, I know, has been endorsed by Captain R. F. Burton - but Burton would endorse anything that was uncomplimentary to the African. I know not which to wonder at most - the impudence of Monteiro or the credulity of his stupid readers.' It has to be remembered, too, that Burton-like views were entertained by many of Stanley's white collaborators and contemporaries on the Congo: the missionary Bentley described the Bolobo as innately cruel, drunk and immoral, while Liebrechts considered that the intelligence of the African was used mainly for evil purposes.

But Stanley was not just impressed by the innate goodness of the black man; this could after all be subsumed in paternalism with the added rider 'until corrupted, just like children'. He declared himself fully convinced of the African's intellectual equality with the white man. Among the Irebu in June 1883 he listened to a brilliant piece of narration from an African storyteller: 'The story as a story was capitally related; as a comedy it was surpassingly well done and proved that in this faraway part of Africa there must have been many a Shakespeare and Milton, who have mutely and ingloriously died unwept, unhonoured and unsung by the ignorant civilised world.' And as for ability in business: 'In the management of a bargain I should back the Congoese native against Jew or Christian, Parsee or Banyan, in all the round world. Unthinking men may perhaps say cleverness at barter, and shrewdness in trade, consort not with their unsophisticated condition and degraded customs. Unsophisticated is the very last term I should ever apply to an African child or man in connection with the knowledge of how to trade ... I have seen a child of eight do more tricks of trade in an hour than the cleverest European trader on the Congo could do in a month.' Stanley was a Victorian paternalist only in that he was convinced of the superiority of European culture.

Any assessment of Stanley as 'man of Africa' must deal with his impact on indigenous societies and the reputation he left behind. Yet this is peculiarly difficult to gauge and quantify. Generalising, we may say that his effect was greater the longer he stayed in a given locality (as in the Congo in 1879-84) or when he came into contact with the more solid tribal organisations like that of Mutesa. But properly to measure the force of his advent on aboriginal societies, we need to set him in a context defined by general African views about the white man and his qualities and powers.

The most common basic view entertained in nineteenth-century Africa about whites when they were encountered, before familiarity bred cynicism and envious contempt, was that they came from the land of the dead, were spirits and could therefore work magic spells. On one linguistic analysis 'Mpoto' - 'the land of the white man' - really means 'the land of the dead'. So, for example, the missionary Grenfell working on the Juapa in 1885 was called 'Bedimo' ('ghost'). Charles Bateman who worked for Leopold on the Kasai reported that the Bashilele people called him 'Chienvu' - the reincarnation of a former chief of that name. Associated with this was the idea that white men had powers over death since they came from the land of the dead itself. Harry Johnston and Lt. Orban were once asked by a chief to send back a man from his village who had just died. Another gloss on the almost universal belief that white faces were the mark of a spirit was the idea that to work for such spirits in itself meant death. This engendered a general fear but also the sanguine attitude that the white man could control the weather at will; Bateman, arriving at a strange village in the middle of a thunderstorm, once claimed to have started it so as to impress the villagers with his power.

Tying in whites with the spirits of dead ancestors produced some interesting results. The horrors of the slave trade could be palliated by the notion that slaves went to America, died, then as spirits worked at producing sums of wealth unknown in the land of the living. When the distinction between Europe and America began to impinge, a different variant appeared. This was that when rich Africans died they went to Europe and became white. The cloth with which they were buried was their merchandise when they came back to trade, so the differential wealth of European and African traders could be explained in magical terms.

Another belief about whites was closely associated with the usual mode of their arrival - aboard steamers. It was widely believed that the pale-faced strangers lived beneath the sea, where they wove cloth in great quantities. It has been suggested that this belief arose because Africans would see an approaching ship mast first, then hull and only finally the entire ship. The first steamers the Bangala saw made them think that their owners were water kings, Lohengrins of the Equator, and that the ships were drawn by huge fish or hippos; the engine room was envisaged as a vast casserole where food was prepared. But the steamers - 'Kumba' as Mata Buiki called them - were not the only source of wonderment to the Bangala. Since they often saw the white men go down to the bottom of the ship to get pearls, mitakos and other merchandise, they believed that the men of the Mpoto (the West) descended into the bowels of the steamer to open up a door and thence fetch their treasures up from the bottom of the river. A variant on this farther downriver was that it was water-sprites, distinct from the white man, who wove the cloth they possessed. This was why when Stanley arrived, the Bangala at first hesitated to trade with him; they feared that if they accepted his gifts, the Likundu or evil spirit would restrict their wealth in future to those exact gifts.

The steamer motif also fed into the notion of whites as spirits since the steamer gave them the power to go away and come back again at great speed. In 1883 the first name the Bangala gave to Stanley was Midjiji (Ghost). This was all part of the general African disbelief in physical laws in favour of magic. But it was clear that the coming of the powerful strangers was received with gloom. One of the most powerful African myths was that of a golden age before the coming of the white man. In this era all animals lived together peacefully. But the golden age was shattered by man's sinfulness: animals turned and rent one another and the final apocalypse was denoted by the coming of the Ibanza or white wizards. Yet, as with most myths of the apocalypse (Norse Ragnarok for example), the gloom was lightened by hopes of a new age, when the elements or wild animals would destroy the interlopers and herald the dawn of a new Eden. The hope was sparked by the high mortality of Europeans in Africa which eventually prompted a more sophisticated response from the Congo peoples: that Europe must be a very unsavoury place indeed, since its inhabitants preferred death by disease in Central Africa.

The white man, then, at the very least was perceived as a being with enormous knowledge and talents deriving from magic or superior fetish. In an ironical but poetically justified inversion of European cultural chauvinism, Africans actually expressed surprise that the strangers had human feelings! To some extent the worst fears about whites in this regard were laid to rest when the first white women and children appeared on the Congo - a convincing proof of normality.

All the great African explorers left behind them traces in the local folklore of their coming and a reputation that could vary from sandiness to aggression and brutality, as in the case of Livingstone and Sir Samuel Baker respectively. Speke too had made a very favourable impression on the tribes with whom he came in contact; this was confirmed by Livingstone, and Frank Pocock in 1876 reported that Speke was 'all the rage' in Uganda and Karagwe. Some have gone so far as to assert that he was the most popular of all European explorers in Central Africa. Stanley's name, as might be expected, excited mixed reactions. Where he was compelled by the momentum and logistics of his expeditions to press forward at great speed, clearing the way with Sniders or Winchesters, his reputation tended to be that of a fearsome demon. When he was able to build up the trust of the locals slowly and over a long period, a very different picture emerged in the local folklore.

An awareness of place and time is all-important in assessing Stanley's niche in African folk memories. On the Livingstone expedition Stanley made little impact on Nyamweziland. Like Burton and Speke before him (significantly Speke's great reputation was in Uganda rather than Tanzania), he was not really distinguishable from an Arab. The first white man to make an impression in the Tanganyika lands was Philippe Broyon; only on the second Stanley expedition did his name begin to be whispered.

On the 1874-7 expedition Stanley came into contact with major African rulers like Mutesa and Mirambo, who were clearly impressed by him. In general, the higher the level of social organisation, the better the records of Stanley's visits - hence his name lived on in Uganda and Unyoro, especially as he tarried there longer than elsewhere on the Through the Dark Continent journey. Lesser chieftains tended to be intimidated by the size of his columns; these both bred envy and created serious pressure on precarious food supplies. Naturally, all the Stanley variables were interrelated: the sense of urgency which did not permit a leisurely, peaceful progress was a function of the size of his parties, and this in turn was a function of the lavish sums with which he had been equipped by Bennett. And the endurance of his name in Buganda was itself part of a process whereby the solid structure of Mutesa's social system owed something to the presence at his court of knowledgeable, sophisticated aliens, whether Arab or European. The only caveat that should be entered against the persistence of Stanley's reputation in Uganda was, as he pointed out in the early 1880s, that the story of his time with Mutesa in 1875 was attenuated by the rapid turnover of court personnel: 'almost all the notables of the country mentioned in Through the Dark Continent have perished and those who were at that time mere pages at the court occupy their positions.'

But it was during his arduous five years founding Leopold's Congo state that Stanley's reputation among Africans acquired a stability and fixity. His fame was mixed, with some oral traditions emphasising his dark side, others his positive aspects. Simplifying, we can whittle down the different, heterogeneous strands to three: Stanley was a hard and ruthless man, he was just, he was wealthy. Interestingly and characteristically, Stanley was as indifferent to his reputation among Africans as he was to the criticisms of him at home by white liberals. When Herbert Ward asked him what impression the arrival of his flotilla had made in 1879 on the tribes of the Lower Congo, Stanley replied insouciantly: 'In this world we can't stop to think about the impressions we create - no time for that sort of thing.'

The hardness and ruthlessness are well attested. Stanley's wangwana said to Livingstone's servants at Ujiji: 'Your master is a good man - a very good man; he does not beat you, for he has a kind heart; but ours - oh! he is sharp - hot as fire.' Many an African who had tasted the lash from 'the little master' could tell the same story. In the 1920s there were still Africans alive who had known Stanley and could provide vivid testimony to his hardness. Despite the lack of overt hostilities, the 1883 expedition by Stanley's flotilla to Stanley Falls, and his demonstration of the power of the Krupps gun, left him with a local reputation as an aggressor, second only to Tippu Tip in ferocity. Later, on the Emin Pasha expedition, oral tradition credited him with having cut a swath of destruction through the Ituri rain-forest. Col. George Williamson, a US Civil War veteran in the service of Leopold's Congo in the late 1880s, reported that Stanley's name 'produced a shudder among the simple folk when mentioned; they remember his broken promises, his copious profanity, his hot temper, his heavy blows, his severe and rigorous measures by which they were mulcted of their lands.' The missionaries too testified to the fear of Stanley and his henchmen that pervaded the Congo basin.

But this aspect of Stanley should be seen in perspective. Congo missionaries were riven with factionalism. One clique strongly supported Stanley and all his works and depended for their success on his support. Naturally the 'out' groups exaggerated his notoriety among the tribes for their own purposes. Much of the fear engendered by whites on the Congo arose after Stanley had left the area and the full brutality of Leopold's minions was unleashed. The problem here was that the term Bula Matari was widely used to denote both Stanley himself and the Association he represented, so that any atrocities committed by the Belgians tended to be laid at the door of Bula Matari. And there is no serious question that Stanley could be compared with genuine men of blood like the German Karl Peters who finally fulfilled Stanley's fantasy of violent revenge against the 'insolent' Gogo by machine-gunning them in droves. Known to Africans as Mkonowa-Damu - 'the man with the blood-stained hands' - Peters was eventually recalled as Imperial High Commissioner (Kilimanjaro district), asis brutality revolted even the not normally squeamish German authorities in Berlin.

But against the 'forceful' aspect of Stanley can be set his reputation for justice. Three witnesses will suffice, all of them admirers, but critical ones, of the explorer. The missionary A. M. Mackay reported: 'Whenever I find myself in Stanley's track, I find his treatment of the natives had invariably been such as to win from them the highest respect for the face of a white man.' Ward found that his name 'acted as a talisman throughout the Congo country. By millions of these savages his name is uttered with respect almost akin to fear.' And this was Harry Johnston's verdict: 'No disparaging word has ever in my hearing fallen from the lips of an African. He was generous, kindly, sympathetic and just, only severe to wrongdoers; absolutely uncured with that odious British pride and snobbishness which seals up the black men's sympathies and confidences.'

The two strands of harshness and fairness represented Stanley's Janus face, and he sometimes traded on this ambiguity to achieve his goals. He was helped in this by the fact that he had appeared on the Congo in two very different guises: in 1877 as the Ibanza, sailing in canoes, dealing out death from a hundred bullets and crushing all who stood in his path; and in 1880-83 as Bula Matari, the dispenser of trade goods, the Solonic law-giver, the Solomonic arbitrator. It was a mammoth task to persuade the tribes that the two men were one and the same. For the African a man's very identity was guaranteed by his enduring characteristics: his pacific or bellicose nature, whether he travelled in a canoe or in 'the house that walks on water', and so on. How could Bula Matari and Tandelay be one and the same? The Ibanza of 1877 had traded in brass rods while Bula Matari traded in bales of cloth. The only judicious conclusion was that Tandelay, the first to appear on the river, had been sent by Bula Matari; this meant that Tandelay was merely Bula Matari's vizier or First Minister. Stanley turned this incredulity to his own advantage when settling the Irebu civil war in 1883. Reluctantly 'conceding the truth', he warned the Irebu that although he, Bula Matari, was a man of peace, if they did not compose their differences, he would summon his war-chief Tandelay from the lower river to return with his host of deadly 'lightning sticks'.

Which of the two faces of Stanley - that of Tandelay or of Bula Matari - dominated in African consciousness is hard to determine but one good 'control' in elucidating how the Africans actually felt about him was in the degree of fidelity and loyalty they were prepared to give him. Wissmann thought that the ultimate test of an African explorer, given the hardships produced by the necessary evil of porterage, was whether his porters were prepared, in the main, to stick by him. No explorer could expect a nil or even low rate of desertion but, when all allowances have been made, Stanley scores remarkably highly in this area. The key to this was that he actually liked Africans. He had no time for those, like Thys and Bateman, who maintained that the African was feckless and shiftless, with no thought for the morrow, treacherous (always ready to make alliances with the white man to defeat rivals), and gluttonous. To a greater extent than any African traveller after Livingstone (except perhaps Weeks) he genuinely enjoyed the company of his 'dark companions'.

The third aspect of Stanley's reputation among Africans - that of a man of wealth - is perhaps the most securely anchored in the evidence of oral tradition and, arguably, the most important. The combination of the mysterious and impressive steamers and the plethora of trade goods they disgorged were irresistible. Stanley related the mixture of awe and cupidity with which the Irebu greeted En Avant. They thought its paddle-wheels must be turned by some twenty men concealed at the bottom of the ship. More sophisticated observers guessed that the secret must be the 'big pot' (the boiler) because the engineer was forever stoking up the fire. But what was he cooking there?' 'Perhaps,' concluded the Irebu, 'if we had also big pots in our canoes, and we had some of the white man's medicine, we need not toil any more with tired arms at our paddles, and suffer from aches and pains in our shoulders.'

Wealth was crucial in establishing the reputation of the white man in general and Stanley in particular. In Usukuma in 1889 Stanley, driving vast herds of cattle through East Africa with the Emin Pasha column, acquired the prestige of being a harbinger of meat and plenty. The local folklore said that for this reason, if he ever returned, men would flock to him. Among

344

the Bangala Stanley had a reputation as a man who introduced the mitako or brass rod as a unit of currency, thus contriving a dual system, for before the Bangala used the manyango (copper).Riches were considered all but definitional of the white man. For this very reason the Congo missionaries initially had a thin time of it, for they were white men without wealth. Only when their medical expertise became widely known did they win favour.

Africans could never understand the secret of European wealth, for they operated on a kind of proto-Marxist labour theory of value, in terms of which, with limited human labour to add to natural resources, the store of wealth available to a community could grow only slowly. With barter too they were limited to a circulation of existing goods. Totally alien was the Western notion of the creation of 'wealth' by credit, of buying stocks 'on margin' or creating an intrinsically non-existent effective demand by devices like credit cards. Exploitation in the classical economic sense they would learn from the whites and then only when they were its victims. Hardly surprisingly, then, when Stanley tried to explain to the Irebu how a complex Western trading system worked they were mystified and exclaimed: 'We know how to trade but our wealth does not increase.' Convinced that the total wealth of an area could not be augmented by trade, they concluded that Stanley's wealth was a purely personal attribute of the man himself which could be explained only in magical terms. It was a short step from this to the belief that Europeans could distribute gifts in unlimited quantities without growing poorer.

The stories and legends about Stanley that survive in African oral tradition almost invariably fasten on one or more of this trio of attributes: hardness, justice, wealth. But the full blast of the legend of Bula Matari was felt in those societies where Stanley had irrupted like a thunderbolt (Soko, Bangala, Irebu, etc). Where he was a distant figure, his local fame was a faraway echo of this. A good example was at Manteke which was founded in 1879 by Henry Richards of the LIM but which Stanley himself did not visit until 1883. Here he was simply known in oral tradition as 'the second white man'. Yet along the Congo proper his fame was such that oral histories dated events around his coming in 1877 much as we might use 1066 or 1789 as historical markers. Glave mentions that if a thief was hauled before a village council for stealing a chicken, he would give an account of his personal history by invoking the universally known formula: 'Arlekaki Tendele mboka bis kaza kala' - 'When Stanley passed our village a long time ago.'

This brings us to a consideration of the most famous name by which Stanley was known in Africa - Bula Matari (properly Matadi) - 'the breaker of rocks'. Both Stanley and his wife were immensely proud of this sobriquet which seemed to connote the Nietzschean morality of strenuousness by which the great explorer lived; the fame of the name was such that a tributary of the Upper Congo was named for it - Maia Boula Matari. The appellation sped through Central Africa by bush telegraph, to the point where in Ujiji by 1882 there was already a legend that this was where 'Father David' had met the 'Stone Breaker'. But in fact the Congolese did not really intend it to refer to the sledgehammer incident at Vivi and still less to the dynamiting of Ngomi mountain. Instead it was meant to denote a ruthless individual whose head was so hard that he could break rocks with it. When other evidence suggests that the Bangala - Stanley's 'Ashanti of the Upper Congo' - were thoroughly cowed and genuinely frightened by him, the balance of the Sirius-like ambiguity of Stanley's reputation seems to tip decisively towards the dark side. On the other hand there is this testimony from the independent Congo's first Prime Minister Patrice Lumumba - scarcely a man one would have imagined with much sympathy for Leopold's right- hand man: 'Stanley gave us peace, human dignity, improved our standard of living, developed our intelligence, made our spirit evolve.'

The question of the impact of Stanley on African society is a different one, more elastic and imponderable and subdividing into direct and indirect effects. But something of the same rule of thumb holds good: his impact was the greatest where he stayed longest. Arguably though, the relationship with advanced African societies is the inverse from the reputational situation, for Stanley and those who came after him were able to transform weaker social systems miraculously and almost overnight, whereas the stronger, more cohesive societies resisted the incursions of the West much longer. Uganda still held its own in the late 1880s while Kabba Rega of the Bunyoro fought gallant guerrilla warfare against the colonising power right through the 1890s.

While Stanley was still a technical explorer, his impact was as limited as that of any other occasional visitor to the great African courts; as has been well said, 'These men, and even Livingstone, were customarily regarded in a light similar to that in which the court of Imperial China examined envoys from the West.' But when he returned to the Congo in 1879 as the standard-bearer of Western civilisation and the harbinger of its motor-force, capitalism, the dislocating effect on traditional society was immediately apparent. Unwittingly, Stanley was delivering Central Africa to the rapacious maw of the most blatant system of exploitation the world had seen since the Ancient World. The rate of change was astonishing. According to Thys, the Bangala were transformed out of all recognition between 1877 and 1887. Even those who had no inkling of the later horrors to be unleashed on the Congo in the form of 'red rubber' and the official terrorism of Leopold's corporate 'Free State' noticed the rapidity of change. First the economic system of the Congo was transmogrified; then the older customs and modalities were broken down to produce a social system functional to Leopold's desire for plunder.

The first effect was the simplest. By bringing in large amounts of brass, Stanley and his European aides caused a devaluation of the brass rod currency even as they introduced it to tribes where it had been unknown before. In the 1880s the mitako became shorter and prices rose. The value of the brass rod was declining in proportion to its length, causing general price inflation; at the same time prices were fluctuating in real terms because of changing supply and demand in response to the arrival of European traders. After the Berlin Conference the Great Powers, hand in hand with private trading concerns, made a concerted effort to strangle native competitors. On the Congo the impetus to drive the Bobangi out of business by any means necessary reached the point where bloodshed was inevitable, and duly followed in the late 1880s and early 1890s.

Stanley himself played a part in this process. In 1883 he gave medals and payment in kind to the chiefs of Kinkanza to make them local managers and suppliers of labour, especially porters. The payment was a pig and a goat to those in the existing tribal hierarchy. But when some of the chiefs protested that the medals were 'bad medicine' and refused to co-operate, Stanley simply went behind their backs and supplanted them with more pliant individuals who were prepared to play the Association's game. This tied tribal hierarchies to a cash nexus rather than old customs and traditions and eventually had the effect of replacing matrilineal succession by succession through the deceased chiefs younger brother or sister's son. Stanley was impatient with any local customs or folkways that interfered with his purposes. One of the traditions on the Lower Congo was the maintenance of political clientele- age through the import and distribution of alcohol. When a chief demanded rum in return for his services, Stanley was able to seek general European legitimation for his destruction of the ancient ways by portraying the chief as a bibulous, boozy scoundrel.

The Congolese were well aware of the threat to their traditional way of life posed by the presence of white men trading as far up as Stanley Pool and then breaking into their monopolies on the Upper Congo. They threatened to disrupt the so-called 'Great Congo Commerce' - the flow of trade from the coast to Stanley Pool and beyond, whereby ivory was exchanged for goods imported by the European traders at the Atlantic estuary to the Congo. The Berlin Treaty of 1885 removed the last barrier to the process. The Free State declared itself the owner of all land not actually in use by the 'natives' and reserved for itself the definition of 'use'. While formal slavery was abolished, corvee and the requisitioning of labour was introduced. Local traders were crushed, the tribal chiefs bought off by making them 'managers'. Local cults were suppressed in favour of Christianity, and in return decades of sleeping sickness was ushered in. The Africans meanwhile were denied assimilation into the capitalist, bureaucratic and industrial institutions at any level except the most menial. But their very social structure made unity against the Europeans difficult, and the division of labour ruled indigenous modernisation on the Japanese model out of court. The only solution, as the great African chief Mirambo saw clearly, was to unite all of East and Central Africa under a handful of paramount chiefs, perhaps himself, Mutesa and Kabba Rega, to form a formidable and impenetrable military block. But until such a day came, Mirambo could see no alternative to an alliance of convenience with Tippu Tip and the hated Arabs.

Such were the momentous consequences of Stanley's epic 1877 voyage down the Congo. Yet his indirect impact was even more startling. He was the first explorer to force a switch of trade from the historic long-distance trade routes, largely because by his very success in venturing into the unknown in 1876 and conquering all obstacles he opened the door to Tippu Tip and his slavers. This, if anything, was the indictment that Hyndmans and others should have brought in 1878 instead of nitpicking over the technicalities of Bumbire. Until Stanley opened up the Congo and the Aruwimi, the tribes lived in security from Tippu Tip and his Arabs. By the mid-1880s Tippu was using his 'Manyema hordes' to crush the Soko and other peoples in the Stanley Falls area. The London press were later to pick up this point and contrast the responsible patient twenty-year stint Kirk had put in with Barghash with Stanley's glory-hunting, publicity-seeking forced marches, all guns blazing. Stanley, it was alleged, should have stayed in one area as Kirk and Livingstone did, 'but Stanley had other work to do'.

When Stanley proceeded to the 'rescue' of Emin in Equatoria, the more perceptive analysts pointed out that the effect of that expedition would be to open Equatoria to to the slavers. But it seems unnecessarily harsh to blame Stanley for consequences that he could not have foreseen. Once again we are in the quagmire of Popper's 'unintended effects'. Even Livingstone himself fell foul of this particular trap. His blockade-breaking in 1858 when he used a show of force to browbeat chief Tengani into opening up the Shire River also had the effect of letting the slavers in. But Stanley's indirect impact was far more significant than this, for by removing the barrier to Tippu Tip and the Nyangwe Arabs Stanley triggered a minor version of the disastrous menace of southern Africa in the early nineteenth century. Once on the Congo, Tippu Tip's Arabs penetrated every tributary and byway and were soon in collision with the mighty Luba empire of Katanga.

Stanley's impact becomes even more significant if we regard the long-distance trade that he so disastrously affected as an 'African mode of production' analogous to the Asiatic mode that Marx explicitly recognised. It has been trenchantly argued that long-distance trade was itself a mode of production, possibly the dominant mode of production in pre-colonial Africa. Here we return in effect to the debate on wealth between Stanley and the Irebu and its implications. According to the Western view, a mode of production by definition must produce a surplus value. Long-distance trade, on the other hand, is a mere transfer of wealth from one society to another. Here we confront a clear conflict between traditional and Western notions of what constitutes wealth. A proper assessment of Stanley's indirect impact must await a more comprehensive resolution of this technical issue.

The question of Stanley's relationship to imperialism is easier to resolve, for the golden age of his explorations antedated both imperialism proper and the 'scramble for Africa'. Stanley was an imperialist in the 1890s but his active career was then over and his place had been taken in Africa by active exponents of empire like Lugard, Rhodes and Milner. Stanley is best seen as a precursor of imperialism, a man who laid foundations that were later used by others for different purposes. He could scarcely be considered an imperialist in any of the classical senses, since no European nation recognised its 'manifest destiny' in Africa until after the Berlin Conference, and the 'scramble' was arguably triggered by Leopold's own dreams of personal empire. As Lord Salisbury recorded: 'When I left the Foreign Office in 1880, nobody thought about Africa. When I returned to it in 1885, the nations of Europe were almost quarrelling with each other as to the various portions of Africa which they could obtain.'

Economic imperialism - the notion of colonies as a necessary outlet for the export of surplus capital, so as to prevent a domestic crisis of under-consumption - lay almost twenty years in the future. Besides, Leopold's motive was not the health of Belgian capitalism but his own aggrandisement. His unlocking of the Congo was part of a massive scheme of personal booty: 'The Congolese system was too viciously wasteful, too recklessly short-term in its conception, to deserve even the term of exploitation. It was no more than a prolonged raid for plunder. 'As a final irony, Leopold came to Africa by accident after disappointment in the Philippines and elsewhere. The idiosyncratic nature of the monarch's enterprise in the Congo partly accounted for its unhappy history. The classical model of economic imperialism required stability as a precondition for foreign investment. But Leopold was merely interested in turning himself into a combination of absolute monarch and Rockefeller. So far from being an agent of imperialism, Stanley was merely used as 'a decoy by a subtler mind than his, and became the unconscious instrument of the most colossal invasion of human rights the world has ever witnessed.'

But if Stanley was the mere agent of a royal plunderer, the relationship was an uneasy one. He was Hercules to Leopold's Eurystheus and the fraught relationship of official master and employee showed that Stanley was an unruly and unreliable subordinate. He wanted to go slowly in the Congo and build on solid foundations; Leopold wanted him to rush ahead and plant the flag of the Association everywhere along the Congo, be the foothold never so precarious. Leopold dreamed of sucking out from Central Africa vast wealth that would enable him to be the most powerful man on earth, with the charisma of kings and the dollars of Carnegie. Stanley looked forward to the day when the Union Jack would flutter over the domains that he had discovered. Both men needed each other. In the early days only Stanley could have secured the foothold for Leopold's undisclosed Promethean ambitions in Africa. Yet only Leopold could send Stanley back to the continent that had made him. He had come to the end of the line with Bennett and knew that he was too controversial a figure in England to be employed by the RGS on any of its expeditions. Stanley was the sorcerer's apprentice. The position he and Leopold found themselves in may be likened to the mutual exploitation of the German Nazis and the giant German corporations (Krupps, I. G. Farben), each trying to mould the other to its own purposes. When Stanley most truly became an agent of imperialism, by contrast, was when he turned away from Leopold and embraced Mackinnon and the British East Africa Company.

But as a precursor of imperialism, Stanley did demonstrate in a spectacular way that Western technology was a vital necessary condition for the conquest and subjugation of Africa. Few people ever gave more convincing proof of the saying current at the time among the wangwana: 'Bunduki sultani ya bara bard - 'The gun is the Sultan of Africa. 'The period of Stanley's active life in Africa (1870-90) saw the most spectacular revolution in firearms technology in history.

The switch from muzzle-loading rifles to breech-loaders - a key element in the Prussian victory over Austria in 1866 - also dramatically widened the technological gap between European and non-western peoples. It accounted for the British victory over the Ashanti in 1873 after two campaign defeats on level technology and the final defeat of the aboriginal peoples and the closing of the frontier in both North and South America. The key rifles of this type were the French chassepot (famous from the Franco-Prussian War), the Sniders used by Stanley in 1874-7 d the American Martini-Henry and Peabody-Martinis. All these used metallic cartridge cases and steel barrels instead of iron as in the older weapons and could be quickly reloaded from a prone position.

But the breech-loader was scarcely perfected when the first repeating or magazine rifle was introduced. The first, the Winchester, was used by the Turks in the war against Russia in 1877-8. In all these small-bore magazine rifles the use of smokeless powder became the norm. The discarded breech-loaders then entered Africa in large numbers, with the Europeans able to maintain their technological gap. Stanley found Emin's troops in 1889 armed with breech-loaders. This development alarmed Europe's pro-consuls. Kirk's successor at Zanzibar, Euan-Smith, told Lord Rosebery in 1888 that if a large-scale arms trade in breech-loaders developed in East Africa, pacification of the indigenous inhabitants would be impossible. The scale of the problem can be appreciated when it is realised that in 1885-1902 a million firearms and four million pounds of gunpowder, plus millions of caps and rounds of ammunition, entered the German and British spheres of influence in East Africa.

After the pilot Winchester came the Mauser (1884), the Mannlicher (1885), the Lee-Metford (1888) and the French Leber. Meanwhile there was significant development in another sphere: the machine gun, which made its debut with the Gatling in the American Civil War. Stanley took a Krupps variant of this to the Congo in 1883. But the real breakthrough came in 1884 with the first machine gun to be operated by propellant gases instead of a hand crank. The gun, patented by Hiram S. Maxim in 1884 and adopted by the British army in 1889, contained only one barrel. Since smokeless cartridges were consistent in their energy output, the loading could be done by gas pressure or by recoil instead of with a crank. The Maxim, unlike the Gatling and its derivatives, was light enough for infantry to carry, it could be set up inconspicuously, and it spat out bullets at a rate of eleven per second; its sole drawback was that it could really be used only as a defensive weapon. Stanley was always at the very forefront of weapons technology, for he took a Maxim gun with him to Africa in 1887 - a full two years before it came into use with the British army. There can be no serious question but that Stanley's reputation on the Congo derived in part from the awesome weapons he was able to deploy.

There is a final area where the justifiability of imperialism, the impact of Stanley and the morality of Western penetration of Africa all merge. Stanley always tried to legitimate his involvement in Leopold's shadowy schemes on the grounds that by his nation-building in the Congo he was walking in Livingstone's footsteps and liberating Africa from slavery. But did the indigenous African see it like that? The fact was that it was the Europeans' wealth and military power that impressed the African most, not their religion and culture. By and large Africans genuinely respected Arabs, even when they feared and envied them. The slave trade, such an anathema in Western eyes, was merely an extension of the domestic slavery sanctioned by tribal custom. Islam too was attractive: unlike Christianity, it was untouched by racial bias and it accepted the African perception of the role of women. Islam and African tribalism were at one in accepting a plurality of wives and a general chattel status for females; the Muslim religion itself required no more than the mouthing of a few rote-learned words. Best of all, Islam put prestigious firearms in its converts' hands and the Muslim paradise, with its four luscious virgins assigned to each male member of the faithful, was infinitely more appealing than the anaemic and ethereal Christian heaven.

Moreover, on any analysis the Arabs did more for the African than Leopold and his henchmen did. The Arabs taught the more advanced tribes administration. With scribes working in Arabic, they were able to offer enlightened local rulers the elements of a modern bureaucracy. They spread Swahili as a common language through East and Central Africa. They were responsible for a revolution in African diet, having introduced mango, orange and avocado trees, beans, onions, garlic and tomatoes to the continent. Indeed some British colonial administrators later regretted that the Arabs had not established an empire over the entire area, thus providing the incoming European overlords with a sophisticated class with which to collaborate.

These issues formed the subject matter of a number of debates Tippu Tip conducted in the 1880s with Europeans, notably Vangele and Becker. Tippu spoke with contempt of the great zeal Europeans had to abolish at once everything that it had taken the Arabs and Africans centuries to build up. He challenged Becker to explain to him the difference between African slavery and Russian serfdom. In his view, his own slaves had a better deal than the proletariat of Europe's cities. At least, slaves as they were, they had full bellies, while the European employee, if he was lucky not enough to find employment and be tied to a master, had the 'freedom' to languish from lack of proper payment and the 'privilege' of watching his children die of starvation. Tippu made the further point that Christian arguments about the dignity of freedom were so much humbug in a continent where a slave could be happy while the 'free' tribesman was at the behest of some murderous chieftain. There was far less racial prejudice between Arab and black than between the white man and the black man; he himself would not treat a black slave the way he had seen Stanley treating his own whites. You Christians believe in the morality of work, he taunted, yet the black man left to himself is lazy and prefers to steal his bread rather than earn it. How then did Christians square 'freedom' with the 'morality of work'? His final point was that European aspirations for the eventual independence of Africa were, if not false and hypocritical, a recipe for disaster: 'Independence for the African is nothing else but licence, theft, brigandage, debauchery, madness and misery. Just see what will happen in the future."

These views could perhaps be dismissed as the self-serving statements of a merciless slaver, if the later record of Leopold's Congo did not far eclipse in ferocity anything Tippu had been able to compass. Yet even as they stood, they received support from some more thoughtful observers in Europe. In 1888 the journalist E. Belfort Bax wrote in the London Star.

Would that the English democracy at least could be made to take sufficient interest in this African question to see the infamous transactions of philanthropists and explorers through all their cant of anti-slavery and the like. Would that one could bring down to them the fact that the Arab slave trade at its worst is but an idyllic dream compared to the state of things which Mr Chamberlain recommends as a panacea for the slave trade - to wit, the forcing of civilisation, i.e. modern capitalism in its worst form, upon an unwilling and primitive population accustomed to simple conditions of life. Everyone that has gone into the business in the least knows well enough that the whole business of Stanley, Emin & Co is being machined by a ring of capitalists greedy for cheap labour, cheap ivory and markets in which to shunt cheap home-made goods. The Arab slave trade, besides being a convenient handle to disguise the nature of the undertakings in question, is as far as it goes often really an obstacle to their immediate success. Hence the exaggerated and highly coloured pictures we are daily receiving of the horrors of the slave trade.

There was a moral dimension here similar to the one Marx famously explored when examining the coming of capitalism in India. While at one level one hailed the destruction of benighted superstitions like that of Hanuman the monkey (or in this case the African slave trade), one deplored the ruthless and inhuman way in which traditional societies were eviscerated in order to integrate them with an international capitalist system. It was typical of Stanley the ruthless technocrat that such moral dilemmas never arose in his mental universe, or if they did they were at once discarded as mere armchair abstractions, a waste of time for the man who would master the 'woodenheaded world'.

Chapter Eight

FROM Berlin Leopold's nagging about the Congo book followed Stanley to Brussels and back to Sackville Street. At the beginning of March Stanley had an interview with the King about the book. Leopold was still concerned that if recalcitrant officers were named, future would-be recruits would be deterred from African service. Stanley found the monarch's behaviour boorish and added a waspish aside in a letter to Sanford that the implicit portrait of the King in his book would do nothing to enhance his reputation. As it turned out, Stanley scored a minor satisfaction, since Leopold's final corrections arrived too late to be included in the book. Moreover, the order to emphasise in the preface that he was still in the King's service seemed to Stanley to sort ill with the general prescription for maximum discretion.

The final proofs and corrections were in his editor Marston's hands on 23 April 1885 after some particularly troublesome work on the Congo maps. These last-minute corrections were done at Newstead Abbey in Nottingham, where he was visiting the Webbs whom he had not seen for seven years. He had other claims on his time too: Dualla had left him to get married after six years' service and he was on the look-out for a young Somali aged between sixteen and twenty with a knowledge of English. But the interlude was a pleasant one, as he told Mackinnon: 'It is an unequalled treat for me to breathe a little country air after my close confinement in London and Berlin ... oh dear! England is lovely, and it is a crime in L. Low & Co. my publishers to keep me indoors proofreading - it is only a wee bit more cool than on Congo today, and everything looks so lovely.' His antennae ever sensitive to any change in ambience, Stanley soon sensed the only tiny cloud on the horizon: 'Mrs Webb, though she is not quite so cordial as in old times to me for some reason, is a model lady fit to sit in the presence of queens. 'From Newstead Stanley proceeded to Liverpool to embark on a transatlantic visit for a trip to the USA about which he was remarkably cagey to Mackinnon, saying no more than that it was business not pleasure. What had happened was that his American publisher Harper had warned him that a Philadelphia rival was putting out a pirated edition of the Congo book, since the rights of foreign authors were not protected in the USA. It turned out that Stanley had not after all been through the necessary formalities to be considered a US citizen; mistakenly he assumed that service in the Civil War and the oath of allegiance he took then were enough. It was therefore necessary to present himself to the proper authorities in the USA for a formal naturalisation process. The trip was a typical Stanley lightning in-and-out affair. He left Liverpool on 23 April, obtained his citizenship papers on 15th May and on 25th May was back in London.

Finding no word awaiting him there from Brussels on his future employment in Africa, Stanley now started to fret. He had arranged all his baggage and even bought two donkeys on the assumption of an imminent return to Africa. Well, when was this return to take place? He had expressed some anxiety on this score even before he left for the USA as he told Sanford: 'May I ask at what time the Association requires me to go to the Congo? I had a curious letter from Count Borchgrave the other day who said he noted I had not mentioned a word about my engagement while Col. Strauch at Berlin asked me not to mention the fact on account of the hostility by French and Portuguese. What does it all mean?'

What it all meant was that, unknown to Stanley, France and Portugal had agreed to recognise the Association at Berlin only when given personal guarantees from Leopold that Stanley would never be sent back to the Congo. Since Brazza was still in Central Africa, this was France's way of getting its revenge on the man who had outwitted and humiliated their national hero. It is also the clearest and most remarkable testimony to Stanley's importance in the struggle for mastery in Africa. Leopold naturally did not tell Stanley that he had bargained away the explorer's future to secure his own ends and raised no objection to the gloss Stanley put on the leave of absence granted to him - that is to say, that when it ended on 1st June 1885 he would immediately return to the Congo. The only answer the explorer received to his enquiry was a curt two-liner from Borchgrave that his services would not be needed for quite some time.

Stanley wrote back sternly to point out all he was doing for the Congo Free State in England. He mentioned the 'intolerable expense' (some £500) of getting all his tropical kit together, ready to leave for Africa at a moment's notice. This time the reply was a resounding silence. On 24th June Stanley wrote again, this time to Leopold to complain of Borchgrave's stalling. He was not favoured with a direct reply, but four days later Borchgrave wrote another short note to the effect that it was impossible to say exactly when the explorer would be sent back to Africa. Strauch was tempted to tell Stanley flat out that he could never return to Africa under Association auspices because of opposition from France and Portugal. But Leopold's reflex action was secretiveness, so he opted for keeping Stanley on ice. He explained to Strauch that it was not a good idea to reveal to Stanley the pledge he had given the French and Portuguese; he needed him as a second string to his bow in case Brussels had to send him back, for example, if de Winton fell ill or key men like Janssen and Valcke succumbed to fever or the climate. Strauch disagreed and favoured sending Stanley out anyway. Leopold clinched the debate by pointing out that Stanley could only go out to the Congo if he was put in the picture about the royal pledge to France and Portugal, and if he knew that, he would (justifiably) feel so hurt and resentful that his future utility and loyalty would be in question.

Meanwhile in the privacy of his journal Stanley fumed at the treatment meted out to him. 'How long am I to remain a victim to suspense? Are my expenses in vain? Does the King wish to send me to the Congo or does he not? Is it true, as I have heard, that the French stipulated before signing the treaty with the Association, that I was not to return to the Congo?' He felt very bitter that Sanford had persuaded him to renew his contract that he had then cut short all his engagements in England and even crossed to the USA incognito, while all the time Leopold was playing false with him. It was clear that the King's attitude was: 'We are grateful for past services of Mr Stanley but we think we can carry out the administration and all further work on the Congo without further aid from him.' Stanley professed not to care whether he went back to Africa or not; what mattered was certainty and predictability. If he knew for certain he was not wanted he could make money out of lecturing; he accordingly decided to take Borchgrave's letter as a prolonged extension of leave.

He therefore kept a high profile in the relevant English circles. If ever he felt unwilling to fulfil a social engagement, he hinted darkly that Leopold had given him secret orders not to attend. Sometimes the cry of wolf concealed a real wolf. Such was the case when Baroness Burdett-Coutts pressed him to attend a meeting at which the British government's 'betrayal' of Gordon in the Sudan would be discussed. Stanley was always willing to wade into any discussion on Gordon but on this occasion he received explicit orders from Brussels that as an employee of the Congo state he had to steer well clear of this particular controversy. Stanley therefore picked and chose what parties to attend and which contacts to make, using Leopold as the perfect excuse. He accepted honours from the Baptist Missionary Society for his support in the Congo. He addressed the Anti-Slavery Society. He received ovations at the RGS anniversary dinner on 8th June, and attended the reading of de Winton's paper on the Congo the day before. He corresponded with Cardinal Manning about a Gordon memorial; the Catholic Church had condemned the policy of non-intervention in the Sudan, as it meant leaving the peoples there to savagery.

But overall Stanley was a deeply unhappy man. Not only, it seemed, had Leopold double-crossed him, but the King was also dragging his feet over the project dearest to Stanley's heart: a Congo railway. Stanley's feverish interest in this amounted at times to obsession. He drew up a detailed scheme for a 5 2-mile track between Vivi and Isangila on the right bank to get round the most fearsome cataracts, and another 95-mile track to link Manyanga and Stanley Pool on the left bank. At their meeting in Brussels in March 1885 Leopold gave Stanley permission to take soundings in England and, if possible, to form a syndicate to finance the 150 miles of track. In concert with Hutton and Mackinnon he soon managed to raise £400,000; a detailed synopsis was despatched to Brussels and won the King's qualified approval.

But Leopold, as ever, was playing a double game. He wrestled with the problem of how to sign an agreement with British capitalists to get the much-needed railway while maintaining political control. The problem was that the proposed railway company would have to be given land concessions to lay track and total rights along the railroad. Leopold solved the dilemma by stalling Stanley's syndicate with a provisional agreement while he cast about for ways of raising the money himself.

Even for a past master of tergiversation and prevarication, Leopold excelled himself in 1885. First he delayed answering Hutton for two months. Then he told the syndicators that the matter could go no further until a report from a Belgian survey team was received. But Stanley kept up the pressure, maintaining a high profile in the English press for the idea of a narrow-gauge Congo railway while trying to pin Leopold down to details. Leopold then uncoiled a fresh serpent of problems. He wriggled ingeniously with the idea that any dispute between the state and the railway company be settled according to the law of the Free State; since the Congo constitution had not yet been drawn up, this amounted to offering the syndicate a pig in a poke. Then he added a further layer of obfuscation by insisting that the company buy the rails for the track in Belgium; this elicited the perfectly reasonable answer that this was a matter for the contractors. Only in 1886 did he finally throw off the mask and reject the British syndicate's proposals on the (spurious) ground that a railway monopoly was contrary to the Berlin Act and that an agreement with the railway company would compromise the sovereignty of the new Congo state. The real reason for his opposition was that by now there were Belgian capitalists interested in the railway project. The Belgian syndicate was led by thirty-seven-year-old Captain Albert Thys who, by a dynamism rivalling Stanley's, managed to raise one million francs to form the Compagnie du Congo pour le Commerce et l'Industrie (CCI). By the time Stanley had departed on the Emin Pasha expedition, in May 1887, Thys had set out for the Congo to implement Stanley's brainchild. After a year's energetic work there he replaced Strauch as Administrator-General of the Association.

Leopold's strategy was high-risk. He needed capital to sustain the infant Congo state but was unwilling to relinquish his own iron grip on the territory. Since the Berlin Act forbade import duties and Leopold (as a further sop to the humanitarians) had banned the sale of alcohol in his African domain, bankruptcy loomed by 1886. The original idea of a 20-million franc lottery in France, agreed at Berlin, went into abeyance with Ferry's fall from power. Turning down the British railway syndicate and stalling for time until a Belgian company was in place was an act of fanaticism or courage, depending on one's point of view. Once again 1887 proved Leopold's lucky year, for a bond issue was arranged in the nick of time. The King persuaded the Belgian government to authorise an issue of 150 million francs' worth of premium bonds, eighty million of which were to be offered on the French bourse. A guarantee for prospective shareholders was provided by the moral support of a consortium, including the Banque Nationale (the Belgian state issuing bank).

It can be seen that Stanley was a small cog in the mighty wheel of Leopold's machinations. Nevertheless, in Stanley's inner world the refusal to send him back to the Congo and the underhand way the King had scuttled all his hard work on the railway was tantamount to betrayal. However measured his later statements, he never really forgave the monarch for his treatment in 1885-6. That was bad enough. But the twelve months from July 1885 on also brought Stanley bitter disappointment and unhappiness in his private life, making this period in his life in many ways the nadir of his career. It is not clear why, after so many years in the emotional wilderness, Stanley should have decided on his return from the Congo in 1884 that he needed a wife. Perhaps he felt that his social position in Anglo-Saxon society could only be secure if he possessed the outward trappings of respectability. Perhaps the guilt at the repressed homosexual side of his personality was becoming too great to bear. Or perhaps the desperate need for affection (existing side by side with a morbid fear of any woman who might provide it) began to overwhelm him. Whatever the reason, certain it is that on his return to Europe Stanley was actively looking around for a partner, as he informed Leopold during the 'debriefing' sessions of September 1884.

His first fumbling overtures nearly brought disaster. Much of the evidence has been suppressed or destroyed but, reading between the lines, it is clear that he was the victim of a blackmail attempt from a woman, almost certainly involving a paternity suit. At the end of December 1884 he wrote to inform his friend Alexander Bruce that he had cancelled all his engagements and would appear no more before the British public; he intended to make a permanent abode in Belgium 'where ... I shall at last be able to live without the fear of an absurd and ridiculous scandal instigated by a demented woman ... I cannot permit myself to be dragged to a police court at the instigation of every woman that has a mania ... I have examined the whole affair thoroughly, and I find that although two minutes would be sufficient to prove the whole thing a fraud, yet as it cost me from 1872 to 1878 to disprove the effect of Sir H. Rawlinson's impudent letter to The Times, a dozen years might elapse before I should be able to recover the lost ground in the esteem of those who at present profess esteem.' Worst of all was the thought of the field day his enemies would have: 'Cameron and Markham will be in their glory.'

The affair was somehow hushed up, or the woman did not go through with her threat. It is easy to see how Stanley could have been prey for a blackmailer, for in the company of women he was impossibly gauche and reserved. He explained the problem himself in a letter in August 1884: 'I have lived with men, not women, and it is the man's intense ruggedness, plainness, directness, that I have contracted by sheer force of circumstance ... I wish to say, my dear friend, that I am absolutely uncomfortable when speaking to a woman, unless she is such a rare one that she will let me hear some common sense. The fact is, I can't talk to women. In their presence I am just as much of a hypocrite as any other man, and it galls me that I must act and be affected, and parody myself... It is such a false position that I do not care to put myself into it.'

One woman who qualified as a 'rare one' was the German writer and painter Marie von Bunsen, to whom Stanley was introduced shortly after his dinner with Bismarck. Scion of a diplomatic family, she spoke perfect

English so was able to make a shrewder assessment of him than would otherwise have been possible. At first sight she found Stanley disappointing: he was short, broad, circular with a tanned face, keen dark eyes (the whites were rather yellow), grizzled hair, short moustache and strongly marked features. 'His manners at first seemed more than simple; he hardly looked at me and sat down uncouthly. I talked for all I was worth and tried every kind of topic; he hardly responded.'

Two days later at the American Thanksgiving festivities Stanley was virtually dragged up to her by Sanford. He mumbled in his aloof, indifferent, stiff way that he was to have the pleasure of taking her in to dinner. This time she was able to pierce the carapace of reserve to some extent. She found that he had no small talk or witty conversation and spoke as if giving a public lecture. He told her of the affectionate nature of Africans, of how the beauties of nature made up for loneliness in the Dark Continent, of his ordeal because of the apathy of his white companions, and that the Bible and Shakespeare were his constant companions. He was especially bitter about his treatment in 1872 and 1878 and said that when nobody believed he had found Livingstone tears rolled down his cheeks. After the dinner Sanford congratulated Marie on her marvellous success in getting Stanley to come out of his shell. Several people later told her that Stanley had been interested in her as a possible wife, though her overall opinion was not sufficiently favourable. She never recanted the judgement passed after the first meeting: 'He impressed me as being of the tough Conquistadores type with the outward habit of a disgruntled farmer and the phraseology and vocabulary of an American journalist.'

Marie von Bunsen was clearly too formidable a woman for someone with Stanley's problems, so predictably the encounter led nowhere. Back in England Stanley took to conducting a postal flirtation with an Austrian woman who had written to him through his publishers but would not reveal her name. But with both sides boxing clever and neither giving anything away this brush with 'The Unknown Madame or Mademoiselle' also came to nothing. Stanley became despondent at the thought that though he could tame Africa and subdue the most ferocious chieftains, he could make no progress with women. It even caused him anguish to dwell on others' marital felicity. In July 1885 he wrote to Sanford: 'Don't for pure charity conjure up beatific visions of domestic bliss. I have always maintained your right divine to be proud and happy, but it is unkind to twit a doomed bachelor like myself.'

But in June 1885 Stanley's fortunes suddenly took an unexpected turn. Gertrude Tennant, widow of a wealthy landowner and sometime Tory MP for St Albans, ran one of the fashionable London salons, where political, artistic and literary celebrities mingled. Aged sixty-six (she died at ninety-nine in 1918), she was one of Victorian London's grandes dames, and Edwin Arnold of the Daily Telegraph was a frequent visitor at her soirees. At her daughter's suggestion, she asked Arnold to bring Stanley with him to dinner on 24th June. Stanley accepted the invitation but, as it turned out,

Arnold himself could not attend, so his place was filled by no less a person than Gladstone. At dinner Gertrude Tennants's daughter Dorothy (always known as 'Dolly') sat between Africa's greatest explorer and the 'Grand Old Man'.

Dorothy Tennant was the only woman of any importance in Stanley's actual life (as opposed to the fantasies he wove around Virginia Ambella, Katie Gough-Roberts and Alice Pike). Edwin Arnold described her as 'tall and statuesque, handsome in face and figure. She moved like some goddess of old story.' Aged thirty-four and single at the time of the dinner engagement, she was in her own way as much an oddball as Stanley himself. She kept a detailed diary, addressed to her father who had died a dozen years before. The normal form of ending her daily entry was to sign off 'Goodnight, dearest' or 'Goodnight my darling'. It would doubtless be facile to talk of an 'Electra complex', especially since Dorothy was abnormally close to her own mother, even to the point of sleeping in the same room, but there was undoubtedly something more than a little eccentric about Dolly. It is surely significant that one of her contacts in the art world, Sir John Millais, used her as the model for a painting called No! which shows a girl on the point of sending off a letter rejecting a proposal of marriage.

For as well as being a society hostess Dolly was an amateur painter of some repute; her work was hung in the Royal Academy in the late 1880s. She specialised in painting Grecian nymphs and London urchins, the latter a subject doubtless suggested to her through her activities on the outer fringes of Beatrice Webb's Fabian circle. Her canvases seldom exceeded a foot in height but she mounted them in gilt frames so deeply recessed that it was said that the beholder had an immediate sense of distance. Her London gamins were taken straight from the street; she would offer them a good dinner and a cash 'tip' to pose for her. The urchins' naivety charmed her. Once when the door to her house was opened by a flunkey, one of the lads asked Dolly: 'Why does your brother dress in that rummy way?' The same boy, having eaten dinner, told her in full innocence: 'My eye, but yer mother can cook!'

Such was the woman who distracted Stanley's attention from Gladstone, with whom, in any case, he never got on. The evening was a great success. 'What a charming lady Miss Dorothy is!' Stanley wrote to Arnold. She for her part reacted in what can only be described as an overripe way. Her diary that evening 'told her father': 'So much for succeeding. I am astonished at succeeding. Oh God help me. Do help me. What am I to do?' She wrote to tell Stanley he should feel free to call at Richmond Terrace any time he wished.

The Tennant establishment in Richmond Terrace was situated in a cul-de-sac, prolonging the line of Downing Street towards the Victoria Embankment. It was eminently peaceful: only the clip-clop of hooves, the jingle of bells on the bridles of cab horses or the sound of a steamer siren on the Thames occasionally punctuated the tranquillity. Stanley was nothing to return, but Dolly began by overplaying her hand. She slipped from the formality of 'Dear Mr Stanley' to 'My dear Bula Matari' before the reserved Stanley was ready for such familiarity. She had to return to 'Dear Mr Stanley' before he was tempted to return. Partially to make amends, she wrote to propose an oil-painting of his head: 'I would let you be very comfortable, you shall smoke ... and feel just as though you were in your own tent.'

Stanley accepted, but before the sittings could begin he had to keep a prior engagement with Mackinnon in Balinakill. He did not enjoy the interlude, apart from the one-night stopover in Glasgow with the Bruces. He suffered from facial pain, a recrudescence of the toothache in Brussels in November 1882, and found the damp, cold climate on Mackinnon's estate completely unsuited to him. He was glad to return to London and the company of the Tennants. With some reservations Stanley approached the double doors of Richmond Terrace by a short flight of stone steps with a fanlight above. In the hall was a gaslight, then the vestibule opened out into lofty rooms with vast mantelpieces and velvet, tasselled curtains, which were drawn across the fireplaces in summer. She took him through the library to the left of the entrance hall, through the dining-room and to her 'birdcage', a small room which she used as a studio. Here Stanley sat while she painted, and a friendship developed.

Dolly left a full physical description of Stanley, and her close scrutiny and painterly eye make it worth having as a detailed record of the explorer at the age of forty-three. She found him both older and younger than his years in looks with an erect carriage, deep chest and thick short arms. He had small hands with short, round, broad-tipped, round-cushioned fingers, and short, thick legs. He had a short, well-proportioned nose, lips that were at once sensitive and determined, and a very big head, with a well-shaped forehead and thick throat. Whenever he entered a room full of people he held his head slightly tilted backwards, in a self-conscious posture.

His chin is very square and would be a beautiful chin but for a slight thickening come to form an under chin, not of superfluous fat, but rather the muscular throat of a man prematurely aged ... his face is somewhat marked, I should say by exposure to sun, by fever, by responsibility, by anxiety. His smile is what the French call 'caressant', his eyes look tender and sorrowful, he laughs softly, and just a little self-consciously, as he throws his head on one side ... He uses his hands very much when talking, not violently, for he is calm deliberation in person, but he slowly emphasises or illustrates what he is saying with his hand. When excited, he raises his arm and brings down a fist with spasmodic strength. Like all observers of Stanley, Dolly was most impressed by his eyes: The eyes are mysterious, his look most expressive and most searching. His look has something intense and penetrating. The upper lid, or rather brow beneath the eyebrow, tilts over the eye, giving a sort of earnest grandeur to his expression. The white of his eye is troubled and murky, slightly bloodshot, and yet the eye shines out clear, with the observance of some keen-sighted bird who is watching you, listening to you rather with the eye than with the ear.

The intimacy deepened that afternoon to the point where Stanley told her about Alice Pike. He had just finished telling her the story when her mother came in, spoke about the oddity of Gordon's never marrying and concluded: 'I am sure he must have been jilted by some girl in the past of whom no one has heard yet.' Stanley's and Dolly's eyes met as if to say, 'What a coincidence!' Stanley's conclusion, expressed to Alexander Bruce, was 'Barkis is willing, but she may not be.' Dolly, though, was deeply touched: 'I wish Alice had died because then, though separate he could have thought of her with love, and he would not have mistrusted mankind. I felt so sorry for him, not because of this only, but there is a loneliness and disappointment about his life which he will not allow. 'By the time of the second sitting two days later, Stanley was confiding to her his bitterness about Leopold and the myopic Belgian xenophobia. He boasted that he had written his Congo book in stretches of eighteen hours' writing at a time. After a long session from 11 a.m. to 2.30 p.m. Stanley came very close to hinting what was in his mind: 'I feel in the depths of my heart that I have been denied what I should have enjoyed with rapture - see, I have no house, no one of my own to care for me. 'The sittings went on until mid-August when the Tennants departed London for the season. Stanley occupied himself with moving into his new chambers at 160 New Bond Street which he had rented unfurnished, then spent £900 doing them up to his own taste. Then, at the beginning of September, he departed for a holiday in Switzerland. At Ostend, before proceeding, he cabled ahead to request an interview with Leopold, but this was refused. He was at Zurich, Lausanne, Berne, Fribourg and Geneva in a densely packed two-week trip which he claimed did wonders for him: 'I feel quite set up. Muscles dense and hard, appetite excellent, carriage firm and stout.' Then he heard from Leopold, who claimed to have been waiting for news from England, when all members of Stanley's syndicate in England had been waiting for him. From Geneva Stanley took the express to Paris and thence to Brussels where he had an audience with the King, and meetings with Van Neuss, Thys and Van Etvelde, Administrator for Foreign Affairs of the Congo State. By coincidence, just before he left Geneva he received a letter from Sanford, advising him to abandon his celibate state and think about marriage. Stanley replied with typical secretiveness: 'Where are the pretty girls you wrote me about? I have not seen one to talk to.' But after his talks in Brussels his mood seems to have darkened for he wrote again to Sanford in more sombre vein. 'I cannot be punished more than I have already. With the womankind Fate has decreed that I shall have little to do in this world, perhaps because I am reserved for exquisite pleasure in the next.'

Fortunately the correspondence with Dolly enables us to chart the reasons for the change of mood. Dolly wrote to him from Staffordshire to tell him she was going to visit Newcastle. Stanley replied from Switzerland with lengthy screeds and later, from Belgium, with ironic amusement at an incognito visit he had made to the Congo Exhibition in Antwerp: 'I have no correspondent living that I should take the trouble to write to so lengthily but yourself.' But meanwhile in Newcastle Dolly had met Burt, MP for Morpeth, the only ex-miner in the House of Commons, who took her down a mine and explained the pitiful conditions in which his brethren worked. Dolly wrote to Stanley: 'I felt glad to know what I felt intuitively somehow, that the future of England depends upon the working man.'

Stanley was displeased with Dolly's enthusiasm for the proletariat. He always had a strong antipathy to socialism, hardly surprisingly in the case of one who had come so far from the workhouse, since such individuals invariably feel that 'levelling down' diminishes their own status and achievements. Stanley's understanding of socialism was in any case elementary: he equated it with the technically classless primitive societies of Africa before the rise of a State in which the task of government becomes the responsibility of full-time officials - in this respect at least he would have agreed with Engels on the meaning of class. He wrote back to Dolly with a homily about the superiority of Nature to human society - a clear hint that he thought social inequality a manifestation as natural as gravity. And he 'punished' her by an inconsequential flirtation with Jeanne Orianne, daughter of the commander of the Belgian Gendarmerie Nationale.

But Dorothy Tennant was a spirited woman. She struck back by some acerbic remarks on Leopold that went beyond anything Stanley would have permitted himself. And she defiantly reiterated her commitment to the cause of the common man: 'The coming elections somewhat excite me. Politics are dangerously fascinating, even putting aside all the higher considerations. If I were a man I would throw myself into the arena, fight for the people and deserve the title of "Procurator of the Poor". As it is, I look on eagerly and hopefully.'

The incipient storm between them blew itself out. While Dolly and her mother relaxed at Hunstanton in Norfolk, Stanley on his return from Brussels headed north again. After short stops at Manchester and Glasgow, he joined Mackinnon in Tarbert to help him with electioneering - for the electorate had now broadened considerably following the 1884 Franchise Act. Then it was on to Balinakill for relaxation and excursions on the loch in Mackinnon's steamer. On his return to London his letter of thanks for the holiday was exuberant. He claimed his lungs and entire body had been renewed and strengthened, that he was taking to his letter-writing chores like a duckling to a pond and was quite prepared for eighteen hours a day of desk work. 'Nothing in all my past life equals it [viz. the holiday]. It has been one long enjoyable and joyous holiday, cold winds, wet weather, wet decks and wet feet notwithstanding. '

The fact that he got back to London and immediately collapsed with a bilious attack and raging headache tells a slightly different story, as does his world-weary missive to Sanford: 'I have no plans. I am simply trifling my time in unproductive work, dining out being among them. 'November

1885 was not a good month for Stanley. He should have been basking in the generally favourable reception of his Congo book. Though the story lacked the brazen drama of his previous books on Africa, Leopold's pruning and blue-pencilling had at least prevented Stanley's worst excesses in the way of personal attacks on rivals and critics. Even Kirk received the book well: 'You cannot read Stanley's book without imagining what the position of these natives should have been left to such masters as were at Vivi.'

There were, however, two vociferous critics of the book. Peschuel-Loesche resented the unflattering (but accurate) picture Stanley had painted of his Congo work and published a polemical anti-Stanley pamphlet in Germany. Leopold advised Stanley that he would have it answered by his German friends, that Stanley was on no account to enter the fray and that he was to avoid public discussion 'with a man so inferior to yourself as Peschuel-Loesche'. But Stanley had already entered the public arena to joust with his second critic - the American Tisdel who had stormed out of the US delegation to the Berlin Conference the year before. Tisdel had made an extended trip to the Congo in 1885 and now launched a splenetic attack on Stanley as a fantasist, a man who was using his reputation as an explorer to mislead and bamboozle the gullible over the alleged mineral wealth and natural resources of the Upper Congo. When this broadside produced no response, Tisdel twisted the knife in the wound. He cited a long list of authorities including de Winton, Parminter, Verney Cameron and Chavannes (Brazza's secretary) who disagreed with Stanley's estimates and added, as if privy to great secrets: 'If His Majesty the King of the Belgians will relieve me from the bond of secrecy imposed by him at my last audience, I shall not hesitate to give some interesting facts communicated to me by His Majesty.'

This was too much for Stanley. Leopold or no Leopold, he was not going to stand idly by and see himself defamed. His problem was that he could not positively assert that the Upper Congo was a land flowing with milk and honey. So he resorted to nitpicking and personal abuse of Tisdel. Of Tisdel's report he said: 'It fills about twelve and a half pages of the consular reports, yet I have discovered that there are over fifty errors which are either the result of ignorance or caused by an unworthy motive of some kind.'

It was a relief for Stanley to renew his visits to Richmond Terrace, once Dolly and her mother had completed their peregrinations. On 23 November Stanley went to tea and held court among a bevy of admiring young men. Dolly noted: 'We all sat round Stanley. I like to hear his deep decisive voice, his commanding enunciation.' As for Stanley, the real object of his visits was as far away as ever from being achieved. He had revealed his true motives earlier in the year to Bruce:

Do you think I am making any progress in this affaire du coeuri I cannot see it. I am easily rebuffed and very sensitive. If she proposed to me it might be very different but I have to propose to her, do you know I rather think I will not have the courage. And then, there is a mother in this case, and I am rather afraid of her. I think it would be a boon to shy people like myself, if there were no such people as mothers. I find them sadly in the way. Having brought eligible people up - they insist on interfering at the wrong time. My bachelorhood is solely due to these mothers.

The letter was a classic of self-deception and transference of guilt. The only mother to whom his bachelorhood was due was his own.

But Stanley was in earnest about advancing his suit, however timid it might be. He took the advice of Baroness Van Dornop and slept with a piece of wedding cake under his pillow 'with all the firm belief of childhood in the goodness of Santa Claus'. The charm seemed to work, for in December 1885 there were definite signs of progress in the relationship. Fascinated by the name 'Bula Matari', Dolly had made for him a tiny silver token for his watch chain with a monogram bearing the legend of a Greek capital delta crossed with a T. Another invisible Rubicon seemed to be crossed when Dolly consented to come with her mother to tea at Stanley's rooms at 160 New Bond Street, although the explorer was so terrified at the thought of being alone with the 'Queen of Ragamuffins' (as he affectionately termed Dolly) and her mother that he pressed Mackinnon into service as a kind of male chaperone and minder.

Yet he would have been less pleased if he could have glimpsed the contents of Dolly's diary. On 7th January 1886 she attended Millais's wedding and noted: 'I wonder whether I shall ever marry. I do not see anyone I would wish to marry.' She claimed to need a wise, hardworking and tall (!) man; some of her male friends had two of the three attributes but none all three (it is clear which Stanley did not possess!). She drew up a short list of possible, on which were Arnold, Stanley and a M. Coquelin, 'whom I now see and hear from rarely, it is true'. But despite finding no one eligible, she confessed to a 'fierce longing to be understood and cared for'.

For all that, the deepening friendship with Stanley continued. On 9th January the explorer paid another visit to Richmond Terrace, and again Dolly put him under the microscope of her minute observation. Once more she noted the cold, silent, disdainful public persona - a veneer that concealed a tenderness he dared not show, marked by a strong feeling for children, slaves and the oppressed or dispossessed. She noted that he habitually spoke slowly, tensely and emphatically; the timbre of his voice was agreeable, he had a slight American accent, and he had a mannerism whereby he strongly accentuated the last syllable of words. 'He comes into a room with his head thrown backwards and a rather curious step. He says "good day" to you with great solemnity and ceremony, bowing whenever you offer him a chair.'

Obliged to reciprocate the Tennants' hospitality, Stanley increasingly sought the avuncular support of Mackinnon to coach him in the small change of etiquette in polite society. A gift of cheese from the Scotsman produced a typical response: 'it will do to put on the table and show my lady friends what a friend I have in the north.' Gradually Mackinnon himself became a regular feature at the Tennants' dinner parties whenever he was in London. The first such invitation showed Stanley in - nervous, half-facetious mood, fretting about whether Mackinnon and Dolly would get on: 'Miss Dorothy does not know much about big ships though she has undertaken a picture where there is a sailor standing near a shroud bidding goodbye to his native land.' Stanley meanwhile honed his social graces to perfection by inviting other guests to his rooms in New Bond Street. A frequent visitor was Mrs French Sheldon, an admirer seven years his junior, qualified as a physician and married to a wealthy American businessman. A letter to her in January shows Stanley trying to be a man of the salon: 'Mrs Dickens and the Misses Roche are invited to tea on Sunday afternoon at 4.30 p.m. Won't you and "Shell" [Mr Sheldon] come and bring Mr Wellcome also, that we may not be outnumbered by the young of the fair sex.'

In private with Dolly, Stanley continued to fume about his treatment by Leopold - the 'weak stomached' monarch, as he described him to Mackinnon. His frustration and anger reached a peak in January 1886 following a prolonged but abortive meeting with the King (together with Hutton and Mackinnon) in which he attempted to disentangle the layers of obfuscation Leopold was throwing around the Congo railway project. During these discussions Leopold deliberately made no mention of Stanley's personal position. On 16th January Stanley wrote a personal letter to Leopold that expressed real anger about his own treatment, the delays to the railway proposal, and most of all about the fact that he was barred from Africa. He mentioned the expense he had already been put to, Leopold's implicit acceptance that he would be returning to the Congo by pressing him to renew his contract, and the rumours of a gathering Anglophone xenophobia in the work of the Association. This alarmed British capitalists and prevented their investing in the railway syndicate. Stanley ended by reminding the King of the promise he had made as far back as 1878 - that if the Congo venture prospered, Stanley would be named Director-General of the State, and asked for a clear and unambiguous reply about his future.

Leopold hated it if anyone pointed the finger at him and accused him, even implicitly, of duplicity. Stanley's letter was perfectly justified, but Leopold reacted to it as if Stanley had made reference to the King's debaucheries or the virgins he liked to deflower in the Palace. The tone of injured innocence in the reply has an emetic quality: 'The King has been surprised by your reply and grieved to see you doubt his sentiments towards you.' Stanley ought not to listen to calumnies about the Congo nor credit the easy canard that he had enemies at the Belgian court. As proof of this, Leopold offered to prolong his contract into the 1890s; he reiterated that he did intend to use him again in the Congo but could not fix a date as yet.

This assuaged but did not satisfy Stanley. The King, he felt, should make a clean breast of it and admit that he could not employ Stanley in a Belgian colony because of domestic public opinion. Not that Stanley would accept even that judgement: how could he harm the nation he had built himself? 'It is as much my child as it is the King's.' Anyone who observed the failure of the German Loango expedition in 1873-5, and the perennial Dutch opposition to any foreign penetration in the area, could not but come to the judicious conclusion that by Stanley, and by Stanley alone, was the Free State created, certainly not by the Belgian mediocrities Leopold had sent out to help him.

So in private Stanley fumed. The letter from Leopold confirmed all his worst fears about the 'Belgianising' of the Congo. This posed serious problems for him. He could not serve under a Belgian, for was he not Bula Matari? At the age of forty-five, he was aware that time was running out. Did Leopold seriously think that £1000 a year could compensate for the awesome ordeal of his five years in the Congo? If he was to be condemned to indolence and atrophy by not being able to return to Africa, no amount of money could compensate for the loss. But publicly Stanley returned tokens of fealty and confidence in the King.

There was scant sympathy for Stanley's plight in Brussels. Among Leopold's courtiers there was a widespread but usually unspoken view that the 'American' was already too big for his famous African boots. When Stanley wrote to thank Leopold for the extension of his contract until 1895, and the award of the Grand Order of Leopold, he still expressed an expectation of returning to Africa. Count Devaux was sufficiently taken aback by Stanley's 'impertinence' to send the following to Mackinnon, noteworthy for its arch insinuation of Leopold's sexual excesses in the closing remarks: Stanley wrote a very polite letter this time to thank the King for his Order. I am sorry to hear that he is unwell and I am convinced that his dyeing his hair has something to do with it. I have seen so many brains and stomachs affected by the dyeing of the hair. He does not seem to me to have a right and fair appreciation of his situation. In the first place there is certainly some difficulty for the King to say now and at once what he will do with him. It may be that he is more necessary here than in Africa for some time on account of the railway affair. On the other hand the Congo is being transformed into a new shape ... It is not very easy in such a state of things to decide what precisely Stanley's [role] may be in the course of time. One thing is certain - the exploring period is over or very nearly so. Stanley is no more to be a pioneer. He must now get into the garments of a state's man [sic]. I don't see why he frets in that way and why he does not confide in the King who after all has not treated him so badly. There is certainly no man in Belgium who has been treated the like of it.

Devaux's letter mixes nonsense and shrewdness in a perplexing manner.

It was true that Stanley was ill: since the beginning of January he had been ill almost constantly with gastritis and indigestion. He himself blamed the malady on incessant letter-writing and desk work, which meant no exercise and hence poor health. That was certainly a more plausible

FREANK McLYNN

scenario than Devaux's absurdities about hair-dyes. But the real reason was
hinted at later in the Count's letter. Not only was Stanley the victim of
Leopold's deviousness and duplicity; there was also in Stanley's mind the
fear that his day was over, that even if he was sent back to Africa it would
be in some tiresome administrative capacity, that the days of exploring new
segments of the 'Dark Continent' were already in the past.

In February Stanley's ill-health gave cause for concern. He spent one
wretched evening at dinner at the Tennants' with Gladstone (now Prime
Minister) and Mackinnon, but scarcely touched his food; he later told Dolly
that the mere sight of it nauseated him. When the two Tennant ladies went
to visit him next day, they found he had been ill all night; the grande dame
had to play Florence Nightingale. After two weeks without significant
improvement, Stanley's doctors recommended a trip to Mediterranean
sunshine.

At the beginning of March Stanley set out for Nice but on the road to
Folkestone, he had a dangerous relapse of stomach inflammation. A local
doctor got him strong enough to return to London, where Sir William
Jenner, the eminent physician, tended him. It was decided that sea air
would do the patient good, so Stanley departed for the Granville Hotel in
Ramsgate to convalesce prior to continuing his European trip. After three
days in Ramsgate his London doctor was convinced that a complete cure
had been affected and departed for London; all pain in Stanley's stomach
had disappeared. The explorer put himself on a strict, salubrious regime.
He had a fine suite of rooms overlooking the Channel and there he slept
soundly for seven to eight hours every night. He was on a milk diet and
told Dolly that since the beginning of March he had lost 27 pounds: 'Congo
weight without the Congo fibre!' He walked for three to four hours a day,
'laying in a good stock of ozone'. Indeed the only after-effect of his sound
sleep was a slight stiffness in his joints from all the walking. 'I stick to my
milk diet, as I am still timid of taking anything that might possibly renew
the agony suffered at Folkestone.'

But there was no escaping the exigencies of Leopold, even when he was
ill or convalescent. After leaving him unconsulted for months, the King
suddenly reactivated his faithful agent in England at the very time stomach
cramps were bringing him to a standstill on the Folkestone road. For the
monarch's interest had been awakened by Gladstone's speech at the
culmination of the Commons debate on the Sudan, in which the GOM
made it clear he wanted no British confrontation with the mahdiya.
Leopold saw a chance to get by the back door into the mansion whose front
door Bismarck had slammed in his face at the Berlin Conference. Covering
his tracks as ever, he asked Stanley to write to Brussels, as it were
spontaneously, proposing that the Congo State lease the Sudan at an annual
subsidy of £200,000. Leopold would pledge himself to put down the
Mahdi's followers and remit to Egypt the annual revenue of £600,000
which used to be paid to Cairo before Mohammed Ahmed cut the umbilical
cord. Stanley was to play up the 'saving savages for Christianity' angle and

368

word the letter in such a way that Leopold could present it to the British as an unsolicited suggestion coming from an African expert.

The resultant Stanley letter, written in Ramsgate, was a minor masterpiece of dissimulation. He began by claiming that the Sudan had fascinated him ever since he met Linant de Bellefonds in 1875, d that if Verney Cameron had solved the Lualaba/Congo riddle, he himself would have gone north to join hands with Gordon. There followed an unusual (from Stanley) encomium for Gordon's 'rightdoing' in the Sudan and a typical lecture from Stanley the geographer, in which he pointed out that Equatoria province was as near to the Congo as to the Nile and that Cairo itself was nearer to Europe than to Gordon's former gubernatorial domain. He argued that the obstacles that beset Gessi and Baker did not exist on the Congo, and that with the Sudan in the grip of the Mahdists, Christianity's only hope was the annexation of Equatoria by Leopold. He underlined the fact (all-important to Leopold) that under Gordon the Sudan returned revenue to the Khedive, of which £70,000 was clear profit. Stanley then 'besought' Leopold to use his formidable military capacity and suggested that if Britain baulked at outright annexation, a deal could be cooked up whereby Leopold did the job and presented the bill to Egypt.

Here was an embarrassing poser for Stanley's fellow-diner at the Tennants', William Ewart Gladstone. He handed the letter to the Foreign Secretary, with a note scrawled in the margin: 'What answer does Lord Rosebery advise?' Rosebery was a good match for Leopold, as his answering minute shows. 'That we do not contemplate any further operations in the Sudan ourselves and that it was mainly the method in which that surplus of £70,000 was extracted that led to the Sudan rebellion.'

Once he had recovered his health at Ramsgate, Stanley returned to London, packed his effects and was on the 8 a.m. train out of London on 23rd March. He arrived in Nice at 5 p.m. the next day. Ironically, 24th March 1886 saw the last of his mother Elizabeth Parry. Stanley had kept in touch spasmodically over the years, and saw her last in August 1884 at the Langham Hotel in London just before he crossed to Belgium to confer with Leopold. The same Dr Pierce who had delivered Stanley in 1841 attended her at death and buried her in Bodlewydden churchyard. When he heard of her death, Stanley at once sent a cheque to clear Dr Pierce's account and defray all funeral expenses. So passed the woman who more than any other person was responsible for Stanley's twilight sexual identity.

At the Hotel des Anglais in Nice Stanley discovered Flaubert's Salammbo for the first time. His old friend Edward King, who wrote the preface to a new English translation, dedicated the edition to him, in the hope that he would find this dark African tale of interest. King knew his target. Stanley was enraptured; he found the book better than all other historical novels he had devoured, among them Ivanhoe, Ben-Hur and The Last Days of Pompeii f He was in good spirits generally. He joined a family of Scots from Dumbarton for prayers and psalm-singing, protesting that his piety was sincere, and was entranced by the Mediterranean, which he pronounced a panacea for all who were ill: 'I who knew it so well and had gaily toyed with the sunshine and sea of these shores when younger - how could I have forgotten it?'

Continuing on his tour, Stanley reached the Hotel d'Italie in Florence on 3 April and spent the weekend there exploring and 'walking his feet off. Stanley was bowled over by Florence; not even Ruskin, he said, could do justice to its beauties - but he was taken aback by the contrasting squalor and filth of its inhabitants and the prevalence of fleas. His letter to Mackinnon on 6 April is full of violent mood swings, one moment enthusiastic about some architectural masterpiece, the next curmudgeonly and pessimistic: 'I wonder whether you have carried with you this thought. That whenever God has been most gracious to man or most bountiful of his creating, there we find man most regardless of them.' He speaks of his hope that Italian sunshine will mean the end of the dark days of his illness, then touches on the subject that almost certainly triggered them in the first place. He says he could have been spared all this suffering {italics mine} if Leopold had been only as generous to him as he was to the wangwana and simply given him indefinite leave, so that he could have enjoyed himself.

On 7 April he left Florence for Rome, where he stayed at the Hotel Costanzi. He enjoyed the sightseeing immensely - for all his globetrotting this was his first visit to the Eternal City. He drove along the Old Appian Way to the catacombs of St Sebastian, distinctly put out by the pious Latin mumblings of the monks in his party. Crossing the Tiber put him in mind of a favourite author, Macaulay. The sheer weight of antiquity overwhelmed him: 'One comes across such grotesque scenes at Jerusalem, in Egypt, in Uganda and in Rome, but our true feelings in the presence of graves, tombs and memorials of the dead may not be spoken.' But Rome also showed the dark side of Stanley. He entangled himself in a somewhat absurd verbal campaign of vilification of Gladstone. The trigger was a letter from Dolly in which she declared she was turning against the idea of Home Rule and distancing herself from the GOM. This plugged into an inferno of pent-up hatred for Gladstone that had been festering in Stanley's mind. In successive letters to Dolly and Mackinnon he inveighed against the 'treason' involved in espousing Home Rule: 'after the public utterance of the vile treason, Mr Gladstone can never be regarded by me more than as a traitor to his own country.'

After a final banquet given him in Rome by Prince Teano, who introduced him to a princess 'who I think excels the famous Greek Helen in beauty', Stanley departed for Naples on 12 April and stayed there for ten days, visiting Pompeii, Herculaneum and Ischia. He spent the best part of his letters to Dolly in further attacks on Gladstone; he was not even prepared to concede him the eloquence his political enemies credited him with. But Dolly gave as good as she got; to some extent the correspondence was a return of their clash the previous year over the working class and indeed at the end of her long, impassioned defence of Gladstone's integrity she conflated the two themes. Stanley had jeered at the 'levelling down' involved in the extension of the franchise by the 1884 Act. Not so, she replied, it was simply giving the counties what the boroughs already enjoyed. She also condemned Stanley's 'elitism' (though the term did not exist then): 'I can speak from experience of the capability of the Welsh miner and the Northumberland miner to vote intelligently - I should say that these men were more thoughtful and earnest than thousands in the towns who before were privileged to vote.'

Stanley replied with a long apologia for his position, laced with heavy irony: 'I have received your admirable defence of Mr Gladstone with wondering eyes and bated breath. What power there is in faith. While any was left in me I also was brave and strong in the cause of the good and true.'

Stanley had soured the effect of limpid Mediterranean sunlight by his gratuitous verbal assault on Gladstone. Suddenly, as if it were nemesis for his hubris, the tour itself went sour on him. When he arrived in Milan from Naples, he found that his protective cover was blown and the incognito was no more. Instead of being able to wander alone in ancient ruins, he found himself lionised by Milanese society, so that he could not even manage to see the sights properly. He was given a reception by the town council and the geographical society and showered with medals and diplomas: 'My neck became quite limp with bowing so much - and my back has a faint lumbago feeling still.' He was bitter that the Italians would not leave him alone; like many who dream of fame when young, he found that the reality turned to ashes in his mouth. And because he was Bula Matari, who had braved the rigours of Africa, it was thought that no physical feat was beyond him. He railed at the necessity of having to climb up 400 steps to the top of the duomo, which left him with 'fever of the muscles ... yet what could I do? Strangers fancy that because I crossed Africa I could easily go up the Duomo . .. my dear Mackinnon, pray take a friend's advice. Don't cross Africa if you can possibly live without doing it - for if you come back safe, your friends will ask you to become a member of Alpine clubs, and Lawn Tennis clubs and other muscle-fever clubs.'

Stanley decamped from Milan as soon as politeness permitted and went up to a hotel at Menaggio on Lake Como. But here too he had no peace; there was always someone at his elbow, nudging him with 'That is Bellagio,' 'This is Menaggio.' His bland description to Mackinnon masks the real anger he expressed to Dolly: 'The Milanese and Comoese were getting too exuberantly hospitable altogether for a convalescent, and so I had to depart from Italy by express.'

From Lake Como he took the express through St Gothard to Paris, where he sought protective cover in his beloved Hotel Meurice. His mood was grim, for he now felt that his vacation had been ruined: 'All Europe is crowded. The hotels, the lakes, the trains, each public conveyance and caravanserai - and the people talk of depression of trade. Why, Paris is full. The Grand Hotel and the Hotel du Louvre turn people away, and they say the times are dull and out of joint. Why, I never saw the times so gay or so prosperous. People find money to throw away, despite its reported universal scarcity.'

The curmudgeonly mood continued when he returned to London in the first week of May. He was reunited with Dolly at a Thames-side lunch aboard Mackinnon's ship Manora, but a week later at Richmond Terrace, at lunch with James Bryce and others, Stanley was the only one present who opposed Home rule. Dolly's attempt to convert him to the cause failed, as her cryptic diary entry hints: 'People are very passionate on the subject, frantically for or against. 'There was bad news waiting for him, quite apart from Leopold's continued foot-dragging on the Congo railway scheme. At Stanley Falls station Captain Deane, who had replaced Wester, had allowed himself to become embroiled in open confrontation with Tippu Tip. Deane refused to give up a woman who had fled from the Manyema to the station for his protection. When the Arabs made threats, Deane opened up on them with the Krupps gun. This was arrant stupidity. Heavily outnumbered, Deane and the garrison could put up only token resistance when Tippu Tip ordered the post sacked in retaliation; Deane was lucky to escape with his life.

Stanley spent a dull and frustrating June in London before he and Mackinnon decided to take another trip across the Channel to see if they could ginger up the railway proceedings. They paused on the way back to take the waters at Hombourg-les-bains. Their luck was in on 15th July, for an hour after their crossing on a smooth sea to Dover, a ferocious gale blew up and raged along the Channel. From London the two men proceeded to Scotland. They embarked at Greenock on one of Mackinnon's steamers for a house party at Balinakill for fifty guests, including Dolly and her mother. The party was followed by a cruise around the Scottish Isles. The Tennants enjoyed Scotland so much that they stayed on, visiting friends, when Stanley left for London.

It was the proximity to Dorothy Tennant on the cruise that finally decided Stanley to nerve himself up and ask for her hand. In mid-August he took the plunge. 'I wrote a letter to Miss T,' his journal records cryptically. But he dithered for two days before he signed and dated it and sent it off to Scotland. The letter, which reads at times like a Jane Austen parody, reveals Stanley at his most gauche and vulnerable.

You have dropped phrases in my hearing which have induced me to think that possibly I did not love in vain; if I have misconstrued them the punishment is mine . . . knowing how woefully ignorant I am of women's ways, I restrained myself, lest by giving expression to the ardour that possessed me, I should unknowingly give offence to one I had learned to esteem, admire and love with all my heart and soul .. . Thus I went to you and came away, visit after visit, always perplexed and doubting, never certain of anything, but that you were the noblest and brightest of your sex and that I loved you ... You are in need of nothing. I cannot advantage you in anything, therein I am poor, helpless, trembling. I am only rich in love of you, filled with admiration for your royal beauty ... I have sat and brooded for hours over the possibilities and impossibilities, which confidence alternating with diffidence pictured ... For all the world I would not wound your feelings, nor offend any delicate susceptibilities. Nevertheless, bear without offence this declaration of mine, and tell me honestly, and candidly, to put an end to this exasperating doubt of mine . . . When I leave you I become miserable and unfit for company, and memory of you obscures all things else.

The letter was not well planned. Stanley said nothing about his future African plans and made the tactical error of agreeing to be bound without demur to whatever decision Dolly made. The answer was rejection. The letter turning down his proposal does not survive (almost certainly because Dolly later destroyed it) and she appears to have given no specific reasons. Stanley suspected that it was his origins and early life that told against him, but almost certainly this is rationalisation. It is most likely that a number of different considerations weighed with Dolly. In the first place she was not 'in love' with Stanley, as her diary entries show clearly, and she was perhaps a little young for a hard-headed marriage of convenience. She realised that she and Stanley were poles apart on a number of important issues of fundamental principle (Gladstone, the workers, etc.), and that marriage to such a strong-willed man would mean submerging the independent part of her personality. Also, she wanted a 'proper' marriage and did not relish being an explorer's 'grass widow'. In their many conversations Stanley had repeatedly expressed the hope of returning to Africa. She might have been prepared to consider him if he had been willing to promise never to return to Africa, but he would not. A judicious conclusion would seem to be that neither party felt old enough to set down on the other's terms.

The rejection from Dolly coincided with the final collapse of hopes for the railway syndicate. Leopold was able to throw off the mask as soon as he had a consortium of Belgian capitalists in place. Not even a flying visit to Brussels and a personal plea to Leopold from Stanley could alter his resolution, and on 13th September the news that the contract would be awarded to a Belgian consortium was made official." Leopold's action was a particular blow, for Stanley had told Dolly melodramatically that he would go abroad if his suit was turned down. Ignoring the fact that he could have been put on the spot if Leopold had called him for African service and Dolly had accepted him, he poured out his bitterness about both tormentors to Mackinnon: I have been living ever since my book left my hands last year in a fool's paradise. That woman entrapped me with her gush, and her fulsome adulations, her knick-knacks inscribed with a 'Remember Me', her sweet-scented notes written with a certain literary touch which seemed to me a cunning compliment to myself - as I detected a certain kind of effort, her pointed attentions to me ... on leaving her presence I was buoyed up with some letter or despatch from Brussels which kept me on the stretch of expectation always. 'We do not know exactly when we shall need you, but we shall let you know - my dear Mr Stanley - in ample time to prepare.' So I lived, constantly hoping, hoping here and hoping there - and after all both have come to nothing. I look back with regret that nearly sixteen months of my life have been lost through these artful people."

Bitterly disappointed and taking the collapse of the railway project as the last straw in his disillusionment with Leopold, Stanley sought oblivion in work. He signed a contract with the impresario Major Pond for an American lecture tour that would net him £40,000; this would be followed by a tour of Australia that would bring in a similar amount."But first, remembering the debacle of his lectures in the USA in late 1872, he would try out his material on English audiences. Beginning at Harrogate on 29th September, Stanley swept through the country for a month, enthralling audiences with the most exciting yarns he could produce on the Dark Continent. When the tour ended in London on 5th November, he crossed to Queenstown to take the steamship Baltic to the USA. Departing on 17 November he was in New York for his first speaking engagements on the 27th and 29th, at the Lotus Club and Chickering Hall.

At the back of his mind Stanley still nursed the hope that a summons would come to recall him to his work in Africa. Before he left on the Baltic, he had been told by Mackinnon that there was a project afoot to send an expedition to bring Emin Pasha, governor of Equatoria, out of Africa and the grip of the Mahdists. This was grist to Stanley's mill, for he had always wanted to lead an expedition into the northern, eastern or north-eastern corners of the Congo, to discover new resources and fix the national boundary. He told Mackinnon that if the project took shape he was ready to put himself at its head 'at a moment's notice . . . without hope of fee or reward', regardless of the financial losses he might have to take from cancellation of his American tour.

December saw Stanley in Massachusetts and Connecticut. His old friend Mark Twain went to Boston to introduce him on the lecture rostrum and entertained him 'rather elaborately' at Hartford, where Stanley also lectured on the 8th. Twain suggested to Stanley that he write an autobiography while he was on tour. With his stenographic abilities, he could write it in just 105 days, while riding the cars and the book should net him $50,000. But on 11th December at St Johnsburg, Vermont, Stanley received the telegram he yearned for. Mackinnon's cable told him the Emin Pasha expedition was on, and the committee had offered him the leadership. Stanley telegraphed his acceptance immediately, booked passage, and was back in England on Christmas Eve, ready for the greatest challenge of his life.

Chapter Nine

EQUATORIA province was a ghost from the past for Stanley. It was in 1875, while at Mutesa's court, that his sphere of influence and that of Gordon had intersected. And now in December 1886, Gordon's successor as governor of the province, Emin Pasha, was to draw him back to the area and, for the first time since 1877, take him into unexplored regions of Africa.

Equatoria was an Egyptian province in the extreme south of the Sudan, where the Nile emerges from Lake Albert. It was Khedive Ismail of Aida fame who first tried to establish effective control over the area. Sir Samuel Baker was appointed its governor from 1870 to 1873, followed by the even more illustrious figure of Gordon, who was governor from 1873 to 1876. Both men set themselves in vain to extirpate slave trading in the area. Primitive technology and transport, the ineffectiveness of local armies and the vast distances involved made this a hopeless task. After the rapid incumbencies of two American and one Egyptian governors, the man known to history as Emin Pasha was appointed to the office in 1878.

Emin Pasha was no more the governor's real name than Henry M. Stanley was his would-be rescuer's. He was born Eduard Carl Oscar Theodor Schnitzler in Silesia in 1840. After qualifying as a doctor, Schnitzler left Prussia to seek a new life in an alien culture. He entered Turkish service as a medical officer and travelled widely through the Ottoman Empire. Thereafter he always referred to himself as Emin Bay. In some ways he was a Prussian epigone of Burton. Like him he had an unquenchable love of the exotic and was an outstanding linguist. He spoke French, English, German, Italian, modern Greek, Turkish, Albanian and (most importantly) Arabic and several African languages. He was also a man of unquenchable scientific curiosity, a highly talented botanist and zoologist.

In 1875 he came to Khartoum as a physician. The following year Gordon invited him to become chief medical officer in Equatoria. His great success with the Africans - for he was completely devoid of feelings of European superiority - led Gordon to recommend him as governor. But Emin Pasha was unlucky. His tenure of office was immensely complicated by the great Mahdist uprising which began in 1882. The Mahdi's victory over the forces of Hicks Pasha in 1883 ended effective Egyptian rule in the Sudan. It was followed by the disaster of Gordon's relief expedition to Khartoum, culminating in Gordon's death there in January 1885.

Cut off in Equatoria, Emin decided to retreat to the extreme south of the province, where he reckoned himself safe from the ravages of the mahdiya. In July 1885 he arrived at Wadelai station, where he made his headquarters. Wadelai was on the west bank of the Nile, about 35 miles north of Lake Albert, and was chosen to enable Emin to maintain contact with Zanzibar. The first cause of the Emin Pasha expedition can be located in the letters

Emin proceeded to pour out to his east-coast contacts and especially Alexander Mackay, the leading Church Missionary Society agent in Buganda. Mackay persuaded Emin to stay put in Equatoria, on the grounds that there was a good chance his beleaguered enclave would be annexed by the British. This heartened Emin, who saw the British Empire as civilisation's best hope. He had no confidence in his fellow-countrymen, and still less in Leopold's Belgians; the Congo State was anathema to him, and in 1883 he had tried to extend Egyptian dominion into the Mangbetu country, expressly to pre-empt the encroachment of the Association.

Mackay forwarded Emin's letters to British officials in Zanzibar, who passed them on to London. They were full of pleas for help from the British. Still feeling guilty about their failure to rescue Gordon in 1884-5, sections of the British elite, with press and popular backing, began to toy with the idea of an expedition to snatch Emin from the jaws of the Mahdists, thus gaining at least token satisfaction for their murder of a great British hero. The idea of Emin as a 'second Gordon' began to be promoted by The Times and other organs. Extension of British influence inland made sense to men like Mackay and Frederick Holm- wood (Acting British Consul-General at Zanzibar); they had long argued for abandoning the traditional policy of supremacy on the coast in favour of concentration on the upper Nile and the Lake Victoria region.

Yet the decision-makers at the highest reaches in British politics were not at all keen on the idea. Gladstone in 1886 reiterated his resistance to any idea of reviving a British military presence in the Sudan, even under camouflaged Anglo-Belgian auspices. When the Home Rule crisis brought about the fall of the GOM, the Tory Prime Minister who took over, Lord Salisbury, proved equally hostile. If Emin had to be rescued, he reasoned, and Emin was a German, why then it was Berlin's business and nobody else's. Moreover, if a private expedition under Stanley's direction was financed by British capitalists, Salisbury wanted it clearly understood that there was no question of the British government's bailing out Stanley if he got into trouble; he would be as much on his own as the Christians in Buganda had been after Bishop Hannington's assassination in 1885.

But Salisbury was led to modify his originally vociferous opposition by four main considerations. In the first place, Mackinnon argued that here was a golden opportunity for British businessmen to avenge themselves on Leopold's perfidy over the railway syndicate. Not only was there a possibility of huge profits if the cache of ivory Emin reportedly had at Wadelai could be transported to the coast; in the long term, important commercial concessions could be wrestled from the tribes for British trading companies in East Africa. Secondly, after the massacre of Christians at the Kabaka's court, Buganda seemed a 'busted flush'; British interest in East Africa needed a new focus and Equatoria could well be it. Thirdly, Sir Evelyn Baring (British Consul-General in Cairo) pointed out that the relief of Emin was important for Egyptian interests and self-respect; whereas the Egyptian government lacked the resources to bring

Emin out itself, it would be willing to provide £10,000 towards an Emin Pasha relief expedition to be headed by Stanley. But it was the fourth argument that really weighed with Salisbury. African colonialism after 1884 represented the outer projection of European conflicts and incontestably the new interest the Germans were showing in East Africa was worrying. Mackinnon and Sir James Fergusson at the Foreign Office plugged away at the motif that the Emin relief project could turn the flank of Bismarck's offensive in Africa. Reluctantly Salisbury acquiesced in the idea of an expedition, provided it was not under the auspices of Her Majesty's Government. The combination of Mackinnon's money and the Egyptian subvention enabled Salisbury to get himself off the hook on which he was impaled by public opinion, without lifting an official finger.

While Stanley was in America, Mackinnon set up an Emin Pasha relief expedition committee and began feasibility studies. Stanley had promised him that the cost of the expedition would not exceed £20,000 and Mackinnon was confident that he, Hutton and his other financial contacts could raise the money. In return for this outlay they could hope to establish their commercial position in East Africa by opening a direct trade route to Victoria Nyanza and the Sudan. It was not far-fetched to expect that these territories could be governed under charter in the same way as the Royal Niger Company operated; on the way to relieve Emin, Stanley was to negotiate treaties and concessions with the chiefs between Mombasa and Wadelai.

But was Stanley the right man to head the expedition? Some thought the Scottish explorer Joseph Thomson had good claims and Thomson himself pressed hard to be considered as an alternative to Stanley. It was in vain. Mackinnon's was the dominant role on the EPRE committee, and he was determined that to Stanley would go the palm. Thomson was bitterly disappointed by the decision and spitefully pointed out that he was being passed over in favour of an American citizen. For a while he sulked and raged, then reflected and offered himself as Stanley's second-in-command. Stanley claimed to have supported him for this but, whatever the case, Thomson was turned down. It is interesting in the light of Thomson's assiduous propaganda portraying himself as the man of peace as against Stanley's man of war, that the CMS missionary Mackay thought that Stanley was far the better choice. He wrote to Emin as follows: 'Whether Stanley or Thomson will be in charge of the caravan I cannot of course say. Most probably the former . .. Thomson has, I fear, more inclination for mere exploration than for relieving those in trouble.'

So by the time Stanley docked in SS Allen at Southampton on Christmas Eve 1886, preparations for the Emin Pasha relief expedition were already well advanced. Stanley was given full discretion over the expedition's personnel, organisation and equipment. The only remaining major question was which route the expedition would take. Ever the precision, Stanley had already sketched out a number of possible itineraries, with the costs attaching to each. Some of these routes were unlikely, such as the one through Abyssinia or the direct route through hostile Buganda. More promising was the idea of sailing up die Zambezi and the Shire Rivers to Lake Nyasa, thence to Lake Tanganyika, a south-north crossing, and then on to Lake Albert and Wadelai; the problem here was the probability of large-scale desertions. Thomson's 1883-4 route through Masailand, from Mombasa to the north-east end of Lake Victoria, thence through Bunyoro to Wadelai, was on paper the best of all, but Stanley felt he would not be able to get through without severe and sustained fighting. An itinerary from Bagamoyo to Wadelai via the south side of Lake Victoria was vulnerable to the charge of trying to annex German territory.

On 29th December, at a meeting of the EPRE committee in Stanley's rooms at New Bond Street (attended by Mackinnon, de Winton, the explorer Grant, A. J. Kinnaird and the Hon. Guy Dawnay), Stanley expressed his reservations about all these routes on the ground that the desertion rate would be unacceptably high. Instead he proposed sailing from Zanzibar to the Congo mouth, steaming upriver to Stanley Falls and then cutting across to Lake Albert. This would trim the manpower and materiel requirements back to 600 porters and fifteen whaleboats, whereas for his second choice (Bagamoyo to Wadelai via Lake Victoria) he would need 800 carriers, fifty transport donkeys, twelve riding animals and a steel boat. But the committee plumped for Stanley's second choice, for two main reasons: the Sultan of Zanzibar was known to be hostile to the Congo Free State and would veto the recruitment of porters for use on a Congo route; and the expedition would become snarled up in Free State affairs and thus unable to promote British interests.

It now remained for Stanley to cross to Brussels to get Leopold to release him from his contract; if the King played dog in the manger, there would be no Emin relief expedition, at least not with Stanley at its head. Stanley had already foreseen difficulties here and had attempted to make straight the ways with a formal request to be allowed to lead the expedition. He recapitulated the unhappy history of his employment with Leopold since the passing of the 'deadline' for further African service in June 1885, especially since the disappointment over the railway he would have expected to hear something but 'nothing but a cold disappointing silence'.

Leopold was in two minds about Stanley's application. Though he knew all about Stanley's antecedent unhappiness, and had even half expected a request from Stanley to be released from his contract, he was still toying with the idea of putting the explorer in command of a punitive expedition to regain Stanley Falls and march on the Arab capital of Nyangwe. Strauch felt that the Free State did not yet have the resources for a successful war on the Arabs. But Leopold's overall sentiment on Stanley's arrival back from the New World was to turn down his request for the Emin Pasha command in return for a firm commitment to send him with a major military expedition against the Congo Arabs.

Belgian public opinion, in so far as it was at all engaged by Leopold's African exploits, naturally assumed that, since Stanley was in the King's service, it must have been the monarch who summoned him back from the USA for work on the Congo. Perhaps the plan that Stanley had put to the King in September 1884 - of extending the Congo State's boundaries to Equatoria and paying the costs by the rubber and ivory the expedition could uplift - was about to be revived under the pretext of 'rescuing' Emin. The analysts were not far wrong. Strauch had vetoed the original plan on the grounds of difficulty and expense but, with money from Mackinnon and the Egyptian government seemingly sloshing around in London, perhaps this time Leopold could pull off a coup by sending a Belgian expedition under Stanley to relieve Emin in return for a subsidy of, say, £60,000.

Immediately after the EPRE committee meeting on 29th December, Stanley took the evening train to Calais and arrived in Brussels at 6.30 a.m. on the 30th. Three hours later he was in conclave with Leopold. Stanley summed up the tension at the beginning of the meeting as follows: 'It was a harrowing meeting .. . since the close of the Berlin Conference in February 1885 - the King has been keeping me on tenterhooks ... in a few minutes I let him perceive how much he had wounded me by this curious conduct of his.' Leopold was emollient. He told Stanley he always wanted to send him back to Africa and hinted, without being explicit, that it was French opposition that had prevented him. 'Well, Mr Stanley, I confess it has been hard upon you but it could not be helped. Circumstances were such that I could not employ you as I had intended. Haut politique, you know, to which we must all bend.'

After these soothing preliminaries, the King came straight to the point. He could release Stanley from his contract only if the Emin expedition proceeded up the Congo. The nimble-minded Leopold had already worked out that it was quite possible to achieve his Equatoria ambitions without contributing a penny himself - always the scenario he liked best. If Mackinnon and the other paymasters accepted these terms, he was willing to postpone the 'important mission' he intended to entrust to Stanley. Leopold's confirming letter to the EPRE committee was uncompromising: extra expense notwithstanding, the committee would either have to send Stanley out via the Congo or find another leader. Mackinnon and his associates had no realistic option but to accept the itinerary imposed on them. Stanley received his formal instructions a few days later: 'The Congo State has nothing to gain by the expedition for the relief of Emin Pasha passing through its territory. The King has suggested this road merely so as to lend your services to the expedition, which it would be impossible for him to do were the expedition to proceed by the eastern coast.'

Back in London at the New Year, Stanley tested the waters in Foreign Office circles with regard to Leopold's demands. On 5th January he saw Sir Percy Anderson and argued Leopold's case as follows: they would be using river borne transport to within 500 miles of their goal, the itinerary was quicker and would allay German fears; most of all, the Kabaka, hearing of the expedition's approach, would be constrained from harming

English and French missionaries. Anderson promised to consult Lord Iddesleigh (the Foreign Secretary) and let Stanley have an answer on the 8th. All roads led back to Iddesleigh. When Stanley approached Admiral Sir Francis Sullivan about using a Royal Navy ship to get the expedition to the Congo, the Admiralty simply replied that it was awaiting its cue from the Foreign Office.

Meanwhile Stanley and the EPRE committee had to sift through the hundreds of applications to join the expedition; more than eighty were received on New Year's Day alone. By the end of the first week of 1887, some of the officers had been selected. After very strong representations on behalf of Major Edmund Barttelot and Lt. William Stairs, Stanley agreed to take them provided Lord Wolseley raised no objection and gave them a good reference. A. J. Mountney Jephson was on the point of being rejected by the committee when he produced his 'ace in the hole' - a donation by his patroness the Comtesse de Noailles of £1000 towards the expedition. Even so, de Winton, a powerful voice on the committee, thought Jephson was too much of a 'masher' to stand up to the rigours of Central Africa. Stanley's dissenting opinion is interesting, underlining once again his mania about neatness and personal appearance, as well as being self-contradictory: 'I differ with him for I don't think how a man dresses matters a bit. It depends on the nature of the man within them [sic], I am positive that the skulker and the malingerer affects the mean dress mostly while the dandy white or dandy black have always stood up to the mark.'

Other additions to the expeditionary personnel including J. Rose Troup, Captain Nelson and James Jameson, another man who was taken on only after subscribing £1000 to the expedition. Among those turned down were Sir Claude de Crespigny and the Marquis of Queensberry. The Foreign Office meanwhile requested Holmwood in Zanzibar to recruit immediately up to 500 wangwana. Arrangements were made with Baring in Cairo for the free issue of 400 Remington rifles and ammunition, plus 200 loads of ammunition to be taken to Emin. Mackinnon's steamship line had to provide all the ocean shipping for the run from Zanzibar to the Congo and for the transport of ammunition to Zanzibar, after P & O declined to carry such an explosive cargo. The Zanzibar mail ship was diverted to carry supplies, and the Eastern Telegraph Company offered to transmit all the expedition's cables at half-rate. Stanley himself sent orders ahead to Zanzibar to collect large quantities of cloth handkerchiefs, beads, wire, brass, iron and copper for trade in Africa. In the end the expedition set out with 27,262 yards of cloth, 3600 pounds of beads and forty porter-loads of choice provisions from Fortnum and Mason's.

The most impressive aspect of the expedition was the amount and quality of firearms it took with it. Altogether there were 510 Remington rifles with 100,000 rounds, fifty Winchester repeaters with 50,000 cartridges, 2 tons of gunpowder, 350,000 percussion caps, 30,000 Gatling cartridges and 35,000 special Remington cartridges. In addition the very latest addition to the arsenal of conquest was donated: a Maxim machine gun, which could fire 600 rounds a minute as against a maximum of 200 by any other machine gun. Stanley and Stairs went to inspect the gun in the grounds of Hiram Maxim's residence at Thurlow Lodge, Norwood. After trying out the firing mechanism, Stanley declared himself delighted. He put Stairs in charge of the gun and said that it 'would be of valuable service in helping civilisation to overcome barbarism'.

Other offers were not so welcome. The African Lakes Company offered the expedition full facilities if it would adopt the Zambezi-Tanganyika route, but it turned out their 'facilities' were virtually nil: 'This is sheer impudence,' thundered Stanley, 'or are they fishing for advertisement.' Nor were the personnel coming forward very much to Stanley's liking. One who perplexed him was William Bonny, a former army sergeant, who was one of the very first to volunteer for the expedition. After three weeks of agonising Stanley made his decision. On 7th January he wrote in his journal: 'Have finally agreed to accept William Bonny as Doctor's Assistant. It is much against my will, but I have been unable to resist his pertinacity... there is a peculiar stodginess about the man that prevents me from anticipating any valuable service from him.'

By the end of the first week in January, Sir Julian Pauncefoote at the Foreign Office was able to tell him that the Remingtons and ammunition had already left Suez for Zanzibar. But just when all appeared to be proceeding smoothly, Leopold put another spoke in the wheel. He announced that he could not put all his Congo steamers at the disposal of the expedition, as he would need some for the normal business of the Congo State. The EPRE committee declared this new condition unacceptable and sent a special courier to Leopold with a letter to ask exactly what he was prepared to give. This was a blow to Stanley. The committee was already hostile to the Congo itinerary and now here was Leopold with his nitpicking Fabian tactics ruining the one solid merit the Congo route had; it was essential for Stanley to have all his flotilla for the journey up to Stanley Falls. He made it clear that he would not commit himself to taking the Congo route until Leopold put all his steamers at his disposal and he no longer had to worry about water transport.

Leopold sent the EPRE committee assurances of his support, but couched in terms that were still not entirely unambiguous. It was only after Stanley's second interview with him, on 15th January, that this aspect of things was cleared up to the explorer's satisfaction and he wrenched from the King a statement of full backing for the expedition. Now it was time to square the Foreign Office. Unfortunately the promised interview with the Foreign Secretary never took place, for the day before it was due to happen Lord Iddesleigh dropped dead from a heart attack. However, it was known that Iddesleigh had favoured the Congo route, since it spared him from angry representations from the French and Germans.

On 13th January Stanley went with Baroness Burdett-Coutts to receive the freedom of the City of London. Then he travelled Dover-Ostend en route to Brussels to beard the (literally) bearded lion in its Brussels den; he was accompanied as far as Dover by Barttelot, who was going on ahead to Egypt. On the 15th he had a two-hour audience with Leopold, when they spoke mainly of Tippu Tip. The King seemed to harbour a murderous spite against the Arab leader for the sacking of Stanley Falls station and wanted to pursue him to the death. Stanley pointed out that in the present state of Free State resources that was a pipe dream. Much better would be to use Tippu Tip for the monarch's own ends. Stanley suggested biding time - revenge is a dish best eaten cold - but meanwhile offering Tippu (who would be referred to in correspondence as 'Number One') the governorship of Stanley Falls under the Belgian flag. Leopold acquiesced grudgingly. For once he had revealed the dark side of his personality, as Stanley noted: 'Though His Majesty is about as perfect a gentleman as I have ever seen, yet even he, considerate and just as his nature is - is not without vindictiveness. 'It was typical of Stanley's love of playing one side off against the other that he allowed no hint of the proposed arrangement with Tippu Tip to reach British ears, so that the Foreign Office remained apprehensive that Leopold intended to use the Emin expedition to recapture Stanley Falls from the Arabs.

Stanley left Brussels at 5.30 p.m. on 15th January and was back in London early next morning. But if he thought to compensate for the nights sleeping 'on the cars' he was disappointed. At 2 a.m. on the morning of the 17th he was aroused from his sleep by an insistent hammering on the door of his apartments in 160 New Bond Street. At the door was a policeman to tell him that Rose Troup was in gaol for assaulting a brother constable. Since Troup was to be tried before a magistrate at 10 am, on the 17th and knew that a man of Stanley's reputation would tip the scales in his favour, he requested his presence. Piqued by this intrusion on his repose, Stanley sent Hoffmann with a note to de Winton, asking him to assume the onus.

On the 18th Stanley travelled with de Winton to Sandringham to see the Prince of Wales. They had tea, a visit to a model dairy, dinner, then Stanley with the aid of maps gave a fifteen-minute talk on the itinerary to the dozen or so guests, before retiring for billiards and cigars. In the morning the Prince said goodbye very amiably and made him a present of a silver cigar case. That evening in London there was a farewell banquet at Burlington House, and afterwards the Webbs of Newstead appeared to wish him a personal Godspeed.

On 20th January the rest of Stanley's officers left England in the Navarino: Nelson, Jephson and Stairs in charge of the Maxim gun (Barttelotwas already in Egypt). Also due to depart was the troublesome black boy Baruti, whom Stanley intended to return to his Soko kinsmen. In charge of Baruti Stanley had placed Bonny, so that it was a shock when James Grant the explorer returned from Fenchurch Station with the black boy in tow and the news that Bonny had left him at the station for hours, hungry and cold, after depositing him on the platform and saying he would be back in a few moments. Next day Bonny appeared and Stanley taxed him with his misdemeanour. At first Bonny tried bluster and said the date on de Winton's instructions had been wrong. 'This won't wash,' replied Stanley laconically. 'Where did you go?' Bonny's next version was that, as he had never seen the Crown Jewels and could well die in Africa, he had gone to the Tower of London on a sudden impulse. Realising that this was a cock and bull story, Stanley's instinct was to sack Bonny then and there but his hand was stayed by the reflection that as yet the expedition had no doctor. He therefore contented himself with a severe warning to Bonny that one further such 'mistake' would lead to his being sued as a runaway. There was an Australian steamer at Plymouth which was scheduled to be at Suez before the Navarino. Stanley ordered Bonny to catch it forthwith.

On the evening of the 21st, after dining with Mackinnon, Stanley drove to Charing Cross Station for departure on the high adventure of rescuing Emin. He was seen off by large cheering crowds, who pestered him to know when he would return. 'As soon as I can,' was the laconic reply. The trio of de Winton, Mackinnon and Hutton accompanied him as far as Cannon Street, then he was left alone with Hoffmann, Baruti and his own reflections. Stanley reached Brindisi at 4 a.m. on 24th January, to find a telegram from James Gordon Bennett asking him to carry his yacht club flag across Africa! 'I cannot refuse him, though it is a ridiculous whim.' At Brindisi he embarked on the P & O steamer Tanjore for Alexandria.

He was at Alexandria at 6 a.m. on 27th January. There surgeon T.H. Parke volunteered his services as expeditionary medical officer. To test his resolve Stanley gave him a somewhat abrasive answer: 'If you care to, follow me to Cairo, and I will talk further with you. I have not the time to argue with you here.' At 10 a.m. he took the train for Cairo, where he was met at the station by Evelyn Baring, effectively Viceroy in Egypt. On the way to his house Baring told him that the German explorers Schweinfurth and Junkers had influenced the Prime Minister, Nubar Pasha, against the Congo route on the ground that it would take too long. Nubar and the Khedive were also worried that the expedition now seemed to be a purely exploratory venture, in no way concerned with Egyptian prestige, and they therefore failed to see why they should foot the bill.

Stanley in lordly fashion replied that de Winton, Grant and other experienced people had endorsed the Congo route and that he preferred their opinion to the Germans'. A meeting that evening with Schweinfurth did nothing to palliate Stanley's distaste; he contrasted himself, the disinterested rescuer of Emin, with Schweinfurth, an axe-grinder of German imperialism. He repeated that he wanted to avoid fighting - his reputation as warmonger was bad enough already - but that an east-coast approach would certainly mean conflict, with the people of Ankole, Karagwe and Bunyoro at least.

Next morning Stanley breakfasted with Nubar Pasha and Mason Bay, the circumnavigator of Lake Albert in 1877. Nubar agreed to write to Emin to order him to pull out of Equatoria, since the Egyptians could no longer afford to sustain him there. But it became clear that the rumours were true and the Egyptians were threatening to withdraw their offer of £10,000. Stanley fared better with the second German, Junker, whom he was able to talk round to the Congo route. The two conversed for many hours; in his report of the meeting Stanley gives a valuable clue as to what may have made the rapport possible: 'He seems a quiet little man, about 5' 5" high [!] with a Russo-German cast of features ... he impressed me as a frank and honest man and I am sure his book will be interesting.'

But both Schweinfurth and Junker thought that the presence of the Maxim and the Remingtons meant that Stanley intended to cut a path of destruction to Emin, which demonstrated to Stanley's satisfaction that they possessed no judgement outside their own narrow field: 'We carry African currency to buy food, arms to defend our charges and wits to use as occasion might need.' This led him into a disquisition on the use of force. He noted that press reports had Emin fighting his way out to Uganda to general praise: 'it is strange that the press is willing to applaud Emin for using force to come out while it is very ready to condemn me if I use force to reach him.' He reserved the right to use force and claimed that, as the territory of the Congo State extended as far as Lake Albert, it was nobody's business but Leopold's if he did. He ended his apologia by using the arguments of Bentham, whom he habitually derided. It was necessary on this expedition to weigh up the greatest good of the greatest number, not just Emin's men against hostiles but present losses against future gains: 'I fancy the posterity of the present wild Aruwimi tribes will have reason to rejoice that the unreasoning portion of their ancestors retired before our rifles.'

Next day Stanley dined with General Stephenson, Commander-in Chief of British forces in Egypt. Present also were Junker, Schweinfurth, Valentine Baker and others. Junker provided a character sketch of Emin and warned that he would be most unlikely to withdraw from Equatoria even if ordered. Junker's portrait made it clear that Emin was no hero, merely a prudent and conscientious scholar and administrator. Coffee with Mason Bay next day tended to confirm this negative picture of Emin. Baker expressed doubts about the Remington ammunition sent to Zanzibar and suggested that the Egyptians would not be above palming him off with already condemned cartridges.

On the first day of February Baring took Stanley to see the Khedive: 'a short, stout man like his father Ismail, good-looking, and I should say amiable.' Although Stanley later claimed to have 'won round' the Khedive and Nubar to the Congo route, the truth was that Lord Salisbury had ordered Baring to override the Egyptians and give the Emin expedition his full support. It was behind-the-scenes pressure by Baring that effected the conversion Stanley attributed to his own eloquence. It was agreed that, whereas the Khedive basically wanted Emin to return, he left it open to the Pasha to sever his Egyptian connections if he wished to stay on in Africa.

After the audience with the Khedive, Baring took Stanley on to General Grenfell's to test the quality of the ammunition. Grenfell professed himself astonished at Baker's allegations and said he would carry out exhaustive examinations immediately. As a result of the tests, Stanley wired Mackinnon for 50,000 rounds of fresh ammunition.

Next day he breakfasted with the Khedive: 'at table he showed a pleasant side of character. His laugh is hearty and good-natured. He protests his patriotism.' The Khedive gave him a letter for Emin which promoted him to Brigadier-General but also allowed him to decide his own fate, with the proviso that if he stayed on in Africa it was on his own head.

Stanley's work in Egypt was now finished and at 11.45 a.m. on 3rd February he left Cairo for Suez. Huge crowds saw him off; the sixty-one Sudanese troops recruited for the expedition by Baring came marching to the railway station with flags flying and music playing. At Zagazig he was joined by Parke, whom he had finally decided to take on as the expedition physician. Jameson joined them at Ismailia. All paths were now converging on the Navarino. Bonny and Baruti were expected on the Garonne at Suez and at Aden Barttelot would join them. The party would then be complete, except for Rose Troup and a few others who were proceeding directly from Liverpool to the Congo.

This time all went to plan. Bonny and Baruti arrived at Suez on 4th February. The combined party (Stairs, Jephson, Jameson, Nelson, Parke, Bonny, Baruti, Hoffmann, the Syrian Assad Ferran and sixty-one Sudanese) sailed in the Navarino for Aden to pick up Barttelot. Stairs whiled away the boredom of the cruise down the Egyptian littoral by drilling the Sudanese. Hoffmann meanwhile was heard to enquire if it was really the Red Sea down which they were steaming. 'Yes,' replied Stanley. 'Well, sir, it looks more like a black sea than a red one,' was his ingenuous answer.

They arrived at Aden in the small hours of 12th February and changed ships, as the Navarino was going on to Bombay. Barttelot came on board the new steamer SS Oriental with twelve Somalis whom he had engaged.

Also, Stanley was held to his absurd promise to Gordon Bennett when the agent of the British India line brought him the flags left behind by the Herald proprietor.

They steamed down to Zanzibar, stopping en route at Lamu and Mombasa. At Lamu they saw, at the entrance to the harbour, a pile of human skeletons, said to be the result of a battle between the Somalis and Gallas (respectively the clients of the British and Germans) which the Somalis won. They also received word of the German Oscar Lenz who had just crossed Africa. Lenz had originally been sent out to rescue Emin and had proceeded up the Congo as far as Stanley Falls. Finding himself unable to obtain men there, he had made his way back via Lake Tanganyika and Zanzibar. It always irritated Stanley when anyone else achieved a trans-Africa journey, so not surprisingly his journal reference is suitably waspish: 'Having failed in his purposes he will doubtless visit the Congo with his blame - at least it has been the habit of all failures of late.'

At Mombasa, reached on 21st February, Stanley noted that the best place for the Mackinnon concession he was trying to wring from the Sultan would be on the right-hand side of the northern entrance to the harbour. But the Oriental made but a short stop here and pressed on to anchor in Zanzibar roads at midday on the 22nd. The expedition transferred to berths on the Madura, which was to take them round the Cape and to the Congo. Stanley himself lodged with Consul-General Holmwood.

There could be no mistaking the changes that had come over Zanzibar since his last visit eight years earlier. Cables had been laid to Aden, Mozambique and Cape Town. There was a broad carriageway in the centre of the town, full of horses and carriages, and many new buildings, including a palace and a clock tower. Hoffman was entranced: 'Along the wide, well-made streets of the city, lit by oil-lamps, went stately horses and carriages. I could see steam-rollers, lamp-posts, shop-fronts, all as modern and ordinary-looking as possible. Save for the hordes of black men clustering down on the quayside, and the rich, tropical vegetation, we might have been arriving at an English port.'

But it was the warships at anchor in the bay that denoted the more profound change, a change in the entire political complexion of the area. Bismarck's late bid for colonies was already producing sensational results. In 1884 Peters led a small party into the East African interior and concluded twelve treaties in six weeks in which the chiefs alienated land 'for all time'. After the Treaty of Berlin, the Kaiser (on 27th February 1885) issued a charter extending his 'protection' to all the Peters territory. Peters then formed a German East African Company and transferred to it the treaty rights of 1884. Barghash protested vehemently to the Kaiser; in answer five German warships anchored in Zanzibar roads in August 1885. Kirk meanwhile had been ordered by London to encourage Barghash to accept a German protectorate; in view of the French threat to Egypt and the success of the Mahdi in the Sudan, Gladstone wanted no quarrel with Bismarck. In 1886 a joint Franco-British-German commission investigated the Sultan's claims to territories in East Africa; following German pressure the three commissioners recommended that the Sultan should be allowed to possess merely the ports on the mainland and a ten-mile coastal strip opposite Zanzibar.

Almost the first person Stanley met in Zanzibar was Tippu Tip, whom he had last seen in December 1876. Tippu had aged a lot in ten years: his hair was iron-grey and his beard white but at 6 foot 2 inches he still had a commanding presence and, with Barghash's castration by the Germans, was the power in Africa between Lake Tanganyika and the Upper Congo. Tippu had been in Zanzibar since November 1886 discussing the implications of the Berlin Act with the Sultan. Barghash had confided in him the possibility of having to withdraw to Manyema from Zanzibar if German pressure became too great.

The news of the sack of Stanley Falls station after the imprudent action of Captain Deane had appalled Tippu and his first thought was that he ought to travel to Belgium to discuss differences with Leopold. On arrival in Zanzibar, finding Barghash a spent force, he was compelled to assume the mantle of Arab leadership himself and began negotiations with Holmwood. He warned him that the Arabs of the interior would resist to the death any attempt by Europeans to wrest their possessions from them by force. On the other hand, he welcomed British help in composing his differences with the Belgians, even suggesting that the Association appoint a competent officer to deal with Arab relations.

Tippu Tip's position was immensely complicated. In general he liked Europeans and had had satisfactory meetings and conversations with Cameron, Vangele and Becker. But he could not abide Stanley at any price. Stanley he saw as a congenital liar, a man without a shred of honour or integrity, one who went back on his word, did not keep his bargains and was a worse slave driver to his men than any official slaver. His only use for Africans, said Tippu, was as human sacrifices; when he was not using them as cannon fodder, he was hurling them into the darkness of Tartarean forests from which they could not extricate themselves. Beyond this, Tippu had a personal grudge against Stanley. In 1876, when Stanley launched into the unknown north of Vinya-Niara, Tippu had prophesied that the white man would never be seen again. His triumphant emergence at the Congo mouth had led to loss of face and credibility for the Arab leader. It was partly Stanley's role as Leopold's agent in the Congo and partly Deane's headstrong aggression that made Tippu Tip so angry with the Belgians, and there was no question but that he was strong enough to maintain himself against all comers in Central Africa.

Such was the situation when the two men met on 22nd February. Superficially all was politeness. Stanley began by offering Tippu the governorship of Stanley Falls under Belgian auspices, as agreed with Leopold on 15th January, under the mistaken impression that the Arab leader was short of money. Tippu asked, reasonably enough: 'How can you give me what's already mine? What do you want in that country anyway?' Patiently Stanley explained the terms of the 1885 Berlin Treaty. Tippu snorted with contempt. What right had Europe to take his country and give it to Leopold? Stanley shrugged: as for that, Tippu should ask the Sultan or the Consul-General; he himself had nothing to say on the matter.

Tippu then calmed down and asked why Leopold wanted him. Stanley argued that Tippu and Leopold had a common interest in keeping out other white interlopers. The only conditions the Belgian King exacted were flying the flag of the Congo State, allowing a Belgian resident, and prohibiting the slave trade between Stanley Pool and Stanley Falls. In return, Tippu would receive a salary of £30 a month as governor of the Falls. Most importantly, Stanley wanted to hire 600 porters from him at $30 a head, with a $1000 bonus payable on successful completion of the hiring; this made $19,000 in all apart from the monthly salary from Leopold - surely a better deal than an uncertain war against the Belgians. Tippu hesitated about accepting. He went away and consulted with Barghash. Was not the salary insulting and derisory? Barghash advised that it would be wise to accept even if the Belgians were paying a third of the amount, for as governor at Stanley Falls, Tippu Tip could still command the destinies of Central Africa.

Tippu returned for further talks with Stanley. The sticking point seemed to be that Tippu did not want Leopold to extend as far as Stanley Falls but Leopold was insistent on it. Disappointed that the proffered money did not seem to be having the desired effect, Stanley warned that if Leopold could not extend as far as Stanley Falls, his Congo State would collapse. If that happened, France would step in to fill the vacuum and would have no compunction about sending a major army of conquest up the Congo. This point, made with forceful asseveration, chimed in with Barghash's advice. With great reluctance Tippu agreed to Stanley's terms. He had other motives, revealed later. The principal one was concern for his commercial future. German pressure was already leading to Zanzibar's downfall and a steep decline in Arab profits from the Congo trade. By this concession to the Europeans, Tippu hoped to open a new pipeline for his trade into Equatoria. On 24th February he signed a contract with Stanley. Barghash witnessed the signing and gave presents to the two signatories: a gold watch and 2000 rupees to Tippu and a diamond-embossed ring to Stanley.

When this contract became public knowledge in Europe, Stanley was vilified by liberal opinion for doing deals with a known slaver. But in his own terms he had pulled off a great coup. Forced to proceed by the Congo route by Leopold, Stanley knew that he faced well-nigh insuperable labour problems unless he had Tippu Tip's co-operation in securing porters. Without this co-operation, he would have to give the Arabs at Stanley Falls a wide berth, since it was far too dangerous for European interests to run the risk that the expedition's vast arsenal of arms and ammunition might fall into Tippu's hands. In a word, despite Stanley's bluster to the EPRE committee, it was Tippu and Tippu alone who made the Congo route a viable proposition.

But the agreement with Tippu Tip was not the only fruit of Stanley's brief sojourn in Zanzibar. There was also the question of the Mackinnon concession. On 23rd February Stanley had a private audience with the Sultan on this subject. As he drove to the palace, many of his old followers among the wangwana lined the route and called out: 'Yes, it is he!' Stanley was bored, as ever, with protocol at Barghash's now increasingly fairy-tale court, so he came to the point very quickly, presented his credentials from Mackinnon and the letter in which Mackinnon asked for a commercial concession as a counterpoise to the Germans. Stanley played the German card very skilfully; he warned the Sultan that when he returned in three years' time he fully expected to find Zanzibar part of German territory. He advanced an argument peculiarly calculated to appeal to the weak and vacillating Barghash: even if he did not trust Mackinnon, why not simply play off the British against the Germans? His eloquence found its mark. Holmwood had been plugging the selfsame line even before Stanley's arrival, so it was not difficult to persuade Barghash to come to an 'in principle' agreement.

After a farewell dinner at the consulate on the 24th, the Madura weighed anchor next morning, groaning with human bodies. Tippu Tip was to accompany the expedition to Stanley Falls to be installed as governor and took a hundred of his men on the voyage. In addition, 623 wangwana, two Syrians and twelve Somalis drew four months' pay in advance and were then marched straight to the ship to prevent bounty-jumping. Together with nine Europeans and sixty Sudanese, all in all some 800 passengers thronged the gangways of the steamer on its passage south. It was perhaps hardly surprising that just two hours after clearing Zanzibar harbour, a ferocious battle broke out between the Sudanese and the wangwana. Stanley's officers had to wade in among the combatants with clubs to restore order.

When the vendetta between the two groups was temporarily settled by physical separation, with the Zanzibaris in the fore quarters and the Sudanese in the aft, Stanley had the leisure to reflect on the calibre of officer he was taking with him to Central Africa. Rose Troup, who had worked for Stanley in the Congo, was travelling out directly. James Jameson, who had virtually bought his ticket with the £1000 subscription, was the most delicate-looking of the party. Obsessed with natural history he seemed of no great force of character, amiable and quiet: 'still the same nice fellow we saw, there is not a grain of change in him - he is sociable and good.' The twenty-one-year-old Lt. Stairs of the Royal Engineers Stanley found much more impressive mentally. He was painstaking and industrious, and was already making real efforts to communicate with his men by learning Swahili. Nervous, excitable, warm-tempered, Stairs 'is a splendid fellow, painstaking, ready, thoughtful and industrious - is an invaluable addition to the staff.'

The thirty-eight-year-old Captain R. H. Nelson of Methuen's Horse, a veteran of the Zulu war, likewise elicited little comment from Stanley, except to say that he was modest, unpretentious, good-natured and undistinguished. Surgeon Parke, too, was damned with faint praise. A charming gentle-mannered Irishman, he sometimes gave Stanley the impression that English was not his native language and that he was not over-bright - a verdict he was later to reverse.

But from the very earliest days the two officers who most engaged Stanley's attention were Mountney Jephson and Barttelot, the second- in-command. Stanley began to note his antipathy towards Barttelot as early as 26th February, when he noticed his deputy's tendency to exceed his authority and usurp functions reserved for the expedition's leader. There was nothing wrong with his physical courage: a major in the 7th Fusiliers, he was a veteran of the Second Afghan War and Wolseley's Sudan campaign and, at twenty-seven, was tough, wiry and a born fighter. But outside his knowledge of army life in Africa and the tropics, he was an ignoramus, a pure military automaton who did not read or think. The combination of fussiness and autocracy in Barttelot overcame the obvious advantage (in Stanley's eyes) of his short stature - he was just 5 foot 4 inches tall. 'Barttelot is a little too eager and will have to be restrained. He is a little unsound in discipline, and there is a lurking aggressiveness in him which may lead to open rupture - unless a thorough African rupture makes him more amenable. There is plenty of work in him, but you can well understand how lovely this quality would be if it were according to orders. The most valuable man to me would be him who also had Barttelot's spirit and go in him and could come and ask if such and such work had not better be done. It at once suggests thoughtfulness and willingness, besides proper respect.' Jephson, who was different from all the others in having no previous experience of tropical travelling or soldiering, quickly won Stanley's esteem. He was plucky and very strong and distinguished himself during the brawl between the Sudanese and Zanzibaris. He was a great reader, had a fine memory and possessed the art of small talk. As he was socially well connected, it was not surprising to find him and Barttelot, with a host of mutual friends, boon companions in the Madura. But where Stanley took an almost instant dislike to Barttelot, conversely he took an immediate shine to the twenty-seven-year old Jephson, who had the added advantage of not being too tall (5 foot 7 inches in his shoes, as Stanley, always obsessed with other men's height, records): 'There is a great deal in Jephson the thin-voiced whose manner is so affectedly deprecatory. His manner is actually fierce when aroused, his face becomes dangerously set and fixed ... [he is] gallant and plucky. But he is a man of whims and humours, thin-skinned - awfully so - prone to nourish resentment - and remember small grievances. I believe he has a keen scent for the latter, would in fact scent a grievance where you would least expect one. This comes from too much feminine society, because manliness would despise pettiness - which is a fault with prettiness and over self-admiration. Jephson will be either made or marred if he is with this expedition long.'

But if Stanley disliked Barttelot and was fond of Jephson, the man who intrigued him most in the whole party was William Bonny, the forty-year old former sergeant of the Army Medical Department. Enigmatic and well-travelled (everything from soldiering in South Africa to coffee planting in Brazil), Bonny had already fallen foul of Stanley over the Baruti business. Stanley oscillated between not knowing what to make of him and fearing that he would be his most mistaken appointment. Certainly he had stood the heat so far better than any of the whites. So at this stage Stanley contented himself with an anodyne assessment: 'Bonny is the soldier. He is not initiative [sic]. He seems to have been under a martinet's drill ... is Tommy Atkins par excellence, stolid and steady, with not an idea in his head, beyond so many months will give him so many months' pay.'

The passage from Zanzibar to the Cape also gave Stanley the opportunity to ponder the many 'contradictions' in the enterprise on which he was launched. Very different interests were at play on this expedition, all of them apparently irreconcilable. First there was the British position. Mackinnon, baulked of a railway on the Congo, had now decisively switched his attention to East Africa and wanted to ape Leopold by making his British East Africa Company a second Association - that is to say, he wanted treaties with East African chiefs and trade stations on the Congo model. To this end he was prepared to use Emin as his agent if the Pasha agreed to come out of Equatoria. Salisbury, for his part, thought Mackinnon's ideas chimerical but saw the need to counter German influence in East Africa. The Egyptians, having lost the Sudan to the Mahdists and unable to persuade the British to reconquer it for them, wanted to retain a foothold in Equatoria or, at the very least, retrieve some prestige by getting Emin and the Egyptian garrisons back to Cairo.

Secondly, there was Leopold. The King wanted to extend the boundaries of his Congo State to the Nile and to this end was prepared to create Emin governor of a new Belgian enclave on the Upper Congo/ Nile watershed. The monarch wanted a harbour on one of the great lakes and a secure military bastion against possible invasion by the Mahdists. He claimed to see no conflict between his ends and those of Mackinnon and the British, but this was almost certainly an example of the King's bogus naivety. There was a conflict between Mackinnon's aims and Leopold's, and between the ends of both these men and the Egyptians, and not just in the sense that a Congo itinerary for the relief expedition seemed to tip the balance in favour of Congo interests over East African ones. Which side was Stanley on? Almost certainly the answer is, his own. He did not confide the scope of Mackinnon's ambitions to Leopold, nor Leopold's offer to Emin to Mackinnon, though enough must have slipped out to make the King realise wearily that of the rival bids for Emin's services that of the British magnate would probably beat his. Stanley was playing both ends against the middle, manoeuvring for personal advantage. Ever the opportunist, Stanley's main aim was the enhancement of his own reputation and glory, though if he had to choose between the interests of the two men, he was psychologically likely to opt for Mackinnon, for Leopold had hurt and humiliated him in 1885-6 and the Scotsman had not. The itinerary he proposed to take, outward up the Congo and homeward through East Africa, seemed an acceptable compromise between the exigencies of Leopold and Mackinnon but was in fact most clearly calculated to help Stanley. It is a tribute to his often-derided political skills that he had won over general opinion to this mixed route by the time he left London.

The international prospect was already impossibly cloudy. Even France became involved; it entertained a deep suspicion of the real motives of the Emin Pasha expedition and suspected Anglo-Belgian collusion to carve up the uncharted and unclaimed areas of Central Africa. The suspicion was reinforced in 1888 when, with no news from Stanley, there was talk of a fresh British relief expedition; the French suspected that Stanley's 'disappearance' was part of a previously concerted plot to allow the British to send large-scale military forces to the area.

Yet even apart from all these considerations, there were two obvious jokers in the expeditionary pack, as Stanley shrewdly saw. One was the huge cache of ivory Emin was supposed to have at Wadelai. It was the prospect of laying hands on this that made subscriptions to the EPRE committee so plentiful. Yet Stanley the master administrator quickly did some sums on the Madura that exposed the hollowness of such hopes. Junker had estimated Emin's ivory store at 75 tons, worth £60,000 at 8-shillings a ton. This seemed a fortune well worth possessing. But a realistic logistical assessment soon showed the treasure to be located in cloud-cuckoo-land. If each of Tippu Tip's porters realistically carried a load of 38 pounds apiece, only £6600 worth would be brought to the Falls. Once deductions of £3800 had been made for transport, pay and bonuses, only £2800 would remain, on which freight and other charges would be payable. Unless the ivory fetched an unexpectedly high price in Europe, even a couple of round trips would not realise more than £6000. Therefore the high profits envisaged by armchair speculators in Europe would not materialise.

Even more of an imponderable factor was Emin himself. The relief expedition was always bedevilled by a fundamental ambiguity and uncertainty about what exactly 'relief meant. Did it mean that Stanley was to escort Emin and his Egyptian troops back to Cairo, or did it imply merely the delivery of supplies and ammunition? The problem, as Stanley saw it, was that if Emin accepted none of the three propositions put to him, from the Khedive, Leopold or Mackinnon, what was his position then? 'If he refuses all three, then he and his force must undertake an independent role, and live on the country as they best can and Emin will be a kind of white Mirambo living on violence and cattle lifting. What a prospect for Gordon's lieutenant!'

Stanley would not have been reassured if he could have read Emin's correspondence while the expedition laboriously threaded its way towards him. All Emin's letters to Kirk, Felkin, Mackay and others seemed to contain the recurrent phrase 'Help us quickly or we perish.' But this did not mean, as Stanley so consistently presumed it did, that Emin wished to leave Africa. What he wanted was to stay in Africa because he personally loved the continent, preferably under the British protectorate that Kirk and Mackay had long urged on him as his best chance in the future. Emin was high in his praise for Stanley when he heard he was on his way. 'I have always felt the greatest admiration for Mr Stanley as an explorer; his intrepidity, his pluck and his kindly regard for his followers have always commended my hearty sympathies.' But he made it clear that he had no intention of following Stanley out of Africa; his reading of the relief expedition was that Stanley would deliver the stores and ammunition and then depart: 'If, however, the people in Great Britain think that as soon as Stanley or Thomson comes I shall return with them, they greatly err. I have passed twelve years of my life here, and would it be right of me to desert my post as soon as the opportunity for escape presented itself? I shall remain with my people until I see perfectly clearly that their future and the future of our country is safe. 'From December 1886 until April 1888 both the men with assumed names lived in a twilight world of mutual misunderstanding that was eventually to have explosive effects.

Chapter Ten

HE Madura slowly made its way south, past Mayotte Island of the Comoro group. Stanley made sure all his officers had specific tasks to occupy their time. Parke had overall responsibility for the Sudanese, Bonny was in charge of the donkeys and goats, while Stairs, Nelson, Jephson, Jameson and Rose Troup were in charge of 117 wangwana each. Barttelot's task was to deliver rations in gross to each officer daily, for distribution to his group. Every day a muster was held to allow the officers to familiarise themselves with the men. And from 26th February to 4th March Parke vaccinated everyone on board against smallpox.

Annoyed that all the officers seemed to be keeping journals, Stanley by and large held himself aloof from them. He spent most of his time with Tippu Tip and Jephson. Already rumours were running around the ship of Tippu's animus towards Stanley, how Stanley on leaving him in 1876 had promised to make him a rich man but instead sent him his photograph! Stanley broached the subject of Tippu's discontents, only to find the Arab raging about the conduct of Captain Deane. This was an old bone of contention. Tippu had brought three Krupps shells to Zanzibar and ostentatiously produced them to Stanley as proof of the type of bombardment his men had sustained from Stanley Falls station. Stanley tried to pour oil on troubled waters; was Tippu really going to generalise about white men from the consequences of a single hothead's exaggerated sense of 'honour' over a woman; was this not another instance of the phenomenon Tippu himself must often have seen, the 'young buck' on the rampage? He pointed out to Tippu that once he was governor of Stanley Falls, there would be no need to see the white men he so disliked.

Stanley had given Tippu Tip and his ninety-six followers free passage all the way from Zanzibar to Stanley Falls on the calculation that it would not then be open to the Arabs to try to persuade the wangwana to desert. His attitude to Tippu was generally cynical and even at this stage of the expedition he was planning to double-cross him if that became necessary. 'If there is no ivory, I shall be indebted to Tippu Tip for the sum of £3600 ... at the same time I shall not risk the expedition for the sake of ivory.'

But it was Jephson with whom Stanley spent most of his spare time. Jephson found Stanley remarkably quick at grasping ideas and astonishingly lucid in his capacity to express them: 'he has such a wonderful gift of word painting . .. such a keen sense of the ridiculous. 'Again, as with Livingstone, Burton, Bruce and many others, we observe Stanley's natural rapport with fellow-Celts, as opposed to the born and bred Englishman. The Jephsons of Mallow were, like the Burtons, an Anglo-Irish family. But Jephson soon learned that there was a dark side to Stanley and a diary entry on 28th February indicates the general drift: I had a great argument with Stanley. He seemed to think that the only thing worth doing was to succeed, no matter how, in anything you undertook and that success was everything, whilst I contended that failure was sometimes a nobler thing than success - circumstances made it so . . . Stanley seems to have no sort of patience with anything which does not succeed. Of course such a feeling is splendid, how could great things be done without a great deal of that feeling, still if one has only that feeling it leads to a great deal of injustice and intolerance towards other people who have not been so lucky in succeeding as he has done.

The Madura reached Cape Town on 8th March after a cruel buffeting in high seas around Durban and Port Elizabeth. They took on ammunition, coal, stores and livestock, bearing in mind that on the ten-day run to the mouth of the Congo they would consume x 20 sheep and goats. Stanley went ashore for a short walk but so many people stopped and stared at him that after buying a few books he was glad to retreat to the security of the ship. His distaste for Cape Town was underlined when a deputation of humanitarians from the Chamber of Commerce came aboard to seek assurances that he was not planning to massacre the indigenous peoples he encountered. Stanley replied tartly that he had no intention of robbing Africans or seizing their food and goods; the Remingtons were there as a 'failsafe' weapon, just in case he had to force passage through to Wadelai.

The sensation of Cape Town was Tippu Tip, whom Stanley had allowed to go ashore in company with Hoffmann provided the party took no photographs - already Stanley was wary of possible future rival memoirs. It was not just his height but the retinue of his wives (thirty-five of the ninety-six followers were Tippu's women) that excited the curiosity of Cape journalists. Tippu Tip himself was enormously impressed by his first real view of white civilisation; until now, he admitted, he had thought all white men fools. In the light of Tippu's remarks about the chaos into which Africa would descend if blacks were ever given their independence, there is considerable dramatic irony in his admiration for the artefacts of South Africa.

Jameson, the lover of flowers and wildlife, brought back to the ship from his shore excursion a number of dogs, conjuring memories of the five Stanley had taken with him in 1874-7. Stanley chose a male fox terrier and Jephson a white mongrel. 'I have named mine "Randy",' Stanley wrote, 'after Randolph Churchill because of his stirring speech at Bradford in 1886, with the sentiments of which I heartily agreed. Jephson called his "Bill Sikes", for his low breeding and sullen looks. 'But it was soon Jephson's turn to reveal his dark side. After just four days he grew tired of his pet for being smelly and low-bred and for being ribbed about him by his messmates. He tied two iron bars to the dog and dropped him from a port-hole. Stanley was always sentimental (though not necessarily compassionate) about animals, and the incident upset him: 'Meek and voiceless creatures like Bill Sikes are often the subject of contumely in this world, then people get an idea in their heads, that their existence is intolerable and exercise a pressure against them, until they are crowded out.'

The Madura weighed anchor at 5.30 p.m. on 10th March and began to creep up the western coast of South Africa; again there was stormy weather immediately after leaving the Cape but, mercifully, this soon abated. On the 14th there occurred the first death among the wang- wana, from dysentery. As on the trip down to the Cape, Stanley spent much time closeted with Tippu Tip, and hammered out with him an agreement that once at Leopoldville, Tippu would go on ahead, collect the promised porters, and rejoin Stanley at Yambuya village, at the confluence of the Congo and Aruwimi. The only jarring note at present was the strong antipathy Stanley felt for Tippu's favourite son-in-law, Salim bin Masoud.

On 18th March 1887 the expedition arrived at Banana to find that the telegraph cable had recently broken, so that neither Stanley's cables nor Leopold's instructions had arrived and nothing was ready for them. After disembarking its vast quantities of humans and materiel, the. Madura continued on its ocean-going way. For the 108-mile voyage to Matadi (on the opposite bank from Vivi) Stanley chartered from the Dutch and English trading companies the river-steamers Albuquerque and K. A. Niemann and the paddle-boat Serpa Pinto. The agents of the English house depressed his officers with tales of the Congo authorities' incompetence and food shortages ahead. This irritated Stanley, already 'decidedly grouchy' after the initial bad news. Fred Puleston, who met him at Banana, found Stanley extremely reserved and brusque, pessimistic, obsessed with the coming trial but full of forebodings. He snapped at Puleston and his two English companions: 'I am surprised that you gentlemen do not invite my men ashore and ask them to point out their last resting places.'

At Boma Stanley's mood darkened further. Liebrechts had succeeded de Winton as governor of the Congo State, but downriver Valcke and Parminter held undisputed sway. After their antecedent turbulent relationship, it was not surprising that Valcke was cordial but awkward with Stanley and seemed to delight in giving him the bad news of famine and steamer shortages at Leopoldville. 'Valcke I feel sure has vented some malice in so glibly giving me such an extinguisher. For a junior to find himself in power, and able to thwart his once formidable senior, would be more than human not to let his gentle malice be exercised . . . Valcke's malice peeped out (and I am sure he must have felt good) when he said, "And I have to remind you, Mr Stanley, that the boats were only to assist you if they could be given without prejudice to the service of the State." '

Stanley proceeded upriver to Matadi, fuming inwardly at the obstacles in his path. If only half of what Valcke had told him was true, it was quite obvious that Leopold was hampering the expedition rather than helping it. He oscillated between blaming Leopold for duplicity and censuring the EPRE committee for not having opted for the Congo route in the first place. But at all events, 'our prospects are of the blackest.'

At Matadi the scattered segments of the expedition reunited. A Portuguese gunboat brought in Barttelot and the Sudanese and Jephson and his quota of the wangrvana. Nelson and Jameson marched their contingents overland, while Valcke and Parminter brought the rest of the Zanzibaris up to Matadi in Association boats. Then Valcke translated the orders he had received from Strauch. The only commitment seemed to be to provide the steamer Stanley and a lighter. Stanley raged inwardly when he thought of the time the EPRE committee had spent trying to ensure that Leopold could not pull the stunt he now seemed to have pulled. He particularly bridled at the statement that the committee 'solicited the aid of the King'; but for Leopold's obstinate intervention, the expedition would have set out from Bagamoyo on the east coast route! 'I observe that Valcke is not so much to blame as Strauch, though I still fancy that "putting a spoke in our wheel" has given him a great delight.'

At Matadi too Puleston met Barttelot for the first time. He noticed that he and Stanley did not get on; they were too much alike, both impatient and domineering. Given Stanley's foul humour, Puleston had a strong intuition that something would go badly wrong on the expedition. It did not take a person of exceptional insight to intuit that. Every item of bad news Stanley received seemed to whip him into a frenzy. When the missionary Comber offered to lend him the steamer Peace, then at Stanley Pool, but with certain restrictions, Stanley noted angrily in his journal: 'I am becoming suspicious of both State and missionaries. There is a false ring about their promises.'

It was doubtless the deep anger and frustration Stanley felt that turned the overland march to Leopoldville into a nightmare experience for all. It was the rainy season when they set out on 25th March to follow the south bank route overland to Stanley Pool, and many of the party were new to the perils of heat, swamps and crocodiles. The caravan route, which wound round the thirty-two cataracts between Matadi and Stanley Pool, was a mere footpath, 40 inches wide, winding through grass several feet high. In the early stages of the march there was no particular shortage of food, though the descent of 800 armed men on small villages taxed their resources as well as causing some alarm. Stanley had issued a 25-day iron ration, but his men supplemented this by bartering blue beads, brass wire and cloth handkerchiefs for a wide variety of foodstuffs: pigs, fowl, goats, fresh and smoked fish, hippo meat, eggs, potatoes, nuts, shrimps, even rats and locusts. There was also abundant sugar-cane, tobacco and palm-wine, while pineapples were in European terms literally ten a penny.

But the Sudanese found the going tougher than they had expected. They also regarded portering as beneath their military dignity and were mutinous and insolent. Barttelot, in charge of them, complained that Major Chernside, who recruited them in Egypt, must have deliberately picked out the greatest scoundrels he could find. Barttelot answered their recalcitrance with brutality. He struck and punched them and threw the ringleaders into the river, so that their clothes drifted off downstream and their ammunition was spoiled. Stanley reprimanded his second-in command: 'The Sudanese are rather trying to get along with, being of stubborn temper and sulky. Still, it is early times to maul people and I had to admonish Barttelot and to explain to him that we must not expect too much from the people at the outset.'

Every morning camp was struck early and pitched again in the early afternoon. The column was already beginning to straggle and often different contingents made separate camps for the night. There was rising mortality. Within a week of arriving at Banana nine of the wangwana had died, most of them from Nelson's company - a fact which Stanley attributed to their having been located near the boilers on the Madura. Stanley himself was very ill, being attacked by both diarrhoea and bilious fever. Two officers established themselves in his estimation at this time, surgeon Parke by his assiduous attentions and Jephson by jumping into a stream to guide the bearers of the hammock containing the prostrate expedition chief.

On 28th March the column ran into a caravan headed by Herbert Ward, whom Stanley had recruited for Congo service in 1884. After three years in the Congo State Ward was preparing to leave for Europe when he heard of the Emin Pasha expedition from the missionary Charles Ingham. Knowing of the shortage of porters, he collected 300 men and intersected Stanley's party, offering to place the porters at Stanley's service provided he himself was taken on. His account of the meeting provides a graphic account of the Emin Relief expedition on the march:

I had broken camp early one morning, and was marching rapidly along ahead of my caravan, when in the distance coming over the brow of a hill I saw a tall Sudanese soldier bearing Gordon Bennett's yacht flag. Behind him, astride of a fine henna-stained mule, whose silver-plated strappings shone in the morning sun, was Henry M. Stanley, attired in his famous African costume. Following immediately in the rear were his personal servants, Somalis with their curious braided waistcoats and white robes. Then came Zanzibaris with their blankets, water-bottles, ammunition belts and guns. Stalwart Sudanese soldiers with dark-hooded coats, their rifles on their backs, and innumerable straps and leather belts around their bodies; and Zanzibari porters bearing iron-bound boxes of ammunition, to which were fastened axes and shovels as well as their little bundles of clothing, which were rolled up in coarse sandy-coloured blankets ... At one point a steel whale-boat was being carried in sections, suspended from poles which were each borne by four men; donkeys heavily laden with sacks of rice were next met with, and a little further on the women of Tippoo-Tib's harem, their faces partly concealed and their bodies draped in gaudily- covered cloths; then at intervals along the line of march an English officer with whom, of course, I exchanged friendly salutations; then several large-horned African goats, driven by saucy little Zanzibari boys. A short distance further on, an abrupt turn of the narrow footpath brought into view the dignified form of the renowned Tippoo-Tib, as he strolled along majestically in his flowing Arab robes of dazzling whiteness, and carrying over left shoulder a richly-decorated sabre, which was an emblem of his office conferred on him by H. H. the Sultan of Zanzibar.

Yet this impressive parade masked an ever-escalating brutality. On 3 April there was another fight between the Sudanese and the wangwana. The Zanzibaris were having to lug 65 pounds of ammunition, four days' rations of rice and their own kit, while the haughty Sudanese carried their rifles only. While the wangwana stuck to their task stoically, the Sudanese were always complaining. To avoid further conflicts Stanley had to order Barttelot to keep his Sudanese a day's march ahead of the Zanzibaris. He was already regretting having brought the Sudanese along. They were meant to be an earnest of Egypt's intentions towards Emin and his garrison, but nobody had warned Stanley how pig-headed and contumacious they were.

Problems with the Sudanese continued. At Banza Mateka mission station, run by Mr and Mrs Richards (two of the few Congo missionaries for whom Stanley had any time), and again at Lukungu station, four days' rations of potatoes, bananas, Indian corn and palm nuts had been assembled for the expedition, but the Sudanese simply gorged their supplies, then threatened to desert if they were not given more food.

Stanley often pondered what his position would be if the Sudanese actually did desert en masse, but meanwhile he had discipline problems on all sides, not just involving the unruly men of the Sudan. The wangwana came to him with complaints that Nelson was striking them crippling blows on the legs and shins; Stanley had to reprimand Nelson. But Stanley employed different standards according to whether it was he or his officers who did the chastising. Barttelot recorded with relish:

'Stanley as rearguard got on Ai. He flogged loafers and they all kicked amazingly.' Parke, usually uncritical of Stanley, confirmed that he speeded up the daily rate of march by flogging loiterers. Jameson, who had originally regarded beating porters as not fit work for white men, changed his tune after a while and recorded this verdict on Stanley's flagellation exploits in the rearguard: 'How he did lay his stick about the lazy ones, and the Somali whacked away too! It was a sight for sore eyes to see the lame, sick, halt and the blind running with their loads as if they were feathers; and I was delighted to see some of my men catch it hot, after I had been told by Mr Stanley himself not to strike them.'

But predictably the worst offenders against Stanley's disciplinary code were always the Sudanese, and it was on this issue that Stanley first came into serious conflict with Barttelot. On 5 April one of the Sudanese soldiers came to Stanley to show him a black eye - the effect of a punch from the Major. Stanley sent for Barttelot and rebuked him. The Major did not deny the punch but said he was taking his cue from Stanley. 'I have seen you do it.'

Stanley glared at him for a moment, until he was satisfied that the response was spontaneous and not a calculated piece of insolence. Then he gave Barttelot a lecture on the difference between his 'exemplary' violence and the Major's gratuitous brutality. He pointed out that his own punishments were always public, proclaimed and explained: 'I sometimes affect a great rage, or I taunt them with irony but I don't pitch into them like a pugilist. Besides, I speak their dialect perfectly. I give them notice that I am coming and if they don't scamper I call out to their headmen to start them. There is method in what I do, and no scars are left.'

Barttelot listened to the homily in silence, but there was something about his 'body language' Stanley did not care for. He decided to seek an early pretext to take the Major down a peg or two. Meanwhile Stanley took out his anger on another target. This time it was Bonny, who had been out of favour ever since the Baruti/Tower of London incident. On the pretext that Bonny's marching was sloppy and mechanical, Stanley humiliated him in front of his charges by calling out: 'Hello, Bonny, wake up, my son. You will mistake the mouth of a hippopotamus for a doorway if you go on nodding in that way.'

On 8 April the Sudanese again threatened mutiny. Stanley warned them that if they deserted, he would give the order in the country around that these were Bula Matari's enemies and should be shot on sight. When the Syrian Assas Farran claimed to be exempt from the daily chores imposed on the Sudanese, Stanley dubbed him ringleader of the troubles and threatened to spit him with a bayonet. In an attempt to pour oil on troubled waters, Barttelot apologised to Stanley for the problems the Sudanese were causing, but Stanley rounded on him and said all was the fault of the Major's poor leadership. If he had to shoot the Sudanese for desertion, he, Stanley, would see to it that Barttelot's name was blackened with Lord Wolseley. When Barttelot blazed defiance at this threat, Stanley picked out the laziest of the Sudanese and ordered the Major to take them on ahead to Leopoldville by forced marches, threatening dire sanctions if they lost a single load. The order was a clear, calculated act of vindictiveness, as judicious onlookers admitted.

The nightmare continued. By mid-April the expedition was sustaining losses on every day's march: from illness, desertion, and pilfering of rifles, ammunition and stores. Fever was cutting a swathe through the remaining Sudanese, and Hoffmann was delirious with it. The Sudanese were both skeletal in appearance and beyond the control of their officers; only the fear of Stanley drove them on. When a third box of Remington ammunition was lost in Parke's company, Stanley had to reprimand Parke, one of his favourites. Salim bin Masoud gave further evidence of fractiousness by an altercation with Jephson (he had already clashed with Stairs) in the course of which Jephson threatened to throw the Arab into the river. Tippu Tip intervened to silence his refractory subordinate but then complained to Stanley of Jephson's behaviour. When Stanley called Jephson in for a talking-to, he in turn did not respond well to his leader's admonitions.

On top of all this came a letter from Liebrechts at Leopoldville, which showed how deeply the EPRE committee had been gulled by Leopold. There was also a grudging missive from Bendey about the loan of the Peace, whose tone Stanley bitterly resented after all he had done for his mission. The stress of all this found Stanley at his most irrational and punitive. First he humiliated Jameson in front of his men, in the process making him the victim of the most barefaced duplicity. Stanley had ordered Jameson, over his protests, to flog on the sick. When one of the chiefs fell ill on the march, Jameson urged him on, whereat Stanley rushed up with surgeon Parke and proceeded to play the part of the concerned, compassionate leader as against Jameson's brute. It was a frequent Stanley ploy on this expedition to give secret orders to his officers to act in a draconian way, then to intervene himself in compassionate guise as the angel to their devil; if necessary, Stanley would take the wangwand's side against his own officers, even when they had merely faithfully carried out his orders. This was pathology itself: Stanley was determined there would be no Frank Pococks, with a special relationship with the men of Zanzibar, on this expedition.

18 April was a black day even on this dark-limned trek. Three separate incidents revealed Stanley at the very limits of rationality. When yet another box of ammunition went missing. Stanley arbitrarily identified one of the porters as the culprit and gave him a hundred lashes. Even while he was being beaten, the man protested that his ammunition box was in camp, which later was proved to be the case. Jephson remarked cryptically: 'It was rather an extreme measure but he knows best what to do, I suppose.' Stanley then proceeded to chain and padlock all the chiefs or porters together, and lectured the trussed wangwana on how such ammunition losses in 1877 would have meant their death by firing squad. Seeing Jameson looking on disapprovingly, Stanley warned him that if any more such losses occurred, Jameson would be dismissed. Jameson went to Stanley's tent afterwards and protested bitterly about this censure.

Next Stanley summoned Jephson to his presence and warned him that he would not allow the expedition to be jeopardised through the shortcomings of its officers. He was disgusted with his officers' racialism and their talk of 'niggers' and so on. But if he made Jephson the official recipient of the proof of his toughness, it was Baruti who (literally) received the sharp end that day. When Hoffmann came in to tell his employer that Baruti could not be found to carry the master's lunch basket, Stanley ordered the boy found and flogged. Baruti, who had already in London demonstrated his martial spirit, and was now a strapping lad of fifteen, tried to resist the flogging, whereat Stanley took out his hunting knife and threatened to rip him up if he did not submit to his punishment. Stanley then laid on with the whip himself.

On 20 April the main column caught up with Barttelot's tardy Sudanese. Disgusted at their slow progress, Stanley ordered them to halt and to forgo the privilege of marching a day ahead of the porters. On the other hand, he warned Barttelot that he would be held personally responsible for any fisticuffs between the Sudanese and the wangwana. At this Barttelot fell into a towering rage. Two men with volcanic tempers were glowering at each other but, as ever, Stanley could see just one point of view: 'The Major's temper is not improving, and if he's thwarted in the least, he gets extremely saucy. One of these days I shall have to put a bridle on his fluent tongue, for an outburst of bad temper is sure to provoke, in the end, something similar in others if too oft indulged.' Barttelot tried to strike back at the leader by initiating a whispering campaign. When Stanley accused his officers of opening the Fortnum and Mason's box, Barttelot noised it about that this was to mask the fact that Stanley was surreptitiously helping himself to the luxury goods.

At last, on 21 April, the month-long ordeal was over and the expedition trooped despondently into Leopoldville. For the last six days of the march Stanley had enjoyed the company of a man later to become both famous and infamous: Roger Casement. Casement, then aged twenty-three, was in Congo service as superintendent of the boiler irons for the steamer Florida. 'He is a good specimen of the capable Englishman,' noted Stanley. But the expedition itself already presented a tatterdemalion picture: the losses from death, desertion, pilfering and wastage had been severe. The strong liquor imbibed at Lukunga station came close to killing some of the white men. Hoffmann had had three attacks of fever in a month, but with no chance to convalesce - since his master halted for the illness of no man save himself - he had kept himself going with doses of quinine so strong that he was temporarily struck deaf.

Nevertheless, Stanley was determined to enter Leopoldville in heroic style. He mounted his Europeans on the fine Muscat donkeys they had brought from Zanzibar and had Tippu Tip march at his side, resplendent in a white fez and yellow djoho. He belittled his heavy losses by saying that if he had taken the eastern route to Wadelai, he would already have lost over a hundred men through death, sickness or desertion.

But what he found in Leopoldville appalled him. The extent of Leopold's perfidy became clear. His much-trumpeted 'help' was revealed as a sham. There were no steamers to take the expedition on upriver. No preparations had been made, even though Leopold had insisted on the Congo route. Even worse, famine was raging throughout the Stanley Pool area. There was adequate food for only about one-third of the expeditionary force. Food shortages were partly a result of the Association's already growing reputation for brutality which had driven many of the indigenous food producers into the bush. But they were also due to the fecklessness of the missionaries who had not planted a single crop of bananas, rice or maize since Stanley had been in Leopoldville three years earlier, despite the fertility of the soil; they existed on hippo meat and their motto seemed to be 'Let be everything - struggle no longer.'

There was a pressing need for the expedition to get out of the Stanley Pool orbit and into the Upper Congo where they could reasonably hope for more abundant food supplies. This meant requisitioning the available shipping in Leopoldville and environs. Accordingly, Stanley's first call was on Bentley of the Baptist Missionary Society to get final agreement to hiring the Peace. When Bentley raised difficulties on grounds of deficient parts for the steamer, Stanley became angry. Suspecting that the missionaries had deliberately sabotaged the craft so as not to have to lend it, he raged at Bentley: 'If any disaster befell the expedition through the delay, it would be laid to the account of the Baptist Missionary Society.'

The Baptist Missionaries had always supported Stanley. If they were reluctant to charter their steamer, how much more resistant would the Livingstone Inland Mission be, for this society had always opposed Stanley and held itself aloof from all his endeavours. Since the end of 1884 the LIM had had its own steamer Henry Reed at Stanley Pool, a rival to the Peace of the BMS. It was this ship that Stanley was now determined to get his hands on. But Dr Sims and Mr Billington proved tough adversaries. When Barttelot and Jephson visited them to negotiate for the loan of the Henry Reed, Billington claimed that the ship needed to be painted and that in any case he needed it to go downstream, as he was to be married shortly. Sims tried to negotiate a quid pro quo whereby he would be allowed to accompany the expedition to Stanley Falls to set up a mission there. When this was refused, both men flatly turned down the request. Billington added insult to injury by claiming that he had consulted the Bible and found therein an injunction not to assist the Emin expedition.

Stanley's anger came bursting out of every fissure at this response. He rehearsed the many favours he had done the LIM. In 1881 he had saved their missionaries Clarke and Lanceley from starvation. Again, in 1883 Sims, after trying vainly to negotiate on his own account with the Stanley Pool chiefs, approached Stanley for an LIM site, which was granted. In 1884 he extended the grounds belonging to that mission and even gave permission for a branch mission at Equator station. Now he asked a favour from them, this was how it was requited! All his bitterness came pouring out: 'Mr Billington was only hungering after the carnal pleasures of marriage with a person whom he never saw before . . . what cantankerous, ungrateful people these missionaries are!'

On the evening of 22 April Stanley, together with Jephson and Barttelot, dined with governor Liebrechts. Patiently Stanley explained his position to Liebrechts and put him in the picture on the new Brussels policy towards Tippu Tip. He made the point forcefully to Liebrechts that if his expedition was forced to stay at the Pool for lack of river transport, he could not guarantee their good behaviour. He also hinted darkly that if necessary he would seize the steamers by force and defy the Congo State to oppose his 800 Remington-wielding men. Liebrechts was in a peculiarly difficult position. He knew that Leopold was in fact double-crossing Stanley, since the King, foreseeing that Stanley might try to commandeer Henry Reed, had ordered Valcke to take the ship on an exploration of the Ubangi, to pre-empt its use by the Emin expedition. As so often, Stanley's hard-driving methods meant that he was on the spot before the order could be implemented. But Liebrechts also knew that Stanley was well capable of carrying out his threat. Also, it was clear that total starvation would soon overtake Leopoldville if this huge force was allowed to remain.

Stanley left Liebrechts' table confident that he had sold his message well: 'I think Liebrechts is on our side but we shall see.' Next morning he sent him an official letter, formally requesting the requisitioning of the Peace, Henry Reed and Florida, so as to remove the threat of famine and disorder from Leopoldville; he was willing to pay double the normal hiring rate (i.e. £100 per month). Liebrechts responded swiftly to this and signed the necessary order. Billington responded to this by removing the valves and pistons of the Henry Reed but, unluckily for him, one of the locals found them and informed Stanley.

The seizure of the missionary steamers was a typical example of Stanley's ruthlessness and iron resolve. Later Liebrechts tried to pretend that the decision was forced on him by Stanley, but Rose Troup, who witnessed all the negotiations, quite correctly pointed out that it was not possible for the governor to shirk responsibility for his own signature. Nevertheless the boldness of his action shook the protocol-minded European residents of Leopoldville. So alarmed were the missionaries that Bentley asked the British consul at Loanda to register the Peace so that thenceforth they could invoke British protection against requisitioning. Stanley smirked in triumph and wrote in heavy irony: 'Billington can now proceed to marry his bride with the consciousness that in his absence the mission is making money.' He sealed his triumph with an acidulous letter to The Times inveighing against 'ingrates' among the missionaries. Billington, though, was predictably heartbroken: 'If it is possible to love an inanimate object, I love the Henry Reed. And now to think she should be committed to the hands of such ruthless "ne'er do wells" and become the habitation of whoremongers and harlots.'

Stanley additionally secured the Florida - a vessel belonging to the Sanford Exploring Expedition, which Sanford against Stanley's advice had set up in December 1886 in disillusionment with Leopold; this seizure too was controversial, and when Stanley later damaged the Florida, Sanford sued his erstwhile comrades in the EPRE committee. The proximate cause of Stanley's getting his hands on Florida was that it was in the charge of his old friend Swinburne at Kinshassa. Its acquisition meant he had a viable flotilla at last. He invited Casement to a champagne breakfast to celebrate the launching of the Florida. The explorer sat on an old camp chair outside a hut, his bronzed features lit up by the bright, piercing eyes. They ate cold roast fowl, brown ship's biscuit and milk less tea. Then Stanley opened the champagne and puffed contentedly on his cigar. A little later at Kinshassa the two men met up again, and Casement rather boldly asked Stanley if it was possible for a white man to travel unarmed through Africa, as Caillie had done in North Africa in the 1820s. Stanley was, as ever, scathing about such hypothetical and counter-factuals: 'You might perform the journey from Matadi to the Pool on stilts, Mr Casement, and I have no doubt you could accomplish the remainder of the distance on your head if you liked to devote enough time to it, but what good you would derive from it, or anyone else, when you emerged at Zanzibar, I don't really know.'

Tippu Tip meanwhile was finding profitable employment in quizzing

Ngalyema about the ivory trade of the Central Congo. Ngalyema greeted his 'brother' Bula Matari effusively, but his long list of complaints about the increasing savagery of the white men at the Pool bored Stanley; he was glad to hand the chieftain over to Tippu.

On 25 April Stanley struck camp and marched overland to Kinshassa, after holding a muster that revealed a loss of fifty-seven men, thirty-eight Remingtons and 50 per cent of their implements (axes, spades, shovels, etc.) during the twenty-eight-day march on the Lower Congo. Stanley rationalised this by claiming that most of the losses accrued from bounty-jumping, and that the desertion rate would have been many times greater on the eastern route.

While Barttelot and Parke with 153 men took the one officially authorised steamer, the Stanley, upriver, at Kinshassa the leader supervised the overhaul of the Florida. Stanley was still in sour mood, angry that his chief ship's engineer was ill with fever: 'It is hard lines for me when I have paid him wages from London to Leopoldville and a first class passage, drawing four months' pay for nothing and the first day he is wanted, he falls ill.' But Casement, noticing that the dog Randy's tail was docked, asked what had befallen him and received a bizarre tale. Tired of the Spartan fare on the slog to Leopoldville, Stanley one night cut off the dog's tail and made soup out of it for him and Nelson. They then served up the cooked tail for Randy to eat, and the fox terrier demolished his own tail in short order!

At last, on 1st May, the flotilla was ready to start upriver. With three commandeered ships under his aegis, Stanley allowed himself to feel slight confidence. The feeling was reinforced by a conviction that nature and the elements were on his side. Although it was the rainy season, there was fine weather every morning and the rain, as if on cue, began to fall only at around 2 p.m. The river was neither too high nor too low, tornadoes occurred solely in the evenings when they were safely moored. Even the riverside pests, mosquitoes, gadflies, tsetses, crocodiles and hippos, did not seem so vicious as on previous occasions. The only minor hitch was that they had to return to Leopoldville for repairs to the Peace's boilers and rudder, which continued to give them trouble.

On 5th May they caught up with Parke and Barttelot at Mswata; they had arrived four days earlier to lay in a store of provisions. There was more trouble with the Peace and from 7 to 10th May additionally they had to carry out extensive repairs on the Stanley. But when the flotilla got under way, it made an impressive sight. First came the Henry Reed, carrying fifty men and a hundred loads and towing two barges containing another fifty men. Next in line was the Stanley, carrying 160 men, 400 loads and six donkeys, and towing the Florida, which contained 160 men, a hundred loads, and six donkeys. Bringing up the rear was the Peace, with fifty men, a hundred loads, towing two barges with thirty-five men. All in all there were 590 men, 700 loads and twelve donkeys. Yet even this armada did not exhaust the complement of expeditionary materiel and manpower.

Stanley had to leave two depots of stores and men behind. The first, to his intense chagrin, was left in charge of Rose Troup. The second, under Ward and Bonny, was at Bolobo station.

After fattening up on the abundant food at Bolobo station, where he left the least healthy of his men, Stanley took the flotilla on to Equator Station, where he met up with another of his old favourites, E. J. Glave, and Alphonse Vangele. But just before they arrived at Equator an incident had occurred which seemed to cast doubt on the entire future of the Emin project.

By the common consent of all who participated in the expedition, a pall of gloom hung over the flotilla as it slowly beat up the Congo. The wangwana could not always be prevented from raiding villages, looting and pillaging. But to prevent this meant flogging and beating, for which many of the officers had no heart. To make matters worse, no word of encouragement or praise ever emanated from Stanley's lips. He had a talent for always finding something to criticise, for ignoring ninety-nine good things to fasten on the one bad one. Barttelot testified: 'the harder we worked, the glummer Stanley looked. After a long march, no smile from him or word of any sort, except to say, "You have lost a box" or some sneer of that sort.' Stanley also consistently sided with the Africans against their officers, while reserving the right to mete out condign punishment to any wangwana who displeased him. He was domineering and autocratic and always took his meals alone in his own tent at night. He had none of the qualities of true leadership, of inspiring men to an esprit de corps. No one would ever have called him with affection, as Shackleton's men called their leader, 'the boss'.

Stanley's version of this state of affairs was that since most quarrels started from trivial causes - because people in close confinement got on each other's nerves - the best policy for himself was to eliminate the possible triggers. As for failure to praise, Stanley made a virtue of this and claimed that with professionals praise was unnecessary. But these protestations masked the fact that Stanley shunned intimacy, never had any close friends, and found it next to impossible to relate to another human being as an equal. The instinct to dominate was too strong. Significantly, of all his officers he got on best with Parke, a physician of some ingenuity in whom there was a hard core of professionalism for Stanley to respect. On the other hand, Parke was temperamentally a respecter of authority, any authority. Stanley was the leader, and for Parke that was good enough. His account of his time with Stanley is Panglossian in tone and slides over some of the more unsavoury incidents on the expedition with an enviable myopic facility.

Stanley's jottings on his officers' qualities, as the flotilla continued on the Upper Congo voyage, are most revealing of his state of mind. He saw clearly that none of them had a particle of affection for him, but they had by and large given him prompt and implicit obedience, which was what he wanted most. 'I can get love any time I ask for it, but in this daily struggle against all forms of death, it is the confidence that whatever strength there may be in my force, it is mine to wield, direct and guide, when and how it is needed, and on the instant.'

Nelson he found too querulous and 'would gladly add violence to a talk'. His one reservation about Parke was that he was too much under Nelson's influence. At this stage he had a warm feeling for Stairs, though he noted his acerbity and ability to wound with a telling word. Bonny was largely a write-off in Stanley's mind; it had been a grievous mistake to let himself be imposed on by the man's pleadings. Barttelot was suffering from the culture shock of Africa and the conviction that there was a war brewing between England and Russia, which he would miss through this adventure with the 'niggers'. As for Jephson, Stanley's attitude at this stage was amused contempt: 'Were I to open even a chink for jaw I think we should soon become a befuddled debating society. Jephson, I know, is chock full of effervescent gabble which if I were to uncork would be my death.'

These comments help to illuminate the acrimonious clashes that came to a head as the flotilla neared Equator. At Mswata on 5th May one of the best wangwana headmen came to complain that Barttelot had taken to prodding 'malingerers' with a spiked stick and showed the wounds he himself had sustained. Stanley immediately sent for Barttelot and remonstrated with him. Stung by the criticism, Barttelot poured out a flood of bitterness about the tasks he was expected to perform on the expedition. Stanley tried to sidestep the altercation by remarking that there were better ways of punishing a man than poking at him with a spiked stick, which could kill or disable. When Barttelot wanted to argue the point, Stanley fixed him with one of the steely glares that had faced down Ngalyema, Mata Buiki and a dozen others. 'Let us drop the subject right here,' Stanley said icily. 'I have said my say.'

A week later Stanley confided to Stairs that he was thinking of leaving behind a Rear Column when he got to the Aruwimi River. At Leopoldville Stanley had told Liebrechts that he had not yet decided between three routes to Wadelai: via the Oubangi-Welle; via Stanley Falls and the Mboura; or up the Aruwimi. But in fact all along he had favoured the Aruwimi approach; he simply wanted to play his cards close to his chest and keep the Congo State guessing. The question was, who should command the Rear Column? Stanley wanted Stairs but he also intended to leave Barttelot behind as a punishment for his unsatisfactory behaviour. Stairs, reasonably enough, pointed out that he, an army lieutenant, could not command a major, whatever Stanley's wishes. Very well, asked Stanley, who will stay with Barttelot? You? Stairs answered firmly that he would rather be sent home. Jephson, then? No, said Stairs, there would be a furious row within twenty-four hours. Who then? Stairs recommended leaving Jameson as Barttelot's second-in-command, assisted by Bonny; Ward and Rose Troup would bring their contingents up to base camp later, when the Stanley was sent downstream to fetch them.

This seemed good advice to Stanley. Next day he told Barttelot of his decision. The Major, naturally, was much cast down and read the move, correctly, as punishment. Stanley tried to sugar the pill by saying that the halt at base camp would not last long - only until Tippu Tip supplied the promised porters. But Barttelot was secretly very angry. It was clear to him that he and Jameson were personae non gratae: 'it is my belief, if he thought he could get rid of us, he would; he sticks at nothing.'

Yet on 20th May, when the most serious breakdown in communication yet between Stanley and his officers took place, Barttelot found himself in the unusual role of peacemaker. The problem arose from gross indiscipline on the 15th when both Sudanese and Zanzibaris ran amok and looted a village about 12 miles north of Bolobo. Jephson and Stairs, hitherto among Stanley's favourites, began to confiscate all the goods they could identify as looted. When the wangwana resisted this 'expropriation', Jephson lost his temper at their impudence and hurled some of their food and bedding overboard. Since this happened on the Stanley, the leader summoned Jephson and Stairs to give an account of themselves. A bizarre altercation then took place at voice-tops, since Stanley was standing on the deck of the Peace, calling out to his two officers on shore.

Stanley began by asking Stairs for his version. Stairs in some exasperation pointed out that he and Jephson were forever having to beat back the Zanzibaris from looting villages; this particular incident was only one of several. Stanley then repeated the wangwanals charges of routine and gratuitous violence. At this Stairs lost patience: 'Oh well, if you like to believe them in preference to what I say, you are welcome to do so. You will only be acting according to your custom.' Stanley then called to Parke to witness the sequel. He called Jephson forward. Jephson approached the bank with pallid face and blazing eyes.

Stanley bawled out impatiently to Jephson to give his side of the story. Jephson yelled back at him. 'You are not to shout at me in that way, sir!' At this Stanley exploded and he railed at Jephson. 'You goddam son of a sea-cook! You damned ass, you're tired of me, of the expedition, and of my men. Go into the bush, get, I've done with you. And you too, Lieutenant Stairs, you and I will part today; you're tired of me, sir, I can see. Get away into the bush!' Next Stanley boomed out to the wangwana that if either Stairs or Jephson gave another order, they were to be tied to trees. Seeing the look of contempt on Jephson's face, Stanley then

completely lost control. 'If you want to fight, goddam you, I'll give you a bellyful. If I were only where you are, I'd go for you. It's lucky for you I am where I am, you goddam impudent puppy.'

This torrent of rage can be seen as mixture of stress, anxiety, fear of failure, unconscious resentment of Jephson's 'silver spoon' and paranoid delusion, though Stanley, typically, rationalised it as a case of his officers 'trying it on'. But he was clearly shaken by his own over-reaction, for when Barttelot came to see him around noon to ask if the decision about Jephson and Stairs was irrevocable, Stanley hesitated and said: 'As regards myself it is.' Barttelot thought he detected a measure of bluster in the words and pressed on with his self-appointed task as mediator. Stanley asked him to sit down, then launched into self-justification. First of all, he wished to say that nobody was indispensable, except Parke, and if anyone wished to join the dismissed duo, he was free to do so. All he was trying to do was to train a new generation of explorers to take over from him, since he himself was getting old. He took the opportunity to criticise his officers sharply; they did not know the country or the language, knew nothing of man management and relied on violence alone; but for the presence of Bula Matari the expedition would already have disintegrated.

Calmly and uncharacteristically, Barttelot rolled with the punches. When Stanley insisted that the confrontation with Stairs and Jephson had been a 'set-up', Barttelot denied that there were any cabals and assured him that Jephson and Stairs both deeply regretted what had happened. In that case, snapped Stanley, they should come and apologise. Barttelot departed, and a little later Jephson and Stairs came to apologise. Stanley 'magnanimously' reinstated them and summoned the headmen of the wangwana to tell them that the 'little masters' were once again in command and that their policy on looting must be heeded. Writing up the incident that night in his journal, Stanley recorded surprise at Barttelot's admirably statesmanlike behaviour; he was the very last person Stanley would have imagined as a mediator. He sensed, too, that he himself by contrast had appeared to disadvantage.

His suspicions were certainly shared by his officers, all of whom were disgusted that Stairs and Jephson had been obliged to apologise for a fiasco that was entirely of Stanley's making. Jameson recorded his verdict in stupefied incredulity.

'I had no idea until today what an extremely dangerous man Stanley was. Could there be anything more inciting to mutiny than what he had told the Zanzibaris? He forgets one thing, however: that if they dared to lift a hand to one of us, there would be a terrible lot of them shot, which would rather weaken his expedition. It is a curious fact, when one thinks over it, that the very men who complained to Mr Stanley ought, by his own orders, issued when we left the Pool, to have been severely flogged.' Barttelot concurred with this estimate. 'The missionaries, two of them, who heard the disturbance, and the captain and engineer of the Peace, never heard such language or witnessed such a disgraceful scene before. I believe this is Stanley's method of carrying on in Central Africa, but I had judged him pretty well before, and was not surprised so much at his conduct.'

At Equator station Stanley found more to excite his contempt, not just the missionaries from the LIM but Vangele's taste for administration over exploration. When Stanley proposed to him an exploration of the Welle, Vangele reacted coolly. Stanley recorded scornfully in his journal: 'that is the way with most men. They crave for chances of distinction. The opportunity comes and they turn their heads away. It is too perilous a job! Well, nothing great was ever achieved without braving danger, or incurring trouble and pains.'

By 30th May the expedition was at Bangala station, 547 miles above Leopoldville, 892 miles from the Atlantic, with just 488 more miles to the planned base camp at Aruwimi rapids. After the initial problems with the Peace, including an occasion when Stanley gashed her forward section by running her on to a reef, the steamers had settled down to a slow chug, which involved huge woodcutting details at night for fuel, In the end the engineer on the Peace got her into effective running order by capping the upper safety valve so as to stop steam escaping. But Stanley was worried that he was now badly behind schedule. He had expected the entire expedition to be completed by December 1887, within the budget of £20,000 even though many in Britain had warned that he was being absurdly sanguine in such an estimate. He claimed in Cairo that he could get to Wadelai via the Congo in 157 days from Zanzibar, yet already a hundred of those days had passed. Even if he got to the Aruwimi rapids in sixteen days, he would still be 360 miles from Lake Albert - leaving him an average of 12 miles' marching a day to reach his target on time, which he frankly conceded was impossible.

It was time for some sober, realistic calculations and Bangala, with its ample food supplies, was a good place for reflections and lucubration. Van Kerkhoven, the station chief, was away but Baert, his deputy, entertained them liberally. Stanley marvelled at the transformation of Bangala in ten years. Cannibalism, the ordeal by poison and the sacrifice of slaves to a dead chief were all things of the past, and Stanley could comfort himself with the thought that he had been Providence's chosen agent to bring light into such darkness. It was in eupeptic spirits that he sat down with Tippu Tip and Barttelot to plan the next stage of the expedition.

The gist of Stanley's talk with Tippu Tip concerned the number of porters needed to bring the cache of ivory out of Equatoria and the exact logistics of this - dotting the 'i's and crossing the 't's of their Zanzibar agreement. Barttelot received orders to accompany Tippu to Stanley Falls to supervise his formal induction as governor and to bring back the first of the porters. Stanley himself would set up base camp at Yambuya, 96 miles up the Aruwimi past its confluence with the Congo, where the Aruwimi cataracts began.

Stanley's voyage to Yambuya was accomplished without incident and he arrived at the village on 15th June. At the Aruwimi confluence Baruti was reunited with his kinsfolk among the Soko. On board the Peace he called out to one of the tribesmen milling around in canoes that he was the youth's brother. The young man was sceptical until Baruti told him that he had a bite mark on his arm under the tattoo where he had been mauled by a crocodile when a little boy. The two brothers then embraced heartily. Stanley commented: 'Some say the African has no love, no gratitude, no affection, but there is a sight that speaks for itself.'

On 16th June, at river journey's end, Stanley took his flotilla across to the south bank of the Aruwimi and asked permission to billet in the village of Yambuya. The tribesmen were reluctant and a palaver began. But when he seemed to be getting nowhere after a couple of hours. Stanley lost patience and ordered a forced occupation of the village. The landing of the armed rvangwana was accompanied by a cacophony from the steamship whistles, designed to inspire fear. When the defenders broke and fled, Stanley, now mindful of public opinion in England, rewrote the incident so as to make it appear that the locals were overawed by the steamer whistles alone.

Stanley next converted the abandoned village into a heavily fortified camp, surrounded by a ditch and a double wooden palisade. He fretted about the fact that he was eight days behind schedule, 'all owing to the wretched little steamer the Peace' and its allegedly incompetent crew and engineer. Naturally he did not mention that he had been in error by underestimating the length of time the expedition would take or that he himself had caused a major delay near Bolobo by running the steamer on to a reef. But he did recognise that failure to conciliate the local Tungu peoples put their future food supply at risk and he dreaded to think what kind of a fist Barttelot would make of conciliating fractious tribesmen. It seemed the last straw when his protégé Baruti decamped with two Winchesters."

Nelson and Jephson were kept busy collecting wood to fuel the Stanley and Florida for the return trip, to pick up Rose Troup, Ward, Bonny and their contingents. Parke lost caste in the leader's eyes by telling a story which revealed that he was incapable of remembering the simplest orders - an ominous sign. But most of all, as the days slipped by and there was no word from Barttelot, Stanley began to fear that he might have been the victim of treachery by Tippu Tip at Stanley Falls. Or else, the Major's hot temper - epitomised by an infamous pistol-whipping of a mutinous Somali during the Gordon relief expedition - had erupted and caused an armed clash with the Arabs and Manyema at the Falls."

But if there had been any treachery, it was on Stanley's side. Yet again Tippu Tip had allowed himself to be duped. His disenchantment began immediately on arrival at Stanley Falls. There was a serious clash with the local tribesmen. Tippu called on Barttelot to help him put a defiant village to the torch. Barttelot replied that he had strict orders from Stanley not to become involved in quarrels between blacks and Arabs."This angered Tippu, but his rage grew when he asked for the supplies of gunpowder Stanley had promised him for the arming of his men. Barttelot said he had none; all the powder had been left with Rose Troup at Kinshassa. This was a clear breach of the agreement with Stanley. He put it to Barttelot that since there was no powder at the Falls, and his men were already hard put to defend themselves against hostiles, how could they possibly come up and join Barttelot and the Rear Column at Yambuya? That was a practical point; the morality of 'no powder, therefore no porters' spoke for itself."

There was yet another aspect to Stanley's failure to keep his side of the bargain. There was already considerable resistance among the Manyema to the idea of helping Stanley and the Emin expedition. Tippu's deal with

Stanley was as fiercely criticised by his own people as a 'sell-out' to the Europeans as it had been in Europe on the grounds of its being a Faustian compact with a slaver. Said bin Habib, the local magnate, refused to recall his raiding parties at Tippu's request when the Arab tried faithfully to implement the terms of his governorship."Tippu could perhaps have made his writ run if he had brought the gunpowder but failure to do so seriously dented his credibility with the Manyema. In despair at his humiliation Tippu later threatened to return to Leopoldville for his powder, bill Stanley and return with the ordnance, or else return to Zanzibar in disgust if the material was not handed over. Tippu was particularly incensed at Stanley's duplicity, for he had noticed all the way along the route to Stanley Pool how cheap gunpowder was; he could have bought any amount on his own account. But on the Upper Congo it was scarce and if he tried to obtain some immediately from Stanley at Yambuya, he knew that the explorer would try to drive a sky-high bargain for its sale.

If the failure to give Tippu his gunpowder was the hinge on which the entire fate of the Rear Column turned - and Stanley must have known that without it Tippu would not meet his side of the deal and send porters - whatever possessed Stanley to act in such a self-destructive way? Here we enter the world of what Leopold liked to refer to so glibly as haute politique. Stanley knew very well that if he gave Tippu Tip the gunpowder, he himself would fall from grace in the Belgian monarch's eyes, as it would postpone the day of reckoning between the Belgians and the Congo Arabs. On the other hand, if he failed to deliver the powder and thus fell foul of Tippu Tip, the Rear Column would be doomed to impotence. The fiasco that later attended the Rear Column was, then, a direct result of Stanley's duplicity, of his attempt to have his cake and eat it. Stanley knew this very well, but later tried to cover his tracks so that the finger of indictment could not point back to him.

Barttelot made his way back to Yambuya in some consternation, angry that Stanley's explicit orders had wrong footed him with Tippu. He was even angrier when he learned from his brother officers that Stanley had been worrying about his safety; he took that as a slur on his military abilities. But Stanley trumped his ace by working himself into a fine lather over the fact that Tippu would not perform on a promise; in Stanley's world it was perfectly permissible for him to demand 600 porters now while Tippu waited for ever for his powder. Stanley's frustration was increased by the realisation that his fears about the food supply were beginning to be borne out; for six days before Barttelot's arrival, Stanley and his officers had had nothing to eat except rice, beans and manioc.

A pall of gloom hung over the base camp. Iskander, one of the two Syrians, died of exhaustion following repeated attacks of malarial fever. While the Peace and the Henry Reed were prepared for departure, Stanley sat down with Barttelot to brief him on his duties while the Advance Column was away. He stressed that the camp would have to be well defended at all times, for there was a potential threat from the Arabs as well as the Tungu. He cautioned the Major against undue pugnacity, but the interview on 25th June (lasting from 2 to 4 p.m.) did not impress Stanley with his intellectual qualities.

But there was more to be said for Barttelot's position than Stanley allowed. Again and again the Major pressed him about Tippu Tip's reliability. Stanley obliquely hinted that that was why he had not supplied him with gunpowder, keeping his own arrangements with Leopold right out of the conversation. He reverted to his original itinerary, as agreed in London. A quick dash to Lake Albert would lead to a meeting with Emin about the end of July or a little later. The refugees and the ivory would return to the Congo estuary, while Stanley and the wangwana pressed on through East Africa to Zanzibar. Stanley himself would return to base camp to pick up the united Rear Column before completing the trans-African journey.

Yet Barttelot remained unclear about his orders. Was he to wait at Yambuya for the reinforcements from Ward and Rose Troup and the 500-600 porters promised by Tippu Tip, or should he attempt to follow Stanley? Stanley knew well enough that without aid from Tippu, the Rear Column could not advance. He also realised that his own actions had made such aid unlikely, to say the least. But he struck a histrionic posture and declared that if the Arab would not 'co-operate', they could manage without him. This was a rationalisation of the fact that Stanley had already decided to press on to Lake Albert without waiting for Tippu. He expected to arrive back at Yambuya in November, then take the Rear Column back to Lake Albert with him - all predicated on the idea that the journey to the lake would take no more than two months.

Stanley's journal makes it quite clear that he expected Barttelot to await his return some time in November 1887. In normal circumstances, his grotesque underestimate of the difficulties that lay ahead would have been plain to see and he would have been convicted nem.con. of the very amateurish incompetence he so excoriated in others. But Stanley was nothing if not lucky, and now luck played into his hands in such a way that he was able later, after a fashion, to cover the traces of his own spectacular blunder. For Barttelot now pleaded and cajoled to be allowed to follow in the leader's footsteps if certain conditions obtained. Stanley relented and agreed to blaze a trail for Barttelot to follow. But he was only definitely to follow if Tippu Tip provided the full complement of porters - a contingency Stanley knew to be next to impossible.

To underline his instructions, Stanley laid out four hypothetical cases. Barttelot had full authority to advance when the steamers returned with Troup, Ward and the rest of the Rear Column and all 600 porters arrived from Tippu Tip. If the Arab supplied part of this force, Barttelot was to use his discretion about advancing. Nothing was said about the scenario where Tippu provided no porters - which Stanley must have known was the most likely outcome. It was clear that marching in relays would involve Barttelot's having to throw away too many loads, so the logic of the 'no porter' situation was that Barttelot would have to remain in Yambuya. This was anyway Stanley's original wish, for he authorised Barttelot to remain in base camp, whatever the circumstances, if he thought it best. This was the unequivocal implication of his parting words to Barttelot: 'Goodbye, Major, I shall find you here in November when I return.'

By toying with the idea that he might after all follow his leader, Barttelot unwittingly opened a Pandora's box of ambiguity and uncertainty. This enabled Stanley when writing his public account of the expedition 'In Darkest Africa' to cover up his own poor judgement and leadership by asserting that he always imagined Barttelot would follow him and was flabbergasted when he did not. Stanley was never more 'economical with the truth' than when rewriting the history of his final conferences at base camp in June 1887.

Chapter Eleven

ON 28th June 1887 Stanley and the vanguard left Yambuya for the unknown. They were plunging into the uncharted 'Dark Continent' just as fully as in December 1876 when Stanley left Tippu Tip at Vinya-Niara. 389 men with 360 rifles descended into the gloom of the Ituri forests. Behind them lay the Rear Column proper at base camp with 130 men under Barttelot and Jameson, plus another 131 under Ward at Bolobo. Bonny was left behind as 'doctor' to the Rear Column. With Stanley went Stairs, Nelson, Parke and Jephson. Stanley had revised his optimistic forecasts of being able to march 12 miles a day, and had now set a realistic target of the end of December as the date when he would be at the shores of Lake Albert.

Stanley was not to know that he was embarking on his most taxing and hellish expedition yet. His 1887 plunge into the Ituri rain forest was the most dreadful ordeal any European explorer of nineteenth-century Africa ever faced. Less than half of the expedition's manpower would survive, and for much of the time the survival of the rest of them was touch and go. The problem was that the Ituri had never been crossed by Europeans, yet Stanley's scant intelligence led him to believe that after a few weeks' march the forest would give way to parkland, enabling him to make the sort of daily progress he had clocked up in 1874-7.

But in fact the Ituri was a green hell of 50,000 square miles. Rivers like the Ituri (the Upper Aruwimi) flowed from the plateau of the Nile/ Congo watershed through a dense forest of tangled vegetation, matted lianas and oozing, clotted undergrowth that exhaled noxious miasmata and squelched underfoot. Lofty forest giants reached a great height and formed an overarching canopy through which shafts of sunlight seldom penetrated. Marching in such conditions was a hot, sticky, steamy affair, like being permanently in a Turkish bath. They had to use machetes to hack their way through the impacted, interpenetrated undergrowth; even the donkeys shivered with fever.

On the first day they experienced temperatures of 86°F in the forest. More worryingly, there were immediate signs of hostility. The first village they came to was deserted and the ground was bristling with skewers, the points turned upwards to cut and gouge the feet of the intruders. Stanley divided his force into two columns, then sent the first forward on a kind of minesweeping operation, while the other column covered them with the Remingtons. While the work of plucking up the skewers was in progress, the men were assailed by a cloud of tiny arrows.

On the second day out, Stairs became very ill. Some spears were thrown into the camp perimeter at night, showing that the hostile tribesmen must have penetrated well within the picket lines. Next day the agonisingly slow advance continued. Every time one of the wangwana climbed a horse or mule to see if skewers lay ahead in their path, arrows whined and whistled past his ear. At 3 a.m. on the morning of 1st July the entire encampment was aroused by the howling of a madman, shrieking that the strangers were not welcome and would be enslaved.

Progress was so slow that on the 2nd Stanley decided to make for the river bank and follow it past the rapids. Stanley's contempt for Parke's naivety continued; the surgeon assured them that forest bees had no sting but had scarcely uttered the opinion before he was badly stung himself. On 4th July they struck the Aruwimi River, only to be ambushed a second time by the Bahungi people, this time hidden in overhanging trees. A second fight took place; when the enemy fled, the expedition found a goat tethered in an abandoned canoe - this provided a welcome meat ration for the leader and his officers.

So far the hostility had been explicable on the grounds that Stanley and his men had been mistaken for Arab slavers; the cane skewer was the main line of indigenous defence against them. When Stanley launched a Lady Alice-style portable steel boat (carried in sections) on the river, this inference was strengthened. There was almost immediately a river fight between the expedition boat party, containing twenty men, and a flotilla of eleven canoes. Under steady Remington fire, the locals abandoned their canoes and fled. After a day's halt in a camp by the riverside, amid swarms of multi-coloured butterflies, Stanley divided his men into a land and a boat party. Stanley travelled by boat, while Jephson commanded the land contingent.

The river here was about 800 yards wide. There were crocodiles in abundance in the water, but no hippopotami, which Stanley attributed to the lack of edible grass. The march routine was four hours' progress between 6.30 and 10.30 a.m., two hours' rest, then marching again until 3.30p.m. Already many of the men were suffering colds from a rain storm. Dejection and demoralisation were beginning to creep in: 'So many impediments are met - impervious swamps, stiff thorny undergrowth and a bewildering mass of creepers and lianas, creeks, sloughs etc. so that our progress is but one mile an hour.' Every yard had to be fought for by the billhooks of forty pioneers in temperatures that were still as high as 96°F at 4 p.m. On the other hand, the boat could complete a day's land journey in two hours.

On 10th July they came to Banalya, a cluster of seven villages near the rapids. Again Stanley ordered a few days' rest, for even those who had departed Yambuya strong and healthy now looked jaded. In Banalya, as elsewhere in the Ituri, the villagers fled to the opposite bank with their goats and valuables. The expedition then occupied the huts and ate the abandoned manioc. The rest enabled Stairs to recover his health after fourteen days of being carried in a litter. Stanley noted the poverty of bird life here as compared with the Congo. But the awesome forest itself revived the feelings he had first experienced north of Nyangwe in 1876:

What attracts my wonder in these terrible forests is the venerable ancientness of Time, and how with deathly stillness, it can speak to my heart of my own utter nothingness, and unimportance of no more worth, note, or use than that to add my body - a little heap of corruption among the dead leaves, the withered and withering branches. The atmosphere appears to me weighted with an eloquent dumb history which I read, and hear, and see and inhale until the cell and smallest vein on my body feels its influence, and out of which it has driven for the time all remembrance of self, all knowledge of identity, perception of visible things or matter, all extraneous consciousness to give place to the overwhelming fact.

On 13th July they pressed on to another settlement at a bend in the river. Again Stanley had to call a halt because of the pelting tropical downpour and the exhaustion of his men. No meat was to be had at any price. On all his expeditions so far Stanley had been able to count on eating meat at least twice a week, but in the Ituri there seemed nothing available but roots, manioc and vegetables. Though many tracks of elephant, buffalo and wild boar criss-crossed their track, they never sighted any game. Quite apart from the difficulty of traversing the Ituri rain forest, Stanley had overestimated the resources likely to be available to him under its sunless canopy. The population of the forest was about 3.75 per square kilometre at this time. This very sparse population lived at subsistence level, so there was no surplus to trade with European travellers.

By mid-July, the river party had grown in size to five canoes and the steel boats, carrying seventy-four men and 120 loads. As Stanley's supply of canoes increased, so did his sick list to fill them. Inevitably he ascribed this tendency to malingering. But given the fury of the elements, this was an unnecessary hypothesis. Between 16th and 17th July it rained seventeen hours non-stop. Morale was plummeting all the time: the men had no meat, their clothes were sopping wet and most were unable to sleep through the incessant downpour. Most demoralised of all was the handful of Somalis, to the point where they lacked the spirit even to light a fire.

They continued to creep slowly along the river. Some days the land party could manage no more than 400 yards' progress from dawn to dusk! Stanley cursed himself for not having brought the fifteen whaleboats, which would have enabled him to cover 20 miles a day. All along the river their approach was signalled by the sonorous booming of drums fashioned from hollow logs: 'the absence of all other sounds lends peculiar power to their voices and the boom of their drums.' They took their first casualties on 20th July when two of the wangwana went missing with two rifles, almost certainly killed while straggling.

Stanley's officers were all performing well, with the exception of Parke, who lost his way in the forest when he was officer of the day in charge of pioneers. Stanley was especially pleased with Jephson, who had made an almost incredible (Stanley's word) transition from the London man-about-town to seasoned African explorer in a mere six months. His direction of pioneers was exceptionally able. This detachment of forty sickle- and machete-wielding veterans had the toughest job in the expedition. Every morning it left camp half an hour ahead of the column to clear the way through the jungle.

Further slight lightening of the gloom came when they started to move beyond the orbit of the Aruwimi slavers. Here the only non-indigenous peoples were Manyema brigands who burnt villages barbarously and fought fire with fire by planting the local pathways with poisoned skewers. There was a slight thawing in the unremitting hostility that had attended the expedition so far. The local people were the Bali and the Bira. They would call out to Stanley's party: 'Go up river, oh son of the sea. We suffer also for we have no food.' Just occasionally, though, Stanley was able to barter for some chickens and eggs.

The roofs of the huts the expedition stayed in were infested with rats, mice and beetles, but there was a worse threat to frayed nerves in this part of the rain forest: a plague of bees and wasps. On 25th July they experienced the worst these insects could do. From the clouds of wasps above one of the Aruwimi cataracts, Stanley dubbed it Wasp Rapids. That morning they set out from their camp near an elephants' watering hole to negotiate the cataracts. While the boats were in the most dangerous part of a narrow boiling channel, one of the men steadied himself by grasping at a branch overhead, and accidentally disturbed a wasps' nest. The angry insects at once sallied out to punish the intruders. The sequel was terrible. The churning, seething river was as wild as the sea and required all their attention, but meanwhile the wasps were at them, inflicting horrible bites. The wangwana had no choice but to endure stoically the most frightful wounds. With their eyes glued to the water, they were forced to allow the insects to settle and sink their jaws into skin. Stanley and Jephson, fully clothed, fared better than their dark companions. At last, some 200 yards beyond the rapids, the wasps left them as suddenly as they had come. In the 'post-mortem', Hoffmann was held to be to blame for having made a sudden movement in the canoe that forced the Zanzibari to cling on to the branch overhead; he was the object of much bitter laughter. The remaining wangwana had the ingenuity to find another route past the wasps, but the Sudanese and Somalis, blithely reckoning that lightning would not strike twice, suffered a second ferocious attack on their passage through the rapids.

The sufferings sustained from these aerial tormentors necessitated another halt. Stanley's coxswain was in a high fever from wasp stings, and squadrons of forest bees continued to zoom and dive around them. The sole consolation was that the bees' and wasps' mastery of the lower skies seemed to have scared off the mosquitoes, for there were few of these on the river.

A visit from the chief of the Bira seemed to open up the possibility of large-scale trading with the locals, but their extortionate demands led the wangwana to begin selling axes, billhooks, machetes and even cartridges for food. Stanley took a prisoner to enforce better bartering terms and, as a second string to his bow, sent 170 men under Nelson, Jephson and Parke across the river to try to find an alternative source of supply. Some supplies were brought back but not before an incident when one of the Zanzibaris

fell into an elephant pit. His cries brought the locals
running, he shot one of them, and the man fell across the pit, making a kind of human awning.

By the beginning of August, Stanley had fourteen canoes and the steel boat at his disposal, enough to convey three-quarters of all their baggage. He ordered the canoes lashed together in twos and, after stowing ten days' provisions on board, he set off upriver. But the Somalis and Sudanese at once revealed themselves to be useless canoeists. The Somalis were attacked by hornets, abandoned their canoe and lay down depressed on the river bank until Stanley's bodyguard got them to their feet by lashing them with switches. The Sudanese fared even worse. They managed to capsize two canoes, containing twelve rifles and ten loads of beads and ammunition. Fortunately, Stanley's divers dredged up six of the rifles and all the ammunition.

Hard on the heels of this misfortune came the first death through heart failure, the loss of a further straggler and the demise of an exhausted donkey. The stench of death was all around them; the mounds of decaying corpses in one deserted village kept them at arm's length, lying on the forest floor instead of in the huts. Next it was the turn of Stairs' men to capsize canoes. Two boatloads of guns and trade goods went to the bottom. Jephson's divers recovered thirteen cases of ammunition and five rifles, but even so the losses were serious: seven Remingtons, two boxes of Maxim ammunition, five cases of cowries, four of beads and one of copper wire. Since leaving Yambuya, they had now lost fifteen rifles. Stanley's usual punishment for those who lost canoes was to put them in the overland party.

On 4th August they reached the obstacle of Panga Falls, but though these were 20 feet high, they had got to the bottom of them by the afternoon. Stairs, who had been put in charge of the pioneers for his misfortune with the canoes, retrieved his reputation by valiant man- hauling of canoes overland round the cataracts. But on the way to Nejambi rapids another canoe capsized, with a loss of eleven rifles and nine bales (though all but two of the rifles were later recovered).

By 9th August food shortages were again becoming acute. Stanley sent out three detachments in different directions to forage. They brought back barely enough food for one day, and a Zanzibari was wounded in the throat by an arrow into the bargain. Another of the rvangwana died of dysentery and several more were at death's door. An attack from a hippo could be shrugged off, but by now the rapids were so difficult that the land party was starting to get into camp before the river party. On the 12th another Zanzibari died of gunshot wounds - probably suicide. Stanley himself was going down with fever and awoke every morning with aching limbs. There was now a desperate need of food.

With hungry bellies and a daily lengthening sick list, the last thing the expedition needed was a clash with hostile tribesmen. Yet at Avissiba rapids on 13th August they had to stand and fight their grimmest battle so far. The wangwana blazed away madly at the hostiles, who replied with showers of arrows, one of which wounded Stairs just below the heart. Some of the wangwana made a flank attack and captured a flock of seven goats, but their shooting had not been accurate enough to dent the attackers' confidence. A pep-talk from Stanley that night did the trick. When the Avissiba peoples renewed their onslaught next day, 300 rounds of accurate firing rapidly thinned their ranks: 'a few straight shots had effected in a few minutes what the indiscriminate and wasteful firing of the day before had not.'

Heaps of enemy slaughtered did not compensate in Stanley's mind for the seven wounded in his own party in the two fights and the close call of Stairs, who had to have the poison from the arrow wound sucked out by Parke. And still there was no solution to the gnawing food shortages. On 14th August, tired of the wangwana's ineffectual and unpunctual foraging, Stanley sent out Parke, Jephson and Nelson on a major reconnaissance for provisions. While he continued along the first-class track on the river bank (even though Stairs was seriously wounded, Stanley would not stop), he sent this foraging column inland with the orders to bring back food at all costs. All the time his sick list grew; two more wangwana died of dysentery. Even the man of iron was beginning to despair: 'I am not running despair [sic], but if I give rein to my fancy, I see a very dark outlook indeed ... If 389 picked men, such as we were when we left Yambuya, are unable to march to Lake Albert, how can Major Barttelot with 250 men make his way through this endless forest?' He estimated that he was still no more than a third of the way to the lake shore.

On 18th August, with no word from Jephson's party yet, Stanley sent out scouts to investigate. The news they brought back filled him with apprehension. Instead of looping round and swinging back south towards the river, Jephson had lost his bearings and was heading diagonally away from them in a north-easterly direction; each day that passed increased the gap between the two forces. Railing at the stupidity of his officers, he summoned his most reliable headman Saad Tato and sent him out with another party to intercept the Jephson caravan and guide it back to the river.

A sick and dispirited Stanley waited anxiously while the death toll around him mounted. Two of his men died of tetanus from the arrow wounds and another of dysentery. On 18th August there was another pelting tropical storm; 'had we not enough afflictions without this pelting rain?' By the 20th he was beginning to fear the worst; he was sure that Jephson's judgement was not good enough to deal with any serious problems that might have befallen his column. But after six days he was more resigned than angry: 'I am not as savage with Jephson now. I think his sufferings must be as great as mine are. Had he returned on the second or third day there would have been a scene.

At last, at 5 p.m. on the 21st Saad Tato led back the bedraggled Jephson column, which itself had sustained three fatalities (two from arrow wounds, one from dysentery). The entire episode had been a monumental error on Jephson's part, and Saad Tato's rescuing party itself had been in danger and had skirmished with hostile bands. Stanley's relief was so great that his reception of Jephson was mild. The young man recorded in his diary: 'I expected to be met by reproaches and angry words but Stanley was very quiet and nice about my having led the expedition astray.'

Stanley at once helped Parke to tend the wounded. The most serious cases were those who had taken arrows in the throat or windpipe. Even when the poison was sucked clear instantly, death from lockjaw could follow. With his manpower being eroded, and not yet half-way to his goal, Stanley was apprehensive but no longer depressed, as he had been when both Jephson's and Saad Tato's parties were away and in danger. Attending the sick 'must have exorcised a malign influence over me ... the last few days had begun to fill me with a doubt of the expedition.'

The united party marched to the foot of Mabengu rapids and camped there. A general muster showed 373 still alive, but fifty-seven of these were sick. Morale was low, the men were exhausted and the struggle for food was too protracted. Indiscipline was increasing. When they found food at the Nepoko rapids on the 26th, the men would not be warned not to overindulge and gorged and stuffed themselves. When this was followed by the wild firing off of guns in camp, Stanley issued a warning that future offenders against the code of conduct would be severely punished. But the very next day the land and river parties failed to link up. Stanley's mood was savage: 'A native who would surrender was shot this afternoon. He had a dozen freshly poisoned arrows and a bundle of "corked" slugs in canoe.'

And still all around them loomed the dark, forbidding Ituri. Hoffmann recorded his awestruck impressions. The mighty African forest, with its gigantic trees through which scarcely a ray of light could penetrate, with its tangled, thorny undergrowth, seemed to do everything in its power to impede our progress. We had to cut our path every inch of the way with bill-hooks, knives and axes, through the close network of creepers, through the fleshy tendrils of lianas, through the thick plantations of sugar-cane. Crossing deep swamps, we had to keep a wary eye open for motionless objects on the edge of the water; objects which looked like logs of wood but were more probably lurking crocodiles, and pick our way carefully among the razor-edged oyster shells that were strewn across the bank.

On the last day of August Stanley was supervising the cutting of a track past the rapids so that they could portage their boats when a scout came running into camp breathlessly to announce that Emin Pasha was approaching. 'Emin' turned out to be a Manyema Arab in a canoe with nine slaves. The Manyema spent a night with them and explained that ahead lay an Arab settlement at the village of Ugarrowa's, headed by Abed bin Salim. Next morning they were gone before daybreak, leaving behind them the body of a murdered seven-year-old boy and with five Zanzibari deserters.

The coming of the Manyema and their precipitate departure made two things clear to Stanley. One was that the burned and deserted villages the expedition had encountered had not been examples of spontaneous abandonment. It was clear that the locals would regard his party as slavers, so that hopes of food were vain. He would have to act like the Manyema themselves to avoid starvation. Hence the pattern of occupied villages, appropriated canoes, food seized at gunpoint, women and children held as hostages in a cycle of ruthlessness that appalled Jephson and opened his eyes to his leader's true nature.

The second implication of the proximity of the Manyema was that there was now an incentive for their kin the wangwana to desert. Immediately after the coming of the Manyema party Stanley noted a growing propensity to desertion by men taking away arms and ammunition. Six men, three rifles, three boxes of ammunition and a tin of biscuits went missing the day after the Manyema decamped. Next day was even worse: five men unaccounted for, a box of cloths and a box each of Remington and Winchester ammunition vanished. So far he had avoided draconian punishments when the deserters were brought back, but he realised that once he left the river and carriers were at a premium, this problem would become acute. Unless the dribble of manpower ceased, he would be forced to employ capital punishment to preserve his own credibility. He summoned the rvangwana headmen, who were against severity but could suggest no concrete way to arrest the tide of desertion. 'It is getting patent daily that severe measures will have to be adopted to stop this desertion and theft of ammunition - we have now lost five boxes of ammunition by theft and are short of 48 rifles - almost a rifle per day.'

When four more deserters were reported on 4th September, Stanley was reduced to removing the rifle springs of men he considered unreliable, in the hope that would-be absconders would think twice about decamping with useless rifles. He also tried to staunch the haemorrhage of ammunition by appointing a special overseer of cartridges and powder. Insult was added to injury when a man was caught red-handed trying to desert with one of the Fortnum and Mason's boxes. Stanley wanted to hang him but the most the headmen would agree to was that, like other deserters, he should be put in chains. Jephson showed himself more of a hardliner on this occasion even than his boss: 'If I were Stanley I should hang the man whether the chiefs wished it or not, he will never stop desertion until he does.'

But still the desperate food shortage continued. Stanley's men found a woman with two children hiding in the bush, who was able to impart the name of her tribe but also confirmed that there was no food to be had in the forest. By 12th September no one had eaten for three days. The men were walking skeletons: 'Achmet the Somali is reported to be dying. It is a wonder that he has lived so long, being a dreadful object of bones, covered with a skin.' When they camped by Hippo Rapids - so called for the large numbers of hippopotami there - Stanley tried in vain to bag one for the pot. In desperation, Stanley got off a shot at a bull elephant but succeeded only in wounding him.

And still the skirmishing continued. The arrows being fired at them were getting longer - now around 20 inches in length. The wangwana shot dead two warriors who glided by in a canoe, but other similar craft floated past, causing fears for the fate of any stragglers. Another Zanzibari pioneer was bitten by a snake as he cleared a way through the bush. On 14th September two further desertions were recorded - thirty men had now gone missing since the muster roll of 23rd August when Jephson's column returned.

At last, on 16th September, gunshots signalled that contact had been made with the Manyema of Ugarrowa's. Later that day Stanley came into the adobe settlement (containing 300 people and eighty guns) and greeted Ugarrowa, who as a boy had accompanied Speke and Grant on their expedition of 1860-63. Stanley made camp on the left bank facing Ugarrowa's and pondered his next move. The first disappointment was to learn that the food supply was exiguous here too. But he at least secured enough for a few days. Until his departure on the 19th, he was in negotiations with Ugarrowa for the care of fifty-six sick and dying men he intended to leave behind at the settlement. He also wrote a letter to Barttelot, which he hired Ugarrowa's people to deliver to Yambuya; however, the couriers were turned back at Wasp Rapids by the hostility of the tribesmen.

Ugarrowa showed Stanley his cache of ivory and gave him his first sight of the Mbuti pygmy people. He also co-operated in a scheme to cut down the desertion rate. First Ugarrowa warned the wangwana that he would not harbour any refugees from the column once it moved on. Then he was an amused spectator while Stanley and the Zanzibari headmen enacted a charade. Stanley condemned one of the chained deserters to death as an example to the others. The headmen then begged and besought him to commute the sentence. With much theatricality Stanley 'allowed himself to be persuaded' and the man was set free. The friends of the condemned were so overcome with emotion that they set up a cry of fidelity to Stanley, promising to follow him unswervingly to Lake Albert: 'Death to him who leaves Bula Matari!' arose the chant.

Sadly it was a case of 'the devil a monk'. The very next day after the departure from Ugarrowa's three deserters were brought in. Ugarrowa, furious that his words had not been heeded, flogged the men and sent them back to Stanley in chains. This time Stanley felt he had no choice but to go through with the execution; if desertions continued at the September rate, there would be nobody left by the end of the year. Stanley called his men together for a general assembly and addressed them. He argued that the deserters had to die for the general good and the safety of all. Lots would be drawn, and whichever of the three drew the fatal number would be hanged by the other two. So it was done. The unfortunate victim, Mabruki by name, was selected; the other two, still chained, hauled him up. All hands witnessed the execution. But the hanging proved a messy business. The first tree-bough over which they strung the rope snapped under Mabruki's weight. He had to be strung up a second time and died within two minutes. The sight of the hanged man was so sickening that Stanley decided to exercise mercy with the other two and commuted their sentences, to relief and satisfaction from the wangwana.

After just five days into the wilderness after Ugarrowa's, having left fifty-six sick behind there, Stanley found himself with another fifty ailing men on his hands. Hunger was again a problem and there was a desperate need of fresh meat. They were in elephant country now and Stanley comforted himself with the idea of bringing down a tusker to provide the entire party with steaks. They could hear hundreds of the great beasts trumpeting in the forest, but could seldom get near them, as the noise of the human caravan frightened them off. Stanley managed to get off a shot at one but merely wounded it. A few days later Stairs wounded another, was charged by it and almost gored. In partial compensation a few days later he found a gazelle trapped in a game pit. Also, a captive woman was brought in who swore that slightly inland there was a great abundance of plantain.

As hunger oppressed them, so too did the dank gloom of the mighty forest. Stanley described it as a wall of trees, extending the distance from Inverness to Plymouth, lashed together with an impenetrable undergrowth of creepers, some 12 inches in diameter. Temperatures ranged from $80°$ to 92 F. Rotting vegetation and the trunks of fallen forest giants were 'buried in masses of creepers of the most vivid green, netted by hundreds of lianas, and ten fathoms' length of calamus. Then every mile or so the dark, sluggish, winding creeks . . . covered over with lilies, with a sickly perfume strangely mixed with a nauseous effluvium of pitch-black mud.'

Hardly surprisingly, the river party, even after struggling with boiling rapids, frequently got far ahead of the land contingent. For this reason, and because navigation by canoe was becoming increasingly difficult, Stanley proposed abandoning the river. They were having too many narrow escapes. On 4th October the boat was nearly wrecked and a canoe was swept twice beneath the waves. But Uledi (of Through the Dark Continent fame), volunteered to be a pathfinder canoeist. However, one decision Stanley did take at this time. With a half-starved force and a mounting desertion rate - the hanging of Mabruki had had only momentary exemplary effect - Stanley lacked the capability to carry the sick in litters. He therefore resolved to leave behind Nelson, who was ill with ulcerous feet and legs, together with fifty-two other sick men and eighty-one loads, while the main column pressed on to the nearest Arab settlement.

The decision to abandon Nelson was the most signal example so far of Stanley's utter ruthlessness and it caused consternation in the minds of the other officers. But it solved nothing. Three days after leaving Nelson and his party behind, Stanley held a muster, which recorded 213 souls present (as opposed to 224 on the 6th). Eleven men had deserted in three days, all of them crazed with hunger. There were numerous traces of game now: wart-hogs, buffalo, antelope, elephants, but though Stairs, Jephson and Stanley all tried their hand at tracking these animals they had no luck. Stanley managed to wound an elephant but it got away.

Desperately hungry, and intermittently attacked by wasps and showers of torrential rain, Stanley confessed he had never encountered hardship like this on any of his previous expeditions. The marvel was that Randy the terrier was still going strong. But the leader's journal is eloquent of the most frightful anxiety they all felt as death by starvation began to loom as a distinct possibility.

10th October. A few only of foragers across river have returned. They bring nothing having found nothing ... I ate my last bean, last grain of Indian corn and of rice, and very last portion of everything solid foreign to this soil and this morning the horrid emptiness of the stomach gave me real anxiety and had to be filled with something lest the muscles exercise upon itself... I tried a handful of potato leaves, bruised fine, with a beautiful fruit large as a prize pear . . . and a cake made by a captive woman of the wood bean flour.

11th October.
Our weakness is most pitiable - but there is courage in our people yet.
12TH October. Nine have died since yesterday.
The expedition was now so debilitated that when men deserted with guns and ammunition, Stanley was too dispirited to send posses after them. Even the 'beautiful fruit' turned out to be an illusion, for Hoffmann who ate it ravenously was then violently sick. In agonies of hunger the officers tortured themselves with the devising of haute cuisine menus. None of them had ever before realised the importance of food; as Stanley remarked: 'prayer precedes meat but praise comes after.'

By 15th October it was clear to all that death was not far away. Stanley left a party on the river in the boat and himself struck north into the forest. After a terrible day's march, he killed and ate his sick donkey. That night he overheard the wangwana talking; they were all convinced they would die and that hope of striking an Arab station was illusory. Randy was now getting weaker and weaker. Stanley dared not feed him scraps, for the Zanzibaris would have murdered him if they thought he was getting anything they could eat. When Stanley let the terrier wander free in the forest, he frequently returned with signs of combat with some denizen of the gloom. The only bright spot was the stoicism and endurance of his officers, though this was variable. The only man who never criticised the leader with a look or gesture was Parke. Jephson was tough but mutable, while as for Stairs: 'I do not quite believe him to be friendly. Sometimes I catch something in his looks which forbids me let myself go in over praise.'

On the 17th their hopes were buoyed up by questioning of a forest dweller who revealed that there was an Arab post just one day's journey away. Next morning, after a chilling trek in thick, cold mist, they heard singing and shouting in the distance. As the mist cleared they found themselves in a clearing on the outskirts of the town of Iota, surrounded by people jabbering away excitedly in Arabic and Swahili. They were saved. After thirteen days without any food grown by man, 192 men had survived.

It turned out that Ipoto was under the command of a runaway Zanzibari slave called Kilonga-Longa, a rival of Ugarrowa. The Manyema here had far outstripped Tippu Tip in devastation of the environment. The coming of the Arabs on the Upper Congo and Aruwimi had produced ecological disaster. It was their depredations that had brought the expedition to the brink of disaster from starvation. Tippu Tip, Ugarrowa, Kilonga-Longa - it all formed a pattern: 'Half a dozen resolute men, aided by their hundreds of bandits, have divided about three-fourths of the great Upper Congo forest for the sole purpose of murder, and becoming heirs to a few hundred tusks of ivory.'

At first Stanley and his men were well received and treated hospitably. The wangwana gorged themselves to the point where their stomachs reacted negatively to the overeating. But when it became clear that the expedition had nothing to offer in return for its demands, the Manyema attitude hardened. They refused to part with food except for trade goods and threatened to shoot any of Stanley's men found pillaging their plantations. In response the wangwana began to sell their clothes, then their ammunition changed hands within three days. Stanley realised with alarm that the Manyema were trying to disarm the expedition by buying up its rifles and cartridges. Stanley began by bluster, demanding that the Manyema return the rifles. When they ignored the request, he turned his anger on his men. He held a muster and sentenced to twenty-five lashes anyone who could not produce his gun and ammunition. One man was flogged on the spot. Yet immediately afterwards word was brought that yet another man had sold his rifle for food. This time Stanley hanged the culprit, one Jumah, as an example to the others. This show of 'strength' finally impressed the Manyema and they agreed to return five of the rifles.

Relations with the Manyema continued tense. One of the wangwana was speared to death while raiding a cornfield, and Stanley gave another a public flogging of 200 lashes for stealing. Stanley's sadistic side emerges in his bland comments on the affair: 'the scars will last on his body till death, and for the time being he is utterly disabled.' Fortunately for Stanley his negotiations with the grasping Manyema were materially assisted when Uledi and the river party came in, for Uledi was a master diplomat. While Stanley was confined to bed for a day with a slight fever, Uledi traded enough goods to enable a forward march to be made.

Stanley's mood at Ipoto was deep black. Jephson recorded: 'We see very little of Stanley, he stays in his hut all day and we remain near ours. This evening he came up whilst we were at dinner and remarked that we seemed to be doing very well in the way of food, we told him that except the coffee, everything we were eating we had bought with our own clothes - he turned the subject violently.' The leader's anxiety now centred on the abandoned Nelson. By 26th October he had an agreement with the Manyema that they would assist Jephson to go back and find Nelson. The party would consist of forty wangwana and thirty Manyema. To seal the pact Stanley made brotherhood with Ismaili, the most important of the headmen (Kilonga-

Longa was absent), and signed an agreement with him, witnessed by Parke.

Next Stanley told his officers what his plans were. While Jephson accompanied the relief party back to find Nelson, he would press on. Parke would remain at Ipoto to tend Nelson and the other sick when they came in. Jephson asked and got permission to follow the leader once he had rescued Nelson. Stanley agreed, provided Parke remained in Ipoto with Nelson and the sick. For greater protection he would leave the Maxim gun behind. He himself would return for them in three months. Parke did not relish the prospect of a further period of short commons among the treacherous Manyema, but accepted without demur. Privately he was bitter that Stanley was leaving him and the sick as, in effect, hostages, at the whim of Kilonga-Longa - hostages moreover who stood more chance of being relieved by Barttelot and the Rear Column than by Stanley himself.

Jephson was even more disgusted at the dispositions Stanley suggested, and the disgust showed. On the 26th Stanley doled out Nelson's food for six days - a good-sized plateful of coarse hard flour and one small chicken. Jephson describes the sequel: 'When this was brought in, he remarked that it was an ample allowance for that time. I said nothing but I think my face must have expressed the disgust I felt at the scandalous smallness and meanness of the allowance, for a few minutes after the food was taken away to my hut, he sent another small chicken for me to take on - it was very fortunate for me and for Nelson as well that I had sold my clothes for food, we should have been on short commons indeed had we depended entirely on Stanley.'

On 28th October Stanley himself marched on from Ipoto through heavy rain, accompanied by Manyema guides. Their insolence towards the wangwana irked Stanley and he seethed inwardly, but he had to curb his tongue, since Jephson, Parke and Nelson were all in the power of the Manyema. Everything about Ipoto had angered Stanley. When would the European powers combine to bridle Arab arrogance and clear the slavers out of Central Africa? The first essential step was a treaty to ban the sale of gunpowder. 'It is simply incredible that because ivory is required for ornaments or billiard balls, the rich heart of Africa should be laid waste at this late year of the nineteenth century, signalised as it has been by so much advance, that populations, tribes and nations should be utterly destroyed. Whom after all does this bloody seizure of ivory enrich? Only a few dozens of half-castes, Arabs and Negros, who, if due justice were dealt to them, should be made to sweat out the remainder of their piratical lives in the severest penal servitude.'

Stanley and his men stumbled and fell over prominent tree roots. To get to the village of Bukiri they had to cross a log 'bridge', 20 feet high, between the edge of the forest and the village. But gradually the going improved. The forest was more open, so that they could cover one and a half miles an hour as opposed to half a mile an hour in the depths of the Ituri. For the first time billhooks were not constantly needed. They enjoyed brilliant sunshine every day and a thunderstorm at night. After crossing the confluence of the Ituri and the Epuru, they entered a well-populated area, the domain of the Balese tribe. Once past the dreadful orbit of the Manyema, food was plentiful again. They could get bananas, corn, goats, chickens, flour and beans: 'for the first time since leaving the Congo we were assured of being able to fill the ravenous stomachs of all our followers.'

The one blot on the horizon was the insolence of Khamis, chief of the Manyema guides. Tension grew between the Manyema and the wangwana, especially after Khamis slapped Saad Tato in the face. Stanley asked his headmen not to retaliate for the moment but to bide their time. The time came on 10 November, as their pace quickened to two miles an hour over firmer ground which absorbed the rain. To the sounds of crashing timber all around them as forest giants breathed their last, Stanley warned Khamis that since they were now out of Ismaili's territory, henceforth the wangwana had his blessing to retaliate for any slight.

On 10 November Stanley called a halt while Khamis and a mixed party of Manyema and wangwana scouted ahead for food. Stanley was so plagued by fleas that he pitched his tent in the middle of a village street to try to be rid of them. Four days later Khamis came back, laden with flocks of goats; he had sent on his own men to loot and pillage, since Stanley had forbidden the Zanzibaris to do so. After a day's gorging, Khamis and his men left without fulfilling their contract to escort the expedition to Lake Albert. They left behind a store of ivory, which Stanley sent after them, to remove any pretext for Khamis to 'badmouth' the white man with Ismaili.

Scarcely had Khamis left than Jephson came into camp. Cunningly foreseeing that it would take Barttelot nine months to cover the ground Stanley had marched in three, Jephson had made it a point of understanding that he be allowed to escape the anathema of beggary into which Stanley had cast Parke and Nelson. His mood when leaving Ipoto on 26th October was grim: 'I know Stanley will make no allowance for these difficulties even if he allows there are any, he always slangs one indiscriminately so one must just make up one's mind to grin and bear it.' Three days later he found Nelson, who told him he had been unable to sleep at night because of anxiety ever since the others left him. This was hardly surprising. Only five of the fifty-two men who had been left with him were alive and two of those were dying; of the others seventeen were dead and the rest had deserted.

After burying thirteen boxes of ammunition, Jephson and Nelson arrived back at Ipoto on 3rd November. Nelson soon found that his plight had improved only marginally. Stanley had made no arrangements with the Manyema chiefs to feed his officers. Stairs, in charge of the Maxim gun, had had to sell his clothes. Parke was particularly incensed that Stanley had not even bothered to say goodbye to him. As Jephson remarked bitterly: 'It is really quite wonderful how little Stanley seems to care about the welfare of his officers, he seems to take no interest whatever in what they do or how they manage to get on. I think it is a mistake his having European officers under him, he should merely have Zanzibari chiefs and see to all the work himself.'

Not surprisingly, then, when Jephson and his forty-eight men caught up with the main column, the letters he brought from Parke and Nelson were full of bitterness and recrimination towards their leader. Nelson upbraided Stanley for having made no arrangements for their food at Ipoto: 'What are we do to do? Die of hunger? Surely we deserve a little better treatment than this . . . what would people at home say?' Stanley waved the point aside. He snapped only when Parke's letter told him that Ismaili was already trying to evade the terms of his sworn contract. 'If ever a man had cause to pity himself, I have!' he exclaimed.

Next day he sent out Stairs to reconnoitre the route. One of the wangwana named Simba was wounded in a fracas with the locals, then blew his own brains out, to the disgust of his comrades who said he was too poor to have the presumption to commit suicide. Uledi came in with more news about Ismaili's bad behaviour, and a muster on 23rd November produced just 175 men - 285 had left Ugarrowa's. Stanley felt some remorse about his treatment of the people of Ibwiri. They had treated the expedition well, but the wangwana had requited their kindness with looting and pillaging.

On the 24th the expedition marched on from Ibwiri. Food was still plentiful and the forest became less dense. By the 30th they were trekking through mixed country, part forest, part parkland. Stanley delighted in the new sensations: a new specimen of arrow, 2 foot 6 inches long with a spear-shaped three-inch point; the most plentiful tobacco crops he had yet seen in Africa; and his first sighting of black cattle with a white face. On 3rd December they reached the main Ituri River and finally on 4th December they emerged well and truly from the forest gloom. The five-month Hobbesian war of all against all was over. Stanley describes the moment. 'We emerged upon the plains, and the deadly gloomy forest was behind us. After one hundred and sixty days' continuous gloom, we saw the light of the broad day shining all around us and making all things beautiful. We thought we had never seen grass so green or country so lovely. The men literally yelled and leaped with joy, and raced over the ground with their burdens. Ah, this was the old spirit of former expeditions successfully completed all of a sudden revived.'

They proceeded across the rolling plain, largely untroubled by the heavy rain. Stanley looked forward now to seeing Lake Albert which had intrigued him ever since he read Philip Gosse's book during the 1882-3 home leave from the Congo. In particular he wanted to see the 'large donkey' which Harry Johnston later identified as the okapi. But just when they thought they had left all cares behind them, they ran into the stiffest indigenous military resistance so far. At first the people Stanley calls the 'Abunguma' watched them sullenly as they crossed the eastern Ituri by a suspension bridge, which would admit just one man at a time. Then came skirmishing and a half-hearted night attack on the camp. Finally, when the expedition got to the foot of Mount Mazamboni, the Abunguma, 'the most populous tribe since the Bangala', decided that matters had gone far enough.

On 9th December the expedition was camped on a strong position on a hilltop, fortified by a thorn boma. Stanley decided not to move until the locals made friends with them or, alternatively, until they were taught the power of European technology. When all peace negotiations broke down, Stanley ordered a punitive sortie. He divided his force into three. Jephson and thirty riflemen were told off to the left, Uledi detached to the right, while Stairs led the centre. Stairs and his men confronted the enemy across a broad stream. The crackle of gunfire echoed across the undulating grasslands. At first the tribesmen faced the onslaught bravely, and loosed showers of arrows at their tormentors, confident in the watery barrier between the two forces. Seeing this, Stairs ordered the charge and led his men across the stream in a rousing onslaught. They gained the far bank and opened up a withering fire on the now faltering tribesmen. They pursued them into banana plantations and villages which they put to the torch. Uledi meanwhile had discovered a path leading along a mountain spur and after ascending 500 feet came on to and above the right flank of the enemy. Catching them in a natural killing ground, they opened up with the Winchesters and did awesome execution. Finally Jephson's party emerged from the left ravine, effectively catching the hostiles between three fires. It was a classically successful textbook military exercise.

Chief Mazamboni next announced he would make a final decision for peace or war after seeing the quality of Stanley's trade goods. Two yards of scarlet cloth and a dozen brass rods, however, proved less than efficacious, so battle was resumed. Between 9th and 13th December four more pitched battles took place, with the enemy trying to cut off the rearguard and taking severe punishment from the Winchesters in the process. On the 12th Stanley himself killed a man who was yelling on a hillside with a shot fired from fully 600 yards away.

On 13th December Mazamboni's men followed them at a respectful distance, out of rifle range, as the column threaded its way down to the lake shore. Excitement was running high with the Europeans. Stanley described the situation. 'At 1 p.m. we resumed our march. Fifteen minutes later I cried out, "Prepare yourselves for a sight of the Nyanza." The men murmured and doubted and said, "Why does the master continually talk to us in this way? Nyanza indeed! Is not this a plain and can we not see mountains at least four days' march ahead of us?" At 1.30p.m. the Albert Nyanza was below them. Now it was my turn to jeer and scoff at the doubters, but as I was about to ask them what they saw, so many came to kiss my hands and beg my pardon, that I could not say a word.'

But the euphoria of gazing down from the plateau on to the great lake soon turned to puzzlement and disillusionment. Where was Emin with his levies? Questioning of the peoples by the lakeside revealed that they had not seen a white man since Mason Bay's circumnavigation ten years earlier. This awakened Stanley's worst fear: that Emin might meanwhile have made his own way to Zanzibar, thus destroying the point of the expedition. He did some quick calculations. It would take four days to get to Wadelai by water, but he had no canoes, so the point was academic. By land it would take twenty-five days, and because of his aggressive policy towards the Lake Albert peoples he would probably have to fight all the way. With only forty-seven cases of cartridges left, a running fight all the way to Wadelai would leave them with just twenty-five cases to hand over to Emin - a plain absurdity for a 'relief expedition.

So it was that, paradoxically, the Emin Pasha relief expedition was in need of relief itself. On 14th December Stanley informed his officers that for the time being the search for Emin would have to be abandoned. He proposed returning to Ibwiri, building a fortified camp, then sending out detachments to gather up all the far-flung pockets of manpower along the trail, Parke and Nelson at Ipoto, the men at Ugarrowa's, and so on, even to the Rear Column itself. Once the entire expedition was reunited at Ibwiri, they could make a second, more determined attempt to find Emin.

This announcement caused his officers intense disappointment. Stairs and Jephson argued that this meant turning back on the very brink of success. Jephson pleaded to be allowed to cross the lake to Wadelai, but Stanley rejected this as too risky." As reinforcement for his decision he pointed to the continuing hostility of the lakeside peoples; by day they were sullen and suspicious and by night they went in for sneak attacks on the camp. How could the expedition guarantee its food supply in these conditions?

The decision to retreat contained some rationality, but only on premises which themselves logically precluded the original decision to split the expedition and leave behind the Rear Column. In his fanatical desire to reach Lake Albert at any cost - and fanatical is the only word to describe such a blithe failure to think through the consequences of his actions - Stanley swept aside inconvenient facts and obvious considerations which returned at the lakeside to strike him with force. It may be, as has been suggested, that Stanley was embarrassed to meet Emin with his expedition in its current ragged state, but this hardly explains the disappointment at not meeting the Pasha at the lake. More likely, having redoubled his efforts as he lost sight of his goal, simply to brave out the horrors of the Ituri, Stanley found himself driven on by the 'automatic pilot' of constant action and did not stop to correlate means and ends until he reached the notional 'end' of his journey.

Retreat to Ibwiri meant further clashes with Mazamboni's truculent people. Some part of the motive for Mazamboni's aggression comes through in the verbal exchanges recorded on 15th December. 'A man and his wife came within a bow shot from the shore . ... "Which way did you come from? Ituri? Ah, that proves you to be wicked people. Who ever heard of good people coming from that direction? If you were not wicked people you would have brought a big boat like the other white man and

shot hippopotamus like the other man." ' This was the Bula Matari/
Tandelay syndrome in reverse. Mason, who had arrived in a steamer, was
a good man, a man of wealth. Stanley, who had arrived on foot and with
no wealth, was bad.

The retreat turned out to be every bit as perilous as Stairs and Jephson
had feared when arguing against it to Stanley. They were detained at first
by a severe rainstorm, but when they got under way they were at once
plagued by a shower of arrows from small marauding parties.
Mazamboni's men no longer offered combat in pitched battles, but adopted
a kind of guerrilla, hit-and-run warfare. In response Stanley tried to burn
off the attackers by long forced marches. In addition to the usual day's
travel, he insisted on a further five hours' trekking from 5 to 10 p.m. At the
end of this the exhausted wangwana would simply flop on the grass and
sleep where they lay, the cold nights of the grasslands notwithstanding.
Mazamboni's men constantly nudged and prodded the rear, moving in at
the first opportunity to spear the sick and straggling. Even hunting was
difficult. There was an abundance of game, especially kudu and
hartebeeste, which was easy to kill, but there was the ever-present danger
of ambush to the hunters.

Stanley was not the kind of man to take la petite guerre lying down. His
patience snapped when he saw a sick straggler being speared about 500
yards behind the column. He decided to ambush the ambushers. Saad Tato
and four of the best sharpshooters were positioned behind a rock for an
ambuscade. They poured lead into their pursuers and momentarily shook
their resolve.

Next day things seemed to be looking up with the lucky find of a vast
store of grain and beans, enough to provide every man with five days'
provisions. But just as the officers were congratulating themselves on this
piece of serendipity, Stanley through his binoculars spotted a fresh ambush
in tall grass. He swerved the line of the column away, and his sharpshooters
again foiled an enemy attempt to fall on the rear. Tired of this war of
attrition, and unable to afford the steady drip-drip in loss of men and
ammunition, Stanley decided on a policy of search and destroy. He sent
out a mobile column of eighty of his best men to plunder every village
around, strip it of its livestock, then burn it to the ground. Mazamboni's
men took to watching the expedition from afar and giving it a wide berth.

By 23rd December they were at the main ford of the eastern Ituri. Now
on the borders of the Balese country, Stanley was startled to find that the
locals had destroyed all bridges and taken away all canoes. To cross the
river, he had his men construct a crude suspension bridge as far as an island
in mid-river. A violent hailstorm assailed them while they were crossing,
but the bridgehead on the island gave them a toehold. There they
constructed rafts of banana stalks to get them to the other side.

Through his interpreters, Stanley warned the locals that he would be
returning and if the bridges were still down there would be a reckoning.
This 'Christmas message' was pure Stanley. 'Those unacquainted with

these people might think we should be grateful for crossing and march off without molesting them. I have the best will in the world to do so, and if but a child came and expressed regret, I would forgive all but if I go and leave them unpunished, my people will certainly suffer, and I shall bear the loss.'

By noon of 26th December they were all on the far side of the Ituri River. Little else disturbed the tenor of their march for the next two weeks, and on 6th January they came to the familiar approaches of Ibwiri.

Chapter Twelve

THEY found Ibwiri abandoned but with plenty of food in store. This, together with a stash of fine wooden boards, gave Stanley the incentive to build a stockade camp. By 18th January 1888 the stockade, henceforth known as Fort Bodo, was complete. The main problem about the fort was its infestation by rats, fleas, mosquitoes and, above all, red ants. These were a constant menace in the Ituri forest, as Stanley noted: 'to the living the red ants are a nuisance. Twenty times a day while on a march we have to cross their columns and then only do the Zanzibaris break into the double quick to avoid them - but woe betide the unlucky man who stumbles and falls over their lines." But the ants were not only a danger to moving columns. They seemed particularly attracted to Ipoto, as Parke recalled on 19th January: 'A column of ants, of about four inches in width, and densely marshalled, has now been continuously passing through my tent for nearly twenty-four hours. So the length appears to be unlimited.' But troublesome as the red ants were, they were not so deadly as the black variety. Marching in military squares 12-15 inches wide and 100 feet long, black ants were more likely to eat anything in their path than live and let live.

Once the stockade was completed, Stanley despatched Stairs to Ipoto to rescue Nelson and Parke. Whatever the provocation, he was not to open fire on the Manyema unless they had actually spilt the blood of expedition personnel. Stairs returned on 8th February with the tattered remnants of the Ipoto contingent, the steel boat and the Maxim gun. There were just sixteen survivors. Eleven men had died of starvation and the Manyema had tried to starve out the others to get their guns. Parke and Nelson shocked Stanley by their appearance, Nelson particularly so: (he) 'walks like an old man of ninety. Yet he eats well and would naturally eat much more if food was properly cooked and of European quality."

Picking up from camp gossip that the British officers felt very angry at his cavalier attitude to their sufferings, Stanley insisted that Parke and Nelson write an official account of their time at Ipoto. This was a typical Stanley tactic. He always liked his officers to write down their version of any controversial incident, defying them in effect to criticise him. If they criticised him, he would find means to victimise them. If they did not, but complained later, Stanley would use the 'official account' to which they had signed their names to rebut any criticism of himself. Stanley also suspected Stairs of manoeuvring behind the scenes to influence the wangwana headmen. When he proposed returning to look for Barttelot and the Rear Column, the Zanzibari chiefs opposed the idea and exhorted him to try to find Emin once more. Stanley was in a ticklish spot. He had urged his men forward on gruelling forced marches with the promise of meeting the Pasha at Lake Albert; but when they got there, the locals said they knew nothing of any white man. There was an issue of credibility here that Stanley was trying to duck; he could not face the embarrassment of a second fruitless search for Emin.

He therefore opted for a middle-of-the-road strategy. He sent out Stairs again, this time to bring up the men who had been left behind at Ugarrowa's and Barttelot's Rear Column, on the assumption that Barttelot 'must' by now have got as far as Ugarrowa's. Stairs departed on 16th February. Two days later Stanley complained of a large glandular swelling on his left arm, and next day he was attacked by a violent pain in his stomach and the familiar symptoms of African fever. The pains spread to the abdomen, liver and gall bladder. Parke, who was in constant attendance, examined him and found inflammation of the left auxiliary gland. He made a general diagnosis of impacted gallstone and aggravated African fever - the very same illness that had brought Stanley to the brink of death on three previous occasions (one of them in New Bond Street). Stanley was in a critical condition from 19th February to 16th March.

Stanley had only a confused recollection of that time. He could not praise his physician enough - 'Dr Parke has been most assiduous in attention and gentle as a woman in his ministrations' - but in his conscious intervals he was violent, unpredictable and raged at his officers mercilessly. In one of his fits of anger he hit Hoffmann over the head with a stick. Hovering near death, in his lucid moments while sipping soup or having poultices applied, he lashed out physically and verbally at all in sight. He told Jephson he was guilty of 'overweening pride - pride of birth and pride of self and suggested that instead of his soft life he should have spent three years before the mast by the time he was eighteen. He also spoke of himself in a way that drew stupefied incredulity from Jephson: 'He made himself out to be a St John for gentleness, a Solomon for wisdom, a Job for patience and a model of truth. Whereas I do not suppose a more impatient, a more untended and more untruthful man than Stanley could exist. He is most violent in his words and actions, the slightest little thing is sufficient to work him into a frenzy of rage, his sense of what is honourable is of the haziest description and he is certainly a most untruthful character - "o wid some power the giftie gie us".' '

By 13th March Stanley was able to walk for the first time in three weeks. Parke lanced the tumour in his arm, out of which a great mass of pus discharged. On 16th March he took his first extended walk without being supported and thereafter convalesced rapidly. By the 25th of the month he was well enough to travel. Stanley decided to return to the lake to try once more to make contact with Emin, without waiting for Stairs to return. The cultivation in the fields around Ford Bodo had produced prodigious results, so that there was no longer any worry over food supplies.

On 2 April Stanley, Jephson, Parke and 126 men with the steel boat set out for the return march to Lake Albert; Nelson and another forty-nine invalids were left behind at Fort Bodo. The expedition was unopposed at the Ituri except for a handful of warriors who shot a few arrows at them, which fell short, then retired. On 11th April they emerged from the forest into the grassland. The switch from darkness or twilight to brilliant sunshine was hailed with shouts of joy, by none more so than Parke, who had endured 289 days in the fuliginous gloom of the rain forest. The euphoria of the experience led Parke into one of his rare moments of indiscretion: 'Dr Parke and Mr Jephson not taking the advice of the Zanzibaris respecting the light-coloured tobacco leaves, smoked them and became qualmish and uncomfortable therefrom.'

Next day, when they occupied a Besse village, the locals tried to counterattack but were quickly dispersed by a skirmishing line of sharpshooters. East of Besse they lost their way and had to steer straight across the grassland to the Undussuma peak, scene of their struggle with Mazamboni's on 10-11th December the previous year. Stanley put out peace feelers to Mazamboni and this time his overtures were reciprocated. Mazamboni's men explained that the hostilities were another case of mistaken identity. The area in which they lived was a favourite target for Kabba Rega's raiders from Bunyoro; Stanley's men had been mistaken for them. The explanation led to a general reconciliation. First Mazamboni's courtiers apologised for the events of last December. Then Stanley made blood brothers with Mazamboni himself.

Mazamboni then introduced Stanley to the other tribal leaders of the area: Gavira and Kavalli. Between them the three chiefs controlled a large area extending from the lake shore to the neighbouring plateau and the grasslands to the west. As he learned more, Stanley made interesting ethnological discoveries relating to the power politics of the region. It seemed that two entirely different tribes coexisted on the grassland. A Hamitic race of hunters and warriors had begun to encroach on the preserves of the agricultural matrilineal peoples sometime in the eighth or ninth century AD and had achieved total conquest by the beginning of the seventeenth century. These taller, slimmer Hamitic peoples (called by Stanley the Bakuma), characterised by longer heads, narrow noses and thin lips, lorded it over the original Babira (of Bantu stock). But masters and servants were forced into a closer symbiosis by the ever-present threat from Kabba Rega and his warriors.

All three chiefs had news of Emin. Mazamboni told him that someone answering the Pasha's description - 'Malleju' ('the bearded one') - had been on the lake since Stanley's visit. At Kavalli's the young chief actually handed over a packet that Emin had left behind. The letter was wrapped in an oilcloth and a fragment of The Times for April 1886. What had happened was that Emin, under threat from both Kabba Rega and the Mahdists, at first received garbled reports in Wadelai of a white man raiding the area on the western shores of Lake Albert. He had assumed that this could not be Stanley(!). When the reports became too insistent to be ignored, Emin and a detachment of his soldiers sailed south from Wadelai to Mswa on the south-western corner of the lake at the end of January. But interrogation of the lakeside peoples threw up the same unsatisfactory answers that Stanley had received a month before. Just in case it was Stanley that was looking for him, Emin left a letter with Kavalli. He did not have the resources for a full-scale search for Stanley and, between Kabba Rega and the Mahdists, had problems enough in his own province. The letter he left behind asked Stanley to send a messenger to the northwest shore of the lake, where he would be picked up by one of Emin's steamers. The letter came as a very great relief to Stanley's officers, tired as they were of chasing shadows, though Stanley himself remarked sourly that it was a very cool message indeed from a man supposed to be in the last extremity.

Stanley at once ordered Jephson and Parke to launch the steel boat Advance on Lake Albert and go in search of Emin. From Mswa Jephson sent a note to Wadelai to tell Emin that this was indeed the Stanley expedition. Emin at once ordered his steamers south. On 27 April Jephson and Emin met at Mswa. Emin was effusive in his thanks to the British for their efforts; Jephson for his part was deeply impressed by the intelligence and sincerity of the Pasha; he contrasted his humanity and popularity with the ruthlessness and aura of fear that surrounded Stanley. It only remained now for Jephson to escort Emin back for a meeting with Stanley that would, on paper, emulate the sensation of the 1871 Ujiji meeting with Livingstone.

Stanley meanwhile left Kavalli's camp at Bundi, 5000 feet above sealevel, overlooking the southern end of Lake Albert, for the descent to the lake itself. Katonza and Komubi, the chiefs who had harassed the expedition at the lake shore on 13-16th December, hearing that the trio of most powerful chieftains had made obeisance to Stanley, followed suit and made their submission; again their excuse for previous hostilities was that they thought Stanley's men were Kabba Rega's.

They descended to the lake which, like Lakes Tanganyika and Victoria, was alive with crocodiles. Stanley amused himself by placing pieces of meat on the roof of a conical hut, just an arm's length away, and noting the boldness of the kites, who would swoop down, grab the meat and fly away before anyone could touch them. He was beginning to warm to Lake Albert's peculiar charms: 'I have often smiled at the rhapsody of Sir Samuel [Baker] on his discovery of the Albert Nyanza, perhaps oftener after Mason's mysteriously brusque way of circumscribing its "illimitability", but I can feel with him now some sympathy despite its known length and breadth.' But Stanley still felt angry that Emin had not taken proper steps to meet them in December, which could have saved them five days' fighting and four months' loss of time. His mood was fluctuating and temper uncertain, and Jephson recorded a typical incident just before he left for Mswa: 'Stanley got in a great rage with the men today and as they were not working as well as they might he fired at two of them, he just grazed the heel of one of the men and took a piece off about the size of a sixpence, a quarter of an inch more would have shattered the bone of the foot and made him lame for life; Stanley really is not responsible for what he does when he gets into these fits of passion.'

On 29 April Jephson, Emin and his friend and confidant Captain Casati loaded the steamer Khedive with provisions and livestock and took the

Advance in tow. That evening on the lake shore Stanley saw through his field glasses a large steamer approaching. At 8 p.m. the trio rowed ashore. The wangwana were so excited that they fired off their guns in welcome. A bespectacled figure walked up to Stanley's tent and said in excellent English: 'I owe you a thousand thanks, Mr Stanley. I really do not know how to express my thanks to you.' Stanley replied: 'Ah, you are Emin Pasha. Do not mention thanks, but come in and sit down. It is so dark out here we cannot see each other.'

In his journal Stanley provided a fuller account of the historic meeting:

At the door of the tent we stood and a wax candle threw light on the scene. I expected to see a tall thin military-looking figure in faded Egyptian uniform, but instead of it I saw a small spare figure in a well-kept fez and a clean suit of snowy cotton drilling, well ironed and of perfect fit. A dark lively beard bordered a face of a Magyar cast though a pair of spectacles lent it somewhat the appearance of an Italian, or Spanish appearance. There was not a trace in it of ill-health, or anxiety - it rather indicated good condition of body and peace of mind. Emin did not look his age (forty-eight) but nearer thirty to thirty-five. Casati, though younger, looked gaunt, care-worn, anxious and aged. He too wore a suit of clean Egyptian cotton and a fez.

Five bottles of champagne had been given to Stanley at Stanley Pool to toast the occasion of his meeting with Emin. Unlike at the famous meeting with Livingstone, this time Stanley did not forget them, possibly because two had already been opened to celebrate the first sighting of Lake Albert. The remaining three bottles were now uncorked and the five Europeans sat talking and drinking far into the night.

With the first great European Africanist Stanley had 'found' there was instant rapport. With Emin there was an equally immediate failure to communicate. As soon as Jephson handed him Stanley's letter at Mswa, Emin recorded in his diary that he had no intention of leaving his province. Yet during the first day's conversation he made no mention of this. Stanley began by revealing that the Khedive's orders were that if the Pasha stayed in Equatoria, he did so at his own risk. Stanley then tried to sway him in favour of returning by asking him what would happen when he grew old or died. Emin said his problem was that he could not leave unless he had carriers for the women and children of the Egyptian garrison. They can walk, riposted Stanley brusquely. Emin then raised difficulties about food supplies. By mutual agreement the

subject was deferred. Stanley noted with some irritation: 'I am unable to gather from long conversation with Emin Pasha his future intentions. When a return is proposed to him, he taps his knee, shakes his head and smiles in a kind of "we shall see" manner. I do not think he can make up his mind easily to leave this country, where he has lived like a king.'

In retrospect it is hard not to be fanciful and contrast the noonday meeting with Livingstone at Ujiji (on the eastern shore of a lake) with this encounter in darkness and candle-light (on the western shore of a different lake). Even the words 'we cannot see each other' were to prove prophetic. Almost all the variables that made the Livingstone/Stanley meeting result so happily were different in this case. True, Emin was just 5 foot 7 inches tall, so did not present a threat at this level - Stanley, ever-obsessive about the height of men he met, noted down the stature of Emin and Casati on two different occasions. But Livingstone had been a devout Christian, whereas Emin had embraced the Islamic faith. Emin was a brilliant linguist, botanist and zoologist - an academic, in a word - while Stanley never truly mastered any language other than English and had the plain man's impatience with sciences that did not have an immediate pragmatic value. The perfect choice of explorer to 'rescue' Emin, if he had only been twenty years younger, was the linguist and orientalist Sir Richard Burton.

There was a sense in which Emin and Stanley were at once too alike and too unlike. They were alike in that both were rootless individuals who had reinvented themselves. Eduard Schnitzer had become Emin Pasha; John Rowlands had become Henry Stanley. Both had denied their origins and found fame and solace in Africa - African exploration always contained this element of a desire to return in effect to childhood and so transmogrify the experiences of actual childhood. But there the similarities ended. It was no accident that Stanley's 'socialisation' should have been in the America of the expanding frontier and 'manifest destiny'. He represented the aggressive, thrusting, technologically superior West, contemptuous of 'inferior' cultures and desirous of making them over, via Christianity, capitalism or overt imperialism, to the comforting embraces of 'civilisation'. Emin, by contrast, had explicitly chosen to be a man of the East, a man ready to submit to Fate, kismet, baraka, the will of Allah. For Emin everything was written; for Stanley nothing was. Stanley was all energy, incessant activity and the will to dominate. Emin's nature showed itself in indecision, changes of mind, procrastination, a tendency to let matters drift or problems solve themselves, to attain his ends indirectly or by intrigue rather than by bluster or brute force.

Emin was far superior morally - in his concern for others and his genuine love of Africa (whereas Stanley loved Africa for what it gave him). But Stanley's Promethean will made things happen in situations where Emin could only wring his hands.

On 30 April the two contingents marched to Nsabe to make permanent camp further along the lake. Stanley thought the wangwana cut a much more impressive figure than Emin's Sudanese. While Emin sent out for more food and bearers - there was no game nearby - Stanley handed over the Remington ammunition and suggested that the joint forces dig in behind an entrenchment, in case Kabba Rega, with his 1500 riflemen, decided to try conclusions. The Khedive steamed off to bring up reinforcements, while Saad Tato and the best of the hunters scattered far and wide in search of prey. Then the two leaders settled in for a further round of talks.

The talks proved very difficult. At first Stanley brought the maximum pressure to bear to get the Pasha to return to England, or at least Egypt. Emin finally came clean and admitted that he did not want to leave, especially having regard to the people in his care. He adduced the new argument that if he ordered the Egyptians and Sudanese to pull out, they might mutiny. Stanley in reply tried psychological warfare, speaking of the need for the Pasha to make a will for, depending on whether the Mahdists or Kabba Rega killed him first, he would need to leave his accumulated back-pay to someone. But Emin was tenacious. All he wanted was the ammunition and supplies to maintain himself where he was. His soldiers did not want to leave Equatoria and he did not want to leave them. Besides, they could have withdrawn to the east coast at any time since the Mahdiya started.

In the back of both men's minds were unstated considerations and motives. After the trauma of 1872, Stanley did not want to return to England a second time without his 'quarry', perhaps to be accused once more of being a fraud and impostor. Emin, on his side, was shocked and appalled at the small scale and general condition of a 'relief expedition' which seemed to be in need of relief itself. Stalemate ensued.

On 3rd May Stanley tried again. Reluctantly he unveiled the two possible commissions for Emin if he stayed in Africa, from Leopold and Mackinnon. Since, he argued, Egypt lacked the military resources ever again to be able to control Equatoria, the choice for any rational man in Emin's situation had to narrow to these two. Leopold's offer, made orally to Stanley, was for Emin to remain governor of Equatoria under the aegis of the Congo State. Emin turned the offer down flat. He argued that the idea was implausible for a number of reasons. He himself could not change flags without the Khedive's permission as he was in the service of Egypt. Moreover, distance and logistics meant that the Congo could not help Equatoria against the Mahdists or Kabba Rega; they had their own dispute with the Congo Arabs to settle and could not even defend Stanley Falls!

What about the British, Emin asked? Did they not have an interest in Equatoria? The snag here, Stanley confided, was that Equatoria was 500 miles too far inland. Unless Britain undertook the conquest of Uganda, an east-coast corridor to Equatoria was too perilous; no government would be prepared to make expensive outlays on such an indefensible province. This was the point at which he introduced the Mackinnon scheme. He proposed that Emin and the elite of his troops should accompany the expedition to the Kavirondo area of Lake Victoria, there to be established as the nucleus of Mackinnon's British East Africa Company. Without bringing pressure to bear on Emin, he advised him that this was a far better offer than Leopold's. If Emin accepted, once he was established in Kavirondo, Stanley would lead the relief expedition through Masailand to the coast and then get formal approval for the actions he had taken as Mackinnon's plenipotentiary.

This proposal allowed Emin the leeway to stall that he had been seeking throughout the talks. He said that a decision was possible only after he had consulted his Sudanese, for he could not be seen to be, nor did he wish to incur the charge that he was, running out on them. Emin's real motive was to find a plausible pretext to stay on. Stanley tried to cut the Gordian knot by sounding Casati on his opinion, for Casati's view was known to have great weight with Emin. However, this tactic foundered on the obvious rock that Casati understood no English and his French was even worse than Stanley's. Besides, he had his own reasons for disliking Stanley. He was at Kabba Rega's court, just starting to make progress in negotiations with that potentate, when news of the Emin expedition arrived in Bunyoro. Kabba Rega read this development as an attempt by the combined European and Egyptian forces to conquer Buganda and Bunyoro. Casati was lucky to escape the kingdom with his life.

It was left that Emin would tour Equatoria seeking the opinions of his soldiers on a return to Egypt, while Stanley went back to find his Rear Guard. Should the Sudanese prove reluctant, as was most likely Emin would try to win them over to Mackinnon's Kavirondo scheme. At this stage Stanley was very keen that Emin should opt for this solution, and spoke in grandiloquent terms of the Imperial British East Africa Company. This had a capital of £400,000 already subscribed, there were plans for a railway from the east coast to Lake Victoria, and the IBEA would soon become a second East India Company.

How plausible was the Mackinnon solution? According to Stanley, some Egyptian officers came to his tent on 4th May to tell him that they wanted to go back home, never mind Lake Victoria, but 'the Pasha does not want to return - he is happy with his travels about the country and bird studies and such things but we . .. wish to return.' This seems to be a case either of Stanley deceiving himself or misunderstanding what he was told. Emin, who knew his men's minds intimately, realised that they did not want to move anywhere. He had tried to persuade them before to trek off south towards safety or home but they had refused; it seemed, then, that even the Lake Victoria idea was a pipedream. Besides, Sudanese morale was poor. They had expected an army of deliverance and found instead a motley gallimaufry of scarecrows. To counteract the poor image his 'relief expedition had presented, Emin wanted Stanley to come with him on the provincial tour. But Stanley was now obsessed with the fate of the Rear Guard, so offered to send Jephson instead.

Emin stayed with Stanley almost a month, and their political discussions petered out after the first week. Much of the rest of the time Emin spent telling Stanley bizarre stories about Gordon's period as governor and his notorious eccentricities. He revealed that the hero of the British people was an opium addict and attributed to this habit his sexual abstinence, for opium was said to make men impotent, as was the root of the Lymphaca lotus, with which Gordon also dosed himself. Stanley always liked it if someone played the iconoclast with Gordon's reputation but Emin unwittingly deepened Stanley's dislike for his Islamic deviancy, when he said, as though between normal heterosexual males: 'I cannot conceive how mortal man could restrain himself from sexual intercourse.'

Stanley's distaste and resentment for Emin deepened over their time together. He was most annoyed to find that the Pasha was not in desperate straits, so that there had been no real need for the Advance Column to put itself under such pressure to reach him. In this way Stanley transferred the guilt for his own hard driving, which had caused so many fatalities, on to Emin himself. Also, it was quite clear that assembling Emin's people for the putative march to Lake Victoria was going to take a very long time. To salve his angry feelings, Stanley allowed himself to be patronising in his journal about Emin's scientific flair and curiosity: 'The Pasha is so exceedingly industrious that all kinds of work seem agreeable to him. It is pleasant to observe at his quarters aneroids laid out in shade but truly exposed to air, thermometers, dry and wet bulbs properly arranged . . . His journals are a marvel of neatness and fine writing as though he aimed at obtaining a prize for order, neatness and accuracy. Such a man as this would be invaluable for such expeditions as I have led since 1874.'

In other respects the sojourn at Nsabe was a pleasant one. Saad Tato and his young assistant Mabruki performed wonders on the big game trail. They bagged two buffalo on their first day out, but not before one of them had gored Mabruki. Next day Saad Tato shot four roan antelopes, amply replenishing the meat supply. When food supplies again started to run low, towards the end of the second week of May, the wangwana started to loot and pillage. The local Balegga refused to take their incursions lying down, and in one raid two of them were killed and another two badly wounded. Two days later another of the wangwana was found dead and his Winchester missing. Stanley remained uncertain how to react to these events: 'I am never quite satisfied as to the manner of these accidents, whether the natives or the Zanzibaris are the aggressors. The latter relate with exceeding plausibility their version of the matter, but they are such adepts in the art of lying that I am frequently bewildered.'

On 14th May the Khedive returned with supplies. Emin gave gifts of cloth to Stanley and his officers. His apparent affluence served to rub salt in Stanley's wounds, since he had left his own reserve supply of clothing at Yambuya with the Rear Column. But one worrying sign was observed when the Khedive arrived. Instead of possessing natural authority, Emin seemed to be reduced to pleading and wheedling with his men to get them to do his bidding. If there was one thing Stanley despised in a leader, it was a man who coaxed and cajoled his followers instead of browbeating and overawing them. But Emin's methods seemed to work. He sent the Khedive back to Wadelai and it returned on 22nd May with its sister ship the Nyasa and a reinforcement of eighty Sudanese soldiers.

The stay at Nsabe also provided Stanley with the unwonted luxury of reflection on the grandeur of nature in Africa. On 6 May a ferocious storm blew across the lake, churning up the whole face of the Albert into foam, spray and white rollers. A week later they were hit by a tornado. Nights in Africa always particularly intrigued Stanley and the STANLEY:

SORCERER'S APPRENTICE Emin expedition prompted him to a vintage Stanley purple passage:

By nine o'clock the men, overcome by fatigue, would be asleep; silence ensued, broken only by sputtering fire-logs, flights of night-jars, hoarse notes from great bats, croakings of frogs, cricket-cheeps, falling of trees or branches, a shriek from some prowling chimpanzee, a howl from a peevish monkey, and the continual gasping cry of the lemur. But during many nights, we would sit shivering under ceaseless torrents of rain, watching the forky flames of the lightning, and listening to the stunning and repeated roars of the thunder- cannonade.

An aspect of nature not so welcome was the discovery of two small brown snakes of a coppery tint in his tent on the morning of 20th May. Perhaps by an association of ideas he made Emin a parting present of two mongooses. Stanley was irritated by Emin's less than gracious acceptance, for he complained that in general the animals were a nuisance; they knocked over instruments and spilled ink. They also had a mania for eggs, to which they reacted like dogs to aniseed.

On 23rd May the wangmana entertained Emin and his men to a farewell dance. Stanley and the Pasha made their final plans for a rendezvous later that year. In eight months' time Stanley's entire force would muster at Fort Bodo, ready for a march to Lake Albert, where Emin would have assembled all his people for the journey to Lake Victoria. All ideas of taking Emin's cache of ivory back via the Congo were laid aside. Stanley made his farewells to Emin, then briefed Jephson, who was to accompany the Pasha, privately. He was to use all his powers of persuasion to convince the garrison to return to Egypt, insinuating that they would not be paid unless they reported to Cairo.

To show his good faith, Emin made Stanley a parting present of 130 Madi carriers from Equatoria. Superficially, the two men parted on good terms. Stanley's force departed for Fort Bodo on the morning of 24th May. But a short way along the road the Madis deserted en bloc and fired a shower of arrows at Stanley's men as a Parthian shot. Parke dropped one of them in his tracks with a well-aimed rifle shot, but this simply precipitated the flight of the deserters.

The day had begun badly, but a little later a great silvery-topped mountain peak was pointed out to Stanley. This was the Ruwenzori, the fabled 'Mountains of the Moon', a staple of African legend since the days of Ptolemy. All ancient accounts of the source of the Nile spoke of its headwaters being located around a lake system and a range of snow-capped mountains. Until 1888 no such mountains had been found in the lake areas, though the discovery of Kilimanjaro by the Germans alerted the more perceptive geographers that the old stories might contain a grain of truth. Stanley later claimed that he had succeeded in getting the first recorded sight of the Mountains of the Moon by a European. But in fact Jephson and Parke had seen it first, on 20th April while on their way to Lake Albert with the boat. Parke records in throwaway manner the true first sighting of the Ruwenzori: 'On the march we distinctly saw mow on the top of a huge mountain situated to the south-west of our position. As this was a curious and unexpected sight, we halted the caravan to have a good view. Some of the Zanzibaris tried to persuade us that the white covering which decorated this mountain was salt) but Jephson and myself were satisfied that it was snow.' But it was ever Stanley's practice to belittle the achievements of other explorers or to downgrade the feats of his fellow travellers. He did not bat an eyelid when Emin wrote to him: 'Allow me to be the first to congratulate you on your most splendid discovery ... It is wonderful to think how wherever you go, you distance your predecessors by your discoveries.'

Even later that day Stanley was amazed to see Kavalli with 400 warriors hurrying towards them on the road. It transpired that Emin had told the local tribes he was proceeding against Kabba Rega in Bunyoro but, because of the loss of manpower to Stanley, he had to call on their levies to assist him. Stanley was concerned that Emin seemed to be playing straight with nobody: 'His conduct to Kavalli reminds me somewhat of a suspicion that though he is fair in words, he appears to dislike doing what he promises ... Emin strikes me as being rather heedless or weak in carrying out intentions and promises.'

On 26th May Stanley learned that the chiefs Musiri and Kadongo intended to attack his column between Gavira's and Mazamboni's. This was very bad news, for he had just 111 rifles and ten rounds each to reach Fort Bodo, 125 miles away. To make every shot count, he decided he would have to 'take out' the two hostile chiefs successively: 'it was held by Thomas Carlyle that it was the highest wisdom to know and believe that the greatest thing which necessity ordered to be done was the wisest, the best and the only thing wanted there.' Fortunately at this moment a further eighty-two Madis, sent by Emin to replace the deserters, caught up with him at the foot of the plateau. He decided to rope them together, then untie them when he had placed three or four hostile tribes between himself and Emin. Next he carried out a precision raid on Kadongo's village which succeeded perfectly. On the road to Gavira's after the raid they ran into Mazamboni's brother. Stanley impressed on him that the expedition expected Mazamboni's aid in chastising Musiri. Fortune was with Stanley that day. On arrival at Gavira he found the eponymous chief ready to join in the attack; then, an hour after sunset, Mazamboni himself came in with 1000 warriors. With this powerful force, Stanley swooped on Musiri's village. He found another empty village. Forewarned of the attack, Musiri's men had decamped and taken their herds. But there was a full granary to reward the assailants, and Stanley was jubilant that he had brushed yet another enemy from his flank without any waste or ammunition.

The victory war dance that followed contained the finest music and the most impressive balletics Stanley had seen so far, and was crowned by a message of submission from Musiri. After taking detailed notes on the ethnology of the area, Stanley pressed on to Bodo at a great pace. After their mauling in April, the Besse people left them well alone. On 4th June they were at the Ituri and the expedition members, some 224 strong (with 101 Madis and 111 wangwana), began to drive across the river the livestock Mazamboni had given them. Suddenly a large crocodile appeared and started to make for the swimming cattle, its saurian head held above the water as if intending to swallow a cow or donkey. Stanley fired at the marauder and appeared to score a direct hit, for the crocodile at once sank beneath the waters and troubled them no more.

On 8th June they entered Fort Bodo to find Stairs awaiting them. He had experienced another nightmare journey back through the rain forest to fetch the sick and ailing from Ugarrowa's. Only fourteen of the fifty-six left behind remained after the trek to Fort Bodo. This meant that of the 389 souls Stanley had led away from Yambuya a year before, just 169 remained. Stanley was alarmed at the physical condition of the men at Bodo. Ahead of them loomed a 1000-mile return march, which only the fittest could hope to survive. He spent a week handpicking 107 volunteers, each carrying twenty-five days' supply of Indian corn. To cut down on baggage and loss through sickness, he intended to march to the Rear Column himself, with no white companions. But first he had to make sure Fort Bodo was well defended against any conceivable combination of Manyema and tribesmen. He fortified it strongly and put Stairs in command. This elevation gave Stairs the boldness to suggest that perhaps the non-appearance of the Rear Column at Ugarrowa's was because the Belgians had detained the Stanley downriver. Stanley scouted the suggestion. If anyone was to blame, the prime candidates were Barttelot and Tippu Tip. He recorded his intuition that the entire Emin Pasha relief expedition was ill-starred: 'Evil hangs over this forest as a pall over the dead; it is like a region accursed for crimes; whoever enters within its circle becomes subject to divine wrath.'

The more Stanley brooded over the course of the expedition - and brood he did all the way from Nsabe to Fort Bodo - the less satisfactory everything seemed to him. There could be no denying that splitting the expedition and leaving a Rear Column had been an egregious error. That was bad enough, but the misalliance with Emin seemed even worse the more he pondered it. In the course of their numerous conversations Emin had been unable to hide his disappointment that the 'relief expedition provided neither a secure route to the coast, nor ammunition and other goods in sufficient quantities to enable him to maintain himself in his province, nor even a guarantee from Egypt or Britain of Equatoria's continuing existence. From Emin's point of view, the arrival of the so-called relief expedition was simply a further drain on his resources, and in its laughably inadequate size and resources it affected adversely his credibility in Equatoria - especially as Stanley refused to show himself in person and unfurl the legendary banner of Bula Matari.

From Stanley's point of view, Emin's lack of grip on his province was deeply worrying. He seemed shot through with weakness and false pride. He also seemed to be labouring under the illusion that the relief expedition had been sent out because of his reputation as a scientist, not because he was perceived as the man who had inherited Gordon's mantle and was heroically holding out against the Mahdi's dervishes. How else explain his curious remark to Casati regarding the specimens he had sent to the British Museum: 'Who would have thought that a bird and a butterfly would have proved so useful to my people?' This sort of thing excited Stanley's particular derision. He had the man of action's contempt for visionaries, dreamers and practitioners of theoretical or non-applied sciences and repeated the familiar charges that the scientific mentality cared more for abstractions than feelings and for 'Man' than flesh and blood human beings. The seeds of the later apocalyptical breakdown in relations between the two men were already there in May 1888.

On 16th June, taking 208 of the 283 men at Fort Bodo, Stanley set out for Yambuya, by now desperately anxious about the fate of the Rear Column. Stairs and Nelson were left behind to await Emin and Jephson, prior to the general rendezvous on Lake Albert. With Stanley were Hoffmann, 1x3 wangwana and 95 Madi porters. Parke was to accompany them as far as Ipoto to bring back the loads left there. Stanley took such a large body with him to Yambuya on the best-case scenario that the non-appearance of the Rear Column was solely due to Tippu Tip's not having kept his word about the carriers. Even so, he hoped that Barttelot had some at least of the promised men, otherwise the full impedimenta of the expedition could not be brought to Lake Albert.

But deep down Stanley was apprehensive that some far worse disaster than Tippu Tip's non-feesance had overtaken the Rear Column: mass desertions, the foundering of steamers, maybe even an attack on Yambuya by Tippu and the Manyema. But he told Parke that whatever he found, he would go no farther west than Yambuya. If Rose Troup, Ward and Bonny had failed to arrive with their loads, that was the end of the matter; in no circumstances would he go down to Stanley Pool after them.

The march back to Ipoto was as gruelling as Stanley had feared, though accomplished in a much shorter time than the outward journey. 'The cries of the leaders indicate the nature of the obstacles to be met through the forest. We hear "red ants afoot!; a stump! spikes! a pitfall to right! a burrow to left! thorns! Those ants! lo, a tripping creeper, ware nettles! A log below! a hole! slippery beneath! Look out for mud! Those ants! red ants on march! Ware ants! a log! spikes below!"'

At Ipoto, reached on 22nd June, the healthy, well-fed appearance of Stanley and his men frightened Kilonga-Longa and his Manyema into an apology for their previous behaviour. Nineteen out of thirty of the purloined Remingtons were brought to Stanley, though only fifty of the 3000 cartridges were returned. Stanley had no time to chastise the Manyema so, accepting their apologies, and leaving Parke behind, he plunged into the forest again on 25th June. They ferried across the Ituri in canoes, entered the previous October's wilderness and reached Nelson's starvation camp. Only the hope of meeting Barttelot drove them on through the green hell. But Stanley was pleased with progress. A distance it took them thirteen days to cover in October 1887 when starving they could now cover in four days with full bellies.

At Nelson's camp they dug up the buried stores and ammunition, which were still in good condition. On 29th June they left the river route to take a shorter, inland route, steering south-westerly by compass through the trackless woods. On 2nd July they struck the Lenda River and crossed by a tree bridge. But on the other side the pattern of starvation, desertion and sneak attacks by poisoned arrows reasserted itself. The first to drop in their tracks through hunger were the Madi carriers, who had jettisoned their corn supplies to lighten their loads. Other Madis, unused to the forest, were severely wounded in the foot by spikes and had to be carried. Whenever the expedition came upon a plantain plantation they would rush upon it and devour it like locusts.

On 7th July they were tormented by a tropical downpour. As Stanley made camp in the pelting rain 'in the bosom of the unrevised woods' he decided that his decision to strike inland had been a mistake. When next day he found some women who offered to guide him to Ugarrowa's, he jumped at the chance. But after three days' hewing and hacking at the unyielding jungle, they found themselves back at the camp they had occupied three days earlier, exactly where they had encountered their 'guides'. Seeing that they had expended so much energy merely to walk in a circle, the wangwana declared the women traitors and called for their execution. Stanley resisted the call, took further bearings and two days later steered them by compass to their old camp on the Ituri opposite Ugarrowa's.

Ugarrowa's itself they found deserted; the chief had returned to Stanley Pool to sell his huge stock of ivory. They were now in desperate straits from hunger. Not only was the village where they had hoped to replenish their supplies an abandoned husk, but when they pressed on to Aruwimi Falls they found that Ugarrowa's men had eaten all the food in the area on their westward trek. By great good fortune the expedition located a single plantain plantation, which gave them the wherewithal for a few more days' marching. Setting out on 16th July, in seven hours they got to the rapids above Navabi Falls and found their old camp at Avamburi landing place. It was full of the skulls of refugees from Ugarrowa's marauders. Since several of the Madi had also joined the ranks of the dead, Stanley halted here for two days and buried the dead in a mass grave.

After a seven-hour march they came on 20th July to camp above Bafaido cataract. Here another Matadi, whose foot was skewered, lay down and took a stoical farewell of his comrades. Finding a store of canoes, Stanley embarked the expedition and started to negotiate the cataract. They made just 2 miles' progress next day, which they spent battling the rapids - which claimed another two men in its boiling waters. A further two wangwana, who went absent without leave to look for plantains, were cut down by the local tribesmen.

By 25th July they were at the Bavikai rapids at the mouth of the Nepoko River. Stanley was growing weak from lack of meat, having subsisted for so long on a diet of bananas and plantains. Hearing from the spies he habitually kept among the wangwana that the Zanzibaris had been having considerable luck catching and eating goats and chickens, he issued an order that any meat caught must be brought to him. In this way he soon tasted his first fowl for weeks and quickly felt restored in vigour.

But always the horrors of the terrain oppressed him. On 26th July he recorded his impressions in his journal:

I was never so sensible to the evils of forest marching as on this day - my own condition of body being so reduced owing to the mean and miserable diet of vegetables on which I was forced to subsist made me more than usually sympathetic. At this time there were about 30 naked Madis in the last stages of life, their former ebon black was changed to an ashy grey hue ... Almost every individual among them is the victim of some hideous disease, tumours, scorched backs, foetid ulcers, are common, others are afflicted with chronic dysentery, and a wretched debility caused by insufficient food ... the ground was rank with vegetable corruption, the atmosphere heated, stifling dank, and pregnant with the seeds of decay of myriads of insects, leaves, plants, twigs and branches.

On 27th July they portaged their canoes over Avugadu rapids and pressed on to Mabengu. Armies of bats swarmed around them at night. By the end of the month they reached Avisibba, scene of the battle with the cannibals with poisoned arrows a year before. They found the remains of their deserters from that time, who had been killed and eaten. A forlorn little girl they happened on spoke of a major engagement between the Avisibba people and Ugarrowa's men, who had passed that way a few days before.

After camping at an island above Nejambi rapids, Stanley ordered the canoes passed through the cataracts on the left-hand channel. Some of the wangwana tried getting through on the right-hand branch and were swept away and drowned. The next obstacle was Panga Falls, which also had to be portaged. They struggled to complete the task in pouring rain but by 5th August had a flotilla of nineteen canoes below the falls. They now entered the area where they had encountered the stiffest armed resistance on the outward march. Sure enough, dozens of skirmishes ensued, and the wangwana took casualties from poisoned arrows. By now fresh traces of Ugarrowa's men were everywhere in the form of gutted villages and devastated fields. Stanley decided to overtake Ugarrowa by rapid passage on the river. He split his force, gave thirty-five to his chief guide Rashid to take overland, then pressed on with his flotilla of canoes to overtake Ugarrowa at Wasp Rapids.

On 10 August Stanley's men caught up with Ugarrowa's force. It consisted of fifty-seven loaded canoes, and among their number were the couriers Stairs had sent from Ugarrowa's to get news of the Rear Column. Driven back by local resistance at Avisibba with the loss of four of their number, the couriers had sought refuge in the bosom of the Manyema marauders. Ugarrowa himself received Stanley with great kindness and sympathy, and provided him with canoes enough to take his entire party downriver. Stanley waited until Rashid and the land party arrived, then embarked his entire force on 12th August.

Persistent drumming followed them to the Mariri rapids, but the hostiles kept their distance. Floating past their outward land camps, they came to Bunganeta Island. Stanley now recognised all the landmarks and, sixty days out from Fort Bodo and just 90 miles from Yambuya, congratulated himself on his rate of progress. His original estimated time of arrival at Yambuya had been 3rd September, so he was two weeks ahead of schedule. But still there was neither sign nor word of the Rear Column.

Suddenly, on 17th August, Stanley rounded a bend in the Aruwimi River near the village of Banalya and saw a European-style encampment. Through his field glasses he made out white clothes and a red flag. He ordered his canoeists to paddle with all their might for the shore. As he got closer, Stanley saw that the camp was stockaded. At the gate Bonny suddenly appeared. There followed a dramatic dialogue.

'Well, Bonny, how are you? Where is the Major? Sick, I suppose?' 'The Major is dead, sir.'

'Dead! Good God! How dead? Fever?'

'No, sir, he was shot.'

'By whom?'

'By the Manyema-Tippu Tib's people.'

'Good heavens! Well, where is Jameson?'

'At Stanley Falls.'

'What is he doing there in the name of goodness?'

'He went to obtain more carriers.'

'Well then, where is Mr Ward, or Mr Troup?'

'Mr Ward is at Bangala.'

'Bangala! Bangala! what can he be doing there?'

'Yes, sir, he is at Bangala, and Mr Troup has been invalided home some months ago.'

This bare recital did not do justice to the gruesome facts. Within hours Stanley learned that the Rear Column had been overcome by disaster so complete that he, the superstitious Welshman, was inclined to attribute its collapse to the forces of darkness and the malign work of the Evil One.

13

WHEN Stanley marched from Yambuya into the unknown horrors of the Ituri forest on 28th June 1887, he left behind him the latent elements of potential tragedy. The origo mali was Leopold. Since the King had not provided a flotilla of boats so that the expedition could proceed together, Stanley was forced to leave behind at Leopoldville the bulk of his ammunition. This meant that once at Yambuya Stanley could not fulfil his side of the bargain with Tippu Tip and give him the gunpowder he required. Since Tippu in turn refused to implement his side of the contract unilaterally, there were not enough porters for the entire expedition to proceed, even though it had already dropped astern two separate detachments, under Rose Troup at Kinshassa, and Ward at Bolobo. Everything would still have worked out well if Stanley had returned as promised in November 1887, or even if he had returned six months later. But his lamentable underestimation of the difficulties he would face in getting to Emin, and the ambiguity and imprecision of the orders he left with Barttelot, combined to produce a disaster which gave new meaning to the cliché about 'The Dark Continent'. Jephson once said of the Emin Pasha expedition: 'the whole story is a very dark one, as dark as any of the many dark stories connected with African travel.' Within this darkness, the experience of the Rear Column counts as the ninth circle of hell.

Yet perhaps Stanley's worst mistake of all was the appointment of Barttelot to command the Rear Column. In retrospect, as Stanley later saw, Barttelot was wholly unsuited by temperament to exercise a difficult command in conditions of maximum stress. Hot-tempered and autocratic, Barttelot could get on with none of the other officers except Jameson. He also continued to smart at the humiliation, as he saw it, of being left behind at Yambuya by Stanley as a punishment. Additionally, he hated and was hated by the 1vangwana. The word 'nigger' was never far from Barttelot's lips and he had actually been reprimanded on this score by Stanley himself. 'He was completely at sea when dealing with the black' was Ward's verdict. Rose Troup put it more strongly: 'It did not take me long to discover that he had an intense hatred for anything in the shape of a black man, for he made no disguise of the fact. His hatred was so marked that I was seized with great misgivings concerning his future dealings with them, more particularly when he would have to handle Tippu Tib's men.'

Six weeks after Stanley's departure, on 14th August, the Stanley brought both Ward's and Troup's contingents up to Yambuya, but not before the rear of the Rear Guard had itself come close to disaster. With men packed on her like sardines, the Stanley hit a reef while coming upriver. The fore compartments filled with water and had the bulkheads not been watertight, the ship and its complement would have gone to the bottom in seconds. They were a long way from the shore, with a fast current running, but there was no panic, largely because the men did not realise the danger they were in. Troup got the men off in canoes and spent a nervous night aboard himself. Next day the canoes had to take off 150 loads before the Stanley got off the sandbank; then three days were spent fitting a new plate.

Once the detachments were united at Yambuya, Barttelot had to face the fact that he had under his command the dregs of the expedition: the malingerers, skrimshankers, troublemakers and the genuinely sick; Stanley had taken the manpower's gold and left the dross. Out of 271 men at Yambuya, perhaps 165 were in a condition for porterage. In camp were 660 loads, 493 of which had been brought up by Troup. There were four times as many loads as men, so real progress was only possible when Tippu Tip sent his bearers. By the time the Stanley arrived, there was no sign of them.

Stanley had told Barttelot he would return in November. The Major's wisest course, then, was to sit tight and wait for the leader to return. But his force was beset by illness and food shortages - the only readily available source of nutrition was manioc, which grew in abundance around the camp. There was a danger that inactivity and inanition would finish off the Rear Guard before Stanley returned. Stanley had permitted Barttelot to follow in his footsteps if Tippu Tip supplied all 600 of the promised porters. If he merely supplied some, he had left it open to Barttelot to make a very slow advance using relays of porters. Barttelot's real problem was to decide how long he should wait for Tippu to supply the promised men.

These, then, were the adverse conditions confronting the Rear Column. They were condemned to enforced idleness and food shortages, they were beset by sickness and a hostile environment, uncertain both of Stanley's return and Tippu's intentions. In addition, they were commanded by a racialist martinet, who was at daggers drawn with most of his officers, and who was a harsh and unyielding disciplinarian. The mixture was inherently combustible.

A further decline in their fortunes became apparent the day after the arrival of the Stanley when the presence of a force of Manyema in close vicinity to the stockaded camp became known. These Manyema were raiders and slavers, operating independently of Tippu Tip. They were a threat to the Rear Column, not so much directly as because they diverted the precious supplies of fish, palm oil and other foodstuffs from the local villages to their own camp and threatened the locals with death if they traded with the expedition instead. Barttelot interviewed the headman of these Manyema, who told him that Tippu Tip had already sent the promised 500 porters to Yambuya, but that opposition from hostile tribesmen had first detained, then finally dispersed, them when their gunpowder ran out.

Barttelot at once decided to send Jameson and Ward to consult with Tippu Tip at Stanley Falls. After a five-day journey they arrived, were treated with conspicuous friendliness by Tippu, and sent on their way with a promise that he would let them have more men, though possibly not as many as in the original party. He sent back his nephew Selim bin Mohammed to take over as chief of the Manyema encampment, so that relations between the two camps could be conducted through official channels.

The two men returned, confident that the porters would soon be with them. Ward collapsed with an attack of dysentery that kept him hors de combat for six weeks, to Barttelot's disgust. He noted in his diary: 'Ward a little better, he ain't much of a chap.' Barttelot hated Ward for his intellectual superiority and his genuine feeling for, and ability to get on with, the Africans he so detested.

But as the weeks went by, and no carriers arrived from Stanley Falls, Barttelot began to fret over the presence of the nearby Manyema. Not only were they a threat to his food supplies and a standing reproach to him - since they massacred the locals with impunity and when these appealed to him for protection, Barttelot found himself frustrated and impotent, bound by Stanley's 'non-intervention' instructions - but their free and easy lifestyle tempted the wangwana to desertion. In response Barttelot's discipline became more and more draconian.

A never-ending cycle of brutality began. Two Zanzibari deserters, Bartholomew and Msa, were given 150 and 100 lashes respectively. What this meant can be gauged from Glave's description of a Congo flogging:

The chicotte of raw hippo hide, especially a new one, trimmed like a corkscrew, with edges like knife-blades, and as hard as wood, is a terrible weapon, and a few blows bring blood; not more than 25 blows should be given unless the offence is very serious. Though we persuade ourselves that the African's skin is very tough, it needs an extraordinary constitution to withstand the terrible punishment of 100 blows; generally the victim is in a state of insensibility after 25 or 30 blows. At the first blow he yells abominably; then quiets down, and is a mere groaning, quivering body till the operation is over, when the culprit stumbles away, often with gashes which will endure a lifetime ... I conscientiously believe that a man who receives 100 blows is often nearly killed, and has his spirit broken for life.

Having survived this ordeal, the two men deserted again, were recaptured, and sentenced to further punishment. Msa received 150 lashes, and Bartholomew was given the 'lenient' punishment of 75 strokes, since he was still tender from the previous flogging. Next it was the turn of the Sudanese to taste Barttelot's wrath. The theft of a goat led to the arrest of the Sudanese soldier Burgari Mohammed. He received 150 strokes then, since he had tried to implicate another man, was fined nine months' pay and sentenced to another flogging as soon as he had recovered from the first one. Until then he had to walk up and down in the sun every day in chains. Burgari escaped, was recaptured, and tried for desertion. The death penalty was proposed. Jameson and Troup argued against this, but Ward and Bonny were for it, so the luckless Sudanese was executed by firing squad.

An even more notorious instance of brutality concerned the wangwana interpreter John Henry, who made the mistake of stealing Barttelot's revolver. Barttelot at once sentenced him to be shot, but the wangwana threatened to desert in a body if the execution was carried out. After a furious altercation in which Barttelot fumed, blustered and threatened the Zanzibaris with excommunication from their native island, he 'commuted' the sentence to 300 lashes. John Henry died from the effects of the savage flogging two days later."

Troup, Ward and Jameson were by and large civilised and

compassionate men, but Barttelot had a rival for brutality in Bonny. Shortly after Stanley returned to Banlaya, Stanley inspected the victim of one of Bonny's 150-lashes sentences, for theft. One of the sick was emitting a noisome foetor and Stanley asked to see the man's 'ulcer'. He lifted his loin cloth for an answer and 'the sight was enough to sicken a hyena, even. Never in my life have I seen anything so awful. The seating parts or buttocks were two deep hollows in which maggots swarmed and a saucer might easily have been put into either hollow.'

At the beginning of October, with Ward still ill and Bonny down with fever, Barttelot decided on another visit to Stanley Falls. He took Troup with him to try to beard Tippu Tip in his lair. Tippu told them that local manpower was now exhausted on his own slaving and ivory expeditions; the porters would have to come from Kasongo, in the heartland of Tippu's 'empire', a month's journey upriver towards Nyangwe. At the beginning of November the two white men returned to Yambuya with empty hands, save for a herd of goats and flock of chickens. T0 keep up the pressure, Barttelot ordered the recently recovered Ward up to Stanley Falls to complain about the behaviour of the local Manyema. He found that Tippu had already departed for Kasongo, ostensibly to find the porters.

By December the Yambuya camp of the Rear Column was a shambles. The white men took it in turns to succumb to rheumatism, fever and biliousness. Thirty-one wangwana had already died of malnutrition and scurvy and the effects of eating raw or improperly cooked manioc. The manioc tuber contains a form of cyanide, and only careful preparation and cooking can eliminate the poison. The tired and listless wangwana had no time for such niceties. The result was giddiness, fainting, stomach cramps and nausea in the short term; in the long run the results were degeneration of nervous tissue, paralysis of the optic nerve and blindness. Salim bin Rashid, one of Stanley's veterans, confirmed that it was the unremitting diet of manioc that helped to explain why Stanley found only sixty out of 271 alive when he returned to Yambuya in August 1888. 'There is another thing I wished to say and that is, we have been wondering why we who belong to the continent should die and the white men who are strangers to it should live. When we were on the Congo and other journeys, it was the white men who died and not we. Now, it is we who die, a hundred blacks to one white. No, master, the cause of death is in the food. The white men had meat of goat and fowl and fish and lived, and we who had nothing but manioc died.'

Christmas passed and New Year 1888 dawned, and still no news from Stanley. Barttelot was now beside himself with anxiety and frustration. He discussed the possibility of advancing without any of Tippu Tip's porters, but Rose Troup, the expedition's transport specialist, advised him that with their existing manpower it would take twelve days to advance 4 miles. For want of anything better to do, Barttelot decided on a fourth excursion to Stanley Falls. This time he took Jameson and the Syrian interpreter Assad Farran with him. In mid-February 1888 they reached Stanley Falls to find that Tippu Tip was still absent in Kasongo. Barttelot decided to send Jameson downriver to find him, this time with an additional request for 400 fighting men.

Back at Yambuya in March 1888 Barttelot revealed the thinking behind the request for fighting men. He now intended to take a flying column in search of Stanley, accompanied by Tippu Tip's warriors, while the rest of the Rear Column retired under Rose Troup to Stanley Falls station. The snag was that this was directly contrary to Stanley's orders. So Barttelot decided to send Ward down to the Atlantic coast to cable the relief committee for further instructions. This was a peculiarly eccentric decision, both because whatever the committee replied it would not materially affect the basic problems he confronted at Yambuya and because, if his own plans worked out, he would anyway not be there to receive the answer telegraphed to Ward. The official Barttelot explanation was that the committee might have news of Stanley from the Zanzibar coast and might want to withdraw the entire expedition. The real reason for Barttelot's action was pathological.

By spring of 1888 there were clear signs that the stress of inactivity and uncertainty at Yambuya was beginning to unhinge Barttelot. Without Ward and Jameson to guide him, he lurched into pointless, angry confrontations with Selim Mohammed and the Manyema. Troup's sickness began to exasperate him: 'Troup, sick as per usual' was a typical diary entry. In April a rip-roaring row between Troup and Barttelot led to Troup's retiring to his tent for six weeks in an Achilles-like sulk. Bonny described the confrontation: 'There was a big row between Barttelot and Troup, each accusing the other of certain things. Barttelot charged Troup with being a drunkard and having been in police courts, etc., Troup charging Barttelot with having been kicked out of the Egyptian army, etc. . . . Barttelot ordered Troup to leave the camp. Troup said, "You are not head of this expedition." '

Another example of Barttelot's unbalanced mental state was his decision to send all Stanley's effects downriver as part of the process of freeing the would-be 'flying column' from unnecessary baggage. Not only did Barttelot send down to Bangala Stanley's spare sets of compasses and maps and the provisions which had been hauled up from the Atlantic at such cost: he even sent down Stanley's spare clothes and his favourite pair of trousers!

But worst of all examples of Barttelot's paranoia was his increasing preoccupation with poison. He became obsessed with the fact that all five of Stanley's white comrades on his first two expeditions had perished and began to concoct a theory that Stanley had deliberately made away with them. One day Barttelot was discussing the drowning of Frank Pocock with Bonny. ' "The Major asked me ... if I did not think you to be a poisoner like Palmer of Rugeley and I asked why. 'It is odd, you know,' he said, 'that not one of his white companions ever returned home from his expedition, and I suspect that he did away with them to hide the truth.' " '

The reflection led by an association of ideas to the notion of getting rid of his chief tormentor among the Manyema. Barttelot told Bonny one day: 'I want to poison that nigger Selim bin Mohammed.' Bonny was so alarmed at this that he took all dangerous drugs out of his medicine chest and hid them.

This is the context in which Barttelot's extraordinary order to Ward should be seen. The nearest place from which a cable could be sent to the Emin Pasha relief committee was 1500 miles away: the Portuguese posts of Sao Thome or St Paul de Loanda. The journey there was arduous and, on the first stretch to Bangala, perilous since the route lay through unstudied areas. It is not stretching a point to imagine that Barttelot may genuinely have hoped Ward would not survive. There seems to have been a peculiar animus by Barttelot towards Ward. Bonny claimed that Jameson inflamed the Major against Ward by hinting to him that Ward had embezzled brass rods for his personal profit, but the true evil genius of this whispering campaign is likely to have been Bonny himself.

But whatever the genesis of Barttelot's paranoia and hatred, there could be no mistaking its reality. Four days after setting out, Ward was overtaken at the Lomami River settlement by an extraordinary letter from Barttelot, which read as follows: 'WARD -1 am sending this to warn you to be very careful in the manner you behave below - I mean as regards pecuniary matters. I shall require at your hands a receipted bill for everything you spend, and should you be unable to purchase the champagne and the watch, you will not draw that £20. The slightest attempt at any nonsense I shall be down upon you for. I have given you a position of trust, so see that you do not abuse it. You will send me a receipt of this letter, EDMUND M. BERTHELOT, Major.' Ward replied, 'Consider letter gross insult and will demand explanation and satisfaction on my return.'

Despite the insult, Ward behaved heroically. The journey downriver was far the worst in his three and a half years' Congo service: there were heavy thunderstorms every day, he had to canoe on rivers engorged with rain and trek through grass 18-20 feet high. When he got to St Paul de Loanda and cabled the EPRE committee, the answer came back, predictably: obey Stanley's orders.

Ward then hastened to return. He was at Stanley Pool on 1st June, caught the steamer En Avant for the upriver journey and on 3rd July met Rose Troup coming downriver, on his way home after being manoeuvred by Barttelot into requesting sick leave. The captain of Troup's ship handed Ward another amazing missive from Barttelot: 'SIR - On arrival at Bangala you will report yourself to the chief of the station, and take over the stores from him belonging to the Expedition. You will remain at Bangala till you receive orders from the Committee concerning yourself and the loads .. . On no account will you leave Bangala while you remain in the service of the Expedition, till you receive orders from home . . . Should you bring a telegram of recall for me, you will make arrangements with the chief of Bangala to forward it to the Falls, where a messenger awaits it. You will not, however, send any other message after me, nor will you on any account leave Bangala station unless you receive orders to that effect from the Committee - EDMUND M. BERTHELOT' That was effectively the end of the Emin Pasha expedition for Herbert Ward.

Barttelot's friend Jameson meanwhile had a superficially more placid journey, to see Tippu Tip in Kasongo, but the consequences were even more sensational than Ward's abortive journey. Jameson got a very warm welcome from Tippu, for he was one of the few Europeans the Arab really liked, by contrast with Barttelot, whom he detested cordially, even more so than he did Stanley. In fact Tippu even confided in Jameson that, as far as he was concerned, his contract to supply carriers was with Stanley, not Barttelot, therefore the Major had nothing to do with the matter. Another of Tippu's grievances, extensively aired during the time at Kasongo, was that the Belgians had sent no representatives or 'residents' to visit him at Stanley Falls with his insignia of office; other wealthy Arabs, such as Said bin Habib, openly scoffed at this 'gubernatorial office' that provided Tippu with no visible signs of authority and at the Belgians who did not even deign to send a steamer to visit their 'governor'.

At last, on 5th May 1888, Tippu started back to Stanley Falls with his good friend Jameson, to see if he could at last get the Rear Column under way. But at Riba-Riba, an Arab settlement half-way to Stanley Falls, an event occurred that would ever afterwards besmirch the memory of the Emin Pasha expedition. The date was 11th May. Tippu and Jameson had been discussing cannibalism, and Jameson ventured to suggest that the whole idea was an invention, a 'traveller's tale' or tall story. Tippu looked solemn and reiterated that the practice was a daily reality. The sequel is described by Jameson:

He then said something to an Arab called Ali seated next to him, who turned round to me and said, 'Give me a bit of cloth and see.' I sent my boy for six handkerchiefs, thinking it was all a joke, and that they were not in earnest, but presently a man appeared, leading a young girl of about ten years old by the hand, and then I witnessed the most horribly sickening sight I am ever likely to see in my life. He plunged a knife quickly into her breast twice, and she fell on her face, turning over on her side. Three men then ran forward, and began to cut up the body of the girl; finally her head was cut off, and not a particle remained, each man taking his piece away down to the river to wash it. The most extraordinary thing was that the girl never uttered a sound, nor struggled until she fell. Until the last moment, I could not believe that they were in earnest. I have heard many stories of this kind since I have been in this country, but never could believe them, and I would never have been such a beast as to witness this, but that I could not bring myself to believe that it was anything save a ruse to get money out of me, until the last moment.

The girl was a slave captured from a village close to this town, and the cannibals were Wacusu slaves, and natives of this place, called Mculusi. When I went home I tried to make some small sketches of the scene while still fresh in my memory, not that it is ever likely to fade from it. No one here seemed to be in the least astonished at it.

Meanwhile at Yambuya, Barttelot's anxiety and paranoia was increasing daily. He became convinced that the Manyema under Selim bin Mohammed were planning an attack on Yambuya. His diary for early April is peppered with anxious remarks: 'Salem means mischief.' 'Things look black.' 'Perhaps my days are numbered.' He decided on yet another visit to Stanley Falls, this time to enlist the help of Tippu's deputy Bwana Nzige in the 'coming conflict' with Selim. Nzige assured him he would recall Selim, if that would put his mind at rest. Twenty-four hours later Barttelot set out on the return journey. On arrival he found there had been no Arab attack nor any serious pretence of one. When Selim came to tell him that he had been recalled, even this clear evidence of Arab good faith did not satisfy Barttelot. Like all in the grip of paranoid delusion, he simply used evidence contrary to his illusory thesis as inverted supports for the initial paranoia. Hence: 'Salem Mohammed came to see me, and told me he was going away down river ... this may be a blind. I have sent men out to watch him.'

It is worth stressing the absurdity of Barttelot's fears. If either Tippu or Selim had wished to destroy the Rear Guard encampment at Yambuya, they could have done so easily. Tippu Tip later reacted with anger to the suggestion that he had deliberately sabotaged the Rear Column. He pointed out that if he had so wished, he could have wiped out the entire expedition, Stanley included; it was not his policy to hinder someone he disliked, he simply killed them.

On 8th May another dimension was added to the complex relationships between the Arabs at Stanley Falls and the Europeans at Yambuya. The Belgians finally put in an appearance in the shape of the steamer AIA, conveying Lt. Van Kerkhoven and the engineer Werner, together with the escort Ward had left at Bangala. It was almost as though the Congo State had exercised telepathy and picked up Tippu Tip's bitter complaints to Jameson. After three days at Yambuya, AIA steamed off to Stanley Falls. A few days later Barttelot too decided to make yet another visit to the Falls, to await Jameson's return. On 22nd May Tippu Tip and Jameson arrived to find the Major and Van Kerkhoven ready to talk serious business.

Tippu Tip at once informed Barttelot that he could let him have 400 men, not the 800 originally promised, provided they were not asked to carry loads heavier than 40 pounds per man. This was a shock to Barttelot, but next day all was explained. The Belgians were attempting to divert the spread of Tippu's sphere of influence towards Bangala by putting him in the picture about the Mobangi-Welle River, allegedly rich in ivory. Tippu played both sides against the middle. He told Barttelot that Belgian pressure meant he would have to detach half of the 800 porters for use in this expansion towards the north. But he told Van Kerkhoven that he saw right through the Belgian's game. He would not be distracted from his own plans to pacify the Congo as far down as Bangala. The discussions between the Belgian and the Arab became strained, then heated, until by 7th June word was all over the Falls that there had been the most frightful row between Tippu and Van Kerkhoven. Tippu declared that as inheritor of the Sultan's mantle he intended effective occupation of the Upper Congo territories. Van Kerkhoven replied that he would shoot any man of Tippu's who ventured near Bangala.

Faced with these cross-cutting rhythms, Barttelot made one of his few sensible decisions and accepted that the 400 porters represented all that he could hope to get from Tippu Tip. He and Jameson cut across country with Muni Somai, the Manyema headman who was to lead the porters into the Ituri for them. They had contracted him for £1000 and guaranteed the sum personally, in the case the EPRE committee raised a cavil. Tippu Tip and Van Kerkhoven made a stately progress to Yambuya (which the Arab had not yet visited) on that. On the way they met the Stanley, bringing the Belgian 'resident' for Stanley Falls, M. Haneuse. The Stanley then followed them up the Aruwimi to Yambuya. The Belgian purpose in sending Haneuse was not to boost Tippu's status at the Falls and to support him against recalcitrant Arab rivals; it was simply to spy on him, against the day Leopold was ready for his decisive military move.

Once at Yambuya Barttelot and Jameson put in a week's strenuous labour to make all ready for the advance into the Ituri. But Barttelot's problems with Tippu Tip were not over yet. On 7th June, when the expedition was all but ready to depart, Tippu examined the loads for the Manyema and found them a few pounds overweight (the heaviest was 45 pounds). He refused to allow the bearers to proceed unless the loads were repacked at the agreed weight of 40 pounds. This apparent nitpicking was the Arab's revenge for Barttelot's failure to complete his side of Stanley's agreement. He did indeed hand over the promised gunpowder, but the ammunition caps were found to be 80 per cent faulty. Not only could they not be delivered to Tippu; Jameson and Barttelot actually had to buy 40,000 new ones from the Arab!

At this eleventh-hour intervention from Tippu, all Barttelot's pent-up wrath burst forth. Vangele witnessed the sequel. He described Barttelot as raging at Tippu Tip like the successive waves of the sea battering at a storm-tossed ship. Barttelot's behaviour was brutal and arrogant. Tippu Tip blinked his eyes nervously but behaved correctly. Apparently, though, he had ordered his men to shoot the Major if he laid hands on him. All Barttelot's rage was in vain. Tippu insisted that the loads be disbanded and repacked, even though this meant in many cases that airtight tins of powder and cartridges had to be opened and soldered up again. But finally all was completed to general satisfaction. On Monday 11th June, Barttelot, Bonny and Jameson marched out of Yambuya in Stanley's tracks, almost a year after his departure. With them went twenty-two Sudanese, 115 wangwana, 430 Manyema and 150 camp followers (women and slaves).

One final action Barttelot took before leaving. Jameson had complained to him that Assad Farran, the Syrian interpreter, was a venal man of no fixed loyalties. Barttelot dismissed him on the grounds that he was utterly useless and a valetudinarian. He made Assad sign a statement in which he swore not to divulge any information about the expedition, but Barttelot and Jameson had unknowingly made a very powerful enemy, a man who in the future was to contribute materially to sustaining Stanley's version of the Rear Guard disaster against that of its chief and second-in command.

One of the pressures contributing to Barttelot's eventual mental breakdown was the apprehension that Stanley and the entire Advance Column had perished. When a whole year passed without anything being heard of Stanley by the outside world, European opinion began to share Barttelot's fears. Many newspapers confidently reported that Stanley was dead. The fear was that he had been lured to his death by the Arabs; his previous experience would not have made him proof against such perfidy, since it was all with African kings, not slavers. This canard led to a fully-fledged debate between the leading Africanists on Stanley's likely fate. The Egyptian government felt convinced that he was dead. Joseph Thomson, the man passed over for leadership of the expedition, declared: 'I unhesitatingly express my conviction that he and his entire party have been annihilated to the west of the Albert Nyanza,' (doubtless the wish was father to the thought). Circumstantial evidence of Stanley's death seemed provided by reports that the Mahdists had taken white men prisoner, and that some Snider rifles had been captured, until someone pointed out that Stanley had taken no Sniders on this expedition, only Remingtons and Winchesters. Joseph Thomson proceeded to trump his own ace by saying that Stanley could not have been taken prisoner by the Mahdists, since he had already been massacred in the Ituri forest.

These fears were not shared by the more thoughtful British analysts. Harry Johnston thought that the explanation was that opposition from forest tribes had turned Stanley northward into the Upper Welle. Cameron too was convinced Stanley was still alive, as were de Winton, Mackinnon and the other members of the EPRE committee. In France official pessimism was tempered by Brazza's view that Stanley had gone to the White Nile and was making treaties there. But the greatest consensus in favour of Stanley's survival was found among Austrian and German geographers and explorers, all of whom, except for Peters, thought he was safe. Wissmann was all along confident that Stanley was not dead, on the grounds that if he was, some news of this would already have surfaced in Africa. The man in the best position to know the likely truth, Rose Troup, now returning convalescent from the Congo, hinted that he could say a lot, had he not been gagged by the terms of the engagement of the EPRE officers, which forbade them to utter on the subject until six months after Stanley had published his own account. He did, however, allow himself to comment that he was too much of a believer in Stanley's pluck, willpower and, above all, luck, to think that he had perished. But he added ominously - a hint of the controversies to come - 'Though I am not afraid for Stanley, I am for his fellow white men. Somehow or other, Stanley has got a singular knack of always coming back alone.'

But the uncertainty that was entertained by everybody in Europe, including Leopold and Queen Victoria, soon led to a conviction that a second Emin Pasha relief expedition should be sent out. The Germans scented a golden opportunity to extend their sphere of interest westward to Lake Albert, and a German expedition was prepared under Peters and Wissmann. The Belgian explorer Jacques Becker also laid plans for a journey to the Congo to learn what had happened to Stanley; Leopold meanwhile concluded that his best hope of furthering his Congo interests lay in throwing in his lot with the German expedition. All this activity caused a flurry in London. Sir Samuel Baker warned of the blow to British prestige if the Germans finally succeeded in relieving Emin, and talk arose of a second British Emin relief expedition under Joseph Thomson, routed through Masailand.

But already in the columns of the British press a backlash against the whole idea of the Emin Pasha relief expedition and ventures like it was beginning to be discernible. The pointlessness of relieving someone who had constantly asserted that he did not wish to be relieved, and the baneful indirect consequences of opening up further segments of Africa to the slave traders, were frequently stressed. De Winton and the EPRE committee were increasingly forced on to the defensive. De Winton wrote many letters to The Times to defend the Congo itinerary and to divert attention towards the threat from the Peters/Wissmann expedition: 'what use is the German expedition? Is another nation to reap the harvest sown with British blood and British treasure?'

The tone of the criticisms was increasingly severe. The Cork Examiner saw the Emin expedition as simply an excuse for gigantic plunder. In 1889 anxiety about the eventual fate of the expedition and criticism of it continued, especially when Stanley's first despatches began to be received. Stanley's admission that he had hanged men caused as much furore as the Bumbire incident a dozen years before, and again the query arose, under what authority or sanction of international law Stanley had ordered these executions. Others criticised the tone of his despatches:

' "He has sustained heavy losses of men" - as though he and not the poor fellows themselves deserved pity on account of their deaths.' A devastatingly cynical article appeared in the London press in April 1889: It is impossible not to admire Mr Stanley's pluck and endurance. But I venture to question the use of marches like his into the interior of Africa. The plea was that Emin Pasha wished to be relieved. He does not want to be. He is only desirous to be left alone. What benefit, then, is it to the cause of civilisation that a white man should hire a vast number of carriers and undertake an expedition, in which half of them die of fatigue, and some are hanged for wishing to desert, in order to force his way through tribes by burning their villages and shooting them? The net result seems to be that it has been discovered that one lake is not so deep as it was a hundred years ago, that another lake lies to the south of the first, that there is a very dense forest, mainly inhabited by dwarfs, on the road to these lakes, and that somewhere in the vicinity of this forest there is a high mountain (hitherto unknown), the top of which is covered with snow. All this is, no doubt, interesting. But is it worth impressing carriers who die of fatigue or are hanged, shooting dwarfs, and destroying villages? I should like to hear a carrier or a dwarf on the subject.

Yet all this was mild beside the controversy over Barttelot's brutality which broke out when Assad Farran, the Syrian interpreter dismissed by the Major as 'quite useless', arrived in Hull on 18th September 1888. His detailed allegations against Barttelot created a sensation. He also told the story of Jameson's sketching the cannibal feast. Immediately the Barttelot family, the EPRE committee and other interested parties sprang into action to deny the allegations and state that they were actuated merely by spite and hatred because Barttelot had dismissed Farran. In Paris Brazza proposed to deal with the issue by racial prejudice. No one should take Farran's word for anything, he declared, as he was a Syrian: 'They are, as a rule, an arrogant, offensive lot, with very little breeding and even less probity.' As for Jameson's having taken part in a cannibal feast, that was a bagatelle; these were common on the Congo and in any case how was he supposed to stop it?

Pressure was brought on Assad Farran by Burdett-Coutts of the EPRE to retract his remarks. It was pointed out to him that in his contract was an article stating that he would forfeit six months' pay if he criticised any of the expedition's leaders. Since Farran arrived without a shirt on his back, it did not take much persuading to get him to withdraw his charges. The letter of retraction read as follows: 'I, Assad Farran, late interpreter with the Emin Pasha relief expedition, declare that the alleged severities towards his men of which Major Barttelot has been accused were an exercise of discipline which was rendered absolutely necessary, in the interests of the expedition, by the circumstances in which Major Barttelot was placed at the camp at Yambuya, and by the mutinous conduct of his men.'

This 'confession' at once caused uproar in the press. The Liverpool Echo wanted to know whether money had changed hands to exact this retraction, and whether Farran had been sufficiently independent to speak the truth. It also pointed up the absurdity of the EPRE committee's actions. If Farran was a pathological liar, as the Barttelot family alleged, what was the point or value in Burdett-Coutts' getting him to retract and sign a fresh statement, one so obviously drafted by the said Burdett- Coutts? The Star pointed out that all the way from Hull to London Farran had talked most freely about Barttelot's barbarities; only under threats from the EPRE committee did his story change. It expressed its impatience with the rhodomontade about 'absolutely necessary discipline'. The only serious question was whether Barttelot had in fact behaved in the barbarous way Farran charged. But the greatest absurdity in the committee's actions was pointed out by a correspondent in Pall Mall. Having quoted the letter of retraction, the writer went on: 'The Committee of the Emin Pasha Relief Expedition have not, it is clear, much sense of humour ... For a native interpreter, who was dismissed by Major Barttelot as an "utterly useless" and "very inferior" fellow, Assad Farran has a very pretty English style, and a really gratifying sense of English "discipline".'

As yet, however, the Emin expedition was merely controversial, not notorious. The row over Barttelot's severities and Jameson's actions, the question marks over Stanley's judgement or the motives of the expedition's authors raised in 1888-9 but the advance ripples of a tsunami of excoriation that would overwhelm Stanley and his collaborators in 1890.

When Barttelot marched out of Yambuya on 11st June, he was not so acutely aware as Jameson that he was in for big problems with the Manyema. The particular individuals Tippu Tip had got together were insufficiently socialised in Arab ways, so that neither Tippu himself nor the headman actually on the march, Muni Somai, had much control over them. They were utterly unsuitable for the role Barttelot had cast them in. They found the work uncongenial, refused to move on for days on end, and generally took the line that they would proceed only on their own terms. There was considerable friction between the Manyema and the wangwana. The wangwana despised them for carrying lesser loads, but feared their numbers and their cannibalism. Soon the march was wracked with familiar problems: there were fights between the two factions of carriers, the trackers lost their way, there were threats against the lives of the Europeans, and a smallpox epidemic broke out. On the fourth day of the march fourteen of the wangwana deserted with twelve of the most precious loads.

By this time Barttelot was, by common consent, no longer truly responsible for his actions. He decided to return to Stanley Falls (yet again!) to acquire chains with which to fetter the runaways and deserters. After a 300-mile trip in eight days Barttelot reappeared at the Falls to Tippu's stupefaction. He obtained the chains and in addition requested and received sixty-eight replacement porters. By 15th July he was back with his main column at Banalya, where Bonny (acting commander) had brought it to camp. Jameson was still five days in the rear with the tardy Manyema.

Barttelot now entered a period of steep mental decline. When his boy servant Soudi tried to desert, the Major kicked him and beat him so badly that the boy died of his injuries. He took to going about the camp with a pointed stick, jabbing and poking the men with it. Bonny relates that he actually beat a man to death with it. He took to facing out the recalcitrant Manyema by staring at them and showing his big front teeth in a hideous rictus; on one occasion a Manyema woman annoyed him, so he bit her in the shoulder. On 17th July Manyema began to celebrate the Festival of the Moon and began firing their guns off wildly. One of the shots narrowly missed Barttelot and the Major chose to take the incident as an assassination attempt. He caught the offender and punished him severely.

At about 10p.m. on 18th July an insistent drumming began, accompanied by the noise of singing. Barttelot sent his boy to stop the noise. It ceased. But early on the morning of the 19th a Manyema woman started beating a drum and singing. This time the Major sent some Sudanese out to quell the disturbance. Hearing firing commence, Barttelot got out of bed and snatched up his revolver, telling all within earshot that he would shoot the first man he found firing. Barttelot pushed his way through the crowds of Manyema to where the offending woman was beating the drum and singing. He ordered her to stop. Just then a shot rang out from a loophole in a house opposite, occupied by Sanga, the husband of the woman. The bullet passed through Barttelot's heart; death was instantaneous.

From the screaming that ensued, Bonny feared a general massacre was imminent. But when the noise ceased, he ventured out, saw what had happened, examined the corpse and buried it in the forest, after sewing the body in a blanket. Then he sent a note to Jameson to tell him what had occurred. Jameson hurried up to Banalya, made a note of the goods still unlooted - for Sudanese, Tvangtvana and Manyema alike had gone on the rampage in the confusion after the murder - then hurried to Stanley Falls to request help in the apprehension of Sanga.

Uncertain what to do next, once at the Falls Jameson consulted his friend Tippu. To his amazement, Tippu jumped out of his chair and said dramatically: 'Give me £20,000 and I and my people will go with you, find Mr Stanley, and relieve Emin Bay.' This was a demand so steep as to amount almost to extortion, but as Jameson saw it he had little option. Without the Manyema the expedition could not go forward, but only Tippu Tip in person could overawe them and get them to do their duty. Jameson agreed to the sum in principle, but decided to descend to Bangala to see whether the committee's telegram to Ward contained any guidance or leeway that might enable him to agree to the sum requested without footing the bill himself.

First, however, he had to attend the trial of Sanga. Caught hiding in the forest, Sanga was conveyed to Stanley Falls for trial. The hearing took place on 7th August before a tribunal consisting of Tippu Tip, M. Haneuse, M. Baert and two other minor Belgian functionaries. After Jameson's evidence, there was little defence Sanga could mount. Tippu had advised Sanga that his only chance was to plead that there had been a general Manyema conspiracy to assassinate Barttelot, and that he had been assigned to carry out the deed. Sanga, however, chose to stick to the truth: that he had shot the Major because he seemed to be menacing his wife. The court found him guilty by unanimous verdict and he was taken out and executed by firing squad.

Jameson now prepared to depart for Bangala. But the Belgians, who had heard of Tippu Tip's plans to accompany the expedition to Equatoria, began to think of their own insecure position if he departed, and protested that as governor of the Falls he had a duty not to leave his post; his contract with Stanley was to supply the expedition with porters, not go on it himself. They insisted that if Jameson found no positive instructions at Bangala, he would have to descend to Banana to cable Brussels for Tippu's furlough.

Tippu Tip was ever afterwards convinced that the Belgians had poisoned Jameson to ensure that such permission could never be forthcoming. There is certainly something mysterious about Jameson's last days. He left Stanley Falls in good health on 9th August and on the 17th he died in Ward's arms at Bangala, officially from haematitic fever. The other possibility is that Jameson, learning at the Falls that Assad Farran's tale about the cannibal feast was all over the Congo and would soon be the talk of Europe, simply lost the will to live. But his sudden death added yet another strange twist to the already macabre story of the Rear Column.

Stanley certainly perceived it in this light. Later he was to reflect on the occult 'synchronicity' of the date 17th August 1888 - for on that day he arrived at Banalya to discover the chaotic world of the Rear Column, Jameson died at Bangala, while far away in Equatoria Emin and Jephson were taken prisoner by the Mahdists. As he recorded with the superstitious awe of the true Celt: 'This is all very uncanny if you think of it. There is a supernatural diablerie operating which surpasses the conception and attainment of a mortal man.'

STANLEY'S immediate reaction to the guilt he felt when Bonny recounted the sombre tale of the Rear Column was to claim that Barttelot was always supposed to follow him as soon as possible and he could not make out why this had not happened. Why, he asked, had Barttelot only started in June 1888 on a journey he should have begun in August 1887? The seven visits to Stanley Falls by Barttelot and his comrades accounted for 1200 miles of travelling which could have been spent on forward marching. To Jameson (now dead) he wrote: 'I cannot make out why the Major, you, Troup and Ward have been so demented ... all of you seem to have acted like madmen.' To Mackinnon he told the same story, preparing the ground for the music he would have to face when he returned home: 'My opinion is that the entire lot - except Bonny - have shown themselves utterly incompetent and lack brains altogether. They had positive instructions from me what to do. The first report from deserters settled them. From that time to my meeting with them they have acted like madmen.'

He then began to grill Bonny for information that would redound to the discredit of Barttelot. Naturally, this was not difficult to find. In the light of Barttelot's conduct, he asked, why did not Jameson or Bonny, or somebody, relieve the Major of command? Bonny replied, reasonably enough, that anyone trying to take over could have been arrested and shot as a mutineer. He attributed his own survival to the favour Barttelot showed him for keeping his mouth shut. Jameson, additionally, had his own reasons for not opposing Barttelot. Barttelot knew all about the cannibal incident - indeed, so did everyone on the Congo - and had it to hold over Jameson. Finally, even if they had relieved Barttelot of command, they would have had his blood on their hands, since the wangwana, no longer in fear of the firing squad, would have murdered the man they hated so at the first opportunity.

What about the wangwana, Stanley persisted. Why were they not given at least occasional supplies of meat to arrest their death toll? Surely Barttelot could have bartered rods and beads to get a meat supply? Ah, said Bonny, the Major expressly refused to do this, so as to punish the Zanzibaris for pilfering axes and other tools and selling them. What was in the Major's mind, asked Stanley. Bonny replied that he was obsessed with 'kudos', chafed at being Stanley's Number Two and so tried to find out as much as he could to Stanley's detriment. His abiding hope was that if he waited long enough, news would come through that Stanley had perished in the forest; he would then take command of the expedition, find Emin, and become one of the youngest colonels in the British army.

Bonny's analysis chimed in perfectly with Stanley's own reading of Barttelot. He had reprimanded the Major on the way upriver for his insatiable hunger for kudos and had quoted him the couplet:

Not once or twice in our fair island story
Has the path of duty and honour been the road to glory.

It was a long-standing Stanley motif that, influenced by Bentham (who found the word 'duty' 'disagreeable and repulsive'), the English cared more for kudos than duty. All his officers on the expedition dreamed of winning a Victoria Cross or Albert Medal, but were not prepared for a diet of rice and beans which might actually be the means of achieving those honours. Barttelot, in Stanley's analysis, had foolishly set himself on a collision course with Tippu Tip, when real politic meant that without Tippu there would not just be no expedition, but not even any Yambuya encampment. If Tippu could be faulted, it was in having promised more than he could deliver - when he was cool and dispassionate, as opposed to when he was making propaganda, Stanley could see that the provision of 600 carriers was a tall order. With these thoughts in mind, Stanley proceeded to a justification of his own conduct vis-a-vis the Rear Column.

I parted from the Major in the confident belief that he was inflexibly resolved to march eastward soon after the arrival of the expected steamers. His face was aglow with resolution, his grip was firm as he clasped my hand and wished me his farewell. He was such a simple, honest, active soldier that none of us in the Advance had any doubt of him. He was a man who hated meanness, dawdling, shirking, malingering ... of a small figure, wiry and tough - with a square resolute face on which courage was writ large - he was the very ideal of a jockey of Mars, a good type of those who rode so gamely with Cardigan, through the flames of Muscovy's cannon ... He was a gentleman and always bore something subtle about him that marked him as one. Proud and decided, fastidious and severe but upright and sternly just. It's a perfect riddle to me why such a man as this yielded to the fascination of Tippu Tip and broke his promise.

It is interesting that at this stage in the expedition Stanley was disposed to absolve Tippu Tip from all blame. Indeed the letter he wrote on the 17th, inviting the Arab to join him, was cordiality itself. 'Emin Pasha has ivory in abundance, cattle by thousands, sheep, goats, fowls and food of every kind. We found him to be a very good and kind man ... If you go with me it is well. If you do not go with me it is well also .. . whatever you have to say to me, my ears will be open with a good heart, as it has always been towards you.' Stanley thought he knew the right bait with which to attract Tippu, but the Arab, having had a possible £20,000 snatched from his grasp by Jameson's death, had no intention of following Stanley gratis.

Three days after his arrival at Banalya, Stanley moved from Banalya to a camp at Bunganyeta Island in the River Aruwimi, about 14 miles upstream. Stanley's aim was to separate the wangwana from the Manyema, who were now riddled with smallpox. Here Stanley brooded on another matter. Rashid had found a letter lying in water which turned out to be a confidential letter from Stairs to Barttelot, sent from Fort Bodo in June. The dispatch had been entrusted to Wadi Mambruki, who drowned. When the wangwana fished his cartridge pouch on to the shore, they found the message inside. In the letter Stairs bitterly criticised Stanley for his insouciance towards his sick officers. He accused him of needless brutality, raiding villages in reprisal for a few harmless flights of arrows, and forever reserving the best provisions for himself. Its comments were notably hard-hitting:

Stanley has got the name all about these parts of being the meanest man ever given life. It's pretty well true . . . Stanley treated us all from first to last in a perfectly damnable manner as regards food; he has at times had all sorts of things given him, not one of which we ever got unless one of us went and shamed him out of the thing. Emin gave him a devil of a lot of whisky and tobacco for us which we have not seen, and so on, till every one of us have quite given up any idea of ever getting anything from him .. . Stanley will chisel like the mischief and want all the provisions for himself at Yambuya; he gives in at once, though, if he is stuck up to on this point.

Bonny was soon able to attest the truth of these observations. On Bunganyeta Island he fell ill and asked Stanley if he could have some goat or chicken. Stanley said he had no meat but on the very next day he killed a goat and pointedly offered Bonny none. But Stanley always based his selfishness on the small print of the officers' contract which spoke of a 'fair share' of European provisions. This did not mean an equal share with the leader; in every army the general drew more allowances than the brigadier, and so on. Stanley failed to realise that in his punctiliousness he was actually conceding the substance of Stairs' indictment.

The short march to Bunganyeta had revealed to Stanley the low morale and wretched equipment of his men. For a week he tried to build them up into a credible fighting force for the long trek through the forest gloom to Fort Bodo. Then on 29th August the expedition set out. Stanley had 462 men and 254 guns. 283 of the men were carriers. He divided them into a land party and a river party. There were just enough men to carry all the loads.

They got through Mariri rapids and were at south Mupe on 4th September when Tippu Tip's emissary Selim bin Mohammed caught up with them to say that Tippu would not be coming with them, and that he was in no way responsible for the disaster that had overcome the Rear Column. Finding that his honeyed words had had no effect on Tippu, Stanley lost his temper. He raged at Selim that whereas Tippu could not hurt him, he could hurt Tippu, so that he might like to reconsider the question of following him. Then the wangwana headmen came to Stanley to say that Selim had been trying to inveigle the Manyema back to Stanley Falls. Selim promised to return with Tippu's further answer within forty days. Stanley said this was humbug: the Arabs had no intention of keeping their word and had caught up with him simply to lure the Manyema away. Selim asked if he could take away the Manyema who wished to leave. Stanley adroitly turned the tables on him: since he was supposed to be returning in forty days, he could pick them up then.

Stanley's analysis - correct as it turned out - was that although the Arabs were cold-blooded killers, they would only murder white men or other Arabs if motives of revenge were afoot. This meant that he had seen the last of Tippu and his men. The sight of Selim bin Mohammed triggered memories in Bonny of Barttelot's obsession with him. He told Stanley that Barttelot had prepared petrol at Yambuya, ready to pour over all the stores and ammunition ready for ignition if it came to a last stand, so that 'those accursed Arabs' would gain nothing by their treachery.

Next day Stanley discovered that the Madis were going down with smallpox after contact with the Manyema at Banalya. The wangwana had been inoculated on the Madura but were not proof against general debility. The first desertions began, followed by the first deaths from hostile action: two of the Zanzibaris went on a raid on a Batundu village and were slain. A few days later a party of nine scavengers (five Manyema, three wangwana and a Sudanese) were ambushed and speared to death.

On 8th September they were at 'Elephant Playground' and on the 11th at Wasp Rapids. Here Stanley waited for the land party to come in, before making a new division of forces. 192 expedition members would proceed by canoe while 262 went overland. But heavy losses continued to be taken. On the 13th a canoe capsized and two boxes of powder and beans went to the bottom. One of Emin's Madis sustained a bad wound from a spear launched at his back by a crouching tribesman. Primitive surgery revealed that none of his vital organs were harmed, so Bonny simply stitched him up again.

The toll from smallpox and hostile action continued. On 18th September one of Stanley's best men, Jabu, was shot dead by an arrow from a hidden tribesman. On the 20th another Madi was speared in the woods and a Manyema woman received an arrow in the groin from which she later died. A Zanzibari dropped dead in his tracks from weakness, bringing the death toll for that one day to three. On the 21st another two wangwana were killed. During September additionally three men had been drowned in the Ituri and one committed suicide by drowning to avoid the ravages of smallpox. His most daring foragers, including one Stanley refers to as 'a veritable Jack Cade', usually returned from their raids with horrible wounds from poisoned arrows.

Initially Stanley was puzzled at the continuous hostility on the Ngula River in September and the showers of poisoned arrows that daily assailed the river column. He made the best of it by telling himself that at least he did not have to administer the death penalty for desertion- the locals were doing that for him. Questioning of prisoners revealed that the new boldness and aggression of the people on this stretch of the journey - who had given him no trouble on the first journey - were due to their successes against Ugarrowa's party earlier in the year.

Stanley did not crack on the pace in the early stages, so as to give his men a chance to collect food against the great barren wilderness ahead, but even so they found victuals hard to come by. The craving for meat led on 16th September to a swimming race between an entire company of his men and a bush antelope, but when they caught it and speared it, it proved far too small to make any difference to hundreds of meat-hungry mouths.

And still the fatalities went on. A 100-strong foraging party returned on 22nd September, laden with bananas, but there were many stragglers left in the forest. 'Till long past midnight, guns were fired as signals and great ivory horns sounded loud blasts which travelled through the glades with continued rolling echoes.' When a muster was held, four more men were discovered dying in agony from arrows coated with poison. During the first forty-nine days of this march Stanley lost forty-four men killed - an average of almost one a day.

They portaged their way slowly past Panga Falls and Nejambi rapids to Avisibba and Engwedde - the stretch of river with its numerous islets that gave them so much trouble the first time. A local woman gave birth squatting on the river bank; the wangwana recommended that the child be killed there and then. By the 30th they were at the upper rapids of Avugadu. Stanley noted in his journal: 'If I were twenty-five years younger I might live to see this primeval forest widely open and this track of mine a broad highway.' Still the missiles continued. Two of the arrow-wounded recovered well, but a Manyema woman who had taken seven pointed shafts in the back died, to the grief of the husband. Stanley noted the incident down as further evidence against those who claimed Africans had no feelings.

Stanley's mood during this first month in the wilderness, as they were subjected to the swathes of smallpox (sometimes fifteen fresh cases in a single day) and the attrition of enemy arrows, was black and sombre. When a second wangrvana committed suicide by hurling himself into the rapids, Stanley simply remarked coldly: 'He was one of the most worthless men in the expedition. ... I have fourteen or fifteen men of no earthly use to us, themselves or anybody else ... Most of these people suffer from indigestion which has induced debility. Good food or a daily allowance of meat would soon cure them, but alas we have none of these

things.' His harshness is also shown by an explicit linking of himself to the exploitation of Africa. He quoted Sir James Mackintosh and said the words could equally well apply to Central Africa: 'Not an acre of land has been brought into cultivation in the wilds of Siberia, or on the shores of the Mississippi which has not widened the market for British industry.'

And still he fumed away about the intercepted letter from Stairs. It particularly riled him that Stairs had said his officers had to hide their illnesses from him, for to be ill was a crime. He chewed over the phrases 'the meanest man', 'a cheat', 'a bad lot'. To assuage his anger he took to inviting Bonny to his tent for long sessions of gossip and debate. Under pressure from Stanley, Bonny admitted that his January 1887 story about leaving Baruti to visit the Tower of London was a phoney. He was in fact trying to avoid his third wife, who he discovered had married him bigamously, and who was trying to waylay him at the station. When Bonny decamped, the woman stood guard over Baruti until the 'white-haired gentleman' rescued him, when she gave up. What had happened to the other two wives, Stanley queried. Both dead, Bonny told him.

'A third wife!' said Stanley. 'There must be something fascinating about you for the women. I have not been able to get one wife yet and you have had three. Well, well, there is no accounting for women's tastes, is there?' Bonny then further admitted that when Stanley had openly chided him for his listlessness on the journey between Matadi and Stanley Pool he had actually been under the influence of opium. Further probing elicited the intelligence that Bonny was a genuine opium addict; he had picked up the habit in India and now smoked it every day. Stanley confided in his journal that he had misjudged Bonny: 'A man who has succeeded in securing three wives to himself must be a man of character.'

Moving up to the confluence of the Ngaya with the Ituri, at Little Rapids, in early October they were assailed by a tornado. Further attacks from poisoned arrows persuaded Stanley to cross to the south bank of the Ituri, but in another fight with the forest peoples a man was wounded with a poisoned shaft. On 10th October they had a bizarre encounter. A dense cloud of moths, extending from the water's face to the forest canopy, 80 feet high, blanketed the entire expedition, flying at a rate of 3 knots. The cloud was 'so dense that before it overtook us we thought that it was a fog, or, as scarcely possible, a thick fall of lavender-coloured snow.'

They proceeded through Hippo Broads to Amiri rapids, where a Zanzibari headman was so badly stung by wasps that he despaired of life. Stanley dosed him with carbonate of ammonium while Bonny injected him with a hypodermic. The man made a good recovery, but ominously there were now signs that the wangwana's immunity against smallpox was beginning to fail.

By the second week of October Stanley was tiring of Bonny's company, even though the ex-sergeant provided him with someone to moan to about

Hoffmann's shortcomings: 'Stanley said that every man on the expedition had a better character than his servant William who was a fearful thief and liar.' But Bonny himself soon came under the verbal lash. Stanley told him that after nearly two years' service with the expedition, there was no evidence that his services had any value, and that an automaton would have done just as well. Faced with this onslaught, Bonny did what he always did when Stanley was in this mood: he diverted him on to the subject of Barttelot's crazed behaviour, especially his action in sending Stanley's precious effects downriver. But he recorded ruefully in his diary: 'Of course I must believe that the man [Stanley] treats me with the greatest contempt... he is just the man for the work he has undertaken but he should be alone or without white men.'

Stanley's negative attitude to Bonny did not improve when he discovered that the sergeant had appropriated Barttelot's notorious pointed stick and was using it to chastise the men in his detachment. After he had severely wounded one of the wangwana with it, the man broke it across his knee and swore that but for Allah he would have retaliated directly on Bonny. Stanley haled Bonny before him and reprimanded him for unnecessary brutality; this one incident gave him a very clear light on what daily life at Yambuya must have been like.

Disciplinary problems were mounting too. Stanley had taken two milch goats with him for their milk, but one night three of the wangwana overpowered the goatherd and slaughtered the animals for their meat. Stanley punished them with twenty-four strokes of the switch each, followed by fettering in the chain gang. He felt positively murderous that this act of indiscipline had deprived him of milk for the rest of the trek.

After Amiri rapids there were more losses through enemy action. Out of twelve foragers sent ahead of the main body, three returned wounded and two were posted missing, believed dead. They now began a march through a land empty of food, sustained by the thought that they had ten days' rations in hand. On 23rd October they came to Ugarrowa's which, as on the inward 1888 journey, was deserted: 'A crop of rice seemed to be growing in the big courtyard but the grains had all been picked by the birds.'

On 25th October they moved to a camp opposite the mouth of the Lenda River. The Ituri was in full flood, so that even crossing a creek entailed a soaking. A terrible storm battered at them. They were 160 miles from the grassland, and so far had existed mainly on roast plantain. Stanley looked forward to the pleasures of being free of insect bites, especially from the ubiquitous red ants. The only consolation was relative immunity from snakes. After 24,000 miles of travelling, only two men had been bitten by serpents, neither fatally. But whenever they cleared the ground in the forest, they realised the danger they had fortunately escaped. Whip snakes, puff-adders and horned snakes were killed in numbers. The Ituri itself swarmed with water snakes and in the forest were tiny snakes akin to the Indian krait, no longer than earthworms but supremely venomous and greatly feared by the locals. Around Fort Bodo, additionally, there were pythons and fanged ground snakes.'

On the 27th Stanley took the fateful decision to take a more northerly route to Lake Albert, avoiding Ford Bodo altogether. This was despite the fact that provisions were already running low and ahead of them stretched the uninhabited track of forest which contained Nelson's 'starvation camp' and where they had all suffered so fearfully before. In the ensuing days they captured a number of pygmies (whom Stanley weighed and measured for his Victorian 'scientific' public), who told them that the Manyema had stripped the region of food. The clearing at Andaki on 2nd November confirmed the bad news. They cut their way with billhooks through overgrown plantations choked with weeds. They were lucky to find an elephant track running parallel to the Thuru River, along which they made good progress - lucky, because at this point the river itself was impassable because of the rapids whose roaring they heard all around them in the forest gloom.

By 4th November Stanley was growing anxious. Food supplies were running very low, there were thirty men on the sick list with ulcers, tumours, smallpox and fever, the desertion rate was growing, and stragglers were being left behind on the trail. When Stanley detailed two Sudanese to carry Osmani, a member of Emin Pasha's bodyguard, as he was feverish, he was found next morning quite dead, in circumstances that suggested to Stanley that the Sudanese had simply strangled him to be rid of the burden. Bonny was worse than useless. When he was not flogging the men, he had other non-expeditionary matters on his mind.

He had found himself a Manyema concubine, whom he wanted to take with him even on foraging forays; Stanley's dislike of both Bonny and sexuality dictated a firm refusal.

Starvation now threatened. 'I am getting more and more anxious. This is the fifth day since we had food supplies, which means for many two days' hunger.' Despite the wangwana's fatalistic 'Inshallah', Stanley knew the end was not far away. He ordered a halt while a large party of foragers was sent out. To keep up his men's spirits, on the 8th he distributed a cupful of flour to each man, and surveyed the sorry state of his expedition:

Not long ago most of these men, now crippled with wide'-spreading ulcers, tortured with pain and emaciated from hunger, were fine robust fellows, but disease and hunger have made terrible ravages among them. Some few of them have been skewered in the feet, by the deadly native skewers in the plantations, other in their heedless scramble over the logs in the clearings have abraded their shins, others have had their feet gashed by oyster shells in the creeks they forded, and these wounds through dirt have become ravenous ulcers. Constant showers, morning dews, wading through mud have also had ill-effects. The fatigue of burdens and the heat - it was 94°F. yesterday, have compelled them to fling themselves down anywhere for rest and the sudden chill of the damp ground has caused many a fever, which rendered them incapable of looking after their rations.

When the foragers did not return to 'starvation camp' after a week, Stanley came as close to cracking as he had ever been in all his African travels. Taking Hoffmann and a party of men with him, he set out in a desperate search for the missing foragers. He also took a loaded revolver and a full dose of poison, determined to commit suicide if he could not find them. But the day after leaving 'starvation camp' Stanley's party ran into their comrades, bringing back up to five days' supplies of plantain. Stanley had learned a bitter lesson. From now on there would be no attempts at short cuts, they would cleave to the route they knew. He ordered a return to the river, prior to striking for Fort Bodo.

When they reached Kilonga-Longa's ferry, they found the hostile tribes had destroyed all the canoes and the river was in full flood. They began to follow the Ihuru River northwards along an elephant track: 'this forest is a little more open than that we have lately passed through.' But momentary joy in the beautiful effect caused in the forest by the rays of the afternoon sun was cut short by the intelligence that the chief of the Manyema had jettisoned four loads (67 pounds) of the precious European provisions. There was nothing he could do about it now, but Stanley swore vengeance for later. The Manyema had brought nothing but trouble. Among other diseases caught by contact with them was mumps, now in evidence as the small pox epidemic waned.

Porters continued to die but the loads remained the same. Every one of his porters was now ill from an endless list of maladies: ulcers, body pains, headaches, rheumatism, fever, gastritis, and many other ailments. Some respite was afforded in mid-month by the finding of a huge plantation of bananas but, still under intermittent arrow fire from the hostile forest-dwellers, Stanley on 17th November ordered Bonny ahead to try to find a ferry over the Ihuru.

On the 20th came fresh armed conflict, between Stanley's rearguard and a tribal regiment. The hostiles fled under a lashing of lead from the Remingtons, leaving behind one dead and two wounded. Next day the pangs of hunger began to grip them once more. Stanley confessed that he was feeling half-crazed from the effects of not having tasted meat for a month: 'I cannot help thinking that vegetarians would soon abandon a vegetable diet were they subjected to our experiences in this forest. The strength of us whites soon declines if we are without meat for some days.'

Bonny returned without success in his hunt for a ford across the river. Stanley's personal relations with him remained cross-grained and sour. He was still irked by his diary-keeping (a rival record) and warned him that if he was to be shot by accident (!) the survival of his diary might depend on its freedom from personal anecdote. When Bonny asked why they always displayed Gordon Bennett's yacht club flag, Stanley told him that it was his understanding in 1886 that Mackinnon had arranged for Bennett to foot the expenses of the expedition. It was on that understanding that he had accepted its leadership and carried Bennett's flag across Africa, only to learn later that the Herald proprietor had not contributed a penny to the expedition.

22nd November saw the expedition again seriously short of food. A heavy shower of rain contributed to the general demoralisation, and there were further desertions. A soup made from two gallons of water and two tins of Liebig meat extract provided but temporary relief for aching stomachs. Some of the men were by now truly maddened by hunger pangs. A Madi managed to crawl to Stanley's tent, attracted by the light of a candle.

Hearing him groan, Stanley rushed out and found a naked body writhing around in the mud, seemingly incapable of purposive movement. When the man saw the candle flame, his pupils dilated and he attempted to grasp the light with his hands. He was lifted up and taken to the campfire where he eventually recovered.

With the men on their last legs, they were scarcely able to repel another attack, which left one tribesman dead and two wounded. Fortunately the foraging party returned at noon on the 24th with forty-six loads of plantain and a goat which was used to make a thirty-gallon stew. As so often, Stanley's men made themselves sick with overindulgence. It was a recurring pattern on these expeditions for the porters to throw away their reserve provisions after a 'blow-out', then to find themselves starving three days later.

At last, on 1st December, Bonny found a place where a pontoon bridge could be thrown across the Dui River. Bonny and Rashid performed heroically in constructing the bridge, and the expedition crossed over. Still attacks continued. At the beginning of December a Manyema and Bonny's African servant succumbed to poisoned arrows. And now starvation as severe as that just after Ugarrowa's once again overtook them. The news that Bonny had at last located the Ihuru River was not enough to lift the general gloom that hung over the camp. They were once again in a 'starvation camp', once again awaiting the return of a desperate foraging mission. All their provisions were exhausted, largely because his men had trusted the word of a local woman who told them there was a village with food nearby.

By 14th December the foragers had been absent six days and hopes of survival were again fading. A young boy died and the condition of the other followers was most disheartening. Two more Madis expired and the last surviving Somali was on the point of terminal collapse. Stanley broke open the officers' box, took out the scanty contents and mixed them with water in a tin bath to make a thin gruel. But the words with which Stanley described his compassion betrayed a remarkable imperviousness to the suffering around him: 'These constant sights acted on my nerves until I began to feel not only moral sympathy, but physical as well, as though there was a contagious weakness' (italics mine).

Stanley agonised about whether to wait for the overdue foragers and so risk starvation or strike into the jungle after them. In the end Bonny volunteered to stay behind with ten men and ten days' provisions while

Stanley and the others went in search of the foraging party. A council was called which adopted the plan. After slaughtering the only remaining goat to make soup as sustenance for the trek to come, Stanley led out sixty-five souls on the search for their lost comrades. Bonny was left with twelve men, twelve women and forty-five sick with instructions to maintain strong defences. In all minds was the unstated conviction that the leader was engaged in a forlorn quest. At I p.m. on the 14th Stanley led out his bedraggled column. He considered himself doomed as surely as when he had determined on suicide the month before. The situation he left behind him was piteous, for 'the sick and feeble were condemned inasmuch as it was impossible to do the slightest service for them in the difficulty we were in. They could not follow us to obtain food, nor could they share the meagre diet necessary for the garrison of the camp and the preservation of goods.'

Stanley's contingent spent the night of the 15th in the open forest. Next morning they arose stiffly from an unsettled sleep amid the dew. Soon after resuming the march Stanley heard voices in the distance and called for silence. Within minutes his men were embracing the returning foragers. Again they had escaped death by a whisker. After gorging themselves on bananas and plantains, the united force arrived back in 'starvation camp' at 2.30 p.m. on the 16th.

With stomachs replenished, they struck out towards the Ihuru River, then followed its course to Fort Bodo, which they reached on 20th December. It had been a very near-run thing. The fatalities were horrific. Between Banalya and Fort Bodo, Stanley had lost 105 persons out of the 462 that left with him at the end of August. He himself was down to 127 pounds in weight, having lost 50 pounds since arriving in Africa. Parke described the arrival of the bedraggled survivors as follows: 'Mr Stanley looked cadaverous and ragged to an extreme degree - and I never felt so forcibly as now how much this man was sacrificing in the carrying out of a terribly heavy duty which he had imposed upon himself. He might very well have been living in luxury within the pale of the most advanced civilisation, housed in some of its most sumptuous mansions, and clothed with its choicest raiment, and here he was, I had never before so fully believed in Stanley's unflinching earnestness of purpose and unswerving sense of duty.'

Fort Bodo did not exactly provide the relief from care Stanley had been looking for. Although Stairs had local matters well in hand, Jephson had not arrived and there was no news from him. Word of the death of Randy in June did not improve the leader's temper. He set about putting his subordinates in their place. Stairs he punished for his 'treachery' by giving him all the dirty work to do. On Christmas Day he sent him out on a foraging expedition and, when he returned from this, sent him out again to seize enough canoes for the Ituri crossing. Hoffmann was already in disgrace after being caught red-handed in theft in the Ituri. After his first act of stealing, Stanley simply reprimanded him and purged his anger by flogging six of his men who had not fallen in quickly enough. After the second, Hoffmann had to sign a confession, in Bonny's presence, that he was guilty of theft and lying.

Stanley's most turbulent relationship was with Bonny. He enjoyed the sergeant's 'rough diamond' qualities and his quickness in debate and sometimes engaged him in discussions about the Bible, Wolseley or Gordon. He was particularly amused at a discussion between the two medical men Parke and Bonny about the appropriateness of the phrase 'landing in the water' - a subject which arose when Bonny was giving his eyewitness account of the sinking of the Princess Alice in the Thames in September 1878. But most of the time Stanley was markedly antagonistic to Bonny. On his return to 'starvation camp' with the foragers on 16th December, Stanley gratuitously told Bonny he regretted giving him fifteen cups of rice on 9th October. He continued to be irritated by the sergeant's keeping a journal and reminded him of the 'six-month' clause in his contract, adding with asperity that he would do better to keep his mind on the day-to-day work of the expedition. Bonny retaliated next day by asking permission to travel to the Welle River and thence to the Congo and home. Stanley dismissed the suggestion as ludicrous. He took it as proof that Bonny was no better than the other failures in the Rear Column. He accused Bonny of being both useless in general and cruel in particular. He had often heard Bonny's ferocious floggings and accused him of 'the deliberate and ferocious murder - it deserves that name' of a Sudanese soldier who had stolen a piece of meat.

Bonny's request led Stanley to call all his officers together and make a general speech about the pitfalls of the search for kudos - the flaw that had destroyed Barttelot. The unconscious motive for his speech was his intense dislike for the idea that anyone but himself should explore new regions. Then, after resting at Fort Bodo over Christmas, he established a camp at Kandehore on the far side of the Ituri River, and began to transfer the loads from Fort Bodo in stages, still occasionally under attack from showers of arrows. Repeated marches got the loads to the edge of the grasslands - there were not enough men to move the stuff all in one go. There he left Stairs and Parke with the sick and the loads and pressed on to Mazamboni's country. At Mazamboni's he received a letter from Jephson to say that he was at Kavalli's. Jephson's letter also explained the zigzag pattern of his fortunes since parting from Stanley in May 1888. It soon became clear why he had not been at Fort Bodo.

Emin's garrisons had imagined that Stanley was bringing large-scale assistance but the shock Emin and Casati felt when they saw the bedraggled 'relief expedition sent ripples back into Equatoria province. Rumours about their future fuelled the uncertainty felt by the Sudanese and Egyptian soldiers. When word came through that they might have to withdraw altogether, Emin's garrisons burst into revolt. When Emin and Jephson arrived back in Equatoria to drum up support for the Kavirondo scheme, they were arrested. The rebel council then formally deposed Emin, and for some time his life and that of Jephson hung in the balance. Unable to agree on their next move, the rebel leaders were rapidly approaching stalemate when the Mahdists took a hand. The ripple effect of Stanley's expedition had by now reached Khartoum, where the Khalifa too imagined it to be a major military enterprise, presaging an attempt to reconquer the Sudan. Abdullah's hordes swept into Equatoria.

In panic at this new development the rebel officers released Emin and Jephson, who retreated to the south of the province. While pitched battles were fought between the Sudanese garrisons and the Mahdists, Emin and Jephson tried to get ready the people who wished to leave the province, as agreed with Stanley. By the end of 1888 Equatoria presented a confused state: the north of the province was in Mahdist hands, the middle sector was held by the rebels who had deposed Emin, while the ex-governor himself maintained a toehold in the extreme south.

All this would have been enough to convince any rational man that Jephson had excuse enough for not adhering to Stanley's schedule. But instead of accepting that all actions have unintended consequences, that no one can predict the future, that at least the imbroglio in Equatoria was not on a par with the chaos of the Rear Column's year in Yambuya, Stanley raged at the failure of the world to conform with his minutely laid plans. There is a volume of egocentricity, and a smidgen of madness too, in the way Stanley reacted to Jephson's tale as simply a perverse and malicious refusal by Equatoria province to do his bidding. All Stanley could see was Jephson's 'indecision': 'If I had hesitated at Banalya, very likely I should still be waiting for Jameson and Ward, with my own men dying by dozens. Are the Pasha, Casati and yourself to share the same fate? If you are still victims of indecision, then a long goodnight to you all.' With heavy irony he asked Jephson to wait at Kavalli's 'if you consider yourself still a member of the expedition subject to my orders.' After an immensely long screed, Stanley thought it better to add a postscript. But instead of toning down any of what he had said before, he added a series of gratuitous and patronising remarks about members of the Rear Column: 'Jameson paid a thousand pounds to accompany us. Well, you see, he disobeyed orders and we left him to ponder the things he had done. Ward, you know, was very eager to accompany us, but he disobeyed orders and was left at Bangala, a victim to his craving for novel adventures. Barttelot, poor fellow, was mad for Kudos, but he has lost his life and all - a victim to perverseness. Now don't you be perverse, but obey, and set my order to you as a frontlet between the eyes, and all, with God's gracious help, will end well.

Jephson's mild remarks in his diary on the receipt of this missive considerably understate the case against Stanley: 'His letter to me is in many ways greatly wanting in common sense and I think the way he speaks about the officers of the Rear Guard is not very pleasant.' The only thing that can be pleaded in mitigation of Stanley's brutal letter - and even then it can only be partial mitigation - is that he was still reeling from the horrors of his third and worst journey through the black and green inferno of the Ituri (he was the only white man, apart from Hoffmann, to make the journey thrice). As he told Mackinnon: 'this has been the nearest approach to absolute starvation in all my African experience.'

The horrors of the Ituri made him determined that at all cost he would strike for home by the eastward route. But the presence of large numbers of Kabba Rega's men on his flank in that case meant he had to have the extra protection of some at least of Emin's Sudanese. This reinforced his original conviction that, having returned once without his quarry (Livingstone) and had been reviled as a consequence, he would not go back empty-handed a second time. Emin, who was a much shrewder judge of human beings than Stanley imagined, already knew what was in Stanley's mind. He felt bitter that Stanley's coming had not only brought him no aid or comfort but had actually precipitated both the revolt in Equatoria and the Mahdist offensive there. Angrily he reflected on the pressures Stanley was bringing to bear to effect a complete withdrawal from his beloved province: 'For him everything depends on whether he is able to take me along, for only then, when people could actually see me, would his expedition be regarded as totally successful. To Stanley's chagrin, when he went on the expedition to find Livingstone, he experienced what it meant to leave behind in Africa the main object of his expedition. This time he would rather perish than leave without me! Therefore Stanley urged Jephson, during his own absence, to try everything to persuade me to leave. So, here again, we have only egoism under the guise of philanthropy.'

Stanley for his part was determined both to force Emin to go with him and to avoid any further encounters with the Ituri. At Mazamboni's he was able to allow himself the luxury of recollecting in tranquillity the African forest that he would never see again and its peculiar moods and noises: 'No stillness even at midnight. Never-ending clicking of crickets and the chorus of frogs. Also a distinct audible movement of insects, creeping, crawling, hopping or biting some crisp material. Doleful and oft-repeated cries of the lemur, calculated to disturb the nerves of the timid. A tribe of monkeys may be migrating or a solitary chimp assuring himself by striking at trees. Sometimes a dead tree falls with a startling crackle or booming fall. The decayed branches of trees often fall down. This can often make the forest echo with a crash like a musket shot. 'Such memories were to become increasingly distant. In January 1889 Stanley set his face away from the primeval-mysterious blackness of the African forest and towards the dappled sunlight of Africa's vast plains and grasslands.

Chapter Fifteen

JANUARY 1889 was a fallow month for Stanley. While he waited for a reply from Jephson, he established base camp at Kavalli's in rolling country that reminded Bonny of the Transvaal, where he had served earlier. The sick list of 124 remained in Ituri ferry camp under Stairs' command - clearly this was further punishment for Stairs' 'impudent' letter to Barttelot. When Kabba Rega's allies the Balegga massed to attack the white man's camp, 1500 of Gavira's men with sixty rifles met them on a mountain overlooking the lake and, after sharp resistance, put them to flight.

With the Balegga on his flank as an irritating gadfly, Stanley ordered Nelson to deputise for Stairs and test the Maxim gun. Like all machine guns this proved unreliable and did not work satisfactorily. One obvious defect was that the canvas-belt contracted when wet, making it difficult to introduce cartridges. Another was that the tin which contained the water for keeping the barrel cool was detachable and could be lost. If this one item was lost through theft or accident, the entire gun was useless. The Maxim's one great advantage was that it was very light and could be carried by just four men even during a forced march. The Remingtons too were a superior weapon; unlike their 'rival' the Martini- Henry rifle, they did not have a tendency to jam.

On 28th January Stanley celebrated his birthday and allowed himself some self-congratulation: 'I am forty-eight years old today. If I were asked whether the privations of the last two years had affected permanently my physical vigour and elasticity - I should feel bound to say that at present I am not conscious of it.' His mood alternated between buoyancy and anger. On the one hand he was aware that prising Emin Pasha out of Central Africa was not going to be easy and he raged at the Pasha's 'ingratitude'. On the other, he was quietly confident that he would eventually manage to winkle Emin out of his stronghold. Since the news of the revolt in Equatoria his intentions had changed. It was no longer feasible to imagine that Emin, with his diminished resources, could establish himself at Kavirondo. This meant that he had to take the Pasha to Zanzibar, by force if need be. Gone was the jaunty insouciance in the Ituri forest, when Stanley had declared he did not care whether Emin returned or stayed, as instanced by this jotting by Bonny: 'Stanley said yesterday that Pasha thinks that some of the Expedition members would like to stay with him. Well, let them as far as I am concerned. I should not care if the lot remained with him.'

But what Stanley said in the depth of the Ituri, when he was uncertain whether he would survive, was one thing. His view of the matter when he reached the grasslands and learned of the revolt in Equatoria was quite another. Jephson was not the only one who felt the full force of Stanley's wrath in January 1889. Emin also received a letter, dated 17th January, asking for a reply within twenty days as to his intentions: did he, or Casati, or others intend to proceed to the coast, for Stanley's expedition could not be expected to remain inactive at Kavalli's indefinitely.

This letter, and the insulting one to Jephson, caught up with the pair on 26th January at Tunguru, where they had fled from Wadelai in December. Emin replied next day, accepting the fresh ammunition and gunpowder Stanley had brought him from Yambuya, but renouncing further aid, since Stanley's ultimatum precluded the gathering of all those Sudanese and Egyptians who might want to take advantage of the offer of an escort to Zanzibar. He bade Stanley adieu and wished him a safe homeward journey. It was quite clear he had no real intention of accompanying the expedition. Jephson then said goodbye to Emin and prepared to return to his leader's side at Kavalli's. The idea that this was farewell rather than au revoir hung in the air between him and Emin, though Casati promised he would bring the Pasha down to talk to Stanley within a few days.

On 6th February Jephson arrived at Kavalli's and gave Stanley a full report of his nine months with Emin. According to Jephson, the Pasha's soldiers were eager to leave Equatoria: 'no one keeps Emin Pasha back but Emin Pasha himself.' Jephson also added a piece of information which Stanley stored up for future use: he told him that most of Emin's Egyptian officers were 'animals who have been sent from Khartoum for nefarious practices'. Stanley was scathing about Jephson's good opinion of Emin personally and pondered the 'riddle' the Pasha was presenting. Why did he want to try to hang on by the skin of his teeth in Equatoria,

when his officers had made it clear by their revolt that they did not want him?

Stanley now decided that he would force Emin to accompany him. He dashed off an angry, threatening letter, but Jephson persuaded him not to send it and compose instead something more diplomatic. Stanley then sat down and incited a despatch 'after a style which probably Chesterfield himself would have admitted was the proper thing, which my friend Jephson pronounced was "charming" "nice" and "exquisitely sweet".'" The gist of this epistolary 'masterpiece' was a request that Emin extricate himself from Tunguru and come down to Mswa for a further conference. Meanwhile Jephson ingratiated himself with Stanley by a story purporting to show that the real obstacle to Emin's falling in with Stanley's plans was his eminence grise and evil genius Casati. Jephson's report, as filtered through Stanley, ran as follows:

I find Casati more impossible than ever. I asked him whether he would go with us tomorrow, and he replied he would rather wait. I then asked, 'How many loads have you?'

'Oh,' he answered, 'you know I have very few things. All my things were taken by Kabba Rega; perhaps I may want eighty carriers.'

Vita the apothecary wants forty carriers, and Marco the Greek trader wants sixty, so at this rate our Zanzibaris will be killed between here and Kavalli's. The Pasha remonstrated with Casati for taking all his grinding-stones, earthen jars, bedsteads for his boys and women, etc., upon which he said: 'Mr Stanley has offered to take all our loads.'

So pleased was Stanley with this tale that he invited Jephson to take his meals with him, an honour that had never before been extended either to Jephson or to any of the other officers. He confided his fears that Mahdists would take advantage of Emin's softness to infiltrate themselves into his party and thence into the expedition's camp. Already he was preparing a master strategy to force Emin to come with him, and this notion of betrayal and treachery by a fifth column was central to it.

At bottom Stanley wanted to bear away Emin to the coast as a trophy, both to avoid a repeat of the 1872 experience when he had returned without Livingstone and to salvage something from an expedition whose failure and notoriety so far would surely breed a multitude of questions in England. Emin would not consent to go unless his conscience was clear about 'his people'. But a horde of ragged Egyptian civilians and assorted hangers-on would be a drain on the expedition's resources and would create no very favourable impression on arrival in Zanzibar. Stanley had to find the equilibrium point: just enough followers for Emin to feel justified in leaving, but not so many that they acted as a drag on the chain to the expedition.

To a large extent Emin played into his hands. Having decided not to leave his province, he should have remained deaf to the siren songs from Kavalli's. But on 13th February he wrote to inform Stanley that he had arrived at Nsabe. The reason for his journey was to accompany Selim Bay and some of his other Sudanese officers, who wanted Stanley's assistance against the Mahdists, and needed Emin as an interpreter. Stanley at once sent Jephson down to the lake to escort Emin's party back to Kavalli's. On 17th February a large party trooped into Stanley's camp. With Emin were Casati, Marco, Vita Hassan, Hawashi Effendi and Osman Latif, plus the first detachment of genuine refugees, those who were prepared to accompany Stanley to the coast. Additionally, Selim Aga and a deputation of officers came to discuss joint operations against the Khalifa.

At the first interview, where Emin acted as interpreter, Stanley made it plain that the officers could expect no help from him in Equatoria. He told them their choice was simple: either remain and survive on their own devices, or accompany him to the coast. Selim and the officers then asked for sixty days' grace in which to prepare their families and effects for the march to the coast. Stanley answered simply that all who wished to go with him should assemble at Kavalli's. Again Stanley was playing a double game. He needed a minimum of sixty soldiers to stiffen his force against possible attacks from Kabba Rega, so was prepared to temporise to acquire them; but he never had any intention of escorting out the entire loyal Equatoria garrison. Emin was anyway doubtful that Selim and the others actually would follow Stanley out of Central Africa.

Selim departed with an assurance that the expedition would wait at Kavalli's until all those who wished to avail themselves of the safe-conduct to Zanzibar and Egypt had assembled there. The wangwana were now given the unwelcome task of transporting the baggage belonging to Emin's party from the lake shore to base camp at Kavalli's. Meanwhile the other contingents trickled in: Nelson and his column, and Stairs with the Ituri camp convalescents, another twelve of whom had died.

To sustain the increasing numbers of people arriving to occupy the 190 huts at Kavalli's - by 18th February there were over 500 and this quickly rose to over 1000 - Stanley sent out raiding parties to requisition cattle and supplies. He was ruthless in his collecting, raiding and burning surrounding villages if they resisted. For these distasteful forays he tended to use Stairs - his punishment for the Barttelot letter continued.

But the real bone of contention at Kavalli's was the baggage of the refugees which the wangwana were supposed to haul up from the lake shore to the plateau. Friction soon arose between the men of Zanzibar and the arrogant Egyptians and Sudanese, who treated the wangwana as their personal servants. Even more seriously, Emin's followers had completely ignored Stanley's injunction to keep their baggage to an absolute minimum. 'That was a rash promise of mine to convey all their property,' Stanley remarked ruefully. Emin had demanded 380 loads for himself, Casati, Vita Hassan and Marco the Greek, but in the event this total was exceeded. Casati brought eighty loads, Marco sixty and Vita Hassan forty, but Hawashi Effendi, the Egyptian officer who had commanded at Dufile before the Equatoria rebellion, arrived with ninety-four. Not only did most of this comprise bric-a-brac and rubbish, but there were items that could not be condensed into loads: 10 gallon jars for making raki, wooden bedsteads, 20-gallon copper cooking pots and grinding stones weighing 80 pounds each.

Two reports from Stanley illustrate the problem. 'There is an old Saratoga trunk, which was borne by two men. I tried to lift one end of it, and from its weight I should say it contains stones or treasure. What a story that old trunk could tell since it left Cairo! How many poor natives has it killed? How much anguish has it caused? The Zanzibaris smile grimly at the preposterously large size of the boxes they have to carry. They declare there are thousands of such cumbrous articles yet, and that they will be kept here for ten years.'

Again, on 22nd February: 'Marco the Greek merchant reached camp today with Bonny's escort. He is a fine, manly looking fellow. He has also an eye to comfort I see. In his train are domestics carrying parrots, pigeons, bedsteads for himself and harem, heavy Persian carpets, oxhide mats . . . and, oh horror, he has also brought three hundredweight of stone to grind corn with, as though the natives here could not lend us any number of stones. He has also brought ten-gallon pots to make beer in, and for use as water vessels. If all the refugees are similarly encumbered, we shall, I fear, be employed for months carrying this litter.'

To help solve the problem of baggage transport Stanley started to exert leverage on the local tribes. His raids for cattle became more extensive. On one day alone Stairs brought in 125 head and their protesting owners. Stanley purloined more cattle than he needed to feed the swelling throng at Kavalli's in order to achieve a corvee. The tribesmen were told they could have their cattle back if they helped in transporting the loads from the lake shore up the escarpment.

But Stanley was playing a subtle game as he got the impedimenta of Emin and his followers hauled up the plateau. For a start, it was unnecessary for all the effects to be taken to Kavalli's ready for sorting for the march to the coast. The sorting process could, and should, have been done at the lake shore. Moreover, Stanley could have requisitioned vast amounts of local labour by blackmail. But he did neither of these things. He recruited just enough local labour to ensure that the wangwana were not overwhelmed by their burdens, but not so much that their onerous task was relieved and their complaints stifled. He intended to screw up Zanzibari anger to such a pitch against the Egyptian and Sudanese ingrates that when he finally played his trump card, the wangwana would be willing and zealous collaborators. The Machiavellian ploy worked. Discontent and demoralisation among the porters grew. The headmen remonstrated with Stanley, but he feigned impotence: 'I am aware of what is going on. But what can we do? These people are our guests. We are bound to help them as much as possible. We indeed came here for that purpose.'

By 10th March the Zanzibaris were at the point of open mutiny. Nelson's contingent was sent for yet another back-breaking trip to Lake Albert to bring back sacks of grinding stones and heavy pots. The men's patience snapped and they mutinied. Some of the mutineers called out, with reference to the Egyptians and Sudanese: 'Shoot them all and let us go to Mazamboni's!' The wangwana expected that Stanley would take their side, as he had done in many similar situations, even against white men. But Stanley ordered the disloyal men to fall into line. He then disarmed them of their rifles, gave the eight ringleaders sixty lashes each and a further five to twelve lashes to thirty of their boldest accomplices. He then roped them all together back to back against the flag post and left them there all day until they had apologised. Hassan Bakani was given ten strokes of a cane for going absent without leave, and was so aggrieved that he threatened to shoot himself, as another of the wangwana had done a few days previously. He rushed into his hut to find his gun, and it took the strength of five men to restrain him. Tensions were mounting noticeably in camp, but all was grist to Stanley's mill.

One interested observer of Stanley's methods was Casati, who 'read' Stanley earlier and more shrewdly than his friend Emin. He left an account of10May which is much what the rabbit would leave if it could record its encounter with the snake:

The punishment was inflicted in a bold, frank, confident manner; and to one of the guilty men, who in a frightened faint voice answered the call, he said in a grave voice, while blows rained down: 'My name is Stanley Bula Matari and not only Ibrahim like yours.' Stanley is a man remarkable for strength of character, resolution, promptness of thought and iron will, Jealous of his own authority, he does not tolerate exterior influences nor ask advice. Difficulties do not deter him, disasters do not dismay him. With an extraordinary readiness of mind he improvises means, and draws himself out of a difficulty; absolute and severe in the execution of his duty, he is not always prudent, or free from hasty and erroneous judgements. Irresolution and hesitation irritate him, disturbing his accustomed gravity; his countenance being usually serious. Reserved, laconic and not very sociable, he does not awaken sympathy; but on closer acquaintance he is found very agreeable, from the frankness of his manner, his brilliant conversation, and his gentlemanly courtesy.

On 28th February Emin, who had gone with Selim back to Equatoria, returned with his loads and his six-year-old daughter Ferida, fruit of a union with an Abyssinian woman lately dead. Stanley always had a soft spot for children and was much taken with the pretty little six-year-old with large beautiful black eyes and the 'colour of a Portuguese'. But for Emin himself, though his overt relations were cordial at this stage, he entertained nothing but contempt. Stanley regarded him as a materialist, suffused with 'scientism', far more interested in the skulls of the dead than the fortunes of the living: 'He certainly has but little sympathy for anyone but himself and I fancy his best friendship does not extend beyond verbal expression . . . Emin has not taken any interest in a single Zanzibar or Sudanese in this expedition ... as regards any particle of what is divine that may be found in them, Emin simply yawns - though always politely.'

He even saw fit to compare Emin to Bonny - only a person of Stanley's purblind prejudices could have produced such a grotesque equation. Stanley was rapidly losing patience with Bonny's routine brutality to his servants which, despite the sergeant's protestations of innocence, he had been able to verify with his own eyes. Of Bonny he said: 'Barring one man I knew when a boy, the most cantankerous fellow I have ever met. Black man equally with the white falls under his displeasure.' Then came the ludicrous comparison with the gentle Emin: 'It is in this curious way of showing how aggrieved he is, that the Pasha, for reasons even more puerile than those of Bonny, closely resembles him. One grievance is linked to another, until the chain of grievances becomes portentously long and one day I become suddenly aware of the fact that I am an unspeakable tyrant, and altogether too wicked to breathe the same air with them.'

Stanley's murderous hatred of Emin, because the Pasha had dared to oppose his will to his own, and because he refused the 'privilege' of being forced out of the province Stanley was supposed to be coming to 'relieve', and was not suitably 'grateful', found expression in obsessive point-scoring against the supposed imbecility of all the whites who surrounded him. Parke, the man who had saved his life, Stanley described as an intellectual simpleton away from his medical textbooks; he scoffed at the ignorance of a man who thought that Arthur Young, the eighteenth-century traveller, had been up the Congo! But always it was Emin who was the chief focus of his derision. Stanley contrasted himself with the Pasha by saying that Emin wished to know only the Africans' external measurements and dimensions while he wanted to probe the secrets of their souls; for this reason Emin was absurdly trustful where he, Stanley, was sceptical and cynical. As time went on, his interest in the taxonomy of birds and fossils drew from Stanley a neurotic irritation:

I never see him handle these subjects which consume his time and occupy him so absorbingly without being reminded of a model housewife. The way he holds them up to view is finicky - with the little finger of his hand uplifted. He is painfully clean and dainty in his habits. His handwriting is so minute as to require a magnifying glass to read. His journals are scrupulously free from blots, as they may well be from the manner he holds his pen, and the deliberate care with which he dips it into the ink. His delicate and slender fingers are naturally fitted for delicate and dainty tasks, for handling the fittings of a watch, fine needlework, or to put the finishing touches to a miniature. He is so short-sighted that though he writes so minutely, he cannot see the face of a man twelve paces off, and I think his nature is such that he finds more interest in an ant than in an elephant, in the colours of a butterfly than in the moods betrayed by a man's face. A true naturalist would find as much interest in the greater as in the lesser.

As the stream of refugees trickled in, the March pattern of daily life at Kavalli's followed February's but in enhanced form. In one day Stairs and Jephson requisitioned 310 head of cattle. The expedition made periodic forays into the territory of the Baragga, to cow these allies of Kabba Rega and uplift cattle, as also against the Milindra people, old enemies of Emin and Casati. They discovered chimpanzees in the Baregga hills, so all the white men (including Emin) went picnicking there to collect zoological specimens. Emin Pasha had already assembled an impressive collection of local fauna and flora, including the original chimpanzee skull that first triggered the excursion. But it was this very collection that so irked Stanley. Emin spent all his time with it and none with his people. This explained why he had not a particle of control over them and, by extension, why Equatoria province was in such a mess when Stanley arrived. But all of Emin's actions played into Stanley's hands. He told the rvangwana he sympathised with their plight and agreed with them about Egyptian arrogance: 'It is riling also to see the Egyptian officers congregating in special groups each day, smoking their cigarettes and making their reflections on our slavishness.'

15th March brought the denouement at Kavalli's a stage nearer. Stairs arrived from the lake with Shukri Aga, another of Emin's senior officers and second only to Selim Bay in importance. Shukri conferred with Stanley and Emin on the flexibility of Stanley's original twenty-day deadline as vouchsafed to Selim Bay. Difficult negotiations ensued all that day, at the end of which Stanley set a definite date of 10 April for the departure of the expedition on the homeward trek. Stanley wanted Shukri to sign a written document, but instead Shukri gave him his hand as a sign that his promise would be kept religiously, without a written pledge.

Stanley's mood continued grim. At a general inspection on the 20th some of the men's rifles were found to be in an execrable state. Stanley ordered them cleaned and primed on pain of severe flogging; he could not risk misfiring Winchesters and Remingtons if it came to a shoot-out with Kabba Rega's 1500 riflemen who, Stanley discovered to his horror, were armed with Sniders, Henry-Martinis and Jocelyn and Stars - firearms individually not that much inferior to his own and wielded by a force that would outnumber his effectives by some three to one. Bonny too was becoming a running sore. 'Bonny has been engaged in another miserable squabble with the Zanzibaris about a female servant. He is so aggressive and positive in his disputes that he requires to be silenced sharply in order that the other side may be heard. I believe he is deteriorating rapidly.'

On 26th March Emin received a letter from Selim Bay to say that there had been a further mutiny at Wadelai. This meant that it was no longer possible for those loyal to Emin to maintain themselves in the province, so that they would now certainly be accompanying the expedition. The only snag was that, owing to uncertainties in the war-torn province, more time was needed. The 'twenty-day' deadline, and even the extension granted to Shukri Aga until 10 April, was no longer feasible. Stanley reacted to this news much as he had reacted to Jephson's story of the earlier revolt in Equatoria: it was simply an excuse or a pretext for delay or incompetence and did not merit further consideration.

Yet this time Stanley's impatience was a Machiavellian pose. He had never had the slightest intention of waiting for Selim Bay and his levies, delay or no delay, and had deliberately set a deadline which Selim could not meet. Genuine relief for the stricken province of Equatoria was the last thing on Stanley's mind. He needed Emin as his trophy and a sprinkling of his troops to make the expedition viable against Kabba Rega's raiders. Anything more than that was an encumbrance and an irrelevance. Now Selim had played into his hands and given him the excuse to do what he intended to do anyway. With the deadline fixed and irrevocable, the remaining part of Stanley's strategy could be implemented: an internal coup d'etat that would leave Emin shorn of all power and influence even over his own troops.

Emin was an ingenu fallen among rogues. Throughout February and March his journal is full of entries bespeaking respect for Stanley's dynamism and leadership qualities. When he received Selim's letter, with its intelligence that all the garrison would now follow Stanley and Emin out of Equatoria, he went to Stanley's tent with the good news, beaming with joy. 'What did I tell you?' he said. 'You see, I was right! I was sure they would all come.' He was shocked to find that Stanley did not view the news in the same light at all. Stanley was adamant that whatever Selim said, the expedition would move out on the morning of 10 April. He explained that he had a duty to the EPRE committee, which was spending

£400 a month just to keep the expedition ticking over in Africa, and to his officers who were keen to return to their normal careers. All this could not be set aside for the convenience of Selim and his men. Stanley thus revealed to anyone more perceptive than Emin one prong of his double-toothed strategy. The other he then hinted at by saying that in any case he suspected the good faith of the men Selim was bringing back; their most likely motive was to overpower the expedition and seize rifles.

At this Emin started to hedge and asked for an extension of the deadline. Otherwise, he averred, he simply would not know what to tell his own officers. Stanley proposed calling a full council of his officers to discuss the matter. When Stairs, Nelson, Parke and Jephson were assembled, Stanley addressed them in a nudging speech, which hinted very strongly at the answer he wanted them to give Emin. He rehearsed the incompetence of the Pasha's men, spoke of their traitorousness and unreliability, and hinted at Emin's own gullibility and incompetence. Emin had had nine months to organise an exodus, yet when the expedition returned from the horrors of the Ituri, it found Emin and Jephson the prisoners of Mahdist sympathisers. He pointed out the Pasha had originally accepted that twenty days constituted 'reasonable time' for Selim to return, yet in thirty days he had managed to get no farther than Tunguru with one-sixteenth of his men. Shukri Aga was also well behind schedule at Mswa. The original twenty days had been extended to forty-four, yet still the Egyptians pleaded for more time. Then Stanley played the ace he was to use continuously for the next fortnight: the fear of conspiracy. There were already conspirators in the camp, awaiting their opportunities to seize the expedition's goods and rifles in the Mahdi's name. If they waited for Selim, all they would do would be to strengthen the hand of this faction. Was there, then, a case for extending the deadline beyond10April?

One by one the officers said there was not. Emin then asked if he could reasonably be acquitted of the charge of having abandoned his people if he marched out on10April without waiting for Selim. All but Nelson overruled this objection. Nelson alone seemed keen to sustain the argument that a hasty departure would mean a failure in duty towards the Equatoria garrisons, but Stanley silenced him with an angry look.

Stanley's hectoring performance at the 'conference' was a tour de force of insulting behaviour and specious logic. Emin had had to sit through a rant, in which he and his people were excoriated as being either traitors or imbeciles. Stanley's illogicality almost defied belief. His listeners were expected to accept both that the men Selim and Shukri were gathering were Mahdists to a man, actuated by a desire to destroy the encampment at Kavalli's, and that it was still worth waiting for them until10April! It was almost a textbook demonstration of the leader's insincerity and bad faith. Parke had often been derided by Stanley as an ignoramus, but he was not so stupid that he could not put two and two together and see that there was something badly wrong with his leader's logic.

When his officers dispersed, Stanley asked Emin to wait behind for a few more private words. To sugar the unpalatable pill, he revived the idea of Emin's becoming Leopold's governor on the lower Congo, but this time contingent on his returning to Zanzibar first. As an alternative, there was the prospect of being governor of Mombasa under Mackinnon's IBEA company, at a salary of £700-800 a year. It remained unclear whether the Egyptian and Sudanese troops could also be employed by Mackinnon, but in any case they were primarily an Egyptian government responsibility; Emin, by contrast, had been given carte blanche by Cairo - he could either return there or make his way to any new appointment. Significantly, Stanley did not raise the question of the original Kavirondo offer and Emin, after the Equatoria revolt more suppliant than independent entity, was too embarrassed to mention it.

But Emin was now disgusted and disillusioned with Stanley. Not only had he been subjected to a barrage of direct insult and wounding innuendo but, for the first time, he began to get the measure of Stanley's breathtaking duplicity. He asked for time to consider and swept from the tent. Typically, Stanley carried self-deception and mendacity into his own private journal. All he could see, or claimed to see, was Emin's ingratitude. 'We believed when we volunteered for this work that we should be met with open arms. We were received with indifference, we were led to doubt whether any people wished to depart . .. instead of meeting with a number of people only too anxious to leave Africa, it was questionable whether there would be any, except a few Egyptian clerks.'

By the end of March the wangwana had completed the transfer of effects from the lake. Nelson came up from the lake with 132 men - the mutinous company that Stanley had cowed on the tenth. In six weeks they had conveyed 1355 loads to Kavalli's. The number of refugees at the camp stood at nearly 600. Jephson came in with fifty-six locally recruited carriers. The cattle raids continued, but the supply was beginning to dwindle. By now the scavenging parties were returning with fifty or sixty cows per foray, as against an average of several hundred a month before. On 1st April Stanley despatched Stairs (inevitably!) to Mazamboni's to form an advance depot for the onward trek.

On 31th March Emin returned with Casati to express serious reservations about proceeding with Stanley. A long debate ensued, ranging over political and ethical theory, dealing with law, duty, honour and morality. Ever the practical man, Stanley despised this sort of disputation. He thought that Emin and Casati were dishonest and were simply casting around for a philosophical peg on which to hang a decision they had already taken on quite other grounds. Emin was adamant that his men would do all in all as he would. Stanley begged leave to differ and thought that only about half would be swayed by the Pasha. The Egyptians and Sudanese had no intention of yielding to Emin's authority in any true sense but would play along with him for their own purposes. Once again, Stanley's journals are full of contempt and barely-contained rage towards the Pasha. 'Should any accidental violence be the consequence of our delay

487

- the whole must be attributed to Emin Pasha, inasmuch as he is the sole cause of our having been delayed so long here . . . the least apparent submission of his people to the Pasha makes him run over with love towards them, though to any of us here it is a base farce. 'By now Stanley was beginning to identify Casati as the principal obstacle to his plans: 'The Pasha pays great respect to Casati's opinion, who is only a reflection of the Pasha himself.' Stanley began to get Casati more firmly in his sights when Emin again came to say that Casati had advised him to stay with his people. 'What people, please?' asked Stanley sardonically. Did the Pasha mean the people who had already revolted and gone over to the Mahdists or did he refer to those who intended future treachery? Emin shrugged and suggested that Stanley should talk to Casati via an interpreter. As expected, this interview revealed an adamantine resolve on Casati's part to stay put and an unshakeable conviction that the pledge Emin had given his officers at Mswa overrode anything Stanley had elicited from him by browbeating. Stanley objected that Emin's troops did not seem to see it that way. Casati said that a commander should never abandon his post. Agreed, retorted Stanley, as long as his troops don't rebel. And what about the countervailing duty to the Khedive? None of this budged the Italian one inch. For a while Casati usurped Emin's role in Stanley's journals as 'Public Enemy Number One'.

What I have gleaned hitherto of Casati's character is that in some points he resembles the Pasha. He is more African than Emin even, for Emin has some regard for his dignity, while Casati appears to have none. He hobnobs with the Egyptian clerks and officers daily, takes coffee and smokes with them while in his dress he is as slovenly as a European could well be. I have only seen him at a distance, he has not ventured to exchange the ordinary courtesies of the day with any of us. His household consists of nine blacks and were it not for his colour, there would be no difference between master and servant - such is the equality preserved in his house. At first I was much affected by it - as it was so anomalous - but we have got used to it by this. His choice of a hut also among the Egyptian rabble, the whispers of the Pasha about his eccentricities, the fondness he shows for a black female child - have all contributed, unconsciously, to cause him to lose caste among us. I may be misjudging him, but he certainly is an odd character.

Stanley's particular animus was aroused by the fact that every time Emin went to confer with Casati, he came away depressed and wanting to stay on. What was Casati's motive, he wondered? 'Can it be that life in Italy was harder than we have any conception of? That the fleshpots of Wadelai appear to him preferable? ... I am quite content in my own mind with the surmise that life in Italy, after the freedom, licence and gratuitous bounties of Equatoria, has no charms for Captain Casati, but it is the case of Emin that always puzzles me.'

This was a reference to a conversation when Emin told him he would prefer to be, like Livingstone, an unfettered rover of the great African spaces. He would be quite happy never again to be subject to the stifling conventions of Europe, if he could just get regular newspaper reports from Europe. 'No,' said Emin, 'I don't wish to return to Europe, I remember its restrictions, its tiresome etiquette, and the pettiness of its bye-laws. I could not breathe in an over-ruled atmosphere after the freedom of Africa. Oh yes, I know what the return to Cairo means. I should have plenty of sugared phrases for a short time and then be relegated to the corner of a coffee house, and soon forgotten. None of that, thank you, for me.'

On the evening of 3 April Emin came to Stanley's tent for another chat. They talked for an hour, between 5.30 and 6.30. Emin told him that all but four of his servants had declined to go on with him, and one of those was accompanying Emin merely in hopes of recapturing a stepdaughter whom Casati had taken into his household and treated like a pet. Stanley was interested in anything that concerned the man now considered Emin's evil genius and asked for further details. Emin explained that the soldier in question was not the girl's natural father, so Casati denied his rights in the case. Emin deplored Casati's obstinacy and feared that the brooding stepfather meant him no good. All this was yet another consequence of the 'morbid attachment of Casati to his servants male and female'.

But Emin soon proved to be tarnished with the selfsame fault, if fault it was. About an hour after Emin had left him, Stanley happened to be passing the Pasha's tent. Inside he heard a furious row going on; his own name was mentioned several times. Shortly afterwards Mohammed Effendi, whom Stanley had identified as the disputant with Emin, came striding up to him with a crowd of followers to demand 'justice'. Patiently Stanley began to unravel the dispute. It turned out that Mohammed's wife had fled to Emin's protection and was now Ferida's nurse. Mohammed wanted her back. Stanley promised a decision when he had heard all sides to the story. First he summoned the wife, who said she had left her husband because of his brutality. Then he sent for Emin, who stressed how important the woman was to his daughter's well-being. Stanley asked to be given binding powers in the case and Emin acquiesced. Stanley promised a decision next morning.

This judgement of Solomon took the form of a written contract to regularise marital behaviour. The woman was to return to her husband, provided he apologised to Emin. She was to continue to attend Ferida by day, then return to her husband by night. Mohammed himself was pledged not to beat her or call on her services during the day. Even so, Emin had to command her several times to return to her husband before she reluctantly consented to do so. Stanley advised Mohammed to tie her up until she came to heel. At the end of the interview, the woman finally took down her veil and Stanley saw that she was very beautiful. 'I little expected to have such an interesting and beautiful female figure in any book of travels of mine.'

Stanley had long been casting about for a pretext to deprive Emin of any independent power and reduce him to a cipher. The opportunity came at last when the boy Sali, Stanley's spy, reported that there had been an attempted theft of rifles, and that only two out of fifty-one of Emin's men intended to accompany him. Stanley now resurrected the spectre of Mahdist conspiracy. His frequent hint that the men Selim and Shukri Aga wished to bring into camp were fifth columnists was now extended to the proposition that the enemy was already within, and that the attempted theft of rifles portended a general mutiny in the camp, in advance of the arrival of the other 'Mahdists'. To understand Stanley's actions on 5 April 1889, we have to understand that the obsession about 'conspiracy' denotes, not paranoia, but hard-headed calculation.

That morning Stanley stormed into Emin's tent and accused his people of being on the brink of mutiny. There was a vile and murderous plot afoot, said Stanley, which only the efficiency of his secret agents had forestalled. As a result, Emin and all the Egyptians and Sudanese would be immediately evacuated to a camp 3 miles away, and then allowed to accompany the expedition only when they had taken a formal oath of allegiance. Emin was too stunned to ask the obvious questions: how many rifles had been stolen, come to that, had any been stolen, did not the whole structure of 'conspiracy' rest on the say-so of Sali? Instead he feebly asked to be allowed to consult Casati. Stanley insisted he had to have an answer right there and then. The wangwana would that very day go round the camp to announce an immediate departure. All who resided or dragged their heels would be expelled from the camp. Alternatively, the Pasha might like to set out that very day with an advance guard, leaving Stanley to deal with the 'mutineers'.

'The Pasha during all this time was shaking his head in that exasperatingly melancholy manner - which has always seemed to me to betray the pitiable weakness of character which has wrecked the fine forces of men he commanded.' Emin said he could not consider the first possibility, of being expelled from camp. As for the second, he was not ready to move out at a moment's notice, his schedule was predicated on the agreed departure date on the 10th. Very well, Stanley persisted, what do you suggest? Emin repeated that he could not be ready before the 10th. At this Stanley lost his temper and said he was tired of the Pasha's excuses. He had been packing for fifteen days and was still not ready, did not like Stanley's proposals but could suggest nothing himself. Stanley stamped his foot on the ground and said in a convulsed voice: 'I leave you to God, and the blood which will now flow must fall upon your own head!' After several more angry exchanges - which Emin described as being like scenes in a madhouse - Stanley stormed out of the tent in a rage, exclaiming: 'I am resolved, Pasha, I am resolved.'

At this Emin took fright and came running out of the tent after Stanley to ask what he could do to make matters right. Brusquely Stanley informed him that the time for pacific solutions was past. He ordered him to sound the trumpet for general muster. When, after ten minutes, there was no sign of the Egyptians and Sudanese, Stanley sounded the alarm signal and ordered Jephson to take No.1 Company with sticks and beat out every single one of Emin's men on to the square. Now at last the reason for Stanley's apparent harshness towards the wangwana as they protested about lugging the heavy loads from the lake became clear. He had tuned them to a fine pitch of indignation, so that they were now more than willing to fall on their tormentors from Equatoria. The men of Zanzibar laid about them with gusto. The release involved in such an unexpected revenge led to many sore heads and aching limbs on the other side. The wangwana blocked all exits from the camp, pulled down tents around the ears of the laggardly, and laid bare heaps of merchandise and cases of ammunition. Stanley went into his tent and re-emerged almost at once, rifle in hand and cartridge pouch on his belt. Emin too disappeared into his tent and came out with long field boots on, as if he was ready to march. 'For the first time in years the Egyptians and Sudanese had to form a decent line. Not until they had formed it with military precision was a word said to them.'

When Emin's men were standing apprehensively to attention, Stanley pitched into them with a flood of rhetoric. Looking straight at Osman Latif, whom he suspected of being the leader of the Egyptian opposition, Stanley said he had heard the men of Equatoria were anxious to prove their mettle. Well, if they wanted a fight they could have one right now. Stanley worked himself up into a lather and shrieked at them. 'If you have the courage, point your gun at my breast. I am alone and unarmed.' Blind fury made him unaware of the palpable absurdity of the statement. Not only did he have a Winchester rifle in his hand, but behind him was a solid wall of wangwana, their guns pointing at the Egyptians and Sudanese, their trigger fingers itching to avenge the many slights they had taken on the chin throughout February and March. When Osman Latif denied that there was any conspiracy, Stanley lashed out again. In that case, what is the meaning of your arrogant behaviour, the theft of rifles, the plots, and the threats not to accompany Emin? He wound up in minatory vein. 'My orders alone are to be obeyed here, and whoever resists I will kill him with this gun, and trample him under my feet. Whoever intends to start and follow me, let him pass to this side. 'Stanley then ordered all who intended to accompany Emin to step to one side. All did so, out of fear of being shot dead on the spot. Next Emin's servants were sent for. All likewise stepped aside, with the exception of Selour, whom Emin identified as the chief conspirator. Stanley pretended that he wished Selour taken out and shot immediately. What about a trial, protested Emin. We can have a trial if you will consent to point out the other conspirators, Stanley replied. Emin was reduced to defusing Stanley's rage by pointing out other 'conspirators' who were placed under arrest. Histrionically making an effort to calm himself, Stanley told the other men on the square that any further sign of rebellion or revolt would be dealt with by the firing squad.

The dramatic events of 5 April represented a kind of coup d'etat, in which Stanley, using an entirely fabricated conspiracy theory, gelded Emin Pasha and thoroughly browbeat and subdued his men. To achieve this, he used the pent-up anger of the wangwana, who by obeying the leader's orders so willingly (for their own ends) simply gave a massive demonstration of Stanley's naked power. He had effectively manipulated all actors in the drama. His officers, after initial puzzlement, backed his actions once the 'details' of the 'conspiracy' were divulged. Emin himself was left both shaken by the revelation of the true nature of the man he had to deal with and shaking with rage at his own humiliation. 'Today for the first time in my life I have been covered with insults,' he told Casati. 'Stanley has passed every limit of courtesy, but I have promised not to speak, so can say no more.' In the privacy of his journal he raged at the treatment meted out to him. Still accepting the reality of the conspiracy, he noted with bitter irony, redolent of the usual contempt of the academic for the Grub Street scribbler, that Stanley could have made his point 'with fewer scenic effects and journalistic rhetoric . . . Stanley is created to converse with Zanzibaris, he should never include Europeans on his expeditions.' But he decided to tread carefully. After the day's traumatic events Jephson had a private word with him. He warned him not to make the mistake of thinking that the day's insult was the utmost Stanley could do if provoked; the Pasha had not yet plumbed the depths of the man nor realised the extremes of which he was capable.

Yet what Jephson saw as high drama and Emin as tragedy, Stanley, secure in his overwhelming victory, was inclined in retrospect to view as farce. He had decisively broken the will of Emin and Casati and the 'effete' Egyptians, whose long slothfulness in Equatoria had made them incapable of fight or opposing their wishes to his. The tone of Stanley's reflections that night establishes beyond question that the entire 'conspiracy' was a charade and that his rage was pure histrionics - but significantly the kind of thespian performance only available to one who could tap in at will to a reservoir of anger stored up since childhood.

The farce is over and has succeeded admirably, for I think the Pasha's followers are pretty thoroughly impressed. Even the Pasha himself wakened up and the acted vigour has been like champagne to him. Once I came near breaking down and spoiling all by laughing. Osman Latif Effendi's wrinkled old mother - who must be somewhere between seventy-five and eighty years old - came up to me in the midst of my tragic display and jabbered Arabic most volubly to me, as though I were a born Arab, upon which with an impatient wave of the hand I said to her in English, 'Get out of this, this is not the place for old women.' She lifted up her hands in horror, gave a little shriek and cried 'A Allah' in such terms of terror that I came near betraying the fact that my sternness was only affected [italics mine]. Everyone else guffawed loudly at the poor old thing as she beat a hasty retreat from the terrible scene.

Next day a kind of appalled tranquillity lay over the camp. Emin Pasha was incommunicado on the grounds of ill-health (he was broken and depressed), while Casati was no longer speaking to him because Stanley had found in favour of the soldier in the matter of the little girl Casati claimed as ward. But there were clear signs that the Egyptians, doubtless in fear of their lives, were at last making serious preparations to march.

In an attempt to defuse tensions, now that he had got his way, when Mazamboni's men came to entertain them with a farewell dance on the 8th, Stanley arranged a fight between the Sudanese champion and Zanzibari challengers. The idea seemed decidedly risky to Bonny: 'I think Stanley committed a grave blunder in thus furnishing such a breach of discipline which might have ended in a general rising of Arabs against Zanzibaris. I was never more surprised in my life when the fight was ordered by Stanley.'

But once again Stanley proved a shrewd judge of men. He used the occasion to display his 'even-handedness', thus convincing the Sudanese that he was not an automatic ally of the wangwana. Omar, a giant of a Sudanese sergeant, took on three Zanzibaris in a duel with clubs and laid them all out. The enraged wangwana then rushed him, which gave Stanley and his officers an opportunity to intervene and separate the combatants. The Zanzibaris responsible for ordering the assault were placed in the guardhouse. Selour was sentenced to two dozen lashes for using a shovel during the fracas. On the other hand, Omar was sentenced to carry a box of ammunition on his head until the wounds of the men he had knocked out healed. The same sentence was visited on three more of his countrymen. Amazingly, this 'solomonic' judgement, ending an affray Stanley had himself ordered, was received with general approbation.

No obstacle now remained to the expedition's departure for the east coast. On 10 April, as agreed, it threaded its way out of Kavalli's. The caravan was 1510 strong, including 230 wangwana, 130 Manyema, 350 plateau tribesmen, 200 of Kavalli's people plus 600 of Emin's followers, including 268 women and 105 children, and requiring 397 carriers for their effects. Nelson, commanding the Rear Guard, had orders to fire the encampment as he left it. The resulting inferno could be seen for miles.

What Stanley described as a 'splendid blaze' was not viewed in that light by Selim Bay when he finally staggered in to Kavalli's to find a gutted husk. Despite many letters pleading for an extension because of the revolt at Wadelai, Stanley ignored all Selim's correspondence and left him to his own devices. When Selim moved down to Kavalli's, his force of ninety men and 300 women and children was repeatedly attacked by the plateau tribes in revenge for Stanley's humiliating cattle raids and the forced labour Stanley had requisitioned for carrying his loads. If any of these porters deserted, Stanley simply carried out further raids to make up the numbers. The upshot was that Selim was marooned at Kavalli's until 1891 when Emin returned, now in German service. Selim refused to speak to him for his 1889 'treachery' and told the Pasha's companion Stuhlmann that, unlike the perfidious Emin, he remained an Egyptian subject, bound to the government in Cairo, not an adventurer who sold his birthright for a mess of pottage.

Wherever Stanley went, it seemed, he left a trail of destruction, not just in the form of smoking villages and dead tribesmen but in the ravages he made in personal relationships and the feelings between man and man.

Just three days after the hurried departure of the expedition, Stanley fell seriously ill with gastritis. The column came to a halt at Mazamboni's. What neither the pleas of Selim Bay nor the exhortations of Emin could bring about Stanley's illness now achieved. Parke injected his patient with morphine but could not hover over him in attendance as he had done the year before. Soon after the inception of Stanley's malady, Parke, Jephson and Bonny all went down with fever, making the last two-thirds of April another limbo period.

Relations between the humiliated Emin and Casati and the British remained tense. Particular resentment was felt that the duo did not bother to visit their fellow white men when sick. Parke noted acidulously on 26 April: 'Captain Casati is very retired; he has never come over to this camp, even to enquire for Mr Stanley or any of us.' Emin, however, sent further messages asking Stanley to wait until Selim came up. This merely served to rile the valetudinarian Stanley, who conducted further versions of a conspiracy theory, this time one in which Selim was in league with a fifth column already on the march, which had instructions to slow down its rate of progress. It seemed to have escaped him that the only thing slowing down the expedition was his own illness. Nevertheless, from his sickbed Stanley gave orders, over Emin's protests, that the Pasha's followers should have the mainsprings removed from their rifles.

Further bad feeling was caused when Emin refused to abide by the decision of a court martial that the ringleaders in the 'plot' should be executed by firing squad. He tried to pass the buck to Stanley by asking for wangwana sharpshooters to do the deed. Not wishing to widen the rift between the two sections of the expedition, Stanley refused the request and told Emin to get his own men to do it. Emin said he had no men who could shoot well enough to dispatch the victims humanely and used this as an excuse to commute the sentences to flogging. Even Jephson started to lose patience with the Pasha at this point. He felt he had been made a fool of, and made to serve on a six-hour court martial for no purpose.

It was probably this background that made Stanley determined that the next delinquent, whosoever it proved to be, would face the supreme penalty. When Stairs - who continued to get the dirty work - returned with the deserter Rehan, who was guilty in addition of theft of rifles and incitement to desert, Stanley was insistent that he had to die. In his published account of the expedition, Stanley claimed he advised a non-capital punishment, but this is inconsistent both with other eyewitness reports and with the general context; only Stanley was likely to have pressed for a death sentence, certainly not Emin, and the only one of his officers likely to have argued for hanging (Bonny) had no influence.

Stanley, still on a milk and water diet and unable to stand, dragged himself to the court martial, held in open session, at which Rehan was sentenced to death by a tribunal composed of Stairs, Nelson, Jephson and

Parke; the leader cunningly took no direct part himself. Stanley offered to spare him if any of his vpangwana colleagues spoke up for him but, after 5 April, everyone was edgy and suspected Stanley of wishing to identify 'conspirators'. More than anything, it was the atmosphere of witch-hunt in the camp that doomed Rehan. Stanley turned this tragedy too to his own benefit by insisting that all Emin Pasha's men attend the execution, so that they could witness his 'impartiality'.

The actual execution contained echoes of the first hanging in the Ituri forest, in September 1887. The rope used for the lynching - for such in effect it was - had become so rotten with exposure to wet and damp that it broke when Rehan had been hoisted about a foot from the ground. Four plies were then spliced together for the second attempt. While all this went on, Rehan displayed not a scintilla of hope but looked on, apathetic and indifferent. The renovated noose was then attached and the victim was drawn up to a height of some 14 feet from the ground, in which position the body was left suspended for the night.

Emin continued more enigmatic than ever. There are even signs that he had decided to play the Stanley game of obfuscation back at him. He complained of lack of carriers, then when Stairs went to investigate the problem, Emin told him that his people did not deserve any help, but that if Stairs was short of the odd porter, he would send him a slave or two! Emin's behaviour gradually alienated his erstwhile allies among Stanley's officers. Even Jephson found the Pasha offhand, rude and ungrateful. Ruefully he recorded his reappraisal. 'The Pasha is in his way as dangerous a man as Stanley and tried to put one in very nasty positions; only he does it in a meaner and more ungenerous way than Stanley does, and that is saying a good deal. For the past three days I have not gone to see the Pasha. I can no longer trust myself to remain quiet under his rudeness.'

The wheel came full circle when the man Stanley had once likened Emin to emerged as a virulent critic. 'Bonny, after falling foul of every white in the expedition with abuse, gave me his opinion of the Pasha which is the reverse of flattering. They have fallen out about the birds they collect and Bonny is dissatisfied with his share. It seems that he shoots the birds and the Pasha's people prepare them, and in consideration of shooting them he obtains half the collection. He is so angry that he calls the Pasha a vile swindler!'

Emin's raw state after the mauling from Stanley on 5 April is attested to from a variety of sources. Casati was no longer speaking to him. Next Emin compounded this misfortune by turning on Vita Hassan the apothecary and accusing him of having instigated Mohammed Effendi to make the scene at Kavalli's which ended with Stanley's judgement of Solomon and the return of his wife on a nocturnal basis. Nor was Emin's state of mind improved when Stanley came to him with circumstantial evidence that one of his officers (Ibrahim Effendi Eltram) was a traitor - the most obviously bad apple in a thoroughly rotten barrel, as Stanley put it. His correspondence was said to prove that Selim Bay too was a traitor, who wished to detain the caravan only to deliver it to the Mahdists. Stanley then rubbed salt in the wound by adding as a Parthian shot that he would have acted against the 'mutineers' long before 5 April, but for fear of humiliating the Pasha! Stanley's version was that the events of 5 April were forced on him as soon as he realised that Emin was virtually alone in his desire to leave. This was gall of a high order. Not only had Emin not desired to leave, but the humiliation on the 5th had been consummate. One can only speculate on Stanley's actions had he not been constrained by 'consideration' for the Pasha's feelings!

Of course this was yet another example of Stanley's spectacular ability to lie even to himself. We can form some idea of how far Stanley's polished publications were from the raw actuality. In 'In Darkest Africa' there is no entry corresponding to Stanley's entry under 6th May in the 'Personal Journal' of the Emin Pasha expedition - the journal that Stanley considered publishing later. This journal entry deals with the

arrival of Shukri Aga and tells how he returned from a raid with twenty-eight prisoners in tow. The 'Personal Journal' entry is as follows: 'I am getting pretty sick of these Egyptians. I would rather they themselves should perish than that they should harm these people who have been so loyal and good to us.' Thus does Stanley portray himself as the true humanitarian, sickened by the brutality he sees around him. But the original undoctored journal puts a very different slant on this event. Here Stanley says that the 'bush people' deserve no mercy but they could well be left alone but for the excessive demands and rapacity of the Egyptians and their families. His main objection to such raids is not their inhumanity but the trouble they lead to - a pragmatic rather than humanitarian consideration. The original unvarnished diary entry read as follows: 'I really think they had better die rather than we should unnecessarily inflict misery or common injustice even to beings so low in the human scale as bush people [italics mine].'

At last, on 8th May, Stanley felt well enough to press on from Mazamboni's, though for the first few days of the journey he was carried in a hammock made of hide. Again he refused to heed the Pasha's entreaties that he should wait for Selim Bay. And he refused to extend to Jephson the care he had lavished on himself. From 10th to 27th May Jephson lay ill with a fever that oscillated between 102 and i05°F. But where Stanley had been in the cool of a tent at Mazamboni's, Jephson was jolted and jarred in an unwieldy hammock borne by clumsy porters.

Once on his feet, Stanley strode purposefully at the head of the column, a pipe in his mouth, a stick in his hand, guiding the destinies of 1500 people with his adamantine will. Ahead of him was thrown out a party of wangwana scouts with local guides. Behind Stanley and his men came Jephson and his company, then Emin and his people, escorted by another company. The families of the Egyptian officials, their servants, carriers and dependants, plus the Manyema recruited at Yambuya, were in the rear. Last of all came the rearguard, alternating between Nelson's and Stairs' company. The march began at sunrise and continued until 11 a.m. without halts. By that time the head of the column would have reached the night's resting place, but usually the rearguard did not get in until 4 p.m.

The pace was the usual blistering one set by Stanley in his African journeys and within days stragglers and sick were being left behind, many of them cursing the day they had first heard of the Emin Pasha relief expedition. Pleas for stopovers were met with the argument that since even three or four days' rest would do little to alleviate the misery of the worst cases of illness, it was press on or abandon the march altogether. Part of the reason for Stanley's haste was to make sure that Selim Bay and his party could not catch up. If they did, Stanley had a contingency plan ready. He would disarm them as traitors and, if they objected, attack them as foes.

For all that, the first few days of the march were the easiest. Since Mazamboni was escorting them to the limits of his territory with 300 warriors, the expedition was allowed free range in the luxurious banana and plantain plantations. In return Mazamboni received forty head of cattle and sixteen tusks of ivory, averaging 52 pounds each. Then they began a slow ascent to a spur above the Balegga valley. On their left rose the slopes of mountains, a range 70 miles along, among which the snowy peak of Ruwenzori was clearly visible. To their right, in a westerly direction, the forest, black as night, kept company with them. They were seldom out of sight of the advancing capes and receding bays of the dark wooded mass. Once on the spur they saw how narrowly they had avoided being swallowed up by the forest. They continued the climb to the uplands at 5000 feet.

Seeing that the Egyptians marched at half his rate and abused the officers he sent back to hurry them on, Stanley predicted heavy casualties once they ran into enemy forces. The first brushes came sooner than he expected. As soon as Mazamboni's warriors turned back at the frontier, on 10th May, Kabba Rega's elite warasura warriors saw their chance. While bathing in the river, Emin's men were attacked. Fire was returned and three of the enemy killed, though not before they had shot Casati's servant Okili dead through the head.

Now deep in enemy country, Stanley sent out two heavily armed parties of 120 men each to forage, one under Stairs, the other under Nelson and Bonny. The main column slogged on through a cloud of mist, the product of a violent rainstorm on the night of the 4th. Already on the march there were clear signs of man's inhumanity to man. The rearguard executed a man for 'spying' without even referring the matter to Stanley. Bonny told of a baby abandoned in tears on the road by one of Emin Pasha's women. Stanley asked what Bonny had done about it. 'Why, I left it there. What else could I have done with it?' Stanley gave him a withering look. Even by his own lights Bonny was stupid, for Stanley was sentimental about children and would have given the sergeant money for the child. The sentimentality comes out clearly in a eulogy Stanley delivered on the boy Tukabi who absconded twice from his father to join the expedition, as he wanted to see the land where guns and gunpowder were made. 'Such a boy as this must be a wonderful fellow. I ought to mention that he appears to be a singularly bright little fellow with very intelligent eyes.'

The expedition was now heading south into the valley of the Semliki, the river that linked Lakes Albert and Edward. All of this was land that no white man had seen before. 'From the temperate and enjoyable climate of the regions west of Lake Albert we descended into the hot-house atmosphere of the Semliki valley - a nearly 3000 feet lower level. Night and day were equally oppressively warm and close and one or two of us suffered greatly in consequence.' Stairs, Jephson and Bonny were the main victims, but Stanley himself suffered from a high temperature and a two-day fever.

As they wound their way down into the valley, Nelson came to meet them with news that Kabba Rega's forces were massing on the far side of the Semliki to dispute passage and had taken all the canoes. The situation required all Stanley's skill. Through his binoculars he spotted an unguarded canoe on the other side of the river. Under covering fire Saad Tato and Uledi swam across and retrieved it. Saad Tato received an arrow wound and had to be patched up by Parke, but at least the pair had succeeded in bringing back the precious canoe. While the warasura fired showers of arrows at them, Bonny and the five best shots in the expedition paddled across and established themselves in a beachhead. The canoe was sent back and further detachments of half a dozen men were ferried across in relays. The beachhead became a genuine bridgehead and some fifty crack shots were pouring lead into Kabba Rega's warriors. Stanley found two more canoes and stepped up the ferrying. On the afternoon of the 18th an arrow attack by the warasura on the canoe ferries led to a general engagement with Nelson's one-hundred strong company, in which Kabba Rega's men were completely routed. By the afternoon of 19th May, 1168 souls, 610 loads of baggage, 235 cattle and three canoe-loads of sheep and goats were safely across the Semliki.

But on the other side it took the expedition five days (three of marching, two of rest) to get just 16 miles inland from the Semliki. One day they marched for six hours through quagmires of mud in the thick, gloomy forest of Awamba, which Stanley found in many ways worse than the Ituri because of its excessive humidity. One village was so badly infested with gnats that he regretted occupying it almost at once. His irritability found a focus in Bonny. 'I had to reprimand Bonny, gently, in consideration of his pluck at the Semliki ferry, for choosing the best house in the village for himself when it should have been reserved for the Pasha. He replied that as Jephson had taken all the milk he thought it was to be every man for himself. Jephson being so pitifully weak after his long bout of illness, I had to tell him not to presume so much.'

But it was the Egyptians who most excited Stanley's scorn during the gruelling march on the other side of the Semliki. They would start the day well, then collapse after about an hour. Utterly unaccustomed to a rainy zone and the effect of precipitation on the roads, the Egyptians floundered through the quagmires in an agony of misery and demoralisation, only making progress at all because the rearguard whipped and prodded them on. One Egyptian, sapped by 12 miles of mud, sat down on the road and refused to go any further, saying he would prefer to die. Women abandoned their children in woods off the trail where they could not be seen or heard. Stanley was the terminus for a never-ending stream of complaints, from the rearguard at their thankless task in chasing up the laggardly Egyptians, and from the Egyptians, via Emin, who complained of cruel usage by Stanley's officers. Stanley noted bitterly. 'I wonder what the well-fed sentimentalists of England would say were they in my place on such a day as this! It is cruel work altogether, cruel for the rearguard who wish to get to camp, and rest out of the rain and mud and the fatigue of waiting and urging on men who break out into insolent abuse of them in return for their well-meant efforts ... the number of women with infants and small children straggling in the mud, wet to the skin, and hungry, give a heartrending aspect to the expedition.'

Matters came to a head when another Egyptian called Hamdan tried the 'sit-down strike' method on Nelson in the rear. Nelson simply left him there, with the result that that night rumour flew the Egyptian camp that Nelson had shot Hamdan. Stanley decided to have it out with Emin. Not surprisingly, he found the Pasha still smarting under the impact of 5 April. Emin said he had witnessed with his own eyes the cruelty of Stanley's officers towards his own people. Stung by this aspersion, Stanley asked cuttingly why Emin did not take fifty men and act as the rearguard, and see how he liked going without food for twelve hours only to be cursed for his pains. Emin snapped back at him: 'I wish to God I had not consented to come with this expedition.' 'I quite believe you,' replied Stanley with heavy irony, 'though for what sane reason only God and yourself know.' Emin glowered at him and accused him of taking the expedition on much too fast, without sufficient halts. Stanley stalked off but got his revenge that night in a choice journal entry in which he rehearsed all Emin Pasha's sins. Babies had been thrown into the woods, women left behind and Egyptians abandoned on the road, but Emin took no interest whatever. Immune to the splendours of Ruwenzori, uninterested in the natural phenomena of hot springs, salt lakes or even the pygmies, Emin's gaze lit only on birds, beetles and butterflies. Stanley fed the line to Hoffmann, who faithfully reproduced it in his book. 'His gallant rescuer might be dying, his men might all desert him, but bring him a rare bird, an unknown beetle, a strange flower, and he would immediately become wrapped in a sort of divine ecstasy from which it was impossible to rouse him.'

Stanley's response to the sufferings in his rear was typical. He made the sentimental gesture of having all the children brought to the space around his tent at night, for greater security, then regretted the gesture when their crying kept him awake all night. Then he looked around for a focus for the anger he felt towards the Pasha; by an association of ideas natural to him his choice fell on Bonny, who had allowed large numbers of the cattle to stray while they were in his charge. Bonny evidently replied to the reprimand with a form of 'dumb insolence', for Stanley recorded: 'His bearing often puzzles me. It is not what could with justice be called insolent or defiant, but it suggests that everybody is in the wrong but himself - and that if he liked he could prove unutterable things to everyone's discomfiture.'

Some respite from hardship was offered at Ugarama, where the people were delighted to hear that Stanley's herds of cattle had been seized from the allies of Kabba Rega. Here food was plentiful, since terraces were cultivated up to a height of 8000 feet. There was a great abundance of fruit, millet, yams, corn and sweet potatoes. Then it was an easy passage until the end of the month through Batama and Bukoko. But one untoward event soured the more favourable turn of events. Two separate parties went out skirmishing, the wangwana for game and the Manyema for ivory. Mistaking each other for enemies, they became involved in a fratricidal shoot-out that left a man killed and eleven wounded. Suppressing his anger, Stanley consented to accept an apology from Kilonga-Longa's men. But his mood did not improve when there was yet another erroneous armed clash on 30th May, this time between Shukri Aga and the locals who had mistaken his men for warasura. Altogether fatalities amounted to four killed and eight wounded in the expeditionary personnel.

By the first week in June, the supply of livestock was down to 104 cattle and thirty sheep and goats; neither the forest nor the rank grass of the Ruwenzori suited the beasts. They were now splashing through cold streams, at their nearest point yet to the snow-capped Ruwenzori - which the pygmies regarded as the seat of their gods. Stanley decided to send out a party to attempt an ascent of the lofty peak. His first choice to lead the climbing party was Jephson, but Jephson no sooner recovered from one fever than he went down with another. Nelson was the fittest officer to hand - he had even gained ten pounds in weight since leaving Mazamboni's - but since he now did the job of two officers, Stanley could not spare him. Reluctantly, he decided to send Stairs, who was still in disgrace and normally the expedition's white dogsbody.

Emin and Stairs set out to conquer Ruwenzori. Emin's weak lungs forced him back after just 1000 feet of steep climbing, but Stairs managed to get to nearly 11,000 feet before lack of oxygen forced him back. The main column meanwhile descended the precipitous walls of the Rami-Lulu gorge, traversed the narrow level, then ascended the wall-like slope on the other side. They entered a forest, whose variety exceeded the Ituri but which, like the Ituri, contained numerous hostile peoples. A Madi chief was speared on the first day, and skirmishing continued until Stanley pitched camp in a dry forest glade and opened negotiations with the local Bakonjo people. He discovered that the local Konjo and Nande tribes had retreated into the forest to escape the superior Hamitic peoples. But when the Bakonjo learned that Stanley's expedition were sworn enemies of the

Bunyoro, they welcomed them with open arms and sought their help against their ancient foes. Soon the Konjo were fast friends and provided an escort through Mtsora and Muhamba, the edge of the lowlands.

Before beginning the ascent of the next range of mountains, Stanley tried to guard against the possibility of massacre in the rear by forming Emin Pasha's men into a company of fifty-four riflemen. Predictably the attempt foundered on Egyptian sullen un-cooperativeness. Casati asked for his servant to be excused and Stanley rashly consented. Then all the other Egyptians joined in refusing to release their servants. Angrily Stanley ordered the arrest of Vita Hassan, Marco the Greek and Basili, the chief clerk. Emin, who stood to lose his bodyguard of six armed retainers, went to Stanley to complain.

Stanley received his overtures coldly and said that if everyone took the same selfish attitude, there would soon be no defence left. Just then Shukri Aga came in to say that the Egyptians were regarding Emin's request as a test case and would not co-operate if Stanley made special concessions to the Pasha. 'I see your example has been speedily followed,' said Stanley sardonically. 'If you were unwilling to control this rabble, why did you bring them with you?' Emin shrugged and said he could not stop them. Stanley asked him if he wanted to see his people massacred. Emin replied: 'I don't care for that and I cannot help whatever may happen. I must have my own people. I dare say they are very sorry they came along, and I am very sorry I ever came too.' Stanley accused him of being an ingrate. Emin stormed off in a rage. His parting words were: 'Do as you please and you may leave me behind any time you like.' 'No,' Stanley shouted after him, 'it is as you please.' Both men were in a towering rage. Emin turned on his heels and repeated; 'I think you had better leave me here, I wish you had never come to help me.' Stanley bawled back at him: 'You are a most thankless and ungrateful man. 'Once again Stanley had won a propaganda victory over the Pasha, for all his officers, especially those who toiled in the rearguard, approved Stanley's actions and felt that Emin's refusal to co-operate was unreasonable. He also won his point and formed the recalcitrant Egyptians into a rifle squad.

On 15th June the expedition left the plain and began the ascent into the mountains. The landscape reminded Stanley of the lower Alps as viewed from Berne. Next day they descended a long hill to the River Ruvehari in the plain of eastern Usongara. Stanley remarked on the poor condition of their cattle and Nelson told him this was due to Bonny's incompetence. Stanley summoned Bonny to his tent and got Nelson to repeat the charge. When he heard the accusation, Bonny rounded on Nelson and called him a 'damn liar' and a 'professional vilifier'. 'He had charged Stairs to him of being afraid of his men, Jephson of being the cad of the expedition, Dr Parke of being ignorant of his duties and of being unprofessional, that he had said the most horrible things of the Pasha, though he was glad to dine with him, and had not even spared me.'

At this obvious instance of pure malevolence, Stanley told Bonny to shut up. Even if everything he said was true, it was irrelevant to the charge and did not excuse his neglect of the cattle. He ordered Bonny to apologise to Nelson. Instead of doing so, Bonny lashed out and landed a blow. Within seconds the two men were writhing around on the floor of the tent, punching and gouging. Stanley fired a shot with his revolver to bring them to their senses, then ordered them to their feet. They obeyed sheepishly. Again Stanley ordered Bonny to apologise and again he refused. Stanley ordered him to be confined in his tent under close arrest. When Bonny had been marched off, Stanley apologised to Nelson for the sergeant's behaviour.

Even more than previously, Bonny was proving a thorn in Stanley's flesh. He could not understand why the man had such an exalted opinion of himself. He was plucky, was a good bridge builder, he kept his records methodically, and to his credit he had his behaviour in 'starvation camp' in late 1888 and the courageous way he crossed the Semliki into a possible ambush. But on the debit side he was hopeless at managing blacks, had an ungovernable temper, was churlish, vindictive, sly and vain. Stanley decided to keep him in isolation for a few days as a 'cooling-off period.

The march east was already threatening to turn into a full-blown nightmare. Not a day passed without some personnel problem; the external threats almost came as a relief. He learned that the Egyptians had captured ten local women for the satisfaction of their lusts and ordered them released. 'Who was responsible for this behaviour I did not think it was polite to enquire too closely, as I do not wish my journal-keeping friends here to know things of this kind which would not reflect on the expedition as a whole.' One small consolation was that just after he had taken a photograph of Ruwenzori, Emin came to apologise for the behaviour of his men. The two shook hands and Stanley said that as far as he was concerned all disputes between them were now closed. But when Emin asked to be released to go his own way, Stanley refused.

As the expedition approached Rusesse, a herd of twenty-five cattle was taken into its possession. Then they trekked on to Katwe, where Stanley discovered the salt lake of Katwe and the saline flats around. Here they ran into a large party of musketeers and spearmen belonging to Ruvara, a vassal of Kabba Rega's. These warriors were routed after a short, sharp fight, following which a flotilla of canoes belonging to Ruvara's foes approached to offer friendship if Stanley would burn Katwe village. He was happy to oblige. In return chief Kakuri, Ruvara's rival and enemy, appeared next day with food, which enabled the expedition to rest while Stanley explored Lake Katwe. Circumnavigating the lake in a canoe on 18th June, Stanley saw a large black panther slaking its thirst at the lakeside, but was unable to approach close enough to get off a shot.

On 20th June they pressed on from Katwe, skirting the salt lake, then proceeded over a plain flat as a billiard table to Muhoyka, a village equidistant from the lake and the mountain: 'a dry and hot land, the ground was baked hard, the grass was scorched - the sun, but for the everlasting thick haze, would have been intolerable.' On the other hand, marching on the plains involved no thorns, stones, roots or red ants. When they reached the River Rukoki the vanguard received a volley from Kabba Rega's musketeers who lay hidden in ambuscade in a thick brake of reedy cane. Stanley ordered a charge which soon drove the warasura pell-mell from the rushes. Then he sent Nelson's company, one hundred strong, out with his local allies to track the enemy and overhaul then. After a 12-mile pursuit without finding them, Nelson broke off and returned to the column.

On 25th June they crossed the Nsongi River and began plodding into the uplands. There was desultory firing at them from warasura on hilltops, but the real threat to the expedition came from a quite different source. Ague and fever caused by drinking adulterated rainwater decimated the expedition. 200 persons reported sick. Stanley himself was prostrate for four days, with a temperature as high as i04°F. Emin, Parke, Jephson and Hoffmann also succumbed. As if sensing that the expedition's pulse had faltered, on 28th June the warasura launched their fiercest attack yet on the rearguard. They took heavy casualties from the repeating rifles and sheered away suddenly. This proved to be the last serious encounter with Kabba Rega's raiders.

With fever still running through its ranks, the expedition descended to the level terrace at the foot of the eastern walls of the basin of Lake Edward. By now they had travelled along the northern, north-western and eastern coast of Lake Edward. They were received with friendship and hospitality by the local chief, and Stanley used the halt to discuss the future path to Zanzibar. Situated as they now were on the borders of Ankole, they had three choices: they could strike across Buganda; go the long way round via Ruanda and Lake Tanganyika; or traverse Ankole south-west to the southern tip of Lake Victoria, then follow Stanley's 1874-5 route to Bagamoyo. Since Buganda was known to be in turmoil and Ruanda was an unknown quantity, it was thought best to opt for the Lake Victoria route.

On 4th July they left Lake Edward. The level plain assumed a rolling character, dotted with trees. Soon they were among hills, trekking on an upward gradient. Stanley approached Ankole, ruled by Ntare, with some apprehension. But the king proved just as fearful of the expedition. He was suitably impressed by the power of the Maxim gun, the expedition's numbers were not such that his territory would be laid waste, provided he got rid of it quickly, and besides Stanley had checked his own enemies, the warasura. As a result, a kind of non-aggression pact was agreed and Stanley received permission to cross Ankole. He later claimed, mendaciously, to have been ceded all sovereign rights in Ankole by Ntare.

After warning his men to be on their best behaviour, since they were now among friends, Stanley commenced the climb up to the pass of Kinyamagara. Then the expedition descended into a long winding valley running parallel with the eastern shore of Lake Edward. On 10th July they reached Katara in a land teeming with lions and leopards. At night a hyena dragged off one of the goats. At Katara an event pregnant with significance for the future took place. A delegation of Christian rebels approached him to solicit his help in deposing Kabaka Karema and replacing him with Mwanga. But Stanley was dubious. He knew very well that Mwanga was the author of the murder of Bishop Hannington in 1885 and he doubted the sincerity of his conversion to Christianity. So Stanley stalled, promising an answer when he had traversed Ankole.

With Emin, Casati, Stairs and Jephson all prostrate with fever, Stanley was irked to find that his old nemesis Bonny, one of the few with the constitution to fight off the diseases of Africa, was up to his old tricks. Stanley haled him in for another ferocious dressing-down over the loss of twenty-four cattle, caused when Bonny abandoned his post. But Bonny was as insolent as ever. 'He shrugs his shoulders, departs to bed and acts as though it were no concern of his that the cattle perish or are lost. Yet there is no man on this expedition, white or black, who will make more clamour, or grumble more fiercely, if his rations are in the least stinted.' This raises the obvious question: why did Stanley put up with him? Almost certainly the answer is that he already foresaw the furore that would break out in England over the expedition and wanted Bonny's evidence against Barttelot as a reserve weapon,

Bonny's particular imbecility was simply one species of a widespread genus in the expedition. It passed Stanley's understanding how his men could go in for petty pilfering after they had been treated so well by the people of Ankole, themselves not far from the bread line. Here were over 1000 people, living free, with no hongo, tax or blackmail being levied. The innate goodness of the African was daily apparent. One day a feverish Bonny fell into a ditch. A passing African spearman could have killed him with impunity, but instead went and fetched a half-gallon gourd of fresh milk, gave it to Bonny to drink, then helped him from the ditch and on his way. Apart from Stairs, who had a genuine rapport with Africans, his officers seemed unable to reciprocate these friendly feelings, but complained if Stanley reined in their brutality and whispered that he preferred blacks to whites. Well, enough was enough, Stanley concluded. The next case of looting would be visited with exemplary punishment.

The expedition wound through hill country and through a pass in the Ruampara mountains into the narrow, winding Niamianja valley - a land stiff with cattle. All the leading expedition members were constantly up and down with fever; Stanley suffered another three-day bout from 17th to 20th July. 'The ascent to the eastern plateau was marked by an increase of cold and many an evil consequence, fevers, colds, catarrhs, dysenteries and paralyses. Several times we ascended to over 1000 feet above the sea, to be punished with agues, which prostrated black and white by scores. In the early mornings at this altitude hoar-frost was common - blackberries were common in north-western Ankole, 5200 feet above sea level.'

At Niamianja village the rearguard was menaced by tribesmen, but Uchunku, the prince-royal of Ankole, coming fortuitously on the scene for a blood-brotherhood ceremony with Stanley, chased them off. But the favourable conditions experienced during the crossing of Ankole seduced Emin's men into a bad mistake. Some Nubians deserted and four Egyptian officers, tired of the rigours of the march, asked permission to stay behind. Clearly foreseeing the consequences, Stanley agreed. No sooner was the rearguard safely gone, than the locals set on them and stripped them naked.

This was not the only such incident on the march through Ankole. Some children who were left behind by Emin's people were immediately seized and enslaved by the locals. Jephson, once in Stanley's words a 'confirmed Feminist', was becoming more and more disillusioned over the Pasha's indifference to the fate of his people. 'Gordon spoke truly when he said a man should return to Europe every three years, otherwise his sense of morality (in the broad sense of the word) would gradually adapt itself to that of the country in which he lived. The Pasha is a striking example of the truth of Gordon's remark. Someone defines morality as a tissue to the growth of which a hot climate is not conducive. I think it was Lord Beaconsfield.' Jephson was becoming sickened by all the barbarism he saw on the march that seemed to leave Emin unscathed. Not only were laden porters cuffed, pummelled and lashed by their Egyptian and Sudanese overlords, but their treatment of women was supremely callous. 'Poor women, young girls from twelve or thirteen, with ulcered limbs, heated with fever, and footsore, would be seen miles away from the column, loaded down with sheer rubbish, that neither had value nor use for anyone.'

After the blood-brotherhood ceremony with Uchunku, Stanley gave the prince a demonstration of the power of the Maxim gun. Its rapid bring sent Uchunku into boyish ecstasies and he had to clap his hand over his mouth to suppress his delight. But Stanley's officers were already impatient to be away from Ankole. The huts in which they received hospitality were alive with rats, bugs and fleas, so that they turned out in the morning like boiled lobsters - an invariable concomitant of sleeping in huts rather than tents. The rats had a playful habit of dropping from the ceiling on to sleeping men, sometimes right on top of their noses.

But, as they prepared to cross the Alexandra Nile, just 125 yards wide, in the valley of Mavona, prior to entry into Karagwe, Stanley had more serious matters to ponder. A second deputation from the Uganda Christians arrived to solicit aid in their civil war. Stanley later rewrote the incident so that it appeared he had been lobbied only by the Christians of Ankole. In fact it was the Christians of Uganda and Mwanga himself who asked for aid. Stanley's decisive refusal to become involved provoked yet another angry scene between himself and Emin, who urged him to take the expedition to their aid. Stanley again lost his temper and raged at Emin. 'We are much too weak. You do not know Uganda, if you think that with our force we could go to Buganda.' Emin then volunteered to go with just his own people, but Stanley vetoed that suggestion too. Only afterwards, when he learned that he had fluffed a chance of extending British influence into Buganda, thus leaving the way open for the Germans, did Stanley doctor his account of this incident.

Almost as soon as the expedition had set foot on the soil of Karagwe, a leopard carried off one of the Manyema women. In Stanley's mind the bad omen was soon occluded by the familiarity of the surroundings. Here were the Magata hot springs he had visited in 1876, and here too he was welcomed by chiefs and headmen who had known him then. It was also one of the few areas of Africa where rhinos throve in abundance - again echoing the experience in 1876. Stanley saw three of the beasts feeding on a hill and fired at them, only to see them gallop off unharmed. The Nubian hunters had better luck and downed four of the pachyderms. They brought a baby rhino into camp as a mascot, but it proved so aggressive that it had to be despatched forthwith.

They began climbing again, along the grassy ridges of the Ruanda borders, making for Kafurro. In Karagwe they were received with the same kindness as in Ankole, but Stanley's boasts about his friendship with the king drew a contemptuous diary entry from Jephson: 'All this talk of kings and emperors and princes of the royal blood, with their residences, courts and palaces sounds all very well in books of travel, but it is nothing but bosh and it conveys a very false idea to the people for whose instruction the book is published.'

Mutual contempt was very much in the air on the trek through Karagwe. Casati became so ill that he had to be carried in a hammock by six bearers. Emin purged his bad feelings towards his old friend by confiding in Stanley during the evening halts what he termed Casati's 'weirdness'. Casati would never ask the women of his household to do any work for him, since they were widows and he did not want to incur the charge of exploiting husbandless women. Casati also regularly gave his property away to his black followers and burdened himself with the care of a little black girl who was no relation.

But Emin's disenchantment with Casati was merely at an abstract level. It was otherwise with Stanley's feelings for Hoffmann and Bonny which reached breaking point as the expedition threaded its way up and down the Karagwe hills. It was now clear to all that Hoffmann was a kleptomaniac who spent all his time trying to maximise the theft of as many items as possible from the widest possible range of people. A board of inquiry was convened to consider his conduct. He was found guilty and dismissed from the expedition, but allowed to draw rations as far as the coast. Stanley itched to do the same with Bonny who 'gives me as much trouble in his way as a dozen Hoffmanns'. But Bonny was too valuable to Stanley to ditch in this way.

On they plodded, over dreary wastes of sere grass on mountain and valley, prey to flailing sleet and bitter cold. On 10 August they descended 800 feet to the narrow basin at the head of Urigi Lake and next day left the confines of Karagwe. There was now heavy mortality and loss through desertion; a muster revealed only 800 left out of the 1500 who had quit Kavalli's. One of the wangwana decamped into the wilds even with thirty months' pay owing to him. In the rearguard Stairs and his men found

Emin's people so exhausted that they had to build grass fires and revive them in the warmth before they were fit to continue.

All this took place in Karagwe where, by the generosity of the rulers, the expedition enjoyed free living. Once they crossed into Kavari, problems of dearth and morale were accentuated, and this led directly to one of the most ugly incidents in the entire eastward crossing of Africa. At the village of Mutara on 12th August, a Sudanese soldier shot one of the locals dead and wounded two others during a looting raid. The tribal elders formed a deputation and came to Stanley to complain. He ordered all the Sudanese mustered and asked them to point out the culprit. At first there was a conspiracy of silence, but then he threatened to impound their accumulated pay at Zanzibar to make good the villagers' losses. At this the Sudanese informed on the culprit, one Fathel Mullah. Stanley handed him over to the tribesmen to do what they wished with him, justifying his action as follows: 'If we get a reputation for being predatory and violent after the manner of Fathel Mullah, the chances of the expedition's reaching the coast will be scant.'

Stanley described the incident in his book, but had the effrontery to add: 'He was marched away and we never knew what became of him. 'In fact the man was put to death with hideous tortures, as Stanley knew. The full reality of this unsavoury incident is conveyed in two descriptions, respectively by Parke and Jephson. Parke described the sequel to Stanley's unsolomonic judgement.

They greedily rushed upon him and seized him - as only savages can do - with eyes blazing with demoniacal delight, and a horrible grin of vindictive satisfaction displaying their white ivory-like teeth, which gnashed with the rage they were about to quench in his blood. It was a horribly thrilling sight to see him dragged off by his captors. He had a most scoundrelly-looking face, and they hauled him off, in spite of his abject entreaties, to spear him to death, as is their custom, for it is 'blood for blood' with these people. He certainly was an atrocious ruffian, and thoroughly deserved his horrible doom; still it was a dreadful scene as he was brought off to receive the treatment that awaited him at the hands of the executioners.

And here is Jephson's sombre assessment:

The guides tell us that the natives will all collect tonight from the villages round and have a feast and drink quantities of pombe. They will have the prisoner bound in their midst and the women will all insult and beat him and when the men have drunk sufficient pombe to madden them, they will rush on him in a body and hew him to pieces. That is their custom. A horrible fate certainly, I cannot conceive a much worse fate, but it is a fate he has brought on himself and one which he richly deserves.

Only Casati grasped that there was a pathological element in Stanley's behaviour. How could the man who claimed to have inherited Livingstone's mande sanction the savagery of lax talionist. If he wanted to appease the tribal elders and mete out exemplary punishment, he should himself have had Fathel executed by firing squad. To explain such mindless cruelty, the word 'sadism' hovers in the air. It was as if Stanley's hatred for Emin and his people finally found a focus in a single sacrificial victim. Emin was urged to intervene to plead for clemency, but was too broken by his many scarring conflicts with Stanley to have the stomach for the task.

The despondent expedition trekked east from Lake Urigi to the base of the Unya-Matundu plateau, then up to Kimwani where they were well received by chief Kajumba. On 15th August they came in sight of Lake Victoria. A quick survey of its south-western fringes confirmed that the lake was even larger than Speke and Stanley's original estimates. They began a march across flat land from which the lake had receded twenty-five years before. This was lion country and at night many of the beasts roared at a respectful distance from their camp fires. Stanley patted himself on the back at the thought that 'Providence' had cleared a path for him through territories that had been ravaged by civil war in 1887-8.

In this land of Uzuija the general health of the expedition began to pick up and fevers became less common. But losses of cattle were frequent, through Bonny's incompetence. Stanley recorded his disgust: 'A master at shirking duty, a framer of plausible excuses whenever addressed upon any palpable dereliction of duty. He is simply unteachable, and yet he always bears himself as though he were undeniably right, whatever fault he may be convicted of.'

At Amranda above Lake Victoria they turned east for the English mission station at Usambiro. On 28th August they were met by Alexander Mackay, the Scottish missionary, himself an accomplished amateur explorer. Stanley took to Mackay straight away and called him a 'second Livingstone'. Mackay was a man of small stature (inevitably Stanley noted the detail!), with long brown hair and a rich auburn beard, dressed in white linen and a Tyrolese felt hat. It was doubtless the likeness to Livingstone that made Stanley go overboard for him, since it was a long time since he had allowed himself to praise a man so. 'God knows, he has passed through hard times in Uganda - when his bishop was murdered, his pupils tortured to death, and the Uganda hero turned his eye of death on him. And yet I see why the little man did not flinch, and his blue eyes unblinkingly regarded the monster. Brave little Mackay! Spirits of his kind, whatever the size of their bodies may be, cannot be daunted or cast down.'

At Usambiro mission station the expedition remained from 28th August to 17th September for rest and recuperation. It was very necessary. Parke was down with ophthalmia that stayed with him until the coast and prevented him from completing his diary. All were exhausted and famished. But Stanley, at Mackay's behest, had to deal harshly with some of the expeditionary personnel who started selling slaves to the locals. He mustered the entire party and warned that anyone found guilty of this offence would be kept in chains as far as the coast, then turned over to the consul for imprisonment.

There was plenty of food at Usambiro, and Stanley often contrasted the groaning board of dinner at night with the fare in 'starvation camp' in the Ituri. He began to catch up with the news, some of which had unfavourable implications for his expedition. Anglo-German rivalry in East Africa was now at fever pitch, and Peters had been sent out from Berlin with a fully equipped force to rescue Emin. The EPRE committee in London had also sent out a second British expedition to the east coast to find Emin, on the assumption that Stanley was lost. Stanley was incensed at this, as it seemed a slur on his own abilities: 'I certainly must blame those responsible for sending Jackson to relieve me at Wadelai, before they heard that I needed relief.'

His anger at these two developments helps to explain how firmly he set his face against any collaborationist endeavours, even when vehemently urged by Mackay. Mackay wanted the Jackson and Stanley expeditions to unite, then intervene in Uganda, replacing Kalema (backed by the Moslems and Arab slave traders) with Mwanga and the Christians and incidentally blocking German expansion. Thus would religion and trade go hand in hand: 'If you have Buganda you have the lake, and there you will find the only market for ivory.' But Stanley reiterated his implacable opposition to the idea of intervening in Buganda, and he warned that the Jackson expedition, unless armed to the teeth, would be at risk not just from Kalema but also from the Mahdists and Kabba Rega.

Stanley was now more than ever determined to take Emin to the coast, so that it could be clearly seen that it was he, not Jackson or Peters, who had rescued Emin. He feared that Emin had pro-German sympathies and would defect to Peters if the expedition made contact with the Germans. If Stanley collaborated with Jackson, he also feared that his lustre would be dimmed and his glory halved. Nor would Stanley consent to halt at Usambiro against the day that clearer light could be shed on the increasing complexities of East Africa. When Mackay asked him to remain until rumours of a war between German forces and Arab slavers could be verified, Stanley refused adamantly.

But Emin saw a chance now to force Stanley to show himself in his true colours. He sought him out and resurrected the Kavirondo project, now, with the coming of the Jackson expedition, eminently feasible. Blandly Emin asked when he and his people could expect to be escorted to the north-eastern corner of Lake Victoria. It took Stanley a moment to recover self-possession, then he answered that the proposal had been made originally only on the premise that Emin would withdraw sufficient men from Equatoria to make the project viable.

'Then am I to understand you refuse to keep your promise?' Emin asked.

'I beg your pardon, Pasha, but you force me to say that I made no promise to take you alone there.'

'It does not matter, Mr Stanley. I knew you would never keep your promise and besides my life is always at my own disposal and I can end it when I like.'

'May I ask what you mean by that, Pasha?'

Emin made no verbal reply, but Stanley claimed that his intention was clear from the look on his face. He asked Emin what terrible secret he possessed that made him take that tone. The Pasha made no reply but stalked from the tent.

The first two weeks of September were spent catching up on press reportage of the Emin relief expedition. For the first time Stanley realised how unfavourable was the publicity at home. He began to jockey for position in the post-mortem stakes that were certain to come. He demoted much of his correspondence to blistering attacks on Emin, portraying him as both an ingrate and a comic-cuts short-sighted naturalist who had not been worth the trouble of saving. Emin replied in kind in his correspondence. Learning that the Jackson expedition was on the north-eastern shore of Lake Victoria, Stanley laid plans for his own caravan to leave Usambiro before Jackson could meet him or hand him any new orders. He left behind a cold dry letter. This drew from Peters the comment: 'Not a greeting to his countrymen, not a word of counsel or of suggestion to Jackson and his colleagues!'

After a sumptuous dinner, complete with rare wines, given in their honour by Mackay on 14th September, the officers mustered the expedition and found just 559 souls ready for departure to the coast - little more than a third remained of the crowd who had left Kavalli's in April. On the 18th they trekked out of the mission station in a south-easterly direction; Mackay accompanied them for a mile on the road. Despite Stanley's pleadings, he declined to accompany them to the coast, preferring, like Livingstone, to remain with his work in Africa.

The week after leaving Usambiro turned out to be the most perilous in the entire homeward journey. In February 1875 Stanley had crossed Usukuma without major hazard and with simply routine payments of doti. But now he ran into stiff opposition. Perhaps this was partly due to the fact that his earlier crossing of Sukumuland had been at the height of the rainy season, whereas now he marched in the boiling sun. Perhaps too the spread of trade goods and firearms had made the Sukuma peoples at once more avaricious and belligerent. The plethora of missionaries between Bagamoyo and Lake Victoria had inflated the going price for bongo from ten cloths to the equivalent of £270 for three days' transit. Whatever the reason, it was here that the expedition encountered the toughest military challenge in the entire three years. 'That first week's journey southwards from Msalala and Lake Victoria was in some ways the most terrible part of the expedition,' Hoffmann recalled. At first Stanley was inclined to shrug off the showers of arrows desultorily loosed in their direction as simple high spirits. But he changed his tune after a narrow escape at the village of Ikoma. Mackay had told them that the English ivory trader Stokes had a store of European provisions there. Expecting the inhabitants to be friendly, Stanley neglected to take the usual precautions and stumbled into an ambush. Desperate hand-to- hand fighting ensued, in which Stanley had his rifle almost torn from his hands until two of the wangwana came to his aid. So far from obtaining provisions, the expedition had to fight its way out of the village, leaving ten dead, to avoid being overwhelmed.

A three-day running fight ensued: 'the entire population appeared to have turned out to obstruct, annoy and assault the column at any favourable point or opportunity.' In one skirmish seven of the Sukuma people were killed; in another, Stanley's men captured 130 head of cattle and goats. And all the time overhead the sun shone with extraordinary fervour. The faces of the defenders were baked and their lips cracked with the heat. The grass along the route was so short that the roots themselves were eaten by their hungry animals. A thunderstorm on the afternoon of the 23rd came as a welcome relief.

The climax of the testing fight in Sukumaland came on the afternoon of the 24th. Three separate enemy detachments approached, intending to attack on right, left and centre. The caravan was now short of food and water and Stanley's patience was at snapping point. He ordered his men to form a square, with women, children and non-combatants inside the laager. Then he brought up the Maxim gun. Waiting until the enemy had advanced to within 300 yards, he gave the order to open up. The Maxim raked along the enemy ranks, dropping warriors by the dozen. After this devastating exhibition, the Sukuma peoples kept their distance. They tracked the column from afar, yelling war-cries and firing off flintlock muskets into the air.

Tired and hungry, in need of water and rest, after seven nerve- wracking days the expedition entered the territory of the friendly Sinyanga and dropped the enemy astern. Stanley's relief was palpable. 'This September will be memorable with us for the many crosses we have had to bear. Its earlier days stand out as in a dream. They were so pleasant and our anticipations were delightful. Alas, five days' fighting, sufferings from thirst, the heat of the sun which focused all its power directly on us, the vile water, all combined with this day's particular fatigues and rank offensive smells to try our temper greatly.'

For the first few days of October Stanley was sick. After a halt to accommodate the leader, the expedition pressed on through Usongo and Singwizi. Their track led through scrub plains and thorny jungles, and the pace finally saw off Osman Latif s old mother, who had been carried in a hammock all the way from Lake Albert. Predators abounded, and Stanley gave this account of a typical night: 'Lions, jackals and the brays of our donkeys made this night hideous and few of us had any sleep despite fatigue.'

On 18th October two French missionaries from Bukumbi, Fathers Schynse and Girault, overtook the column and sought permission to accompany it to the coast. Next day the Manyema fell in with a caravan belonging to Tippu Tip and started west on their homeward journey. By this time the rate of progress of the expedition had slowed down and its composition was different from the force that left Lake Albert. First came

Stanley and two companies of mangwana. A third Zanzibari company formed the rearguard. In the middle were the Wanyamwezi porters Stanley had recently recruited and the racial pot-pourri that made up the tired and huddled masses from Wadelai - such of them as still survived. The Sudanese had now been given the task of herding the cattle, down to eighty head.

They were heading directly south-east through a country teeming with lions, all the more plentiful now since a Masai invasion had scared off the indigenous Ikungu hunters. There were many giraffes which the lions preyed on, and Stanley's hunters 'bagged' one of the beasts for a communal supper. Also to be seen were packs of wild dogs, ferocious enough to bring down a solitary lion unprotected by his pride. As if this was not enough, four tribes of bandits were known to infest the region. And above all there was the unremitting heat. 'The sandy paths through the jungle on account of the great heat are almost unbearable to the carriers of the caravan. The thorns have also been a nuisance and our people are not at all happy looking. Though they are not stinted in meal and meat, they mostly all look seedy and thin.'

Schynse noted that there was bad blood in the expedition between the Europeans and particular animus against the 'pile of corrupt and useless Egyptians'. But he himself took comfort from the fact that the chief of the Kabarata who had insulted him last year was very subdued in the presence of such a large caravan and assured Stanley that he was the white man's best friend. Schynse also learned the reason for the Sudanese keenness to drove the donkeys, goats and cows through the heat, despite their (the Sudanese) reputation for idleness. Meat supply apart, all domestic animals cost four times as much at the coast as in Usukuma.

On 26th October the expedition reached the territory of Stanley's old enemies, the Wagogo. At once thefts and skirmishes became commonplace. The Sudanese lost their goats in one raid. When Stanley tried to buy the predators off with ivory, they demanded wood. His men cried out for him to give them lead, but he settled for twenty-six doti of cloth. The trek through Ugogo's red soil was as tedious as on the three previous occasions Stanley had traversed their territory. The Gogo peoples alternated outrageous hongo demands with the barefaced theft of guns. Stanley recorded ruefully: 'Ugogo has been a bitter land to travellers for generations. In the whole of Africa there are few people so insolent. However, it is not likely I shall ever see Ugogo again, but I should esteem it an agreeable task to bring this people to a sense of their long wrong-doings.'

The expedition wound its way down from the plateau for the eight-day crossing of the vast and arid Ugogo plain. As they picked their way across rocky terrain, they were assailed by taunting Wagogo, by wind, dust and thirst. Even when they pitched their tents under baobab trees they were assaulted by clouds of red dust. In Nyangwira, the most populous part of Ugogo, Stanley again bowed the head and paid a substantial hongo to the one-eyed ruler Mukenge. There were some tense moments while Stanley bartered in a grove of palm trees near the chieftain's kraal. Stanley did not want to have to swivel the Maxim gun into action for a few doti, while Mukenge hesitated to attack such a large caravan.

It is a bitter irony that Stanley, so often under attack in England for over-reaction to tribal 'impudence', should on this occasion have been singled out by Peters for a different and opposite kind of criticism. The bloodthirsty Peters, who later solved the Gogo 'problem' by slaughtering them in hundreds, accused Stanley of egregious weakness, especially given that he had a Maxim gun with him. When Mukenge redoubled his demand for hongo, Peters argued, Stanley should have used the opportunity to take the strut out of him. Instead Stanley meekly sent him four times the usual doti. This was a bad mistake, Peters thought, since it inculcated the idea that whites would always pay tribute; if a large expedition containing nine white men bowed the knee, what hope was there for other travellers?

Schynse too was intrigued as to why Stanley, who according to Emin was a man of force and blood, should have swallowed Gogo 'insolence'. One afternoon as Stanley sat under a tree smoking his pipe while his tent was being erected, Schynse raised the matter with him. Stanley said they were near journey's end and he had too many women and sick in the column to make it worthwhile engaging the Wagogo; had any of the tribes further inland tried his patience in this way, it would have been a different story, however. 'If this was the beginning of the expedition, I'd give them a hongo in lead,' he confided. 'After fifty-three skirmishes, I'm philosophical. I'd like to come back here and sort them out. I don't mind paying normal hongo but the Wagogo are thieves. They still try to stop us getting water, in spite of the hongo, the chief reckons he's not responsible for anything.'

But even Stanley in pacific mood had his sticking point. When the Gogo people tried to deny the caravan the use of their wells, Stanley set men with loaded guns to impress the point that he must have an unimpeded water supply. The Wagogo backed off, asking only that the waterholes where they took their own herds should be inviolate.

After Nyangwira Stanley struck off from the main caravan route to try to avoid excessive demands for tribute. Their route was still determined by waterholes, and food was short unless they wished to pay the Wagogo's extortionate prices. The soil was a sandy gravel and Stanley marvelled that the cattle remained in a good condition, even though he could not make out what they found to eat. At night they camped on hills and eminences and at day descended into the acacia-dotted plain - so flat that in the rainy season it was completely waterlogged.

On 8th November they came to the border of Ugogo and Masailand. Stanley turned sharply south-east, with a chain of hills flanking him to the north, then crossed the chain when it turned south. Ahead of them was only the final plateau. But as they passed through this no man's land where the population was part Masai, part Gogo and part Wanyamwezi they sustained the fiercest enemy attack since the last week in September. Masai raiders came charging in on the camp in search of cattle. Surprisingly, this time it was the wangwana who panicked and the Sudanese who held firm. A steady fire which dropped two warriors in their tracks broke up the assault within minutes."

Next day they passed the Masai encampment. Yesterday's would-be plunderers watched them go sullenly. They crossed the Kambi plain, breasted another chain of hills and descended into another plain where they made out the distant flags of Mpwapwa. Mpwapwa was now the extreme eastern outpost of German power. There to meet them was Lt. Schmidt of the Imperial German Army, who commanded a garrison of four whites and one hundred Zulu mercenaries. Schmidt broke out champagne for them. For the first time since Kavalli's Emin unbent and looked happy. Stanley caught up with international press comment and sent off a shoal of letters.

After pausing for a couple of days to allow Schmidt to attend his second-in-command who was ill with dysentery, the expedition set out again. Since this part of East Africa was now recognised as German territory, the rest of the journey was supposed to be in the nature of a triumphal tour, in which Schmidt would show off his guests. The first few days of the march, up and down hills, were taxing but once they entered Usagara proper they found it a paradise after Ugogo. The presence of German troops had produced a new deference towards whites, so that the expedition no longer went in fear of enemies, but enjoyed the placid spectacle of teeming herds of buffalo, gazelle and antelope.

On they went, through places familiar to Stanley from 1874 and his very first African journey in search of Livingstone eighteen years earlier: Makata, Simbambwenni, Mrogoro. 'The change in the aspect of the country since we touched the slopes dropping down to the Mukondokwa valley is marvellous. Instead of the dry and arid outlook on either hand and thorny jungles we have come among slopes and plains bedecked with lilies, which effuse a delightful fragrance.'

Stanley was already nervous that the presence of Schmidt and the Germans might lure Emin away and even questioned the Pasha about his future intentions on 17th November. But there was one welcome slice of serendipity for Stanley from the German presence. On 22nd November Schmidt began to distribute to the whites the European provisions that Wissmann, German commander-in-chief in East Africa, had forwarded. Tired of waiting his turn, Bonny pushed to the front to demand his share in his customary bully-boy style. To Stanley's delight, Schmidt gave him the most ferocious tongue-lashing. How dared Bonny claim as of right something which was given by the Germans as a gift and over which he, Schmidt, had absolute prerogative? What Stanley, for his own prudential reasons, dared not do the Germans now did for him.

On 29th November, just a few miles from the coast, at Mswa, Stanley ran into a younger version of himself in the form of Thomas Stevens, reporter for the New York World. When Stevens, whose previous exploits included trying to cycle across Africa and riding a mustang across Russia, arrived in Zanzibar, Wissmann told him he would not be allowed to interview Stanley on the march, as this privilege was reserved for German correspondents. With Stanley-like persistence, Stevens crossed from Zanzibar to Bagamoyo, only to be taken prisoner by Wissman's assistant Baron Gravenreuth, who released him after he had given his word of honour he would not try to find Stanley. The officer in charge of Stevens, admiring his pluck, released him from his parole, with the result that Stevens raced ahead to Mswa and scooped both the German correspondents and his rival Vizetelly, who had been sent out to 'find' Stanley by Gordon Bennett and the New York Herald.

Stevens described the scene at Mswa: 'Big tents and little tents, groups of little grass huts which the African porter or soldier constructs for himself at every camp, were scattered over a large space, on a gentle slope, between the thorny environs of a hidden village and a dry ravine. Egyptian flags, crescent and stars on a red ground, floated lazily from tent-poles.' He secured the first interview with Stanley, but Vizetelly was able to scoop him later by offering Stanley £2000 for the first published interview. Stanley never allowed sentiment to interfere with business. He took Gordon Bennett's money while having an infinite personal preference for Stevens.

In 2nd December Stanley gave a celebratory dinner for his officers and Emin and Casati. Next day the Pasha seemed to have mellowed sufficiently to make a chat feasible. Now that he was at the coast, Emin seemed to have lost his irritability and eremitic propensities. He told Stanley that he had half decided to accompany Casati to Naples where they could build a villa. Appropriately enough, to signal journey's end, their conversation was interrupted by the booming of the cannon at Zanzibar which could be heard across the channel and inland. Next day Wissmann himself appeared on the other side of the Kingani with horses for the ride to Bagamoyo. Leaving the expedition to catch them up later, Stanley, Emin and Wissmann rode to Bagamoyo, where they arrived at 11.30 a.m. on 4th December. After nearly three years in which he had aged thrice that amount, Stanley once again gazed on the limpid waters of the Indian Ocean.

Chapter Seventeen

IN Bagamoyo Wissmann had prepared a sumptuous banquet for the home comers. He had his own reasons for being delighted at the arrival of Stanley with Emin, since it cut the ground from under his compatriot and rival Peters who, having got a head start on him, was nonetheless denied the glittering prize of having 'rescued' Emin.' The banquet was laid out in an upper room and the guests included Emin and Casati, Stanley and his officers, the German and British consuls, representatives of the two East Africa companies, and the captains of the German naval squadron that hovered in Zanzibar waters to remind the Sultan of the time of day.

Stanley went to the banquet at 7.30 that evening (4th December) and virtually collided with Emin on the stairs. He noted that Emin was flushed with wine, but attributed this to the fact that the Kaiser had sent him a telegram of congratulation and awarded him the Order of the Crown. Upstairs, to the strains of a mediocre orchestra, there were many champagne toasts and the cables of congratulation to the expedition were read out. Unnoticed, Emin slipped from the room. The next thing Stanley observed was his 'eyes and ears' Sali running into the room, calling out that the Pasha was dead. It turned out that Emin had gone into the next room and stepped out of a window 15 feet above the ground. His fall was not, as Sali first reported it, fatal but it could well have been but for a steep lean-to roof below the window which broke his fall. Schmidt had then been summoned. He found Emin unconscious, badly bruised and bleeding from the ears. After failing to rouse the Pasha by dowsing him with cold water, Schmidt sent for a stretcher party. By the time Sali arrived at the upper room with the news, Emin was ensconced in the German hospital with severe concussion and a suspected fracture of the skull.

The official version of this unfortunate accident was that Emin, notoriously short-sighted, had mistaken a low window for a door. But Stanley was convinced that Emin's fall was a suicide attempt. 'It is true that he had partaken freely of champagne that day but just a minute before the accident - as we call it - he had delivered a perfectly sensible - even brilliant speech ... the balcony wall was quite three feet high, and as it was freshly built, it bore the marks of his heels. If he did not purposely climb on that wall, it is an absolute mystery to me how the mortar had the impress of his heel.' What, then, could the motive be?

Stanley had long suspected that Emin's habitual vacillation, his desire to remain in the province that had repudiated him, his foot-dragging on the return journey, especially at Mackay's mission station, his reluctance to return to Egypt even to collect his £6000 back pay - all this pointed to a hidden motive. This motive he claimed to have uncovered on arrival in Bagamoyo in December 1889. There waiting for Emin was a letter from the wife he had abandoned in Silesia in 1875, taking all her money and valuables and leaving her destitute. Her attempts to pursue him through the courts had failed because Emin had hidden himself away in Equatoria, safe from European judicial processes. But Stanley's 'rescue' had dragged him back unwillingly into the orbit of civilisation to face the censure of the world. By all accounts, the letter from Emin's wife did not make pleasant reading.

The truth of all this is probably impossible to retrieve, but Emin's accident - if accident it was - removed him at a stroke from British influence and delivered him to his fellow-countrymen, to whose cause he was anyway inclining. Stanley at first demanded that Emin be transferred to Zanzibar on a British warship, but the Germans insisted their patient was too ill to be moved. Typically, Stanley then washed his hands of Emin. He paid a perfunctory visit to him in hospital and was satisfied from the fact that the Pasha shook his head that he did not have a fractured skull. Then he departed for Zanzibar, where after a 2 Vi-hour crossing he landed at 11.30 a.m. on 6th December. Parke and Jephson stayed behind a bit longer to tend to Emin; before departing for Zanzibar Jephson solemnly renewed his old friendship with the Pasha and urged him to return with them to Egypt. Emin said he would never forget that Jephson had been his comrade in captivity in Equatoria in 1888 but sentiment alone could not induce him to go to Egypt.

In Zanzibar Stanley found a further shoal of telegrams awaiting him, from Leopold, Gordon Bennett, Queen Victoria, Kaiser Wilhelm and many others. The Kaiser managed to reinforce his claim to East Africa even as he congratulated the hero: 'that your way home led you through territories placed under my flag, gives me great satisfaction.' Queen Victoria had all along followed the epic journey with great interest. Now she indicated her pleasure in the clearest possible terms: 'STANLEY, Zanzibar. My thoughts are often with you and your brave followers, whose dangers and hardships are now at an end. Once more I heartily congratulate all, including the survivors of the gallant Zanzibaris who displayed such devotion and fortitude during your marvellous Expedition. Trust Emin progresses favourably. VRI.'

In Zanzibar Stanley was the guest of the new consul Euan-Smith, who behaved towards Stanley impeccably while being in other respects just as cross-grained an individual as his predecessor Kirk. Stanley spent until 29th December writing an official report of the expedition that Euan-Smith would forward to London. He did, however, make the unStanley-like mistake of visiting Parke in hospital - Parke was now down with blackwater fever. The result was a Christmas spent in bed with fever himself.

From time to time he made efforts to prise Emin out of his bolthole in Bagamoyo. Both the Pasha and Casati declined passage on the official Egyptian ship which arrived at Bagamoyo to pick up the Sudanese and Egyptian survivors of the African crossing. When Stanley sent Sali across the straits to find out how Emin was getting on, he saw further evidence that the Germans were playing the same trick he himself had used to secure

Emin - a form of compassionate arrest. When Sali handed Stanley's letter to a German officer, the officer ordered Sali out of Bagamoyo and threatened him with hanging if he was found there again. Stanley sent Stairs and Jephson over to verify the tale and dissuade Emin from accepting service with the Germans. Neither man was able to speak to the Pasha save in the presence of four German officers. Emin was further incensed against Stanley by the reports reaching him of Stanley's unflattering character portrait and he repaid the 'compliment' in kind. Stanley fumed at the unfortunate consequences of Emin's fall. Apart from the 'trophy' motivation, Stanley wanted Emin out of East Africa for another reason. He was still hoping that Mackinnon would invite him to lead an expedition from the IBEA base at Mombasa to set up on Lake Victoria the kind of stations he had established for Leopold on the Congo. If Emin joined German service, there was a good chance that the combination would forestall him.

Euan-Smith watched his guest with a kind of awed fascination. He noted the uneasy relations between Stanley and his officers and the antipathy for Emin. To end the slave trade Stanley argued for an arms embargo to Africa by all European powers and a railway from Mombasa to Lake Victoria. But the consul evidently found the company of his guest bracing and stimulating: 'Stanley has now been a guest in my house for nearly a month and we have talked "Africa" until the most unpronounceable names are now familiar in every mouth as household words. His hair is as white as snow. When first I saw him he looked dreadfully use and done up but the rest and good living have worked a wonderful change for the better in his appearance.'

Two events of significance took place before Stanley departed for Mombasa on 29th December. The first was of the nature of the 'dog that barked in the night'. The future great man of Africa Frederick Lugard made a point of avoiding him. 'Between ourselves I did not care greatly about meeting Stanley. Letters of his that I had seen [not published] had made me feel disinclined to fall down and worship him, so I went up country again.' This was a straw in the wind, indicating that Stanley's reputation was about to go into a nosedive in English elite circles.

The second represented one of Stanley's more serious miscalculations. He decided to institute a suit against Tippu Tip, alleging breach of contract for his failure to provide Barttelot with porters at Yambuya. He lodged an indictment in consular court asking to have Tippu Tip's assets in Zanzibar (some £10,000) frozen pending the outcome of the suit. The court decided that the suit could not proceed without the Sultan's consent, as Tippu Tip was his subject. On 23rd December the Sultan gave his consent and the suit proceeded. A hearing was fixed for 26th December. But since Tippu was absent and his son Sef bin Mohammed refused to appear in his place, consular judge Cracknall decided that Tippu should be given six months' grace, from the date of reception of a subpoena, to appear and answer the charges. Stanley could not wait either, so he left a written deposition countersigned by Bonny, dated 27th December. The court placed under injunction the £10,000 paid by Becker to Tippu's agents for the sale of ivory. Informed opinion in Zanzibar held that Stanley's litigiousness would merely alienate the Arab to the German side.

Hearing of this development, Leopold craftily saw a possibility for Belgian expansion at the expense of the Germans. He wrote to Tippu to ask him to visit Brussels for talks; in return Leopold would see that the damages suit was waived. He had consulted legal and African experts about the affair, who assured him that the contract with Stanley was so vaguely worded that it could not possibly constitute grounds for a lawsuit. Tippu received Leopold's letter before the subpoena from Zanzibar and was predictably angry. His hatred towards Stanley was now at white heat. In 1891 he grudgingly came to Zanzibar to defend himself against the charges. At Bagamoyo he met Stairs and Moloney en route to Katanga. Tippu denounced Stanley as the most notorious liar on the continent and warned that if he returned to the Congo or East Africa again, he would be at high risk of assassination.

On arrival in Zanzibar Tippu Tip hired a lawyer who easily rebutted Stanley's charges and entered a countersuit for reimbursement of all goods provided to the Emin expedition by Tippu. Over Stanley's enraged protests, it was decided to seek accommodation. Both sides withdrew their suits, and so the ill-advised litigation ended. Mackinnon was so disillusioned with Stanley over his precipitate suit (entered into without consultation with the EPRE committee) that he refrained from offering him further employment.

On 29th December Euan-Smith accompanied Stanley on a warship across to Mombasa, where he was to take passage to Egypt. 'It has been very pleasant having Stanley with us for the last three weeks. We have done our best to fatten him up. I think he has really enjoyed himself, though he is looking forward immensely to the reception which awaits him in Europe. He is wonderfully well and hearty and I can see that he is quite prepared to come out to Africa again should fitting work be found for him.'

On New Year's Day 1890 Stanley with his four officers and Bonny, plus the ubiquitous Sali, boarded the steamer Katoria for Suez. Stanley was still suffering from a cold he had picked up in Zanzibar and the infected lungs plagued him for three weeks. The very idea of writing a book on the Emin expedition filled him with dread in Zanzibar as he completed its 'synopsis' in the form of the official report to Euan-Smith. He told himself he would take the first steps once at sea, but on the Katoria he was given a y x 5V2 foot stateroom, into which he had to squeeze his seven boxes. Serious work would have been impossible even if he was not liable to disturbance every few minutes from the waiters.

Eight days later the ship was at Aden and on 13th January they were at Suez. Here Bonny was expected to take his leave of the others, but he insisted on being put up in Cairo at the expedition's expense despite a fierce rebuke from Stanley. In Zanzibar Bonny had distinguished himself at the Grand Hotel by conduct that was far from exemplary. 'There is a good deal of drinking going on, and rows alternate with fevers,' Stanley recorded laconically over Christmas 1889. But Bonny went on to higher things. A fist-fight with a Dr Charlesworth landed him behind bars, from which he was released only on the understanding that he was forthwith permanently expelled from Zanzibar. It was a tremendous relief for Stanley when Bonny finally quit Cairo on 25th January. 'A specious rogue' was Stanley's final summing-up, but he realised that he was also a rogue whose testimony he might well need in the future.

As the Katoria came to anchor at Suez, Stanley stood on the quarterdeck, dressed in grey tweed. His figure was very much slighter than it had been when he was last here three years earlier. His close-cut hair was now almost completely white and threw into relief the bronzed face, hard-set lips and cold grey eyes. He spent the night of 13th January at the British India Agency, then at 7 a.m. next morning boarded a special train that whisked them all to Cairo. They arrived on one of the wettest days ever known in the Egyptian capital. Water was 2 feet deep in some streets. At the station to meet them were Sir Evelyn and Lady Baring, Sir Francis and Lady Grenfell and a host of ambassadors and Egyptian dignitaries. Stanley was then conveyed in a private carriage to the Khedive's residence, where they discussed Emin at length. Then it was on to Shepheard's Hotel where, because of the flooding, planks had to be laid from Stanley's carriage to the fourth step of the hotel entrance which led straight on to the veranda. In the evening there was a banquet attended by the ailing Nubar Pasha. Stanley replied to the toast with a motif he was to develop further in his book In Darkest Africa, alleging that his success was due to 'the finger of that Great Power - call it chance, fate, Providence or what you will.'

After a period of socialising, rest, and posing for group photographs with his officers, on 25th January Stanley started work on the book that would eventually become In Darkest Africa. But finding the atmosphere at Shepheard's Hotel uncongenial, on 1st February he moved to the Hotel Villa Victoria to begin concentrated work.

From the very earliest days Stanley's friend and editor Edward Marston had seen that the controversy surrounding the Emin Pasha expedition would make Stanley's account of it a potential bestseller. He had to beat off severe competition to retain the British rights. The competition for the American rights to the book was also very severe. In the end it narrowed down to a two-horse race, between Harper Bros and Scribner Bros. After sealed bids had been invited, the palm went to Scribners, who paid a £40,000 advance. Given that huge sums of money hung on the outcome of his labours, Stanley asked Marston to come to Cairo so that he could be on hand for daily consultations.

Marston found Stanley ensconced at the Hotel Villa Victoria, situated in the most beautiful part of Cairo, near the Ezbekiyeh Gardens. Surrounded on all sides by fine, newly built mansions, the Villa Victoria comprised three separate buildings, forming three sides of a quadrangle, in the centre of which was a garden of huge palms and orange trees, criss-crossed by walks. One of the orange trees, laden with ripe fruit, looked straight into Stanley's workroom. In the very centre of the garden was a fountain surrounded by tropical and oriental plants; Marston thought it a veritable lotus-land. Stanley was in the part of the hotel farthest from the street, in a fine suite of rooms on the ground floor, very handsomely furnished in the oriental style. There was a large lofty reception room and an equally large and gracious dining-room. Here Stanley girded his loins for the writing of his magnum opus?

Stanley approached the task with trepidation. 'I knew not how to begin. Like Elihu, my memory was full of matter, and I desired to write that I might be refreshed; but there was no vent. My right hand had lost its cunning and the art of composition was lost by long disuse.' He found it hard to hit his old stride again. Sometimes he could write nine folios an hour, at others he could scarcely manage a hundred words. But gradually the old skill returned and he started to cruise at his old speed. He had copious notes and diaries to write from, and from 8 a.m. to 11 p.m. every day he toiled away, hardly ever going out, even for a stroll in the gardens. He wrote at a tremendous pace, never stopping to amend or blot, and throwing the wet sheets away from him as soon as they were finished. As he frequently forgot to number his sheets, it was laborious to piece the day's work together again. He had an eccentric habit of lying on the floor while writing, resting on his left elbow while scribbling with his right hand. Stanley was able to take the strain of this all day long, where most people would soon have become exhausted through muscle tension.

But the barriers to Stanley's completion of the herculean task were not just physical and mechanical. Psychologically, he faced the daunting task of exculpating himself from responsibility in the many dark incidents that had besmirched the image of the expedition. The Rear Column disaster aside, there was the appalling casualty list to explain. 708 wangwana set out with Stanley from Zanzibar in February 1887. Only 210 returned in December 1889. Of 555 of Emin's followers who had joined him at Kavalli's, only 290 reached the coast. Of the sixty Sudanese whom Stanley had taken to the Congo only twelve survived and one only of the thirteen Somalis lived to tell the tale. Ulcers, fevers, fatigue, debility, abandonment, straggling and skirmishes had done for the rest.

Arguably Jackson had achieved more with less cost, less pomp and less bloodshed. The greatest irony was that not a pound of Equatoria's rich hoard of ivory ever reached the coast. Emin told Father Schynse with great bitterness that the lust for ivory had always been the main motive of Stanley and Mackinnon. This might well have been true of Mackinnon, but if so he was sorely disappointed. Most of it was dumped into the Nile during the civil disturbances in Equatoria and the rest passed into the hands of the Mahdists. Against this were some substantial achievements in exploration and geography: the Ituri, the Semliki, Ruwenzori, etc., but scarcely enough to atone for the fearful loss of life.

Stanley naturally skated lightly over the dark side of the expedition, except when to deal with it was unavoidable, as with the Rear Column, in which case he threw the blame for the fiasco on to anyone and everyone but himself. He presented the expedition as an achievement in the heroic mould. By the middle of February he was in full flight with the writing. 'I am sailing now right ahead with scudding sails set, and fair weather. Two months' more steady work will see me through. If I had this book on my back in England, I should be unfit to go into society.'

For two months Stanley rarely ventured out of his room even for a stroll in the garden. He refused to go for a drive with Parke and on the one occasion he consented to an excursion to the Nile, with Marston, he was so restless and preoccupied that after half an hour Marston was glad to let him flee back to his sanctuary. At lunch and dinner he would be agreeably chatty for an hour then disappear to his cloister. The only drink he touched was Apollinaris water laced with a tablespoonful of brandy. His abstemiousness led him to neglect his rare lunch and dinner guests, as he never thought to offer them anything to drink. Nothing irritated him more than a tap at the door when he was working. He sometimes glared tigerishly even at Marston, who was of necessity a frequent and privileged intruder. He terrified Sali by roaring in agony if ever the black boy brought him a telegram, so that in the end Sali simply poked the offending cable into the room on the end of a bamboo pole and bolted. Stanley excused his curmudgeonly behaviour like this: 'When my work is accomplished, then I will talk with you, laugh with you and play with you or ride with you to your heart's content, but let me alone now for heaven's sake.'

The one intrusion on his time Stanley permitted was to Miss E. M. Merrick, who had been commissioned by Sir John Elliott and the RGS to paint his portrait. Even so, he was an impatient sitter, alternating between taciturnity and garrulousness. And he fussed over the details. When the sittings were over, he would place a large looking-glass next to the portrait to compare his likeness. Next time Miss Merrick would be handed notes on which would be written instructions: 'Nose not straight enough', 'Forehead too low', 'Hair too grey', etc. He was inordinately vain about his eyes. 'Take care of my eyes,' he told her, 'for Stanley's eyes are known all over the world.' On one occasion he consented to give an interview to a Belgian journalist while he was sitting but soon regretted it. He became exasperated with the questions about his private life and boomed at the questioner: 'If people would only try and discover what Stanley has done and not who Stanley is, they would be saving themselves much time and trouble.'

As he hit his stride and the writing progressed more fluently, Stanley became impatient of any and every interruption, however necessary. He wrote tetchily to Mackinnon: 'There are a lot of idlers in Cairo who pester one to death, sit with one for half an hour for nothing. I have not a word to say to them except monosyllables - and it is quite amusing to watch one resolved to bore me to the utmost limits and I resolved to be patient.' But for many of the interruptions from Marston Stanley had only himself to blame. All the photographs he had taken in Africa turned out to be either under- or over-exposed. He had not written the first few chapters (before Marston arrived) in copying ink. And he clashed with Marston's artist Joseph Bell, who insisted on naturalistic accuracy in the illustrations. On one occasion Bell and Stanley were discussing an illustration of a porter crossing a river with a donkey.

'Did the porter carry a rifle?' asked Bell.

'Of course,' replied Stanley.

'And in what hand did he carry the rifle,' Bell pressed him, 'seeing that one hand is already engaged in guiding and helping the donkey and the other in swimming for dear life?' Stanley scowled at him. He had no sense of humour where his own glory and reputation were involved.

At last, after fifty days, the task was completed. The 900-page book, compiled from 903 foolscap sheets of manuscript, had been written at the rate of 8000 words a day. Since in the same time Stanley had also written 400 letters and fired off one hundred telegrams, it is hardly surprising that the writing of the book was hailed by many journalists as a more astounding feat than the expedition itself.

Most of the writing time not spent on the book during February-March 1890 was devoted to analyses of the officers who had accompanied him through the valley of the shadow of death. Although Stanley liked Parke best at a personal level - because he had not breathed a word of criticism of his leader - the man he considered the best officer was Stairs, and he now regretted that he had not placed him in command of the Rear Column, Barttelot's seniority notwithstanding. Stairs was remarkably quick at getting the hang of things; he could improvise and think on his feet. Most of all, he was the one white whom the Africans truly respected: 'He was a man to them with a big "M", with his superior wits ever on the alert, sharp, active, ready, with every sense at instant command. 'Nelson, too, made great strides and at the end was physically the toughest of them all. As yet, however, Stanley was ambivalent about Jephson. His generosity and sociability were offset by hotheadedness. Jephson operated on a short fuse; hence his nickname among the Africans 'Bubu-rika' ('the cheetah') - denoting his tendency to spring at them if they did not obey instantly. 'He has a deal to learn yet before he is capable of commanding men.' But Stanley admitted his besetting fault as a commander when he confessed to Mackinnon: 'I never permitted myself in Africa to indulge in laudation of any act however well done. 'But even beyond these jottings, Stanley did manage to deal with an avalanche of letters and telegrams in Cairo, sometimes by having Marston answer for him. In other cases he had no choice but to take pen in hand himself. There was the suit against Tippu Tip to deal with, the question of payment and compensation for the survivors of the expedition, wrangling with Sanford over the lease of the Florida and considerable routine correspondence with the EPRE committee. Stanley was glad when the burden of writing was lifted and he was able to take ship for the French Riviera at the end of March.

At Cannes he was Mackinnon's guest on board his yacht. Then he took the train to Belgium there for a week in April he was treated by Leopold and the Belgians almost as though he were a visiting head of state. All of this he had dreaded and he endured it with an inner loathing. 'I am angry with myself that, conscious of my physical and mental unfitness for such a life, I do not utter a decided "no" and depart to leave myself in some quite retreat.' Yet even in Belgium the vista was not unclouded for, with In Darkest Africa yet unpublished, Stanley was propelled into the headlines as a stalking horse in the growing Anglo-German rivalry over East Africa.

In allying himself with Mackinnon, Stanley became involved in a head-on clash between German ambitions for an African colony running east-west across the continent and the idea of the map painted red from the Cape to Cairo which was the dream of Mackinnon, Harry Johnston and Cecil Rhodes. Although Stanley was not an ideological imperialist as they were, he did believe in annexing valuable territories, and it was his proud boast at the end of the Emin expedition that he had made treaties with six different rulers through whose lands he passed on the march from Lake Albert, ceding suzerainty to Britain.

But the Germans challenged the validity of the 'treaties', pointing out (rightly) that non-aggression pacts and blood-brotherhood ceremonies were not the same things as treaties yielding sovereignty. Stanley was asked to justify his claim to have signed treaties. He produced two different arguments. One was that he had had to make the treaties informally, since Emin and Casati were with him. The other was that his call for the annexation of the territories was made independently of his agreement with the chiefs.

The issue came to a head after the Peters expedition into the interior of East Africa, in the course of which he signed a formal treaty with Mwanga, pretender to the Ugandan throne - the man who had unsuccessfully solicited Stanley's assistance. The English and German press whipped up the Stanley-Peters rivalry into a re-run of the Stanley-Brazza affair a decade earlier. It was alleged in England that Peters' pretensions in Uganda were bogus in the light of the Stanley treaties. Stanley meanwhile claimed that everything between the Aruwimi and the eastern shores of Lakes Victoria and Tanganyika was British by right of effective occupation, viz., his marches during the Emin expedition.

The position of the protagonists, Peters and Stanley, was immensely complicated by the lukewarm support each man received from his respective government. Stanley lamented that he could not compete with Peters if he had support from Berlin while Mackinnon had none from London. But in fact opinion in Berlin was very far from monolithic. Bismarck's line was that Germany already had enough African possessions and in any case he did not want friction with Britain just because Stanley and Peters wished to re-run the Stanley-Brazza game. London's view was that Stanley's 'treaties' would have to be watertight in international law before the Empire took on Germany over the issue. Both the sorcerers' apprentices tugged at the leash. Peters claimed it was an open secret that the German Emin Pasha expedition was a colonialising enterprise. Stanley aggravated the situation by making inflammatory speeches about the disputed territory in the lake country.

Both Lord Salisbury in England and Bismarck in Germany wanted to play down their rivalries in East Africa. Hatzfeldt, the German ambassador in London, assured Salisbury that Uganda and Wadelai and all places to the east and north of Lake Victoria were outside the sphere of German colonial ambition. But behind the scenes in both countries powerful forces manoeuvred to bring about a head-on collision. On both sides the Royal Family was inclined to take the hawkish view. The young Kaiser Wilhelm was sympathetic to Peters, and when he dismissed Bismarck later in 1890 he was inclined to give 'the German Stanley' his head. Opponents of Salisbury's 'softly-softly' approach warned Queen Victoria that to allow Germany to dominate the Lake Tanganyika region might lead to a dip in the Tory government's popularity so disastrous that the dreaded Gladstone would be returned to power. Salisbury found himself having to write private memoranda to the Queen, explaining his opposition to Stanley's ideas.

When Stanley arrived back in England at the end of 1890, the pace of controversy hotted up. In speech after speech he warned that the Salisbury government was letting slip a great opportunity in East Africa. The combative Salisbury, after taking discreet soundings from Leopold, decided to hit back. In a speech at the Merchant Taylors' Banquet on 22nd May 1890 he poked fun at the 'African lion' then at the very height of his popularity.

Mr Stanley has warned you that the British government is doing terrible things - that it has surrendered vast forests and tremendous mountains and great kingdoms which he has offered the British public to occupy; and he gives you mysterious hints in order that you may interfere in time or - if you do not interfere - that you may be satisfied to submit to his threat that the Company with which he is connected will abandon Africa to its fate.

But in fact all the time Stanley was speaking with forked tongue. To his large audiences he spoke of the chances being squandered after he had laid the foundation with his treaties. Yet to the Foreign Office he conceded that he had no written treaties that would stand up in international law. When the Germans challenged Stanley to make good his boasts, the Foreign Office intervened to say that Stanley was irrelevant; he was a private explorer, not a British official, so that nothing he did could bind the British government.

This official smokescreen masked considerable irritation in Whitehall that Stanley had embarrassed the government and brought it into collision with Germany on the strength of a will o' the wisp. Sir Percy Anderson of the Foreign Office produced the underestimate of the year when he minuted with regard to the conflicting claims: 'If there is a liar about (and there must be one), I should be surprised to learn that it is Stanley, though of course it may be.' The likelihood that Stanley was the liar became certainty when Stanley produced the map of his journeys in 'In Darkest Africa'. It became clear that the larger British pretensions could not be sustained even on the basis of first possession. Mackinnon suffered yet another disappointment in his famous protégé.

There was considerable irony here. At Bagamoyo Stanley had told the reporter Stevens that hardly anyone except himself kept promises. 'Mr Stanley said also, that he believes that in every profession and every walk of life, simple, straightforward truth always triumphs over falsehood and deceit.' He went on to say that the secret of Bismarck's success was that he never lied, and that his truth-telling was received with incredulity by other diplomats. Apart from the grotesque humbug of Stanley's presenting himself as a mythical George Washington, one can only smirk at the retrospective insight that it was Bismarck himself who a few months later was the victim of Stanley's penchant for 'expedient exaggerations'.

The Anglo-German dispute of 1890 over East Africa was settled in the end, not by rhetoric or propaganda from Stanley or anyone else, but, predictably, by haute politique. This time Britain won the battle for spheres of influence in East Africa. Faced with a possible war with France and Russia, Berlin needed British support. In return for the cession of Heligoland to Germany, the Kaiser consented to a British sphere of influence from Uganda to the Congo boundaries and a British protectorate in Zanzibar. The entire area between Mozambique and the British sphere of influence became German East Africa - virtually identical to the Tanganyika of the post-World War One mandated territory, except that German East Africa included Ruanda-Urundi.

One final consequence of the Anglo-German conflict in 1890 and Stanley's role in it was that Emin Pasha threw in his lot with his compatriots. Since Stanley had beaten Peters to the punch by getting to Emin first, the only way the Germans could retrieve their laurels was by suborning Emin in turn away from the British. The paths to this objective were made straight by Stanley's sustained jeers and jibes at Emin, which not only further enraged the Pasha against Stanley and all his works but destroyed Emin's credibility with Mackinnon and the IBEA Company.

Yet there is evidence that Emin was reluctant to become a German agent. On 13th March 1890, now fully recovered from his injuries, he had a long conversation with Euan-Smith. He began by rehearsing the history of his dealings with Stanley. He confirmed that he had turned down the idea of service with Leopold, since he remained convinced that the Congo State would either collapse or fall into the hands of the French. He attacked Stanley for failing to honour the Kavirondo promise, not allowing him to join the Jackson expedition, and for failing to help Mwanga in Uganda. He lamented the fact that Stanley's calumnies had ended his chances of working for Mackinnon's IBEA Company and he was considering writing a book to present his side of the case.

In fact it was not Stanley's opposition that damned Emin. Both Euan-Smith and Kirk had independently come to the conclusion that Emin as a British agent would be more liability than asset. Even as they spoke, Euan-Smith had within his gift the post of Administrator-in-Chief of the IBEA Company, and Mackinnon himself was in favour of the appointment, as an irritated journal entry from Stanley shows clearly. But Euan-Smith thought Emin utterly unsuitable for the post, and in this opinion he was backed by Kirk, finally in full agreement with Stanley about something. Kirk wrote: 'I am glad we are rid of Emin - he has been a grossly exaggerated man and would have been to us a fearful encumbrance - I have little doubt he will become more German than the Germans themselves - for after all he is I believe or was a German Jew and one with not a particularly bright record until he got on under Gordon. Of course he is a remarkable man and a scientific man but no administrator.'

The sequel was predictable. Unless he was to return to Europe - which he always refused adamantly to do - Emin now had no choice but to accept the service which Wissmann offered him at £1000 a year. Wissmann coaxed Emin into a substantial propaganda assault against Stanley and the British. First, Emin wrote to the Sultan to complain about the personal discourtesy meted out to him by the British. Next he wrote a letter dissociating himself from Stanley's suit against Tippu Tip. Since the German intention was obviously to swing the injured Tippu over to their cause, Stanley was forced to advise Euan-Smith that the only way to trump Germany's ace was by abandoning the lawsuit and freeing Tippu's assets so that he would not be permanently alienated. He neglected to point out that the entire mess involving both Tippu and Emin had arisen in the first place because of his own injudicious treatment of them.

When it was learned in London that Emin had entered the service of Britain's rivals after so much blood and treasure had been spent by the British in getting him out of Equatoria, there was a predictable outcry.

At this stage the version that Emin was a mere ingrate was almost universally accepted, for Stanley was riding high in popular esteem. Even Stanley saw that Emin's service with Germany turned his expedition into a thing of farce, though he could never admit this publicly. But in the short term the 'betrayal' played into his hands by stoking the fires of anti-German feeling in England. Only when the full Emin expedition scandal broke in the columns of British newspapers at the end of 1890 did the more thoughtful analysts attempt a reappraisal.

Emin got his wish to become, like Livingstone, a wanderer over Africa. If his fall at Bagamoyo on the evening of 4th December 1889 was, as Stanley suspected, a form of death-wish, Emin's unconscious desires soon found fulfilment. In October 1892 he was deep in the Ituri forest when he became the first victim of the imminent war between Leopold's Congo and the Arab slavers. On the orders of the Arab chief Kibonge he was murdered while under a safe-conduct. But the cynics maintained that after 1889 Emin was always a mere shadow of his former self, that he had been 'killed' in all but physical form by Stanley's brutal treatment of him. Stanley's fall from grace was like Lucifer's. He had begun his career by revering the one true man of Africa in his era, and ended it by destroying another such rara avis - surely the appropriate term, given Emin's predilections. Stanley's life was now in steep decline in more senses than one.

Chapter Eighteen

STANLEY arrived at Dover from Belgium on 26 April 1890 to be greeted by the Mayor and Corporation as 'Henry Mortlake Stanley'. The pressmen who were there to accompany him on the train journey to London found him looking very bored. With snow-white hair and a 'Chinaman complexion' like unburnt clay, he puffed away phlegmatically at his cigar. Once in London he had a string of social engagements to fulfil, the most important of which were with the Royal Family.

As early as February de Winton had written to him about the immense interest in his affairs by Queen Victoria and her family. Leopold too was primed to let the Queen know the very second Stanley had completed his private talks in Brussels. Consequently, Stanley's first social engagement was at Sandringham where, in company with Mackinnon, de Winton and Parke, he gave an after-dinner lecture on Africa to the future George V. On 3rd May he attended a reception at St James's Hall in the presence of the Prince of Wales and other royalty. Finally, on the 6th he was received at Windsor Castle in private audience by the Queen herself. She found him more prepossessing than in 1872 but still remarkably cagey about his future plans. But Victoria was swept along by the current Stanley-mania. Not only did she commission a portrait of Stanley's head from the painter Angeli, but she toyed with awarding him a knighthood then and there. De Winton advised her that it would be better to wait until after the publication of In Darkest Africa, as the book was likely to be controversial. So she contented herself with sending him a jewelled portrait of herself.

The diary of engagements gave Stanley scarcely a moment of leisure. A reception by the EPRE committee was followed by a banquet and speech at the Royal Geographical Society. Then came dinners and banquets from a variety of sources: the Corporation of London (who gave him the freedom of the City); the Turners' Company, the Chamber of Commerce, the Merchant Taylors, the Fishmongers' Company, the Savage Club, the Society of Expatriate Americans. In the speeches he gave to these assemblies, Stanley largely followed the line he had given to Vizetelly of the New York Herald at Msua, stressing the discoveries on the Aruwimi and in the Ituri, the attempted ascent of Ruwenzori, the charting of Lake Albert and Lake Edward. The providential theme was again well to the fore: 'A veritable divinity seems to have hedged us while we journeyed ... a higher plan than mine . .. the vulgar will call it luck, unbelievers will call it chance but deep down in each heart remains a feeling, that of a verity there are more things in heaven and earth than are dreamed of in common philosophy .. . their [his companions] diet has been all the time what the legal serfs of Sing Sing would have declared infamous and abominable and yet they live.'

In the speech to the Royal Geographical Society he concentrated on the gains of the expedition, anticipating the criticism to come. Apart from the new discoveries, he had unlocked huge quantities of rubber and gum to trade, had opened up the farthest recesses of the Dark Continent to Christianity and had established that in the Aruwimi there were 10,000 million more trees than mankind knew about before. Not all his listeners were that impressed by this hectoring way with statistics. One journalist reported acidly: 'Except that it will furnish some new Catullus with a fresh comparison for his demand of kisses from some new Lesbia, we see nothing particularly interesting in the 10,000 millions. 'May, June and July 1890 saw Stanley's reputation at its apogee. For now the few voices raised in opposition were crying in a wilderness. John Burns, later to be the first working-class Cabinet Minister in Britain, waxed incandescent at the proposal to give Stanley the freedom of the newly constituted London County Council, and John Bright made a vigorous defence against Stanley's contemptuous attack on the Quakers' work in Africa. But almost everyone else joined in the uncritical adulation for a great expedition successfully accomplished. The sensation continued with the publication of In Darkest Africa on 28th June. This was a bestseller that outstripped by far the considerable success of his earlier books. 150,000 copies were sold, and impresarios in North America and Australia at once began clamouring for the explorer's presence in the lecture halls. Stanley spent June in a triumphal progress through Scotland. He collected the freedoms of Edinburgh, Glasgow, Dundee, Aberdeen and Manchester, and attended degree ceremonies at Edinburgh and Oxford where he was awarded the honorary LLD and DCL respectively. The conferring of similar doctorates at Durham and Cambridge was held over until the autumn to accommodate his bulging engagement calendar.

Among those who had watched with trepidation Stanley's perilous three-year odyssey in Central Africa and followed the many newspaper accounts of his death was Dorothy Tennant, the woman who had rejected his marriage proposal in 1886. On Stanley's return she ventured a wish to see him. She began the letter formally but ended with 'Bula Matari, do not be too proud to come.' He did not answer this, but on 3rd May at a crowded party she tried again. She grasped his hand and whispered, 'Come to me.' But he rebuffed her coldly: 'It is hard to say it - I must decline the pleasure of approaching you . . . you will do wisely and well to leave me alone.' On 6th May she made a further overture, explaining that she just wished to say goodbye and to tell him that his letter of proposal in 1886 had always been sacred to her.

What I wrote to you in '86 was only true in this sense. Suppose a wild, uncultivated tract of land and suppose that one day this land is ploughed up and sown with corn. If the field could speak it might say: 'I have never borne corn, I do not bear corn, I shall never bear corn.' And yet all the while the wheat lies hidden in its bosom. When you were gone, when you were out of reach, I slowly realised what you had become to me, and then great anguish filled me. I then made myself a vow that I would train myself to strive to become wiser and stronger, better, gentler and then, when you came back I would see you and tell you all quite simply, and say 'Truly I have never cared for anyone but you. I did not know it when you wrote to me, for till you wrote the possibility of your caring for me had never even occurred to me. But at that time I was not worthy of your love. Now I believe I am, let me help you and take care of you, and be everything in the world to you.' But there was vanity in this, for it presupposed your still caring for me.

Stanley replied from Windsor, where he was the guest of Queen Victoria. He explained that he had been humiliated in 1886 as if he had been a base-born churl in the presence of a queen. 'I worshipped you as a goddess and the goddess spurned me ... please take this as an explanation, and not as recrimination . . . had such possibilities approached me in 1886, I would have been delirious with joy, nothing in all the wide world would have been so blissful.'

On 7th May the two met at an evening party. Dolly told him she would be his wife if he still loved her. But now it was Stanley that was playing hard to get. He replied curtly next day: 'let us be good friends.' This cold douche thrown in her face made her redouble her efforts. She wrote again, explaining that she realised what he meant to her only after he had departed on the Emin expedition. She had taken a vow to make herself morally and spiritually worthy of him, which was why she now accepted an equal pain in rejection to that he had suffered in 1886. 'Oh Bula Matari, listen to me. If I made you suffer I have expiated the wrong done. Remember the difference between us. You were a man, you knew more of life, you had loved before. I was a girl unacquainted with love . . . Yours was only a flower, a rose you say which I crushed. But my love is a flame which will never die, it began so small a spark you could not see it light, now it burns like the altar flame never to be extinguished [her underlining].'

Having received the obeisance he required, Stanley allowed himself to admit to his emotional need for a wife. On 13th May he made a formal proposal of marriage. The note containing this reached her at Richmond Terrace at 4.30 that afternoon. She wrote back at once.

My own beloved Bula-Matari,

It is all true - and not a dream and I am really to be yours. If you did but know how I love you, how intensely I love you. I am afraid of my joy, after so much unhappiness it seems too much light.

Next day she called on him at 34 De Vere Mansions and after a short talk, they agreed to make their engagement public. Two days later Stanley came to see her mother and brought along a diamond engagement ring for Dolly. The news travelled swiftly among the London socialites. Baroness Burdett-Coutts at once invited the explorer's fiancée to the Turners' banquet. The following Wednesday Dolly and her mother attended a party at the Foreign Office, then withdrew from society to prepare for the wedding. Press reporting of the event tended to be on the waspish side. Many, then and later, asserted that Dorothy Tennant was too good for Stanley. Others drew attention to Dolly's opportunism. Apparently a picture she was exhibiting shortly before the engagement had been priced at £200. The secretary of the gallery received an offer of £170 and wrote to Dolly to advise her to take it. He was surprised

to receive a curt note by return, ordering him to accept not a penny less than £200. Then he read in the press of the engagement to Stanley and everything fell into place.

Great fun was also had with Stanley's admission to the Savage Club that in Africa he had been as chaste as Galahad. One columnist remarked: 'An interesting fact, doubtless, and very comforting, maybe, to the wife of his bosom: but of what public concern? Who cares much whether he preserved his virtue intact or ran riot in the jungle?' Private comment too tended to be critical. Beatrice Webb, an acquaintance of Dolly's, found the public engagement vulgar. Frank Harris, told that the charming Dorothy Tennant was to marry the 'lion of the season', remarked that a truer description was that she was about to marry the king of beasts, for Stanley always seemed to him a force without a conscience.

More tact and sensitivity was shown by Frederick Myers, the English poet and founder-member of the Society for Psychical Research, who had married Dolly's sister Eveleen in 1880. He wrote at once with his congratulations and an assessment of his sister-in-law. He found her spoiled, impetuous and not always wise. Against this she offered, as few other women did, cheerful, loving, helpful and intelligent companionship. Welcoming Stanley as his brother-in-law he went on: 'You will understand that it is not your fame that makes me feel this. Nothing would be more disagreeable to me, as an intimate member of the Richmond Terrace group, than to have a new and overwhelming fame and importance suddenly plunged down beside me in the family, unless that man were one whom I could myself honour and care for his personal and private qualities.'

What assessment can we make of this whirlwind courtship and engagement? Is very clear in retrospect that in 1886 Stanley had unconsciously willed the rejection that Dorothy Tennant had meted out to him, just as he had done earlier with Virginia Ambella, Katie Gough-Roberts and Alice Pike. This is the hidden subtext of the letters where he had seemed to go out of his way to pick fights with her over Gladstone and the working man. This was part of the syndrome of simultaneous attraction and repulsion that characterised all Stanley's dealings with women. He had not counted, however, on the boomerang effect of Dolly's conversion while he was on the road to Wadelai. The torrent of poignant regret and damned emotion she released on him swept away his defences for the moment. But the unconscious was to strike back before the wedding, as we shall see.

Dolly in her own way was as much a psychoanalytical study as her would-be husband. There is something bizarre and disconcerting about the way she refers to herself in 1886 (when she was thirty-four) as a 'girl'; arrested development seems a mild term in the circumstances. And there is surely much unconscious significance in the symbolism of the field of corn. 'I have never borne corn, I do not bear corn, I never shall bear corn [her underlining].' This seems to denote either an admission of barrenness or a morbid fear of childbirth and points forward to the scarcely surprising eventuality that her marriage with Stanley was childless. The unconscious impetus of her feelings towards Stanley seems to be the need to find a surrogate father, after years of corresponding with the dead original.

I sometimes realise how little I really know of life, and passions and tragedies and all the turmoil. Thank God you will take care of me and shield me and keep me from harm. I dread the world, the real world. Of course, the world of London parties is only like play-acting. What I shirk from is dealing with the rough outside world, being deceived by people. I see by reading and observing how people drift into being bad and miserable. I hate the world. Oh keep me close to you, put your arms around me. Don't think I can stand alone. People here called me 'self-sufficing', they say I am independent, I did not invite confidences. But it was not really so, only I felt there was more dignity in standing aloof so long as I could not, would not, lean for ever on anyone I met. But you are beside me now, my rock, my prop, my bulwark against the great breakers of life.

Dolly's implicit conditions for the marriage contained the unspoken assumption that it meant the end of his career as African explorer. Harry Johnston, his old friend and admirer, was urging this consummation on both partners in the run-up period to the marriage. On 6th June he wrote to Stanley as follows: 'Go no more to Africa. You have now secured - surely - enough glory for your lifetime and for history. Sit down therefore and enjoy yourself for the rest of your natural life. I called you once in a magazine article "The Napoleon Bonaparte of exploration". Well, you have now won your Austerlitz. Stop short and do not risk a Moscow or a Waterloo.'

In similar vein he addressed Dolly a little later. 'I am so glad you are going to marry him, and I think you will be happy in so doing if [three times underlined] you don't go to Africa. Don't go to Africa [three times underlined]. Your mission is to reconcile Stanley to England, where he must reside as "Agent General" for Africa. Stanley must go into Parliament and you must help him, nurse him, encourage him, entertain for him, and generally be that real helpmeet to him that only a good wife can be. So will his career meet with its true fruition.'

Dolly replied the same day. 'The future lies before me a dark unexplored continent. I have never questioned Mr Stanley about it - but - I confess to you - I have my hidden away fears. I dread Africa. I have read far too much about it not to dread Africa. But if he must return - I go with him. If duty urges him to return I shall not dare dissuade him. Your words therefore greatly console me. You make me hope that possibly he may not consider it his bounden duty to return to Africa.'

As the day scheduled for the wedding drew closer, the unconscious 'failsafe' mechanism which would ensure an escape from actual intimacy, rather than the fantasy of the 'ideal woman', was triggered. Stanley felt violently ill and there was doubt whether the ceremony could proceed as planned. The official diagnosis was gastritis, but why the explorer should have been attacked at this precise time, rather than in Cairo when he was under enormous pressure to finish his book, was not explained. Certainly his letter to Mackinnon at the beginning of July hardly indicates coup de foudre. 'Were she the ugliest little mortal in existence, I think I would marry her, provided I could get some excuse for breaking away from this weary, frivolous world of writers of letters upon nothing.'

Until the very morning of 12th July, a question mark hung over the wedding. Then on the morning itself Stanley struggled out of bed and, supported by Parke, tottered into the carriage that would take him to Westminster Abbey. Despite the drenching rain, huge crowds had gathered outside the Abbey to witness the event; the police had great difficulty controlling them. Inside, every one of the Abbey seats was taken. 5000 people had been refused admission tickets, but even so many a leading light of London society was reduced to standing in the aisles. Among those present were Gladstone, the Lord Chancellor, the Speaker of the House of Commons, dozens of dukes and duchesses and, as groomsmen, Parke, Stairs, Jephson, Nelson and even Bonny. There were representatives of the military and exploring worlds. The ceremony was conducted by two Deans and a Bishop and the Master of Trinity, Cambridge, gave the marriage address. Best man was Leopold's representative, the Comte d'Arche.

The first sensation of the day was when Stanley hobbled up to the altar on a walking stick, still too ill to be present in anything but body.

There he sat in an armchair and awaited his bride. Then Dolly swept into the Abbey on the arm of Sir John Millais. She wore a dress of white silk and satin and from her neck dripped a panoply of jewels: a diamond necklace from Mackinnon, a diamond locket from Queen Victoria, a bracelet from Leopold, and a sapphire and diamond bracelet from Stanley.

Stanley suffered agonies until the service was over. Then he was helped to his carriage outside and the newly-weds drove the short distance to Richmond Terrace, still through immense crowds. 'The police struggled in vain to keep back the fighting, shouting, maddened people,' Dolly wrote in her diary. 'I felt so faint and dreaded seeing some horror, some terrible accident. I closed my eyes and only opened them when I felt the carriage go rather quicker. A reinforcement of mounted police had come to the rescue.'

After an inspection of the wedding presents the couple departed with Parke to Waterloo Station, there to entrain for Hampshire. Louisa, Lady Ashburton, had lent them Melchett Court in the New Forest for the honeymoon, though Stanley continued so ill that he could scarcely write, much less consummate his marriage. Gradually, over a month he began to recover and take walks in the countryside. 'We might be in the great Congo forests for all that we see once we enter the woods.'

The real honeymoon did not take place until August, when the Stanley's departed for Maloja in Switzerland, via London and Paris. And it is at the

Hotel Kursaal in Maloja that we get our first important clues to the reality of the Stanley marriage. The evidence is in two parts. In the first place, Stanley absolutely insisted that he would not go to Switzerland on honeymoon unless Jephson came too as a 'minder'. By now he had fastened on Jephson as yet another in the long series of young male companions he always needed at his side. Not since Albert Christopherson in the Congo had he found a man who fitted the bill so well. Jephson, who was bemused by the request to accompany the honeymooners, but was flattered by Stanley's interest, inadvertently tapped into some of Stanley's deeper feelings when he prodded his leader for assurance of his esteem and affection. Stanley wrote back: 'You remember the crossing of the Lufu . . . well had I been in condition to indulge in a sentiment which was near to the tip of my tongue I think I should have revealed pretty clearly my kindly feelings towards you. You remember your leading the caravan one day ... I came near adding "Come to my arms, Jephson."'

The second part of the evidence is in the form of the cancelled passages in Stanley's private journals. Dorothy Stanley suffered from the disease that seemed to beset the wives of African explorers - for we observe the same syndrome with Isabel Burton, Lady Lugard and the wife of Sir Harry Johnston: a desire to expunge the true record so as to present to the world an idealised version of the husband-hero. The journal recording the events of Stanley's private life contains several passages scored out in ink by Dolly. On one page, however, relating to the honeymoon trip to Switzerland, the ending of one entry is legible: 'I do not regard it wifely, to procure these pleasures, at the cost of making me feel like a monkey in a cage.'

Taken together, the two pieces of honeymoon evidence seem to point to a conclusion that is wholly unsurprising in terms of the sexual profile of Stanley adumbrated below (see pp.394-96). Stanley's schizoid personality, which prevented him from integrating love for a woman with carnality, extended into a bisexual limbo where he was incapable of active participation in either heterosexual or homosexual intercourse. He combined a desperate need for love with a desperate fear of intimacy. Attracted to female beauty and grace, yet horrified by the sexuality of women, Stanley was at the same time incapable of out-and-out homosexuality. The coexisting heterosexual and homosexual impulses both remained at a latent repressed level. When he was finally called upon to satisfy a wife, Stanley in effect broke down and confessed that he considered sex for the beasts. The unconscious motive for getting himself rejected by four different women was made manifest. The presence of Jephson in the selfsame hotel where this tragic marital breakdown was being played out suggests that Stanley used the homosexual elements in his own personality as a kind of rudder to maintain his psychic equilibrium.

But to the outer world Stanley maintained the fiction that his was a blissful marriage. 'Dolly is better than fine gold. She is infinitely better than any conception I had of her. She knows something of everything, and when she does not allow her politeness to restrain her, she is wise in her remarks.' And at the mundane level Stanley enjoyed his time in Switzerland. By chance Sir Richard and Lady Isabel Burton were staying at the same hotel; the two explorers had many stimulating discussions about Africa and their contemporaries, though Dolly found Burton's cynicism and forthrightness hard to adjust to. Stanley also wrote an introduction to Jephson's book on Emin Pasha and the rebellion in Equatoria. Jephson was thrilled at the master's praise and at the prospect that his preface would secure it an American sale. It seems clear that the influence of Jephson and Burton tugged one way and Dolly another, for Stanley told Mackinnon: 'I have no immediate purpose of going to Africa as I am bound by my lecture tour but there might come a time when having fulfilled all my engagements I might think European life too dreary to be endured.'

From Maloja they went south to Lake Como, then on to Milan and Monza where they were met by Casati and his long-time patron Captain Camperio who entertained the Stanleys regally at his delightful country house La Santa near Monza. Casati had mellowed in his attitude to Stanley and was now inclined to agree with him about the shortcomings of his old friend Emin Pasha. After Monza the Stanleys travelled to Geneva, then on for a sentimental stay at the Hotel Meurice in Paris. The European jaunt ended with a four-day working sojourn with Leopold in Ostend.

On 8th October the Stanleys arrived back in England. Jephson related that Parke met them at the station but could hardly get a word out of Stanley as 'he was in such ecstasies at again meeting his mother-in-law'. Given Stanley's normal contemptuous impatience with elderly females, this was a surprising development, but strong bonds had evidently been forged between him and Gertrude Tennant. When Stanley told his would-be mother-in-law of his engagement to her daughter, she advised him that she would not give her consent unless she was taken completely into the family. A tearful scene ended with Stanley giving her carte blanche in his household. This gesture completely won the old lady over. She told Mrs French Sheldon that she loved Stanley as a son and was confident that her daughter would be in safe hands: 'it is a great privilege for any woman to be linked with a character and a career like Mr Stanley's.'

The bonds with Gertrude Tennant were tightened when it was announced that she would accompany her daughter and son-in-law on the coming lecture tour of the USA. An interesting spectacle of dependency ensued. Dolly had her mother at her side and in compensation Stanley took Jephson with him. After degree ceremonies at Cambridge and Durham and visits to Cardiff and Swansea to receive the freedoms of those cities, the Stanleys travelled to Liverpool to take ship for the USA on the White Star liner Teutonic.

On 6th November, in bright sunshine, the SS Teutonic entered the Verrazano narrows at the entrance to New York. Pressmen were taken out to the steamer on a lighter and thronged about Stanley with notebooks and questions. Dolly tried to shield him from their enquiries and draw him away to look at the scenery, sweetly frowning on all who questioned him. But the ploy was stymied almost at once when a thick blanket of fog descended on the Teutonic and she had to feel her way like a blind man up the bay to the White Star Pier.

Major Pond had arranged lectures in i10cities, to recoup the expenses of the aborted 1886 tour. Most of the speaking engagements were in cities on the east coast, and Pond confidently expected an enthusiastic turn-out, especially as controversy over the Emin expedition was reaching its height. In its early stages the tour lived up to expectations. Once again Stanley was lucky. Historians of the West often single out 1890 as the year of the closing of the frontier. Americans now had to look elsewhere for an outlet for their blood-and-thunder impulses which they had hitherto indulged with the tales of Davy Crockett, Wild Bill Hickock and Kit Carson. The 'Dark Continent' provided the perfect focus.

Having been out of the USA (except for lightning visits in 1874, 1885 and 1886) for eighteen years, Stanley was unprepared for the vast changes that had overtaken the country in that time and at first suffered from a form of culture shock. He found the noise and pollution of New York almost intolerable. The streets were criss-crossed with tramlines, telegraph posts with myriad wires cut across the skyline, the city streets were forever being dug up to enable some fresh cable to be laid, and a forest of billboards assailed his eye. Worst of all was the elevated railway. 'The man who invented the hideous "Elevated" deserves to be expelled from civilisation . . . the view from our hotel window shows me the street ploughed up, square blocks of granite lying as far as the eye can see, besides planking, boarding, piles of earth and stacks of bricks. I counted one hundred and seventy-four lines of wire in the air, rows of mast-like telegraph poles, untrimmed and unpainted, in the centre of the American metropolis! What taste!'

The Stanley party toured the eastern seaboard and proceeded into Canada in a special Pullman car named 'Henry M. Stanley'. Stanley chafed at the pace of the lecture circuit. Pond would allow him no rest between engagements and kept the press on his tail, 'sometimes on the car and of both sexes [his underlining].' By Christmas Day 1890 they were in Omaha, which he had known so well in 1867. Then it had been a frontier town of 11-15,000 inhabitants but now it contained 140,000 people and sprawled over ten times the area. As in all the cities Stanley had visited, Omaha manifested in its architecture the new craze for conspicuous consumption which often resulted in houses far superior to anything seen in English cities.

But if Stanley was impressed by the wealth of America, he was much less so by its people. 'With all their inventiveness and gifts for improving dead matter, the living man - the American man himself - black or white does not strike me as having improved at all morally or mentally. He is richer, prouder, more independent in bearing, but he still retains the same rudeness of manner.' He contrasted the modernity of American hotels with their staff. 'The servants are simply the most untrained, undisciplined, loutish and ill-bred of their kind in the world. The newspapers are still the same sensational crime-loving journals I knew long ago, ugly, dirty-looking, preposterously coarse in language, slangy and licentious ... I suppose there are six times more churches in America now than in 1867 but I have been looking anxiously for some moral results of all the preaching and praying - and so far my search has been in vain.' Worst of all aspects of the USA was the noise: 'The noisiest streets in the world. They are really murderous in their intensity - such hissing, grinding and rolling of trams every minute throughout the day or night is most wearing on the nerves.'

They returned to New York for a series of lectures in January. Stanley renewed acquaintance with General Sherman at the Press Club banquet and was saddened a few weeks later in Chicago to hear of his sudden death. By the beginning of February Stanley was seriously regretting having taken on such a strenuous tour. He quarrelled bitterly with his agents about the crushing workload and when Pond refused to relent, decided to hit back in his own way. He was asked to name his own time for a reception at the Chicago Press Club and, though he had three free days in the week, he fixed on Sunday, thus outraging the local religious communities. When Pond put his foot down and insisted on a weekday, Stanley then peevishly limited himself to a mere 12-hour appearance at the reception.

March 1891 saw him in the far West. All the proposed lectures in Texas were cancelled, not because of the Rear Column controversy but because it had been revealed that Stanley deserted the South for the Unionists during the Civil War. In the western states his speaking engagements were far-flung: Omaha, Sioux City, Denver, Colorado Springs, Salt Lake City, San Francisco, Los Angeles, Oakland, Stockton, Sacramento, San Jose, Fresno and Los Angeles again. The Californian newspapers infuriated Stanley by quoting his height as, variously, 5 foot 3 inches and 5 foot 4 inches: 'the truth is I am five feet, five and a half inches in my socks,' he huffed indignantly. But the high spot of the tour for Stanley was when he was able to show Dolly around the scenes of his youth in New Orleans, Chattanooga and Nashville. Thence they returned to New York where Major Pond gave them a farewell dinner at the Lotus Club on 11 April. Four days later they sailed to Liverpool.

The lecture tour had netted Stanley some £12,000 but he found it, particularly in its later stages, a veritable via dolorosa: 'enduring the breaks on my privacy because they are a necessity; each time invoking more patience, and beseeching Time to hurry on its lagging movement that I might once more taste of absolute freedom. Meanwhile, what pleasure I obtain is principally in reading, unless I come to a little town, and can slip, unobserved, out of doors for a walk. I often laugh at the ridiculous aspect of my feelings, as I am compelled to become shifty and cunning, to evade the eager citizens' advances. I feel like Cain, hurrying away with his uneasy conscience after despatching Abel, or a felonious cashier departing with his plunder!'

Immediately on return to England, Stanley sought sanctuary at the South Wales retreat he had acquired - Cadoxton Lodge. By now he had decided that, although the marriage could never be a union of blood and passion, the Tennant connection gave him the serenity and tranquillity he needed; even his mother-in-law Gertrude had stood up wonderfully well to the rigours of American travel. He expressed his satisfaction with Dolly thus: 'I loved her but yet I dreaded after all, for I knew her so little. I feared she was gushing and shallow, and a mere society product. But had she been moulded to fit my nature, she could not have been more perfect than she is. She is always May - sunshine with a promise of rain. She is extremely sunny in disposition, yet sensitive, easily affected by joy or sorrow. She is brimming over with gladness, is gay, sportive, irrepressibly merry, but so quick are her sympathies, that if she sees or hears anything suggestive of pain or sorrow, she seems to yearn to soothe, control and heal. This excessive womanliness is a new thing to me in her, for I had only regarded her brilliant externals.'

Dolly, for her part, though she lacked a passionate lover, at least had someone on whom to lavish the devotion she had hitherto expended on a phantom. Like Isabel Burton, she dedicated herself to building up the legend of her husband, denying, striking down and effacing anything and anyone that contradicted the mythical picture. She also had to suppress her own previous opinions and view of the world so as to fit in with Stanley's. An incident in the first year of her marriage shows how far she had travelled from the ingénue who fretted about the plight of miners and proletarians. The parents of Stanley's 1874-7 companions the Pococks had by 1890 been reduced to terrible straits. At seventy-four Henry Pocock was too infirm to continue his work as a fisherman and his wife, a year older, was going blind. Remembering Stanley's eulogy about 'his brother' Frank, Henry Pocock wrote to Stanley to ask for financial assistance. The letter found him convalescing at Melchett Court after the wedding. On 5th August 1890 Dolly fired off a monumentally insensitive reply: 'Mr Stanley is sorry he cannot assist you - he has so many and great demands on him that he is quite unable to respond to the innumerable appeals made to him for money. Night and day he is assailed, just as though he had a great fortune.'

Incensed at the plight of the elderly Pococks, Henry Smetham took up the cudgels on their behalf in a vigorous campaign in the Chatham and Rochester News. He pointed out that the couple lived in Upnor with a widowed daughter who earned her bread by hard toil and campaigned for a fund that would provide the old folk with 12-15 shillings a week as long as they lived. He added that the amount in question was no more than the cost of firing off a single gun on ceremonial occasions: 'That one should be done and the other neglected is a disgrace to mankind - and what we are pleased to call civilisation - and runs near to blasphemy to that God we hypocritically pretend to serve.'

Smetham's campaign for a Pocock fund threatened to mushroom into a scandal, breaking on the public as it did simultaneously with the most unsavoury revelations about the Emin expedition. Stanley acted quickly, but his letter is a masterpiece of humbug and obfuscation in his familiar style.

Dear Sir,

In Detroit I had the pleasure of meeting a relative of the Pococks, who brought most vividly to my mind the sad end of Francis. I urged my wife to remind me of the matter on reaching London. This she has done, and in consequence I send you £50 towards your needs. The Daily Telegraph and New York Herald, in whose service your son died, should treble the sum, and do something to atone to you for the great loss you sustained.

This was typical of the Stanley method. Do not admit that you are doing something under duress, but claim that it was your idea all along. If a tragedy occurs, the victim is in the service of a newspaper or a committee. If a triumph is achieved, this is because Stanley is the leader. Small wonder that there was little room for Dolly's erstwhile sympathy for the underdog if she wished to live in harmony with her beloved Bula Matari. The Pococks, however, were fortunate. Stanley's gesture started the ball rolling, so that in the end enough was raised to carry the old couple comfortably through the few years remaining to them.

Stanley could afford to be generous, for on top of the income generated by the American tour, he secured another useful £2000 nest-egg on his return by making a similar tour around Great Britain and Ireland. Hull, York, Bradford, Sheffield, Cambridge, Liverpool, Cheltenham, Gloucester, Bristol, Swansea, Caernavon, and Canterbury were just some of the venues in a breathless two-month whistlestop. At last he was free to take a holiday and at the end of July 1891 he travelled with his entourage to his favourite place of relaxation: Switzerland.

This time they were at the Grand Hotel des Alpes in Murren. Stanley did not really care for the altitude of the resort (4900 feet) which was too cold for him. But he enjoyed himself with Gertrude Tennant while Dolly lay in bed with a chill: the two used the latest invention, the telephone, to talk to each other from neighbouring hotels and the now doting mother-in-law told him: 'Bula Matari, you are an angel.' Yet he was an angel destined to fall from grace. One Saturday morning they set off for a picnic at a spot about an hour's drive from the hotel. Stanley was showing Dolly's sister's little boy how Africans threw spears. As he swung round with the projectile, he lost his balance, fell heavily and snapped the fibula near the ankle. He was in great pain and had to wait a long time for a stretcher. He was then taken to hospital where he was flat on his back for three weeks before being allowed up on a pair of crutches, with his broken leg in plaster of Paris. For the rest of his stay in Switzerland he was pushed around in a wheelchair.

It is possible that Stanley's accident might have been triggered by some unconscious self-destructive impulse, for it is curious that a man who had never injured a limb during four different expeditions in Africa totalling a dozen years, in which he had hacked through jungles, waded across swamps and scaled precipitous mountains, should have come to grief in a Swiss glen. Perhaps the trigger can be sought in a depressing encounter with the press just before the fall. Special correspondent Aubrey Stanhope of the New York Herald received orders from Gordon Bennett to go to Switzerland to investigate rumours that the great explorer's marriage was on the rocks. Perhaps someone during the American tour with sensitive antennae had intuited that the marriage was not all it might be, or Stanley himself had let drop some half-clue. At any rate Stanhope did not approach his assignment with much relish; he described it as 'quite the most disagreeable' he had ever been called upon to carry out.

The plucky Stanhope went up the mountain on mule-back to Stanley's eyrie at Murren. When he explained his mission, Stanley exploded with rage. But he was in a difficult position. He could hardly send packing a representative of the newspaper that had made his own fame and fortune. Besides, if he did, Bennett might well decide to stoke up again the embers of the dying Rear Column controversy. Stanhope tried to let him off the hook. 'Suppose,' he suggested, 'you go and ask the women what they say about it. They instinctively know what is best to do in such matters.'

Controlling his anger, Stanley went to consult with his wife and her sister Mrs Myers. They indignantly repudiated the rumour. Stanhope asked for a written statement. Stanley produced the following: 'I have no hesitation in saying that each day of our married life has been one of pure content and unalloyed happiness.' Still Stanhope was not satisfied. Respectfully he pointed out that the affidavit was not countersigned by his wife. Almost at breaking point, Stanley went in to see Dolly and came back with her statement which read as follows: 'I am very much astonished and disgusted with reports in a New York newspaper that my married life is unhappy and that I am separated from my dear husband. It is indeed high time that a stop should be put to such a shameful fabrication. Is there no protection from these newspaper insults?'

Back in England, the Stanleys spent two months at Wimpole Rectory at Royston near Cambridge - placed at the explorer's disposal for the late summer by Lord Hardwicke. As Stanley recovered from the broken leg, he was attacked suddenly by gravel and African fever. His physician Sir Henry Thompson put him on an ascetic diet of vegetables, fruit and poultry; nothing sweet, no red meat and no wine was permitted. Thompson's diagnosis was that because Stanley's stomach got used to the primitive fare of Africa, it could not adjust to the rich food of Europe.

Next it was time for another gruelling lecture tour, this time in Australasia. Dolly had originally decided not to accompany her husband after the unpleasant American experience, but two considerations urged her on. First, Stanley was still hobbling on crutches and would need careful nursing. Secondly, not to go would be to fuel the rumours of separation and infidelity in the Stanley marriage that continued to circulate. Gritting her teeth, Dolly prepared for the journey to the southern hemisphere. After a quick visit to Leopold at Ostend, they boarded the SS Arcadia in the Mediterranean. But not before Stanley was involved in a potentially fatal accident. The train taking them to Brindisi was derailed in Italy; the engine, van and four freight trucks in the front of the train were wrecked (without loss of life) and Stanley's compartment was next to the van. Had this been overturned, it might have gone hard with him as he was still lame and on crutches.

The sea voyage to Australia was long, confining and monotonous. It turned out to have been a bad mistake to pick up the liner in the Mediterranean. The ship was packed to the gunwales, with 345 first-class passengers alone, and all the best staterooms and most comfortable seats in the dining-room had been taken by those who embarked at London. There was just a single one-day stopover, at Colombo. The experience did nothing to whet Dolly's appetite for exotic lecture tours. She complained bitterly about the heat, the weather and the slow pace of shipboard travel.

Stanley began his lectures as soon as they arrived in Australia and delivered one daily except on Sundays. There was plenty of sightseeing to be fitted in also; Dolly was raised momentarily from her gloom by the sight of Sydney Harbour Bridge and by a meeting with the former policeman, now magistrate, who had captured Ned Kelly. But she was deeply unhappy. She lamented that since her marriage she had been in her own home for just three weeks: 'a woman is never at home but at home.'

Stanley followed his usual pattern of rotating three lectures on his most exciting African journeys (omitting his five years with Leopold). He was ten days in Melbourne, three in Ballarat, two in Geelong, then in Brisbane and Sydney (where he encountered the only real press criticism). At the end of the year the Stanleys crossed to New Zealand where they were royally entertained by Sir George Grey, a passionate Stanley admirer. They returned via Tasmania and wound up the Australian tour in Melbourne and Adelaide.

It was an exhausted party that arrived back in England in April 1892. But by now the triumphant African lion of two years ago was in danger of sinking to the level of a pariah dog. Stanley's reputation had sunk to an all-time low following the prolonged controversy over the Emin Pasha expedition and its dark epitome in the form of the Rear Column. Stanley, always a superstitious man, felt almost as though he were confronting the gibbering shades of Barttelot and Jameson and that they clamoured for blood.

Chapter Nineteen

THE Emin Pasha expedition had been controversial ever since its inception but criticism of its various aspects reached the zenith in late 1890 as Stanley began his US tour. Stanley was censured for many different things: the self-regarding and self-justifying account he gave of the expedition in his book; his employment of Tippu Tip as governor of Stanley Falls; the huge loss of life on the expedition; the fact that he had camouflaged an essentially profiteering and freebooting enterprise in a cloak of humanitarianism and religiosity; the unfavourable impact of the expedition on Africa; and, most of all, the scandal of the Rear Column.

To some critics the very 'methodology' of the Emin expedition was wrongheaded. Jackson argued forcefully that Thomson, not Stanley, should have been chosen to lead it. Stanley had grossly exaggerated the perils of Masailand and had used his own peculiar employment contract with Leopold as a lever to force the expedition to proceed by the Congo route. From this one decision came the 'double-cross' by the Belgian state, the horrors of the Ituri and the fiasco of the Rear Column. Peters, the most vociferous critic of Stanley, argued that the original mistake was compounded with numerous other contingent errors made by the leader during the course of the enterprise: the decision to employ Tippu Tip, the failure to assist Mwanga, the mendacious identification of Ruwenzori with the 'Mountains of the Moon' and most of all the use of force to compel Emin to go to Zanzibar. Peters described the Stanley expedition as being 'like working an equation with totally unnecessary circuitous ways and formulas ... neither the ostensible nor the real object has been obtained ... even the Mahdi himself could not have been more injurious to the civilising of the Upper Nile than Stanley has been in reality ... if Stanley had stuck fast in the swamps of the Aruwimi, Emin Pasha would at this day, according to all human calculation, be still in Wadelai in a perfectly secure position ... therefore it must be stated that Stanley's enterprise has been absolutely hurtful in its effects for the general interests of humanity, and for the special interests of England.'

When Stanley published his own account of the expedition in 'In Darkest Africa', the huge commercial success of the book soon gave way to doubts and misgivings engendered by the very tone of the whirlwind fifty-day production. Particular exception was taken to Stanley's insistence that he was the agent of Providence and God's elect, that his survival was evidence of some divine favour. Stanley added to this motif on his American tour when he declared: 'I am back from the gloom of a country much of which is unknown to the glory of One that is the Light of the World.' When Stanley taunted England with no longer possessing any Drakes or Raleighs the London Star retorted: 'He seems to be unaware that since those glorious days of piracy moral ideas have advanced somewhat . . . without stigmatising the Sunday-school sentiments about Providence which Mr

Stanley sent home from time to time for the "unco guide" as necessarily humbug, it is plain, in the light of his general character, that even under the most favourable construction they are only thinly veiled egoism, and that of a very bullying and offensive kind.' Another reviewer queried how the constant references to God's providence were to be squared with the 'supernatural diablerie' Stanley claimed to see at work in the destruction of the Rear Column. The fact was that Stanley left a rearguard full of invalids in the power of an Arab he considered unreliable, in the charge of an inept hot-tempered officer, in the middle of hostile, malaria-ridden country. Surely the thesis of the Evil One was supererogatory? Yet others queried the concomitance of the alleged Christian feeling alongside a ruthless commercial insistence that no other members of the expedition could publish their accounts until six months after Stanley's 'official' version had appeared.

Stanley's references to God and Christianity were considered particularly unacceptable in the light of the ruthless real politic attitude he had displayed during the expedition. Criticism focused on three areas: Stanley's seeming indifference to the slave trade and Tippu Tip's role in it; the fact that the one real concrete result of the expedition was to enlarge the area open to slavers; and the commercial motives behind the expedition.

According to one estimate, three-quarters of the 680 porters used by Stanley on his expedition were slaves. This caused an outcry in the Aborigines' Protection Society in 1890, and Stanley's friend Henry Wellcome had to battle against many angry interruptions at a special meeting of the Society to point out that it was impossible for any African explorer to determine with certainty who were and were not slaves; even Livingstone on occasion had been forced to employ slaves. As for Tippu Tip, this was largely a red herring peddled by men who basked in gross ignorance. The Belgian Vangele had already testified on his return to Brussels that Tippu acted impeccably throughout towards the expedition, despite being under considerable provocation from Barttelot. If any blame attached to the hiring of a known slaver as governor of Stanley Falls, such censure must be laid at Leopold's door, not Stanley's. Stanley also ingeniously conflated Christianity with the decision to use Tippu by quoting the biblical passage that there is more joy in heaven over the one sinner who repents.

The critics were on firmer ground in asserting that Stanley's expedition had blazed a trail for slavers to follow. Until Stanley opened up the Aruwimi and Ituri, the tribes there had held their own against the slavers. His penetration of their forest fastnesses sealed their doom. The same was likely to be true of Equatoria; the only question to be resolved was whether the Arabs and the Manyema or the Mahdists would be master there. Before Stanley's coming Emin ran a successful state in Equatoria. Stanley's advent destroyed all that. What made this so unacceptable was his real politic approach, which seemed to deliver to the West the worst of all possible worlds. In his despatches Stanley took Captain Deane to task for his conflict with the Arabs at Stanley Falls: 'the error of judgement which induced Captain Deane to defy the Arabs for the sake of a lying woman who had fled from her master to avoid punishment.' The Saturday Review took Stanley sternly to task for this. 'We are not rabid against slavery, but we very seriously trust that no Englishman will ever fail to commit similar "errors of judgement".'

The third indictment, that the Emin Pasha expedition had been a 'humanitarian' blind to mask commercial freebooting, was the toughest to rebut. It seems clear that there were two main economic motivations to the expedition, one of short-term profit, the other of longer-term economic imperialism. The short-term objective, seizing the estimated £112,000 worth of ivory that Emin had in Equatoria, was a disastrous failure, but this result did not prevent critics asking whether the British public had not originally been gulled into enthusiastic support for a 'rescue' attempt that was more concerned with retrieving elephants' tusks than a short-sighted Prussian naturalist. The long-term objective was to establish a British commercial empire on the headwaters of the Nile. This was why the offer to set up Emin and his followers at Kavirondo on Lake Victoria had originally been made by Mackinnon. His IBEA Company was to be a means of arresting Germany's progress eastward and Leopold's westward. Of course, the two economic motives overlapped, for Mackinnon hoped to finance the nucleus of his commercial empire out of Emin's ivory.

One of the reasons for the ultimate downfall of the Emin expedition, in terms of its real as opposed to ostensible goals, was that it was a geopolitical mess. Officially designed to tweak the noses of the Mahdists in the Sudan by whisking away Emin from their grasp, the expedition's real purpose was to establish British power unofficially in the Lake Victoria region. The expedition thus faced in three main directions: westward towards the Congo, where it complicated the relations between the Congo State and the Arabs; northward towards the Sudan, the Khalifa and the Mahdists; eastward towards the German sphere of influence. The expedition was consequently embroiled in matters of high politics which could be resolved only by war or nation-state diplomacy. The problem to the west was resolved by the Congo-Arab war of 1893; that to the north by the Omdurman campaign in 1898; that to the east by the Anglo-German accord of 1890. In more senses than one, then, the Emin expedition was a 'mission impossible'. The kind of economic imperialism Mackinnon had in mind needed a much clearer field to operate in than was available to Stanley in 1887-9.

There is another point to be made in fairness to Stanley and against his critics. 'Stanley has triumphed, but Central Africa is darker than ever," was a frequent motif of his enemies. But the same critics were not at all pleased when Jephson argued that the corollary to such criticism was to leave Africa to its own devices; he argued that Emin's regime in Equatoria had paid scant attention to the interests of the indigenous blacks and that, in drawing up a balance sheet on the expedition, it was the fate of the aboriginal peoples that should form the centrepiece. This drew a broadside from the 'Thunderer', though the logic of its leader-writer seemed to have been derived from Lewis Carroll: 'The soil, too, itself has rights, as well as savages who live upon it. If it cannot obtain from its aboriginal occupants the measure of development to which it is entitled by its intrinsic capabilities, it will invite strangers to supply its wants.'

All in all, the controversy over the general consequences of the Emin expedition resulted in a draw or stalemate. Even if it was accepted that the entire idea had been misconceived and foolhardy right from the beginning, this was not something that particularly brought Stanley into the dock. As the leader of the expedition, he was the agent of others, and it was the Mackinnons, Huttons, de Wintons and Burdett-Couttses, to say nothing of Leopold and his ilk, who merited the greater censure. Stanley could have maintained his (scarcely unblemished hitherto) reputation intact, had it not been for the ferocious controversy over the Rear Column that gathered steam towards the end of 1890.

In October and November that year, finally released from the legal shackles that had bound them hitherto, the two most virulent anti-Stanley factions published their accounts. First came the posthumous memoirs of Barttelot, as edited by his family; then followed Rose Troup's account of his time with the Rear Column. The substance of the charge in these books had already been anticipated by Casati. The Italian alleged that it was precisely greed for ivory that had led Stanley to the seemingly inexplicable decision to divide the expedition and leave behind a Rear Column; only thus could he hope to recruit enough porters to fetch out of Equatoria the fabled hoards of ivory: 'Instead of sending an exploring detachment to the lake [Albert] under an expert and daring officer, and remaining himself behind to direct the more important work, thus securing the triumph of the undertaking, his inordinate desire for doing everything himself, and his ardent wish not to let a crumb of glory fall into the lap of others, impelled Stanley (forgetful of the charge which had been entrusted to him and not to others) to give summary orders, placing between himself and the principal column an enormous distance, an impenetrable forest, silence and doubt, for long consecutive months.'

The Barttelot book charged Stanley with 'malignity, ingratitude, desertion and misrepresentation' and drew from the press the clamour that Stanley ought to cancel his US tour to answer the charges. The Birmingham Post described the published Barttelot diaries as leaving the 'impression of the perfectly frank, full and unreserved utterances of an English gentleman'. The battleground had now moved beyond the simple point first advanced in 1889 by the Barttelot family, that Stanley had left the Major imprecise instructions. The charge had become a threefold one: Stanley had misled Barttelot and all his other officers, who thought they were engaged on a humanitarian mission when their real objective was to enrich the Mackinnon IBEA Company; he had made a disastrous error by plunging into the Ituri forest without taking his entire force; he was responsible for what had happened to Barttelot,

since he took all the best men with him, leaving Barttelot with the sick and cripples and the ticklish problem of getting Tippu Tip to provide porters.

Stanley could have met these allegations with a discreet silence or a dignified rejoinder. But this was not his way. At first he tried the tactic of pretending that the Barttelot family's charges were infantile and beneath contempt. If he himself was at fault for appointing Barttelot to command of the Rear Column, 'I would then say that if Major Barttelot had not been born, he surely had never existed, therefore the fault lay with his parents; or, if the British government had not seen fit to elevate this young man to the rank of major, I would not have supposed him to be capable of commanding a few hundred men.'

Since this sophistry failed to blunt the daily criticisms of his leadership, Stanley moved on to phase two of his campaign. He gave an interview to the London correspondent of the New York Herald shortly before his departure for the USA. Looking out over his gold-rimmed spectacles and puffing at a cigar throughout the interview, Stanley claimed to have the hidden story of the Rear Column. He had not revealed it before out of regard for the Barttelot family, but since they had repaid his compassion with vindictiveness, he now wanted to set the record straight. The gist of the matter was that Barttelot had been killed rather than murdered, and he had incontrovertible proof of this in reports from Ward and Bonny. Why, then, did you not divulge this material in 'In Darkest Africa', asked the reporter. I did not want to blacken Barttelot's name, replied Stanley, but in view of the Barttelot family's attitude he now saw that his reticence was misplaced.

The reporter asked him what he meant by saying that Barttelot was killed rather than murdered. Stanley said that if the man who shot Barttelot had been tried before an English jury he would have been found 'not guilty'. When the Herald man pressed him further, Stanley with many a wink and nod asked him to consider what were the grounds in English law for a verdict of 'justifiable homicide'. Without saying so in so many words, Stanley left the clear impression that Sanga had shot Barttelot because the Major had taken his wife into concubinage.

The cunning of this ploy was that it plugged into rumours that had long been current about the sexual behaviour of white men on the Congo. Some even hinted that the inactivity of the Rear Column for eleven months was due to sexual bewitchment by the houris whom Tippu Tip had sent to Yambuya to beguile the whites. But Stanley's critics sensed they had their man in a trap. Since he claimed to have doctored the true evidence about Barttelot when he published In Darkest Africa, it followed that he must have it; he should therefore produce it to substantiate his flimsy story. You can suppress evidence and not make charges, or you can produce your evidence and make charges, the critics pointed out gleefully in anticipation of a decisive victory over Stanley; what you cannot do is make charges and suppress your evidence. It was generally considered that Stanley had gone too far this time and fallen into a trap of his own making.

The row between Stanley and the Barttelot family was the news sensation of autumn 1890. Even Queen Victoria followed it with a horrified fascination though she was later to find the Rear Column story 'too horrible to write about'. The French in particular rubbed their hands in pleasure at this internal crisis in 'perfidious Albion' and called for a lawsuit or tribunal to determine the true facts about the Rear Column. Le Figaro crowed triumphantly: 'Now that an Englishman and not a Frenchman like de Brazza; not a German like Peters and Emin Pasha; not a Russian like Dr Junker; nor an Italian like the Catholic missionaries, but an out and out genuine son of Albion makes accusations against Stanley, the British public condescends to listen.' Foreign criticism simply enraged the British press further against Stanley, who was accused of besmirching Britain and the Empire in the eyes of foreigners.

All Stanley's enemies rushed in for the kill they sensed was imminent. The New York World suggested that Stanley's real motive for abandoning the Rear Column was diplomatic. Stanley was sent to Equatoria to spike Germany's guns. Because he was in a race with the Germans he had to press on at full speed and leave the Rear Column to its fate; additionally, Emin was pulled out of Equatoria to prevent the province from passing under German protection. The French explorer du Chaillu was canvassed for his opinion; it was known that he was angry with Stanley for not having, in 'In Darkest Africa' given him credit for the first discovery of the pygmies. Du Chaillu expressed his opinion forcibly that the motive for Sanga's killing of Barttelot was absurd: 'those blacks do not shoot for their women. On the contrary, they will give them to you with open hands. No black would think of killing a white man for such a trifling offence in Africa.'

The indictment against Stanley seemed overwhelming when Rose Troup brought out his account of the Rear Column within weeks of the life of Barttelot; Troup's would have been the first set of memoirs in the field had not Stanley secured an injunction in line with the six-month clause. But Troup took ample revenge in his book. He bitterly attacked Stanley for leaving Barttelot in charge at Yambuya, for the confusion of his orders. In newspaper interviews he accused Stanley of being muddled in his facts about the Rear Column and relying entirely on hearsay. As for the slaying of Barttelot, Stanley's story about a sexual motive was utter nonsense. The shot was fired at point-blank range and was a spontaneous reaction to the fact that Barttelot raised a club to Sanga's wife. The general consensus on the Troup revelations was that they hammered another nail into the coffin of Stanley's reputation.

Stanley's first reaction was weak. He accused Troup of cowardice in not deposing Barttelot and taking over command, even though he could have been shot for mutiny had he attempted to do so. His appeal to Ward also fell on stony ground. Although Ward when interviewed showed a desire to keep out of the entire controversy, he revealed his hand by speaking of Barttelot's death as 'murder' (rather than 'justifiable homicide' as in the Stanley version) and spoke of the expedition's taking Emin prisoner rather than rescuing him. But in the euphoria of having rebutted the sexual innuendo against Barttelot, Stanley's opponents overlooked the fact that Troup's book was highly critical of Barttelot. This was a dormant volcano waiting to erupt.

Only those who knew not Stanley thought that this would be the end of the affair. The explorer Grant had a shrewder appreciation than most of the likely outcome. 'I have never blamed Stanley, who will come out of it, I have no doubt, with flying colours. He is not the man to put himself in the wrong, and when "scratched" will show desperate fight and quite right too ... the correspondence of the Barttelot family shows them all to be burnt by the same iron - they look upon natives as only fit to be kicked and shot - they would never take a native's word - oh no - Mr Stanley has no right to believe in them!'

With exquisite timing Stanley coaxed all his enemies to reveal themselves by appearing to have no answer to the fresh spate of criticisms. Then he unleashed his Caliban. It will be remembered that none of Bonny's eyewitness accounts had yet seen the light of day. Suddenly, at the end of the first week of November, all Britain reeled under the impact of the new disclosures about Barttelot, made by a man who had actually been present during the darkest days of the Rear Column. Bonny told the world that, far from being a perfect English gentleman, Barttelot was as close to a raving lunatic as anyone outside an asylum could come. He had gone around camp with an evil leer on his face, poking people with a pointed stick. He had kicked the boy Soudi to death and shot a soldier for stealing goat meat. He had beaten one man's brains out and crept up behind a Manyema chief and stabbed him in the back. Finally - which led to his death - he had kicked Sanga's wife in the stomach. In addition, he had accused Stanley of being a poisoner, tasted a bit of potassium cyanide on his tongue to see if it could be detected in coffee, and announced that Stanley had actually murdered the Pocock brothers during the 1874-7 expedition.

Even while the public sat stunned under the impact of this dark tale, the Stanley counterattack began. Numerous anti-Barttelot witnesses came forward to attest to the circumstantial truth of Bonny's account. Captain Stanhope, who had seen Barttelot in action at Yambuya, endorsed the Stanley-Bonny account. A correspondent from Cairo reported that Barttelot's army colleagues who had served with him in Egypt were unanimous that he must have been justly slain. Ward, too, fell into the Stanley trap. Riled that Stanley had accused him also of cowardice in not relieving Barttelot of his command, he started another hare by accusing Governor-General Jannsens of the Congo Free State of incompetence in not sending his idle steamers up the Aruwimi to relieve the Rear Column. This simply had the effect of drawing Jannsens too into the Stanley camp;

he declared roundly that all Congo forces fully supported the Bonny/Stanley story. Stanley's brother-in-law Frederick Myers wrote in triumph to the EPRE committee that a comparison of the Barttelot and Bonny diaries showed the Major as 'a mean and jealous spirit throughout. . . one cannot accept Barttelot as a specimen of the generous though headstrong British officer. He was plainly a spiteful and self-seeking person.'

But the evil genius of Bonny had not yet finished weaving its spell. He pointed out artfully that Barttelot's vile temper at Yambuya had an organic connection with Jameson's monumental error in sketching the cannibal feast, since this story ran up and down the Congo and Barttelot feared that he would be held responsible for his friend's indiscretion and lose his commission. By this time it was two years since the Jameson story had first surfaced, and most of the public had forgotten it, if they had ever known it in the first place. Foreseeing that if the Jameson story again hit the headlines, it would drag the Major down with it, the Barttelot family made the bad mistake of launching an attack on Assad Farran, the Syrian who had first broken the story, calling him a liar who hated the Major 'with true Eastern intensity'. The general bemused reaction was: who is Assad Farran? The Times soon indulged that

curiosity by printing in full Assad Farran's 1888 affidavit on Jameson and Barttelot.

Here was startling ammunition for the pro-Stanley camp, since Farran's account of Barttelot's brutality and Jameson's monstrous act of inhumanity predated by a full two years the public controversy over the Rear Column. Immediately there were signs of a swing back in public opinion in favour of Stanley. In vain did the anti-Stanley faction exclaim that the charges against Jameson were incredible, or recruit Rider Haggard to say that he knew both Stanley and Jameson and would prefer to take the word of the latter. Bigger guns sounded on the Stanley side, confirming the Jameson story in detail. Schweinfurth confirmed Assad Farran's story from his private sources, while the Independence Beige endorsed it from the archives of the Free State and referred readers back to an 1888 issue setting the case out in detail. The French pounced on another glorious chance to rub the noses of the British in the mire. 'These stories certainly interfere with the Biblical varnish with which pious England likes to cover her most selfish enterprises. They make it difficult to continue the campaign of vilification which the British press wages against the proceedings of our countrymen. Ah! if one of them had been guilty of any one of these acts which seem to have constituted the daily life of Mr Stanley, what cries, what fits of anger, what indignant expostulations would have broken out among our virtuous neighbours! . .. Let us compare our countrymen with the English. We have fewer angelic pretensions; but on which side is the spirit of humanity?'

Faced with this powerful backlash, the supporters of Barttelot and Jameson tried to shift the ground of the debate on to the reliability of the sources for the cannibal feast story. One target was the Assad Farran affidavit. 'Before whom was the affidavit sworn? It is a novelty to have that sort of legal business transacted in the heart of Africa. Nor were we aware that the natives of those parts were sufficiently civilised to not only know the meaning of affidavits, but to be capable of drawing them up in their own handwriting.' But this sort of legal nitpicking was effectively disposed of by an Australian correspondent with first-hand knowledge of the Congo. He pointed out that a judicial enquiry would exclude much vital material because of the rules of evidence: 'if all history was to be credited only on such evidence as a judge receives at nisi prius, history would be nearly a blank page.'

In any event, the case for the defence of Jameson was soon blown sky-high by a singular error on the part of the Jameson family. Hoping to clear her late husband's name, the young Mrs Jameson published a private letter in which Jameson admitted to being the (albeit unwitting) cause of the girl's death and cannibalism. Some of Stanley's attackers made a 180-degree turn. The Globe, previously one of Stanley's sternest critics, tore holes in Jameson's defence that he thought the locals simply wanted to get doti from him when they offered a sacrificial victim in return for cloth. 'If that was his belief, it appears extremely singular, to say the least of it, that he should have at once agreed to be victimised.' Nor could it be believed that he gave cloth to all who asked, so he must have done it to satisfy a morbid curiosity. Also, why did he not intervene when the girl was produced?

Further grist was added to the Stanley mill when it was pointed out that the EPRE committee had actually had the private letter to Mrs Jameson in its hands when it forced Assad Farran to make his retraction; in other words it forced him to retract what it already knew to be true. Not surprisingly Myers again pounced. In further letters to Mackinnon he pointed out that it was now universally accepted as a plain fact that Jameson was guilty as charged of the cannibalistic incident. 'It is plain that the diaries were written under the moral influence of Barttelot and coloured by Barttelot's hatred of Stanley.' He scoffed at Andrew Jameson's statement in The Times that his brother had behaved like a gentleman and that there was not a vestige of proof to the contrary. Myers commented: 'one wonders still further in what school of gentility Mr Andrew Jameson's notions have been formed.'

The Jameson family were reluctant to accept the overwhelming verdict that their most distinguished scion had penetrated the heart of darkness. Mrs Ethel Jameson pestered the EPRE committee for all relevant documentation, including Assad Farran's denial under duress that her husband had sketched the cannibal feast. Then she and Andrew, her husband's brother, set out for Zanzibar to try to get a different version from Tippu Tip. Euan-Smith, firmly in the Stanley camp, jauntily reported her arrival in February 1891. 'She is rich, pretty, about 24, and does not seem to object to the notoriety cast on her - she probably will soon write a new book.' Andrew Jameson travelled inland as far as Mpwapwa but with scant results for his cause. Not until Tippu himself arrived in Zanzibar did Mrs Jameson get satisfaction. As loyal to Jameson in death as he had been in life, Tippu roundly denounced Stanley as a liar and said that the cannibal story was an absurd fabrication. Alas, on this occasion it was Stanley who was right and Tippu wrong.

Stanley's counterattack had seen off the Barttelot and Jameson families decisively but his obfuscatory tactics did not entirely escape notice. The New York Herald commented that in the maelstrom of scandal surrounding Barttelot and Jameson, some of the original charges concerning the management of the Rear Column seemed to be slipping from sight. A London commentator put it more trenchantly: 'Mr Stanley came in like a lion last spring. It can hardly be said that he goes out like a lamb, for there is nothing that is very lamb-like in his composition. We must seek some other comparison. Shall we say he goes out like a cuttle-fish, which covers its retreat with a cloud of darkness?'

The truth was that, Samson-like, Stanley was able to pull down the entire temple of the Emin Pasha expedition with him but could not arrest his own crash. Not even his closest friends could exculpate him from negligence or errors in his handling of the Rear Column. The very strongest case for the defence had to contain some criticism. This comes through clearly in the judicious assessment made by Harry Johnston. First he placed Stanley in context as a true Africanist, in contrast to the present Congo officialdom. Next he ventured the conjecture that Barttelot in the latter stages at Yambuya had been insane - a common sequel to fever in the Congo. Then he pointed out that nobody had ever been able to pin on Stanley the charges of terrible brutality that had stuck to Barttelot and he reminded his readers of what those terrible floggings involved. 'It means the man's whole back, shoulders and thighs would be a pulpy mass of churned-up flesh, that the nervous system would receive such a shock that the flogged man would probably die of the effects, if he did not succumb quicker to the injuries sustained by his kidneys and other internal organs, which the flogging over the small of the back would most certainly affect.'

But he blamed Stanley for the imprecision of his orders to the Rear Column. Insofar as they ordered an advance, they were impracticable given the human jetsam he left behind. 'We can scarcely understand how it is he expected the wretched rearguard, under much greater difficulties, to make the same journey seven times over which he had barely succeeded in effecting on the first occasion ... History will . . . say that at worst Mr Stanley made a few regrettable mistakes, and did not bestow sufficient care on the condition in which he left the Rear Guard . . . but that he accomplished magnificently one of the most splendid feats performed in this or any century - the rescue of Emin Pasha and three journeys through the trackless forests of the Congo. History will say of Stanley that he was the Napoleon Bonaparte of African exploration, with all Napoleon's greatness and some of his failings.'

This was essentially the judgement the Emin Pasha committee came to when it drew up its final report. Lavish praise was poured on Stanley, but his handling of the Rear Column was criticised. Predictably, Stanley found this intolerable. He could never bear any criticism, no matter how intermingled and overgrown by praise. He told Mackinnon he found the final report a disgrace and an insult to him and all the survivors. He had been accused in the press of maligning the dead who could not answer back; now the committee had inverted this and by raising nil nisi bonum to a new power, had left him angry and speechless. 'As the pamphlet now stands, it is a condemnation of us who lived, and a defence of those who are dead. The dead do not require any defence, they require sympathy, forgiveness and peace, and the living require only justice. 'To make his displeasure palpable he signed himself 'Yours faithfully' instead of the 'Yours ever' he had used with Mackinnon for a decade; relations continued frosty for a couple of months.

Yet however much he blustered, Stanley could hardly fail to see that the controversy over the Emin expedition had irretrievably tarnished his reputation. His chances of honours in Britain or further commands in Africa had been significantly reduced. As one of his critics remarked in 1891: 'It is improbable that, in any case, he will have the chance of leading another English expedition; but if he ever induces another English gentleman to serve under him, that Englishman's relatives will have a good case for putting him under restraint as a lunatic.'

Worst of all crosses for Stanley to bear was that his religious and devotional sentiments were no longer taken seriously. Early reviewers of his book contrasted his harsh and punitive actions with the religious saturation of the sentiments in which he described his pagan worship of power. Insofar as there was a religious sensibility present, it was that of a Celtic heathen: 'that his belief in the supernatural is strong almost to superstition is evident to anyone who knows him or is familiar with his writings.' Troup's darts were particularly aimed at this aspect of Stanley. He confessed himself surprised at the abundance of providential religiosity in 'In Darkest Africa', as he had seen no signs of either overt Christianity (in the form of prayers) or its implicit variety (in the shape of devoutness or compassion). Indeed he had seen precious little vestige of elementary humanity. Troup once exasperatedly exclaimed that Stanley had no more philanthropy in him than 'my boot'.

Stanley had only himself to blame for the frequent charges of humbug he incurred. He actually had the effrontery to say that he foresaw ultimate good from the Rear Column controversy, since the quest for truth proved European moral superiority!) His Nietzschean high-mindedness also left people cold. The Star described Stanley's 'Gospel of Enterprise' as being cant of the same order as Carnegie's 'Gospel of Wealth'; 'it is impossible to believe that the thinking portion of the working classes have the smallest inclination to make a hero of this man.' But it would be a mistake to set his religious sentiments down to humbug. Stanley's God was always the wrathful chastising Yahweh of the Old Testament, not the Jesus Christ of the New. The conflation Yahweh/Wotan - most appropriate for a Nietzschean - emerges clearly in the kind of missionary he admired. Always it was the men of action, the Livingstones and the Mackays, he preferred, not the preachers or contemplatives.

After the bruising experience of the Rear Column controversy, it was only to be expected that Stanley's later career would be mired in shallows. Since it was the New York Herald that launched Stanley on his career as African explorer, it is appropriate for that organ to have the last word on the tattered shreds of reputation left to Stanley in 1891. 'Whatever else these terrible charges and counter charges may have done or left undone, they have killed African exploration as a profession.' If Stanley was to have any future in Africa, it would have to be sought in the career of another Nietzschean 'superman', someone else who regarded himself as inhabiting a special sphere of morality, beyond good and evil. In the Europe of the 1890s that meant one man: Leopold of Belgium.

Chapter Twenty

THE return of Stanley from the Emin Pasha expedition brought to a head his latent conflict with Leopold. Both were men who understood only power, dominance and manipulation; both therefore were exercised to discover a way to exploit the other. Leopold still laboured under the illusion that it was he, not Mackinnon, who loomed largest in Stanley's future African plans. Stanley fostered the illusion and presented the results of the Emin expedition as a great boon for Leopold's Congo: he had secured peace with the Arabs by appointing Tippu Tip as governor of Stanley Falls; he had demonstrated that a great revenue could be drawn from the Ituri forest; and he had extended the territory of the Free State to Lake Albert. Leopold meanwhile was full of praise for Stanley's Promethean achievements; he told Mackinnon that there was scarcely a single one of Africa's mysteries that Stanley had not solved.

But in their intimate letters and journals the two men told a different story. From the Shepheard's Hotel in Cairo in January 1890 Stanley wrote to tell Mackinnon what he really thought of the King. Explaining that in no circumstances would he ever work for him again, he went on: 'I have strong objections to his ingratitude to me in 1885 and 1886. I do not feel like forgiving him for imprisoning me in my room for two years awaiting orders.' Stanley's anger was increased by the reflection that at forty-nine he was past his peak as an African explorer; in the limbo of 1885, when he was still forty-four, it would have been a different story. 'It may be that he has at last made up his mind to that great mission he has so often referred to verbally and in writing. I think, however, that though he remembers "Time is pressing" when he needs me, he forgets how time has flown with me ... I feel like an old man today.'

Leopold's position was different. He still saw a use for Stanley's abilities, provided he could not interfere with his own nefarious schemes in the Congo State; perhaps a position as viceroy in the as yet unconquered territories of Katanga, Aruwimi or Manyema might be the answer? But Stanley knew Leopold too well by now to consent to be shunted into a backwater; to the monarch's consternation he turned down all such 'minor' African appointments. Next Leopold thought of making Stanley the Belgian plenipotentiary to the 1889-90 anti-slavery conference. Again Stanley rebuffed him, saying he had no interest in a commission that was a mere talking shop and a waste of time. His health was a further barrier, and he would need rest and recuperation before returning to Europe from Egypt.

Leopold, whose spies kept him well informed on all matters, knew very well that Stanley's health was robust - vigorous enough to allow him to work sixteen hours a day on his book. He chose to comment ironically on Stanley's valetudinarian status in Cairo. This irritated Stanley and he noted with asperity in his journal that Leopold was one of those people who never accepted illness as an excuse. When de Vaux, Borchgrave's predecessor, was suffering from kidney disease, Leopold seemed amazed that he could not work like a Trojan. In 1882 and again in 1884 Leopold had been impatient when Stanley was prostrated from the after-effects of African fever. Now, after three years on the Emin expedition, Stanley was again expected to need no rest. 'I fear this promise of a big undertaking is but a bait to draw me home the quicker. 'Here was a case of the biter bit. No one had less sympathy for illness (in others) than Stanley himself; it was but poetic justice that he should suffer under the lash of another autocrat with Erewhonian leanings.

Stanley's instincts on the international conference for the suppression of the slave trade were sound, for this was yet another of Leopold's stalking horses to mask his base economic designs. It will be remembered that in 1887 Leopold had persuaded the Belgian government to authorise a premium bond issue. When the bonds came on the market in February 1888 Leopold had to purchase large numbers of them himself to hold share prices steady. But by the time the second instalment of the premium bond issue was ready to be floated, their quoted opening price was less than the market price of the first batch. Even though the Belgian government offered to purchase them, only a third of the second issue was taken up. By late 1888 it was clear that Leopold could not raise enough on the stock market to pay for the day-to-day administration of the Congo, especially since the only permitted tax (export duties) produced negligible amounts. Meanwhile other financial possibilities were non-starters. Ferry's offer of a 20-million franc lottery in 1885 was not honoured by the incoming Freycinet administration in France and it was not until 1888 that the French Bourse authorised a loan lottery. The Rothschilds turned down Leopold's application for a loan, which led the King to weep crocodile tears over the financial community's lack of confidence in him.

From Leopold's point of view there were some interesting straws in the Congo wind if he could only keep the Free State solvent for a while longer. The Belgian railway group led by Captain Albert Thys (in whose favour Leopold had double-crossed the Hutton/Stanley/Mackinnon consortium in 1886) had by entrepreneurial dynamism raised a million francs and formed a Compagnie du Congo pour le commerce et l'industrie. After a year Strauch was sacked as administrator- general of the EIC and Thys appointed in his place. Following this, Leopold gulled Belgian minister Bernaert into making a 10-million franc loan to the railway syndicate. This, plus help from foreign capital, led to the formation in July 1889 of the Compagnie du Chemin de Fer du Congo (with 71 per cent of the capital from Belgian sources). Additionally three new companies were formed: for trading, cattle-raising, and the purchase of ivory and rubber (Societe Beige du Haut Congo).

To parlay his bets until the potential wealth of the Congo could be released, Leopold advanced a troika of ideas. There was political action to get a direct loan from the Belgian treasury. There was (most important of all for the future) the creation of a new economic system for the production of wealth by the Congo state apparatus itself; alienating 'vacant lands' to the State enabled Leopold to construct a state monopoly. And there was an attempt to revise the clauses of the 1885 Berlin treaty that prohibited the levying of import duties.

As before, Leopold tried his old trick of pretending to be concerned with humanitarian ideals, so as to mask his sordid cupidity. His aim was to set up protectionist barriers in the Congo under the guise of stamping out the slave trade. But Leopold had gulled his audiences once too often. To the King's annoyance the Dutch immediately saw through to his base motives. More seriously, so did Emile Banning, one of the architects of the Berlin treaty and erstwhile admirer and supporter of the King; a decisive rift between the two men followed soon after. This was a serious check to the monarch at the very time that he was beginning to win the propaganda battle for Belgian public opinion and suck the parliament into his Congo quicksands. He needed a powerful opinion-former and who better than Stanley, in early 1890 still the unsullied 'hero' of Emin's rescue, not the tarnished angel he was to appear a year later.

Stanley was quite prepared to play Leopold's games as long as they did not conflict with his own interests. He produced a paean to Leopold that satisfied the King but committed him (Stanley) to nothing. 'What does the greatness of a monarch consist in? If it is the extent of his territory, then the Emperor of Russia is the greatest of all. If it is the splendour and power of military organisation, then William II takes first place. But if royal greatness consists in the wisdom and goodness of a sovereign leading his people with the solicitude of a shepherd watching over his flock, then the greatest sovereign is your own.'

Such was the background when Stanley made his week-long visit to Leopold between 19 and 26 April 1890. The King treated his most famous agent as visiting royalty and used the visit to 'sell' the Congo, pointing out that Stanley on the Emin expedition had discovered groundnuts, tobacco, cattle, copper, iron and gold: 'in the recent scramble we have drawn the winning ticket'. After a day of banquets and junketings the two men got down to serious talking on 20 April. Leopold sat with his back to the window on one side of a marble-topped table. Stanley sat facing him. Time seemed to have stood still since the last audience more than three years earlier, except that Leopold's brown beard was now white from ear to ear and his own hair, then iron-grey, was now 'as white as Snowdon in winter'.

Leopold posed detailed questions about the country between the Aruwimi and Lake Albert. Stanley painted a glowing picture of the rubber to be extracted there and proposed an elephant reserve in the Ituri, where herds would still remain when every single pachyderm had been exterminated elsewhere; it must be stressed that his interest was in the continuance of the ivory trade, not nature conservancy. He also argued that the ferocious tribes of the area could be brought round to white rule by the kind of patient and fair treatment he had shown to the Bangala and the Soko on the Congo.

In the afternoon the subject switched to Emin, and Stanley poured out his now familiar litany of criticism of the ill-fated Pasha. When he mentioned with contempt Emin's excessive liking for women, it is legitimate to assume that the famed libertine and roue Leopold suppressed a smile. When the talks resumed the next day it was Emin's troops, especially the 6000 left behind at Kavalli's under Selim Bay, that most engaged Leopold and he discussed the feasibility of sending Belgian officers to incorporate this legion of the lost into the Congo armies.

In the afternoon Stanley raised the project dearest to his heart: the suppression of Arab slavery and the destruction of Tippu Tip's power between Stanley Falls and Lake Tanganyika. He stressed to Leopold that this was much more important than the proposed Welle exploration and would need no more than 2500 troops to accomplish. Besides, if the slavers were not halted in their tracks they themselves would ascend the Welle and make common cause with the rebels in Equatoria. If this combined force in turn linked arms with the Mahdists, all Africa would be carved in two and all Leopold's plans turned to dust. How long would the total project take, Leopold asked? About a year, Stanley replied, and he felt compelled to add that the lands south of Stanley Falls to Tanganyika were much more valuable commercially than the Nile littoral the King seemed to hanker after.

The morning of the fourth day was spent discussing boundary disputes with the French. At one point Leopold rang a bell and van Kerkhoven, one of Stanley's Congo veterans, came in, to be briefed on Stanley's plans for the occupation of the Welle. In the afternoon Stanley went to the anti-slavery conference in Brussels to give an address on the methods used by the Arab slavers. He told the delegates that the key to suppression of the slave trade was an arms embargo; neither Arab slavery nor Mirambo's empire would have been possible without guns and gunpowder.

It was not until the fifth day of their talks that Leopold finally unveiled his proposed future plans for Stanley. Others could expel the Arabs and deal with the French but 'there is only one man capable of making my secret mission a success and that is Stanley, the great explorer and founder of the Congo State.' Leopold spoke the words artfully with a smile, his arms riding up and down histrionically as he put strong emphasis on certain words. He then revealed that he wanted Stanley to command a military expedition to defeat the Khalifa and take Khartoum.

Stanley's first reaction was that such an idea was a chimera. But would you undertake it if you had sufficient resources, Leopold persisted? Of course, Stanley replied. Leopold went on to assert that he had the money to achieve the project, and make Stanley a rich man into the bargain. Stanley tested out the proposition by telling the King that he would need 12,000 European troops. At this Leopold's face fell and he asked how many black troops could do the job instead. Stanley looked grave and assured the monarch that this would be a task for 50,000 crack troops, all from elite squads.

Can't you do with less, asked a disappointed Leopold. Stanley replied that the absolute minimum would be 5000 whites and 10,000 blacks. A disconsolate Leopold shook his head and said white troops were out of the question but he could rise to 20,000 blacks from the warlike tribes of the Congo. At this Stanley grimaced and pointed out that such men would have to be collected from their tribes, then welded into a fighting force. They would then be fighting the best army in Africa on hostile soil, outnumbered four to one. To achieve success against those odds, four years' hard training would be required, by which time Stanley would be too old to command.

While Leopold was still absorbing this disappointment, Stanley moved in for the knock-out blow. Patiently he explained the logistics of the Congo. Apart from the distances to be covered, there was food, transport and subsistence; even 1000 men would need fifty whaleboats to carry them, to say nothing of the army of porters and back-up staff. Besides, his own experience of white officers on the Congo made Stanley doubtful they would stay a four-year course. For all these reasons the capture of Khartoum from the Congo was an impossibility with Leopold's current resources. If he had 5000 seasoned Egyptian troops, the case might be very different. Then he would seize and fortify Fashoda before pressing on to Abba Island and thence to Omdurman and triumph. Even so, he would be talking about a campaign lasting six years and costing one million pounds sterling.

Leopold was downcast and the disappointment showed in his words. 'I was under the impression that a man like you would have been more eager for such an adventure as the taking of Khartoum than it seems you are. You might have had £100,000 for yourself if you had consented to the enterprise.' Stanley retorted that he was always eager for fame, glory and adventure but he could not do the impossible; it would be unworthy of him to minimise the obstacles to such a project just so as to flatter the King.

Stanley was thoroughly enjoying the chance to revenge himself on his erstwhile reluctant taskmaster and the opportunity was enhanced during the sixth day of his visit. They got down to the business of discussing the boundary between Mackinnon's sphere of influence and the Congo. Mackinnon had proposed the Semliki River but Leopold complained that this gave the British an unfair advantage and twitted Stanley about showing favouritism to Mackinnon. Stanley tried to divert Leopold's attention by asserting that his long-term advantage was best secured in the Ituri forest. But has not all this been devastated by the Arabs, objected Leopold? At present yes, Stanley replied, but the potential once the Arabs have been expelled is enormous.

As Leopold was beginning to suspect, Stanley was indeed manoeuvring to place all the cards in Mackinnon's hands, just as he had promised Mackinnon he would. Even though he saw no necessary territorial conflict between Leopold's claims and those of the IBEA Company, he was determined to give Mackinnon the benefit of every doubt and to ensure that

Selim Bay's men passed into the service of the British, not the Free State. So, even as he paid lip-service to the King in the royal palace, he was avenging himself for the slight that had rankled since 1886. Had Leopold known his man through and through, he would have realised how dangerous it was to make an enemy of Stanley.

The upshot of this six-day conference was the signature of a treaty between Leopold and Mackinnon (dated 24th May 1890, with Stanley signing on behalf of the Congo Free State). This laid out spheres of influence, with the Congo territory extending as far as the Nile at Lado (the Lado enclave) on the left bank, with the IBEA on the right bank commanding territory down to Lake Tanganyika. Leopold also tried to manipulate Anglo-German rivalry to his own advantage by suggesting that German East Africa would be more secure if the Free State's boundaries extended as far as Bahr-el-Ghazal. But both the Mackinnon treaty and the German machinations foundered on the reef of the Anglo-German agreement of June 1890, defining respective interests in East Africa, which gave Britain the western watershed of the Nile. Leopold's response to this was to send the explorer Becker to Tippu Tip with proposals for a secret treaty whereby Tippu would receive 200,000 francs in return for his ivory and the establishment of three ports in the Bahr-el-Ghazal and one on the Nile itself. Tippu flatly refused.

1890-91 saw further developments in Leopold's African designs in which Stanley was a (sometimes unwilling) agent. In July 1890 Leopold published his will, showing the personal 'sacrifices' the King had made for 'la gloire beige'. The Belgian Parliament then voted the King a 25-million franc loan over ten years, interest-free. At the end of ten years Belgium was entitled to repayment in full or annexation of the Congo State. In the same month the Brussels Anti-Slavery Conference ended with a tacit agreement to allow Leopold to undertake the conquest of the Congo Arabs. At the same time, he used Great Power apathy towards the internal slave trade to persuade the international community to let him levy import duties so that he could fight the slavers. Queen Victoria was bombarded with letters to this effect. Stanley was pressed into service too, though unfortunately for the King, his order to Stanley to write to The Times on the issue coincided with the full flowering of the Rear Column controversy. Stanley stalled again. First he asked for documentary evidence on the budgetary shortfall to be made up by import taxes. Leopold claimed that he did not have the necessary documentation in the archives. Next, as a quid pro quo Stanley asked for the official Free State report on Jameson's cannibal feast. Leopold failed to send it on, anxious not to be embroiled in the controversy, so Stanley neglected to write the letter to The Times.

However, Leopold's campaign for import duties was ultimately crowned with success. An agreement was reached in February 1891 that Leopold could levy a 10 per cent ad valorem import duty across the board. But the King's duplicity fooled fewer people as the years went on. When Stanley was again reluctantly persuaded to speak in favour of suppression of the slave trade during his American tour of 1890-91, his critics hit back with the Monroe doctrine and charges of humbug. Aside from the fact that the USA was pledged to avoid entanglements outside the hemisphere, anti-slavery rhetoric from the Europeans was cant - they wanted American resources to help prop up their own economic interests in Africa. Nobody could be less interested in the reality of slavery than Leopold.

But Leopold was determined to extract the last pound of flesh from Stanley's American visit. He asked him to lobby the US Senate on the import duty question and a US-Congo accord. Despite waiving an extradition treaty, the King had not been able to overcome Senate objections. So he suggested a modification of the 1884 US declaration in the form of additional clauses or amendments. He asked Stanley to try to get a special session of the US Senate to ratify all treaties relating to the Congo, using a press campaign ostensibly aimed at other objectives. How, he asked, could anyone in the USA - the home of protectionism - object to a picayune secondary tax of 6 per cent on alcohol? 'What can be done? I know Americans do not like to be bothered with affairs outside their magnificent continent, but they have commercial and other treaties with various powers European and African . . . could you not explain this through the American press without giving it the appearance of being suggested by foreigners, for the United States do not like the counsels of the foreigners.' Stanley carried out the commission perfunctorily with a few interviews with Secretary of State Blaine and other luminaries on Capitol Hill.

Leopold by now easily had enough money to support the existing Congo State. But it was his overweening ambition to expand into Katanga and on to the Nile that first led him to the monstrous evil of the extraction of a super-surplus value. The first step was an order in 1891 prohibiting the indigenous inhabitants of the Congo from hunting elephants for ivory or tapping wild rubber. Instead a state monopoly in these commodities was created. It was Banning, now a ferocious critic of Leopold, who pointed out that such a monopoly was not only against the interest of the native population but was expressly forbidden by the Berlin treaty; the Congo was supposed to be policed by the EIC so that the powers could practise free trade there, so Leopold had no right to be buying and selling through a state monopoly.

After attacks from the powers and within Belgium, Leopold was forced in 1892 to modify his position to the point where the Free State divided the 'vacant lands' into three zones, including one where, theoretically, there would be free trade. In fact in the 'free trade zone' a form of bogus competition went on between Leopold's front companies. This head-on collision between the principles of monopoly and free trade fed into the growing clash between Belgians and Arabs. Leopold had to cut out the private trader and ensure that the Arabs sold only to state agents. Seeing the danger looming, Tippu Tip showed Leopold's letter of instruction to the British consul at Zanzibar. In retaliation, and on the principle of sauce for the goose and gander, the British and Germans continued to offer arms and ammunition in exchange for ivory, despite the Brussels protocol signed in 1890. But by 1893 three and a half million francs' worth of ivory was sold in Antwerp, plus one million francs' worth of rubber (this was to double within two years).

In 1891 Leopold tightened his grip on Katanga. An expedition under Stairs was sent to add the territory to the Congo State. Meanwhile Leopold despatched another expedition under Dhanis to occupy Portuguese territory to the south. An explosive confrontation ensued, in the course of which Leopold worked out a madcap scheme for sending a gunboat up the Tagus to hold Lisbon to ransom. The mission was entrusted to Liebrechts, who refused to implement it on grounds of its inherent insanity. Nevertheless a diplomatic settlement in 1891 left Leopold in possession of much of Dhanis' conquests.

Yet since Katanga's copper would take years to exploit, Leopold again schemed to push his frontiers to the Nile, proving that his proposal to Stanley for a conquest of the Sudan was no isolated flash in the pan. Partly he dreamed of becoming the heir to the Pharaohs. But mostly he coveted the vast elephant herds in the southern Sudan and saw Khartoum as the gateway to the Nile, which would give the Congo State an outlet to the Mediterranean, so that it was approachable from both the Adantic and Mediterranean.

Leopold began by sending van Kerkhoven in command of an expedition up the Welle to Wadelai. Van Kerkhoven himself was killed during the bloody progress to the Nile but his second-in-command Lt. Milz made contact with the survivors of Emin's forces and in October 1890 arrived on the bank of the Nile; his successors, however, were driven off three years later by a revolt among Emin's officers. The next Nile development was in 1892 when Salisbury pressed Leopold to renounce the agreement with Mackinnon. Leopold referred Salisbury disingenuously to a Foreign Office communication of May 1890 appearing to show that the British government had no objection to the accord. Further examination showed that it was commercial rights not sovereignty that was being referred to.

But at this point Leopold received unexpected help when France decided to occupy Fashoda. Britain was now prepared to use Leopold as his forces were in situ. In return for the recognition of the Anglo-German agreement, Leopold was offered the lease of Bahr-al-Ghazal and the left bank of the Nile as far north as Fashoda. Leopold then tried to dicker, so as to get Belgian possession guaranteed as long as Belgium was a monarchy. As a concession the left bank up to Fashoda was leased during Leopold's lifetime and Bahr-al-Ghazal on normal notice. This led to angry reactions from France and Germany. The French objected to the Congolese barrier across her line of advance. The Germans protested at the article which allowed Britain a strip of the Congo territory for the passage of the mythical Cape-Cairo railway. Britain was eventually forced to abandon this corridor. Finally, the 1892 Liberal government refused to allow

Rosebery to support Leopold against France, so in August Leopold signed a new treaty with France, allowing him just the Lado enclave.

Where was Stanley in all this politicking? Once again Leopold looked in vain for any support. In 1892 Stanley, a zealous partisan of Lord Rosebery, was engaged in a long-running feud with Sir William Harcourt over the future of Uganda. Stanley campaigned on Rosebery's side in the press and told the British nation that the East African market for African goods could amount to twelve million consumers. The debate between Rosebery and Harcourt supporters became acrimonious. Horace Waller, Stanley's old adversary from 1872, accused the IBEA Company of supporting the slave trade. Harcourt himself had been one of Stanley's bitterest critics during the Rear Column controversy. When Mackinnon met Harcourt and Bryce at the Stanley's home in Richmond Terrace, the sparks predictably flew. The general opinion of Harcourt in Stanley's circle can be gauged from a remark by Mounteney Jephson: 'Harcourt is a politician who goes whichever way the wind blows, even when there isn't any.' Harcourt responded by hitting below the belt. 'I think it a salutary lesson that the Stanley-Emin relief expedition has opened the eyes of the British public a good deal to the importance of these philanthropic-missionary-civilising pretenders. As long as you keep to simple missionaries attending to their own work or discoverers like Livingstone going unattended amongst the savages they are safe enough. But when you come to militant bishops that want annual expeditions, plundering and robbing and killing right and left, it is quite a different thing.'

In the end, although Gladstone had assured Leopold that Britain would definitely be evacuating Uganda, Rosebery's influence was such that Sir Gerald Portal was sent out to establish a protectorate. Gladstone made the mistake of canvassing Stanley's opinion on this expedition and received for his pains a self-righteous screed about how the government would have done better to listen to him in the first place. As Dorothy Stanley remarked: 'I told Mr Gladstone he might keep the letter, he cannot have liked it much.' And it was typical of Stanley in this mood that he would be cold and aloof with potential allies like Lugard, who came to see him about Uganda, but who was regarded by Stanley as too much of a rival for African prestige.

1893 saw a partial rapprochement between Stanley and Leopold, both because the King was able to turn Stanley's feelings of jealousy towards rival Africanists to his own account and because Leopold was pursuing policies close to Stanley's heart. This was the year Leopold finally unleashed his forces under Dhanis against the Congo Arabs and Stanley gave the King his enthusiastic support. When the Belgians emerged victorious, Stanley took all the credit on himself. 'Few in this country know that I am the prime cause of this advance of the Belgians against the Arab slave-raiders. Indeed, people little realise how I have practically destroyed this terrible slave-trade, by cutting it down at its very roots. I have also been as fatal to Tippu-Tib, Rashid, his nephew, who captured Stanley Falls from Captain Deane, Tippu-Tib's son, Muini Mubala, and lastly Said-bin-Abed ... as if I had led the avengers myself, which I was very much solicited to do.'

The other aspect of the entente between Leopold and Stanley concerned Cecil Rhodes. Ever since the publication of Arnot's Garanganze in 1889, Rhodes had been interested in Katanga's copper. His champion Harry Johnston, who shared his dream of a map of Africa coloured red from the Cape to Cairo, was a fervent champion of the proposed Cape-Cairo railway and in 1890 published maps showing the boundary of the Congo Free State falling short of Katanga. It was this action that led Leopold first to protest to Salisbury and then to send Stairs in 1891 to stage an annexing coup d'etat in Katanga.

In 1893 when Leopold moved against the Congo Arabs, opinion in Britain at first inclined to the view that the King was an invader and aggressor; the British continued to supply the Arabs with guns and ammunition from the east coast. Leopold had the idea that Stanley might be able to energise Cecil Rhodes on the Belgian side in return for a railway concession in Katanga. Stanley replied at once. 'With regard to Mr Cecil Rhodes, I beg to say that my personal acquaintance with him extends only to a three hours' conversation with him while at dinner one day last November, during which he gave me reason to believe that he had long ago conceived a highly flattering impression of me. Since 1890 I had looked forward to this meeting, as both of us had mutual friends, who were good enough to carry to me Mr Rhodes's great admiration for my road-making in the Congo and to convey to him my commendations of Mr Rhodes's abilities as a financier, statesman and imperialist.' He warned Leopold that Rhodes was hostile to the Congo Free State both because of the 1891 Katanga seizure and because of the ideological anti-Leopold fuel supplied by H. H. Johnston.

Leopold replied by return to propose a scheme whereby Rhodes would pressurise the British government to recognise the 1890 Mackinnon treaty, in return for which the King would guarantee him facilities for his trans-Africa telegraph line, possibly including an annual subsidy to maintain the telegraph in Uganda and a defensive treaty against the Mahdists. Stanley duly passed on the offer to Rhodes, but Rhodes's suspicion and dislike of Leopold was too great to be overcome. However, Stanley showed his independence from the King by backing Rhodes to the hilt in his war against Lobengula and the Matabele at the end of the year.

Relations between Stanley and Leopold continued superficially cordial until 1895. If anything, it was Leopold who acted deferentially. His agents tried to place an ailing Bonny in the Congo service on Stanley's recommendation, and the King solicited the explorer's opinion even on such matters as the construction of the new harbour at Heist, near Ostend. But in 1895 a major crisis erupted when the Belgian Captain Lothaire arrested the British trader Charles Stokes in the Congo on charges of gun-running. After a hearing before himself and a brother officer, Lothaire led

Stokes out to an immediate execution. The affair caused a sensation in England and lowered public esteem for Leopold's controversial Congo State even more.

Stanley had met Stokes in Cairo in 1890 and was very fond of him. Alarmed by the outcry in England, Leopold had Liebrechts (now Secretary of the Interior for the Congo State) send Stanley the relevant documents, in hopes that he would make another of his interventions in the columns of The Times. But when Stanley read the transcripts of the 'trial' he was appalled. There had been no proper court martial; Lothaire had acted as judge, jury and executioner. Nor could he see what the pretext for a death sentence was; not even Stanley could be persuaded to see that the illegal sale of a few percussion muskets merited the supreme penalty. White men should never swear away each other's lives in Africa, even if Lothaire's actions were not expressly prohibited by the 1894 Anglo-Congolese treaty. In sum, Lothaire's actions were utterly indefensible and a serious blow for all well-wishers of the Congo State. If the documents he examined ever became public, he warned, the scandal in England would be tremendous.

But although Stanley could not defend Leopold's actions over the Stokes affair, he was psychologically incapable of accepting the flood of atrocity stories that now began to flood out of the Congo, exposing a vista of carnage, murder, rape and mayhem not perceived in Europe since the Thirty Years War. He used the bogus argument that the silence of 'six hundred' missionaries in the Congo meant that conditions there could not be as black as they were painted: 'are all the rest of these missionaries paid by the State to keep silence?' The argument was singularly spurious. There were not 600 missionaries in the Congo and those that there were maintained a discreet silence about atrocities out of fear of the wrath of Leopold.

In 1896 when further horror stories reached Europe, Stanley continued to brush them aside in public. A particularly grave series of allegations was published in September 1896 by Captain Salisbury and Mr Parminter, both of whom had resigned in disgust from service with the Congo State. Stanley did his best to rebut them, but as ever he was a bull in a china shop and the newspapers refused to print his 'refutation' as originally written on the grounds that it contained libellous material. Still in a state of willing disbelief Stanley explained to Leopold his theory that the ancient foe, the Dutch House, was responsible for the black propaganda that was utterly destroying the credibility of the Free State in Britain. But his private letter to Leopold betrayed his conviction that there was substance to the stories. 'I would suggest to Your Majesty that something should be done to prevent the continuous supply of Congo sensations because 1905 is not far off, and people, fed as they are with stories of atrocities, will be apt to believe that some of them must be true and that the State ought to be suppressed in consequence ... if England can be persuaded that the Congo government is a disgrace to civilisation, there will undoubtedly be a third Power which will move for the downfall of the State.' Leopold was sufficiency taken aback by this that he promised to suppress all irregularities in the Congo - needless to say the promise was not kept. Although Stanley continued to support Leopold in public - as for instance in the introduction to Guy Burrows' book on the Congo - privately he characterised Leopold's rapacity as 'an erring and ignorant policy'.

The extent to which the two men were far apart emerged from a meeting in Brussels in April 1897. Stanley suggested as a means of dampening down the chorus of international disapproval of the Free State a High Tribunal to deal with all matters affecting foreign subjects in the Congo. Leopold bridled at the suggestion. This would place power in the hands of men who had no commitment to the Congo State. It would be too expensive and the Tribunal might actually demand that the construction workers be properly fed (this from Leopold's own lips)! Besides, how about other nations accepting such interference? Would it be accepted in Cuba, in the Philippines, in Russia? Suppose France sent judges to British Africa or Ireland; imagine the uproar? No, the root cause of the British press campaign was, and always had been, simple hatred of the Congo State; after all Britain was the very last nation to afford recognition in 1885.

One brushed aside Stanley's careful suggestions at one's peril. Stanley brooded on the latest snub. It seemed all the more unacceptable as, in 1896, after the Italian invasion of Abyssinia collapsed at Adowa, Stanley had backed Leopold's scheme for moving into the Italian sphere of influence in Eritrea and Ethiopia, against the advice of friends like Lord Cromer (formerly Sir Evelyn Baring) who saw straight through the King's machinations. The consequence was that although Stanley continued to follow avidly the advance of the Congo railway (completed in 1898), he had little more to do with Leopold. The last contact between the two was when Stanley approached the King for a contribution towards the planned Livingstone monument. The man who had made a personal fortune of £2 million in six years through unspeakably brutal exploitation and rapacity sent - just £20. If ever there was an evil genius in Stanley's life, capable of darkening an already black inner psyche, it was surely Leopold II, King of the Belgians.

Chapter Twenty-One

ON return from Australia Mrs Stanley determined to distract her husband from further thoughts of Africa by encouraging him in a political career. First she had to clear up the uncertainty about his nationality, which had prevented his being knighted in 1890. Correspondence with Lord Salisbury produced the information that the 1870 Naturalisation Act required a potential British subject to have had five years' residence in the United Kingdom. By the skin of his teeth Stanley established his eligibility; between 1872 and 1892 he had spent five years and twenty weeks domiciled in Great Britain. On 20th May 1892 he took the oath and was readmitted to his native nationality.

With the aid of Alexander Bruce, Dolly then persuaded him to become Liberal-Unionist candidate for North Lambeth in the 1892 election. Ten days before the poll the Stanley bandwagon rolled into action. But Stanley was a disastrous candidate. He consented to speak at working-men's clubs but regarded asking any man for his vote as degrading. Totally lacking the common touch, he was ill at ease and irritable during the campaign. To make matters worse, he fought on a highly reactionary platform on imperialism, social discipline and vehement opposition to Home Rule, which in a constituency like North Lambeth was bound to seem aggressive and confrontational.

His first attempt to woo the voters was a disaster. He was unused to the rough and tumble of political meetings and became disturbed and uncoordinated under a hail of heckling and booing. Sensing that he was losing his temper, the crowd stepped up the booing and taunting until nothing else could be heard. He stopped talking, folded his arms and glared fiercely at his tormentors. Dorothy Stanley, perceiving that the entire campaign stood on the brink of disaster, burst into tears and twice tried to rise to her feet only to sink back into her chair. Her evident distress had an effect on the audience, which started to calm down. But before Stanley could resume his speech, she got to her feet and cried out: 'When all of you and I are dead and forgotten, the name of Stanley will live, be revered and loved.' This outburst was greeted with peals of laughter and cries of 'Shame'. Eventually the police had to eject four hecklers before Stanley could limp through to the end of his speech.

On 27th June he addressed the electors from a cart. Again his reactionary sentiments were in evidence. First came a blistering attack on Gladstone and Home Rule and a corresponding encomium for Joseph Chamberlain. Referring to the movement for an eight-hour day, he said that if he had worked only eight hours a day, he would never have got ahead of the Germans in Africa and added 200,000 square miles of land to British territory. He was just getting down from the cart when he remembered an old political trick. 'I had forgotten my duty. Gentlemen, let me introduce my dearly beloved wife, late Miss Dorothy Tennant. She is a descendant of the greatest liberal the country ever knew - Oliver Cromwell.' In this way he linked his wife, formerly a fervent Gladstone supporter, with the anti-Irish movement, for Cromwell was the most hated figure in Irish historical demonology.

Stanley's opposition to Home Rule won him friends in press circles previously his most severe critics. But it did not impress the electorate. The climax of the campaign came on 29th June when his winding-up meeting in Hawkeston Hall, Lambeth was howled down by the opposition. The platform was stormed, the speakers forced to flee. When Stanley and his wife got into their brougham, the enraged crowd tore off the door of the carriage. The predictable election defeat followed. Much against his will, Stanley allowed Dolly to persuade him to remain as the Liberal-Unionist candidate for the constituency. He accepted a banquet from the Chamberlain faction and pledged himself to their service in the next election. This effectively precluded any African engagements, which was what Dolly had been aiming at all along.

The Stanleys assuaged the bitterness of defeat with a cruise on Mackinnon's yacht through the Scottish lochs to the Clyde. Then Stanley entered a limbo period for some three years, lecturing in England, Scotland and Ireland on African issues and contemporary social questions. His stance on domestic matters was always that of a deep-dyed reactionary. In the 1893 coal strike he launched a bitter attack on the miners: 'if I had any money to spare at the present time, it would not be given to men who were determined to be sulky and who, to spite the coal-owners, preferred to starve.' He wrote on Africa and boosted the sales of his friends' travel books by writing introductions for them.

He developed a fondness for East Anglia and Cambridgeshire. In 1894 a succession of malarial attacks led him to spend more and more time at seaside resorts, first on the Isle of Wight, later at Monte Carlo.

The years 1893-94 also saw the demise of many of his closest friends. First was Sir William Mackinnon who, Stanley alleged, died prematurely of a broken heart after shabby and ungrateful treatment from the British government. Then came the deaths of surgeon Parke, the missionary Charles Ingham and his wife - with both of whom Stanley was particularly friendly, General Beauregard, his old commander at Shiloh, and, most grievous loss of all, Livingstone's son-in-law Alexander Bruce. Few clues remain as to Stanley's private life in this period, after Dolly's excisions. We learn that he helped his brother-in-law F. W. Myers organise a parapsychological conference (he referred to Myers as 'a rare mind') and that Dolly had a superstition which prevented her ever from travelling on a Sunday. It is also clear from her addiction to the drug secephonal that she suffered from chronic insomnia.

1893 was a bad year for Stanley, quite apart from the deaths of so many of his friends. A painting trip to Tuscany, with an itinerary from Turin to Rome via Siena and Florence, ended traumatically just when Stanley thought he had secured a new friendship. John Addington Symonds, the celebrated author and Italianist, met Stanley in Rome and enchanted him with his brilliant conversation. Stanley made a dinner date at the Cafe Roma next day, but two hours later a message came that Symonds had been taken violently ill; he died two days later. Stanley was in bed for a week with shock. The experience turned him against Rome. He complained of the strain on his nerves of the racket from the stone pavements and the effect of the dreaded Roman fever on his health.

He returned home to find another headache awaiting him. When Stanley cut short his American lecture tour in 1886 to head the Emin Pasha expedition, Major Pond, the impresario, had accepted the convenient fiction that Leopold had summoned Stanley back to Europe. The truth of course was that he had returned of his own volition. Now it transpired that another party was involved - a London-based American called Greenleaf Webb Appleton, who now sued for non-payment of fees due after introducing Stanley to Pond. Appleton alleged that only Leopold's contractual lien on Stanley's services justified the cancellation of the 1886 lectures and that it was Mackinnon and the EPRE committee, not Leopold, who had summoned Stanley from the USA; therefore he was bringing an action for breach of contract. Stanley was forced into the humiliating position of having to ask Leopold to lie for him to get himself off the legal hook - this partly explains the change of attitude towards Leopold in evidence after 1893. The case was eventually settled out of court on the judge's ruling that the plaintiff was entitled to commission only on the original 1886 fees, not the enhanced ones for the 1890-91 lecture tour.

1895 was a significant year in Stanley's life. In June Parliament was dissolved and electioneering commenced. On 15th July 1895 Stanley at last secured the prize Dolly was hoping for when he was elected MP for North Lambeth with a majority of 405. But his first weeks in Parliament led to further disillusionment. He complained about the accommodation and the facilities offered to Members and was contemptuous of the intellectual and personal qualities of most of his colleagues. Of all the luminaries of whom he left pen portraits in his diary (Redmond, Dollon, Harcourt, Balfour, Haldane, Austen Chamberlain, Curzon, Dilke), it was Sir Charles Dilke who impressed him most. He even noticed with irritation that the doorkeeper addressed him with the words 'Mr Stanley, I presume.' The mock banter and verbosity of the House irked him and he recorded a particularly damning verdict on 20th August: 'The criminal waste of precious time, devotion to antique customs, the silent endurance of evils, which, by a word, could be swept away, have afforded me much matter of wonder.'

But Stanley was providing a very one-sided picture. The truth was that Parliament did not suit him nor he Parliament. A natural man of action, he believed in solving issues by administrative order or the gun, not by talk and debate. His arguments on all topics outside Africa lacked subtlety and finesse and he was soon marginalised as an obscure backbencher of reactionary stripe, his close-cropped white hair and red face making him a quasi-military archetype of the Colonel Blimp figure. He was a poor public speaker on an election platform, since he lacked the ability to improvise and could only orate in the style of his public lectures. In the House this disability was magnified and he was by common consent an indifferent parliamentarian. His first intervention, on the Sudan, was undistinguished, and when he tried to make an even-handed speech on the Stokes affair, his rhetoric was so boring and prolix that the Speaker cut him off.

After just a month of this Stanley took himself off on a three-month tour of the USA. Starting at New York, he swept through Canada, the West and the South (where he paid his final visit to New Orleans). Outwardly he pretended that the trip had been a success: 'I have but lately returned from a lengthy American tour which I much enjoyed. It has added considerably to my stock of knowledge and made me quite ten pounds heavier.' But in the privacy of his journals he railed against the 'general mediocrity' prevalent in America and the indifference of people to him. He found it hard to adjust to the fact that he was already a virtually forgotten figure.

The significant thing about Stanley's tour to the USA was that Dolly did not accompany him; nor did he accompany her on her 1895 holiday in Switzerland. Again, interestingly, 1895 saw a brief resurgence in Dolly's diary-keeping which she had abandoned on marriage to Stanley. Taken together, all this suggests that the Stanley marriage went through some sort of crisis in 1895. The resolution was interesting, for it took the form of the adoption of a sixteen-month-old child called Denzil, the son of an ex-governess whose husband had died, leaving her penniless. So as to permit the woman to resume her career as a governess, the Stanleys agreed to become the adoptive parents of Denzil. The decision was taken, Stanley explained cryptically, because 'we have concluded we are not to be blessed with children'. The reality was almost certainly that there was no physical basis to the marriage, that it was a union that existed purely on a companionable quasi brother-and-sister level.

After returning from the USA Stanley resumed his increasingly unpalatable duties in the House. His contributions during his five years as a Member became fewer and of decreasing significance. He spoke on the Armenian massacres and on the plans for a reconquest of the Sudan, even clashing with Dilke on the issue on one occasion. He had a few words to say on the railways being built from the Zambezi to Lake Nyasa and through Uganda. But it was perhaps significant of his own parliamentary bankruptcy that his last intervention in the House, in 1900, was on the subject of trustees for liquidated companies and the assignment of debts. Stanley lifted a corner on his essential passivity in a letter to Henry Johnston, with whom he had first discussed the idea of entering Parliament on the Congo in 1883: 'I have not so many illusions as I had in 1883, but if ever there comes a time for honest and straight speaking, I will do my level best, to protect against wrongdoing, meanness and cowardice. I have a fund of warm indignation always in reserve against Dilkism, Laborism and Little Englandism, but I am too old and self-contained to let it out on every occasion, besides we have plenty of good speakers who will be able to deal effectively with the more opinionated opponents, and I would rather listen, than engage in unnecessary discussion.'

However, at the beginning of 1896 Stanley was briefly in demand for his opinion on the Anglo-American crisis over the Venezuela-British Guiana dispute. As a man who had had both nationalities and a career straddling the two great English-speaking nations, Stanley's attitude was, suitably, 'a plague on both your houses'. Otherwise, his journalistic output tended to be limited to questions affecting the future of Africa and the role of the British Empire. He was as much on Joseph Chamberlain's side on the issue of imperialism as he had been over Irish Home Rule; Chamberlain had reciprocated the admiration by appearing as a supporting speaker in North Lambeth during the 1895 campaign. In fact it was arguably the encouragement from Chamberlain that kept him going during the onerous five years in the House. One night he came home from the Commons and announced to Dolly: 'Well, I could live for Balfour, but I could die for Chamberlain. He says what he means to do - and why - and then he does it.'

Meanwhile at Richmond Terrace Dolly endeavoured to turn their home into the kind of salon over which her mother had once presided. Luminaries from the worlds of exploration, politics, the arts and sciences rubbed shoulders with the ageing explorer. Apart from his great friend Mark Twain, Stanley had contacts with Trollope, Ruskin, Sir George Trevelyan, G. A. Henty, Holman Hunt, Sir Frederick Leighton and Auguste Rodin. Among explorers he corresponded with Nansen, Sven Hedin, Gerhard Rohlfs and even Carl Peters and George Schweinfurth. Another visitor was the inveterate diner-out Henry James, who had a line to the Stanleys through their mutual friendship with Garnett Wolseley. James indeed bracketed Stanley with Marco Polo as the two discoverers in history who had had the most wondrous adventures. James was also involved in another Stanley contact. Dolly's mother, then Gertrude Collier, was the daughter of a naval attaché at the British Embassy in Paris. During vacations at Trouville she became a friend of Flaubert's and in 1877 Flaubert introduced her to Alphonse Daudet. When the Daudets came to London in 1895, they knew no one except Henry James and the Tennants, mother and daughter. Through this dual contact they were introduced to Stanley, whose enthusiasm for French literature was marked. Daudet described the set-up at Richmond Terrace. There Stanley held court, surrounded by fanatical admirers and old comrades from his expeditions. Outside this circle Stanley was shunned as a man of ferocity and anger.

Two other views of the Stanley 'court' are available to us. Marie von Bunsen, the woman Stanley had allegedly been attracted to in Berlin in 1884, saw him during an 'at home' in London. 'He was standing in the background, flattened against the wall, embittered, like a whipped dog.' She intended to go across to talk but she was intercepted on the way over and when she looked for him again, he was gone. A more complimentary picture comes from Mark Twain. 'Stanley is magnificently housed in London, in a grand mansion in the midst of the official world right off Downing Street and Whitehall. He had an extraordinary assemblage of brains and fame there to meet me - thirty or forty (both sexes) at dinner, and more than a hundred came in after dinner. Kept it up till after midnight. There were cabinet ministers, ambassadors, admirals, generals, canons, Oxford professors, novelists, playwrights, poets and a number of people equipped with rank and brains.'

But lack of action and frequent illness in 1896 made Stanley increasingly restless. He had a particularly severe attack of malaria during a trip to Spain in June 1896. Fever and gastritis produced alarming symptoms of agonising pain, acute breathlessness and shivering so violent that the bed he lay on would shake and the glass on the table vibrate and ring. A visit to Budapest and Vienna in April 1897 failed to cure his malaise - a mixture of physical illness and boredom - so Dolly looked around for other challenges that would not involve a return to the Congo whose spell she so dreaded. An invitation to be present at the opening of the Bulawayo railway in South Africa in the autumn of 1897 seemed to present a risk-free opportunity to give Stanley the illusion that he was once more a man of action. Dolly worked hard to set up a journey that she could somehow control from afar.

Once again Dolly did not accompany her husband, though this time, with Denzil in her charge, she had an excuse. Instead she rehired Hoffmann, who had rehabilitated himself from disgrace by hard-working service in the Congo in the early 1890s. Hoffmann and Stanley left Southampton on 9th October 1897 in the SS Norman, in company with the Duke of Roxburghe and five other MPs. The voyage turned out to be one of the most disagreeable Stanley had ever made. The ship was packed to the gunwales and the din and cacophony on board from morning until night was almost deafening. The noise continued so disturbing at night that Hoffmann was often obliged to knock on the doors of adjoining cabins to request that Stanley be allowed a little sleep. Stanley also missed Denzil and his feeling for children came through strongly in the very real grief he felt when a nine-month old girl died of meningitis and was buried at sea.

As they neared the Cape, Stanley claimed to be able to smell again the continent he had last seen seven years before. Once at Cape Town they boarded a 'State Pullman' - an ordinary corridor train of six coaches with three persons in a carriage instead of the normal four. This was by far the slowest train journey Stanley had ever made in his life; the 1360 miles to Bulawayo took three days to complete at a top speed of 19 m.p.h. They chugged along through Wellington, Kimberley, Vryburg and Mafeking to Matabeleland but still managed to miss the opening ceremony at Bulawayo, since a train ahead of them ran off the rails and delayed the Pullman for a decisive four hours.

Arriving just in time for the evening's festivities, they found their hotel, the Palace, only half finished. Stanley was lucky enough to get a finished room but Hoffmann was reduced to sleeping in an uncompleted partitioned area. To Stanley's fury Hoffmann disobeyed an explicit instruction about never letting his master's boots out of his sight. Next morning they witnessed a confused melee in the hotel corridor with men struggling to sort out 500 pairs of boots which had all been taken away and cleaned indiscriminately.

All in all, especially as Cecil Rhodes was incommunicado, sulking in his tent after the humiliating failure of the Jameson raid the year before, Stanley found Bulawayo a disappointment. It was a boom town with miners and prospectors arriving daily to look for gold, but the Wild West atmosphere Stanley would have relished thirty years earlier (and did) now left him cold. He set off for Johannesburg and was annoyed when the train was delayed at the Transvaal border while Kruger's officials spent from midnight to dawn combing through the passengers and their luggage. At Vereeniging he consented to an interview with a journalist from the English-speaking Standard and Diggers ' News who wrote up the meeting as 'How I Found Stanley'.

Was the mild silver-haired gentleman ... really the much advertised Mr H. M. Stanley, MP, DCL, LLD, PhD . . . who .. . has through grit and a great deal of attitudinising and mise-en-scene made himself famous ... who discovered Livingstone (when he was not lost), who found Emin when that Equatorial dignity did not want to be found . . . and who has so picturesquely if unconvincingly fulfilled the star turn in the Bulawayo advertising troupe?. . . This is Mr Stanley's first appearance in the Transvaal, and he has been retained by journals paid to deprecate and abuse this country. We will not say that Mr Stanley has a 'Darkest Transvaal' in preparation, but we cannot quite rid ourselves of the suspicion that the Republic will be held up to the world - well, not in the kindliest manner.

The reporter was not wrong. In Johannesburg Stanley listened to the grievances of the Uitlanders and, though he rather despised them, began to be won over to the idea that only armed force could secure the British future in South Africa. On 23rd November he moved on to Pretoria and there, at 5.30 a.m. next day, he had a private interview with Transvaal President Paul Kruger. Kruger was sitting on his step drinking coffee and had set aside half an hour for the audience with the famous explorer before departing on an election campaign. Stanley was impressed by his rugged, rock-like massiveness but less so by the Old-Testament prophet aura of righteousness Kruger exuded. 'He reminded me more than anything else of the huge apes that I saw from time to time while I was pushing through the forests of Central Africa. His forehead was low, with great beetling brows. His eyes were little and half-shut, like a pig's; his huge jaw was hunched on to his shoulders, so that he appeared to have no neck, and a large briarwood pipe was clenched between his teeth ... a rusty, old-fashioned frock-coat, old-fashioned even for the end of the nineteenth century, a crumpled stick in his hand and a little top-hat.'

The interview went wrong as soon as Stanley raised the question of the rights of the Uitlanders in Johannesburg. Kruger became angry: 'his right hand went up and down like a sledgehammer, and from his eyes, small and dull as they were, flashed forth the most implacable resolve that surrender must be on their side, not his.' This was the wrong tone to take with Stanley, for Kruger was in effect stealing his thunder; this was how Stanley liked to deal with those who disagreed with him. From this moment Stanley conceived the most violent detestation for Kruger and became an exponent of a forceful solution to the South African problem. After half an hour of Kruger's 'arrogance', 'vanity' and 'contempt' he came away convinced that Milner, Chamberlain, Salisbury and, indeed, any Englishmen who had not met Kruger were living in a fool's paradise if they thought a pacific solution was possible: 'I had seen enough, and heard more than enough, to convince me that this was an extreme case, which only force could remedy.'

From Pretoria Stanley travelled through the Orange Free State and Natal, took ship from Durban to East London, then went back overland to Cape Town. On his last night there he was given a banquet, then on 15th December embarked on the SS Moor for England. As the outline of Table Mountain merged with the horizon, Stanley watched wistfully from the deck. He told Hoffmann he had a strong premonition that this was his last glimpse of the 'Dark Continent'.

He arrived back in London even more of an imperialist than when he left and began advocating a violent solution to the threat from the Boers. Indeed the story of Stanley's last six years of life can be encapsulated in three themes: his jingoism and passionate advocacy of the South African war; his devotion to his adopted son Denzil; and his increasingly frequent illnesses and ultimate physical decline.

The commitment to the British Empire and his implacable hostility to the Boers is amply documented from a variety of sources. At the beginning of 1899 he felt reasonably confident about imperial prospects though concerned about the growing economic challenge from the USA and worried about American imperialistic tendencies as manifested in the Philippines: 'The year 1899 is starting so smoothly in England . . . we have long ago calmed down about the mad French attempt on the Upper Nile and we are so interested in the Czar's peace circular that we have relaxed our attention to Russian misdoing in China. With Germany we have no questions and America has civilly refrained from twisting our "lion's tail". Old Kruger is probably more concerned with his personal infirmities and the colonists are following their usual orderly habits.' He even felt relaxed enough about British prospects in Africa in 1897-99 to engage in a friendly, though somewhat routine correspondence with the notable traveller in West Africa, Mary Kingsley.

But the outbreak of the South African war in 1899 brought the old lion roaring back into the epistolary and speechmaking fray. He spoke out strongly on the necessity for the war and deplored the 'Stop the War' movement as misguided and unpatriotic. He was tempted by an offer from

Major Pond to tour the USA lecturing on the Transvaal and the war but decided that his parliamentary commitments precluded this. In private he lamented the incompetence that had led to the early British reversals in the war but hoped that Redvers Buller would bring the hated Kruger to his knees. Though the British must be degenerate to have allowed regulars to be chewed up by the raw Boer militia at Ladysmith, at least there was now a resolution of the 'evil humours' that had built up over the past nineteen years and action was being taken that should have been put in hand a decade before. 'No people on earth are so averse to war as we are and so prone to be guided by goody-goody sentiment... if you have interests no amount of sentiment will protect them.' He believed in 'pray to God but keep your powder dry' and despised the beautiful phrase-mongering and impeccable logic of those who spoke 'Johnsonia-Gladstonese . . . direct simple English has no chance in these literate days.'

He continued to lament British disasters in the field until the military tide turned in 1900: 'the Boers are first-class fighters in their way and deserve the utmost credit - but with different generalship they could have been sent flying.' Correspondence from 1901 on the South African war also sees Stanley unwittingly pointing to the future. 'What is this I hear of your experiences with Winston Churchill? You must not be too hard upon him for remember he is very young. A little judicious talk with him would soon set the matter right I think, for excepting on this occasion, he has been distinguished for good sense.'

In the autumn of 1898 Stanley decided to look for a country retreat within striking distance of London. No. 2 Richmond Terrace could hardly have been more convenient for the Commons, and the Welsh haven of Cadoxton Lodge, Neath in South Wales fitted the bill for extended stays away from London. But what he needed now was a medium-range establishment that Denzil could regard as his permanent home and where he could grow up serenely. After viewing twenty houses in Kent, Buckinghamshire, Berkshire and Sussex without finding anything suitable, the Stanleys located a mock-Tudor mansion at Furze Hill, Pirbright, Surrey. The house was set in its own grounds, complete with small lake, pine woods and meadows, but was in need of considerable renovation and redecoration. Draft contracts were exchanged at Christmas 1898 in anticipation of vacant possession the following June. At last on 10th June 1899 the Stanleys moved in. Stanley busied himself with the plans for building a new wing, for landscaping the gardens and installing electric lighting. He transformed one large room into a library and converted the vast entrance hall into a billiards room. In the autumn of 1899 the Stanleys moved in properly. From now on this was their true home, and Richmond Terrace (where Gertrude Tennant remained) was definitely second-best.

At last Stanley had a proper home for his beloved Denzil. His paternal affection for his adopted son shows the more attractive side of Stanley. The older the boy grew, the more attention the explorer paid him. His early jottings on his son show him almost in the vein of the Dickens of Little

Nell vintage. 'Warmest greetings to darling Little Denzil, our own cherub! Possibly I think too much of him. If I were not busy with work and other things, I should undoubtedly dwell too much on him . . . look full into his angelic face, and deep down into those eyes so blue, as if two little orbs formed out of the bluest heaven were there, and bless him with your clean soul, untainted by any other thought than that which wishes him the best God can give him. At present, he is of such as are the beings of God's heaven, purity itself.'

In an attempt to recall his beloved Africa, Stanley gave names to the different parts of the grounds on his Pirbright acreage. The lake was called Stanley Pool, the pine woods the Ituri forest, and so on. Stanley played games of 'Darkest Africa' with Denzil, or else they would trot round the grounds in a carriage and pretend they were in the USA. A letter from Stanley in 1899 gives a charming picture of domestic bliss at Furze Hill (and a hint of contemporary interest in the Dreyfuss case): 'Mrs Tennant if anything looks younger and Mrs Stanley is of such an amiable disposition that time is very partial to her. Baby is thriving. He is getting on to four now and has a predilection for politics. Every morning I take him a ride by train to some distant part of the States - Chicago to San Francisco or to New Orleans and he delights in playing the conductor's part - and calling out "Salt Lake City", "Sacramento" or "Adanta" etc. He believes in Picquart and condemns Esterhazy. 'Soon it was difficult for Stanley to write a personal letter at all without some reference to the 'beloved cherub'. From an early age the Stanleys seem to have encouraged the boy in the profession of arms he was eventually to adopt. The Wellcomes sent him a pistol when he was six at which his eyes opened wide but 'I cannot get his attention because of a new monkey called Mr Puff which he has just received from an admirer.' They also dressed him in the uniform of a Horse Guard and inflamed his anger against the Boers. But Stanley, with his uneasy mixture of fire-eating bellicosity and Christian piety, got his comeuppance on one occasion when he reproached the boy for hating the Boers. 'If they are not wicked people, why do you fight them?' Denzil replied.

William Hoffmann, who was a frequent visitor at Furze Hill after his successful outing to South Africa with Stanley, made the shrewd point that Stanley's adoption of Denzil was in a sense a re-enactment (this time successful) of the adoption of John Rowlands by the Stanleys in New Orleans forty years before. Certainly Stanley's empathy with Denzil seemed to bring out a childlike streak in his last years. Hoffmann would be ushered into the library where a disembodied Stanley voice would order 'Find Me!' After a lengthy and fruitless search a revolving bookcase would swing round to reveal the hidden explorer. This behaviour was highly significant, since in psychological terms it embraced three different strands of the Stanley personality: the excessive secretiveness, the desire to 'have the drop' on other people and the wish to recapture an imaginary lost childhood.

Stanley spent the quiet years at Furze Hill working on his autobiography which, however, never progressed beyond the year 1862. In 1897 he revealed to Marston in effect that his unconscious was sabotaging his attempts to deal with his early years, though at the conscious level he rationalised this as pressure of time. 'It is just the most interesting part from my eighteenth to my twenty-fifty that wants the material which I only can supply. I have tried repeatedly to find an unbroken month or so to add to it, but so sure as I put pen to paper, so sure does a series of engagements interrupt me and compel me to lock it up.' Three years later he told Marston that the book had made no progress because of his political career. Now not only did Stanley not have a political career worth mentioning, but this excuse is singularly feeble from a man who wrote the massive two-volume In Darkest Africa in fifty days. The truth is that, unconsciously, Stanley did not want to finish his autobiography. The years between his eighteenth and twenty-fifth birthdays were painful ones which reflected little credit on him, and he knew it.

In 1898 and 1899 Stanley was busy appealing for funds for the Livingstone monument to be built at Chitambo. Perhaps not entirely coincidentally with his work on this appeal, in June 1899 Dorothy Stanley received the news she had long prayed for. Lord Salisbury wrote to offer Stanley the Grand Cross of the Bath, a higher grade of knighthood than he would have received in 1890 when his nationality was the impediment. When Queen Victoria conferred the decoration a few weeks later she noted in her journal: 'He is grown very old and is rather altered in appearance.'

This was not altogether surprising. Long bouts of illness had made Stanley's thoughts increasingly turn to death. In particular he had the sort of superstitious feeling towards the Emin expedition that survivors of the 1922 Carnarvon expedition had towards the opening of the Tutankhamen tomb. He detected the old 'diablerie' at work that he had detected on arrival at Banalya in August 1888: 'Extraordinary as it may be, those connected with the Emin Relief Expedition steadily diminish in number, as if the very name of the Esau [5/c] had a fatality. Fifteen young and old have already passed away.' In 1902 he made out a death list of the principals which included the following: Mackay (1902), Vita Hassan (1892), Stairs (1892), Emin Pasha (1892), Grant (1892), Mackinnon (1893), Sir Samuel Baker (1893), Parke (1893), Price (1893), Verney Cameron (1894), Joseph Thomson (1895), Charles Stokes (1895), Consul Holmwood (1895), Horace Waller, (1896), Bonny (1899) and Casati (1902).

Memento mori was reinforced by Stanley's precarious and declining health. To have survived the rigours of four long expeditions in Africa when so many of his comrades dropped like flies indicated that Stanley's constitution was ox-like, and it is a reasonable inference that had he spent his career in England, he might have had a Gladstone-like span. But the hundreds of bouts of African fever had worn out even his doughty frame and aged him prematurely. Both his Continental trips in 1898 were visited with illness. First there was a nasty attack of 'flu in Monte Carlo in

February. Then in August, in the Pyrenees, he was again stricken with the mysterious gastro-enteritis that had assailed him in Spain in 1896. He took to his bed in Biarritz, struggled up to Paris where he had a relapse, then staggered back home, where only a starvation diet and assiduous massaging restored him to health. For months he was so ill that he could not sit up in bed.

The year 1900 saw a further sustained period of malady. Stanley was so ill that he could not even imbibe milk. He kept himself alive with white of egg and other spoon victuals. Dolly allayed the pains by injecting him with morphia. Yet in periods of normality he chafed at the strict diet imposed on him, as Dolly revealed to Henry Wellcome. 'How wearying illness is - and it seems such a waste of time - but Stanley is very patient and enduring. If only he were wiser - when I am not there to judge for him.'

The strain of nursing an almost permanent invalid began to tell on Dolly. A decade of life had turned the ingenuous 'girl' into a somewhat grim grande dame. Stanley's granite-hard posture towards the world had affected her, so that her basically weak personality consented to be his creature and to do all in all as he did. The woman who had admired Gladstone's radicalism, fretted about the fate of miners and sympathised with the proletariat was by the turn of the century a neurotic dabbler in potions and astrology. Her weakness and unpopularity with servants comes through in the Wellcome correspondence where it is revealed that while Dolly was nursing Stanley at Richmond Terrace in 1903 'all sorts of robbery and wickedness .. . grew up when Stanley's strong hand was removed by that year of sickness.' The hardness can be inferred from a number of sources. Dolly resented having guests visit Stanley at Furze Hill as it prevented her from taking a holiday. And she took the rather unwomanly stance of supporting vivisection and experiments on living animals; she even told Wellcome that she would like the law amended to make such experimentation easier.

In her quest for potions, elixirs, nostrums and panaceas she had one unexpected ally. Mark Twain was a great believer in the 'Kellgren method' - a form of physiotherapy pioneered by the Swedish physician Dr Kellgren. In 1900 on a visit to London Twain found his old friend bedridden and in agony. He had given up on doctors, having tried sixteen of the best in seventeen years without success. The last one had predicted that the very next attack would kill him. Twain joined with Dolly's sister Eveleen Myers in urging that Kellgren (who had a practice in London) be called in. After some reluctance Dolly did so and the results were miraculous. Stanley sat up in bed, smoked a pipe and ate a hearty meal of bacon and eggs. Twain recorded that Dolly kissed him on both cheeks in gratitude. He laid all the credit at Kellgren's door. 'Today he [Stanley] resumes his seat in the House of Commons a well man. If he had had a doctor he would be under a slab in Westminster Abbey now.'

But it was clear that Stanley was in no state to continue his career as politician. On 26th July 1900 he endured his last parliamentary sitting. His retirement from the House and his making the very last journal entry on 19th December 1901 indicate an awareness that death could not be long delayed, Kellgren notwithstanding. By this time he could not remain in London for more than four weeks at a time as he did not get enough sleep because of the noise. In 1901 he made his last trip abroad to attend Frederick Myers's funeral. His final public appearance was on 9th August 1902 when he attended the coronation of Edward VII. Before the ceremony he wanted to cry off, especially as he had to rise from a sick-bed to attend. Even though he found the pageantry stunning, the uplift was momentary and he had to beat a hasty retreat to convalescence.

By the spring of 1903 Stanley was complaining of giddiness and vertigo in addition to the malarial and gastritis attacks. Dolly went everywhere with him in case he had a fainting fit. But on 13th April he had a stroke, followed by an even more severe one four days later that completely paralysed him down the left side. Tended by four different doctors, he was dosed with ammonia and ether and given hypodermic injections of strychnine and digitalis. Dolly wrote to Wellcome in anguish: 'He cannot turn in bed or lift himself. The eyes do not form together so that when he closes one eye he sees double towards the right. Speech remains impaired by paralysis of cleft lip and jaw . . . owing to weakness and shock and grief he is highly emotional - I have no hopes of his precious life. 'Throughout 1903 Stanley continued in this state, helpless as a baby, still, with his neurotic insistence on order, insisting that he shave himself with his good right hand. His speech was laboured but - just - intelligible to his wife. Weakness and shock made him highly emotional. He was so debilitated that even when lifted from bed into a large armchair and swathed with blankets, he was so exhausted that he had to go back to bed after two hours. Soon there were complications. A bout of malaria led Dolly to cut out all sugar and to substitute Vichy water for champagne and whisky. In the summer his good non-paralysed leg started to swell; cardiac oedema affected the kidneys and caused dropsical swelling. But the great heart beat on and the explorer even seemed to mock death by taking to reading detective stories. Yet the strain on Dolly was bringing her near breaking-point and she began to suffer from severe depression. 'It is difficult - inwardly - always to be cheerful and hopeful, but as long as I can seem so always that is the main thing - and I expect my occasional moods of depression are only because I have been a long time here and I haven't much outlet for energy.'

In August they had a visit from Dr Allart, sometime medical officer at Vivi and Boma, now the Belgian consul in Tenerife. He thought that Stanley was not being moved, rubbed or manipulated enough. Dolly and the nurses accordingly arranged a daily schedule of massage. Additionally, Stanley underwent electric shock treatment but gave up when it seemed to exacerbate his symptoms. Gradually Stanley made a partial recovery. He spent most of the day outside in a wheelchair and by September was able to take a few steps, supported. His speech had returned but fatigue followed any attempt at physical or mental effort or any real concentration of the mind.

In the later autumn of 1903 the Stanleys went up to London and when they returned to Furze Hill for the Easter holidays of 1904 Stanley was able to walk, supported and with a stick, along the station platform - which was far more than he had been able to do the year before. But in April he sustained a bad attack of pleurisy, so bad that Dolly barred the door to visitors. As he recovered from this, he comforted himself with the thought that at death he would surely lie alongside Livingstone in Westminster Abbey. The doctors warned Dolly that his heart was now fading and he could not last long. As if in confirmation of this he said to her at the beginning of May: 'Goodbye, dear, I am going very soon, I have done.' The final death struggle began on 5th May. His mind wandered and his eyes had a faraway look but all was slow and painless. In the last two days of life he murmured many valedictory messages. 'Oh! I want to be free - I want to go into the woods to be free.' 'I want to go home.' At 4 a.m. on 10th May he heard four o'clock striking and said: 'How strange! So that is time! Strange!' He died at 6 a.m. on Tuesday 10th May 1904.

It was generally expected that Stanley would be buried in Westminster Abbey alongside Livingstone, but the Dean, Joseph Armitage Robinson, refused to allow this and declined to enter into reasons for his decision. But correspondence in the Royal Archives reveals the reason. Predictably, Stanley's reputation as a man of blood had told against him, even though it was acknowledged that the idea of burial in the Abbey beside Livingstone had merit and would appeal to the Americans. Thus did the Revd Armitage Robinson explain his decision to the King's private secretary. 'There is not an unmixed feeling among good men whose counsel I have taken as to the claims of H. M. Stanley to be accorded one of the very few vacant spaces in the Abbey. One of our highest geographical authorities lays stress on the violence and even cruelty which marked some of his explorations, and contrasts this with the peaceful successes of other explorers. This chiefly weighed with me in giving my decision to restrict the honour done to him to what I may call second honours, i.e. burial refusal but the first part of the funeral service granted.' This decision could only be overruled by direct intervention from Edward VII, which he declined to make. Dorothy Stanley was left with the clear impression that it was enmity from Sir Clements Markham that had tipped the scale but she braved out the rebuff by declaring that after his marriage Stanley had effectively renounced the world and all its pomp; therefore the rejection meant nothing. Mark Twain's friend William D. Howells put it more forcibly. He said that Stanley was 'refused a grave in Westminster Abbey by a wretched, tyrannical parson'.

Stanley's body was taken from Richmond Terrace to the Abbey for the service then to Pirbright for burial in the churchyard. The pall-bearers in the Abbey were Livingstone Bruce (Livingstone's grandson), Sir Alfred Lyall, Dr Scott Keltie, Sir George Tarban Goldie, the Duke of Abercorn,

Mounteney Jephson, Henry Wellcome and Sir Harry Johnston. Telegrams of condolence poured in: from Lord Kitchener, Lord Cromer, George Bernard Shaw, the polar explorer Peary, and many others. Perhaps the finest tribute came in a letter from Agnes Livingstone Bruce to Jephson: 'I have always felt that Stanley did so much for me personally in risking his life to find my father, and my children have grown up with the same feelings of affection and gratitude towards him.'

Many of those whose lives Stanley had touched were dead already. Of the officers who had accompanied him across Africa on the Emin expedition, only Mounteney Jephson survived him. Jephson married the American Anna Head but could never entirely shake off the strains of fever he had picked up in Africa. After sustained ill health he died in 1908, aged forty-nine. Of the Rear Column veterans Ward survived until 1919 and served with distinction in the Great War. Hoffmann lived on until the late 1920s in increasingly desperate penury and destitution.

Stanley had outlived all the great African explorers. Of the great African proconsuls Lord Cromer (born in the same year) lived until 1917, Sir Harry Johnston until 1927 and Lugard to 1945. Leopold survived to see his Congo State taken over as a colony by Belgium (in 1908) in return for 50 million francs' blood money but not before the Congo had become a byword for savagery and atrocity that shocked and convulsed contemporary Europe.

The women in Stanley's life enjoyed mixed later fortunes. No trace is known to survive of Virginia Ambella, but Katie Gough-Roberts died soon after World War One. The most interesting sequel was that of Alice Pike Barney. She became a patroness of the arts and an amateur painter, and when her husband died she remarried a twenty-six-year-old millionaire artist, twenty-eight years her junior. A five-million-dollar heiress from her first marriage, Alice spoiled and pampered her daughter Natalie, who was later the lover of Colette and the friend of Proust. Alice herself grew bored with the marriage to her second husband Christian Hemmick, who divorced her in 1920 for desertion. Amazingly, the sexagenarian Alice then began a new career as a playwright, wrote eleven plays and won the Drama League of America award for The Lighthouse in 1927. She died in Hollywood, California, in 1931, aged seventy-five.

Yet the brightest torch for Stanley was always carried by Dolly. After his death she emulated Isabel Burton by building up the legend of Bula Matari. All evidence tending to work against the mythical picture she wanted for 'her' Stanley was ruthlessly suppressed. She tricked Katie Gough-Roberts into parting with Stanley's personal letters to her, bribed and browbeat Lewis Noe, dealt harshly and unsympathetically with Hoffmann's pleas for alms, and let it be known that she would go to law readily to defend Stanley's reputation. Her hopes for the heavily edited and doctored Stanley Autobiography, published in 1909, were that it would be a book that would live down the ages. It did not. By the end of Edward VII's reign interest in Stanley was minimal and the book fell still-born from the press.

In 1907 Dolly married again, a forty-year-old Harley Street surgeon called Henry Curtis, sixteen years her junior. But she insisted on retaining the name Lady Stanley, for she knew that her precarious niche in history rested entirely on the fame of her first husband. Looking around for a permanent memorial for Stanley, she instituted a search on Dartmoor for a granite monolith that would be his tombstone. At last she found what she was looking for: a stone 12 feet high by 4 feet wide. This was taken to Pirbright churchyard and erected over the grave. Below a cross cut deep in the top four feet of the monolith was carved the simple legend: HENRY MORTON STANLEY, BULA MATARI 1841-1904, AFRICA.

CONCLUSION

HENRY Morton Stanley was far the greatest of the explorers of Africa. However critical one may be of aspects of his life, his achievements as an explorer are as unassailable as those of Marco Polo or Columbus. To deny this is as absurd as to deny the military skill of the man Stanley most liked to be compared to - Napoleon Bonaparte.' The expedition to find Livingstone was an astonishing achievement for a complete tiro in African exploration. The 1874-7 expedition was an even finer accomplishment, and the descent of the Congo in 1876-7 is one of those journeys that will live for ever in the annals of human discovery. Arguably, the foundation of the Congo Free State was, from the standpoint of history, the most solid memorial of all; Stanley himself cannot be blamed for the black hole into which Leopold and his bloody acolytes later plunged the territory. In the Emin Pasha relief expedition Stanley may well in a technical sense have effected the greatest feat of endurance in all land-based exploration. Certainly it is hard to think of anything that rivals the triple crossing of the Ituri forest or the achievement of the only 'double' in nineteenth-century exploration (the traverse of Africa east-west in 1874-7 and west-east in 1887-9).

This is not to say that Stanley was overall more significant than the explorers he outmatched. He did not have Burton's formidable intellect or literary skill, and still less did he have Livingstone's moral stature. As a genuine Africanist he was excelled not just by Livingstone but also by Emin and by lesser figures like Herbert Ward, who had a far more genuine feeling for the continent and its inhabitants as 'things in themselves'. To paraphrase President Kennedy's famous phrase, we may say that whereas Livingstone, Emin and others were interested in what they could give Africa, Stanley was interested in what Africa could give him. Yet as an observer of Africa Stanley was shrewd and his perceptions of local societies much more acute than his facile critics give him credit for. He had none of the racial prejudice that disfigured the writings of Burton or Sir Samuel Baker; indeed, his white comrades frequently complained that he favoured Africans over them. The writing of African history from oral sources is still in its infancy, but it will be surprising if Stanley does not gain much stature when a proper inventory of tribal accounts is drawn up, especially considering the vast areas of Central Africa in which he was an active presence. Even at the Eurocentric level, if one sees Leopold as the true author of the 'scramble for Africa', one must legitimately concede that Stanley's role was crucial. And his niche in history is also secured by the 'Stanley craze' of the early 1890s, which was a powerful factor in the drive towards the full-blooded version of British imperialism.

Stanley was a man of many and varied talents. He was highly intelligent, extremely well read and a great tribute to the power of auto didacticism. He was an outstanding journalist both in his ability to write fluent first drafts at will and in his 'feel' for a scoop. The Abyssinian triumph might have been enough for a lesser man, but Stanley went on to cap it with the 'finding' of Livingstone at Ujiji - a piece of journalistic opportunism and enterprise unmatched in the nineteenth century. He was also an administrative talent of a very high order, as his iron grip on the infant Congo State from 1879 to 1884 demonstrated. He had a powerful physical presence, was immensely physically courageous, was an inspired amateur military tactician and had the gift that most marks out the successful man of action - an unequalled capacity to improvise. Bracon- nier, his bete noire from the Congo who had no reason to respect him, left this judgement. 'He is a man of sudden resolution and irresolution. Ten minutes before he starts he hardly knows himself whether or where he is going. No one can admire Stanley's qualities more than I. He is a man of iron - easily discouraged indeed, but quick to regain courage; full of dogged will, which is his strength, but a splendid leader.'

His Napoleonic achievements in Africa were complemented by a certain Bonapartism of physical demeanour or rather, given his rolling gait like that of a sailor on land, or a combined Nelson-Napoleon. Harry Johnston, meeting him on the Congo in 1883, spoke of the physical similarity to the French emperor: corpulent, short-legged, and with the same basilisk eye and sense of latent explosive energy that would make any man afraid to laugh at him. One always felt wary respect for Stanley, whether the deeper feelings were those of hero-worship or personal antipathy and detestation.

Stanley, in short, had all the qualities of a great leader save one: he could never inspire his men by direct sympathy so that his aims became theirs automatically, as a Shackleton could. Not only was he unpredictable and unreliable and subject to frequent mood swings, but he was ruthless and inconsiderate to his comrades. When it suited his book, he abandoned his co-workers in Africa without a thought for their safety. In times of scarcity he always got more than his fair share of food and creature comforts, as Braconnier related: 'He treats his white companions as though he were a little king - lives apart, never chums with them, and at certain moments would think it justifiable to sacrifice any one of them for his own safety. I have watched him smoking under his tent, knowing all the time his officers had no tobacco, and it would never occur to him to offer them a pipe.'

Additionally, Stanley doled out grudging praise for good work but produced stinging reproaches for jobs badly done. He had no sense of humour about himself, was hypersensitive to criticism, refused to take blame and always insisted that culpability be assigned elsewhere, declined to take the advice of others, and was a natural authoritarian, insisting on his own way even if all his officers had voted for an opposite course. Anger bubbled away never far from the surface and paranoia revealed itself in over-reaction to those who snubbed him or would not take him seriously. Obsessed with his image, he played down the achievements of other explorers or criticised the findings of those who had gone before him. He was not above claiming for himself discoveries that were in reality first made by his comrades (as in the case of Ruwenzori). He was convinced that he was an Ishmael, with every man's hand turned against him.

This accounted for the blustering, disparaging tone he used with all who were not intimates. It was no accident that Stanley was considered 'no gentleman'; he did not stop at thinking the worst of others but uttered his suspicions in the coarsest possible terms. Thomas Barclay, who saw him at close quarters, said of him: 'Stanley was not a diplomatist. Uncompromising determination was stamped in his features. His angular form and hands were of a piece with truculent manner ... as always we conversed a la Stanley, which meant that his words were final. He was unsympathetic yet fascinating, intensely in earnest and ruthless in his idea of duty yet when off his guard almost sentimentally tender.' This chimed in with Hoffmann's assessment. 'He was on the whole a serious man, not given much to laughter: the hardships he had endured in childhood seemed to have dried up his natural capacity for gaiety. Yet there were times when his dry and witty remarks, his sky allusions to other members of the expedition, made me roar with laughter and convinced me that he was the most entertaining companion possible.'

These contradictory facets of his personality go a long way to explaining the paradoxical aspects of the Stanley expeditions in Africa. The loss of life on his journeys was terrific. On the first two expeditions he lost all five white companions. The death toll during the Free State years (1879-84) excited international comment and worried even Leopold, no shrinking violet or 'bleeding heart' when it came to the expenditure of human life. On the Emin expedition, Jameson and Barttelot succumbed to the tenebrous forces of Africa. Additionally, hundreds of Africans died. Yet the wangwana were always ready to follow him into the unknown. A simple butcher or psychopath could not have inspired their loyalty.

It is the human cost of Stanley's great achievements in African exploration that fills up the debit side of the balance sheet and forces us to probe more deeply into the inner man. This was the sort of examination Stanley always feared and he did his defiant best to hold at bay anyone seeking to understand the demons that drove him. 'On purely personal matters I ought to be better informed than anyone else, and I claim to be able to report them accurately,' he declared with bravado. And again: 'The inner existence, the Me, what does anybody know of? Nay, you may well ask, what do I know? But, granted that I know little of my real self, still I am the best evidence for myself.' But here Stanley protests too much. In psychological terms he was the classic 'resistant subject'. This was the true explanation for his notorious mendacity. Stanley doubtless began his career as a liar to conceal the 'shame' of his illegitimacy and workhouse origins, but in his later life he seems hardly to have been able to distinguish truth from falsehood. His lies had a traumatic origin; the cliché phrase about a 'pathological liar' has scarcely ever been more apt in the description of the life of a great man.

The 'heart of darkness' that was Stanley's psyche suggests a schizoid personality disorder, and the hypothesis hardens all the way along the line of inductive probability when we examine his sexual profile. The schizoid personality classically combines a desperate need for love with a desperate fear of intimacy - exactly the syndrome we observe in Stanley's relations with women. The origin of this malaise lies in the disastrous childhood - the perception of illegitimacy, the guilt about his mother's promiscuity which bred a mortal fear of sexuality, the horrors of casual dalliance and amateur prostitution he observed in St Asaph's workhouse. Typically, the schizoid personality has his true early bonding with an aged relative - in Stanley's case his grandfather Moses Parry - and adult sexual experience is deferred into the mid-twenties and beyond. Retreat into fantasy is the norm, and it is in the realm of fantasy that we should seek the aetiology of Stanley's notorious lies.

Schizoid personalities, though not psychotic, can become dangerous if their fantasy worlds break down. The abandonment of all hope of making loving relationships with real people can kindle the death instinct and fantasies of death. The genetic/environmental inheritance Stanley acquired could in certain other circumstances have turned him into a murderer. But his salvation was the strength of his will and the existence of Africa. Stanley could not make close emotional contacts because he feared that any love he would be given would be withdrawn from him. He pre-empted this possibility by unconsciously willing the destruction of his relationships with women and contriving his own rejection. Unwanted, humiliated, despised, unloved, with huge reservoirs of hostility towards others, Stanley found his salvation in Africa. African exploration provided a means of reconstituting an identity as well as, incidentally, permitting the exercise of homicidal impulses without incurring lethal social consequences.

Another sign of Stanley's basically schizoid personality was his failure to develop a true sense of conscience. Such a sense depends at root on the instilling of a moral sense by loved parents or mentors; strong ties of affectionate dependence then inculcate an 'altruistic' side, by which the individual learns the limits of the pleasure principle - no individual may do everything he or she desires to do. The absence of a father and the wretched inadequacy of his mother took Stanley perilously close to the dictum of Aleister Crowley: 'Do what thou wilt shall be the whole of the law.' Stanley's liking for dining alone and keeping his companions at arm's length denotes the classical schizoid 'lone wolf. Such a man has decided that since nobody cares for him, he in turn will care for nobody; other people are then viewed merely as obstacles to desires or objects of gratification. The combination of powerful impulses linked to an absence of conscience leads to potentially lethal consequences.

Yet no man is purely a textbook case, and although the basic analysis of 'schizoid personality disorder' takes us some way into the psychic world of H.M. Stanley, it provides clues rather an open-sesame master-key. For instance, the classical schizoid route to murder lies through abdication of the will. Stanley by contrast used his immense willpower to integrate the different strands of his personality. Yet the effort left him in a kind of emotional and psychic limbo. One aspect of this was a sort of repressed bisexuality. He was simultaneously attracted to and repelled by the sexuality of women and eventually 'solved' the conflict by a platonic marriage to Dorothy Tennant. The repressed homosexual side of his personality manifested itself in the long line of young males he needed always at his side: Edwin Balch, Edward King, Lewis Noe, Frank Pocock, Albert Christopherson, Mounteney Jephson, plus his servants Kalulu, Selim, Sali and William Hoffmann.

Yet another manifestation of his ambiguous profile and blunted sexuality was sado-masochism. The floggings, the excessive cruelties, the hangings and the abandonment of 'disobedient' men to the mercy of savage tribesmen bespeak something more than the autocratic disciplinarian. The almost willing embrace of hardship and the Grail-like acceptance of pain, especially in the Ituri forest, and the insistence on 'duty' as the supreme moral concept show the other side of the coin, and his own conclusion on his life is surely significant: 'I was not sent into the world to be happy, nor to search for happiness.'

The role of religion in Stanley's inner life is peculiarly hard to pin down. Here is a hostile character-sketch from Frederick Jackson that encapsulates the link between many diverse strands: 'Where he excelled the other great African explorers was as a journalist, a professional journalist, trained in the forceful "take no denial" school of American journalism, with a studied insight into the psychology of his readers. He appears to have been a man with strong religious convictions and he understood the value of quotations from the Bible with a certain section of the public.' The charge of religious humbug was frequently made against Stanley. In the Congo he jokingly told Coquilhat and Vangele that if you wanted to please the English public, you had to talk of God and quote the Bible. But this apparent cynicism need not imply hypocrisy. Stanley's journalistic and entrepreneurial talents mere sharp, but all the evidence suggests he was genuinely Christian in a formal Establishment way, with an added relish of Calvinism, and that he thought of God as his personal guardian. But he was neither the first nor last 'great man' to ally showmanship with a taste for the pious, the devout and the devotional.

What Stanley clearly did believe in was original sin. His sad childhood had made him profoundly sceptical of the innate goodness to be found in human nature, and the anomie of his meteoric rise from the gutter to knight of the realm left him with a worship of power that fed into these pessimistic convictions. In political and social matters Stanley was a rabid reactionary - a phenomenon often observed in those from an impoverished background who eventually climb the greasy pole.

Every individual has a unique psychological configuration, yet comparison can sometimes throw up the illuminating insight. If one sought for a twentieth-century Stanley, one would surely approach closest in the shape of T. E. Lawrence. The same basically schizoid personality is in evidence. Both men were born in illegitimacy in North Wales, both sought other names and identities (Shaw, Ross), both repressed their homosexuality and sought salvation in the open landscapes of an exotic terrain. The famous seduction/rape incident in Deraa finds a pre-echo by transference in Stanley's experience with Noe in Turkey in 1866. In Lawrence's case it was the masochistic side that was more highly developed, as in the floggings self-administered under orders from the 'old man'; in Stanley's it was the sadistic side, most notably evinced by the flogging of Lewis Noe in 1866. Both men were pathological liars, often genuinely unable to distinguish truth from falsehood.

Stanley, it seems, had the greater potential for contentment - he rejected happiness as an end in life - because he had angels of light to succour him, above all Livingstone. It was his tragedy that he chose to heed the Lucifer of the piece - Leopold. Stanley would have done well to follow the example of his great friend Mark Twain, who produced a satire on Leopold and his squalid 'red rubber' State and even promised Conan Doyle on his deathbed that he would give all assistance to the Congo Reform Campaign. Stanley turned his back on the light and embraced the darkness. His marriage almost seems to have recapitulated the process, with Dorothy Tennant before and after the wedding reflecting the Janus face. Casati said of Stanley: 'Men like him are the great exception. A century has- scarcely one such specimen.' In a century that has witnessed a return to the Dark Ages, perhaps we may conclude that, for all his greatness, a Stanley is a luxury we can no longer afford.

NOTES

Guide to abbreviations used in notes.

Add. MSS Additional Manuscripts, British Library AECP Archives Etrangeres, Correspondence Politique AEMD Archives Etrangeres, Memoires et Documents, French Foreign Ministry, Quai d'Orsay APR Archives du Palais Royal, Brussels BL MSS RP Manuscripts in British Library EIHC Essex Institute Historical Collections

HIFL How I Found Livingstone in Central Africa by H. M. Stanley (1872) IDA In Darkest Africa by H. M. Stanley (1890)

JAH Journal of African History

JRGS Journal of the Royal Geographical Society

MP Mackinnon Papers

NLS National Library of Scotland

PRGS Proceedings of the Royal Geographical Society

RA Royal Archives, Windsor Castle

RCS Royal Commonwealth Society

RGS Royal Geographical Society Archives

SFA Stanley Family Archives

TDC Through the Dark Continent by H. M. Stanley (1878)

TNR Tanzania (earlier Tanganyika) Notes and Records UJ Uganda Journal ZA Zanzibar Archives

Printed in Great Britain
by Amazon

0355